Tides of War

Volumes in the history of
international news reporting

by

Robert W. Desmond

The Information Process:
World News Reporting to the Twentieth Century

Windows on the World:
World News Reporting 1900–1920

Crisis and Conflict
World News Reporting 1920–1940

Tides of War
World News Reporting 1940–1945

Tides of War

World News Reporting 1940–1945

Robert W. Desmond

University of Iowa Press Iowa City

University of Iowa Press, Iowa City 52242
© 1984 by Robert W. Desmond. All rights reserved
Printed in the United States of America

Library of Congress Cataloging in Publication Data

Desmond, Robert William, 1900–
  Tides of war.

  Continues: Crisis and conflict. c1982.
  Bibliography: p.
  Includes index.
  1. Foreign news—History—20th century. 2. Reporters and report-
ing—History—20th century. 3. War correspondents. 4. World
War, 1939–1945—Journalists. I. Title.
PN4784.F6D474 1984   070.4'33   84–2504
ISBN 0–87745–125–7

To All Media Representatives who became casualties of military operations during the 1931–1945 period of news reporting

Contents

Foreword

This is the fourth volume in a series of books describing the evolution of international news reporting from the earliest times. The approach is historical, factual, and perhaps journalistic. It is intended as a descriptive rather than critical examination of the media. Neither are the volumes designed for use as textbooks, but as accounts of general interest, yet also of value as references in history, political science, and journalism.

The first volume in this series, *The Information Process* (1978), was subtitled "World Reporting to the Twentieth Century." It sought to explain the means of communication between peoples widely separated in the centuries before paper, ink, and printing existed, and continued to the first years of the present century. By that time, great advances had been made, not only with printing in use throughout most parts of the world but with electrical communications speeding information. Photography added another dimension. The developing education system created a literate public and provided instruction at many levels.

The second volume, *Windows on the World* (1980), bore the subtitle "The Information Process in a Changing Society, 1900–1920." Books relating to "foreign correspondence" had never been numerous prior to the 1920s, except for some biographies and autobiographies and some volumes about "war correspondence." My effort was to give attention to the work of correspondents in reporting the more normal flow of news in a world at peace. Since wars did intrude regularly into the course of human affairs, they were dealt with as elements in the news during the periods covered by these first two volumes, including World War I and the Russian Revolution. Part III of the second volume concentrated upon technical communication advances, electronic journalism, radio, the evolution of the news magazine, photo-journalism, the advancement of photo magazines, and the introduction and development of the "public affairs column." All of these were particularly identified with the decade of the 1930s.

The third volume, *Crisis and Conflict* (1982), describes "World News

Reporting Between Two Wars, 1920–1940." The major concern is with the growing influence of authoritarianism following World War I, with the information media always the first to suffer a loss of freedom. The economic breakdown of 1929–30, with the world depression following, accelerated the authoritarian trend.

This fourth volume, *Tides of War* (1984) describes "World News Reporting, 1940–1945." It begins with an account of Japanese aggression in Manchuria in 1931 to escalate into World War II. It chronicles crises in Europe and Africa fanned into the flames of the Second World War. The book concentrates on events that formed the substance of the news with which the correspondents, photographers, broadcasters, and editors were concerned. The primary purpose here is to describe the media problems, performance, and personnel in the years 1931 to 1945.

Speaking personally, I hope I have added something of value to this volume as drawn from my own activities through the time period. I was in Europe for two intervals of several months each before and shortly after World War I. Then, with about four years of news experience behind me, I went in 1926 to the staff of the Paris edition of the *New York Herald* (now the *International Herald Tribune*). Graduate study in international relations also took me from the United States to Geneva and London.

During the 1930s I was variously news editor in London also for the *Christian Science Monitor,* and concerned with news matters for that newspaper and others in Boston and Washington, the Caribbean area, Rome, and Berlin. An article written from Berlin shortly after the Reichstag fire of 1933, appearing in *Editor & Publisher,* provided the first general account of what was happening to the German press and to foreign correspondents in that country under the Nazi regime.

In the early 1940s, I was on the *New York Times* cable desk in New York, and later wrote and broadcast a regular evening news commentary from a San Francisco radio station through 1942. From 1943 I was in North Africa, Sicily and the mainland of Italy as an officer in the U.S. Army, attached to the military government branch, and at Supreme Headquarters (SHAEF) in London.

These and other experiences before and through the war period provided acquaintanceships among editors and correspondents in a number of countries, permitted me to observe news practices in major cities and capitals, and afforded opportunities to use the resources of the British Museum Library, the Library of Congress, and libraries elsewhere, as well as to form my own extensive collection of material about the international media and news process.

As always, errors of fact or perspective deriving from use of these sources are mine to regret. As always, further, I take this opportunity to thank those persons who have encouraged, assisted, and contributed to the completion of this volume, as of others in the series.

Robert W. Desmond
La Jolla, California

PART I
Again to Arms, 1931–1939

A World in Disarray   1

Hope prevailed among millions following World War I that the conflict's hard lessons might induce the peoples of the earth to cast their
weight upon the side of reason, and so assure permanent peace and well
being for all generations to come.

Added hope rested in the coincidental appearance of what seemed a
mature press organization in many lands, supplemented by a new mira-
cle of radio, to provide a public understanding of current events beyond
anything previously possible. A growth of educational systems, allied
with the media of information, further promised a potential end to illit-
eracy and poverty.

These hopes and expectations of the early 1920s were to prove sadly
naive, as history now makes clear. The fears and personal aspirations of
some in positions of power undid the good purposes of others. Economic events and political ideologies also had so altered the complexion
of the world by 1930 as to lead almost inevitably to conflicts, to measures thwarting constructive procedures, and to limiting the effectiveness of the media in presenting substantial information about matters of
significance.

Seeds of conflict were sown. So began actions of war in Tacna and
Arica and the Chaco areas of South America. More ominously, Japanese forces invaded Manchuria in 1931, to overspread much of China in
what became the unquestioned beginning of World War II, also ending
in Asia in 1945. An Italian military attack on Ethiopia (Abyssinia) in
1935 brought the annexation by Italy of that African country in 1936. In
Spain, an insurrection against the government of the republic, also in
1936, became a full-scale civil war, continuing brutally until 1939. It
provided a testing ground for weapons by Fascist Italy, Nazi Germany,
and Communist Russia—so soon to be engaged in World War II.

Correspondents for the world news media reported from all these battle zones, so far as they were able.

These were preludes or overtures to World War II.

Japanese economic expansion after World War I and especially from 1925–29 had been extensive. The island nation's ships transported finished goods around the world and brought home raw materials to feed its industry. World markets for Japan were suddenly reduced by the economic events of 1929–31, and the disruption of the economy was cause for government and business leaders to fear the growth of Communist sentiment and other political troubles threatening to surface. In 1923, the year of the great earthquake, there had been an attempt to assassinate Crown Prince Hirohito, then acting as regent for his father, Emperor Yoshihito, who died in 1926. Strong anti-American feelings also had been generated in 1924 when the United States abrogated a "gentlemen's agreement" by placing a ban on the immigration of Asians. This was especially resented in Japan, even though not directed specifically at its people.

In building its industrial complex since 1870, Japan had viewed the hundreds of millions of Chinese as a convenient market for its manufactured goods. With its victory over China in the Sino-Japanese War of 1894–95, its victory in the Russo-Japanese War of 1904–05, and its annexation of Korea in 1910, Japan had established a strong position for trade in China, especially in the Manchurian provinces. Manchuria was also a source of raw materials and an area open to emigration, settlement, and exploitation. Since 1905, indeed, Japanese industrialists had owned and operated the South Manchurian Railway and had shared with Czarist Russia and later with the Soviets the control of the Chinese Eastern Railway.

Marshal Chang Tso-lin, military governor of Manchuria since 1911 and a former warlord, became the dominant figure in a triumverate conducting the business of the Chinese Republic at Peking. He was friendly to Japan, supporting that country's interests in Manchuria. For its part, the Japanese government took a conciliatory view of China's Kuomintang (National Peoples Party), which had established a government in Nanking in April 1927. The Kuomintang's intention was to gain control of China, to supplant the weak government in Peking, to unify the nation, and to advance a program of internal development. This program was interrupted in 1927 by a conflict between Mao Tse-tung, influential in a radical wing of the party favoring a Communist government for China. Chiang Kai-shek, military adviser to the deceased Dr. Sun Yat-sen, founder of the republic in 1912, favored a democratic republic and was able to establish his government firmly in Nanking by 1928 and to gain diplomatic recognition from major nations. Mao and the Communist group remained at Hankow, near enough to Nanking to pose a threat to Chiang until 1934, when they made a "long march" northward to Shensi province to establish themselves at Yenan in 1935.

The Japanese response to the aims of the Kuomintang was divided. Some saw in it a threat to Japan's position in Manchuria and prospects for the trade in China it hoped to develop. Japanese troops were sent into China's Shantung province in May 1927 to "protect" Japanese residents. Their real purpose was to block Chinese Nationalist troops from the most direct approach to Peking, which they nevertheless reached in June 1928 and renamed it Peiping (old capital), thus bringing an end to the Chinese Republic of 1912. The Nationalist government at Nanking gained recognition, with Chiang Kai-shek as president and generalissimo of the armed forces.

Marshal Chang Tso-lin, forced out of Peking by approaching Nationalist troops, was killed on June 4, 1928, when his special railroad car was blown up near Mukden in an explosion believed to have been arranged by the Japanese because he was no longer willing to accept their advice and guidance. He was succeeded as military governor of Manchuria by his son, Chang Hsüeh-liang, known as the "young marshal," and who was favorable to the Kuomintang and the Nationalist government.

In May 1929 the Nationalist government charged Soviet Russia with violation of agreements made in 1924 relating to control of the Chinese Eastern Railway. The Moscow government responded by massing Red Army troops on the Manchurian border and there was fighting along the frontier for the next four months, but without a declaration of war.

This border conflict drew sixteen British and U.S. correspondents, most of whom came from Shanghai and Peking, but they were forced to remain at Harbin, with little to report. Among them were James P. Howe of the Associated Press, Demaree Bess of the United Press, John Goette of the International News Service, Frank Oliver of Reuters, and two correspondents of European experience temporarily in the Far East. They were Wilbur Forrest of the *New York Herald Tribune*, and William Philip Simms of the Scripps-Howard newspapers.

In the end, a protocol was signed leaving matters relating to the railroad much as they had been. By then the Nationalist government also concluded that it lacked sufficient military power to force Japan out of Manchuria. In 1930 two new rail lines were planned, however, to compete with the Japanese-owned South Manchurian Railway, and contracts were signed with a Dutch engineering firm to build a harbor to serve one of those lines.

Two years earlier, the Nanking government had been recognized by a dozen foreign nations, nine of whom voluntarily yielded extra-territorial privileges. Great Britain restored control of the port of Wei-hai-wei to

China and put pressure on Japan to withdraw its troops from Shantung. The Chinese mounted a boycott on Japanese goods beginning in 1928 that led Japan to withdraw its troops in May 1929. Trade was resumed in 1930, after the signing of a face-saving tariff agreement, but continuing persistent demands by military and industrial extremists in Japan to bolster the economy included the exploitation of Korea and Manchuria. Two incidents in the summer of 1931 provided a pretext for Japan to move aggressively again in Manchuria.

In the first incident, Korean immigrants in Manchuria came into conflict with Chinese residents. Serious riots followed in Seoul and other cities in Korea against Chinese inhabitants there. The Japanese controlled press was held responsible in both China and Korea because it had published exaggerated accounts and because the Japanese officials in Korea had failed to curb the disorders. A new boycott in China was instituted as a result and the total of Japanese imports fell drastically.

In the second, a Japanese officer, Major Nakamura, was arrested by Chinese troops in western Manchuria and executed or murdered on June 27. Japanese protests drew a denial that any such killing had taken place, and then there was a failure to make arrests, as had been promised. When the news of the killing became public knowledge in Japan on August 17, demonstrations erupted. Japanese military extremists demanded a strong policy toward China, and independently created a third and fateful incident in Manchuria.

The Japanese army stationed near Mukden in southern Manchuria and responsible for the protection of the South Manchurian Railway claimed that Chinese soldiers stationed at Mukden had blown up the railway tracks north of the city during night maneuvers on September 18. Japanese forces immediately attacked Mukden, seized its arsenal, and took control of the city and railroad. There was no clear evidence that the act, if it occurred, had not been perpetrated by the Japanese themselves to provide a pretext for much that was to follow. By the end of 1931, the Japanese had brought all of Manchuria under its control.

For the time being things were quiet in China. It was impossible in late 1931 to foresee what was in prospect there and much less to recognize that the spark had been struck that was to flare into a second world war. The spark at Sarajevo in 1914 had its origin in a political situation, while that at Mukden was an economic one. In Tokyo, Japan abandoned the gold standard in December, devaluing the yen and giving export trade a new stimulus.

On the night that the Japanese army attacked Mukden, William Henry Donald, an adviser to Chiang Kai-shek, telephoned the news of the assault to Demaree Bess at Peiping, where he was United Press bureau chief for north China. Donald, an Australian journalist, was a former Hong Kong editor and a correspondent in China for the *New York Herald.* It happened that Martin Sommers, an able New York newspaperman and formerly with the Paris edition of the *New York Herald,* was in Peiping and Bess persuaded him to go to Mukden for the UP. It took him three days to get there.

Other correspondents arriving as promptly were John Goette for the International News Service and the London *Daily Mail,* Edward Hunter, also of INS, and Morris J. Harris and James A. Mills of the Associated Press, coming from Shanghai and Peiping. Others arrived for news agencies and newspapers of Great Britain and the United States. Writers for the two major Japanese news agencies, Nippon Shimbun Rengo-sha (Rengo) and Nippon Dempo Tsushin-sha (Dentsu), were present, and others for Tokyo and Osaka dailies. The official Chinese Nationalist news agency, Chung Yang Sheh (Central News Agency, or CNA) was not represented because of Japanese military control in the area, but it received reports through the British Reuters agency.

Correspondents making their headquarters in Mukden filed dispatches for transmission to London and New York via the Danish-owned Great Northern Telegraph Company (Det Store Nordiske Telegraf-Selskab) line through Siberia to Copenhagen. The press rate to London was about 30 cents a word, and another 5 cents to New York at the time. The rates from Mukden to Tokyo or Shanghai were moderate, but the transpacific press rate from either of those places to San Francisco was 17 cents, 23 cents to New York, and 28 cents to London. Transmission was slow, subject to delays and also to censorship by the Japanese. Winter weather soon added hardships to coverage in Manchuria.

In Japan, these events were reported to a highly literate people served by a vigorous and well-made newspaper press, although subject to government controls, and also by a small radio network conducted through the Nippon Hoso Kyokai (NHK) or Japan Broadcasting Company formed in 1925. Both the newspapers and the radio stations were provided with a national and world news report from correspondents of the Rengo and Dentsu agencies at major world capitals. Rengo also distributed reports from Reuters and the AP, and Dentsu from the UP and the Central News of London.

The daily newspapers included the nationally distributed *Asahi* of Tokyo, which had an Osaka edition, and claimed a combined circulation larger than for any other newspaper in the world. The Osaka *Mainichi,* with an edition in Kyoto, was another of very large circulation. It was published in association with *Nichi Nichi* of Tokyo, also of large readership. Both papers were distributed nationally. Three other Tokyo dailies of similar distribution were *Yomiuri Shimbun, Hochi Shimbun,* and *Jiji Shimpo*. The *Chugai Shogyo Shimpo* of Tokyo was a respected financial and business daily. The *Japan Advertiser* of Tokyo, owned by U.S. citizen Benjamin W. Fleisher, was the leading English language daily. There was also the British-owned *Japan Chronicle* of Kobe, a government-owned *Japan Times* of Tokyo, and an English-language edition of *Mainichi.*

Foreign correspondents in Japan in the 1930–37 period included Hugh Byas representing the *Times* of London and the *New York Times*; Wilfrid Fleisher, managing editor of the *Japan Advertiser*, but also correspondent for the *New York Herald Tribune*; A. Morgan Young, editor of the *Japan Chronicle,* writing for the *Manchester Guardian,* the *Baltimore Sun*, and papers in Australia; Frank H. Hedges, concluding several years as correspondent for the *Christian Science Monitor*, and followed in 1934 by William Henry Chamberlin, formerly in Moscow for the paper; St. Clair McKelway, writing for the *Chicago Tribune* in 1931–37, and followed by Kenpei Sheba; J. W. T. Mason and Hessell Tiltman for the London *Daily Express*; and Frank G. Smothers in 1936–37 for the *Chicago Daily News.*

News agency correspondents in Tokyo included Malcolm Duncan Kennedy for Reuters. Miles W. (Peg) Vaughn was correspondent for the United Press and director of the agency's Far Eastern service from 1924 to 1934, followed by Raymond Gifford (Ray) Marshall, with Ralph H. Turner and Robert T. Bellaire also in the bureau. Serving the Associated Press at various periods were Max Hill, Glenn Babb, James A. Mills, and Relman (Pat) Morin. James R. Young, a former secretary to Edward W. Scripps, founder of the UP, was Tokyo correspondent for the W. R. Hearst owned International News Service from 1929 to 1941. He also represented Hearst's King Features Syndicate (KFS) and served as business manager of the *Japan Advertiser* in 1931–37.

It had been common for correspondents to move between Tokyo, Shanghai, and Peking, and this movement continued during the 1930s. Correspondents also arrived from other parts of the world as visitors in Japan and China. Thus, Floyd Gibbons, formerly Paris correspondent for the *Chicago Tribune* but a radio personality since 1927, visited Japan in 1931 and China in 1932, writing for INS.

Correspondents in Shanghai observed and reported a Japanese naval action and troop landings there in January 1932. They also reported the destruction of the Chapei district of the city, a workers' residential area, which was pulverized, with thousands killed and wounded. It was the first concentrated air bombing of a populated area. Some 30,000 words of news copy were filed daily to New York alone at a cost of about $4,000 a day during the most intensive period of the campaign. Dramatic photographs taken at considerable risk included motion pictures, some in color.

Japanese control of Manchuria was solidified by proclaiming the area an independent country and renaming it Manchukuo. Other than from Japan, the only diplomatic recognition came from Italy, which sought recognition for its right to control Ethiopia. The Japanese rejected the February 1933 report of the commission from the League of Nations, which had investigated China's complaint against the Japanese aggression. Japan withdrew in May from the League, thus indicating its intention to continue exploitation of Manchukuo and its campaign against China without declaration of war. A truce was arranged that same month with the Japanese by Chiang Kai-shek, who continued to maintain that the Nationalists lacked the military strength to contest the Japanese advance. The generalissimo almost seemed more concerned with crushing the rival Chinese Communist regime under Mao Tse-tung than with stemming the Japanese forces. Continued pressure from Japan on China resulted in concessions by the Chinese government during 1934 and 1935. These were irritating to many Chinese and to foreign interests as well.

By the end of 1935, the general information situation in China had become so difficult that the administrative operations of foreign news agency and newspaper services formerly based in Shanghai's International Settlement had been transferred to Tokyo. Information gathering and its availability was not much more favorable in Japan, where matters had also deteriorated.

The total press representation in those two Asian countries in the 1920s and 1930s did not match the representation in the larger European countries and capitals. Foreign newsmen also were handicapped by a language barrier more difficult to surmount than most. Those lacking a reasonable facility were limited in their sources of information. They were able to work with relative freedom, although often carefully watched, particularly in Japan. There was a disposition on the part of some officials to respond to questions by telling the correspondent what he presumably wished to hear, or what the informant wished him to believe, rather than adhering to fact.

In China, the military advance of the Kuomintang from Canton to Nanking and beyond in 1926–28 and the formation of the Nationalist government in Nanking was of such obvious importance and interest that it demanded coverage by the world press. A reduction in Pacific press rates in 1929 further encouraged such coverage, and the number of western correspondents increased in China. With the establishment of the Nationalist government, those correspondents also expected to find, and did find new and more responsive sources of information. Because the new government was interested in advancing its own acceptance by aiding correspondents, it gave an unprecedented assistance to the vernacular press, as well as to the foreign-language press in the country.

The Kuomintang in 1924 had established the first news agency of any significance in China, Chung Yang Sheh or the Central News Agency (CNA). Under the Nationalist government, it became an official agency, named its own correspondents in China and abroad, and also formed news exchange relationships with the Reuters agency and others. An official vernacular newspaper also was published at Nanking, *Chung Yang Jih Pao* (Central Daily News).

A Central Publicity Board of the Kuomintang party and a Central Publicity Department in the government provided answers to some questions by foreign correspondents and helped arrange interviews with officials. The Ministry of Foreign Affairs (Waichiaopu) set up a Department of Intelligence and Publicity, with a branch office in Shanghai that sometimes was helpful. A Ministry of Communications (Chiaotungpu) also was cooperative. Correspondents soon discovered, however, that the government's policy was to reveal only information deemed favorable, and that even official statements sometimes were inaccurate and unreliable, intended to create a desired impression, with no sure relation to fact. Further, a correspondent, however objective and accurate, might find himself in difficulty if he obtained and reported such facts as the government found inexpedient.[1]

On May 15, 1931, the Nationalist government announced that the Ministry of Communications had established censors in the offices of the foreign commercial communications companies operating within the formerly protected International Settlement at Shanghai. With the contracts for cable and radiotelegraphic service due for reconsideration at that time, relating to service throughout China, some governments yielded to the introduction of an indirect censorship of a kind first used in Argentina the year before. The censorship had three purposes: first to

---

1   Hallett Abend, *New York Times* correspondent, was in disfavor for such reporting in 1929. The government sought to have him deported for what Dr. C. T. Wang, the foreign minister, described in a letter to Nelson T. Johnson, U.S. minister to China, as willful misrepresentation and "insulting" references to the government and people of China.

Abend lived in Shanghai's International Settlement and, under the terms of the extraterritorial treaties, he could neither be expelled nor deported. The case was pending for more than two years, during which time the Foreign Ministry and the government denied Abend certain facilities. He agreed to write a letter expressing his regret that a misunderstanding had occurred. With that letter of April 28, 1931, the Foreign Ministry restored Abend to its "accredited" list of correspondents. At the same time, it released a statement for publication asserting that Abend had expressed regret for "unfair, false news reporting concerning China." That, he had not said, and of that he had not been guilty.

prevent the transmission of reports deemed inexpedient, second to prevent the dissemination of ideas or propaganda that might advance the Chinese Communist cause, and third to avoid aggravating the Japanese government.

After the Mukden attack by the Japanese four months later, the censorship became more strict, and correspondents were never certain that their dispatches had gone through. The Chinese censors also deleted or inserted words, and correspondents were sometimes accused by their home offices of editorializing when a dispatch bore a censor-added reference to "the puppet state of Manchukuo" or to the "puppet" emperor, the former boy-ruler of China forced to abdicate in 1912, but enthroned again in 1934. If words were deleted, the transmission charge on a per word basis might still be for the original total, or if words were inserted the charge might bear the added cost of transmission.

A further complication arose in May 1933 when the Ministry of Foreign Affairs required correspondents to apply to the ministry's Department of Intelligence and Publicity for a certificate of official accreditation for each agency, newspaper, or magazine represented. Weeks of waiting often preceded the issuance of the certificate, which only permitted the correspondent then to apply to the Ministry of Communications for a press card allowing him to send dispatches at press rates from five different locations in China. These restrictions and complications were the cause of some correspondents and administrative functions being removed to Tokyo in 1934.

The position of the press in Japan and the work of the foreign correspondents there also underwent changes after 1930. New obstacles arose after the Manchurian campaign began in 1931. This was partly offset when Toshio Shiratori, a former ambassador to Italy, became chief of the Information Bureau in the Foreign Ministry. Possessed of a sense of news values and having good relations with the military group in Japan, Shiratari possessed more freedom and authority than any previous spokesman for the bureau. His replacement in 1933 was Eiji Amau, whose meetings were far less rewarding and who frequently responded to questions by saying "we have no report" on the subject.

The assassination of two premiers in Japan in 1930 and 1932 by a military group then dominant caused problems for correspondents. Officials and private citizens alike grew cautious about any relationships they might have with foreigners, and especially with foreign correspondents. Police bans against mention in Japanese newspapers of particular subjects, mostly military and diplomatic, and general press controls became steadily more strict. Censors examined all printed matter entering the country, including books and publications in the possession of travelers. Any book with a reference to the Soviet Union or suspected of a Communist connection was almost certain to be confiscated. Newspapers were seized without question and copies of *Time* magazine frequently were taken or scissored. An international incident arose over a caricature of Emperor Hirohito in the U.S. monthly magazine *Vanity Fair* of August 1935.[2]

Even with the restrictions imposed upon the Japanese press, elements in the military group directed physical attacks in the summer of 1935 against the managing director to the Tokyo edition of *Asahi*, the director of *Yomiuri*, and the president of *Jiji Shimpo*, Sanji Muto, who died of wounds. Sand was thrown in the presses of *Hochi*, and when *Asahi* refused to discharge its foreign news editor, Shiro Machida, a national boycott was organized against the paper.

Since 1931 the Japanese government had a growing belief that its position in the field of international information would be improved if a single official news agency served the domestic press and also provided the news of Japan to foreign agencies through the international association of news agencies, or Ring Combination. Two major agencies were then operating in Japan. The Nippon Shimbun Rengo-sha (Rengo), the Associated Press of Japan, was patterned after the Associated Press of the United States. It was owned by eight dailies and provided a national and world service to twenty-six newspapers in Japan and to the Nippon Hoso Kyokai (NHK), Japan Broadcasting Company. It also received support from the Ministry of Foreign Affairs. The second agency, Nippon Dempo Tsushin-sha (Dentsu), Japan Telegraph Agency, was privately owned and virtually as active as Rengo. It also had official status. The NHK was privately owned but became government controlled in 1935. In mid-1936 Rengo and Dentsu were merged as Domei Tsushin-sha (Domei), Allied News Agency, an official agency subsidized by the Ministry of Communication. It was directed by Yukichi Iwanaga, former director of Rengo. He was succeeded upon his death in 1939 by Inosuke Furuno, his associate in Rengo and Domei.

Japan withdrew from the London Naval Conference of 1935 and announced it was building a navy without regard to previous agreements concerning its size. This military domination and policy of aggression in the government caused concern in the Diet and led to a general election on February 20, 1936. Many candidates who were opposed to the aggressive policy were elected and so alarmed an extremist element in the military group that it attempted a *coup d'etat* on February 26. There was

---

2   *Vanity Fair* was denied distribution in Japan because of the ancient taboo regarding disrespect of the emperor. A formal protest was lodged with the U.S. Department of State but no action was taken. Soon after, a protest to the Chinese National government about a reference in the press of that country to the emperor resulted in an apology from Nanking and a fourteen month prison sentence for the responsible editor.

fighting in the streets and the newspaper *Asahi* again received the attention of a wrecking crew. Both Viscount Takahashi, minister of finance
since 1932, and General Jotaro Watanabe of the army general staff,
among others, were killed and more were wounded. The *coup* failed to
place the army in full control and seventeen of the rebels were sentenced
to death by a military court in July.

This "2.26 incident," so-called because of the date, was felt by correspondents in a short censorship imposed upon dispatches leaving Japan.
Cable and wireless circuits were blocked for three or four days, and
telephone calls did not get through to Shanghai or Hong Kong. By November 1936 martial law was in place in Japan and an anti-Comintern
pact signed with Nazi Germany turned the Rome-Berlin Axis into the
Rome-Berlin-Tokyo Axis. New demands on northern China were accompanied by threats of invasion of central China as well.

Editors and staff members of Japanese newspapers were accustomed
to receiving instruction on how to present the news. Following the 2.26
incident, foreign correspondents also began to receive polite but firm
instructions on their reports of military matters and on statements
which might "give the impression that the Japanese are a bellicose people or that the Japanese policy is aggressive."

Correspondents became aware that they were looked upon as spies.
They were tolerated, nevertheless, possibly because some Japanese
journalists abroad then actually were spies. Representatives of the foreign news agencies in the Domei building for the convenience of news
exchange were watched also. Their news sources were brought under
pressure and became suspect for reliability and credibility. Japanese nationals working for the correspondents or for foreign-language papers
were under surveillance, and Japanese employees in the communications offices were told it was unpatriotic to handle messages for foreign
correspondents. In the light of these changes in Tokyo, some correspondents and administrative bureaus were returned to Shanghai.

Foreign correspondents were far more numerous in China than in
Japan, although many served in both countries, as elsewhere in Asia and
the Pacific. Coverage centered in Shanghai's International Settlement,
but Peking was a second highly important post, while others reported
from Tientsin, Nanking, Hankow, Canton, and from the British Crown
Colony of Hong Kong. All of the major news agencies maintained large
bureaus in Shanghai.[3]

---

3   Further details about the press in China and Japan in the 1930s and earlier, and about
foreign representation in those countries are presented in this writer's *Crisis and Conflict:
World News Reporting Between Two Wars, 1920–1940* (1982), *Windows on the World:
The Information Process in a Changing Society, 1900–1920* (1980), and in *The Information Process: World News Reporting to the Twentieth Century* (1978).

There was substantive news to report in China. The Nationalists had gained control of three provinces in the south. The Japanese were firmly established in Hopei province in the north, and the Chinese Communists seemed well established in Shensi, after the long march to Yenan in 1928. In an effort to gain control of all of China, the Japanese made seven secret demands under threat of an invasion. Both the Nationalists and the Chinese Communists wanted Chiang Kai-shek to declare war, but he continued to insist that the government was not militarily prepared to do so. The manner in which these negative issues were reported led the generalissimo to re-establish censorship in October 1936 under the direction of Hollington K. Tong, familiar with journalistic practices both in China and the United States.

In a remarkable episode reported to the world press, Chiang Kai-shek was held as a virtual prisoner by the Chinese Communist group for two weeks in December 1936, again in a futile effort to persuade him to make war on Japan.

Despite the uneasy relationship between the Chinese Communists and the Nationalists, improvements in all levels of domestic life became apparent and the country developed a sense of national unity to a degree never known before. World interest in the events transpiring in China required increased press coverage, as did evolving conditions in Japan.

The facilities for news transmission from both countries improved during 1935–37 and rates were reduced. Part of the improvement was in the opening of radiotelephone service between Shanghai and Tokyo on February 15, 1936, with service extended to Tientsin and to Hong Kong. In November a Tokyo–San Francisco–New York circuit was added, in May 1937 a Hong Kong–San Francisco connection, with ties to London and other parts of the world.

In Tokyo in November 1936, Wilfrid Fleisher, correspondent for the *New York Herald Tribune,* was first to use the radio telephone to transmit directly to New York. The *Herald Tribune* was more enterprising than any other newspaper or news agency in the use of radiotelephony to receive news reports from many parts of the world. Prior to extension of the war in China in 1937, the Japanese did not censor radiotelephone communication because of contractual agreements with the American Telephone & Telegraph Company operating the service.

In Japan, Article 27 of the Press Law was invoked to authorize ministers of the armed services and foreign affairs to shape the issuance of information from their departments. Previous media cooperation on a voluntary basis became mandatory. A wartime censorship imposed in July 1937 also put an effective tight rein on the press and radio. A new but short-lived source of information for foreign correspondents was the Pacific Information Bureau providing a service of translations from

Japanese publications. Responding to government restraint in February 1938, the bureau ceased translation of material deemed not in the Japanese national interest.

Following a sharp renewal of fighting on the night of July 7, 1937, between Chinese and Japanese troops near Peiping, a full-fledged but undeclared war developed. The Japanese seized Peiping and blockaded the Chinese coast. Together the Nationalist forces of Chiang Kai-shek and the Communist forces of Mao Tse-tung strongly resisted the Japanese, but they were defeated in November outside of Shanghai. Much of the city was destroyed and the International Settlement came under Japanese control.

For the first time since the Russo-Japanese War of 1905, Japanese newsmen were authorized by a decree of August 3, 1937, to accompany their troops in China. Some 500 did so and thirteen were killed within the first year. Although fewer in number, Chinese journalists also suffered casualties, but precise details are lacking.

During the bombardment of Shanghai western correspondents were in considerable danger. Anthony James Billingham of the *New York Times* was gravely wounded when a Japanese aerial bomb fell on the Nanking Road within the Settlement, killing 200 people. Abend, bureau chief for the paper, was slightly wounded. They were the first casualties among western correspondents in China, and the first of the developing World War II. The first fatality occurred in November when B. Pembroke Stephens of the London *Daily Telegraph* was killed by machine-gun fire while observing action along the French Bund in Shanghai.

Two others narrowly escaped death in August. Morris J. Harris, then AP bureau chief, survived a bomb explosion that killed about a thousand persons in the Settlement. John B. Powell was a near victim when a bomb struck Sassoon House, where he had his office, and where the United Press bureau was damaged.

Rodolfo Brandt, Acme Newspictures photographer, was severely wounded near Shanghai in October. Another hazard affected Haldore Hansen, of the AP, seized by Japanese soldiers near Paoting, in the north, and held from September 28 until October 12.

The early weeks of 1937 required prompt coverage of such extraordinary events as the bombing of the U.S. Pacific luxury liner *S.S. President Hoover* as it approached Shanghai, and the wounding of the British ambassador to China, fired upon from a Japanese plane as he rode in his official flag-bedecked car on the Nanking-Shanghai Road in September.

Nationalist troops, supported on this rare occasion by a Communist Eighth Route Army, resisted the Japanese attack on Shanghai, but were overwhelmed between August and November of 1937. Attacks upon cities and villages were accompanied by brutality to civilians reminiscent of the Sino-Japanese War of 1894–95. Correspondents witnessed these events, with radio communication in the Settlement providing almost their only link with the rest of the world.

Bombing of Nanking, the Nationalist capital, began in September and the city remained under siege until taken in December. Western correspondents reported the action there, including the destruction of the Central News Agency (CNA) headquarters, with five staff members wounded, and that of the government-operated Central Broadcasting Studio. The final evacuation of Nanking and the slaying of thousands was reported by Archibald T. Steele of the *Chicago Daily News* as "four days of hell." Motion picture films made by Arthur Menken of Paramount Newsreel were flown from Hong Kong to San Francisco by Pan American Airway's "China Clipper" and received early screening in theaters throughout the United States, Canada, Latin America, and Europe.

Other correspondents witnessing the capture of Nanking included F. Tillman Durdin of the *New York Times* with his wife, Margaret Armstrong (Peggy) Durdin, China-born daughter of an American missionary family; Leslie Smith of Reuters; Charles Yates McDaniel, a young American educated at St. John's University, Shanghai, and an AP correspondent; and Sandro Volta of *La Stampa* in Turin, one of Italy's leading dailies.

Seven correspondents evacuated from Nanking were aboard the U.S. gunboat *Panay* on December 13, bound upriver for Hankow, when it was attacked and sunk by Japanese planes. Three U.S. tankers also were sunk in the attack. All four ships were marked as neutral craft and had U.S. flags painted on the superstructures. The Japanese government apologized for the sinkings, and the U.S. government was not then prepared to take any strong position on the matter. Among the correspondents aboard the *Panay*, Sandro Sandri of *La Stampa* was killed. Luigi Barzini, Jr., of *Il Corriere della Sera* of Milan was wounded,[4] as was James Marshall of *Collier's Weekly.* Four others who escaped injury were Colin M. MacDonald of the London *Times,* Weldon James of AP, Norman Soong of the *New York Times* and Wide World Photos, and Norman Alley, a Universal Newsreel cameraman. Alley's films of the attack on the *Panay* were also flown by "China Clipper" to San Francisco, and from there by a special United Airlines flight to New York for processing and distribution. The Alley and Menken films were the first

---

4 Barzini later reported Sandri's death. Volta of *La Stampa*, still in Nanking and unaware of the *Panay* sinking at the time, was berated by his editor in a service message for failure to report his colleague's death. See Philip Knightley, *The First Casualty* (New York, 1975), p. 271.

to portray vividly the kind of air warfare to become tragically familiar in the next few years,[5] and news photos and film clips began to receive wide attention in magazines such as *Life* and other illustrated periodicals. Motion picture newsreels, documentaries, and news photos gave added reality to the years of crisis and war.

Correspondents who had been at Nanking followed the Nationalist government to Hankow, where the English-language *Hankow Herald* was established and edited by Bruno Swartz, an early AP stringer in China. The Trans-Pacific News Service, a former publicity agency, was converted into a general feature service in 1938 as the Chinese News Service. Somewhat informative, it was a government supported propaganda agency.

Those correspondents in Hankow during 1937–38 included Durdin for the *New York Times*; Peter Fleming, the London *Times*; James A. Mills, AP; Doris Reubens, UP; Edna Lee Booker, INS; Agnes Smedley, who had arrived from Yenan and was writing for the *Frankfurter Zeitung*; and Hans Melchers of the German Transozean agency. Two visiting correspondents were Edgar Ansel Mowrer of the *Chicago Daily News*, who was on leave from his post as Paris correspondent, and John Gunther, formerly in Europe for the same newspaper. He was author of the successful book *Inside Europe* (1936), and was in China gathering material for *Inside Asia*, published in 1939.

The cost of coverage in China rose sharply from 1937 as the volume of war news grew. The press rate on messages from Shanghai to New York was 13 cents a word. It was 25 cents at the regular commercial rate, 84 cents at the urgent rate, and 99 cents at a special-rush rate. These differences were significant because the importance of some events, and competition between news agencies led to the filing of a considerable volume of copy at the higher rates to assure prompt transmission. Competition led also to the filing of duplicate messages to be sent by alternate routes to assure the earliest possible delivery.

Earl J. Johnson, general news manager for the United Press in New York, reported that China war reports in September 1937 were costing almost $2,000 a day, the highest figure since World War I. The Associated Press costs for foreign service in July 1937 were $12,000 higher than for July 1936, and were running at about $4,000 a day for news from China and Japan combined, plus photo transmission costs where that was even possible.

Robert Dorman, general manager for Acme Newspictures, a Scripps organization, estimated that pictures from China were more expensive

---

5   Menken also made some of the first motion picture films in Finland and Norway during Russian and German bombings in 1939 and 1940.

to obtain than from any other active news area at the period. The first transmission of a photograph by radio from Tokyo to New York took place in August 1937. Showing a Shanghai bombing scene, it cost $225 to move, required ten hours, plus more time for its retransmission from New York to London.

Staff and travel costs increased steadily from 1931 in the support of assignments, new appointments, and special journeys to China and Japan from other parts of Asia and from the United States and Europe. Roy W. Howard, former president of the United Press, but then director of the Scripps-Howard Newspapers, made the first of several trips to China in 1931–32. Edward W. Beattie, Jr., Frederick Kuh, and Reynolds Packard, all of the UP, traveled from Europe and returned. Wilbur Forrest of the *New York Herald Tribune* was another early visitor. Others included Karl H. Von Wiegand of the Hearst papers, who made two trips from Berlin, H. R. Knickerbocker, and Philip Gibbs, all writing for the INS.

In October 1938, the Japanese military campaign forced the Chinese Nationalist government to leave Hankow. After pausing briefly upriver at Wuchang and then at Changsha, it finally came to rest at the end of the year in Chungking, near the head of the Yangtze River in the interior province of Szechewan, 1,400 miles from Nanking. Still under frequent air attack at Chungking, the Nationalists remained there through the war years. The Chinese Communists remained in the adjacent Shensi province, with headquarters at Yenan.

By then circumstances had changed in Japan, and at the end of 1938 events in Europe were approaching a point of no return, such as had been reached in China.

*The West:
France and
Great Britain*

Europe was deep in economic and political crisis by 1931, with military issues and actions soon to follow. For the British and the French, the victory of 1918 had brought few rewards. Great Britain's prewar industrial and maritime leadership did not revive. Unemployment created internal problems that defied solution, and the vast world empire seemed about to erode, beginning with the partition of Ireland in 1921 and the end of the protectorate in Egypt in 1922. Demands for independence in India grew increasingly persistent. Parliament in 1931 enacted the Statute of Westminster providing for the conversion of the empire into the British Commonwealth of Nations, with the dominions made autonomous. Under severe economic conditions, the unemployed were aided by the "dole" after 1921, and the extreme economic difficulties by 1931 forced the British to abandon the gold standard.

France was equally under economic pressures after World War I. Currency devaluation helped ease the national debt, but at a cost to government bond holders, while social legislation and construction of Maginot Line fortifications to protect the country from another German invasion made demands upon the budget at a time when the world economic depression brought an end to the receipt of the German war reparations. As an earlier and added measure of defense, France was the main force in the formation in 1920–23 of the Little Entente. These alliances with Czechoslovakia, Poland, Rumania, Yugoslavia, Belgium, and later the Soviet Union, were intended to prevent a restoration of the Hapsburg monarchy in Hungary, a spread of communism, and German aggressive power. A 1925 Treaty of Locarno was meant to assure frontiers and to safeguard the peace in Europe. Further safeguards were seen in the admission of Germany to the League of Nations in 1926 and in the Pact of Paris in 1928, wherein twenty-three signatory nations agreed to renounce war as an instrument of national policy.

Neither France nor the other participants were satisfied with the results of the Washington Naval Conference of 1921–22 or the London Naval Conference of 1930. The Anglo-German Naval Conference in 1935 resulted from the Nazi policy of secret rearmament and the frank announcement in the same year of its rejection of the Versailles Treaty. Great Britain made concessions at the conference in recognition that Germany had not been party to any of the previous conferences. This was the first manifestation of a policy of appeasement by the United Kingdom in dealing with Adolf Hitler and the National Socialists.[6] The agreement allowed the Germans to build a navy to 35 percent of the size of the British fleet, and permitted them to build submarines and the warships *Bismarck* and *Tirpitz,* both larger and technically superior to anything in the navies of France, Britain, or the United States. The agreement offended France and cooled its relations with Great Britain, and it encouraged both Hitler and Mussolini to believe they need not fear British opposition to their larger plans. The two dictators made

---

6 This policy of negotiation with Germany through 1939 was supported by Neville Chamberlain, prime minister from 1937–40, by Geoffrey Dawson, editor of the *Times,* by Lord Astor, publisher of the Sunday *Observer,* by Lady Astor, a member of Parliament, and by others. They were sometimes referred to as the "Cliveden set," a name derived from the Astors' estate near Plymouth.

Lord Astor explained the rationale of the policy to this writer and others in a private group as resting in the concept that there was reasonable possibility of reaching agreements with Hitler through acceptable compromises by moving quickly before younger and more extreme elements of the Nazi party gained greater power and made agreement impossible.

a mockery of appeasement, and when it suited him in April 1939 Hitler denounced the 1935 treaty.

The assassination of France's President Paul Doumer in May 1932 was followed in October 1934 by the assassination of Foreign Minister Jean Louis Barthou and King Alexander of Yugoslavia. Barthou had visited the Little Entente countries to counter influences of the Nazi government in Europe and had persuaded the king to visit France. Both were shot to death during a drive through the streets in an open car during the welcoming ceremonies at Marseilles. The assassination was recorded by newsreel cameramen as the sabre of a mounted policeman hacked down the assassin. He was a Macedonian working for Croat revolutionaries based in Hungary and seeking a reorganization of the Yugoslav government. The assassination created a danger of war between Yugoslavia and Hungary, but the intervention of the League of Nations preserved the peace.

The new foreign minister, Pierre Laval, visited Rome in January 1935 seeking to win Italy's support against Germany. As premier in June, he also recognized Italy's interests in East Africa. He concluded a treaty of alliance with the Soviet Union, which was sufficiently disturbed by the German Nazi regime to join the previously scorned League of Nations. In March 1936 German forces moved into the Rhineland, adjacent to the French frontier. Italy annexed Ethiopia in May; civil war began in Spain in July; a Rome-Berlin Axis was proclaimed in October and soon extended to include Tokyo.

These events which loomed as a threat to peace and security in both Asia and Europe brought an improvement of relations between France and Britain. These had suffered because of French objections to British concessions to Germany and British objections to France's concessions to Italy. Further, France failed to support the League of Nations in opposing Italy's move into Ethiopia in 1935–36. But neither nation was prepared to contest Germany's military occupation of the Rhineland, nor to protest the participation of Italy and Germany in the Spanish Civil War in support of Franco, or of the Soviet Union's intervention in support of the Spanish republic. Edouard Daladier's more moderate government formed on April 10, 1938, further restored Anglo-French solidarity, symbolized in a state visit to France by Britain's George VI and Queen Elizabeth in June that year.

In Great Britain, Ramsay MacDonald's coalition government of 1931–35 was succeeded in June of the latter year by a Conservative government formed with Stanley Baldwin as prime minister. King George V died the following January and was succeeded by his eldest son, as Edward VIII. In that summer of 1936, few in Britain were aware that the king was romantically involved with Mrs. Wallis Warfield Simpson, a divorced American woman living in London separately from her second husband. Edward's wish to make a twice-divorced woman his queen in a morganatic marriage was unacceptable to the government or the Church of England, of which the king was nominal head. This constitutional crisis went unreported by the British press or by radio through an unprecedented agreement arranged by the Baldwin government, with the assistance of Lord Beaverbrook, publisher of the London *Daily Express* and the *Evening Standard*. The foreign press reported the matter, and in a further unprecedented action a censorship was applied to such publications reaching British shores. References to the affair were removed or entire publications confiscated. So it was that the public in Britain remained unaware of the crisis until early December. On the tenth, in a radio broadcast, the king announced the first voluntary abdication of a British sovereign. He left England as the Duke of Windsor and married the former Mrs. Simpson in France on June 3, 1937.

Edward was succeeded by his brother, the Duke of York, who became George VI. The coronation on May 17, 1937, was covered by the media more thoroughly than any other such event in history. The press was well represented and every aspect was reported by world-wide short-wave radio broadcasts. Photographers recorded the event from start to finish, and pictures were transmitted electronically across the seas, some in color, and newsreel films were flown to far parts of the earth.

Neville Chamberlain followed Stanley Baldwin as prime minister soon after the coronation. Chamberlain's policy sought a new approach to counter the hazards of Italian and German policy moves. He felt that some concessions to Hitler and Mussolini were not too high a price to pay for peace in Europe. The Chamberlain government continued to shape British foreign policy until May 1940, when the German army overran France and the Low Countries.

Italy and Ethiopia

The Fascist government of Italy headed by Benito Mussolini was aggressive from its establishment in 1922, brooking no opposition to its program and resenting foreign criticism. The Italian press was brought under control of the Fascist party, and the radio medium was turned to propaganda purposes at home and abroad. In May 1932, the press law was amended to require the director or responsible editor of every newspaper or periodical to obtain an annual license to publish, bearing the approval of four authorities: the procurator-general of the Court of Appeal in the district of publication, the Press Office of the Ministry of the Interior, the official Fascist Syndicate of Journalists, and the prefect of the local district. Two violations of the law or two violations of directives were grounds for the dismissal of the responsible editor and for possible suspension of the publication.

In August 1933, Italy made its first move toward the formation of an office for propaganda and public enlightenment, similar to that newly established in Germany. Mussolini's son-in-law, Count Galeazzo Ciano, director of *Il Telegrafo* of Leghorn, became director of the Press Office in the Ministry of the Interior, succeeding Lando Ferretti, and reorganized it as part of the Ministry of Foreign Affairs in September 1934. There it became the Undersecretariat of State for Press and Propaganda with three divisions: Italian press, foreign press, and propaganda. A fourth division, cinematography, was added before the year's end. In June 1935, the organization was advanced to full ministerial status as the Ministry of Press and Propaganda (Il Ministero per la Stampa e la Propaganda). Located on the Via Veneto in Rome, it was a new point of contact and accreditation for foreign correspondents. Ciano soon resigned to participate in the Italian campaign in Ethiopia and was succeeded by Dino Alfieri.

The new name of the ministry did not fully reflect the increased scope of its activities, which included tourism, the theater, cultural exchanges of persons, and the general formation of ideas and opinions. In June 1937, the ministry was again renamed, becoming the Ministry of Popular Culture (Ministero della Cultura Popolare). A foreign press section was added, headed by Guido Rocca, and news conferences were introduced.

Contrary to practices in Moscow, Tokyo, and Berlin in the mid-1930s, foreign newspapers were permitted in Italy, except during two or three brief periods. Nor was any official censorship imposed upon news reports leaving the country until December 1934. Although not recognized at the time, the measure was intended to throw a security blanket over Italy's prospective military move against Ethiopia.

From 1922 until 1934, correspondents in Italy had been assured that there was no censorship on their outgoing dispatches. But they had early become aware that dispatches filed at the communications offices were routed by pneumatic tube to the main post office in Rome and read there by some member of a "board of revision" before actual transmission. Under this system of *revizione* or control, an unobjectionable or routine report would be passed and sent promptly. Otherwise, transmission might be purposely delayed long enough to prevent its arrival in time to meet a deadline, so causing it to be set aside unused or to rob it of news value. This became a kind of indirect censorship.

Under that system, a correspondent had no way of knowing the fate of a dispatch unless he received some query from his home office or checked the stories he sent against what appeared or did not appear in a copy of a newspaper reaching him days or weeks later. Even then, he could not be certain whether the absence of a report meant that it had failed to arrive or had simply been forced out of an edition for lack of space, whether cuts or changes had been made before transmission from Rome, or made by some editor preparing the dispatch for publication.

While Rome still denied any censorship prior to 1934, the *revizione* had become bolder through the years, with cuts and changes added to delays in transmission. If the correspondent complained, the communications office might apologize for the "unaccountable" differences or "errors in transmission," citing technical or administrative difficulties. The correspondent might be reimbursed if the number of words received differed from the number filed. But it was for him to take the initiative in such matters, at some cost in time.

It was usual for a correspondent filing reports in Rome to allow two to five hours for transmission to London or New York, but with no assurance against delays or changes. The use of the telephone from Rome to Paris or London might help meet that problem, but the clarity of telephone communication was not good until after 1930, and the calls, whether at the office or at home, were monitored and even recorded. So long as the government denied the existence of any censorship, there was at least no risk in the use of the telephone. For the same reason, correspondents in Rome felt no hesitation about sending out nonurgent reports in the pockets of accommodating friends or travelers, or of using the mails, and there was no fear of visa complications if they left Italy themselves.

They worked until 1934 under such relative advantages, as contrasted to correspondents in Moscow or Berlin after the Nazi regime began. Even so, pressures existed and multiplied. Decrees in effect since December 1926 making Italian journalists subject to arrest for reports that might be interpreted as hostile to the regime, might also in theory have sent foreign correspondents to jail. That never happened, but correspondents learned to be cautious. They knew they were watched and some whose reports were displeasing to officials were subjected to a variety of harassments. They also were careful of what they said in public. Only two correspondents were expelled in the years between 1922 and 1935. But from that time, the Fascist government followed the example of the Soviet and Nazi governments, with no less than twenty-four expelled from Italy in the three-year period from 1936 to 1939, and others in the years immediately following.

The attitude of the Fascist government toward the foreign correspondent was interpreted by Herbert L. Matthews of the *New York Times* in these words:

> Leave us alone. We are working out a great experiment with 42,000,000 lives and we want no interference, no advice, no condescension. We will be happiest if you do not write anything at all about us, but if you must write something, we insist that it be fair and friendly. You have come here of your own free will; you are accorded the privileges of all foreign guests of Italy and many extra ones because of your profession, and you must, if you want to work here, work with us, and not against us. "Everything for the State; nothing outside the State" goes for you as well as everyone else.[7]

Dino Alfieri, minister of Popular Culture from 1935, countered objections to actions and policies of the government as presented in the world press. He attributed merit to the Italian press itself because, he said, it did not seek "variety in scandal, in exciting the least noble passions and in satisfying unhealthy curiosity" through the publication of crime news and personal references found in the popular press of some other countries. He found nothing improper, however, in articles in the Italian press, or in radio broadcasts, written in what was called "battle style" (*stile battagliero*), peppered with insults and vulgar references to individuals and nations. In justifying it, he said:

> Fascism is undisturbed by discussions or even criticisms and does not seek to escape from a conflict of ideas, especially when that conflict is carried on in good faith, but it cannot tolerate deformations of trust and systematic falsehoods. For this reason, when certain newspapers and certain countries at periodical intervals launch their offensives against Italy, not hesitating to invent the basest lies, the Italian press, as is its right and duty, reacts with vivacity and even violence, which is justified by its lofty comprehension of national dignity and honor.[8]

After about 1937, interviews with Mussolini became rare, and perhaps were arranged as a favor or reward to a correspondent considered to have earned it by writing of the regime in a manner pleasing to Il Duce personally. This system of rewards was an Italian contribution to the methodology of political propaganda later adopted by the Nazi government and others. A second contribution was the establishment by the government of a social club, the Circolo, where correspondents acceptable to the government might meet conveniently in professional companionship. There they might dine well at moderate cost in a period

---

7 *New York Times*, January 13, 1930, p. 2E.
8 Arnaldo Cortesi, *New York Times*, May 19, 1937.

when such amenities were appreciated. This device was adopted also by other authoritarian governments as a means contributing to the control of the media, both foreign and domestic.

In the spring of 1936, Italy succeeded in its campaign to defeat the defending forces of Emperor Haile Selassie in Ethiopia. The country was annexed on May 9 and King Victor Emmanuel III declared emperor. Although Haile Selassie appealed in person to the League of Nations, that body was unable to win full support for effective sanctions against Italy. It could do nothing to restore Ethiopia's independence and the effort cost the League prestige and influence.

When the Italian campaign began in October 1935, correspondents from Italy and other parts of Europe accompanied or followed the troops. Some reporters flew to Addis Ababa to report the war from the Ethiopian side. This was one of the first occasions on which correspondents used air transport to reach the scene of action.

Italian military headquarters was established at Asmara in Eritrea. Ethiopian headquarters were at Harar and at Addis Ababa. Some neutral correspondents were able to report the war from both sides. Although a few had been active during World War I, and two or three had observed the earlier Japanese action in China, the hardships and frustrations encountered in Ethiopia were beyond the experience of most. They were obliged to live roughly under conditions of great heat and dust alternating during the seven months of war with heavy rains and mud, and with malaria and dysentary as constant problems. Food was another problem, especially for those in Ethiopia, as were matters of transportation and communication. A Foreign Press Correspondents Association formed in Addis Ababa had as its chief concern the provision of radio transmission facilities, which were delayed, costly to use, and never wholly adequate or satisfactory. Also, there was so little to do in Addis Ababa most of the time that feuding developed among correspondents.

The war was relatively expensive to cover. Outfitting, transporting, and meeting the requirements of the correspondents involved a substantial outlay. The cost to news agencies and newspapers in the United States was estimated at as much as $4,000 a day, and lasted for almost a year. Reuters later estimated its coverage to have cost about £4,000 (nearly $20,000).

A considerable group of Italian correspondents accompanied the Fascist forces. One was Luigi Barzini, representing the *Corriere della Sera* of Milan. Son of the elder Luigi Barzini, who had represented that paper as recently as World War I, he had been graduated in 1930 from the Columbia University Graduate School of Journalism in New York, and became a traveling correspondent for the the *Corriere* for ten years following. Another was Sandro Sandri, representing Mussolini's *Il Popolo d'Italia,* also of Milan.[9] Some of the Italian correspondents wrote in glowing terms of the war, including the bombing attacks, portrayed as things of beauty rather than of death.

Neutral correspondents with the Italians included Herbert R. (Bud) Ekins of the United Press, formerly in China for that agency; Jacques Barré for the Agence Havas; John T. Whitaker of the *New York Herald Tribune;* James Strachey Barnes of Reuters; and Herbert L. Matthews of the *New York Times,* who also was to spend some time with the Ethiopian defenders. Whitaker, Barnes, and Matthews all later were awarded the Italian War Cross (Croce de Guerra) in May 1936 for "valor in the East African campaign."

Lacking press development, Ethiopia itself provided no coverage. Stringers in Addis Ababa as the war began included Isadore Nebensahl for the Agence Havas; Agop Sivrisarian for the AP; and Alkeos Angelopoulous for INS. The first special correspondent to reach the capital to report the war was Wilfred C. (Will) Barber of the *Chicago Tribune.* He was a former sports writer for the AP, and formerly a member of the staff of the Paris edition of the *New York Herald.* Barber soon became ill from malaria and died at age thirty-two, the only correspondent who did not survive the campaign. He was awarded posthumously a Pulitzer Prize in 1936 citing him for "distinguished service."

George Lowther Steer, representing both the *Times* of London and the *New York Times* in Addis Ababa, was injured, as was Linton Wells of the *New York Herald Tribune.* The latter was present in the capital with his wife, Fay Gillis Wells, who also was injured.

Both James A. Mills of the Associated Press and novelist Evelyn Waugh of the *Daily Mail* had been in Addis Ababa in 1928 to report the coronation of Haile Selassie. They returned in 1935, flying from London with Sir Percival Phillips, the most experienced of war correspondents, representing the *Daily Telegraph.* In the same plane was a negotiator for a consortium of Anglo-American oil companies, who proceeded to sign contracts with the Emperor Haile Selassie by which those companies received rights, good for seventy-five years, to seek and develop oil resources. Substantial annual payments were to be made to the emperor if oil was found. These grants were made on the mistaken assumption that Italy would hesitate to challenge the claims of the companies or invade territories assigned for prospective drilling.

Mills and Phillips produced exclusive news reports about these contracts. Waugh completely missed the story. Not only did the contracts

---

9   Both Barzini and Sandri were together again in the coverage of the war in China in 1937.

fail to restrict Italian military advances, but the agreements antagonized the British and the Americans as a nondiplomatic maneuver. Mills nevertheless received an honorable mention for news enterprise in the Pulitzer Prize awards of 1936.

Waugh had written two novels reflecting his experiences in Ethiopia in 1928, *They Were Still Dancing* and *Black Mischief.* He more than compensated for his failure to get the story of the oil-drilling contracts in 1935 by later producing his own reminiscences of the war coverage, *Waugh in Abyssinia* (1937), in which he made great fun of U.S. correspondents. Waugh also wrote another novel, *Scoop* (1938), satirizing and caricaturing a fictitious but perhaps not wholly unrecognizable correspondent.

Other correspondents in Addis Ababa included J. Walter Collins in charge of war coverage for Reuters; Christian Ozanne for the Agence Havas; Webb Miller for the United Press; Edward J. Neil, Jr., and Andrew Berding for the Associated Press; Hubert R. Knickerbocker for the International News Service; and Floyd Gibbons, an experienced correspondent and radio personality there briefly for the INS.

News agency correspondents reporting from one side or the other for the neutral press included Christopher Holme, Ernest Richard Sheepshanks, and Kenneth Anderson, all for Reuters; Bernard Lavoix of Havas; Hans Shusser of the German official Deutsches Nachrichten Büro; Edward W. Beattie, Jr., Reynolds and Eleanor Packard, Frank Rohrbaugh, and Ben Ames, all of the UP; Karl H. Von Wiegand, Wynant Davis Hubbard, and William C. Chaplin, all for the Hearst Universal Service; Edward Hunter of International News Service; and Patrick Balfour, writing both for INS and for the *Evening Standard* of London.

Other correspondents for individual newspapers included Alan Dick and Lieutenant General Mortimer Durand for the *Daily Telegraph*, Geoffrey Theodore Garratt for the *Manchester Guardian*, Stuart Wallis Emeny for the London *News-Chronicle*, Noel Monks for the *Daily Express*, and Major General John F. C. Fuller and W. H. (Rex) Hartin for the *Daily Mail.* There also were Harold N. Denny and Joseph Israels II for the *New York Times* (Israels later became representative in the United States for Emperor Haile Selassie); William H. Stoneman for the *Chicago Daily News*; Reuben H. Markham for the *Christian Science Monitor*; Robinson McLean for the *Toronto Evening Telegram*; and Allou Cherie for *Paris Soir.*

Still other media representatives were Laurence Stallings, playwright, serving the *New York Times*, the North American Newspaper Alliance, and Fox Movietone newsreel; John Dorad for Paramount Newsreel; Ariel Vargas for Hearst Metrotone News and International News Photos; Ladislas Farago for Wide World Photos, then owned by the *New*

York Times; Joseph Caneva for AP Photos; and Ray Rousseau for Acme Newspictures.

Apart from Eleanor Packard of the UP, at least three other women were in Ethiopia as correspondents. Margareta de Harreros and Edith Marie de Bonneuil both represented *Le Journal* of Paris. Eleanor Meade represented Transradio Press, formed in 1934 in New York as an agency to provide news reports to radio stations.

Following the Ethiopian surrender in May 1936 and the Italian occupation of Addis Ababa, three correspondents were expelled. They were Nebensahl of Havas and Angelopoulous of INS, both stringers, and George Lowther Steer of the *Times* and the *New York Times*.[10] Other correspondents who had been reporting the war, with the exception of some serving the press of Italy, withdrew voluntarily.

The war in Ethiopia barely had ended when in July the Spanish Civil War began. Italy soon joined the Insurgents against the Republic to prevent what was viewed as a potential Communist administration in Spain. Italian "volunteers" were sent to Spain, and Germany intervened in support of the Insurgents. With the additional intervention of Soviet Russia in aid of the Republic, Britain and France began to fear a general European war.

Germany

The financial and industrial crisis that had overtaken Germany since 1930 because of general world economic woes gave new life to what had been a declining appeal of the National Socialist party led by Adolf Hitler, an Austrian-born German army war veteran. Hitler and his party, in objecting to the Treaty of Versailles and capitalizing on the hardships facing the Germans, gained 230 of 608 seats in the Reichstag during the July 1932 election, by far the greatest number for any one party. President von Hindenburg was obliged to name Hitler chancellor on January 30, 1933. Following Hindenburg's death in August 1934, Hitler became president and absolute leader of the Third Reich.

John Maynard Keynes, British economist, in 1919 correctly foresaw that Germany would be unable to meet the demands made upon it by the

---

10 Steer returned to Africa for the *Daily Telegraph* in 1938–39. He became an officer in the British Intelligence Corps when the war began. In 1940, after Ethiopia had been retaken by British forces, he accompanied the exiled Emperor Haile Selassie on his return to Addis Ababa by way of Sudan.

Steer also organized a propaganda campaign contributing to the defeat of Fascist Italy as a wartime ally of Nazi Germany. Late in 1944, while serving in Burma, he was killed in a motor accident.

Treaty of Versailles, and correctly forecast the ill effects the peace treaty could have upon the world economy.[11]

Writing at the same time, Sir Halford Mackinder, eminent British geographer, viewed Germany as occupying a central and dominating position between the Rhine and the frontiers of Russia—the heartland of an area extending as widely to the east and north as the Himalayas, the Yangtze, and the Arctic Ocean. He described this "World Island" as uniting Europe, Asia, and even Africa, and saw it as invulnerable to any attack from the sea.[12]

Mackinder's concept was shared by Professor Karl Haushofer, a former World War I German army major general, who formed and directed a Geopolitical Institute at the University of Munich. The primary concern of the institute was for German domination of the heartland and the world island. Stress was put upon a need for *lebensraum* or "living space" through national expansion, and upon the old German imperial dream of a Berlin-to-Baghdad railway.

As early as 1923, Hitler had discussed the heartland concept with Haushofer, and the idea appealed to the new National Socialist party. Haushofer, through his developing institute, helped steer Hitler into alliance with Italy and Japan. The seizure of Austria and Czechoslovakia in 1938–39 and the German treaty with Soviet Russia in 1939 met with Haushofer's approval, but later doubts about Japan's war on China and the Nazi turn against the Soviet Union in 1941 cost him favor with Hitler. Thus Germany from 1933 was at the center of those forces which shaped world history, both directly and indirectly. Indirectly because the reparations demands were unrealistic and directly because the Nazis advanced policies and practices that were aggressive, unacceptable to the civilized world, and which eventually reached a point of essential resistance.

Hitler's rise from obscurity and his general plan of action was based largely on his awareness of the uses of information-manipulation and propaganda, a subject to which he gave frank and extensive attention in his book, *Mein Kampf*, published in 1925 and made required reading for all loyal Nazis. He had taken note of the uses of propaganda by the German and British governments during World War I, and of methods and devices originated and used in Soviet Russia and Fascist Italy. He himself was an able speaker and a ruthless demagogue. What he had observed and the ideas he had conceived were applied in the advance-

---

11   See John Maynard Keynes, *The Economic Consequences of the Peace* (1919).

12   Mackinder stated in *Democratic Ideals and Reality* (1919) that "who rules the World-Island commands the World." In part to meet this warning, delivered in advance of the book's publication, the Peace Conference approved the creation of buffer states around Germany such as Poland and the Polish corridor, Czechoslovakia, Hungary, and the Baltic republics, and the ban on a union of Austria with Germany.

ment of the Nazi party. Elaborate means were used to shape and control information reaching the German people and, so far as possible, the peoples of the world.

Control of the media was the first essential for a successful exercise of power, as the Communist government of Soviet Russia had demonstrated. Within a week of Hitler's becoming chancellor in 1933, a "Decree for the Protection of the German People" was signed by President Hindenburg. As with many dictatorial moves, it pretended to high purpose and legality, explained in this instance as being intended to prevent the publication of "false news" and "malicious" reports. Within a month, it resulted in the suppression of more than 200 German newspapers and periodicals. A second move came when the Reichstag building was destroyed by fire on February 28, 1933, even then believed to have been the work of Nazis intended to provide a pretext for later restrictive actions.

One such action and the third basic dictatorial move came almost immediately in another decree signed by Hindenburg. It suspended all articles in the Weimar Constitution protecting civil rights, so ending German freedom of speech, freedom of the press, and freedom of association and assembly. Mail could be opened, telegrams examined, telephone conversations monitored and recorded, homes searched, property confiscated, and meetings forbidden.

Two further decrees in March provided for the establishment of a government Ministry of Public Enlightenment and Propaganda (Reichsministerium für Volksaufklärung und Propaganda), a euphemism, but still the first unambiguous pronouncement of propaganda as a function of government. Dr. Paul Joseph Goebbels, a Heidelberg Ph.D. of 1920, a Nazi party member since 1922, and a member of the Reichstag in 1930, held the ministerial portfolio, as he was to do throughout the Nazi regime. The duties of the ministry were defined in a July decree.

Another decree of September 22 established a Reich Culture Chamber (Reichskulturkammer) also headed by Goebbels. It introduced the so-called "Führer principle" into German affairs, meaning in fact an accepted dictatorship requiring an unquestioned loyalty to the leadership. Within the organization there were six separate divisions or "chambers," and ultimately seven: press, radio, theater, music, the arts (painting and sculpture), writers, and motion pictures. Each had its own president and directorate appointed by Goebbels, each exercised full control over its own area, and each was governed under additional specific decrees.

The Reich Press Chamber (Reichspressekammer), for example, was governed by decrees which made effective a detailed press law (Schriftleitergesetz). Comparable to the Fascist press law of Italy, it converted the German press into a "public institution," determined precisely who might work as a journalist, and the conditions under which he might do so. It made all journalists semi-state officials, responsible to the state, rather than to their publishers, editors, or other private interests. The journalist was required, among other things, to keep out of the press anything likely "to weaken the strength of the German Reich at home or abroad, its unity, armament, culture, or economy, or to violate the religious feelings of others."

An honor court supervised the observance of the law. Any journalist found guilty of violations might be punished by fine or imprisonment, and by expulsion from the profession. All licensed journalists, further, were required to join a German Press Federation (Reichsverband der Deutschen Presse), established within the Press Chamber. It was recognized as a public corporation and the official association for editorial workers. Also within the Press Chamber was a German Federation of Bureaus and News Agencies, and a German Federation of Newspaper Publishers.

The Reich Press Chamber was formally established at an inaugural ceremony in the Berlin Philharmonic Hall on November 15, 1933, with Dr. Goebbels officiating. He announced that the president of the chamber would be Max Amann, and that the Führer or Leiter would be Wilhelm Weiss. Amann had served in the same regiment with Hitler during the war and already headed the National Socialist Publishing Association (Zentral Verlag der NSDAP) of Munich, which had produced Hitler's *Mein Kampf* in 1925. Weiss was chief editor of the official Nazi party newspaper, the *Völkischer Beobachter* (National Observer) of Munich. It added an edition in Berlin in 1933 and another in Vienna in 1938.

Dr. Goebbels had said in March 1933 that "the mission of the press should be not merely to inform, but also to instruct. The press of Germany should be a piano upon which the government might play. The press must therefore cooperate with the government, and the government with the press." In this, Goebbels borrowed from the Communist concept that the press should serve an instructional purpose in support of party policies, and he also produced a variation on the musical theme originated by Mussolini in 1926 when he said that he considered "Italian Fascist journalism like an orchestra."

Goebbels called for a press that "should be unified in purpose and complex in the execution of that purpose" or, as he put it on another occasion, "monoform in will, but polyform in the expression of that will." To assure such uniformity of purpose, the Ministry of Propaganda instituted the practice of giving daily instructions to representatives of the Berlin press, conveyed also by telephone to editors in other cities. This was the same practice introduced by the Italian government in 1926, and one also adopted by the Japanese government in 1937. To attain "polyform" expression was more difficult, however, because editors learned to be cautious about departing from exact instructions. The result was that one newspaper on any given day looked and read very much like another.

Additional supervision of information was achieved in December 1933 through the enforced merger of the Wolff-CNB news agency with the younger Telegraphen Union (TU), controlled by Alfred Hugenberg, Krupp steel executive and a Nazi supporter. Out of this merger came the Deutsches Nachrichten Büro (DNB) as the one official agency of the government. Dr. Heinrich Mantler, long director of the Wolff-CNB agency retired, and Otto Mejer, who had headed the Telegraphen Union, became director of the new DNB. The Ring Combination, an association of world and national news agencies operating a news exchange since 1870, was effectively ended in 1933–34. DNB extended its own foreign coverage somewhat to compensate for the loss of that exchange.

The Deutsche Diplomatische-Korrespondenz, a specialized service operated by Wolff to deal with foreign affairs, was continued after 1933 as an adjunct to the Ministry of Foreign Affairs. A somewhat comparable service intended for foreign distribution, the Dienst aus Deutschland (Service from Germany), was erected on the remains of another Wolff subsidiary, Aussenpolitische Korrespondenz.

The Transozean Nachrichten, dating from 1915, was continued after 1933 as a service for the broadcast of reports for use overseas. Originally a World War I propaganda agency, it had been unobjectionable in its postwar role since 1919, but reverted to its original character under the Ministry of Propaganda, with its reports available for use at little or no cost.

To prevent so far as possible the circulation of information and ideas in Germany conflicting with that approved by the Nazi regime, an early ban halted the importation of 254 foreign newspapers and periodicals published in twenty-two countries. This ban was supplemented by another law to the same general purpose in October 1933. It was an offense for German citizens to possess such publications, clippings from them, or material in typewritten or other form taken from them. In addition, no foreign news services were permitted.

In Germany as in Italy, the domestic press was obliged to support a policy determined by the party leadership. Communist and Socialist papers had been suppressed in the first days. Publications under Jewish ownership, and notably a large group of newspapers and periodicals produced by the Ullstein firm in Berlin, were either suppressed or placed under the control of Nazi party members.

A government decree in April 1935 included three orders providing an ostensibly legal basis shaping the operation of publications. First, the orders fixed conditions under which newspapers or periodicals not owned by Nazi party members might continue to appear. Second, they provided that non-Nazi publications might be suppressed in favor of party publications in order "to eliminate unhealthy competitive situations." Third, they provided for the suppression of what was called "the scandal press."

Under the provisions of this decree, Max Amann was able to gain almost complete control of the publishing business in Germany, conducted through the complex activities of the Zentral Verlag der NSDAP and of the Franz Eher Verlag, both under his direction. He enjoyed great personal prosperity, and shared that prosperity with Hitler.

In addition to its official daily newspaper the *Völkischer Beobachter* edited by Weiss, the Nazi party also published *Die Illustrierte Beobachter* of Munich, an illustrated weekly edition of the daily. It added *Die Hitlerjugend* of Berlin, a "Hitler Youth" organization paper, and *Der Arbeitmann*, also of Berlin, a Reich Labor Service paper.

Some Nazi leaders, in addition to Amann, had their own papers. Dr. Goebbels conducted *Der Angriff* (The Attack), a Berlin daily tabloid dating from 1927 and, as late as 1941, he established *Das Reich*, a well printed and rather high quality weekly. Hermann Goering controlled *Der Essener National Zeitung* of Essen; Robert Ley had the *Westdeutscher Beobachter* of Cologne; Julius Streicher published *Der Stürmer* of Nürnberg, a "scandal" paper despite the decree of 1935, notorious for its vulgarity and abusiveness; and Heinrich Himmler, Gestapo chief, published *Das Schwarze Korps* of Berlin the official paper of the Elite S.S. (Storm Trooper) Guards.

The standard of accuracy in the German press and the variety of its content declined greatly after 1933. The similarity of the papers, despite the desire for "polyform expression," discouraged the public interest and circulations fell off. This provided another reason for suspending certain papers. Some that had been among the best, and some that had retained a modicum of independence were suppressed on the pretext that "unhealthy competitive situations" were involved. The *Berliner Tageblatt* and the *Hamburger Nachrichten* disappeared in 1939. The war years brought an end to the prestigious *Frankfurter Zeitung,* the *Deutsche Allgemeine Zeitung* and the *B.Z. am Mittag,* both of Berlin, and to others.

The Nazi government did not conceal the fact that it was "supervising" the press, radio, and films. Officials described the media as "ordered" or "controlled," and the personnel also were controlled. By 1939 more than 1,500 former journalists had been ousted from the practice. German correspondents abroad were not excluded from control. In November 1936 they were ordered to withdraw from foreign or international press clubs or associations. This affected ten German correspondents in the United States, and others in London, Paris, and Rome.

How these influences were extended to the media of Austria and Czechoslovakia will be described in later pages.

The Spanish Civil War, 1936–39

The second Spanish republic was proclaimed in April 1931. It inherited troubles and inequities from the preceding monarchy that the new government could not solve, and it set goals it could not attain. Public discontent resulted in demonstrations and strikes. Efforts to bring about needed reforms led only to further controversies and crises. A new constitution promised rights and privileges, but at the same time a Law for the Defense of the Republic authorized a discretionary suspension of constitutional guarantees, including civil rights. Improvements in education were undertaken and the titles of nobility were abolished in a move toward greater personal equality. Private property was made subject to confiscation and great estates were taken over to grant land to the people. The power of the Catholic Church was challenged and the Jesuit order was proscribed, with its property seized. Under the Defense of the Republic law, private clubs were closed and some associations were dissolved. Meetings were cancelled and newspapers suspended. The net result was less freedom under the republic than under General Miguel Primo de Rivera, who had been premier and dictator in Spain under the monarchy from 1923 to 1930.

The state of the economy and the opposition stirred by property confiscation and action against the church gave rise to nearly a dozen different political parties, among them a Falangist party formed late in 1934. That year had been marked by a general strike and street fighting in Madrid and Barcelona, and the deaths of a thousand Basques and the wounding of three thousand more. Two years before, a Communist rebellion had been crushed with violence. The Falangists reflected the views of the conservative element loyal to the vanished monarchy, of those whose titles had been lost, of those whose property had been confiscated, of those associated with the church, of army and navy officers, and of those dedicated to law and order.

The new constitution of the republic had guaranteed civil liberties, including freedom of the press, but these had not been realized in practice. Premier Manuel Azaña y Dias, at a luncheon of foreign correspondents in Madrid in May 1932, when hope for the republic was high, had promised that there would be full liberty of the press, ascribing to it the duty of finding and reporting the truth, not merely in matters of politics, but in all matters relating to public affairs and the social welfare. Even then, however, he amended this fine statement, as officials had been wont to do in Moscow, Rome, and Berlin, by adding that some foreign newspapers tended to emphasize insignificant incidents, thus giving a distorted impresssion while ignoring "all the immense work being done in this country." This he lamented, because "the people of the world have a right to the truth."

Even as the premier spoke, a stiff censorship limited what the Spanish press itself might publish. In a negation of the constitutional guarantees, newspapers were fined, seized, and suspended for criticism of the republican government. By September 1932, when the International Telegraphic and International Radio Union conferences were taking place in Madrid to review world communications regulations, Alejandro Lerroux, soon to succeed Azaña as premier, was in the contradictory position of being publisher of *La Publicitat,* a Barcelona daily, and president of the Madrid Press Association, while at the same time acting as chief censor of the national press.

Between August and October 1932 some 115 publications of various kinds were ordered to cease publication in Spain, although a number later were permitted to resume. Among them in Madrid were such established dailies as *A BC, La Nación,* and *El Imparcial.* This situation became worse, affecting papers in Barcelona, Valencia, Malaga, Bilboa, and other cities. A press law in force through 1934 and 1935 further restricted information reaching the public, and a new press law in 1935 placed an absolute control on the publications of the country.

Meanwhile, foreign correspondents in Spain were watched, as they had been during the years of the dictatorship. Their reports were censored and their homes sometimes searched. Arrests were common, perhaps simply because they had been seen talking with certain individuals, so bringing them under suspicion. Although there were some resident correspondents in Madrid and Barcelona, it was usual for correspondents based in Paris to visit Spain and then leave to write their reports where they would be free of censorship and personal harassment.

Danger to correspondents was very real during the disorders in 1934. The Havas bureau in Madrid was raked by rifle fire, leading to an official protest by the French government. Many correspondents were caught in cross-fire between troops of the republic and rebellious groups. A correspondent for the London *Daily Express* was arrested late in the year on a charge of sabotage. A Council of Ministers, summoned to discuss his alleged offense, could only conclude with a resolution demanding that the Spanish ambassador in London explain why he had failed to make a complaint to the British government.

Hazards or not, these years brought correspondents for the world press to Spain, some regularly assigned while others made repeated visits. For the agencies, they included Christian Ozanne and Georges Le Lorrain, Agence Havas; Christopher Holme, Reuters; Robert M. Barry, Associated Press, followed by Rex Smith, Alexander H. Uhl, and Clarence Dubose, who died in Madrid in 1931. The United Press was represented by Jean DeGandt, William H. Lander, and Lester Ziffren, later bureau chief in Madrid. Thomas A. Loayza and Edward Hunter were there for the International News Service.

Newspaper correspondents included Lawrence A. Fernsworth representing both the *Times* of London and the *New York Times,* with Barcelona as his headquarters. Frank L. Kluckhohn later served the New York paper in Madrid, with William P. Carney as another staff representative. Ralph E. Forte served the *Chicago Daily News* in Madrid, and Jay Allen, at various periods, served both that paper and the *Chicago Tribune.* Edmond Taylor was a later visitor coming from Paris for the *Tribune.* Henry J. Greenwall visited Spain for the *Daily Express,* F. A. Voigt for the *Manchester Guardian,* and G. Ward Price for the *Daily Mail.* Albin E. Johnson was in Spain for the *New York World* before that paper suspended in 1931, and Leland Stowe was a regular visitor for the *New York Herald Tribune.*

The February 1936 general election in Spain resulted in a Popular Front government viewed by the right-wing parties, including the Falangists, as a proletarian administration verging on socialism or even communism. The nature of reforms begun by the new government resulted in resistance throughout the country which came to a head in the murder on July 12 of José Castillo, a lieutenant in the Assault Guards and a Communist.

Six days later on July 18 an army mutiny led by General Francisco Franco began at Melilla, Spanish Morocco. The mutineers called themselves "Insurgents" and the rebellion spread to Spain proper the next day. Within forty-eight hours the entire country was engaged in a civil war that continued until March 1939 when Republican forces were defeated and a new government was headed by General Franco.

Early efforts by Great Britain, France, the United States, and the League of Nations failed to stop the fighting. The rebellion was supported by the military, the church, the royalists, and the propertied classes. Rallying to the Falangist party and the support of Franco, the Insurgents moved their headquarters to Burgos in north central Spain.

The Republican government headquarters was first in Madrid, until heavy bombing forced it to move to Valencia in 1936 and then to Barcelona in October 1938.

Foreign intervention began in July 1936, with Fascist Italy and Nazi Germany providing men and materials to Franco and the Insurgents. The Republicans received comparable support on a smaller scale from the Soviet Union. Foreign intervention also included an international brigade made up largely of young men from the United States and Great Britain, and some from other countries. Idealists, liberal and often left-leaning, they made their way to Spain in a kind of pilgrimage to do battle against fascism. They reflected an emotional response to a war which caused repercussions throughout much of the world. Some saw the war as a contest between fascism and democracy, others as between democracy and communism, and still others as a contest between the power and privilege of the Catholic church along with those of wealth and position versus the vast majority long deprived of human rights and opportunity.

Frank Kluckhohn of the *New York Times,* with the Insurgents, was the first to get the news out in August by telephone to Gibraltar that Italian and German planes manned by nationals of those countries had reached Franco's forces. The Franco group was displeased by the revelation and the evasion of censorship, and the story almost cost Kluckhohn his life. He was immediately disaccredited by the Insurgents and had to flee from Spain.

Never before had the media been made subject to such pro and con pressures by those whose political and religious beliefs and prejudices were stirred, even though they might be thousands of miles removed from the battle areas. The press and radio as well reported the first air bombings of any European cities, with Madrid repeatedly hit. The media had to report brutalities on both sides exceeding anything known in World War I or to any recent European generations. Many readers and listeners were unable or unwilling to draw a line between such events and the reporting of them, between the facts and the "messenger" conveying those facts, and so sometimes held the media responsible for unpleasant and unwelcome news.

Even the "best" newspapers and news agencies and radio stations or networks were recipients of protests, the targets of public demonstrations and attacks. Religious groups and others sought to persuade advertisers to withdraw their messages from the media, to urge readers to boycott advertisers who continued to use those publications found objectionable. They also opposed those who sponsored radio news programs presenting reports running contrary to the views of local or national organized pressure groups. These prejudices found expression in the very names applied to the contesting forces. Government troops were referred to accurately enough as the "Republicans" or the "government" forces, but they also were called the Loyalists, Patriots, or Reds. The Franco forces were referred to fairly as the Insurgents, Nationalists, or Falangists, but also as the Fascists, Rebels, or Whites.

Almost without reference to what they wrote, and quite apart from considerations of accuracy, any correspondent was almost certain to be accused by some of bias, prejudice, incompetence, falsification, or other sins. Such charges occasionally came even from their own editors at home, perhaps themselves responding to the backlash of pressures being brought to bear by partisans in their own communities.

As if this were not enough, correspondents in Spain faced hardships and the hazards of combat. Four were killed, a number wounded, several captured, some threatened with execution, some jailed, and some expelled. There were difficulties in obtaining information, problems of food, housing, and transportation. There also were problems of censorship and communication, risks to health, and risks of being mistaken for spies and of being jailed and even executed. For some, there were language problems.

The press and radio of Spain was unable to provide accurate or effective coverage of the civil war because of the division and disorder within the country, to say nothing of censorship and controls. The presses of Italy, Germany, and the Soviet Union were subject to their own interests and controls, and actually were not much represented in Spain. They used reports provided by their official news agencies, prepared from such sources as they chose to use or were permitted to use. Almost by default, therefore, coverage of the Spanish Civil War was provided to most of the world by the neutral media of Great Britain, France, and the United States. As neutrals, they were able to report the war from both sides. The group included some correspondents of great experience, a number of whom were recently engaged in coverage of the Italo-Ethiopian War. Others were new to war reporting. Some were in Spain briefly, others for several months, and a few for the entire time.

Lester Ziffren of the United Press bureau in Madrid was the first to flash the news of the outbreak of the civil war in a coded message in July 1936. Lawrence A. Fernsworth returned to cover the war for the *New York Times* and for the *Times* of London. Kluckhohn of the *New York Times* was with the Insurgents during the first month, until forced to leave the country.

The Agence Havas was represented by Christian Ozanne and Georges Le Lorrain. Vincent Sheean, who had written earlier from Spain and Morocco for the *Chicago Tribune,* returned for the North American Newspaper Alliance. Other veterans of correspondence in war and peace who arrived in Spain included Webb Miller, UP; Herbert L. Matthews, *New York Times;* John T. Whitaker, *New York Herald Tribune;* Edward J. Neil, AP; Reynolds Packard, UP; Ernest Richard Sheepshanks, Reuters; H. R. Knickerbocker and Floyd Gibbons, INS; Karl H. Von Wiegand, INS and the Hearst newspapers; Ladislas Farago, *New York Times* and Wide World Photos; George Lowther Steer, the *Times* of London and later for the *Daily Telegraph;* and Sir Percival Phillips, also for the *Daily Telegraph.*

All of these men had reported the Ethiopian war, four had reported World War I, and Phillips, the correspondent of longest experience, began war reporting in the Greco-Turkish conflict of 1897. He only covered the beginning of the Spanish Civil War, however, writing from Tangier, Morocco. Taken ill, he returned to London and died there in January 1937. Von Wiegand, primarily based in Berlin, soon went to the Far East. Gibbons departed to continue his primary assignment of that period as a radio personality, broadcasting general feature programs as well as some news. Miller, another veteran, also had executive and news responsibilities elsewhere for the United Press.

Other experienced correspondents moving into Spain included Leland Stowe and John Elliott, both for the *New York Herald Tribune;* Jay Allen and Alex Small for the *Chicago Tribune;* George Seldes, formerly of the *Tribune* but writing for the *New York Post* and the *Philadelphia Record;* Vernon Bartlett for the London *News-Chronicle;* and Pierre Van Passen for the *Toronto Star.*

H. V. Kaltenborn, a veteran newsman then in the early period of a second career as a radio news reporter and commentator, was in Spain for the Columbia Broadcasting System. He set a precedent by providing a first radio battlefield report. From a haystack near Irún in September 1936, with the sounds of warfare heard in the background, he spoke to a network audience in the United States.

O'Dowd (O.D. or Odie) Gallagher of the *Daily Express* was one of those few correspondents who reported the war from start to finish from both sides, during which he was expelled twice by the Falangist Insurgents. Carney of the *New York Times* was another who saw the war from both sides, but he and his paper became special targets of abuse by some readers in the United States whose emotions were aroused by the issues and who regarded Carney as a spokesman for the Insurgents. Small of the *Chicago Tribune* was a third correspondent to report from both sides and also was expelled by both sides. He narrowly escaped being shot by the Insurgents after a court-martial.

Noel Monks, a former Australian newsman, representing the *Daily Express* in Paris, was another arrested by the Insurgents. Like Small, he was threatened with execution, but then was expelled on Franco's personal order. He later reported the war from the side of the republic. Henry T. Gorrell of the United Press was arrested by Republican soldiers at Toledo and jailed. He was another saved from execution, only to be captured by the Insurgents two weeks later on the Madrid-Valencia road. Alkeos Angelopoulos, an INS stringer in Addis Ababa expelled by the Italians after they occupied that capital, rejoined the INS in Spain, where he was arrested at Valencia and jailed for ten days.

Arthur Koestler of the *News-Chronicle* was one more correspondent on both sides, first with the Insurgents and then with the Republicans. In the latter period, he was captured by the Insurgents after the fall of Malaga in the first winter of the war. Charged with being a spy and sentenced to death by court-martial, he was released only after representations by the British government. Koestler was Hungarian-born and had previous experience as a correspondent for the Ullstein newspapers of Berlin, serving in the Middle East and later in Paris and Berlin. Having become a Communist party member, he had traveled extensively in the Soviet Union and Asia under Soviet sponsorship. He left Germany after the Nazi government was formed. Koestler's Spanish war experiences were recorded in two books, *Spanish Gladiators* (1937), published in the United States as *Dialogue With Death* (1942), and in *The Gladiators* (1939). After severing his relations with the Communist party, he wrote the latter book which also reflected his observations during an adventurous life.[1]

Steer's departure from Spain as London *Times* correspondent in 1937 for *Daily Telegraph* assignments elsewhere was followed by the appointment of Harold A. R. (Hal or Kim) Philby as *Times* correspondent attached to the Franco Falangist headquarters at Burgos. Philby had been there earlier for a small British agency, the London General Press, and remained throughout the war until 1939. He made himself popular with the military and civilian staff, and also with his fellow correspondents. His dispatches to the *Times* were well received in London and were so pleasing to the Falangists that his freedom of movement and his sources of information became exceptional.

Philby was graduated from Trinity College, Cambridge, in 1933 and worked briefly in Vienna as a freelance journalist, then for the monthly *Review of Reviews* in London, and in 1936 had gone to Spain as the war began. At Burgos, his colleagues included Ernest Richard Sheepshanks of Reuters, who had been a friend at Cambridge; Sam Pope Brewer of the *New York Times;* Edward J. Neil, AP; Russell F. Anderson, INS;

---

1 Koestler served in the French and British armies during World War II. He was the author of other books, including *Darkness at Noon* (1940). In 1951, by a special act of Congress, he was granted permanent residence in the United States, where he died in 1983.

and Bradish G. Johnson, Jr., a *Newsweek* photographer. All of them, except for Brewer, were on a road near Teruel early in 1938 when a Republican plane dropped bombs nearby. Johnson was killed outright. The other four were wounded, and Sheepshanks and Neil died later. By order of General Franco, Philby later was awarded the Cross of the Order of Military Merit, a Spanish decoration for bravery on the battlefield.[2]

Other correspondents accredited to one side or the other during the years of the war included Ernest Hemingway. He had deserted news reporting in the mid-1920s for fiction, but wrote as a correspondent with the Republican forces for the NANA, and later was to write a major novel of the war, *For Whom the Bell Tolls* (1940). Martha Gellhorn, whom he married in 1940, was in Spain for *Collier's Weekly* in 1937–38,[3] one of five women engaged in reporting the war. William F. McDermott was another writer for NANA. Matthew Halton was in Spain for the Canadian Broadcasting Corporation, and Robert Capa (André Friedmann), Hungarian-born news photographer, began his career as a

---

2   Only much later, about 1955, did it become clear that Philby had become a Communist agent before his graduation from Cambridge in 1933, and later a double agent. While serving the London General Press and then the *Times* in Spain, he was a secret agent for the Comintern and continued so when representing the *Times* in Berlin during part of 1939. In France, as a war correspondent early in 1940, he became a double agent in the British Secret Service.

At Cambridge, Philby had formed a close friendship with two fellow students, Donald MacLean and Guy Burgess, both also to become Communist agents. Out of the university, Burgess was on the foreign desk at the *Times,* and then a news writer for the BBC. Burgess and MacLean later were with the British Foreign Office, including assignments to Washington, where they also acted as secret agents for the Kremlin. With their espionage activities revealed in the 1950s, both took refuge in Moscow.

Philby continued in journalism after the war. He was in Beirut, writing for the London Sunday *Observer* and covering the Middle East while acting as a triple agent, not only for Moscow and for the British Secret Intelligence Service but also for the Central Intelligence Agency of the United States. Sam Pope Brewer, who had been in Burgos with Philby, also was in Beirut reporting the Middle East for the *New York Times.* In 1958, Brewer's wife divorced him and married Philby in 1959. By then, Burgess and MacLean were living in Moscow, employed by the Soviet government. Shortly after, Philby's complex activities as a secret agent at last were revealed. In 1962 he joined his friends in Moscow, followed there sometime later by his wife.

This almost incredible story is told by E. H. Cookridge in *The Third Man* (1968), and references also appear in William Stevenson's book, *A Man Called Intrepid* (1976). It is told even more fully by Phillip Knightley, with Bruce Page and David Leitch, in *The Philby Conspiracy* (1975) and by Andrew Boyle in *The Fourth Man: The Definitive Account of Kim Philby, Guy Burgess and Donald MacLean and Who Recruited Them to Spy for Russia* (1980).

3   Martha Gellhorn, Hemingway's third wife, continued as a *Collier's* correspondent in Finland (1939), China (1940–41), and in Italy, France, Germany, and England. Following a divorce in 1946, Hemingway married Mary Welsh, formerly Mrs. Noel Monks when both were members of the *Daily Express* bureau in Paris. She also was in wartime London for *Time* magazine. Gellhorn in 1953 became the second wife of Thomas S. Matthews, then editor of *Time.* They were later divorced, and she made her home in London, a writer for the *Guardian*, to the time of her death in 1983.

photo-journalist for *Life* magazine. His wife was killed as she assisted him in the battle zone.

Among other correspondents so far unmentioned, the Agence Havas was represented in Spain during the war by André Chateau and Le Lorrain, who were wounded, Albert Grand, who was arrested, and Jean Rollin, André Vincent, Jean Botto, Martinez Barrio, and Jean d'Hospital. For Reuters, there were Alexander Graeme Clifford, Joseph Swire, Roland Winn, John Allwork, and A. Frank Tinsley.

The Associated Press had H. Edward Knoblaugh, John Lloyd, Richard G. Massock, Charles P. Nutter, Charles Foltz, Jr., Edward Kennedy, Robert B. Parker, Jr., Lloyd Lehrbas, Elmer W. Peterson, James C. Oldfield, Henry Cassidy, Robert Okin, John P. McKnight, Dwight L. Pitkin, and Ramon Blardony. Most were experienced in coverage in Europe, and some in Latin America and Asia.

In the same supplementation of coverage in Spain, the United Press had Jean DeGandt, Leon Kay, Irving Pflaum, Jan Yindrich, Harold Peters, Stephen Wall, Everett Holles, Robert Letts Jones, Burdett Bolloten, Edward G. DePury, and Harold G. Ettlinger. The International News Service had Kenneth T. Downs and William Lee Dixon. The British United Press had Herbert M. Clark.

Correspondents for newspapers, other than those previously mentioned, included Edmond Demaitre for *Excelsior* of Paris; a M. Flash for *Le Journal;* and a M. Delaprée of *Paris-Soir,* who died of wounds received during the bombing of Madrid.

Others for newspapers of the United States included George Axelsson, *New York Times;* James M. (Don) Minifie, Walter B. Kerr, and Robert Neville, *New York Herald Tribune;* Richard Mowrer, *Chicago Daily News;* Frank C. Hanighen, *New York Post;* and Saville R. Davis, *Christian Science Monitor.*

For the British press, the *Morning Post* received reports from Karl Robson. When that paper was merged with the *Daily Telegraph* in 1937, Robson remained as its representative in Spain, but reports also were received from Eric Dawnton, Alan Dick, Mortimer Durand, René MacColl, and B. Pembroke Stephens. The latter was formerly in Berlin, but was reassigned to Shanghai in 1937. Virginia Cowles, U.S.-born, wrote for the *Daily Telegraph,* for the *Sunday Times,* and for the Hearst newspapers in the United States.

For the *Daily Express,* other staffers included Sydney Smith, Hessell Tiltman, formerly in Tokyo, and Keith Scott-Watson, until he switched to the *Daily Herald.* Patrick Balfour wrote for the *Evening Standard.* Henry Buckley was with the Republican forces for the *Times.* Claud Cockburn, using the pseudonym of "Frank Pitcairn," wrote from the Republican side for the Communist party *Daily Worker* in London. The *Daily Mail* received reports from Harold G. Cardozo, Major General H.

F. C. Fuller, Randolph Churchill, son of Winston Churchill, and from U.S.-born Frances Davis. Lorna Wood wrote for the *Manchester Guardian,* and her husband, Joseph Swire, wrote for Reuters.

After nearly three years, the civil war came to an end in March 1939, the forces of the republic surrendering to the superior military power of the Insurgents. Great damage had been done to Madrid and other cities. Thousands of refugees fled the country, mostly to France. Atrocities had occurred on both sides, and many suffered mixed loyalties during the period. More than a million soldiers and civilians were estimated to have been killed in the fighting.

The term "fifth column" or "fifth columnist" was a heritage of the war. It derived from the fact that four columns of the Insurgent army were directed at Madrid. That army also received support from inside the city from Falangist members and sympathizers who were referred to as a "fifth" column. By later definition, it was held to be a group within a country "acting traitorously and subversively" because of sympathy with an enemy.

With the war at an end, a new Spanish Nationalist government under General Franco was formed in Madrid by the Falangists. Franco headed the totalitarian regime until his death in 1975. When the European war began in September 1939, six months after the end of the civil war, Franco declared Spain's neutrality. Considering the assistance given to the Insurgents by Nazi Germany and Fascist Italy, Spain's professed neutrality was regarded with caution and skepticism by Great Britain, France, and the United States.

The Franco regime brought into being within Spain a press and radio organization comparable with those in Fascist Italy and Nazi Germany. The Fabra news agency dating from 1865 had ceased to function in October 1936, ending its long Havas news-exchange relationship. So far as it survived, Fabra was placed in charge of the Republican government's Ministry of Foreign Affairs. Luis Amato, its director in the later years, had taken refuge in France late in August. Interim directors followed, but such world news as reached Spain came mostly by mail and radio, and appeared in print only in small surviving news sheets.

The Falangist party established its own official news agency in 1939. Titled Agencia Efe, it represented a Spanish phonetic rendition of the letter "F." This also had been the initial for the old Fabra agency, for former smaller services, Faro and Febus, and for the Falangist party. With its headquarters in Madrid after the war ended, and with branch offices soon established, Efe received world news for distribution from Italy's Stefani agency, Germany's DNB agency and Transozean service, and some rewritten from the British BBC shortwave broadcasts. Efe thus provided a foreign news report, while domestic news in Spain was gathered and distributed by a CIFRA agency.

The Agencia Mencheta dating from 1882 and specializing in sports news was permitted to resume, and so also was the Agencia Logos, a Catholic news service that had started in 1928. Both were based in Madrid. A beginning was made in the development of radio stations in the larger cities, which became the Network of Stations of the Movement (Red de Emisoras del Movimento), referred to as REM. News for broadcast was received from EFE–CIFRA, but the emphasis was on entertainment.

New papers appeared, and *Arriba,* a Madrid morning paper, was established as the official organ of the Falangist party. It was produced in the former office of *El Sol,* which was suppressed. Some earlier papers reappeared under strict control. Among them were the tabloid *ABC,* featuring illustrations, *Ya,* a Catholic paper, and *Informaciones,* a business daily. All were of Madrid. Six Barcelona papers reappeared, including *La Vanguardia* and the *Diario de Barcelona.* Others resumed in Alicante, Avila, Bilboa, Burgos, Cadiz, Leon, Oviedo, Salamanca, Seville, as well as in other towns. Most were in tabloid format, and the emphasis was on illustrations and entertainment features, rather than on basic or "hard" news.

Although Portugal was under a dictatorial government after 1933, Lisbon gained importance as a news center in the years following because Spain was so embroiled in civil war. It gained further importance when the European war began in 1939. Proclaiming its neutrality, its sincerity was not questioned. Lisbon became a key point in a system of commercial air transport across the Atlantic introduced by Pan American Airways in June 1939, the port of European arrival and departure. Traffic moved to and from New York and South America, from London and cities throughout Europe, and indirectly to and from the Middle East and Asia. Persons of neutral countries and warring countries rubbed elbows in hotels and restaurants. Newspapers and publications of all countries were available, rumors and bits of information were to be picked up, and espionage and propaganda were part of daily life. As never before, staff correspondents for news agencies and newspapers of various countries were assigned to Lisbon.

Conditions in the Soviet Union prior to World War II reflected economic realities as well as interpretations of the Communist ideology, manifested in the brutal and paranoid policies of Josef Stalin. Since becoming head of the party and government following the death of Lenin in 1924, his efforts were directed at consolidating his powers through the elimination of all rivals.

Correspondents found reporting news in the Soviet Union difficult, with roadblocks on every hand to gathering and transmitting information. The people of the nation were equally handicapped in the information made available to them.[1]

A strict censorship had been applied to news matter leaving the Soviet Union since the establishment of the Communist regime. Early in 1939, however, a significant change occurred in that system at a time when Maxim Litvinov was replaced as foreign commissar by Vyacheslav Molotov.

Correspondents were summoned to a night session at the Foreign Commissariat on May 4. There the chief of the Press Department and supervisor of the censorship informed them that, by Molotov's instruction, "from today the preliminary censorship of messages to the foreign press is abolished." Correspondents were warned, however, that each would be held responsible for excluding from his own reports any matter that might be judged hostile to the USSR or injurious to its prestige. This was the first use anywhere of a "responsibility censorship" as a form of control under which a correspondent was expected to censor his own copy.

In August 1939, to the astonishment of nearly all persons, the Soviet Union and Nazi Germany signed nonaggression and trade treaties. A few days later, on September 1, both Germany and the Soviet Union,

---

1 For a detailed account of reporting and the difficulties correspondents faced in the Soviet Union see Desmond, *Crisis and Conflict: World News Reporting Between Two Wars, 1920–1940,* pp. 432–43.

although acting separately, invaded and occupied parts of Poland, so bringing World War II to Europe. In November, the Soviet Red Army also attacked Finland, which surrendered in March 1940. Meantime, the three Baltic Republics had been made part of the Soviet Union.

Eight months after the "responsibility censorship" had been instituted, with no word that it was "temporary," it ended as suddenly as it began. The Foreign Commissariat, on December 29, 1939, explained the suspension as appropriate "because of international conditions and . . . because in the Soviet government's view, results of the abolition of censorship have not been satisfactory to them."

The reinstituted censorship in the Press Department was no longer the "open" censorship of the 1921–39 period. In those years, a correspondent met directly with a censor and might discuss points with him. Under the restored censorship, the censor acted independently and removed any references in reports regarded as affecting the security of the Soviet Union. It was denied that this was in any way a military censorship. "Objective" criticism was not to be barred, correspondents were assured, but neither was any definition offered to indicate what might or might not be regarded as objective. The only concession helpful to the correspondents was a recognition of international regulations approved at the 1932 International Telegraphic Union conference in Madrid whereby a sender was to be notified of any change in a message to be transmitted. Elsewhere, that notification often was delayed, possibly robbing a report of its news value, but in Moscow a censor notified the correspondent promptly by telephone if he objected to some reference. Usually a compromise was reached, but the correspondent also had the right to withdraw the dispatch. Censors were on duty no later than 1 A.M., however, and not again until 10 A.M. Moscow Radio broadcast its Tass agency version of the news at 3 A.M., at least seven hours before correspondents could send out their reports on the same subjects, thus crippling the news value of the dispatches. One western editor cited this Moscow procedure as a "squeeze play" by which correspondents there were denied the opportunity to report the news while it was still news.

---

*Poland to
the Balkans*

Smaller European countries affected by the economic dislocations of the 1930s, and some uneasy about Communist pretentions, also felt threatened after 1933 by the aggressions of the Italian Fascist government and even more by the German Nazi regime. The 1934 uprising of the Austrian Nazis and the assassination of Chancellor Dollfuss, the

Nazi move into the Rhineland in 1936, and the Spanish Civil War, which began in the same year, were all extremely unsettling throughout Europe.

Most countries did little beyond protest the rising sense of insecurity on the continent and in the world. Some sought nonaggression pacts, and Denmark signed such a pact with Germany in 1939, and the adjacent Baltic republics of Latvia and Estonia did the same. A year later, both were occupied by the Soviet Union and Denmark was under Nazi military occupation. Sweden reactivated its military forces but sought to remain neutral as the dangers increased. Finland rejected nonaggression treaties with both the Soviet Union and Germany. Its relationship with the Soviets remained delicate while the rising Nazi element in Finnish politics further complicated matters. A year after the 1939 nonaggression pact between Germany and the Soviet Union, Finland lost territory after a Soviet attack but managed to remain an independent nation.

Poland had regained its identity as a nation after World War I, having been partitioned between Prussia, Austria-Hungary, and Russia in 1795. Internal conflicts were common under the dictatorship of General Joseph Pilsudski, one of the founders of the republic, until his death in 1935. His successor General Edward Smigly-Rydz also exercised a military control and strikes and violence were common during 1937–38.

The Polish government signed a nonaggression "press pact" with Nazi Germany, ostensibly to place a mutual curb upon the publication of hostile material in the newspapers or as broadcast by radio. No such curb was observed by the German media, which continued to attack the Versailles-imposed Polish corridor to the Baltic and the League-administered free city of Danzig. Poland forced Lithuania to open its frontier in 1938, and then moved into the Teschen area of eastern Czechoslovakia early in 1939.

Rumania also had been considerably in the news since the death of King Ferdinand in 1927 and the renunciation of the throne by Crown Prince Carol two years earlier. Under the regency established for five-year-old King Michael I, the National Peasant Party introduced reforms, including abolition of an existing press censorship. But conditions in the country remained unsettled and Prince Carol was asked to assume the throne. At the same time the Iron Guard, a Fascist-oriented and anti-Semitic group, attracted a considerable following. Its opposition to the king led to continued unrest until Carol assumed control of the government in 1938 and suspended the consitution. His dictatorship was opposed by the Iron Guard and the struggle for control of the nation reached a crisis point when Germany gained full control of Czechoslovakia in April 1939.

The Berlin-Moscow treaties in August of that year included designs on Rumania's economy, which ended prospects for good relations with the Soviet Union. Nazi Germany had been angered by Rumanian support given to Czechoslovakia and by an alliance with Poland, and Rumania's support of League of Nations sanctions against Italy during the Ethiopian War had made an enemy of Mussolini. Even though Rumania declared its neutrality at the beginning of World War II, a pro-Nazi cabinet invited a German military mission into the country. King Carol was forced to abdicate by the Iron Guard, and his son at nineteen came to the throne as Michael I.

Coverage of this complex sequence of events in Rumania was reported for the world press by the Agence Havas until 1939, and then by the AP and the UP, both of which sent staff correspondents to Bucharest, as did individual newspapers. The U.S. media gave less attention to the events themselves than to Carol's personal problems, centering around relations with his mistress, Magda Lepescu. The Rumanian press, chiefly a Bucharest press, had limited circulation or influence beyond the country because of the language barriers.

Hungarian economic problems during the 1930s resulted in unsettled political conditions. Extreme right-wing and militaristic views and anti-Semitism gave rise to a Nazi-type Arrow Cross group within the country. Led by Ference Szálasi, this organization was dedicated to a recovery of Hungarian territory lost in the 1919 peace settlements through assignments to Rumania, Czechoslovakia, and Yugoslavia. Admiral Nicholas Horthy, regent since 1920, found himself to be an unwilling candidate for the throne in 1937 when political forces within the country sought to restore the monarchy. In March 1938 the German annexation of Austria placed the Nazi military power on the Hungarian border. Horthy's visit to Berlin soon after was rewarded by a piece of Czechoslovakia and a part of Ruthenia, which gave Hungary a common border with Poland.

Efforts by Hungary to win support from France and Great Britain following the Berlin visit failed. Relations with the Nazis also cooled and, for its own safety, Hungary favored a policy agreeable to the Axis governments. It yielded to German pressure, withdrew from the League of Nations in April 1939, and joined Germany, Italy, and Japan in signing the Anti-Comintern Pact. Although it tried to maintain a strictly neutralist position, it was forced to allow German troops right of passage across its territory in their move into Bulgaria in 1940.

Press coverage in Hungary until 1940 centered in Budapest, with world reports provided through Havas, Wolff (DNB after 1933), AP, UP, and INS, and through stringers and visiting correspondents for newspapers and radio. The general situation was so volatile and confusing that, with public interest also limited, it received generally unsatisfactory treatment in other countries and was not well understood. As in

Rumania and Czechoslovakia as well, the language of the Hungarian press kept it out of general European circulation.

Yugoslavia's internal problems stemmed largely from the differences among the Croatians, Serbians, and the centralized government in Belgrade headed by King Alexander. A new constitution acceptable to the Croatians in 1931 gave promise of a unified country, but the elections of November were disappointing and brought a renewal of the demands by the Croat Peasant party. The king sought reassurance and security through alliances with other countries and from the Nazi regime in Germany then just coming into power in 1933. He signed a Balkan Pact with Bulgaria and Turkey in February 1934 and a trade agreement with Germany in June. France was fearful of this latter action, lest it be a prelude to Yugoslavia's withdrawal from the Little Entente. King Alexander, persuaded to visit France and in Marseilles on October 9, 1934, was assassinated in an open car along with France's Foreign Minister Barthou. The assassin was a Croat then living in Hungary, and the killing raised a threat of war which the League of Nations intervened to prevent.

Although only ten years old, Peter II came to the throne and his father's cousin, Prince Paul, was named regent. In an effort to unify the country and to maintain a neutrality in case of war the regent made economic and cultural concessions to the Croatians. A 1937 treaty seemed to tie Yugoslavia closer to the Rome-Berlin Axis, but in 1939 the Axis supported a military *coup* which overthrew the regent, who fled to Greece. The boy-king escaped to England by means of a British Royal Air Force flying boat.

Bulgaria's political upheavals between the wars were often violent, and frontier incidents continued to create tension with Yugoslavia and Greece. In addition to the impact of the world economic crisis, the country felt the influence of the new Nazi government in Germany as early as 1934. Two years before, Bulgaria had denounced further reparations payments under the Versailles peace treaty, and it refused to join the Balkan Pact of 1934 which supported the payments. A *coup* by army officers forced King Boris to accept a military dictatorship in May 1934. All political parties were abolished and some schools were closed. Students were required to join a youth organization comparable to those in Fascist Italy and Nazi Germany. Political newspapers were suppressed and others placed under censorship. The dictatorship lasted less than a year and the king in January 1935 aligned himself with the Balkan League, which conceded Bulgaria's right to rearm, regardless of the 1919 treaties. Germany supplied rearmament materiel to the country, but Bulgaria did not indicate an acceptance of Nazi concepts. Although it was the recipient of a $10 million loan from Britain and France for rearmament in 1938, German pressure eventually resulted in Bulgaria signing a Tripartite Pact with Germany and Italy in 1941.

Greece had become a republic in 1924 and the political and economic turmoil of the early 1930s caused five changes of government between 1932 and 1935, one attempted *coup d'état,* and a sharply contested presidential election. A revival of royalist sentiment in the country resulted in the return of George II to the throne in November 1935. He supported the League of Nations-sponsored sanctions against Italy for its invasion of Ethiopia in 1935–36, and he also insisted upon a general amnesty for political prisoners. To forestall Communist influence in parliament, the king agreed to a *coup* by General Metaxas, the premier, who proclaimed martial law, dissolved parliament, and instituted a censorship of the press. Greece became a signatory to the Balkan Pact and was on friendly terms with Britain and France on the eve of World War II.

Albania gained its independence from Turkey in 1912 and was a republic from 1925 to 1928. In the latter year it was organized into a kingdom with its former president, Ahmed Bey Zogu, becoming King Zog I. The king's reforms and dictatorial rule created many internal problems. His objection to Italian influence resulted in Italy sending a naval force to the country in 1934 to enforce treaty obligations and further controls, including control of the Albanian military forces and the right of Italians to colonize certain areas. Italian control of trade and finances was established in 1936. King Zog's resistance to an Italian-style Fascist party led Italy to seize control of the country in April 1939, at a time when world attention was focused on Germany's seizure of Czechoslovakia. With the flight of the king and his family to Greece and thence to Turkey, the Albanian assembly voted for union of the country with Italy, which used the territory as a base for an invasion of Greece in 1940.

Turkey became a republic in 1923 and the resultant geographic and political changes brought the country quickly from its ancient caliphate to the beginnings of a modern state. President Mustapha Kemal became known as Kemal Atatürk in 1935, and other personal and place name changes occurred. Constantinople became Istanbul and Angora became Ankara, the new capital. Turkey joined the League of Nations in 1932, and was regarded as a force for peace both in Europe and Asia. Although Islam remained the state religion, the wearing of the fez was forbidden and the veil for women was discouraged. Polygamy was abolished, civil marriage made compulsory, divorce legalized, and other religions recognized. A European system of civil, criminal, and commercial law was introduced. Under the electoral system, women were allowed to vote. The Latin alphabet was used on all printed matter, and was decreed to be used exclusively by 1943.

With the rising crisis in Europe in 1936, Turkey applied to the signators of the 1923 Treaty of Lusanne for the right to refortify the Dardanelles straits. A distrust of Italian intentions in the eastern Mediterranean had led to an earlier decision by Turkey to begin rearmament in 1934. Although it had close trade relations with Germany, Turkey concluded a mutual assistance agreement with Britain and France in June 1939 and remained neutral throughout World War II until its final days. The developments in Greece and Turkey were reported through the 1930s by correspondents and stringers for the news agencies and by resident and visiting correspondents.

Italy and Germany 4

From 1937, the aggressive purpose of Italy, Germany, and Japan had reached a point of no return. Shortwave radio broadcasts from those countries since 1932 had become increasingly hostile to their main propaganda targets of Great Britain, France, and the United States. These broadcasts in appropriate languages were attempts to shape opinion in the Middle East, Asia, and Latin America. Efforts also were made to subvert and control newspapers, particularly in Latin American countries.

France and Great Britain in the mid-1930s tried to counteract the radio propaganda assault by introducing corrective foreign-language broadcasts of their own. Since the United States was being misrepresented in programs broadcast to South America by the Axis powers, to the detriment of the "good neighbor" policy of the Roosevelt administration, the U.S. joined with Britain in establishing "listening posts" to learn more precisely what was being said and to whom.

One result of this effort was the formation by the U.S. government in 1938 of a Division of Cultural Relations in the Department of State. Headed by Dr. Ben Cherrington of the University of Denver, its purpose was to facilitate an inter-American cultural exchange intended to defuse the Axis propaganda. Financial and technical aid also was extended by the U.S. government to private broadcasters to enable them to direct programs to Latin America. It gave its support to monitoring services associated with the Princeton University School of Public and International Affairs in the east and with Stanford University in the west.

As the war began in Europe in 1939, an even more aggressive German propaganda campaign in Latin America induced the United States to form a Council of National Defense in August 1940. It then replaced the Division of Cultural Relations with an Office for the Coordination of Commercial and Cultural Relations Between the American Republics in the Department of State. In July 1941 this became the Office of the Coordinator of Inter-American Affairs (CIAA), headed by Nelson A. Rockefeller. Its function was the formulation and execution of programs to further the national defense and strengthen the bonds between the nations of the Western Hemisphere through radio, press, film, and other appropriate means. With the U.S. entrance into the war in December 1941, this became more simply the Office of Inter-American Affairs (OIAA), still directed by Rockefeller, with much the same purpose. Except for the World War I Committee on Public Information (CPI), headed by George Creel in 1917–18, it was the first and only U.S. government agency holding a propaganda purpose to that time.

In Italy the controlled press by 1937 often indulged in bitter references to the "pluto-democracies," meaning Great Britain, France, and the United States. Leaders in such attacks included Dr. Virginio Gayda, editor of *Il Giornale d'Italia* of Rome, known for its expression of official government views on foreign affairs; Mario Appelius, writer for Mussolini's *Il Popolo d'Italia* of Milan; and Giovanni Ansaldo, editor of *Il Telegrafo* of Leghorn. The latter paper was owned by Count Galeazzo Ciano, Mussolini's son-in-law and by then also minister of foreign affairs.

For correspondents in Italy, sources of news became fewer, less accessible and less reliable. The Foreign Press section, as introduced within the Ministry of Popular Culture in 1937, headed by Guido Rocca, did schedule news conferences. They followed what by then had become a Berlin procedure, but Commendatore Giovanni Bosio, usually conducting the meetings, seldom had anything of news value to communicate. Mussolini had long since ceased to be available for interviews with foreign correspondents, as in the first years, and rarely even to members of the diplomatic corps. Other officials, if seen, were rarely helpful. Rumors, which were plentiful, were almost impossible to prove or disprove. Contradictory versions on some important matters were equally difficult for reporters to clear up.

The growing Fascist sensitivity to world opinion, along with a greater ideological arrogance, produced curious results. A ban on news coverage of the coronation of King George VI in London in May 1937 was an example, with the recall of Italian correspondents and diplomats and the exclusion of British publications from Italy. Another was the arrest of Giovanni Engely, former foreign editor of the staunch party-oriented *Il Lavoro Fascista* of Rome, because he gave a foreign correspondent advance information about Italy's intended December withdrawal from the League of Nations. In May 1938, with Hitler about to visit Rome for a meeting with Mussolini, Jules Sauerwein, the respected director of the substantial foreign service of *Paris Soir,* prepared to cover the event. He was advised, as a "matter of prudence," not to appear in Rome because he had taken a disapproving attitude toward the Rome-Berlin Axis and the recent German annexation of Austria.

Although the Fascist government had refrained from expelling foreign correspondents, with only two forced to leave the country in the thirteen years between 1922 and 1935, expulsion became a serious occupational hazard for newsmen in Italy after that time. No fewer than twenty-four were expelled in the three years between 1936 and 1939, with others in 1940 and later. The first of that group to go was Henry T. Gorrell of the United Press in 1936.

At mid-year in 1938, an anti-Semitic policy paralleling that in Germany was announced for Italy by Dino Alfieri, Minister of Popular Culture, by Roberto Farinacci, former general secretary of the Fascist party, and by Achille Starace, incumbent general secretary. Five foreign correspondents were promptly expelled under the provisions of that policy.

The most notable victim was Dr. Paul Cremona, a British subject born in Malta and educated in England. He was a resident of Italy for seventeen years, dean of the correspondent group, and represented the *Christian Science Monitor.* It was immediately proved that Cremona's family, far from being Jewish, had been Catholic for 300 years. There had been no complaint about his reporting from Italy. Fascist authorities nevertheless refused to admit any error in ordering his expulsion, and Cremona left for London. The other four correspondents expelled were Dr. Edward Kleinerer, a Pole representing the Jewish Telegraph Agency (JTA) of London and New York; Hans Hirschstein, who had written from Rome for the *Neues Wiener Tageblatt* of Vienna until the Nazi seizure of Austria a few months before and then had remained as a representative of the *Jerusalem Post;* Kurt Kornicker, a Milan stringer for Reuters and correspondent there for the *Prager Tageblatt* of Prague; and Otto Kitzinger of the *Pester Lloyd* of Budapest. Although protests were made to the Italian government on behalf of these five men by the Association of Foreign Correspondents in Rome, and also through diplomatic channels, they were obliged to leave the country.

Later in the year, on December 3, 1938, the Fascist government also issued an order effective on January 1 forbidding Italian citizens to work or write for foreign newspapers, news agencies, periodicals, or radio. It was estimated that about 200 persons would be affected throughout Italy, including stringers, photographers, and contributors to technical and general periodicals. Again, protests brought no change in the order.

One of the most prominent correspondents affected was Arnaldo Cortesi, Rome representative of the *New York Times* for seventeen years. He was the son of Salvatore Cortesi, who had retired in 1931 after twenty-nine years as chief of the Associated Press bureau in Rome. Arnaldo Cortesi left Italy and served the *New York Times* in Mexico City and Buenos Aires between 1939 and 1945. Succeeding him for the *New York Times* in Rome in 1939 was Camille M. Cianfarra, former second man in the bureau. He was of Italian heritage, but was unaffected by the order because he was U.S.-born.

Other foreign newspapers and news agencies were obliged to release several assistants from their Rome bureaus under the order. It was arranged, however, that Italians might continue as stringers in five other cities: Milan, Genoa, Naples, Florence, and Venice.

Aside from the five correspondents expelled in 1938 under the anti-Semitic policy, two others were ousted, Frank G. Smothers of the *Chicago Daily News,* and René Bovey of *Le Jour-Echo de Paris,* the *Journal de Genéve,* and Central News of London.

The pace mounted in 1939. Three new subjects calling for discretion on the part of correspondents were identified by Maxwell H. Macartney, Rome correspondent for the London *Times:*

> You never write anything that hints the lira isn't sound. You never write anything that might cast doubts upon the valor of the Italian army. And certainly, at no time, do you dare hint that the Duce is not a Gibraltar of good health.[1]

It was an offense against Mussolini that brought the expulsion in August 1939 of Herbert R. Ekins of the United Press, the twenty-fourth correspondent expelled in less than three years. The UP had distributed a dispatch under a London dateline saying that Mussolini had suffered a heart attack. Fascist authorities held Ekins responsible. Not only was he expelled, but the Rome bureau of the UP was ordered closed, and that of the British United Press as well. Both were reopened six days later, with Reynolds Packard, formerly in Prague, replacing Ekins.

Oliver Guyon of *Le Journal,* Paris, had been expelled earlier in 1939, not because of anything he wrote, but because of information he gave by telephone to the Agence Radio in Paris. The information was not even used by the agency and it was obvious that his telephone call had been monitored.

Others expelled in 1939 included Robert J. Hodel of the Swiss *Neue Zürcher Zeitung,* a former president of the Association of Foreign Correspondents in Italy; David Woodward, London *News-Chronicle;* Paul Gentizon, representing *Le Temps,* Paris, and the *Gazette de Lausanne,* Switzerland; A. E. Guillaume, *Le Jour,* Paris; and Richard Mowrer, *Chicago Daily News.*

A record number of correspondents were in Rome in 1935, with 125 in the membership of the Association of Foreign Correspondents. The

---

1   *Editor & Publisher,* July 15, 1939, p. 18.

largest national group at the time was German, with a sudden increase having followed the Nazi assumption of power. A similar increase had occurred in London and Paris, but there was reason to believe they were not necessarily all *bona fide* correspondents

While Italy was deeply involved in the Spanish Civil War from 1936–39, it also undertook an ambitious armament program in 1937. A naval construction program was added in 1938. The cost of the Ethiopian War and the participation in Spain caused a budgetary problem, a devaluation of the lira, and a rise in taxes. Italy's treaty with Yugoslavia and its support of a demonstration for the cession of Corsica and Tunisia was greatly disturbing to France, and Mussolini's visit to Libya in 1937, with its propaganda appeal to the Arab world, was no less disturbing to Great Britain, as was the Italian position in Spain and its naval pretensions in the Mediterranean. Britain's Prime Minister Neville Chamberlain sought a Mediterranean agreement with Mussolini early in 1938 and ratified it in November, although Italy had not met the terms. A month later in March, Germany annexed Austria without protest from Britain, France, the League of Nations, or Italy. By then, the European situation had become enormously strained, and Chamberlain's expectations were unrealistic beyond belief.

Germany

With Germany and Italy firmly associated in their support of the Spanish Insurgent forces in 1937, the Rome-Berlin Axis was reinforced. Through barter agreements, Germany had established trade relations in the southern European countries. By early 1938, the Nazi party was in position to advance its program bearing upon military, diplomatic, economic, and information procedures.

Hitler himself as president and chancellor assumed direction of the Ministry of War, with General Wilhelm Keitel and General Heinrich Hermann Walther von Brauchitsch in top command. Joachim von Ribbentrop became foreign minister, and Hermann Goering was economic dictator. Goebbels continued as propaganda minister, with Dr. Otto Dietrich, one of Hitler's oldest friends, as Reich press chief, becoming undersecretary. By that time, every government ministry and department had a press officer and the system for information control instituted in 1933 was virtually perfected.

Under this system, the press officer in each division of the government conferred every morning with the head of that division as to what information falling within its area of authority was to be released, what was to be withheld, what might be made known to the German press and radio for guidance but not for use, and what might be made available to foreign reporters. The press officer did not necessarily see reporters himself, much less help them obtain or verify information.

Later in the morning, the press officers of the various ministries and departments gathered for a conference at the Propaganda Ministry, attended by Dietrich or one of his deputies. Each press officer made his report as to what was to be released, and perhaps how it should be treated. These prospective items were approved, rejected, or modified, as Dietrich or his deputy considered appropriate. In this way, the day's budget of news was evolved, notes were taken, and replies to anticipated questions suggested, particularly on sensitive points.

The information to be distributed by the official Deutsches Nachrichten Büro was prepared and placed on the telegraphic circuits. Instructions also went by a special teleprinter network to thirty or more sub-offices of the Propaganda Ministry throughout the Reich for the use or guidance of officials dealing with the press and radio locally. For news originating in those areas, the suboffices usually made the necessary decisions, although Berlin could be queried on doubtful points. These DNB branch offices also forwarded information to Berlin, some for general redistribution as news.

With this groundwork and background in order, the first of three daily news conferences met at the Propaganda Ministry at 11 A.M. It was attended by representatives of the German press and radio, present primarily to receive information supplementing that made available through the DNB, to receive special instructions, and perhaps to ask questions, usually mild and routine. Failure to follow instructions given them in confidence made them subject to punishment, perhaps for treason. This conference usually was brief. If news developed later in the day that might call for a policy decision, the Press Department at the Ministry could be queried for guidance as a safeguard against trouble.

The other two daily conferences at the Propaganda Ministry were primarily for foreign correspondents, although German reporters might attend. A noon conference was intended particularly for representatives of foreign news agencies. The last conference of the day, at 4:45 P.M. was open to all, but intended especially for foreign newspaper and periodical correspondents and for foreign radio reporters.

The conferences held in this fashion since 1933 had not been fruitful. Information was given, but it was largely routine, and many questions were met by the reply, "hier ist nicht bekannt"—the equivalent of "there is no information on that" or of "no comment"—and correspondents tended to ignore the conferences.

Matters improved, however, after Dr. Dietrich became undersecretary and chief of the Press Department in the Propaganda Ministry in January 1938. At the same time, matters also improved at the Foreign Ministry. No regular news conferences had been held there since 1933, and officials questioned informally by correspondents were so cautious in responding, or themselves so inadequately informed that newsmen rarely visited that ministry.

This changed early in 1938. Correspondents received invitations to attend a third conference meeting three days a week at the Foreign Ministry at 5:30 P.M., following the 4:45 P.M. conference at the Propaganda Ministry across the Wilhelmstrasse. The new conferences were conducted by Dr. Karl Bömer, who had been a member of the faculty at the University of Berlin and was associated with the Deutschen Institut für Zeitungskunde, headed by Dr. Emil Dovifat, which was a center for instruction and research in journalism.

Bömer had traveled and lived abroad, and had been a delegate at the Press Congress of the World in Mexico City in August 1931. His English was fluent and colloquial, he was relatively young and his manner informal and friendly. In conducting the tri-weekly news conferences at the Foreign Ministry, it became obvious that he was able to speak with considerable authority. In responding to questions, he was willing to comment upon or to indicate the German reaction to events at home or abroad, and there was less tendency to suppress information. This attitude was refreshing and useful to correspondents.

At the Ministry of Propaganda, Dr. Dietrich sometimes appeared personally at the 4:45 P.M. conference and was high enough in the Nazi hierarchy to respond to questions with confidence and authority. Further improvement came after November 1938. The ministry's Press Department then was reorganized to include a Home Section for German journalists, and a Foreign Section for journalists of other countries. Direction of the Foreign Section was assigned to Dr. Bömer, and from that time he conducted the noonday and afternoon conferences for foreign correspondents at the Propaganda Ministry.

The Foreign Ministry conferences formerly conducted by Bömer were continued under Dr. Paul Schmidt, personal press attaché for Foreign Minister Ribbentrop. If he was absent, the meeting was conducted by one of his assistants, Braun von Stumm or a Herr Loese. The usual procedure was to have four to six officials of the Foreign Ministry seated at a long table at the head of the room. The correspondents present numbered fifteen to twenty-five until the German attack on Poland increased the attendance. The officials of the ministry opened the meetings with announcements, and sometimes gave what amounted to lectures. At times they brought in reports recently published abroad, usually to be termed "false," and refuted. Unlike the German newsmen, foreign reporters asked questions that sometimes made for a lively exchange, perhaps moderately useful in the production of news.

Beginning in June 1939, mimeographed copies of addresses of importance by Hitler and other government leaders were made available to the press and radio in advance. This had happened only rarely before. They were made ready in German, English, French, and Italian, which spared correspondents the delay and difficulties of making translations of material often long and complex, and perhaps under pressure of time to meet deadlines.

The improvements, including the news conferences at the two ministries, still were no substitute for free inquiry. Nor did they wholly meet the correspondents' news requirements. Yet they were somewhat useful because the Nazi government had so reduced other sources of information. Foreign reporters, while less constrained than those of Germany, were confronted thus by something like an advance censorship.

Diplomatic representatives of various countries sometimes were helpful in providing background and clarifying points, but they had to be discreet. The Moscow Radio, supplied with information moving through underground channels, sometimes broadcast detailed and frequently accurate reports of events in Germany within a few hours of their occurrence, even when such events were not reported in Germany itself. But it was difficult or impossible for correspondents to check the accuracy of such reports, to do so promptly, or to get the news past the censorship if they did.

In the same fashion, clandestine publications or newsletters within Germany were too biased to be dependable. Time was required to sift and check rumors, gossip and tips, or to follow up an item appearing in some newspaper. German individuals, however friendly, often were afraid to speak with foreign journalists. Even such established associations as Rotary International were forced to disband, and personal associations within clubs and churches languished, ceased, or were officially forbidden.

Correspondents judged too inquisitive, enterprising, or successful in piercing the Nazi wall of secrecy were courting trouble in a Germany concerned with military security. So the expulsions, common from 1933, continued in 1938–39. There might have been even more, but by 1938 most of those writing from Berlin, as from Moscow and Rome, found it realistic to temper their reporting and so continue their representation, rather than pit themselves against a government otherwise prepared to expel them. In short, they resorted to a self-censorship. Correspondents for the media of smaller countries became hesitant even about asking questions at the Propaganda and Foreign ministries' conferences, lest they be expelled for doing so. They sometimes prevailed upon their colleagues of the British and U.S. press, to ask questions on subjects holding interest primarily for the peoples of those other countries.

Short of expulsion, correspondents in Berlin were subject to other forms of pressure. There were blandishments or disguised bribes in the form of special opportunities to observe newsworthy events, visit selected areas, or to obtain interviews with officials, from Hitler down the list. Correspondents were equally subject to reprimands, however, and also had to be on guard against being tricked into the acceptance and use of false information deliberately planted to trap them into a position the Nazi government then might cite as demonstrating "inaccuracy" and "malice" as a pretext for expulsion.

Self-restraint by correspondents in Berlin was not easy. The Hitler government offended the world by its mistreatment of Jews within its own borders, by its rejection of the League of Nations and other agencies and procedures for the peaceful solution of the world's problems, its revival of a costly and threatening arms race, its participation in the Spanish Civil War, its purposeful use of economic weapons in Europe and Latin America, its generally aggressive propaganda campaigns, and its clear designs upon Poland. Inevitably, the presentation of the bare facts on such topics placed the Nazi regime in an unfavorable light. The German media could be controlled, but not the foreign media, and this was a matter of annoyance in Berlin.

Hitler, addressing the Reichstag in January 1937, advanced the idea that there could be no lasting peace among nations so long as "an international clique is allowed to poison the wells of public opinion." There was no misunderstanding his references to that "clique" as meaning the foreign correspondents in Berlin. He went on to propose the signature between nations of what soon were referred to as "nonaggression press pacts." Under such agreements, the form of a nation's government, the manner of its administration, and the manner in which its press functioned would be of concern to the individual nation alone, and not permissible subjects for any comment by the media of another nation.

The Nazi government actually did conclude press pacts during 1937 with Italy, Hungary, Austria, Poland, and a less formal one with Yugoslavia. Existence of the pacts did not seem to act as a restraint upon the German press, however, which commented adversely on Austria and Poland prior to the annexation of the first in 1938 and an attack upon the second in 1939.

The subject of such press pacts was raised again in September 1937 at the National Socialist Party Congress in Nuremberg. Goebbels and Dietrich charged that the press of other lands was "warmongering" and poisoning public opinion, and that individual correspondents were misrepresenting Germany. Freedom of the press, Dietrich asserted, was "a mask behind which modern bandits, war-mongers and vultures who feed on mankind hide their faces."

Hitler returned to the matter in what was for him a rather conciliatory speech to the Reichstag on February 20, 1938. Referring to Germany and Great Britain and France, he said that "the only thing that has poisoned and injured the common life of these two countries is the utterly unendurable press campaign which in these two countries has existed under the motto 'freedom of personal opinion.' " He went on to say:

> I do not understand it when I am told by foreign statesmen and diplomats that there are no legal possibilities in these countries for putting an end to the lies, for private matters are not at stake. It concerns the problems of the common lives of the peoples and States. We cannot shut our eyes to the consequences of these campaigns for it could so easily come to pass that in certain countries contemptible international lie manufacturers could generate such violent hatred against our country that gradually hostile public opinion would be created among us which the German people would not be able to resist. This is a danger to peace. I am no longer prepared to tolerate unanswered this unbridled slander. From now on we shall answer back and do so with National Socialist thoroughness.[2]

This would have seemed strange talk from the leader of a party and nation whose press in five years had earned a reputation for inaccuracy, for abusiveness, and often for malicious falsehood in references to other nations and peoples. It would have seemed strange talk except for the fact that Hitler himself in discussing propaganda in his book *Mein Kampf* had advanced the "big lie" technique as an effective method of procedure. The point of this was that even a falsehood, if repeated often enough, tended to gain acceptance. His proposal to respond to what he called "unbridled slander" with "national Socialist thoroughness" also was in the same spirit as the Italian Fascist "battle style" of writing already mentioned, and defended by Dino Alfiere, minister of popular culture in that government.

Hitler cited several reports in his speech that were published abroad and that he said were false. If so, it may have been because Germany at that time was alive with rumors that could neither be verified nor disproved under the tight control clamped on information sources by Nazi officials themselves. His references were peppered with accusations of "infamous falsehoods," and he repeated that "the damage wrought by such a press campaign is so great that henceforth we will no longer be willing to tolerate it without stern objections. This crime becomes espe-

---

2 *New York Times,* February 21, 1938.

cially evil when it obviously pursues the goal of driving nations into war."[3]

What Germany wanted, in plain terms, were press treaties that would stifle criticism and effect a censorship of the foreign press and radio to match the control maintained by the German government over its own media.

As a follow-up to Hitler's February 20 address, Dr. Dietrich spoke to a large gathering of diplomats and German and foreign newsmen in Berlin on March 7. Dietrich suggested that nonaggression press treaties be signed on a basis of mutual respect and understanding. He closed with an appeal for international cooperation for a world-wide press peace, in these words.

> We see it as the duty of the foreign correspondent to give his fellow-citizens an unprejudiced and truthful picture of a foreign land and people. Whoever has this conception of his profession can always be sure of our support. We shall not deny him the right of factual criticism. Whoever, however, has personal feelings of dislike or even hatred for the land of which he is a guest, that will bring him into conflict and, perhaps, make impossible objective reporting, should not come to us. By his tendentious writings he harms not only our country but his own also, and becomes the object of a distrust that must eventually lead to a break.
>
> In such cases we have employed expulsion, which is not a National Socialist discovery, but is employed wherever journalists ignore their duty and abuse hospitality. In such cases we have in the past employed expulsion and will employ it in the future.
>
> However, we understand the particular difficulties under which journalists work. We do not believe that every journalist who does not write like a National Socialist is a swine. We recognize that as a member of another people he thinks and feels differently from us, just as we expect Germans abroad to remain constantly conscious of their Germanism.[4]

Magnanimous as he was in conceding that a journalist might not be "a swine" merely because he did not write like a Nazi, Dr. Dietrich still

---

3 This particular Hitler speech, of which the portion dealing with press matters was only a small part, was regarded as so important, because of the mounting crisis in Europe, that the United Press transmitted it in full to the United States and to South America. Running more than 18,000 words, it was one of the longest single press transmissions across the Atlantic to that time. The text, made available in advance through the Ministry of Propaganda, was translated, checked back for accuracy, broken into 75 "takes," and sent on double-trunk teleprinter circuits from Berlin to London, relayed by cable and radiotelegraph circuits to New York and thence to Buenos Aires, with further distribution from both places.

4 Guido Enderis, "Press Amity Pacts Urged by Dietrich," *New York Times,* March 8, 1938; Guido Enderis, "Reich Asks Pacts to Control Press," *New York Times,* March 13, 1938, sec. E, p. 5.

suggested that the concept of liberty of the press was "one of the hollowest of all empty phrases that ever befogged the human mind."

"If newspapers everywhere would not only talk peace, but also keep the peace themselves," he said, "an atmosphere of mutual respect and understanding would be created that, within a few months, would accomplish what decades of futile efforts have failed to accomplish in making a peaceful world."

Dietrich referred to the nonaggression pacts already signed by Germany with Italy, Poland, Hungary, Yugoslavia, and Austria. Such pacts, he said, would be negotiated with other countries whenever the opportunity appeared. He compared such agreements with an agreement to halt the smuggling of cocaine. Lacking such an agreement, however, he repeated Hitler's warning that the Reich would not hesitate to retaliate in kind when it considered itself the victim of misrepresentation abroad.

The Hitler-Dietrich proposals were received scornfully in the United States—the more so when five days after Dietrich spoke German troops marched into Austria, one of the countries with which a press pact had been signed, and made it a part of the German Reich.[5] The proposal was received no less coolly in Great Britain, but the comments were milder in tone. British memories of World War I were keen, yet the nation's military strength in 1938 was such that the Chamberlain government understandably clung to the hope that existing differences in Europe might be peacefully settled. As efforts to "appease" the Fascist and Nazi governments already had been attempted, so some in England felt that Hitler intended to make signature of a nonaggression press pact a condition for a peaceful settlement.

In France and Great Britain, if not in the United States, there was some private recognition that Hitler might indeed have had some reason to question the assertions by political leaders that there were no "legal possibilities" for placing a control upon the press. Hitler must have been aware that the French press had been so manipulated in 1935–36 that it refrained from any serious objection to the Italian invasion and annexation of Ethiopia, and that it had been subject to control on other occasions. He was aware that the British press and radio had been silenced through most of 1936 during the monarchial crisis ultimately leading to the abdication of Edward VIII, and included also a censorship on incoming publications. He knew of the Defense of the Realm Act (DORA) and the Official Secrets Act, both providing for press re-

---

5   The U.S. reaction also was epitomized in a cartoon by Max P. Milians showing an armed Nazi climbing the Statue of Liberty, a bludgeon at his belt and a lash protruding from his pocket. He was inviting "Miss Liberty" to sign a "suggested press censorship pact." The Nazi was saying to her, "You stop telling the truth about me—und I won't print any lies about you! Is it agreed . . . ?"

straints. He knew of the group advocating a policy of "appeasement," with concessions already made to the Nazi government since 1935. He must have been aware that the appeasement policy was supported, within the press organization, by the *Times* and the Sunday *Observer* and possibly the *Daily Telegraph,* leading and influential newspapers. He surely knew that Prime Minister Chamberlain favored negotiation, rather than force, to meet the problems existing in Europe, and that view suggested compromise.

Geoffrey Dawson, editor of the *Times,* had written privately in 1937 that "I do my utmost, night after night, to keep out of the paper anything that might hurt their [the German] susceptibilities." In noting this, Francis Williams in his book *Dangerous Estate* (1957) also reports that Dawson at that period drove Norman Ebbutt, the paper's Berlin correspondent, "to despair by so emasculating his truthful dispatches as to destroy their purpose in reporting the extent of Nazi atrocities and ambitions."[6]

In 1937 the German press was represented in London by about 100 correspondents, far more than ever before. By contrast, there were only about fifteen British correspondents in Berlin. There was reason to believe that most of the German representatives were actually agents watching some 15,000 German refugees then in Great Britain, and that some were engaged in espionage and propaganda activities unrelated to legitimate journalism. The circumstances were such that the British government did take unprecedented action in August when the Home Office notified three German correspondents and the woman secretary of one of them that their permits to reside in Great Britain would be suspended a fortnight later. These were Werner von Crome of the *Berliner Lokal-Anzeiger* and his secretary, Franz Otto Wrede, assistant correspondent for the same paper, and Wolf Dietrick Langen of the Deutsches Nachrichten Büro, who had previously—and rather surprisingly—been expelled from Italy.

By way of retaliation, the German government immediately expelled Norman Ebbutt, correspondent in Berlin since 1925 for the *Times,* and a former president of the Foreign Press Association there. Ebbutt also was attacked in the German press in language that would have been unprintable in Anglo-Saxon newspapers, with his expulsion explained officially as having been based on lying, biased reports. Although the *Times* by tradition had defended its correspondents in any such circumstances and refused to replace a man expelled, Dawson not only had "emasculated" Ebbutt's dispatches but failed to support him. Ebbutt was crushed by the experience and retired. He was soon replaced in Berlin by James Holburn.

---

6 Francis Williams, *Dangerous Estate* (1957), pp. 274–75.

Ebbutt was the seventeenth foreign correspondent ordered to leave Germany between the establishment of the Nazi regime on January 30, 1933, and October 15, 1937. Five others departed voluntarily on the understanding that, if they did so, there would be no expulsion order, and thirteen more left voluntarily because they were Jewish and felt unwelcome and professionally handicapped. Two left because of threats to their safety and one because he was beaten by Nazi hoodlums following attendance at a Hitler speech at the Sportspalast in Berlin.

Although not correspondents, John Walter, son of one of the proprietors of the *Times,* and Rolf Kaltenborn, sixteen-year-old son of H. V. Kaltenborn, CBS radio news commentator, who were traveling together, also suffered violence from Nazis in Berlin. H. V. Kaltenborn himself, arriving in Berlin by air from London in August 1939, was denied the right to remain and was sent back to London on the next plane. Dorothy Thompson, a Berlin correspondent from 1920–28, who returned in August 1934 for the *Saturday Evening Post,* had much the same experience. She was ordered to leave "because of numerous anti-German" references in her writings.

Correspondents expelled included Ivan Bespalow of Tass and Lili Keith of *Izvestia;* both were arrested in Leipzig in September 1933. Noel Panter of the *Daily Express* was arrested in Munich in October. His apartment was searched, his papers confiscated, and he was charged with treason and deported. B. Pembroke Stephens, also of the *Daily Express,* was expelled in 1934 on charges of "news distortion." Others forced to leave in these first years of the Nazi regime included Andreas Rosinger, Tass; Bertil Svahnstrom of the Swedish TT agency; Erwin Wasserbaeck of the official Austrian ANA agency; Karl Robson of the London *Morning Post;* Theodor Steinthal of *Politiken,* Copenhagen; and Mario de Silva of *Il Lavoro Fascista,* Rome.

Among those leaving voluntarily were Edward L. Deuss, chief of the INS bureau in Berlin since 1931; Andreas Hecht, UP; Miles Bouton, *Baltimore Sun;* Oskar Jorgensen, *Social-Demokraten,* Copenhagen; Adolfph Nilsson, *Göteborgs Handels-och Sjöfartstidning;* Erst H. Regensburger, *Neue Zürcher Zeitung;* Erwin Kondor, *Neue Freie Presse,* Vienna; Abram Gartmann and Ilja Tschernjak, *Pravda,* Moscow. Two expelled late in 1937 were Paul Ravoux, a resident journalist in Berlin since 1919 and Agence Havas bureau chief there since 1933, and Herman Boschenstein of the *Basler Nachrichten.*[7]

---

7 A full list of correspondents expelled from Germany or leaving voluntarily between January 1933 and October 1937, with some details of the circumstances, appears in Vernon McKenzie's *Through Turbulent Years* (1938), pp. 237–38 and passim. See also "27 Correspondents Leave Germany Under Pressure of Nazi Regime," *Editor & Publisher,* April 6, 1935.

The problems that beset correspondents in Italy and Germany through 1937 became even more serious in 1938 and 1939. The year 1938 began with the Hitler speech of February and the Dietrich speech of early March, both emphasizing their proposed nonaggression press pacts. This subject was promptly overshadowed, however, by the German annexation of Austria in March, aggression against Czechoslovakia, a Munich conference on September 29, followed in 1939 by the ultimate seizure of Czechoslovakia and a full military attack on Poland, with all of Europe soon at war.

Vienna had been an important European center at least since the time of the Holy Roman Empire. It had been a center for the organized coverage of news of the Austro-Hungarian Empire, and all of southern Europe and the Balkans through much of the nineteenth century and since. Richard D. McMillan of the British United Press described the capital in 1930 as "a city kind to journalists." Perhaps somewhat extravagantly, he said:

> Outrivalling even Paris for gaiety, good-living and Gemeutlichkeit, the old capital of the Hapsburg Empire offered its journalistic wares on a silver platter; and the unfailing plethora of headline jewels was such that any correspondent who was sent to Vienna considered that he had been given the plum foreign assignment in all Europe.

Dr. Kurt Schuschnigg was chancellor of the dictatorial Austrian government since the assassination of Dollfuss in 1934, and he had maintained close relations with Mussolini. An agreement also had been reached with the German government in 1936, after which Schuschnigg undertook to rebuild the Austrian military forces, contrary to the 1919 treaties. His efforts toward restoring the Hapsburg monarchy was opposed by both Italy and Germany, and Austrian Nazi activity in the country resumed under the leadership of Arthur Seyss-Inquart.

German dissatisfaction with his efforts to find guarantees for the safety of Austria through support from Czechoslovakia, France, and the Little Entente, caused Hitler to summon Schuschnigg to a meeting at Berchtesgaden in mid-February 1938. There he was threatened and forced to yield to Nazi demands, which included the release of imprisoned Austrian Nazis, full recognition of the Austrian Nazi party, and the appointment of Seyss-Inquart as minister of interior. He became chancellor upon Schuschnigg's resignation on March 11.[8]

The German army marched into Austria the next day without resistance, and on March 13 Seyss-Inquart proclaimed Austria's union with Germany. On March 14, Hitler arrived in Vienna to take formal possession. A plebiscite on April 10 was reported to have produced a popular vote in Austria of 99.75 percent in favor of union with Germany.

At the time of the German invasion in 1938, Christopher Holme of Reuters gave the world its first news of that event. Paul Lemoult represented the Agence Havas. The German DNB agency understandably was prepared to provide full coverage. Alvin J. Steinkopf was chief of the Associated Press bureau, with Melvin K. Whiteleather, A. D. Stafford, and Louis Matzhold as assistants. Robert Best represented the United Press, and Alfred Trynauer was INS correspondent.

Marcel W. Fodor of the *Manchester Guardian* and the *Chicago Daily News* was dean of the resident foreign press corps and reported the occupation. G. E. R. Gedye reported for the *Daily Telegraph* and the *New York Times*. William L. Shirer, who happened to be present representing the Columbia Broadcasting System, was denied access to any microphone and flew to London to broadcast from there on the night of the invasion. Meanwhile, by telephone he had reached Edward R. Murrow, director of the CBS European service, who was in Warsaw and flew to Vienna. Fergus J. Ferguson, veteran Reuters correspondent, hastened to Vienna from Geneva, and Harry J. Greenwall of the *Daily Express* arrived from Paris.

G. Ward Price of the *Daily Mail* was another correspondent who happened to be in Vienna on the day of the invasion. Lord Rothermere, publisher of the *Daily Mail* since the death in 1922 of his brother, Lord Northcliffe, and Price himself, were commonly regarded in London press circles as personally favorable to the Fascists in Germany and Italy. Price was reported to have spoken to a group of Austrians "in broken German" on the occasion of the occupation, congratulating them and the country on their "hour of happiness." In his book, *Extra-Special Correspondent* (1957), Price continued to insist that the people of Austria showed "delight" at the time of the annexation. This might conceivably have been so had a mutually approved union taken place in 1931, but it was a dubious assessment when it occurred by force in 1938, and far more so in the perspective of 1957.

---

8 Schuschnigg was held under house arrest from March 12 to May 28, at Gestapo headquarters for seventeen months following, and then at Dachau concentration camp until May 1, 1945. For details see William L. Shirer, *The Rise and Fall of the Third Reich* (1960), pp. 352–53, and Schuschnigg's *Austrian Requiem* (1946). Seyss-Inquart was condemned at the Nuremberg war crimes trials and executed in October 1946.

The Germans were quick to place a control over press and radio representatives in Vienna and over communications facilities. Gedye was ordered to leave the city within three days, but then informed the next day that he could remain if he would treat the news as "incidents in an abnormal period." His efforts were obstructed, however, and a week later he was given twenty-four hours to leave, whereupon he went to Prague.

Hitler, on his arrival, proclaimed that Austria and Germany were one. Within a week or ten days most of the foreign reporters had left Vienna, either voluntarily or by order. Robert Best of the UP may have been the only resident correspondent to remain, which he did by choice. As part of Germany, the theory was that news of Austria would clear through Berlin.

Much of what had occurred in Germany following the Nazi assumption of power there in 1933, now occurred in Austria. The Amtliche Nachrichtenstelle Agentur (ANA), the official Austrian news agency since 1922, was closed, and the German DNB agency extended its operations to include Austria. A Vienna edition of the official Nazi newspaper *Völkischer Beobachter* was established. The same general regulations as existed in Germany concerning who might practice journalism and under what conditions were applied in Austria. A change also occurred in the press. Vienna daily newspapers closed included the *Amtliche Weiner Zeitung,* 235 years old, and the *Neue Freie Presse,* a respected daily since 1864. Both were merged with a third, the *Neues Wiener Tageblatt.*

Czecho-slovakia

Even before the Austrian seizure, world attention had been turned to Czechoslovakia as another potential target of German Nazi aggression.

That republic, with a population of about 15 million, was not much larger than Austria, but its agricultural-industrial balance was better and its general economy stronger. Racial and social differences required administration by a coalition government to meet conflicting interests of Bohemian and Moravian elements in the western area of the country, Slovaks in the central part, and Ruthenians in the east. An active member of the League of Nations, the republic also was a member of the Little Entente, along with Rumania, Yugoslavia, and France. Localized Nazi organization appeared most actively in the Sudeten area of the country, a kind of arc around its western edge, populated by about three million Germans or German-speaking persons. Konrad Henlein, with support from Berlin, formed a Sudeten Nazi party and urged union with Germany. From February 1938, this had tacit support from Hitler himself.

Nazi agitation in the Sudeten area continued through 1937, and a full crisis arose between March and May 1938 over a possible German occupation. The German seizure of Austria in March might have served as a precedent. It had the result of placing Germany on three sides of Czechoslovakia. Henlein visited London and Berlin, there were demonstrations and demands, statements and counter-statements, rumors of troop movements and then a massing of German forces on the Sudeten frontier.

Lord Runciman arrived in Prague in August 1938 to talk with Sudeten leaders and others. As part of the British appeasement effort, these talks solved nothing. German troop maneuvers began near the Sudeten border. France called up its reservists. A British fleet concentration was announced. Henlein, after talks with Hitler, rejected Czech compromise proposals.

Britain's Prime Minister Chamberlain flew to Berchtesgaden September 15. There Hitler indicated that he would go to war if necessary to gain the Sudeten area of Czechoslovakia. Chamberlain and Runciman, back in London, were joined there September 18 by France's Premier Daladier and Foreign Minister Georges Bonnet. They all advised Czechoslovakia to accept Hitler's terms without seeking arbitration or further negotiations. The *Times* under Dawson's editorial lead, gave its approval to the German demand. With no prospect of military support from any other country, the Czech government agreed to the German demands on September 21.

A storm of international disapproval had been directed at Germany since the seizure of Austria in March. There had been no response since 1937 to Nazi proposals for the signature of "nonaggression press pacts." Neither of these evidences of disapproval modified the violence of expression by Hitler or other spokesmen for the Berlin government in their demands for control of the Sudeten district of Czechoslovakia.

Chamberlain's second visit with Hitler over the crisis at a meeting at Godesberg on the Rhine near Bonn during September 22–23, 1938, resulted in Hitler raising his demands by claiming additional Czech territory. Demands for Czech territory also arose from Poland and Hungary. After much wavering and indecision, a conference was called at Munich for September 29–30. Chamberlain and Daladier and Hitler and Mussolini, attended by their foreign ministers, Halifax, Bonnet, Ribbentrop, and Ciano, without representation by Czechoslovakia, turned the Sudetenland over to Germany for military occupation the next day. It was understood that the rest of the country would have its frontiers guaranteed by Britain and France and that Hitler would make no further territorial demands in Europe. President Beneš of Czechoslovakia resigned five days after the conference and went to England. Later, he moved to the United States.

The Munich conference was covered by scores of foreign correspondents. In London, Geoffrey Dawson, editor of the *Times,* so "doctored" his parliamentary correspondent's account of a speech of resignation in the House of Commons by the First Lord of the Admiralty, Alfred Duff Cooper, that the correspondent resigned. Dawson, still the appeaser, also forced the paper's central European correspondent, Douglas Reed, to leave the *Times* because his book, *Insanity Fair,* took a negative view of the Munich settlement. Some time later, the *Daily Telegraph* also recognized German sensibilities by dismissing G. E. R. Gedye as its central European correspondent after his book, *Fallen Bastions* (1939), criticized the British government position at Munich.

The French press and radio, possibly at the request of Daladier, had omitted many references that might have offended the Nazi leadership. But Germany itself spent substantial sums, particularly between March and November 1938, to buy the support of venal French journals and journalists, even as the Italian government had done during its Ethiopian venture.

Newspapers published in vulnerable countries adjacent to Germany yielded to direct or implied warnings and were understandably cautious about what they published. The newspapers and periodicals of Italy, Spain, and Japan, as well as of the Soviet Union, each subject to their own government restraints and reflecting the policies of those governments, were not disposed to be critical of Germany. Some newspapers and governments of Latin America were subject to or responsive to German and Italian propaganda and financial manipulation.

Speaking in the House of Commons after the Munich conference, and feeling the criticism of those disapproving its results, Prime Minister Chamberlain remarked that "it is not one of the characteristics of the totalitarian states to foul their own nests!" This was taken by some to mean that he felt a substantial portion of the British press was behaving less admirably than the German press.

The press and radio of the United States were the most outspoken media in the world at this period, and most informative as to Axis activities and policies, but the media of the United Kingdom and the British Commonwealth countries were not far behind. This was an important segment of the international media group and an irritant to the Nazi regime. Speaking at a party congress in Weimar on November 7, 1938, Hitler said that Germany would not disarm until the democracies put an end to "warmongering" against the Reich. This was one of the early uses of that word, which became a cliché in later propaganda campaigns by the Soviet Union.

"In authoritarian states," Hitler said, in another demonstration of the "big lie" technique, "warmongering naturally is not permissible, for their governments are obligated to see to it that there is not any warmongering. But in the democracies the governments have only one duty, that is freedom, and if necessary even to agitate for war!" But as he spoke, Hitler was preparing to complete the Nazi seizure of Czechoslovakia and planning an all-out military attack on Poland.

Mobilization of the Media 5

The rapidly moving sequence of events in Europe during August and September of 1938 brought a mobilization of many of the most experienced reporters in the field of international affairs, representing many countries. Some had been in Austria. They gathered in Prague. They followed the meetings in Berchtesgaden and Godesberg as best they could, and they descended in great numbers upon Munich, even for so brief a meeting of the leaders of four nations as took place there. They came and went between Berlin and Rome, London and Paris. They rallied to report what Leland Stowe of the *New York Herald Tribune* called the approach of Europe and the world to "the thin edge of war." Also, as Stowe said, it was "the first great news event of world-wide significance in which, for days on end and from a half dozen different countries, radio had the whole world by the ears."

Since 1930 shortwave radio broadcasts had been added to the medium wave to provide listeners with general news programs supplemented by very "special events" reported from almost any part of the globe, including the voices of government leaders and other persons of prominence. As transmitted by such networks as the BBC in the United Kingdom, Radiodiffusion Française in France, the NHK in Japan, the NBC, CBS, and MBS in the United States, and others, radio programs were reaching millions of persons by 1938, the largest audiences ever known.

It had become the practice by 1938 to call upon experienced newsmen to report the news by radio, to describe events as they occurred, to "comment" upon events or "analyze" them. Many prepared their own scripts for broadcast, others had scripts prepared for them, or were "news readers," as they were specifically called in Great Britain. Some who were regularly on the air became known by name and by voice, both as heard over local stations and over networks. So also the voices of government leaders and political personalities became familiar to listeners.

One of the experienced newsmen to become a radio journalist and participate in the creation of what was to become known as "electronic journalism" as contrasted to the journalism of print, was H. V. Kaltenborn, broadcasting first for station WJZ in New York in 1922, for the National Broadcasting Company network from 1926–29, for the Columbia Broadcasting System network in 1929–40, and then for NBC again. Thoroughly acquainted with Europe, and a linguist, he also had broadcast from Spain during the civil war, but was usually based in New York. The German seizure of Austria in March 1938, Kaltenborn later said, brought to radio networks a full realization of "the importance of having a competent staff of newspapermen stationed in key capitals of Europe to cover what seemed to be an increasing number of diplomatic crises." This was doubly so from the time of Munich.

Since 1932, when international shortwave radio broadcasting had become technically possible, the BBC, the three networks of the United States, and some other radio organizations had been developing staff representation to provide coverage. Where they lacked that representation, they commonly recruited experienced newspaper and news agency correspondents as stringers to meet such needs as might arise. By the time of the Munich conference, these organizations were well established, and grew stronger from that period.

Kaltenborn himself made history on that occasion. Before, during, and after the Munich conference, he broadcast every aspect of the crisis. With peace in the balance, he lived, ate, and slept for three weeks in the Columbia Broadcasting System studios in New York. His task was to report each development and assess its importance. He made 102 talks of varying length, cutting into programs in progress when necessary to reach listeners over 115 stations affiliated in the network. Nearly all of the talks were without script, "extemporized under a pressure I had never before experienced in seventeen years of broadcasting," he wrote later. "News bulletins were handed me as I talked. Speeches of foreign leaders had to be analyzed and sometimes translated while they were being delivered. . . . I had to keep a constant eye on the control room for signs telling me when I was on or off the air."

With two-way transmissions, hookups and cue-channels by then existing in the advancing techniques of communication, Kaltenborn was able,

> to talk back and forth with newsmen in different foreign countries via transatlantic telephone while all America listened in. On several occasions I was able to transmit to a man stationed in a foreign capital news of which he was entirely unaware because of censorship. . . . All the CBS stations were linked together in such a fashion that by pressing a single button I could read

a news bulletin and make a comment that would be heard throughout the country. Programs of all sorts were periodically interrupted by these news flashes.[1]

In the competition between the three U.S. networks undertaking news coverage in Europe, the National Broadcasting Company had a certain advantage. It had been the first established and had formed contractual agreements enabling it to broadcast from government-owned stations in Germany, France, Great Britain, Italy, and other countries. The very fact that it was called the "National" broadcasting company led some officials in other countries to assume that it had U.S. government sponsorship, and therefore it sometimes was accorded special recognition until the other networks were able to correct that misconception.

The NBC had A. A. Schechter in New York at this period as director of News and Special Events. Fred Bate in London was in charge of European operations. Dr. Max Jordan, a U.S. citizen, but Italian-born and German-educated, and formerly an INS correspondent, was central European correspondent based in Basle, Switzerland. He scored a special triumph at Munich by producing the first report of the concluding four-power agreement.

Paul Archinard was in Paris for the NBC, Philip McKenzie and Charles Lanius were in Rome, with Lanius later in Berlin. There Warren Irvin, Paul Fischer, and Alex Dreier, formerly of the AP bureau, served. Correspondents called upon at times to broadcast for NBC included Reynolds Packard in Rome for UP; G. E. R. Gedye in Prague and Percy J. Philip in Paris, both also with the *New York Times;* John Gunther, formerly with the *Chicago Daily News,* in Europe for the NANA in 1939 and broadcasting during that year from seventeen countries for NBC; and Dorothy Thompson, experienced as a correspondent and a columnist for the *New York Herald Tribune* in 1938, who also broadcast for NBC.

The Columbia Broadcasting System developed an effective foreign coverage by shortwave from 1930, directed from New York by Paul W. White. César Saerchinger, London director of the CBS European service, resigned in 1937 to return to New York. He was replaced by Edward Roscoe Murrow, who had joined the CBS New York staff in 1935 as director of Talks and Special Events. A 1930 graduate of Washington State College in Pullman, Murrow was assistant director during 1932–35 of the Institute of International Education of New York and spent much time in London and elsewhere in Europe.

Returning to London for CBS in 1937, Murrow inherited a small

---

1 H. V. Kaltenborn, *Fifty Fabulous Years* (1950), pp. 209–11.

group of broadcasters. Saerchinger had been an administrator rather than a broadcaster, but Murrow served in both capacities while also traveling about Europe to arrange special broadcasts. His first recruit, as a regular CBS staff news broadcaster, was William L. Shirer. From Coe College in Iowa, Shirer had gone directly to the staff of the Paris edition of the *Chicago Tribune* in 1925. Moving to the staff of the parent paper in 1926, he served until 1933 in Paris and Vienna and ranged as far afield as the Middle East and India, with a side trip to Afghanistan. After a brief period with the Paris edition of the *New York Herald*, he represented the Hearst-owned Universal Service in Berlin from 1935. That service was ended in 1937, however, and he was immediately engaged by Murrow for CBS. Assigned once again to Vienna, he moved to Berlin following the Nazi seizure of Austria.

Shirer reported the German occupation of Austria for CBS in March 1938, although he had to go to London to do so. Murrow, who was in Warsaw when Shirer informed him of the German troop movement, chartered a plane to go to Vienna to report the takeover. Murrow also covered the Munich conference later in the year, the Czech seizure in 1938–39, and broadcast from London throughout World War II, gaining high acclaim for his accounts of Britain's years of valor and torment.

Shirer remained in Berlin until 1940, earning a reputation for his broadcasts, often made under difficulties, and extending to the German occupation of Paris, which he witnessed. Returning then to the United States, he continued as a commentator for CBS, as well as producing a best-seller book, *Berlin Diary: The Journal of a Foreign Correspondent, 1934–1941* (1941), giving him added authority and establishing him in a career divided between radio and authorship, including his classic *Rise and Fall of the Third Reich: A History of Nazi Germany* (1960).

Murrow added other correspondents to the CBS staff in Europe. Thomas B. Grandin, formerly of the INS bureau in Paris, had been manager of the CBS bureau there from 1936 to 1939, and also had broadcast from Rome and Prague. In 1939, he was followed in Paris by Eric Sevareid. A 1935 graduate of the University of Minnesota and a reporter for the *Minneapolis Star*, Sevareid had gone to Paris in 1937, where he worked for the *New York Herald* Paris edition and then for the United Press until he became one of Murrow's early recruits to the CBS service.

The CBS staff was further augmented between 1937 and 1940. When Shirer left Berlin in 1940, he was replaced by Edwin Hartrich. Joseph C. Harsch, then Berlin correspondent for the *Christian Science Monitor*, also broadcast for CBS. Howard K. Smith and Harry Flannery, both in Berlin for the UP, were appointed to CBS, as was Cecil Brown, formerly in Rome for INS. Three Paris correspondents, Lawrence Edward

(Larry) LeSueur of UP, Kenneth T. Downs of INS, and Edmond Taylor, formerly chief of the *Chicago Tribune* bureau, were later recruits, as were Richard C. Hottelet, Charles L. Collingwood, and Walter Cronkite, all formerly of the UP. Maurice Hindus, with Moscow experience and author of books and articles, was called upon for some broadcasts. Albert L. Warner, chief of the *New York Herald Tribune* bureau in Washington, joined CBS in 1939 to broadcast from the capital. Some of these men were to continue in radio and some later in television.

The Mutual Broadcasting System, the youngest of the three U.S. networks, had stations from coast to coast by 1936. Its news operations, as with CBS and NBC, centered in New York, where David Driscoll became director of News and Special Events at the end of the decade. The key stations for MBS were WOR (Newark) and WGN (the *Chicago Tribune* station). John Steele, London correspondent for the *Tribune* since 1919, became London representative for the network in 1935. Sigrid Schultz, Berlin correspondent for the paper, was central European representative, followed by John Paul Dickson. Louis Huot and Waverly Root, formerly of the Paris edition of the *Chicago Tribune,* and then with the UP, represented the MBS in Paris. Patrick Maitland, in eastern Europe and the Balkans for the *Times* of London, was the network representative in that area. William Hillman, former INS chief in Berlin, but then for *Collier's Weekly,* spoke over the MBS stations from various capitals of Europe.

Raymond Gram Swing, formerly in Berlin and London for the *Chicago Daily News* and the *Wall Street Journal,* became New York correspondent for the London *News Chronicle* in 1936–37. He broadcast a weekly "American Commentary" for the BBC, but also became a commentator for MBS, beginning in 1936 and continuing for a decade. His sober, quiet, and informed broadcasts were well liked. As the war began in 1939, they were carried five nights a week over 110 affiliated network stations, were rebroadcast by shortwave station WRUL (Boston) to Australia and New Zealand and went in translation to Latin America, Norway, and other areas of Europe.

Direct coverage by radio correspondents was expensive, particularly as its volume grew in the late 1930s. To report the Munich and Czech crises during the three weeks of September 1938 was estimated to have cost NBC and CBS together about $190,000, including telephone calls and rebates to advertisers for programs cancelled to permit reporting of fast-moving news developments.

Radio stations in various cities of the world, whether or not affiliated with networks, often brought qualified newsmen to comment upon the news. Among others so engaged in New York were Johannes Steel, European-educated and widely traveled foreign editor of the *New York*

Evening Post, speaking over station WMCA, and Major George Fielding Eliot, retired from the U.S. Army, who was military correspondent
for the *New York Herald Tribune* and became a member of the CBS
staff in New York as the European war began.

The BBC in 1936 named Arthur Ernest Baker, former European and
diplomatic correspondent for the *Times,* to administer foreign-language
broadcasts and commentaries as overseas news editor. In that same
year, Ralph Murray became the first BBC special radio correspondent
moving about Europe, and he was at Munich and Prague in 1938. Percy
J. Philip, serving the *New York Times* and the NBC in Paris, also broadcast from there for the BBC, as Swing did from New York. Richard
Dimbleby was another BBC correspondent to gain a reputation for his
broadcasts from Europe. He accompanied King George VI and Queen
Elizabeth on their visit to Canada and the United States in the summer
of 1939.

The Munich conference of September 1938, and the critical days before and after, brought into action a large, élite group of correspondents
gathering from many parts of Europe and from abroad. In retrospect, it
may have been the first example of an international event that was over-
covered. For radio, Murrow, Shirer, and Grandin arrived for CBS, Jordan for NBC, Swing for MBS, Murray for BBC, others for the radio of
France, Germany, and Italy. As noted, Kaltenborn did wonders in New
York.

Those few correspondents who had been regularly assigned to Prague
included Laurence Edmund (Larry) Allen and Roy Porter for the Associated Press, Reynolds and Eleanor Packard and Hans Thomas for the
United Press, and Emil Vadney for the *New York Times.* They had been
joined by some correspondents who had been in Vienna prior to its seizure by the Nazis, including Gedye of the *Daily Telegraph* and *New
York Times,* Fodor of the *Manchester Guardian* and *Chicago Daily
News,* Price of the *Daily Mail,* Steinkopf and Whiteleather of the AP,
Lemoult of Havas, and McMillan of the British United Press.

Stowe of the *New York Herald Tribune,* a Pulitzer Prize winner for
1929, had returned to Europe to report the crisis, as did DeWitt Mackenzie, correspondent in Europe for the AP from 1916 to 1933, foreign
editor in New York, and since 1936 an AP columnist on international
affairs. Karl H. Von Wiegand, a correspondent chiefly in Berlin since
World War I, represented the Hearst Newspapers and the INS.

Walter Duranty, long in Moscow for the *New York Times* and a roving correspondent for the paper, also was in Munich; as were Frederick
T. Birchall, chief European correspondent for the same paper and its
former managing editor; H. R. Knickerbocker of INS, with more than a
decade of European news experience; and Edgar Ansel Mowrer, *Chi-*

cago Daily News, bureau chief since 1915 successively in Rome, Berlin, and Paris. All four were Pulitzer Prize winners.

Other thoroughly experienced correspondents on hand included Kenneth Anderson and Charles Dimont of Reuters; Webb Miller, European manager for the United Press; Sigrid Schultz, long in Berlin for the *Chicago Tribune;* Demaree Bess, Geneva correspondent for the *Christian Science Monitor;* Reuben H. Markham, the *Monitor's* southern European correspondent; Joseph Barnes, Moscow correspondent for the *New York Herald Tribune;* and Wade Werner, AP Moscow bureau chief.

Coming from Berlin, in addition to those mentioned, were Ewan Butler, the London *Times;* Otto D. Tolischus, Guido Enderis, and C. Brooks Peters, all of the *New York Times* bureau; Louis Lochner, AP; Frederick C. Oechsner, UP; Pierre J. (Pete) Huss, INS; Wallace R. Deuel, *Chicago Daily News;* Ralph W. Barnes, *New York Herald Tribune;* and J. Emlyn Williams, *Christian Science Monitor.* Most of them were bureau chiefs.

Arriving from Paris were John Lloyd and Edward Kennedy, AP; Edward DePury, UP; Kenneth T. Downs, INS; Edmond Taylor and Alex Small, *Chicago Tribune;* John Elliott and Walter B. Kerr, *New York Herald Tribune;* Percy J. Philip, *New York Times;* Mallory Browne, *Christian Science Monitor;* and Ralph Izzard, *Daily Mail.* Again, most were bureau heads.

From Rome came G. Stewart Brown and Ralph E. Forte, UP; Richard G. Massock, AP; Frank Gervasi, INS; Arnaldo Cortesi, *New York Times;* James M. (Don) Minifie, *New York Herald Tribune;* and John T. Whitaker, who had switched to the *Chicago Daily News.* Once again, most were bureau chiefs.

From London, among those arriving, mostly bureau heads, were J. Clifford Stark and Fred Vanderschmidt, AP; William Hillman, INS; Edward W. Beattie, Jr., UP; Ferdinand Kuhn, Jr., *New York Times;* William H. Stoneman, *Chicago Daily News;* David Darrah, *Chicago Tribune;* John T. Driscoll, *New York Herald Tribune;* Edward B. Hitchcock and Godfrey Lias, *Christian Science Monitor.*

Still others in Prague and Munich were Léon Rollin, director of foreign service for the Agence Havas; J. Kingsbury Smith, INS; Robert Best, UP; Geoffrey Cox, Selkirk Patton, Donald Mellett and William Morrell, all of the London *Daily Express,* and C. V. R. Thompson, New York correspondent for that paper, but temporarily in Europe; Douglas Reed, *News-Chronicle;* Paul Bretherton, *Daily Mail;* Leonard O. Mosley, *Daily Sketch* and *Sunday Graphic;* Virginia Cowles, *Sunday Times;* and Maurice Hindus, writer for the *Nation* and other magazines, with long experience in Russia.

The press of Germany, France, and Italy was heavily represented, as was that of Czechoslovakia, Holland, and other countries of Europe.

The Munich conference provided an occasion for German photographer Dr. Erich Solomon to demonstrate the effectiveness of the "candid camera" technique in obtaining intimate views of the participants while using only available light without flash. His work with the 35-millimeter camera already had revolutionized news photography.

The settlement reached at Munich placed Germany in a position to dominate Czechoslovakia and the entire Danube area. Correspondents forced out of Prague and Vienna had no easier time in Berlin. A mass expulsion of six British correspondents had occurred there in September 1938 in the midst of the Sudeten crisis. They were Eustace B. F. Wareing, H. C. Greene, and Anthony Mann of the *Daily Telegraph,* Ian C. Colvin and Denis Weaver of the *News-Chronicle,* and Rothay Reynolds of the *Daily Mail.*

Rather surprisingly, the *Times* made a technical protest against this action by withdrawing James Holburn, who had replaced Norman Ebbutt upon his unprotested expulsion in 1937. Holburn returned to Berlin after a short interval but was transferred to Moscow in the late spring of 1939. Mann of the *Daily Telegraph* and Colvin of the *News-Chronicle* were permitted to return to Berlin before the end of the year, but Colvin left voluntarily in April 1939 when his colleague, Hubert D. Harrison, *News-Chronicle* bureau chief since February 1938, was expelled. They were replaced for that paper by David Woodward, who had been expelled from Rome, and P. B. Wadsworth. Keith Scott-Watson, in Danzig for the *Daily Herald,* was expelled from the "free city" in August 1939 by the German secret police on the eve of the Nazi invasion.

More foreign correspondents might have been expelled in the fall-to-spring period of 1938–39 had they not resorted to self-censorship both in seeking news and in writing it. As it was, Kaltenborn's intended visit to Berlin in August 1939 failed when Nazi secret police detained him on arrival at the Tempelhof Airport and sent him directly back to London.[2]

It was in November 1938 that Hitler had complained about "warmongering" by the press and officials in the western democracies. He held such practice impermissible in Germany. Yet the German press was constantly directing shafts at the democracies, many of them aimed at the United States. That same month *Der Angriff,* Dr. Goebbel's semiofficial newspaper, published an article about some of the first U.S. government-sponsored shortwave radio programs broadcast to Latin

---

2   During his absence from New York, Elmer Davis substituted for him as news commentator at CBS. A member of the *New York Times* staff from 1914–24, a writer for *Harper's* monthly and other magazines, and author of books, Davis was then entering upon a new and highly successful career as a radio news analyst.

America, which were intended to counter German and Italian propaganda there. It was headlined "Yankees on the Liepath." The *Berliner Börsen-Zeitung* called the United States a "land of gangsterism," and also referred to the "American lie campaign of anti-German war propaganda in Latin America."

The *Deutsche Allgemeine Zeitung* of Berlin spoke of Victor F. Ridder, publisher of the *New York Journal of Commerce,* as "a traitor to German-Americanism" because he had made an appeal for racial tolerance at a time when anti-Jewish activity was at its height in Germany. *Der Angriff* spoke of "Jewish warmongers" in the United States, and the *Hamburger Fremdenblatt,* in a long article about the "German-American minority," asserted quite falsely that thousands were being persecuted, oppressed, and deprived of work through the action of "Jewish and communistic fellow employees" and because the general public had been "stirred by agitation" to demand their dismissal.

Comparable references in the German press through the years, with information pulled out of context or reshaped to convey an inaccurate impression had an inevitable effect. German visitors to the United States in 1938–39, who had been subjected to misinformation since 1933, arrived with such distorted views that many were unable to comprehend much that they saw and heard, and were unwilling to accept the plain truth for what it was.

Foreign newspapers, periodicals, and books had been excluded in great numbers from the Reich since 1933, and seventy-seven more were specifically excluded in November 1938. This isolated the German people even more from information and ideas that might be contrary to Nazi doctrine. Efforts were added to discourage or prevent the people from hearing foreign-originated radio broadcasts. With information withheld, invented, and distorted, the people were being prepared to accept and support a Nazi war effort.

At almost the same time, Foreign Minister Ribbentrop spoke at a meeting of the Foreign Press Association in Berlin, the correspondents' professional group. He complained that no efforts had been made by "certain governments" during the Munich crisis to induce what he called quieter and objective reporting. "It is our conviction," he said, "that every government, acting in good faith, is in a position to enforce an objective method of reporting." In Berlin, as in Moscow, the term "objectivity" with reference to news reporting was subject to whatever interpretation suited the purpose of the speaker or the regime. Thus the enforced "objective method of reporting" that Ribbentrop expected of the media of the United States, Great Britain, and France, had no essential application to the German press, even though it was admittedly controlled.

Gedye of the *Daily Telegraph* and the *New York Times* was one correspondent who remained in Prague after the Munich settlement. His connection with the *Telegraph* was severed early in 1939 because his book *Fallen Bastions* was critical of British foreign policy and the Munich agreement and was felt to have compromised the paper. The Sudetenland was lost to Germany; parts of Bohemia and Moravia survived in the western part of Czechoslovakia, but in the east, Slovakia and Ruthenia had to give up territory to Hungary and Poland. Internal dissension stirred by Nazi sympathizers in the remnant of Czechoslovakia resulted in the newly elected President Hacha being summoned to Berlin where he agreed under pressure to accept German "protection" for the remainder of the country. These last days of the dissolution of Czechoslovakia as an independent nation were reported without the intensive press and radio coverage at Munich in 1938. They were relatively undramatic except for the entrance of German troops and of Hitler into Prague in March. As part of the German Reich, Czechoslovakia's press and information services were controlled from Berlin and foreign correspondents were excluded from Prague. By this time, Gedye felt he was in personal danger and took refuge in the British Legation until he was able to leave on assignment to Moscow for the *New York Times.*

These mounting tensions were felt in London, where the 100 German press correspondents of 1937 had declined to sixty by January 1938. By April 1939 the force was up again to eighty-three, despite a reduction in the number of German dailies to half the total of 1933 when the Nazi regime began its control of the press. In 1937, the British government expelled four German correspondents and it continued to believe that very few of those resident in London were *bona fide* journalists, but instead were engaged largely in political activities and espionage. Six German correspondents in London were expelled in May 1939, one of whom was R. G. Rosel of the *Essener National Zeitung,* a daily controlled by Hermann Goering.

The low esteem in which the German press was held in informed world opinion, and the lack of trust in Hitler and the Nazi government, did not prevent Dr. Dietrich, undersecretary in the Propaganda Ministry, from making a different approach from that of 1937 to the concept of nonaggression press pacts. The new effort in May 1939 was still an attempt to confuse world opinion to the advantage of the Nazi regime.

A number of German newspapers published a statement that Dr. Dietrich "had offered to put the entire German press at the disposal of a British writer if he [Dietrich] could have in exchange the right to insert in certain British newspapers an informative article about Germany, from the German point of view. His offer was rejected," the report said.

Several days later, Lord Kemsley, publisher of the *Sunday Times,* the *Daily Sketch,* and other newspapers in the United Kingdom, took up Dietrich's proposal. Lord Kemsley was invited to Berlin where late in July he saw both Dietrich and Hitler. Whatever Dietrich may have said in May, he seemed reluctant to discuss in July or to proceed then with the arrangement originally proposed. The time, he said, was inopportune. But on August 21, while at Deauville, France, Kemsley received an article in German from Dietrich. In London the next day, Kemsley was visited by Dr. Hesse, press attaché in the German Embassy. He brought a personal message from Dietrich, Kemsley wrote later, "to say that the article representing Germany's case should be published in Britain before one stating the British case had been sent and published by German papers." The suggestion was unacceptable to Kemsley who reminded Dr. Hesse "that it had always been understood that there should be simultaneous publication of the views on both sides in both countries." Ten days later World War II began with the German attack on Poland and an exchange of articles became irrelevant. Dietrich's reluctance and delaying action in July and August became understandable since by then he knew what was in prospect.[3]

That prospect included the announcement on August 23 that Nazi Germany and Soviet Russia, arch enemies, had signed a nonaggression treaty two days earlier in Moscow. This "Communazi" pact was recognized widely as assurance for both parties that each could pursue his goals without interference from the other. The war in Asia had been underway for eight years when the European war began on September 1, 1939, and the two wars were to become a World War, quite literally, when Japan attacked the United States at Pearl Harbor in 1941.

Correspondents were ready to report the spreading conflict by means of press, radio, and camera in the Far East, the Western Hemisphere, and on the European continent. Those whose countries were at war were limited in their movements by the frontiers of belligerents. Neutral correspondents had far greater scope for coverage in that respect. Because the United States managed to retain its neutrality until late 1941, its media provided extensive coverage until that time.

The U.S. press had only about twenty full-time staffers in Europe in 1914 when World War I began. In 1939, the count was nearer 800.

---

3 Dietrich referred to the subject again in February 1940. He told a group of German editors at Wiesbaden that "Lord Kemsley refused to publish the German viewpoint," adding that Kemsley had not submitted his own promised article. Such was a misrepresentation of the facts. Kemsley responded to Dietrich's assertion a day or two later in a statement published in his *Daily Sketch.* This was the last word on the effort of Nazi leaders to impose some form of control or restraint on the foreign press.

Communications by then were excellent and transportation was as good as the complications of war permitted.

The British press had pioneered in effective international reporting and in war correspondence and was strongly represented, along with the press of the Commonwealth. Beyond that, more countries had their correspondents on the news fronts than ever before. Radio reporting and broadcasting added a new dimension, further supplemented by extensive magazine and photographic/motion picture reportage.

PART II
Blitzkrieg

The War in Europe, 1939–40   6

Armored, mechanized forces of the German Wehrmacht drove eastward across the Polish border from Prussia before 6 A.M. on Friday,
September 1, 1939. Dive bombers of the Luftwaffe loosed coordinated
attacks upon sleeping cities, including Warsaw, about 200 miles from
the frontier. This combined land-air operation was the undeclared
"lightning war" or *blitzkrieg,* a new German contribution to *kultur,* and
one to bring both death and a special kind of hell to countless human
beings in the four and one-half years to follow.

In Warsaw, Lloyd (Larry) Lehrbas of the Associated Press was in the
Hotel Europejski on that morning, with an open telephone line to the
AP bureau in Budapest. To Robert Parker, the agency correspondent
there he gave an eye-witness account of the approach of the German
planes and the first bombing of the city at 9 A.M. In Budapest, Parker
heard the explosions as Lehrbas spoke. His report was relayed to New
York by way of Amsterdam and returned to London and Paris. It was
distributed to all parts of North and South America, reached the rest of
the world, and became the basis for radio news broadcasts.

Because of threats directed at Poland and Danzig by Hitler and the
entire German propaganda organization in the days and weeks preceding the attack, including border incidents since June, some correspondents had moved into those areas. Great Britain and France had assured
support to Poland in the event of a German attack, and most correspondents for the media of those countries had retired from the area.
Indeed, British correspondents in Berlin, on instructions from their embassy, had moved to Denmark on August 24, just after the signature of
the "Communazi" pacts had been revealed. It was hoped that a settlement of the crisis would permit their return, but this proved a false hope.
French correspondents and diplomats left Berlin, as German correspondents and diplomats left London and Paris, following a general
declaration of war on September 3.

This meant that foreign correspondents remaining in Berlin and Warsaw on September 1 were those representing countries still technically neutral. Most numerous and most active in this group were correspondents for the media of the United States.

In addition to Lehrbas, in Warsaw there were Elmer W. Peterson,
also of the AP; Edward W. Beattie, Jr., UP; James E. Brown, INS; and
Edmund Allen, BUP. Sonia Tomara and John H. Walker were present
for the *New York Herald Tribune;* Jerzy Shapiro for the *New York
Times;* Richard Mowrer for the *Chicago Daily News;* and Alex Small
for the *Chicago Tribune.* Although seventeen years in existence, the
highly successful weekly news-magazine *Time* was only beginning to
assign its own correspondents abroad, and Robert Neville, as foreign
editor, had arrived in Warsaw on August 26. James Bryan and Frank
Morton were present as U.S. news photographers. Patrick Maitland of
the *Times* in London was the only British correspondent then present. In
Danzig, the AP had Lynn Heinzerling, the UP had George Kidd, and
INS had Walter Dietzel. The circumstances were such that few radio
broadcasts were possible from Poland because of the speed and destruction marking the German advances. The first broadcast may have been
made over the NBC network by Mendel Mozes, a correspondent for the
Jewish Telegraph Agency. Maitland of the *Times* spoke over the Mutual Broadcasting System.

So long as the Polish government remained in Warsaw, daily news
conferences took place at the Foreign Ministry. Warsaw press communications were interrupted on September 7, and the government and most
correspondents left the city. German motorized columns reached its
suburbs the following day, but the city held out until September 27.
Eleven notes of Chopin's *Polonaise Militaire* were broadcast at regular
intervals from Radio Warsaw in defiant announcement that the city was
still unconquered. On October 5 fighting ended in all of Poland, with the
Germans and Russians establishing controls in their separate sectors.
Meanwhile, a Polish government-in-exile was formed in London on
September 30.

The Polish press never had opportunity to report the German and
Russian attacks. The Soviet press did not undertake to do much more
than publish formal communiqués. Germany was prepared, however,
with combat-correspondents and photographers actually serving as
members of the armed forces in a so-called *Pressekompanie.* They provided the German media and the world with the first reports of the war
from the German side.

The German Propaganda Ministry made it possible about a week
after the September 1 attack for foreign correspondents in Berlin to visit
the Polish front. At least one visiting group was conducted by Dr. Karl
Bömer, head of the Foreign Section in the Propaganda Ministry. Louis

P. Lochner, AP bureau chief in Berlin, was one of the first to be taken on a conducted tour to Poland. A few days later, Frederick C. Oechsner, UP bureau chief,[1] and then Pierre J. Huss, INS chief, visited the area. Others also escorted included Joseph W. Grigg, Jr., UP, who was one of the first to enter Warsaw itself with the German armies; Jack Fleischer, also of the UP Berlin bureau; Joseph Barnes of the *New York Herald Tribune;* and William L. Shirer of CBS. Some moved as far as the Gdynia area and Danzig.

Lehrbas, in leaving Warsaw, was fortunate in being able to drive out with U.S. Ambassador Anthony Joseph Drexel Biddle, Jr. With one or two others, they made a difficult journey to the Rumanian border and reached Bucharest just after the assassination there on September 21 of Premier Calinescu by the Iron Guard. This in itself was a war-related story presaging the German occupation of Rumania to come a year later. On the journey to Bucharest, Lehrbas and his companions encountered Red Army forces moving to Poland, accompanied by Melvin K. Whiteleather of the AP Moscow bureau.

In the first days and weeks of the war in Europe, the radio set a fast pace as a medium of information. Even though immediately subject to censorship in the belligerent countries, it carried the voice of Prime Minister Chamberlain in his September 3 announcement of Great Britain's declaration of war; an address to the Commonwealth countries by George VI; a speech by Adolf Hitler; an address by President Roosevelt; and numerous official statements. It brought late news reports more promptly than was possible through the press, plus analyses and commentaries and descriptions by a new group of radio correspondents, as well as by newsmen brought before the microphones to give eye-witness impressions of a continent at war.

Even before the first shots were fired, German listeners learned from NBC shortwave news bulletins about the Soviet-German trade and nonaggression treaties of August. These were reported four hours before the German government released the news. The MBS, by chance, picked up and reported a German official broadcast on the night of August 31 ordering planes and ships out of a Polish area that would become a theater of war a few hours later. NBC reported the actual German invasion of Poland in advance of any other medium. CBS had the first news of the bombing of Polish towns. NBC reported the first Ger-

---

1 At Czestochowa just on the Polish border, Oechsner was shown twenty-five mutilated bodies of civilians and was told by German officers that they were Germans murdered by Polish civilians. Since there was no way for Oechsner to be sure that they were not Polish civilians murdered by Germans, he refused to accept for use what was presented to him as an atrocity story. Because of this, he was charged by the German conducting officer with "exaggerating your objectivity."

man submarine action, the sinking off Ireland of the outward bound British liner *Athenia* on the first day of the war, with 100 persons lost, including 28 U.S. citizens.

An early radio triumph came on December 17, 1939, far from the center of war. The German pocket-battleship *Graf Spee,* then raiding in the South Atlantic, was pursued and damaged by British naval units. It put in for repairs at the neutral port of Montevideo, but was ordered by the Uruguayan government to leave by December 17 or be interned. The battleship left under protest at 6 P.M. on that Sunday evening, even though British naval vessels were known to be deployed off the coast.

Talbot G. (Jimmy) Bowen, a U.S. motion pictures sales representative in Montevideo and a stringer for NBC, was among those watching the *Graf Spee* from a hillside above the city; he held an open microphone with direct connection to NBC headquarters in New York. As the ship moved down the Plata estuary and passed out to sea, he described the scene. Suddenly, still in view offshore, explosions began to tear the ship apart, crew members went over the side, and the vessel sank in a deliberate scuttling ordered to prevent its capture at sea by British forces. Bowen was able to broadcast an eye-witness account of this event, carried live over the NBC network in the United States in prime time. Later, most of the crew members were interned in Argentina at their own option, but the ship's Captain Hans Langsdorff committed suicide.

There was some question in the United States when the war began as to how much freedom should be granted to radio, which was not covered by the First Amendment to the Constitution assuring freedom to the printed media. The possibility was seen that competition between the three major radio networks then existing might lead to news broadcasts and commentaries rousing public emotions to a dangerous pitch. The Federal Communications Act of 1934 gave power to the president to take control of radio in a national emergency, and President Roosevelt had declared a limited national emergency soon after the war began in Europe.

To avoid any such governmental assumption of control, the National Association of Broadcasters (NAB), representing all networks and stations, established a regulatory code to cover news programs. This stipulated avoidance of "horror, suspense and undue excitement." It ruled out biased comment or news selection and "editorializing" by commentators. It called for "fairness to all belligerents" in handling speeches, proclamations, and official statements for broadcast. All news-roundups and analyses were to be by American citizens, and "analysis" was defined to mean "explaining and evaluating" facts, rumors, and propaganda.

In practice, the radio medium had no trouble in the United States during the war, either before or after the country became a direct participant. It was treated on a par with the press, where censorship was concerned, and it demonstrated such competence and responsibility as to establish itself firmly in the news communication field.

In Great Britain and France as countries at war, there was some disposition to restrict radio and press coverage. In 1939, this was in part because some officials clung to a hope that Hitler himself would seek peace after he had established control over Poland, eliminated the Polish Corridor and the free city of Danzig, and so united East Prussia with the Reich once again. With that hope, they did not wish to see the situation exacerbated by a coverage that might only irritate Hitler. It was a survival of the "appeasement" concept. With it went a strict policy of censorship.

The British government, nevertheless, immediately matched the German Ministry of Public Enlightenment and Propaganda by creating its own cabinet-level Ministry of Information (MOI), with headquarters in a tall structure recently completed in the Bloomsbury district for the University of London.

Plans for such a ministry had been prepared prior to 1938 to meet the need, if war should come. At the time of Munich, it became a "shadow" ministry, with a minister-designate and other directors alerted, but changed more than once before the real ministry was established September 6, 1939, three days after the British declaration of war. The first minister was Lord Macmillan, who had served in the World War I Ministry of Information. Lord Perth, former British ambassador to Italy, was named as director-general. Perth soon moved to another post, and Macmillan was only the first of four ministers.[2] There was frequent change in the staff organization within the ministry during the war, some spurred by complaints from the media.

The MOI was the central channel in London for the distribution of war news and general government news, although each ministry or department was entitled to issue its own news releases as before the war. A wartime censorship was administered by a News and Censorship Department. The censorship was "voluntary" and limited in its application to military information, with no restrictions on political references. A separate Publicity Department was concerned with propaganda. There were twelve MOI regional offices within the United Kingdom.

As the organization took form, working space was provided in the

---

2   The ministers following were Sir John Reith, director-general of the BBC until 1940; Alfred Duff Cooper, formerly secretary of state for war; and Brenden Bracken, formerly parliamentary private secretary to Prime Minister Churchill.

MOI building for British journalists and foreign correspondents. Communications facilities were made available there. A news conference met at 6 P.M. daily in what became known as the Press and Censorship Bureau, and there were background talks on the progress of the war. Other news conferences were scheduled as required, some attended by more than a hundred Allied and neutral correspondents of about twenty-five nations. Copy as written would pass through the Censorship Department. If prepared by correspondents attached to British forces in the field, the copy would go through the appropriate army, navy, or air force censorship, and then through the central Censorship Department in the MOI in London.

Censorship sometimes resulted in delays of perhaps thirty minutes in transmission of dispatches from London to New York in the first days of the war, and of as much as six hours from continental points. London regulations halted the radio transmission of photographs. One result of that policy was that German-originated photos of the Polish invasion sent without delay received full use in much of the world's press.

Described as a voluntary censorship because it had been agreed to by the British press and radio, and because media representatives joined in drafting the code before the war began, it also was a censorship with teeth. The Official Secrets Act of 1911, as amended in 1920, placed limitations on certain subjects, and also provided for memoranda, or so-called "Defense Notices"—"D Notices"—going to the media restricting the use of material viewed as bearing upon national security. The Defense of the Realm Act (DORA), dating from World War I and never repealed, also gave added force to the censorship regulations, with foreign correspondents subject to prosecution equally with British nationals for transgressions. In practice, no such prosecutions ever occurred.

The French government set up an Information Agency when the war began. As the Commissariat Générale d'Information, at the Hotel Continental in Paris, it also performed a censorship function. There was a military censorship administered by the Bureau Central Militaire de la Circulation (B.C.M.C.) based at the Post & Telegraph Office in the Rue de Grenelle.[3]

The French censorship, actually not unlike others, usually eliminated adverse reports. This tended to establish a sense of security among read-

---

3 Edmond Taylor tells of a British correspondent who regarded the Rue de Grenelle censorship as less severe than that at the Continental. One night, however, it censored the first half of a long dispatch he submitted, but passed the second half. He protested, and was invited to take the dispatch to the Continental. He did, and there the first half was passed, but the second half censored out. Taylor tells of another writer whose copy was passed without deletion, but several split infinitives were corrected. See Edmond Taylor, *Strategy of Terror* (1940), p. 213.

ers perhaps unjustified by the facts, and so prevented a realistic appraisal of the war situation by the people and even by officials of the government. The results were to be sadly demonstrated in France.

Gordon Waterfield of Reuters expressed it when he wrote later[4] that "when the censorship only allows through the optimistic portions of an account given by an optimistic general, a wrong impression is given in the world's press." For example, he cited one of his own dispatches stating that while a French army division was holding a sector on the Aisne River the situation was not so satisfactory in another sector on the Somme. After censorship had eliminated the latter reference, the story as published in London on June 1, 1940, gave the impression that "the French tanks were better than the German and that all was right with the world." Since Paris even then was near capture, this was scarcely accurate and it was not what Waterfield was trying to convey.

Early in October 1939, five weeks after the war began, the British War Office accepted the view expressed by General Maurice Gustave Gamelin of the French army and commander of all Allied French and British forces in France, that "it is time to lift the silence which separates the front from the rest of the country."

There had been little war news to report in any case, but under the protection of that silence the Allied forces had established their positions in France and Belgium, including manning the Maginot Line. In October, correspondents were permitted to move out from Paris and London representing the media of France, Great Britain, the United States, and other neutral countries. In their first days, they were entertained at luncheons by the military, put up in hotels, fed very well, and provided with motorcars and conducting officers to help them on visits not only to the Maginot Line but to air units, naval bases, and almost anywhere they wished to go. Whatever they wrote was subject to censorship. The entire procedure was in the tradition of the British Expeditionary Force Headquarters system in France during World War I, except that the number of correspondents was greater. A more important difference was the absence of any battle action to report at the time.

After nearly a week in France and Belgium, Harold N. Denny of the *New York Times* wrote of this latter point. "Hostilities between Britain and Germany are now well along in the second month," he reported, "and not a shot has been fired in anger by the British ground forces now firmly installed on this front. Nor, so far as we can learn, have the Germans made any serious gestures in this way. They have not even sent over reconnoitering airplanes." On October 22, 1939, the cable desk in New York headed this piece, "38 War Reporters Search for a War."

4　Gordon Waterfield, *What Happened to France* (1941), pp. 60–61.

All was not tranquil, however. Poland had been conquered by the end of September. That first month of the war also brought German air and submarine attacks on Allied shipping, with more than 137,000 tons destroyed, plus 42,000 tons of neutral shipping. The *Royal Oak,* one of the greatest of the British battleships, was sunk at anchor at Scapa Flow by a German submarine making a bold raid. The aircraft carrier *Courageous* also was sunk in September. The German luxury liner *Bremen* sailed safely from New York to home waters. German submarine attacks continued, but were countered by British and French naval protection of convoys, with forty-seven German submarines sunk by the end of the year. In December the *Graf Spee* was scuttled at Montevideo.

In addition to German activity in Poland and the Atlantic, there was the Russian move into Poland and the Baltic states and its invasion of Finland on November 30 in a war lasting until March 1940. By contrast, in the west of Europe the quiet that Denny had reported in October continued through the winter. By comparison to the "blitzkrieg" in Poland, this was referred to as the "sitzkrieg" and as the "phony war." Both terms were to become cruelly ironic soon enough.

Through the winter, British and U.S. news agencies and newspapers maintained desks in neutral Holland at Amsterdam, Rotterdam, and The Hague. There they handled news traffic out of Germany, where no advance censorship as yet existed. Copenhagen, Stockholm, Oslo, Bucharest, Budapest, Belgrade, Berne, Lisbon, and Istanbul all became neutral centers of some importance for the gathering of news and for the transmission of news to and from Germany.

Expectation of a possible dramatic clash between French and German forces confronting each other in the elaborately prepared border defenses of the French Maginot Line and along the far less elaborate German Siegfried Line, led some correspondents to move to Luxembourg, then between the lines and precariously neutral. From the Brasseur Hotel in Luxembourg City and from the terrace of the Hotel Bellevue at Remich, they could watch the maneuvers of both the French and the Germans. Neutral correspondents properly escorted could visit either line.

Among correspondents in Luxembourg during the late weeks of 1939 were Walter B. Kerr, *New York Herald Tribune,* Larry Rue, *Chicago Tribune,* and Robert J. Casey, *Chicago Daily News.* Casey arrived in France on a flight from the United States by way of South America and Africa, a new wartime routing. Charles Wertenbacker was present as one of the new overseas representatives for *Time* magazine. Stedman Jones was a *Life* photographer. Eric Sevareid represented CBS, Richard Busvine the *Chicago Times,* and Peter C. Rhodes the UP. Two British correspondents also were there, R. M. P. (Mike) Hawkin for the *Daily Mail,* and Milton Twist for the *Daily Mirror.*

The first move of correspondents with the French army into forward positions east of the Maginot Line occurred on September 21–22. Paul Ward of the *Baltimore Sun,* Edmond Taylor, *Chicago Tribune,* Edgar Ansel Mowrer, *Chicago Daily News,* and Kenneth T. Downs, INS,[5] advanced unescorted onto German soil. William Mellors (Bill) Henry, CBS, and Arthur E. Mann, MBS, with the group as radio correspondents, were the first to broadcast from what was technically the French battlefront, inactive though it was at the time.

The volume of news traffic mounting to a record level as the European war began was to climb ever higher, with the costs of coverage growing fantastically. On September 1, the first day, Press Wireless, Inc., owned by the U.S. press as a transmission service, handled some 150,000 words of news copy from Europe to its New York receiving station on Long Island. The three U.S. news agencies together were filing almost a million words a week from Europe. This was costing the AP about $5,000 a day, approximately twice as much as during most of World War I. The UP communications costs also about doubled, and the INS total set a new record for that agency. These expenses required announcements by the three agencies in 1940 or later of special wartime assessments for those using the services. By mid-1940, CBS and NBC also were spending about $10,000 a week to bring regular "news round-ups" from the capitals of the warring nations. The Mutual Broadcasting System spent somewhat less.

The Associated Press was the only world agency publishing an annual report of total costs for gathering and distributing news and maintaining its staff and network. Unofficial estimates were available for 1942, however, covering the UP and INS. Comparative figures for total maintenance of service in that year were: AP–$12,987,000; UP–$8,628,000; INS–$9,434,000.

Foreign news alone, consisting largely of war news, cost the AP $1,088,210 in 1942. That was up from $757,820 in 1938, and continued rising to $3,539,336 in 1945, the last year of the war, when the total AP costs stood at nearly $17 million.

Newspaper costs for gathering the news are not announced, as a general thing, but it was reported in 1941 that the *New York Times* foreign service in 1940 had cost $708,112. About half of that was for communications charges, bringing more than 5.5 million words into the

---

5 Downs was awarded the first Sigma Delta Chi citation for foreign correspondence because of his 1939 reports from the field.

home office. It also paid for 63 full-time staff correspondents at posts around the world, and included $33,800 for photographs, plus costs for 640 war maps, and payments for AP, UP, and NANA services.[6] In 1941, the costs of *New York Times* reports exceeded $1 million. Even with some return from the sale of that service through syndication, the costs were not recovered, and much less did the *Times* or any other paper make a profit on its own service.

Press and Radio Expansion

The mounting activity on the war fronts brought an increase in the foreign press and radio corps. Media representatives were moved about the world like chessmen on the board. As in China and Japan, correspondents in Europe who had been reporting political and economic and social affairs also became war correspondents. There were shifts and augmentations, but by and large the *dramatis personae* for the media was already in position.

Sir Roderick Jones, chairman of Reuters, said late in August 1939 that "The Reuter organization in Europe is so extensive and has been so long established that little more has been necessary than the strengthening of the main strategic centers with additional staff men."[7] The same could be said, generally, for the British newspapers, and for the French, U.S., and other media in Europe.

The last British correspondents to leave Berlin in August on advice of the embassy apparently were Selkirk Patton of the *Daily Express* and Ralph Izzard of the *Daily Mail.* They went to Copenhagen, there joining Ewan Butler of the *Times* and Anthony Mann of the *Daily Telegraph.* A new Reuters bureau also was formed there. Reuters Amsterdam bureau was enlarged and headed by Gordon Young. Christopher D. R. Lumby of the *Times,* who had served that paper as a correspondent in France during World War I and recently as correspondent in Rome, established himself at Rotterdam, where most of the other British newspapers also had representatives to cover the news from Germany.

After British forces were moved into France by way of Cherbourg in September 1939, Alexander Graeme Clifford, Berlin correspondent for Reuters, went to British headquarters in France as "eye witness" for the entire British, foreign, and overseas press. Martin Herlihy continued to

---

6 See *AP Annual Volumes,* 1939–46; Morris L. Ernst, *The First Freedom* (1946), p. 82; *Editor & Publisher,* May 10, 1941, p. 53; September 23, 1939, pp. 5, 32; August 31, 1940, pp. 3–4, 35.

7 *Editor & Publisher,* September 2, 1939, p. 4.

head the Paris bureau for Reuters. André Glarner was in Paris for Exchange Telegraph. Four British correspondents were chosen by ballot to go to French army headquarters: Nicholas Bodington of Reuters Paris bureau; F. G. H. Salusbury, *Daily Herald;* H. C. Cardozo, *Daily Mail;* and Aubrey Hammond, *Daily Sketch.*

Other British correspondents going to France from London during the first weeks of the war included Ralph N. Walling and A. D. Skene Catling of Reuters; H. A. R. (Kim) Philby, who had been in Spain, and Robert W. Cooper, both for the *Times;* Douglas Williams, Peter Lawless, and Richard Capell, *Daily Telegraph* and *Sunday Times;* E. O'Dowd Gallagher and D. Sefton Delmer, *Daily Express;* G. Ward Price, *Daily Mail;* E. A. Montague, *Manchester Guardian;* Philip Jordan and U.S.-born John Scott,[8] *News-Chronicle;* Charles J. T. Gardner, BBC; J. N. G. Holman and R. S. Roland, Exchange Telegraph; Anthony Gibbs, *Daily Sketch;* Bernard Gray and Thomas E. A. Healy, *Daily Mirror* and *Sunday Pictorial;* G. W. Bryan de Grineau, *Illustrated London News;* Richard D. S. McMillan, British United Press; A. G. A. Harmsworth, Plymouth *Western Morning News;* and J. L. Hodson, Allied Newspapers.

Four news photographers and four newsreel cameramen went to France for British publications and organizations. These were Stanley H. Kessell of the *Times;* Ernest A. Taylor, *Daily Sketch;* Len A. Puttnam, Associated Press of Great Britain; Leslie B. Davies, Sport and General Press; S. R. G. Bonnett, Gaumont-British Newsreel; John W. Cotter, British Movietone News; Ronald Noble, British Pictorial Publications (Universal Newsreel); and Charles R. Martin, Pathé Newsreel.

Commonwealth correspondents who went from London to France included R. A. Monson, Australian Consolidated Press; G. M. Long, *Sydney Morning Herald;* G. Tebbutt, Australian Newspaper Service; and Julius Mockford, Argus South African Newspapers. The Canadian Press (CP) was directed from Toronto by general superintendents J. A. McNeil and Gillis Purcell, and then Charles Bruce, formerly in New York. Samuel S. Robertson was director in London. The staff there was augmented in 1940–41 to include Ross Munro, D. Ernest Burritt, Harold J. Fair, William Stuart, and Foster Barclay. Edwin S. Johnson, former London superintendent and correspondent, returned to Ottawa late in 1940 as military correspondent.

Five correspondents who had been in the United States for the European press, but who happened to be on holiday in their own countries as

---

8   Scott, son of Scott Nearing, U.S. sociologist and educator, who had conducted tour groups in the USSR in the 1920s, had worked as a welder in Russia from 1932–37. He married a Russian and in 1937 was an assistant in the *New York Times* Moscow bureau. He also worked for the Agence Havas and later for *Time* magazine.

the war began remained in those countries. They were Kurt Sell of the German DNB agency; Jean Lagrange, French Agence Havas; Don Iddon, London *Daily Mail;* and Douglass Williams and Denys Smith, both of the *Daily Telegraph.*

For France, the Agence Havas and such newspapers as *Le Petit Parisien, Le Journal, Le Matin, Le Temps,* and *Paris Soir* had correspondents with the armies in the west. German coverage came from DNB correspondents in neutral capitals, from a few individual correspondents for *Völkischer Beobachter* and other newspapers, and from members of the *Pressekompagnie* with the German Wehrmacht. For Italy, the Agenzia Stefani and such newspapers as *Il Corriere della Sera, La Stampa, Il Giornale d'Italia, Il Popolo d'Italia,* and one or two others had their representatives in Germany, France, and Great Britain when the war began. They remained as long as Italy was neutral, until June 1940.

The organizations serving the information media of the United States were well staffed at the beginning of the war and were augmented by correspondents and photographers dispatched to Europe by ship and plane. Representing a neutral country until that status ended in December 1941, the U.S. media provided reports to much of the world from both sides of the battle lines in Europe and Asia.

The Associated Press had Kent Cooper as general manager in New York and Byron Price as executive news editor. John Evans, vastly experienced abroad, was foreign editor, with Glenn Babb as cable desk editor, assisted by Oscar Leiding, C. A. Farnsworth, Tom Yarbrough, Richard G. Harris, and others. DeWitt Mackenzie, with long experience in Europe, soon began a regular column, "The War Today," and later went to the war zone. As chief AP executive in Europe, Milo M. Thompson was stationed in London.

The chiefs of European bureaus for the AP, but subject to change, were Joseph C. Stark, London; John Lloyd, Paris; Louis P. Lochner, Berlin; Richard G. Massock, Rome; Witt Hancock, Moscow; Robert B. Parker, Jr., Budapest; and Elmer Peterson, Warsaw. Staff members in the London bureau included Drew Middleton, Robert Bunnelle, Daniel DeLuce, James C. Oldfield, William McGaffin, J. Reilly O'Sullivan, Thomas F. Hawkins, and British-born G. H. P. Anderson. Staffers in Paris included Henry C. Cassidy, Taylor Henry, and Charles Foltz, Jr. In Berlin there were Fred Vanderschmidt, Robert Okin, Wade Werner, Edwin Shanke, and Melvin K. Whiteleather. Lawrence Edmund (Larry) Allen was in Rome, and Robert St. John and Paul Vadja were in Budapest. In addition, the AP had some 2,500 stringers throughout Europe.

When the war began, Milo Thompson moved from London to Copenhagen, O'Sullivan and Hawkins from London to Amsterdam, De-Luce to Budapest, and Middleton to Paris. Whiteleather moved to Moscow and Cassidy moved from the Paris bureau to join French troops.

The United Press was under Hugh Baillie as president. He happened to be in London at the outbreak of war. Joseph L. Jones was general foreign manager in New York, with Joe Alex Morris as foreign editor, assisted by Louis F. Keemle and Everett R. Holles as day and night cable editors, and Charles M. McCann as overnight cable desk chief. Harrison Salisbury of the Washington bureau later moved to New York to act as foreign editor during the absences of Morris. Edward Leggett Keen, UP vice-president for Europe, and Webb Miller, general manager for Europe, were in London. Also in London were Harry Flory, European news manager, Clifford L. Day, assistant news manager, and Wallace Carroll, manager of the London bureau. Virgil Pinkley, based in Amsterdam, soon took charge of northern European coverage.

Directors of UP bureaus on the continent included Ralph Heinzen in Paris; Frederick C. Oechsner, Berlin; Edward M. Beattie, Jr., Warsaw; and Reynolds Packard, Rome, who was assisted by his wife Eleanor Packard. Staffers for the UP included Meyer Handler and Lawrence Edward (Larry) LeSueur in Paris; Ferdinand Kuh in London; Hans Thomas in Prague; Richard C. Hottelet and George Kidd in Berlin.

Kidd had carried a heavy load there since 1937. Moving about the continent, he was in the Baltic port of Memel, under Lithuanian sovereignty, when it was seized following a Nazi ultimatum in March 1939. His report gave the UP a world beat. He was in Danzig as the European war began in September, then in Copenhagen, and in Belgrade early in 1940. The German seizure of the Netherlands in May 1940 deprived the UP of a useful neutral bureau in Amsterdam, but Kidd conducted a comparable bureau in Zurich until July 1941, when he returned to Berlin.

Harold Peters had replaced Kidd in Copenhagen, remaining until Denmark also was occupied by the Nazis in 1940. He and Henry Gorrell both were then on the move for the agency. Also in Berlin for the UP as the war began was Albion Ross, who had served there in the 1930s for the Philadelphia Public Ledger–New York Post syndicate. He soon left to become foreign editor of the *San Francisco Chronicle*. Robert Best, in the Vienna bureau prior to the Nazi annexation of Austria in March 1938, was one correspondent who contrived to remain there, but his service to the UP was minimal from that time.

Ralph E. Forte, formerly in Rome for the *Chicago Daily News* but with the UP in London when the war began, moved to Glasgow to cover the arrival of survivors of the *Athenia* sinking. Later he was in London,

Zurich, and Madrid. Henry Shapiro, chief of the UP Moscow bureau, on vacation when the war began, returned to the Soviet capital. Peter C. Rhodes was assigned to Luxembourg. Webb Miller went from London to France in September, and Ralph Heinzen went from Paris to the French front, quiet though it was.

Frank H. Fisher was London manager for the British United Press, soon providing service to all London dailies, to the *Manchester Guardian* and *Evening News,* and to the BBC. Edmund Allen of the BUP, upon being driven out of Warsaw, set up in Budapest.

The International News Service under Barry Faris as editor in New York also had J. C. Oestreicher as director of its foreign service. Harry Reynolds was his aide, with Harry Bergman as night assistant cable editor, backed by George Lait, John Edgerton Lee, G. L. (Larry) Meier, and Ed Gottlieb. In Europe, INS had Karl H. Von Wiegand, veteran special writer for the Hearst newspapers, with special familiarity with German affairs. The INS also had H. R. Knickerbocker as a roving correspondent. He was at the French front in September. W. W. (Bill) Chaplin flew from New York to London as the war began, and went immediately to France.

INS bureau chiefs included William Hillman in London, where he also was European manager; Kenneth T. Downs in Paris; Pierre J. (Pete) Huss in Berlin; James E. Brown in Warsaw and then in Budapest; and Percival Winner and Cecil Brown in Rome. J. Kingsbury Smith, former London bureau chief, recuperating from an automobile accident as the war began, returned to Europe upon recovery. Hillman soon left INS to join *Collier's Weekly* as head of a war staff. He was succeeded in London by Charles A. Smith.

Among U.S. newspapers, the *New York Times* received full reports from the major news services and had its own national and international staff and stringer representation. Arthur Hays Sulzberger was publisher, and Edwin L. (Jimmy) James was managing editor in New York. James was former European chief correspondent. Theodore M. Bernstein, in charge of the foreign cable desk, was backstopped by Emanuel R. (Manny) Freedman, Ernest Von Hartz, Gordon Havens, Robert Aura Smith, Walter M. Daniels, John S. Chalmers, Ira Bird, Herman H. Dinsmore, and David Loth. Frederick T. Birchall, former managing editor, was chief European correspondent, with a roving assignment that had him in Berlin from 1932 and in London from 1937 until after the war began.

European bureau chiefs for the *New York Times* were Ferdinand Kuhn, Jr., in London, assisted by Raymond Daniell, Harold N. Denny, Robert P. Post, W. F. Leysmith, and James B. (Scotty) Reston, who had been in the AP bureau in London for two years before joining the *New*

York Times in 1939; Percy J. Philip in Paris, assisted by Lansing Warren, George Axelsson, Camille N. Cianfarra, and Gaston Hanet Archambault; and Guido Enderis in Berlin, assisted by Otto D. Tolischus and C. Brooks Peters.[9] Herbert L. Matthews was in Rome; and G. E. R. Gedye, in Moscow. Jerzy Szapiro had been in Warsaw, backed by Percy Knauth of the Berlin bureau. Carter Brown was in Vienna, Sven Carstensen in Copenhagen, and A. Marcus Tollet, in Helsingfors (Helsinki). Other stringer correspondents were in Europe for the paper.

The *New York Times,* which had been alloting 20 to 25 columns each day to international news, increased that space to 30 or 35 columns. It had become from 1914 a leader in the space given to news of World War I, and its volume of news about World War II and the world was the largest to appear in any newspaper wherever published.

For the *New York Herald Tribune,* Ogden Mills Reid was president and publisher. Mrs. Helen Rogers Reid also was active in its direction. Wilbur Forrest, experienced as a correspondent, was assistant to Reid. Grafton S. Wilcox was managing editor, and John Price was cable editor in New York, assisted by Herbert E. Monahan, Roy Yerger, Frank Waters, and Kenyon Kilbon.In Europe, Laurence Hills, director of the Paris or European edition of the *New York Herald Tribune,* also served as director of the paper's foreign service, with Eric Hawkins as managing editor of that Paris edition.

As *Herald Tribune* bureau chiefs, John Elliott was in Paris as European chief and Walter B. Kerr was Paris chief. Ralph W. Barnes was in London, assisted by J. Edward Angly, Frank R. Kelley, and James Gibson. Joseph Barnes was in Berlin, assisted by Russell Hill; James R. ("Don") Minifie in Rome; Sonia Tomara in Warsaw as the war began in Europe; John Walker of the New York staff also arrived there at that juncture. Wilfrid Fleisher, formerly Tokyo correspondent, was in Stockholm on holiday. Angly went from London to France at that time, and Elliott went from the Paris bureau to the French front.

The *Chicago Daily News,* with Colonel Frank Knox as publisher, had three experienced correspondents in key positions in Chicago. Paul Scott Mowrer was editor, Hal O'Flaherty managing editor, and Carroll Binder foreign editor. In Europe, Edgar Ansel Mowrer was in Paris, assisted by Paul Ghali; William H. Stoneman in London, with Helen Kirkpatrick as diplomatic correspondent; Wallace R. Deuel in Berlin; John T. Whitaker in Rome; Richard Mowrer in Warsaw; and Frank G. Smothers and Marcel W. Fodor were roving correspondents. Kirkpatrick took charge of London coverage in September when Stoneman went to France. Edgar Mowrer moved from the Paris bureau to the

---

9   Not to be confused with Harold Peters of the UPI.

front at the same time. Robert J. Casey of the Chicago staff, a combat veteran of World War I, flew to Lisbon and London, and then went to Luxembourg as a first stop in the war zone, quiet though it still remained.

Leland Stowe, an experienced correspondent of the *New York Herald Tribune* and a Pulitzer Prize winner, joined the *Daily News* staff as the European war began and when the *Herald Tribune* judged him too old at forty to serve as a war correspondent. For the Chicago paper, he flew with Casey to London, and began a distinguished wartime assignment as a roving correspondent.

The *Chicago Tribune* and the tabloid *New York Daily News,* both circulation leaders, were jointly published by cousins Robert R. McCormick and Joseph Medill Patterson. The *Tribune,* with George Scharschug as foreign editor in Chicago and Paul E. Jacoby as assistant, had David Darrah in London, Edmond L. Taylor in Paris, along with Larry Rue and Alex Small; Sigrid Schultz was in Berlin; E. R. Noderer in Rome; Donald Day in Riga; and Sam Pope Brewer in Spain. The sister paper, the *New York Daily News,* had no independent foreign service, but John O'Donnell and his wife Doris Fleeson, both columnists for the *News* in Washington, were in Berlin as the war began. They went to London, where O'Donnell remained briefly and then went to France for a time.

The *Christian Science Monitor* had Roscoe Drummond as executive editor in Boston at the beginning of the war. Walter W. Cunningham, Henry Sowerby, and Charles E. Gratke, all with substantial overseas experience, were foreign editors. Erwin D. Canham, Washington bureau chief, had a comparable background.

In London, Mallory Browne was chief of the *Monitor*'s European service, with John Sidney Braithwaite as administrative manager for Europe on a long-term basis. The London staff included A. Godfrey Lias, Peter Lyne, Ronald Maillard Stead, John May, Harold Hobson, and Melita Spraggs Knowles. J. Emlyn Williams was in Berlin, but was forced to leave because of his British citizenship. He was replaced by Joseph C. Harsch, formerly in the Washington bureau. William Henry Chamberlin, formerly in Moscow and Tokyo, had succeeded Browne and Sisley Huddleston in Paris. Saville R. Davis was in Rome, Reuben H. Markham in the south of Europe, at Sofia, and Edmund Stevens in Stockholm and Moscow.

A number of limited newspaper services operated in the United States during the war. The evening *New York Sun* had Herrick Brown as cable editor in New York. William Bird was in Paris, and British-born Gault MacGowan of the New York staff was in London on holiday as the war began and remained there for the paper. The *New York World Tele-*

gram, a Scripps-Howard newspaper, named Robert E. Dickson, formerly of the *New York Herald* Paris edition, to direct its cable desk. He had special news analyses prepared in Washington by William Philip Simms, foreign editor of the Scripps-Howard Newspaper Alliance and in charge of UP service in France during World War I.

The *Baltimore Sun* had Frank R. Kent, Jr., in Paris, and Paul W. Ward moved out to the French front. The *Wall Street Journal* had G. V. Ormsby in London. William Mellors (Bill) Henry, representing the *Los Angeles Times,* was in France where he also was called upon to speak over the Columbia Broadcasting System network.

The *New York Post,* which had gone through changes since 1933,[10] introduced a new foreign affairs column as the war began. It was written by Paul A. Tierney, assistant managing editor. The paper also arranged to receive the London *News-Chronicle* service.

The *Chicago Times,* an afternoon tabloid established in 1929 by Samuel Emory Thomason, former general manager of the *Chicago Tribune,* was a liberal, nonsensational paper. In 1938 it undertook to provide some direct coverage of international affairs. Gail Borden, its managing editor, went to Europe where he covered the Munich crisis both from Germany and Czechoslovakia. He later went to Tokyo and Shanghai to observe the situation. While in London, Borden engaged Richard Busvine as a correspondent there. Back in Chicago, he named Irving P. Pflaum as foreign editor. A former UP correspondent reporting parts of the Spanish Civil War, Pflaum was assisted by Emmett Deadman.

When the war began in Europe the *Chicago Times* added Denis Weaver, formerly of the *News-Chronicle,* and John Holman to its London staff. Busvine was made a roving correspondent. The paper had Hazel McDonald writing from France, then the only woman correspondent accredited to the French army. Following U.S. entrance to the war in December 1941, Pflaum joined the office of the Coordinator of Information (COI) in Washington and served in government posts there and in Europe throughout the war. Deadman also left to join the U.S. Army Air Force and became a prisoner of war in July 1943 when shot down over Hanover.

Roland Wood succeeded Pflaum as foreign editor of the *Chicago Times* during the war. Bruce Grant, city editor in Chicago, went to London, and Weaver moved from there to Stockholm. Other writers added to the staff as the war continued included Carleton (Bill) Kent, who went

---

10 See details of these changes in Robert W. Desmond, *Crisis and Conflict: World News Reporting Between Two Wars 1920–1940* (Iowa City: University of Iowa Press, 1982), pp. 358–59.

from the Washington bureau to Guadalcanal; Keith Wheeler, also was in the Pacific; Frank Smith, went to U.S. Army headquarters in Australia; and Harrison Forman, formerly in China for the *New York Times,* was in Chungking. James Wellard became a correspondent for the paper in North Africa in 1942. Virginia Hall was in Madrid, B. T. Richardson in Ottawa, and Betty Kirk in Mexico City, where she also represented the *Christian Science Monitor.* Lawrence and Sylvia Martin wrote from Central and South America, and Herbert Clark, formerly in Buenos Aires for the UP, wrote from there for the *Chicago Times.*

Two new dailies were established in the United States during the war years, each with its own foreign service. The first was *PM,* a New York afternoon tabloid beginning June 18, 1940. The paper was written and made up in a semimagazine style, carried no advertising, and was expected to be self-supporting on the basis of circulation revenue. It was conceived and edited by Ralph Ingersoll, experienced as an editor of the *New Yorker, Time,* and *Fortune.* It was financed chiefly by Marshall Field III, then forty-seven and heir to a fortune derived from the Chicago department store bearing his grandfather's name.[11]

With the European war already in progress, *PM* received the UP service, but also sent its own correspondents abroad. Ingersoll himself went to England and Russia, China, Turkey, and Egypt in 1940–42. He interviewed Stalin and Chiang Kai-shek, among others. Classified 1-A in the draft, he volunteered for service at forty-one and entered the army as a private in July 1942, becoming a lieutenant-colonel by 1945.

In Ingersoll's absence, *PM* was conducted by John P. Lewis, managing editor, and Max Lerner, chief editorial writer. Robert Neville, formerly a correspondent for the *New York Herald Tribune* and then foreign editor of *Time* magazine, was foreign editor of *PM* in 1940–41. During that year he went to Vichy, capital of unoccupied France, Berlin, Cairo, and the Philippines. Richard O. Boyer went to Rome, Berlin, and Central America. Carl Wall also wrote from Berlin in 1941, and Carl Randau from Japan. Louis Raemakers, famed Dutch political cartoonist of World War I, reached the United States early in 1940 and drew some cartoons for *PM.* Ben Robertson[12] went to London in 1940 and Moscow in 1942. Neville returned to *Time* magazine in 1941 and was followed as foreign editor of *PM* by Alexander H. Uhl, formerly of the AP.

---

11   Others with an original financial interest in *PM* included John Hay (Jock) Whitney, Dorothy Thompson, George Huntington Hartford II, Philip K. Wrigley, M. Lincoln Schuster, Harry Scherman, Mrs. Louis Gimbel, Marion Rosenwald Stern, Lessing Julius Rosenwald, Garrard Bigelow Winston, and Dwight Deere Wiman.

12   Not to be confused with Sam Robertson of the Canadian Press.

The second new daily in the United States was the *Chicago Sun,* a broadsheet also financed by Marshall Field III, and presenting the only morning competition to the *Chicago Tribune.* In contrast to the *Tribune,* it was planned as a daily friendly to the Democratic administration in Washington, had a far more internationalist view, and was sympathetic to the British position in the war. It was published on a contract basis in the building and from the presses of the afternoon *Chicago Daily News.*

The first issue of the *Sun* appeared on the morning of December 5, 1941, just two days before the Japanese attack at Pearl Harbor drew the United States into the war as a full belligerent. One result was that the *Tribune* became almost equally internationalist and strong in the Allied cause. This deprived the *Sun* of part of its original reason for existence and expectation of popular support. Like *PM* and to an extent like the *Chicago Times,* the *Sun* was forced to recruit staff members from among persons already known for their work. It also arranged to receive service from the United Press and from the North American Newspaper Alliance. The *Sun* was unable to obtain Associated Press service, however, because the *Tribune,* a long-time AP member, objected to that same service being made available to a new paper competitive in the morning field. This *Tribune* objection was effective under the AP by-laws. The *Sun* brought suit and the case reached the United States Supreme Court, where in 1945 the limitation on membership was held to constitute unfair practice, forcing the AP to amend its by-laws. The *Sun* had received the UP service since 1941 and built a foreign and domestic service as well as a war coverage of its own.

The new paper was edited by Rex Smith, formerly managing editor of *Newsweek* and also a former AP correspondent. Hubert R. Knickerbocker, experienced as a European correspondent and a Pulitzer Prize winner in 1931, came from the INS as director of the foreign service. Turner Catledge, in Washington for the *New York Times* since 1929, took charge there for the *Sun.* In its general administration, Silliman Evans, publisher of the *Nashville Tennessean,* took a leave of absence to become publisher of the paper. Frank Taylor, former managing editor of the *St. Louis Star-Times* was assistant publisher. E. Z. Dimitman, formerly of the *Philadelphia Inquirer,* became executive editor.

Rex Smith left the *Sun* in 1942 to join the Army Air Force. Catledge succeeded him as editor-in-chief, but returned to the *New York Times* in 1943. Evans also returned to the Nashville paper, and Field himself became editor and publisher of the *Sun.* Knickerbocker continued as foreign editor, moving about the world also as a correspondent until February 1945. He resigned then to turn to radio news reporting, succeeded on the paper by Ernest Von Hartz, formerly of the *New York Times* cable desk.

The *Chicago Sun* foreign staff during the war years included M. W. Fodor, respected as a correspondent for the *Manchester Guardian* and the *Chicago Daily News* in Vienna until the Nazi seizure of Austria in 1938; J. Edward Angly, formerly of the AP and the *New York Herald Tribune;* Frederick Kuh, formerly chief of the UP bureau in Berlin; Mark T. Gayn, long in the Far East, including service in the foreign news department of the Domei agency in Tokyo from 1934 to 1937, but more recently in New York as foreign news editor of *Time* magazine; Peter D. Whitney, former news editor of the *San Francisco Chronicle;* and such other experienced newsmen as Chester Morrison, Harry Lang, Edd Johnson, John Graham Dowling, W. A. S. Douglas, Cedric Salter, John Mecklin, and John Wilhelm.

Among specialized services in the United States as the European war began in 1939, the North American Newspaper Alliance (NANA) of New York was distributing reports on the international situation by John Gunther, Negley Farson, and Walter Duranty, all known as correspondents and writers on world affairs. It also carried articles by Thomas R. Henry of the *Washington Star,* and by Colonel Frederick Palmer, veteran correspondent and chief censor for the AEF in 1917–18. Background dispatches were provided by Sir Arthur Willert, formerly in Washington for the London *Times* and later chief press officer in the British Foreign Office, and by André Géraud (Pertinax), who had been editorial columnist for *l'Echo de Paris* before the French surrender and his arrival in the United States.

A new service, the Overseas News Agency (ONA) was established in New York in 1940. It worked closely with the Jewish Telegraphic Agency (JTA), of which it was an outgrowth and a subsidiary. Formed to provide interpretative reports, it had as chairman Herbert Bayard Swope, formerly executive editor of the *New York World,* and as vice chairman William Allen White, editor of the *Emporia Gazette* of Kansas and a magazine writer on public affairs and personalities. H. R. Wishengrad, editor of the JTA, was founding editor of the ONA. Directors included George Backer, president of the JTA and then also editor and publisher of the *New York Post,* and Harold K. Guinzberg, president of the Viking Press, New York. Victor M. Bienstock, formerly of the *New York World* and *New York Herald Tribune,* became London representative. After the United States entered the war in December 1941, the ONA sent correspondents to all open theaters of war, women as well as men. ONA copy went by airmail, for the most part. It also distributed political cartoons by the Hungarian artists, Alios Derso and Emery Kelen.

Writers for the ONA included Sir Philip Gibbs, who had distinguished himself as a correspondent during World War I, and Hendrik Willem Van Loon, also a World War I correspondent. Both were known for their books of fiction and nonfiction since that time. Another was Wythe Williams, long in Europe during and after World War I for the *New York Times* and other services, and then editor of the *Greenwich Time* in Connecticut.

From Paris prior to the French surrender of June 1940, Press Alliance distributed special articles. Operated by Paul Winkler, European representative of the Hearst-owned King Features Syndicate, and also head of a French syndicate, Opera Mundi, his service provided contributions by such writers as Emil Lengyel, identified with the *New York Times;* Geneviève Tabouis, political editor of *l'Oeuvre,* a Paris daily; and Alfred Trynauer, for ten years in charge of the INS Vienna bureau until forced out by the German seizure of Austria in 1938.

News photographers and newsreel cameramen came into greater prominence than ever before. When the war began, Acme Newspictures, allied to the United Press and to the Newspaper Enterprise Association (NEA) of Cleveland, all part of the Scripps enterprises, had Robert P. Dorman as general manager in New York. The European staff was headed by Milton Bronner in London and Jean A. Graffis in Paris representing both Acme and NEA. Acme had thirty representatives in European cities and also had the service of Planet News of London, with its own staff of some twenty photographers. Dorman flew to Europe to coordinate the work of the photographers.[13]

The Hearst-owned International News Photos (INP), allied with the International News Service and Universal Service, and directed by Harry Baker as editor in New York, had Walter Hoare in London, Nicholas G. Revay in Paris, George Pahl in Berlin, Umberto Romagnoli in Rome, and Frank Muto in Warsaw. Sam Schulman and Horace Abrahams were sent immediately from New York to Paris at the beginning of the war.

The Associated Press of Great Britain (APGB) handled photos for AP member papers, with six editors and a dozen photographers in London and arrangements with other picture services and freelance photographers. Wide World Photos, then a subsidiary of the *New York Times,* had Emile Barrière in Paris and Leonard Wolfeil in London. It also arranged with professional photographers in many places for such coverage as might be desired.

The illustrated magazines in Great Britain, France, the United States, and Germany depended upon their own photographers, as well as upon existing picture syndicates and freelance photographers. This was true

---

13 Dorman's experience as a news photographer began with the Pershing punitive expedition into Mexico in 1916–17. He was one of the first newsmen to interview and photograph Adolf Hitler in the early 1920s.

especially for such relatively new picture magazines as *Life* and *Look* in New York, *Picture Post* in London, and *Match* in Paris, but it also was true for some of the earlier magazines such as *Collier's Weekly*, the *Saturday Evening Post*, the *Illustrated London News*, and the *Illustrirte Zeitung*.

Life magazine was associated with the news-magazine *Time*, both weeklies, and with the monthly, *Fortune*. All three were under the ownership of Henry R. Luce and used photos, maps, and art work in full measure. When hostilities commenced, they were only beginning to assign or engage their own correspondents abroad, having depended previously for foreign reports and background upon the news agencies, newspapers, and library reference sources. *Newsweek*, the chief competing weekly news magazine in the United States, also developed its own foreign service, and *Collier's* and the *Saturday Evening Post* advanced in that respect, even as they had during World War I.

Collier's in 1938 had engaged Frank Gervasi, formerly of the INS staff in London. Soon after the European war began it also engaged William Hillman in London as European director for INS. The *Saturday Evening Post* had engaged as European representative Demaree C. Bess, formerly of the *Christian Science Monitor* staff. Edgar P. Snow in China for the London *Daily Herald* and *New York Sun* became a writer for the *Saturday Evening Post* in the Far East and then in the Soviet Union.

Time magazine had Walter Graebner in London, where *Life* had John Phillips as a photographer. Louis de Rochemont was in Paris as European manager for *Time, Life,* and for the *March of Time*, a monthly film documentary, of which Sherry Mangan was a staff member. Stephen Laird was in Berlin for *Time;* M. Fillmore Calhoun was engaged in Rome; Thomas D. McEvoy was there as a photographer for *Life;* and Harry Zinder was in Palestine.

Early in August 1939 *Time* had sent Robert Neville to Europe. Charles Wertenbaker of the New York staff succeeded him in October and was based in Paris. With the surrender of the city in June 1940, he returned to New York as foreign news editor and then was war editor until 1943, when he became active as a correspondent again. As Wertenbaker left Paris in 1940, so did Mary Welsh (then Mrs. Noel Monks). Born in the United States and earlier a member of the *Daily News* staff in Chicago, she had become acquainted with Lord Beaverbrook and had worked for his *Daily Express* in London and then in Paris. She was in the London bureau of *Time* after June 1940.[14]

---

14   Mary Welsh became the fourth wife of Ernest Hemingway in March 1946. Martha Gellhorn, whom he married in 1940, was his third wife. Hadley Richardson, his first wife, married in 1921, in 1933 became the wife of Paul Scott Mowrer.

Joseph B. Phillips, formerly in Europe for the *New York Herald Tribune,* returned to New York from Moscow in 1937 to become foreign editor of *Newsweek.* Ernest K. Lindley in Washington and Harold Isaacs in Chungking in 1938 gave further authority to the magazine, but as with *Time,* its foreign coverage was to develop in force only after the United States entered the war in 1941.

The radio medium began to recruit new staff members to report and comment upon the news as it developed each day. For the NBC, Abel Alan Schechter in New York directed the network news and special events broadcasts. Fred Bate in London was in charge of European coverage. Dr. Max Jordan moved from Basel to Berlin and was assisted first by Warren Irvin, formerly in Geneva for the *New York Times,* and later by William C. Kerker. NBC had French-born Paul Archinard in Paris, Philip McKenzie in Rome, and some forty-five other staff and stringer correspondents throughout the world.

John Lloyd, AP bureau chief in Paris, spoke from there on the NBC network, with air raid sirens sounding behind his voice. T. R. Ybarra, an experienced correspondent, broadcast a nightly European news round-up from New York. Dorothy Thompson and John Gunther also spoke from New York. H. V. Kaltenborn transferred from CBS to NBC in 1940 and continued his analyses. Other NBC correspondents at that period included Charles Lanius and David Colin in Rome, John Mac-Vane in London, Martin Agronsky in the Balkans, Helen Hiett in Madrid, and Joan Livingston in Shanghai.

For the Columbia Broadcasting System, Paul W. White, director of the news organization in New York, conferred in London in June 1939 with Edward R. Murrow, European director; William L. Shirer, Berlin correspondent; and Thomas Grandin, Paris correspondent. As the German attack started, Eric Sevareid, formerly of the Paris edition of the *New York Herald Tribune* and of the UP, broadcast regularly from Paris for CBS. Bill Henry, in Europe for the *Los Angeles Times,* added his voice. Charles B. Barber and Cecil Brown in Rome for INS also began broadcasting for CBS. Brown later broadcast from Singapore, Australia, and New York.

Charles Collingwood and Lawrence Edward (Larry) LeSueur, formerly of the UP, joined CBS and traveled widely in Europe and elsewhere. Major George Fielding Eliot, who had resigned from the U.S. Army in 1932 so that he might speak and write without official complications, broadcast for a time from London and later from New York. He also wrote a syndicated military affairs column for the *New York Herald Tribune.* Edwin Hartrich, in Berlin for that paper in 1940, reported from there for CBS when Shirer returned to broadcast from New York. Elmer Davis, formerly of the *New York Times,* succeeded Kaltenborn as news commentator and analyst for CBS when Kaltenborn moved to NBC.

The Mutual Broadcasting System (MBS) had only five correspondents outside the United States when the war began in Europe. John S. Steele was in London, Sigrid Schultz in Berlin, Arthur Mann followed by Waverly Root in Paris, and Peter Tompkins in Rome. William Hillman, then of *Collier's,* and Patrick Maitland of the London *Times* were called upon as needed. David Driscoll in New York headed the news and special events department. Raymond Gram Swing, vastly experienced, broadcast daily from New York over the network.

The British Broadcasting Corporation (BBC) had a staff of news "readers" or broadcasters in London, directed by A. P. Ryan, formerly of the *Daily Telegraph* and the *Manchester Guardian.* Arthur Ernest Barker, formerly of the *Times,* was news editor of the Foreign Language Services introduced in 1938 and extended to include news reports in sixteen languages.

For the BBC, correspondents were actively assigned from the beginning of the European war. Charles J. T. Gardner was with the Royal Air Force in France, Richard Dimbleby was at B.E.F. headquarters, and Chester Wilmot served as a BBC correspondent throughout the war. Edward Ward was in Finland to report the war of 1939–40, in Paris in its last days as a free capital, and later in Libya, where he was captured. Godfrey Talbot also was in Egypt and Libya. Others active for the BBC on various wartime fronts included Anthony Kimmis, John Snagge, Robin Duff, Robert Dunnett, and Frank Gilliard. Alistair Cooke broadcast from the United States, and J. B. Priestley, novelist and playwright, was a regular wartime BBC broadcaster from London.

The experience of many former correspondents and overseas news specialists was enlisted by the BBC before the war or during it. Among them were Vernon Bartlett and Paul Winterton, formerly of the *News-Chronicle;* Darsie R. Gillie and Bernard Moore, formerly of the *Morning Post;* H. D. Harrison and C. F. Whittall, formerly of Reuters; Clifford Hulme, Ralph Parker, and Iverach Macdonald, formerly of the *Times;* N. F. Newsom, former foreign editor of the *Daily Telegraph,* and Hugh Carleton Greene, formerly at European posts for that paper.

The Canadian Broadcasting Corporation (CBC), established in 1936, and the Australian and South African networks had correspondents speaking from Europe. Radio was highly developed in much of Latin America, and most of the warring countries vied to have their programs broadcast or rebroadcast in those countries. The Italian and German radio programs tended to be heavy with propaganda. Efforts were made in Germany and Italy to jam broadcasts from other countries, and otherwise to discourage listeners from paying attention by making it difficult or even illegal for them to do so. Broadcasts in and from Japan and the Soviet Union also had a strong propaganda content.

*   *   *

The power and speed of the German *blitzkrieg* brought the surrender of Warsaw and established control over half of Poland before the end of September 1939. The Red Army captured the eastern half of Poland within the same time and concluded treaties with Estonia, Latvia, and Lithuania in September and October by which Russia was able to establish naval bases, air bases, and military stations in all three of those Baltic republics, soon to be swallowed up by the Soviet Union.

Russia made demands upon Finland in November 1939 for comparable treaty rights, and also called for the withdrawal of Finnish troops mobilized at that country's own frontiers. The government of Finland rejected both demands. In response, the Soviet Union attacked on November 30. Russian planes bombed Helsinki and Red Army troops moved in along the north-south border with the USSR. Naval forces also were employed in the attack. Finnish forces held off Red Army attacks until March 1940 when the so-called Mannerheim Line, maintained under the command of Finnish General Baron Karl Gustav Mannerheim, was broken by Soviet power and the war was soon over. The port city of Viipuri (Viborg) with a population of 54,000 was ceded to the Soviet Union, along with the Karelian Isthmus near Leningrad. In all, Finland lost about 16,000 square miles of territory, resettling the 450,000 population elsewhere in Finland.

Russia's attack on Finland, following its move into eastern Poland and the Baltic republics, seemed to most of the world to be a cynical action. Sympathy went to the small countries, and especially to Finland, with admiration for its gallant resistance. Russia was expelled from the League of Nations as a gesture of disapproval. It was virtually the last action the League was able to take.

The Russo-Finnish War lasting only about three and one-half months was difficult to report. Moscow refused to permit any correspondent from the foreign press to enter its war zone, and all Soviet reports came through the Tass agency. Neither was the Finnish government cooperative in making it possible for correspondents to reach the front areas on its side of the line. The movement of correspondents in a Europe at war was not easy because of complications relating to visas, transportation, and security precautions.[15] Even so, a considerable group of correspondents managed to reach Helsinki. Only a few were permitted to go

---

15   To prevent correspondents of neutral countries changing sides while presumably in possession of military information, British authorities required that those in France with their forces must agree to remain at least three months. When Webb Miller, UP, left France to go to Finland, short of that period, it was only after lengthy negotiations. Then, traveling via London, Amsterdam, and Copenhagen to Helsinki, he had to carry a separate briefcase to accommodate the documents required to cross the various frontiers.

to the combat zone, where they endured 40-below-zero temperatures. Most were obliged to write from well behind the lines, or from Helsinki itself, on the basis of such scraps of information as they were able to obtain. In these circumstances, the reports of the war were generally unsatisfactory, on a day-to-day basis, and sometimes were made worse by inaccurate and misleading headlines prepared by editors thousands of miles away and unfamiliar with the issues and the territory. In one sense, the Russo-Finnish War was technically unrelated to the general European war or to World War II, but was a separate Soviet campaign, somewhat like Italy's earlier campaign in Ethiopia.

Among Anglo-American correspondents in Finland during some part of the war there were Webb Miller, Edward W. Beattie, Jr., Herbert Uexkuell, and Ralph E. Forte, all of UP, plus Norman B. Deuel, who had been moved from Moscow to Helsinki for the UP in September. The AP was represented by Paul Sjoblom, Helsinki correspondent, and by Wade Werner, Thomas F. Hawkins, and Lynn Heinzerling. The INS had Peter de Hemmer Gudme covering the Scandinavian countries, Walter Schwartz, formerly in Copenhagen, and Courtney Terrett, formerly of the *New York World.* Reuters was represented by Gordon Young and Desmond Tighe. James Aldrich, an Australian in Helsinki since 1938 for the Australian Newspaper Services, was engaged by NANA, and William L. White also reported the war for NANA.

For newspapers of the United Kingdom and the United States, Ralph Hewins of the *Daily Mail* was the only correspondent present throughout the entire period of the Russo-Finnish War. Others included W. H. (Rex) Hartin, also of the *Daily Mail;* Geoffrey Cox, *Daily Express;* William Forrest, *News-Chronicle;* Virginia Cowles, *Sunday Times;* Harold N. Denny and Danish-born Karl J. Eskelund, *New York Times;* Walter Kerr, *New York Herald Tribune;* Leland Stowe, *Chicago Daily News;* Richard Busvine, *Chicago Times;* and Donald Day, long in Riga for the *Chicago Tribune.*[16]

In Finland to represent the radio medium were Edward Ward, BBC; Warren Irvin, NBC; and Edwin Hartrich, CBS. William L. White ("Young Bill"), son of William Allen White, broadcast also for CBS while writing for NANA. Frank Muto was in Finland as a photographer for INP, Eric Calcraft for Acme Newspictures, Carl Mydans on an early assignment as a photographer for *Time* and *Life.* Another was Arthur Menken of Paramount Newsreel, who had made films of the evacuation

---

16 Finland joined with Nazi Germany in 1941 to do battle against Soviet Russia, and regained temporarily the territory yielded to Russia in 1940. Day joined the Finnish army in 1942 and in 1943 became a broadcaster in Germany for the Ministry of Propaganda. He was one of eight U.S. citizens later accused of wartime treason.

of Nanking in 1937. Thérèse Bonney of France was the only woman photographer present, and she received a decoration from the Finnish government for her pictures of the resistance.

During the brief war, which ended March 12, 1940, there were approximately one hundred correspondents for various countries in Finland at some time, including some for the Scandinavian press and the German press. Most reports went by telephone to Copenhagen and so to London or other centers for use or relay. No correspondent ever saw a censor during this time, but all news messages were subject to a sharp Finnish censorship before they were permitted to leave the country. Moscow, after proceeding under a "responsibility censorship" since May 1939, had re-established an advance censorship in the Foreign Commissariat Press Department on December 29, 1939.

In Full Fury, 1940

7

Nineteen forty brought war in full fury to Europe. The *sitzkrieg,* or what British wits also had called the Bore War, ended in March 1940.

There had been no occasion for such witticism in China since 1931, nor in Poland or Finland or the Baltic republics since the previous September of 1939. It cannot be said that anybody wanted war in western Europe since that time, but war had been "declared," and war had been expected. A watch had been maintained in Luxembourg, and some correspondents visited the Maginot and the Siegfried lines. Berlin correspondents had been taken to see what the Germans wanted them to see in Poland. Through such visits, and through radio programs and documentary films prepared by the Propaganda Ministry, the Nazis attempted to establish the point that resistance to its armed forces was suicidal.

In London and Paris the organizations that existed at the end of 1939 for the reporting of events and for keeping watch over the "phony war" continued with only a few changes. In London, William H. Stoneman, head of the *Chicago Daily News* bureau, moved to the British Expeditionary Forces headquarters in France in October, with Helen Kirkpatrick assigned to direct the bureau. The United Press sent Clifford L. Day from London to handle traffic developing at Amsterdam. Harold Peters took charge of a comparable relay bureau in Copenhagen, with Edward W. Beattie, Jr., and Howard K. Smith attached to that bureau. Jack Fleischer came from New York in February 1940, and to Stockholm in April and to Berlin in May. The Associated Press had Drew Middleton and G. H. P. Anderson in the London bureau, and James Wesley Gallagher arrived from New York. J. Norman Lodge and Preston Grover also were in the Copenhagen bureau in March 1940.

In London, Basil Henry Liddell Hart, British military correspondent since World War I, became a writer in 1940 for NANA. Allen H. Bill arrived in London for the *Winnipeg Tribune* and other dailies in the Southam Newspapers group. He provided special coverage relating to Canadian troops in England and France at that time.

Quentin Reynolds, a member of *Collier's* staff since 1934, was sent to

Paris in 1939. The *New York Times* assigned Cyrus L. Sulzberger to the Balkans area in 1940. A nephew of Arthur Hays Sulzberger, publisher of the *Times,* he had been in news work since 1934 for the *Pittsburgh Press* and for the United Press in Washington.

The press of Norway and Denmark had representatives in London. Among them were Axel Thorstad of *Dagbladet,* Oslo; Herman K. Lehmkuhl, *Aftenposten,* Oslo; M. Martinsen and Mrs. Lellemer Flem, *Norges Handels og Sjofartstidende,* Oslo; Sven Tillge Rasmussen and Jen Gielstrup, *Politiken;* Terkel M. Terkelson, Sven Ebbeson, and Ebbe Munck, *Berlingske Tidende;* Emil Blytgen-Petersen and Mrs. Ragna Palmer, *National Tidende,* all of Copenhagen.

The savagery of World War II became as apparent in Europe in the spring of 1940 as it already had become in China. In Berlin, plans were completed in March for the invasion of neutral Norway and Denmark on April 9.

Warren Irvin, NBC correspondent, learned of the plan and started from Berlin to Oslo to cover the arrival of German forces. Erik Seidenfaden, editor of *Politiken* of Copenhagen, observed German warships moving north through the Kattegat. He chartered a plane and, at considerable personal risk, flew from Denmark to Norway, saw the German ships approaching the coast, filed a report from Oslo to Copenhagen describing his observations, and then went on to Stockholm. Otto D. Tolischus of the *New York Times* Berlin bureau was in Norway, but left on the night of April 8, a few hours before the invasion began. Nicolas Blaedel, foreign editor of *Berlingske Tidende,* Copenhagen, and a radio commentator, received sufficient warning of the German move into Denmark on the same date to escape to Sweden.

Leland Stowe of the *Chicago Daily News* had gone to Stockholm after the conclusion of the Russo-Finnish War in March. There he and Edmund Stevens, writing for the *Christian Science Monitor,* decided that an important story might develop in Norway relative to a British naval blockade to prevent shipment of Swedish iron ore to Germany by way of the Norwegian port of Narvik, far to the north. They arrived in Oslo on April 8 to follow up this concept, and were present when the German invasion began early the following morning. This gave them a new subject and both filed cables at noon. The AP correspondent in Oslo was able to get out a report that the Germans were arriving. Stowe was able to get out one more short cable before all other news reports were blocked. This gave Stowe the first of six or seven world "beats" on the Norwegian situation during the fortnight to follow.[1]

Desmond Tighe of Reuters arrived in Oslo on the morning of the

---

[1] Stowe describes these experiences in his book, *No Other Road to Freedom* (1940), pp. 64–119. See also Joseph J. Mathews, *Reporting the Wars* (1957), pp. 181–82; "War in Norway," by Leland Stowe, in Curt Riess, ed., *They Were There* (1944), pp. 178–87.

invasion, but left for Stockholm as the Germans began to land, so as to escape capture as a British subject and also to be able to report more freely from Sweden. W. H. (Rex) Hartin of the *Daily Mail* had the same experience. Peter C. Rhodes, UP, and Giles Romilly of the *Daily Express* were in Narvik and witnessed a coordinated arrival of German forces there. Rhodes managed to get across the Swedish border to Abisko, where he flashed news of that phase of the invasion. Romilly, a nephew of Winston Churchill, then still Britain's first lord of the admiralty, was captured.

Details of the Norwegian invasion were rounded up during the next few days by neutral correspondents remaining in the country. Stowe and Irvin of NBC got across the border at the end of the week to Gothenburg and Stockholm, where Stowe was able to dispatch the first comprehensive account of the German surprise move into Norway for use by the *Chicago Daily News.* Other papers subscribing to its syndicated service, including the *Daily Telegraph* of London and several papers in Canada, used the story. He also wrote a long report published in *Life* magazine. Because Irvin was unable to broadcast either from Oslo or Stockholm, Stowe had a world beat on the story.[2] Edmund Stevens, who remained in Norway for another week, was able to add further details on the occupation when he also reached Sweden.

First reports on the coordinated April 9 invasion of Denmark came from Sven Cartensen, *New York Times* correspondent in Copenhagen, who radioed a brief message about noon on that day. This was followed very shortly by a cable to New York from Verner Forchammer of INS. From Stockholm, Exchange Telegraph (Extel) later reported the occupation of Copenhagen and the suspension of communications from that capital. British nationals Selkirk Patton in Copenhagen for the *Daily Express,* Anthony Mann for the *Daily Telegraph,* Stephen House for the Kemsley Allied Newspapers, and W. H. Kelland of Extel were captured and held for the duration of the war. In Berlin at this same time, four Danish correspondents and one Norwegian were arrested and interned.

A few days after these invasions, the British navy landed an Anglo-French-Polish force on the western coast of Norway at Namsos and Andalsnes, with the object of gaining control of Trondheim and intending to get to Narvik.

Neutral correspondents seeking to report this campaign proceeded from Stockholm to Storlein, on the Swedish frontier with Norway and

---

2 Stowe received a Pulitzer Prize in 1930 and the Sigma Delta Chi award for correspondence in 1940 for his reports from Norway. In 1941 he received an Honor Award for Distinguished Service from the University of Missouri.

less than a hundred miles from Trondheim. Swedish officials there would not permit them to cross into Norway.

To avoid this problem, Stowe went to Gäddede, also on the frontier, but about a hundred miles farther north, where a mountain road into Norway had just been completed. He was in the company of correspondents from *Dagens Nyheter, Stockholms Tidningen,* and *Svenska Dagbladet,* all of Stockholm, and a Swedish press photographer, Paul Mylander. Stowe and Mylander crossed into Norway and joined British forces there.

Moving by other routes, Desmond Tighe of Reuters and Ralph Hewins of the *Daily Mail* reached Namsos. So did Barbro Alving, woman correspondent for *Dagens Nyheter,* and Kurt Andersson of *Socialdemokraten,* also of Stockholm, both of whom had reported the Russo-Finnish War. Others to reach Namsos were Betty Wasson of CBS, J. Norman Lodge, AP, and Arthur Menken of Paramount News, who made some of the first newsreel pictures showing Nazi bombing of Norwegian towns.

Meanwhile, the British War Office authorized a number of correspondents to go to that part of Norway occupied by Allied forces. Among them were Geoffrey Cox, New Zealand-born correspondent for the *Daily Express;*[3] Alexander Graeme Clifford, sent from France to Norway for the *Daily Mail;* A. E. Watson, Reuters; James L. Hodson, *Daily Sketch* and Allied Newspapers; Stuart Emeny, *News-Chronicle;* Hugh Carleton Greene, *Daily Telegraph;* Pierre Lyautey, *Le Journal,* representing the French press under a "pool" arrangement; and S. R. G. Bonnett, newsreel photographer for Gaumont-British News.

All of these correspondents were in Norway in June 1940 when the Allied forces there were forced to withdraw, lacking adequate air support or artillery and without proper clothing for snow country. Neither was it possible to provide any relief to Denmark. This was such a blow to the government in Great Britain that on May 10 Chamberlain resigned, replaced as prime minister by Winston Churchill.

Just as Copenhagen had been made a wartime news center, so had Amsterdam, Rotterdam, and The Hague. The German April 9 occupations of both Oslo and of Copenhagen had been orderly and made without resistance or bloodshed. This was far from true when the occupation of Holland began on May 10. Air attacks in the manner of the *blitzkrieg* were followed by the advance of armored forces.

Gordon Young of Reuters and other British newsmen in Holland,

---

3   Cox later joined the British army. He was in Crete in 1941 when German paratroopers landed there. In Washington in 1942, he was *chargé d'affaires* in the New Zealand Legation and a member of the Pacific War Council.

aware of the capture of their four colleagues in Copenhagen a month before, were prepared and managed to escape. Both the British and U.S. news bureaus in Holland were put out of operation almost immediately. U.S. correspondents were in danger from the bombings, but as neutrals were able to return to London or Paris. Among them was Beach Conger of the *New York Herald Tribune,* who had been forced out of Berlin in November because he had reported that "Certain persons have been firmly convinced that Germany intends to invade the Netherlands." Others there included Clifford L. Day in charge of a fifteen-member United Press bureau, and Reilly O'Sullivan and Max Harrelson of the Associated Press. U.S. correspondents entering Holland with German troops included Jack Fleischer of the UP, and E. R. (Al) Noderer of the *Chicago Tribune,* formerly in Italy for that paper.

Two days later, on May 12, 1940, German forces entered Belgium, and those foreign correspondents who were there, chiefly in Brussels, departed ahead of the invaders. Among them were Marcel W. (Mike) Fodor, *Chicago Daily News;* Douglas Williams, *Daily Telegraph;* and Frazier Hunt, back in news work for the INS after some years as an executive and writer for Hearst magazines.

With the Low Countries thus brought quickly under German control—"protection" was the word used in Berlin—the Nazi attack was turned on France. In the classic Von Schlieffen pattern of strategy also used in 1914, the Wehrmacht forces swung north of the Maginot Line, which became a costly defensive nothing, cleared the Channel coast, and then pointed toward Paris. The plan had not worked in 1914, but it worked perfectly in 1940. The replacement of General Gustave Gamelin by General Maxime Weygand as French commander-in-chief made no difference.

Spearheaded by divisions of heavy tanks and supported by dive-bombing planes, the Germans reached the Channel on May 22. During the next week they split the British, French, and Belgian military forces into segments, while streams of civilian refugees choked the roads as they moved westward, away from the approaching Germans.

French and British forces, trapped in a pocket, with their backs to the Channel, suffered heavy losses. Yet nearly 300,000 soldiers of the three armies were evacuated from the Dunkirk beach in France in the last days of May. In an amazing cross-channel operation, a flotilla of small boats from the English shores transported most of the British Expeditionary Force to safety, even though arms and equipment were left behind.

Once in full command of the Channel coast, the German armored divisions and air power was directed toward Paris. The full-scale advance began June 5. The depleted Allied forces could not match the weight of the forty-five German divisions supported from the air. From June 7 the German forces swept west and south. French forces in the Maginot Line were blocked from the rear of that line, and other German forces crossed the Seine to approach Paris.

On June 10 Italy declared war on France and on Great Britain. Italian planes bombed the French naval base at Toulon and the port of Bizerte in Tunisia. On that same day, the French government withdrew from Paris to Tours. Churchill flew to Tours June 11 to rally the French leaders, but it was too late. The French army was split.

On June 14 the German army occupied Paris, and the French government moved again, from Tours to Bordeaux. All of France west and south from Paris was overrun by refugees, many seeking to leave the country. Marshal Henri-Philippe Pétain, one of France's heroes of World War I and at the time ambassador to Spain, was called to the premiership, following Paul Reynaud, who had replaced Daladier in March.

There was discussion of France attempting to continue the war from North Africa, but this was impractical and on June 16 the Pétain government asked an armistice. Hitler set his own terms, which were delivered to France on June 20. In the railway car in Compiègne Forest, where General Ferdinand Foch, allied commander in World War I, had presented Armistice terms to the German emissaries on November 11, 1918, the Germans presented their terms to France's representatives on June 21, 1940. Among those present was Adolf Hitler. The armistice was signed on June 22, and an armistice with Italy was signed in Rome on June 23.

Under the terms of the armistice, the French government headed by Marshal Pétain, was established at Vichy, in the south of France. There a zone was designated to extend in a somewhat irregular form from the French-Swiss border opposite Geneva westward to the Pyrenees, and from the Mediterranean northward to a line not far from Tours. France was authorized to maintain a nominal authority within this area and also over remnants of French army and navy units wherever they might be, and over outlying French territorial possessions—but always subject to instructions from Berlin or from German occupation authorities in Paris.

Along with the fall of France, June of 1940 was a fateful month in other respects. Soviet Russia took advantage of the world's preoccupation with affairs in western Europe to demand and gain control of the Bessarabia and Bukovina sections of Rumania. In July the Soviet Union also formalized its earlier occupation of the Baltic republics and eastern Poland, and annexed these areas as parts of the Soviet Union. Also in June, Rumania's government had come under control of the

Fascist Iron Guard; in August the country lost additional territory in Transylvania to Hungary. General Ion Antonescu established a dictatorship with the help of the Iron Guard in September, and King Carol was forced to abdicate. German troops began to enter the country in October 1940, ostensibly to train Rumanian military elements and to protect the Rumanian oil wells at Ploesti. Actually this was the first move toward an extension of Nazi power in the south of Europe.

Following the French surrender, General Charles DeGaulle, who had been under-secretary of war in Premier Reynaud's cabinet of March–June 1940, had reached England. There he used the facilities of the BBC to announce the formation of a Provisional French National Committee, which he proclaimed to be the true voice of France, dedicated to continuing the war in company with Great Britain. The British government, while recognizing the Vichy government under Pétain, also gave full aid and support to DeGaulle, who proceeded to organize a Free French Army and a Provisional Government of Free France.

Winston Churchill became prime minister in May 1940 and could only tell Parliament and the people that he had "nothing to offer but blood, toil, tears and sweat." Dunkirk followed and then the French surrender, which left Great Britain alone to face Germany and Italy. Hitler fully expected the British to accept a compromise peace, and it was more than a month before he was ready to believe otherwise.

News coverage of war-related events between January and June of 1940 brought hundreds of correspondents, photographers, newsreel cameramen, and broadcasters into action in parts of Europe.

The period from the previous September had been marked by German military and political successes. The news flowed quite freely through Berlin, which was pleased to report its gains and felt no need for censorship, except on photographs and radio scripts prior to broadcast. Since the attack on Poland, most accounts of actual combat operations reported by the German press and radio, and as reported to the world from Berlin, originated with German correspondents also trained as soldiers and sent out as fighting members of the Wehrmacht. The *Pressekompagnie,* or PK, under the command of Lieutenant Colonel Hasso von Wedel, a professional soldier and a member of the General Staff, included reporters, news photographers, motion picture cameramen, cartoonists, radio broadcasters and analysts, artists, and editors.[4]

---

4 Seven members of the PK were killed in the invasion of Poland. During the Norwegian invasion, one company of fifty men and 100 technicians ran into difficulties, and sixteen were killed. These totals of PK casualties were announced in Berlin in April 1940. Between 1939 and 1942 fifty to sixty PK members were killed, wounded, or captured. The Japanese army had such "combat correspondents" in the field in China in 1937. The system was used

When the German invasion of Holland, Belgium, and France began in May 1940, the PK group engaged totalled 200 members with 400 technical assistants. They were in charge of Captain Albert Kost, a political figure, and Oberleutnant Paul Ettighoffer, an essayist, novelist, and poet. Some of the best of the earlier dispatches were Ettighoffer's, with others by Horst Lehmann, representing the *Völkischer Beobachter* and *Der Angriff,* and by Kurt Stolzenberg, Fritz Dettmann, and Walter Müller. Lutz Koch gained a certain reputation in 1942 while reporting with General Erwin Rommel's Afrika Korps in the Libyan campaign.

As the war began in 1939, the foreign press corps in Berlin numbered about 200, even following the departure of British, French, and Polish journalists. Among national groups, the U.S. contingent was the largest and most active, and remained so until it was forced to suspend operations in December 1941. As with the Polish invasion, some correspondents in Berlin also were permitted to move to the west, at times even before the areas in combat had been secured. On the other hand, some correspondents were subjected to official protests and some were expelled.

Eight U.S. correspondents were expelled between September 1939 and early 1941. Others expelled included J. T. Mayer of the Swiss *Neue Zürcher Zeitung* in March 1940. The April-May invasions of Norway, Denmark, Holland, Belgium, and Luxembourg that year meant that correspondents representing the media of those countries in Berlin were immediately taken into custody. Technically, they were to be exchanged later for German correspondents or diplomats in those countries. Since all those countries were under occupation, repatriation became a problem, with internment the only alternative.

The first U.S. correspondent forced to leave Berlin after the outbreak of war was Seymour Beach Conger, Jr.,[5] of the *New York Herald Tribune.* One of his uncensored stories appeared in New York on November 14, 1939, and was prominently displayed in the London press of November 15. It reported the prospective invasion of the Netherlands, and also reported unrest in Germany. Conger's communications privileges were revoked in Berlin on November 18; he was excluded from the news conferences at the Foreign Ministry and the Propaganda Ministry, and officials would give him no information. He was not expelled, but when

---

in the Red Army from 1941, and also by the United States Marines in the Pacific from 1942.

5   The elder son of Seymour Beach Conger, Associated Press correspondent in Germany during 1911–17, he was known as "Beach Conger." A second son, Clinton Beach Conger, was known as "Pat." He represented the United Press in Berlin during the 1930s, and then in Zurich. Unfortunately, their identities were somewhat confused in an earlier volume, *Crisis and Conflict.*

it became clear that he would not be permitted to function as a correspondent he was reassigned by the *Herald Tribune* to its Rome bureau.

The second incident under which a U.S. correspondent was forced out related to Otto Tolischus of the *New York Times.* Some of his dispatches from Germany after the Nazis came to power in 1933 had irked them. His reports in 1939 earned him a Pulitzer Prize in 1940, and were the basis of his book, *They Wanted War* (1940). Tolischus went to Norway and Sweden early in 1940, and while there received a message from the Ministry of Propaganda that he would be permitted to return to Germany for just one day, but then would be expelled. The result was that he left Norway a day before the German invasion of April 9, and then left Germany promptly. He was assigned later to Tokyo and replaced in Berlin by Percival Knauth.

For the *New York Herald Tribune,* Conger had been replaced the previous November by Ralph W. Barnes. There he joined Russell Hill, engaged for work in the Berlin bureau in September as he was about to begin graduate study at Cambridge University on a scholarship awarded him at Columbia University in New York. The appointment of Ralph Barnes was remarkable on two counts. First was that he had been the paper's Berlin bureau chief for four years prior to the beginning of the war in 1939. Expelled at that time and since then directing the London bureau, he was nevertheless readmitted to Germany to succeed Conger. Second, despite the complications of crossing the lines between the warring powers, Barnes was permitted to move from London to Berlin by way of Holland, and to join Hill and also Ed Haffel, by then in the Berlin bureau.

With the German invasion of Holland, Belgium, and Luxembourg occurring May 10, 1940, Barnes was with the German forces moving to the attack on the British at Dunkirk. Louis P. Lochner, AP bureau chief in Berlin, also observed that Channel coast action. Hill, as well, moved with the Wehrmacht. At least four Berlin correspondents later were brought to witness the French surrender ceremony, in the Compiègne Forest on June 22, and at the same time to observe Hitler's jig of triumph captured in photos. These were William L. Shirer, CBS, William C. Kerker, NBC, George Axelsson, *New York Times,* and E. R. Noderer, *Chicago Tribune.* On the day before the signing of the armistice, Barnes and Hill were ordered to leave Germany because of stories they had written. Haffel was allowed to remain in the Berlin bureau.

Barnes' offense had been a reference unrelated to his coverage of the Channel attack. He had written a separate piece on German-Soviet relations in which he suggested, with characteristic prescience, that another year might see the two countries in open warfare, despite the 1939 nonaggression treaties they had signed. He was correct, almost to the day.[6] Had he not been a neutral, his return to London might not have occurred.

Correspondents in Berlin who avoided giving offense to the Nazi leadership were unmolested and might even be accorded some advantages. Journeys were arranged to areas in the east and west to observe battle sites. Restaurant privileges were available at a government-maintained Auslands Klub (Foreign Club) in the Potsdamer Platz, where wartime food rationing was scarcely noticeable. Correspondents were given special opportunities to meet and talk with officials. For example, Karl Von Wiegand in June 1940 was granted the first interview with Hitler since the beginning of the year. Huss of INS was another to interview him. Luncheon invitations were extended to individual correspondents by such press officers as Bömer, Dietrich, and Schmidt, ostensibly to maintain friendly relations, but also with the purpose of trying to establish a viewpoint.

The daily news conferences were informal, and questions were permitted. Also, official war communiqués were distributed, and specialists on specific phases of the military campaigns sometimes were present. Officials were prepared at times to assist correspondents in getting and transmitting information, perhaps even when not altogether favorable to Germany. Communications services usually were good. A direct Berlin–New York radiotelephone service was introduced in June 1940. Shortwave radio broadcasts went out from Berlin, and photos could be airmailed by way of Lisbon for transmission by radio.

---

6 It is not possible to say what the basis may have been or the source for Barnes' assessment of the situation. His integrity and professionalism as a correspondent was beyond question. As this writer can attest on the basis of personal friendship and familiarity with his work, there can be little doubt that he had good reason for writing as he did.

It is known that the German command was planning the attack on the Soviet Union long before it occurred on June 22, 1941. Dr. Karl Bömer, director since 1938 of the Foreign Press Section in the Ministry of Foreign Affairs and spokesman for the Ministry of Propaganda, and at times helpful to this writer and other correspondents, had revealed that the Soviet attack was in prospect after having had one drink too many at a Bulgarian Embassy party in Berlin. The date of the party is uncertain, so this may or may not have been Barnes' source. Whether Bömer's indiscretion became known immediately to officials also is uncertain.

What is certain is that Bömer ceased to appear at ministry news conferences in May 1941. Questions by correspondents as to his whereabouts went unanswered. What later became known was that he had been arrested by the Gestapo. After the attack on the Soviet Union began in June, he was tried and convicted before a People's Court, stripped of all titles, and sentenced to prison. He might have been executed for his offense, but later was released through Hitler's personal agreement on the understanding that he would serve in the army on the Russian front. There with the rank of a lieutenant he was wounded and died in August 1942.

Early in 1940, prior to the campaigns from Norway to France, the Propaganda Ministry made some concessions on news releases and restrictions on military matters. One aspect of this interim policy was the placement of stenographers on the ground floor of the ministry, where correspondents gathered in advance of the late afternoon news conference. They were authorized to write or to copy dispatches for postal transmission on Propaganda Ministry stationery and mail them in ministry envelopes, which no censor would open. All the corresponent had to do was to hand his prewritten copy to a member of the stenographic staff, with the address to which it was to go, and with sufficient postage to cover it. It was understood, however, that such copy might be read before being mailed, and that any report regarded as objectionable would not go out. Thus, again, a self-censorship was involved.

This system was used chiefly by staff or stringer correspondents for publications in smaller countries, especially in Europe. Few U.S. correspondents used it, and they were those making brief visits to Germany, or writing something other than spot news, where a delay in mail delivery was acceptable.

With the German military advances in the spring of 1940, and especially after the victory in France, the official German attitude toward the foreign press and radio representatives began to change. The mail system at the Propaganda Ministry ended, previous efforts to cajole correspondents ceased, and a new arrogance appeared.

As the German drive in Belgium and France gathered momentum, many newsmen and women who had left Paris during the inactive winter months returned. One who did not return and was greatly missed was Webb Miller, United Press general manager for Europe, who had reported nearly every great event for more than two decades. Miller had left France for Finland to report the Russo-Finnish War of November to March. Back in London in the spring, he was waiting for credentials so that he might go to Norway. On May 8 he heard Prime Minister Churchill speak in the House of Commons, and returned to the UP bureau in Bouverie Street to write an account of the session. Sometime after 9 P.M. he boarded a train at Charing Cross Station to go to the country. He had to change trains at Clapham Junction, four miles out of London. Early the next morning his body was found there alongside the tracks.

In trying to reconstruct an event which nobody saw, it was presumed that because of the wartime blackout Miller had failed to realize that the train was not at the Clapham Junction station platform, even though it may have stopped and the time was right. It is believed he opened the door of the carriage to step out but pitched down instead and was killed. After surviving millions of miles of travel by every means, and the hazards of several wars, Webb Miller became the first U.S. correspondent to die in World War II.[7]

Wallace Carroll succeeded Miller in charge of UP activities in London. Edward W. Beattie, Jr., back from Finland and the Balkans for the UP, hastened from London to France, as Miller doubtless would have done in that early period in May to report the German drive. From London also, Drew Middleton, AP, Harold N. Denny, *New York Times,* William H. Stoneman, *Chicago Daily News,* and J. Edward Angly, *New York Herald Tribune,* all returned to France, as did Richard Busvine, *Chicago Times,* and Robert G. Nixon, INS.

For the British press, many correspondents who had gone to France with the British Expeditionary Forces in September and October 1939 were still there in May and June. As in World War I, some were directly attached to the BEF General Headquarters, located first at Arras, then at Lille, back to Arras, and then at Boulogne.

To keep the total number of correspondents within manageable size, the British national newspapers were "paired," as they had been in the 1914–18 period, but in an adaptation by which two newspapers were represented by one correspondent for a period of two months. The correspondent was then changed. The paired newspapers were the *Times* and the *News-Chronicle;* the *Daily Telegraph* and *Daily Mail;* the *Daily Herald* and *Daily Mirror;* the *Daily Express* and *Manchester Guardian;* the *Daily Sketch* and the Allied Newspapers.[8]

In addition there were correspondents for Reuters, Press Association and Exchange Telegraph, two for BBC, and news photographers and newsreel cameramen. In some cases, where the total number of correspondents had to be reduced in the judgment of the military, one correspondent might act as an "Eye Witness" for the entire press, with his dispatches made available to all papers through the Ministry of

---

7   The German DNB agency reported Miller's death and added a "comment" to the dispatch: "For a long time foreign neutrals, again and again, have run up against the dark trace of the British Intelligence Service which, sometimes here, sometimes there, goes about its brutal and shady work. And now Miller, this troublesome neutral witness, has fallen victim to the sinister hand of the secret service."

Nobody accepted this fantastic suggestion. Miller was mourned in London, as in many other places. Funeral services there were attended by U.S. Ambassador Joseph P. Kennedy, representatives of the British Ministry of Information, and many friends. His body was cremated, and the urn buried in June 1940 in Dowagiac, Michigan, his family home. James H. Furay, vice-president of the UP, and others were present, including his widow, Mary, and a son. Miller's estate was appraised in 1941 at more than $62,000. In 1943 Mrs. Miller christened a Liberty ship as the *Webb Miller,* and it carried U.S. forces to Normandy during the D-Day invasion of June 1944.

8   The *Daily Sketch* and *Sunday Times* were owned by Lord Kemsley. The Allied Newspapers, formed in 1924, were a score of others under his ownership in important cities of the United Kingdom.

Information. Adding those representing the foreign media, the press-radio correspondents at the British GHQ in France varied between twenty and fifty.

Conducting officers took the correspondents where they wanted to go, with about thirty cars available for transport. The correspondents were required to be uniformed, with the identifying letter "C" on their caps. Stories were written in triplicate, and about a dozen censors were available to go over copy and explain deletions or changes. A correspondent could appeal a deletion or a "kill" in his copy to the chief censor and to the Director of Military Intelligence, then Major General Mason MacFarland. Following the censorship process, one copy was returned to the correspondent, who usually telephoned his story to London or Paris for use or relay. A second copy went to a censorship officer who listened to the telephone transmission to be certain no unauthorized information was conveyed. The same procedure applied to radio correspondents and their copy or scripts.

Correspondents with the French army were subject to much the same procedures as with the British, except that after the first weeks the censorship was "blind"; that is, they had no knowledge of what happened to their copy once it had been submitted for reading. While the censors might delete parts or kill a whole story, they never inserted any words or phrases.[9] In Paris, Pierre Comert, formerly director of the League of Nations Information Section, was press officer and chief censor in the French headquarters at the Continental Hotel. In the field with the French army in Belgium, Percy J. Philip of the *New York Times* Paris bureau was suspected by Belgians of being a German parachutist because of his unfamiliar correspondent's uniform. This placed him in much the same peril as had beset nonuniformed correspondents in Belgium during the early days of World War I. A similar difficulty confronted John Scott of the *News-Chronicle* and Taylor Henry of the AP.

Paired British correspondents at Arras included Sir Philip Gibbs, famed World War I press veteran, back in harness for the *Daily Sketch* and Allied newspapers and having the sensation, as he said, "of being a ghost and walking among ghosts."

Other paired correspondents were James Lansdale Hodson, who alternated with Gibbs. William Forrest, with experience in Spain, Poland, and coverage of the Russo-Finnish War, arrived in France to replace Philip Jordan for the *Times* and the *News-Chronicle*. Jordan

---

9 The French, however, did change the phrase "Polish corridor" to "Polish Pomerania" in deference to a Polish contention that the area was part of ancient Poland and had not been carved out of German territory after World War I, as Germany contended.

went on to Egypt to alternate with H. A. R. Philby of the *Times*. Douglas Williams of the *Daily Telegraph*, about to return to New York after a holiday in England, remained instead to cover the war for the *Telegraph* and the *Daily Mail* in Holland and Belgium in May. He alternated with Geoffrey Harmsworth and Paul Bewsher of the *Mail*. Bernard Grey represented the *Daily Mirror* and the *Daily Herald*, alternating with F. G. H. Salusbury of the *Daily Herald*. E. A. Montague remained for the *Manchester Guardian* and also represented the *Daily Express*.

A. D. Skene Catling remained for Reuters, paired with Exchange Telegraph, and alternated with Alaric Jacob, formerly in Washington for Reuters. Richard D. S. McMillan remained for the British United Press, and R. A. Monson for the Australian Consolidated Press. Richard Dimbleby and Bernard Stubbs were present for the BBC, with E. M. Sayer as an engineer. F. W. Bayliss represented Paramount News, and Ronald Noble was there for Universal Newsreel. L. A. Puttnam and A. G. Malandine were news photographers, and C. W. Bryan de Grineau was an artist for the *Illustrated London News*.

News of Paris and the French army was reported by a large group of correspondents, many of whom already mentioned had been in Paris before the war began. In addition, the AP staff was augmented by Roy Porter and Robert Okin; the UP by Glen N. Stadler; the *New York Herald Tribune* by Beach Conger, formerly in Berlin and Amsterdam; and the *Chicago Daily News* by M. W. Fodor, formerly in Vienna and the Low Countries. Edmond L. Taylor, *Chicago Tribune* bureau chief, resigned because of a policy difference with Colonel McCormick, publisher of the paper. Taylor joined the CBS staff in Paris in December 1939, replacing Thomas Grandin. Larry Rue succeeded Taylor as the *Tribune* Paris correspondent, until David Darrah came from London, with Rue then taking his post there. Victor Lusinshi was correspondent for MBS. A. J. (Joe) Liebling arrived in Paris for the *New Yorker* magazine, and Frederic K. Abbott, long in Paris for INS, AP, and other services, but originally a film specialist, became Paramount News representative.

For the British media, Courtney T. Young, formerly in Brussels along with Harold King, Gordon Waterfield, and Wilfrid Martin joined Martin Herlihy to represent Reuters in Paris. Peter Flynn and U.S.-born Roger Burr joined André Glarner for Exchange Telegraph. Thomas Cadett, formerly of the *Times*, joined Robert Cooper, C. J. Martin, and E. B. F. Wareing to represent the *Daily Telegraph*. José Shercliff represented the *Daily Herald*, Alexander Werth, the *Manchester Guardian*, and Virginia Cowles, the *Sunday Times*. Jerome Willis wrote for the *Evening Standard*. George Millar represented the

Daily Express in Paris, along with Geoffrey Cox, who returned from Norway. A. L. Easterman, former foreign editor of the *Express,* also was in Paris. George Slocombe, another World War I correspondent, returned to press service and wrote for the *Sunday Express.* Mary Welsh (Mrs. Noel Monks) was in the Paris bureau, while Monks represented the *Daily Mail* at that point, with Hugh Muir as editor of the *Continental Daily Mail.*

As the German attack swept to the Channel coast, the main force of correspondents attached to the BEF was withdrawn to safety on May 21. Those who remained up to the last hours of the BEF at Dunkirk included representatives of the paired British papers: H. A. R. Philby, E. A. Montague, Bernard Grey, J. L. Hodson, and Paul Bewsher. Others were Alaric Jacobs for Reuters and Extel, Bernard Stubbs of the BBC, F. W. Bayliss and Ronald Noble, newsreel men, L. A. Puttnam and E. G. Malandine, news photographers, plus Drew Middleton, AP, Edward W. Beattie, Jr., UP, and R. G. Nixon, INS. Nixon had been attached to the BEF for the U.S. press.

When the force of the *blitzkrieg* was turned toward Paris, a withdrawal of correspondents from there began. While reporting that phase of the war, John Elliott, *New York Herald Tribune,* and William Henry Chamberlin, *Christian Science Monitor,* were injured on the road from Verdun to Paris late in May when their car was hit broadside by a French army truck. Alex Small of the *Chicago Tribune* seemed a favorite target for the German dive-bombers, but somehow escaped injury. With the German troops nearing Paris, it was prudent for British correspondents to depart, as well as some U.S. correspondents who had had trouble with the Nazi regime earlier. These included Edgar Ansel Mowrer of the *Chicago Daily News* and Beach Conger of the *New York Herald Tribune.*

Correspondents were among those fleeing the Germans on the roads westward through France. Some accompanied the French government to Tours on June 11, to Bordeaux on June 14, and ultimately to Vichy. They often were under dive-bomber attack. Pierre Comert, French government press officer and censor, was in the group. Louis Huot, an American citizen in charge of Press Wireless transmission facilities in Paris, managed to take a portable transmitter to Tours and to Bordeaux, making it possible for U.S. correspondents to file copy until the equipment was confiscated by the Germans under the armistice terms. Jean A. Graffis of Acme Newspictures walked the entire distance of 400 miles from Paris to Bordeaux in a period of eleven days. He was frequently forced to take cover from air attacks.

Many of those fleeing from Paris and from France itself, including French journalists, contrived to get sea transport from Bordeaux or to reach Spain or Portugal before the Germans closed the borders, and to fly from there to London or elsewhere. Hugh Muir of the *Continental Daily Mail* and C. J. Martin of the *Daily Telegraph* were among the last of the British news group to leave France. Muir later was in Lisbon for the *Daily Mail.*

Among French journalists leaving the country were André Géraud (Pertinax) of *L'Echo de Paris* and *l'Europe Nouvelle* and a contributor also to the *New York Times* and the *Daily Telegraph;* Geneviève Tabouis (Cassandra), *l'Oeuvre;* Emile Buré, *l'Ordre;* Philippe Barrès, formerly of *Le Matin* and *Paris-Soir;* Henri de Kérillis, editor of *l'Epoque;* Elie Joseph Bois, *Le Petit Parisien;* and Pierre Lazareff, *Paris-Soir.* All reached England, and some went on to the United States.

Eight neutral U. S. correspondents elected to remain in Paris until the Germans arrived. They were Henry Cassidy, Roy Porter, and Robert Okin of the AP; Glen N. Stadler, UP; Walter B. Kerr, *New York Herald Tribune;* Alex Small, *Chicago Tribune;* Demaree Bess, *Saturday Evening Post;* and Sherry Mangan, *Time.* They made themselves known to Eugen Pfeihl, press attaché in the German Embassy in Paris before the war, but now with the army as conducting officer with Berlin correspondents brought to witness the armistice and surrender ceremonies.

German policy was to discourage neutral correspondents undertaking to report from Paris. They preferred that news of unoccupied France reach the world through their own DNB agency and through Berlin. Neutral correspondents, including Swiss, Swedish, and U.S. representatives were requested to leave. Some transferred to Vichy, but most left France for other assignments. Mangan of *Time* was perhaps the last to depart. He remained in Paris until August, when he was expelled. Anne Jungman, twelve years in Paris as science and medical correspondent for the *New York Times,* remained until the U.S. entered the war in 1941, but was constantly watched and was inactive journalistically.

The German occupation of Paris and of most of France from June 1940 brought the suspension of the 105-year-old French Agence Havas and an extensive modification in the world exchange of news. The Ring Combination had ended in 1934, but Havas had continued to occupy an important position in parts of Europe, the Middle East, and Latin America. The Agencia Noticiosa Telegrafica Americana (ANTA), established in Mexico City in 1935, a Havas subsidiary, was subsidized in part by the Mexican government. Reuters tried to keep ANTA going in 1940, but the agency expired in 1943. Reuters also tried to maintain the Havas position in South America, as it had in Europe after the Franco-Prussian War of 1870. It did find some clients, but the U.S. agencies were by then well established in Latin America. They replaced

Havas far more generally in providing world news to the press and radio.

Smaller French agencies and the French press and radio had to make important adjustments under the new regime. Dailies, whether published in Paris or other cities, except in the Vichy area, were under pressure from the German occupation to use news reports provided through the DNB agency or other services under German supervision. Paris dailies that continued to appear during the occupation were suppressed after the war as having been collaborationist.

French journalists out of the country when the surrender occurred, or who escaped, were prompt to recognize a need for a wartime service of news that provided an accurate reflection of a true France. Their efforts centered in Great Britain and later in North Africa.

The Battle of Britain, 1940–41

8

France had surrendered on June 22. England was left alone to battle a fully armed Germany and Italy. The expectation was that the power of the Wehrmacht would be concentrated upon the United Kingdom. Its defenses were low because of its evacuation in disarray from France, where equipment of every sort was abandoned. With German forces poised on the French coast, a cross-Channel invasion was anticipated. Indeed, Germany had Operation Sea Lion planned for just such an occasion.

Hitler found it hard to believe that Britain would fight on alone under the circumstances existing in June 1940, and made no effort to activate Operation Sea Lion. Instead, using his new bases along the French coast, he had the Luftwaffe conduct bombing raids on British ports, towns, cities, and air installations, as though in preparation for an invasion, but with the expectation that a British surrender would be forthcoming.

It was July before Hitler was persuaded that no such surrender was in prospect. Perhaps one thing that convinced him was a July 3 British naval attack upon French war vessels in port at Oran, Algeria. The object was to prevent those ships falling under German control, and preferably to have them join with the British navy. The Vichy government of unoccupied France had broken relations with the British government, and the French in Oran refused either to surrender the ships or to scuttle them. The result was that the British naval force sank or captured most of them. The next day, all French naval ships in other ports then under British control were seized.

Technically, the Battle of Britain began as early as June 18, 1940, the day after France had asked Germany for an armistice. It began in earnest, however, on August 8, when waves of German bombers attacked Dover and other channel ports, airfields, and industrial areas. Worse came on August 15 when a thousand German planes bombed as far north as Scotland, followed by the proclamation of a sea blockade of the British Isles, supported by warships, submarines, and aircraft. A concentrated bombing of London on the night of September 6–7, with about 300 planes raiding the capital, was only the beginning of a "blitz" that brought almost nightly attacks through October and November and continued at intervals until June 1941.

The German bombing was extended to other British cities, such as Birmingham, Manchester, Liverpool, Bristol, Plymouth, Portsmouth, Sheffield, and Southampton. Coventry, a cathedral city, was almost completely destroyed in a mass bombing on November 15, 1940. London suffered particularly damaging raids on December 29 and on May 10–11, 1941. Thousands of persons were killed, more thousands injured, and property damage was beyond calculation. In these months, Britain struck back as best it could. Air attacks were directed at German cities, including Berlin and Essen, and also at Channel ports used by the Germans. The Royal Air Force met the raiding German bombers, many of which were shot down.

The Battle of Britain passed its peak of violence in May 1941, when the Parliament building and the British Museum were among the structures hit in London, not to mention Buckingham Palace itself. At that time, German preparations were being made for the attack on the Soviet Union that was to begin June 22, and air attacks on the British Isles were reduced in number and intensity, except for a "baby blitz" early in 1944.

Submarine attacks on British shipping had continued from 1939, and German undersea craft, sometimes traveling in "wolf packs," sank both Allied and neutral ships in the "Battle of the Atlantic." This became a related part of the Battle of Britain, with losses exceeding 2.3 million tons of shipping merely in the interval between April 1940 and March 1941, and losses continued heavy until brought under limited control in 1943.

As the Battle of Britain began in June 1940, the British information media were prepared to give complete coverage, within the bounds of wartime security, to a threat to the nation of the utmost gravity. Media representatives of allied and neutral countries were present in great numbers. They included those "orphans of the storm," journalists for the Free French, Dutch, Danish, Norwegian, and Belgian media, all now suppressed and under German control. The total correspondent group included many already mentioned as having been in London when the war began in 1939. Some of those had left, but others took their places, although not necessarily strangers to London.

For the U.S. news agencies, the Associated Press staff was augmented by J. Norman Lodge, Eddy Gilmore, formerly in the Washington bureau, William W. White, Alfred E. Wall, Edwin Stout, Dwight Pitkin, William J. Humphreys, Hugh Wagnon, and Edward North, a photographer. The United Press additions included Edward W. Beattie, Jr.,

Edmund Allen Russell, William R. Downs, Jr., G. E. Gregory, Harry Hickingbotham, and Daniel Campbell, who was experienced in Latin America. Arriving for the International News Service were Earl Reeves, who had directed the INS service in London during World War I; Anthony J. Billingham, former *New York Times* correspondent in China, injured in the Shanghai bombing of 1937; H. R. Knickerbocker, George Lait, Robert G. Nixon, Thomas C. Watson, Merrill Mueller, and Frank Butler.

Among newspapers of the United States, the *New York Times* London staff was increased by the arrival of David Anderson, James Mac-Donald, and Craig Thompson. For the *New York Herald Tribune* Ralph W. Barnes had returned to London after his second expulsion from Germany, James M. (Don) Minifie had been in Rome, and Tania Long in Berlin. Others for the *Tribune* were Frank Williams, Joseph Evans, and Whitelaw (Whitey) Reid, son of Ogden Reid, editor and publisher of the paper, later replaced by Carey Longmire, formerly of the Paris edition.

For the *Chicago Tribune,* arrivals in London included veteran correspondent Larry Rue, Stanley Johnstone, who had run the Press Wireless office in Amsterdam but joined the *Tribune,* and Guy Murchie. Dorothy Hewitt joined the *Chicago Daily News* bureau. For *PM,* newly established as a New York daily in June 1940, Ben Robertson arrived as correspondent. Ralph Ingersoll, editor of *PM,* paid a visit to London. Austen Lake arrived in 1941 for the Hearst *Boston Record-American,* crossing the Atlantic with a Canadian troop convoy.

Vincent Sheean and Virginia Cowles arrived for NANA, Paul Manning became London manager for NEA, H. P. Andrews came as a photographer for Acme Newspictures, S. N. Behrman for the *New Yorker* magazine, and Robert Low as a writer for *Liberty* magazine. Eric Sevareid and Larry LeSueur, both of CBS radio, were sent to London from Paris. For news and picture magazines, Mary Welsh, American-born wife of Noel Monks of the *Daily Mail,* escaped with him from Paris. There she had represented the *Daily Express,* but in London she joined the recently opened *Time* magazine bureau. Arthur Menken, news photographer and newsreel cameraman, formerly in China, Finland, and Norway, became a London based representative of *Life.* Will Lang became London picture editor for that magazine. George Rodger and Robert Navarro became photographers for *Life* and for the film documentary, the *March of Time.*

The first attacks in the Battle of Britain came along the Channel coast at Dover and Ramsgate, an area labeled "Hellfire Corner" or "Hell's Corner" because of the air battles joined there. Scores of British, U.S., and other newsmen found spots along the cliffs and elsewhere to watch the planes of the Luftwaffe cross from their bases in France, hardly twenty miles away, sometimes to be engaged almost immediately by planes of the Royal Air Force. So-called barrage balloons, large in size and tethered to fly protectively above Dover and other cities, were intended to keep the bombing planes flying high above the targets.[1]

The Grand Hotel at Dover was an accepted press headquarters until the hotel itself was bombed, destroying about one-third of the building. Guy Murchie of the *Chicago Tribune* survived a four-story fall. Both Murchie and Stanley Johnstone were unhurt, but Edward Dean of the *Daily Mail* was slightly injured. Frank Butler of INS escaped serious injury when hit by machine-gun cartridge cases falling from the skies. James Gemmell of British Paramount News had a close call when a bomb fell three yards away but failed to explode. Whitelaw Reid of the *Herald Tribune* had a similar experience.

Five British newsmen aboard an escort vessel in the Channel in August escaped injury when it was shelled by German guns on the French coast. They were Philip Jordan of the *News-Chronicle* and E. Ross-White, a photographer for that paper, Peter Duffield and photographer H. A. Wallis of the *Daily Mail,* and Jerome Willis of the *Evening Standard.*

In London, as the heavy raids began in September 1940, the entire press-radio-photo organization observed and reported the bombings, often at great personal risk. All Londoners were in danger, but correspondents and photographers frequently were in the streets and on the roofs when perils were greatest. Newspaper buildings and offices in central London were a special target for German bombers. News rooms in some cases were moved to basement shelters, and life tended to go underground when the air raid sirens signalled the approach of bombers. Thousands took refuge in the London underground stations, where bunks were installed. There was little sleep during those nights of September-October 1940 when the raids continued for nine or ten hours as waves of German planes came over. Not only were some newspaper buildings hit, but the homes of some of the members of the news group were damaged or destroyed.

Charles M. Maxwell, a *Daily Sketch* photographer, is believed to have been the first newsman killed in the raids. The *Evening Standard* building may have been the first to receive a direct hit, but production was not stopped. The *Daily Herald* building was slightly damaged, and

---

1 One of the diversions of correspondents at Dover was to give names to the balloons. One they named in jest after Sefton Delmar of the *Daily Express,* who weighed 252 pounds. A film showing correspondents at work in Britain and elsewhere in mid-1940 was released as a *March of Time* documentary in the autumn of that year under the title, "On Foreign Newsfronts."

damage to the gas lines made difficulties for the *Daily Sketch.* The *News-Chronicle* and *Star* press room was badly hit in April 1941. The offices of the AP, UP, and INS were seriously shaken by nearby bomb hits.

The homes of Merrill Mueller and Thomas C. Watson, INS; J. Norman Lodge, AP; Daniel Campbell, G. E. Gregory, and Sidney J. Williams, all of UP, were wrecked. W. F. Leysmith of the *New York Times* was injured in a bombing, and William H. Stoneman, *Chicago Daily News,* narrowly escaped when he was bracketed by three exploding bombs. Campbell of the UP was knocked flat by bomb blasts while watching an attack from the roof of the *News of the World* building, which was also UP headquarters in Bouverie Street, just off Fleet Street. Robert G. Nixon, INS, had the soles of his shoes cut to bits walking over shards of glass in the streets after a night raid, and later was hit by a piece of falling shrapnel.

The main target of the bombings in September 1940 was the London dock area along the Thames estuary. This resulted in vast damage in the crowded East End of London. Every part of London was hit, however, by incendiaries, high explosives, and time bombs, one of which landed in the grounds of Buckingham Palace and exploded with considerable effect. The *Times* building in Victoria Street, or Printing House Square, was seriously damaged by a direct hit in October, but production continued. Broadcasting House, BBC headquarters, received a direct hit and a number of radio technicians and staff members were killed.

One of the most notable reports of this period to reach the United States came in a September CBS broadcast, "London After Dark," arranged by Edward R. Murrow, network chief in the capital. Murrow himself broadcast from Trafalgar Square, describing the searchlights fingering the night sky and the limited traffic. He permitted listeners to hear the wail of the air-raid sirens and the voices of Londoners spending the night in a shelter beneath St. Martins-in-the-Field, the historic church on the Square. Murrow also had nine commentators spotted in various parts of London with portable microphones to provide a varied portrayal of what the bombings meant. Among them were Eric Sevareid, CBS, Robert Bowman, *Liberty* magazine, Vincent Sheean, NANA, and J. B. Priestley of the BBC. For use in later broadcasts, Lawrence Gilliam, BBC features director, employed sound trucks to gather material in London and Liverpool as they were being bombed.

London continued to receive heavy bombing through the 1940–41 fall and winter. Murrow's regularly heard broadcasts beginning with his grimly spoken "This is London" were greatly effective. In a climactic raid on the night of Sunday, December 29, vast damage was done to the "City," or business and financial district, in the vicinity of St. Paul's

Cathedral. That edifice was saved from destruction only by chance and the greatest effort of fire fighters. The Bank of England, the "Old Lady of Threadneedle Street," also survived.

The December raids brought destruction of the CBS headquarters in London. The NBC offices in Electra House on the Thames Embankment were damaged and Fred Bate, chief of the network service, was seriously injured. Charles A. Smith, INS chief, lost his home, and Howard Barry, also of INS, was bombed out of his apartment. Three hits were scored on the Savoy Hotel, where about twenty foreign newsmen lived, among them Ernest Taylor (Ernie) Pyle. A columnist for the Scripps-Howard Newspapers, he was in London for several weeks on his first wartime assignment.

The manner in which the news agencies and newspapers managed to carry on during the raids was described by Charles A. Smith of INS:

> Immediately on the sounding of the air raid alarm . . . a member of the staff goes onto the roof to act as official 'spotter' and reporter. Members of the staff remaining in the office do not immediately take shelter, but don steel . . . helmets . . . continue to work . . . and stand by for further word.
>
> So many of the daylight raids have not been productive of central activity that it would be timewasting to seek shelter on every warning. . . . Immediately there is any sign of unusual activity, a senior staffer usually joins the watcher on the roof. . . . Communication is maintained with the office two floors below by a bell system. One ring . . . means aircraft within hearing; two rings, gunfire in the distance; three rings, German planes approaching; four rings, all-clear sounding.
>
> On the sounding the three alarm signal, all staffers are ordered out of the office into the shelter, and only one senior man . . . keeps watch at an open telephone to the cable company, ready to duck if bomb dropping commences in the vicinity. The roof man . . . comes down after giving the three-alarm and joins those in the shelter.
>
> Usually the period spent in the shelter is very brief, . . . but occasionally in the daytime and usually at night very lengthy periods, sometimes amounting to an hour or more, have to be spent below ground. The nervous tension and strain is of course tremendous . . . since it is only a matter of seconds before a bomber formation first sighted miles away . . . is on top of the building.
>
> Operations are possible from the shelter, but on a restricted basis. We have a large section walled and curtained off . . . about 30 by 20 feet . . . we have a long worktable . . . typewriters . . . chairs . . . several camp-beds, sleeping bags, a first aid kit. . . . Our section is about 20 feet below ground and there are seven floors of concrete and steel constructed building on top. Even so, concussion frequently shakes the place right to its foundations, while incendiaries have caused . . . scares. . . .
>
> By an ingenious system, one of our telephone lines . . . operates . . . independently of the switchboard, which could be destroyed without affect-

ing the special shelter line. Thus we can maintain telephonic contact with the cable companies and outside sources like the M.O.I. during a raid. . . . We also have access to another telephone. . . . Unfortunately, I have not been able to have duplicate . . . teleprinters installed and there is considerable danger in coming up into the cable room every five or ten minutes . . . to collect copy.[2]

The last concentrated bombing of London or other cities during the Battle of Britain occurred in the first two weeks of May 1941, notably on the night of May 10–11. A number of London newspaper offices not previously hit were affected in this series of raids. The House of Commons also was hit and made unusable until after the war, more than four years later. Two U.S. correspondents, Merrill Mueller and George Lait, both of INS, had been injured in raids during April, and a number of others had narrow escapes during May. But the May 10–11 raid was the last on London, until the so-called "little blitz" of 1944, followed by V-2 rocket bombings.

British Forces in the Mediterranean

The London press corps during 1940–41 had relatively little mobility, limiting itself almost entirely to the coverage of the grim Battle of Britain. The strength of the Royal Navy, however, made it possible for Great Britain to exert some power in the Mediterranean, as at Oran and Taranto, and in East Africa. Its effort to provide assistance to Yugoslavia and Greece was less successful. But its success against the Italian forces in Libya between December 1940 and February 1941 brought German parachute troops to Crete and General Rommel's Afrika Korps of Panzer tank divisions and planes to open a desert *blitzkrieg* that drove the British Eighth Army eastward again through Libya and deep into Egypt by the end of April 1941.

Independent of the London press corps, although in some cases moving out from London, correspondents became identified with these other aspects of the war in which Great Britain was battling for its existence beyond the boundaries of the United Kingdom itself. Perhaps the first press representatives ever accredited to the Royal Navy were Alexander Massey (Jock) Anderson, manager of Reuters' Alexandria office, and Laurence Edmund (Larry) Allen, of the Associated Press. Allen went from Rome to Alexandria in May 1940, first to cover British forces

---

2 Charles A. Smith, "When Nazi Bombs Drop on London!" *Quill* (January 1941), pp. 5, 18.

in Egypt, but was accredited also to the navy by September. This, again, must have been a precedent, the first for a foreign newsman.

Following the Italian declaration of war and the French surrender in June 1940, Great Britain was concerned that French naval vessels at Toulon, Oran, Dakar, Alexandria, Martinique, and elsewhere might be added to the Italian and German navies. This led to the British naval attack at Oran, and a less successful move against Dakar in September 1940. In November that year the aircraft carrier *Illustrious* used torpedo planes to destroy Italy's battle fleet at Taranto, and the British navy caused further Italian naval losses between Crete and Greece in March 1941. To supply its Middle East Command in Egypt, the British sent troops and war materials all the way around Africa and through the Red Sea.

German air bases had been established in Sicily, which placed Malta, the nearby British island base in the Mediterranean, under air attack and added new peril for British shipping in the area. Indeed, the *Illustrious* was attacked from the air on January 10, 1941, and nearly sunk, and the cruiser *Southampton* was lost the next day. The British navy sank transports carrying Germans to Crete in March, but British ships also were lost, including the cruisers *Gloucester* and *Fiji* sunk, the battleships *Warspite* and *Valiant* badly damaged, and the aircraft carrier *Formidable* seriously hit.[3]

The wide-ranging sequences of events in southern Europe, the Mediterranean, and the North African areas of Libya and Egypt in 1940 and early 1941 was reported by a large group of correspondents, chiefly for the Anglo–U.S. media.

Anderson and Allen, serving Reuters and the AP, sailed with the British Navy on several missions in the Mediterranean. They were aboard the *Illustrious* in January 1941 when it was attacked by German planes for seven hours while at sea and later at Malta, where it was put out of action. They were in the *Warspite,* Admiral Cunningham's flagship, when it engaged a portion of the Italian fleet just south of Greece in March, and they were present later when Italian ships were bombarded in the Adriatic.

Allen was with a British squadron contesting the landing of German forces on the island of Crete in May 1941. Both Allen and Anderson were aboard the British cruiser *Galatea,* torpedoed in December 1941. Anderson was killed in this action, the first British correspondent to lose his life under combat conditions in the European war. Allen was in the

---

3   A number of the British ships damaged in the Mediterranean, including the *Illustrious* and the *Warspite,* were taken to shipyards in the United States for repair. This introduced some of the first concern with wartime censorship issues and security on the part of the neutral U.S. government.

water for forty-five minutes before he was picked up, unable to swim and dependent upon a half-inflated lifebelt. He was hospitalized in Alexandria, ill with pneumonia, and then returned to the United States for several months of convalescence.[4]

British forces were formed in Egypt to resist an anticipated Italian attack from Libyan bases that began in September 1940. A group of correspondents was accredited to the British Expeditionary Force under General Sir Archibald Wavell's Middle East Command. Swedish and other neutral correspondents sought accreditation then and later to report the desert warfare, but accreditation always was limited to British, British Commonwealth, and U.S. media representatives.

Following Italy's declaration of war on Great Britain in June 1940, British ground forces and two RAF squadrons were transferred from Egypt to Greece. When Italy moved troops from Albania into Greece in October, some correspondents who had been reporting action in Egypt and Libya transferred to Greece. Among them was Ralph W. Barnes of the *New York Herald Tribune*, former chief of the paper's London bureau and recently ordered out of Germany after coverage of the Wehrmacht attack along the Channel coast. Others included Joseph Levy, *New York Times;* Jan H. Yindrich, UP; Edward Kennedy, AP; Edward Ward, *Chicago Times;* Australian-born James Aldridge, NANA; Martin Agronsky, NBC; and Christopher Buckley, *Daily Telegraph.*

Neutral U.S. correspondents and two or three writers for the British press moved in eastern and southern Europe from the time of the occupation of Poland in September 1939. From Warsaw in 1939, Lloyd Lehrbas, AP, and Richard Mowrer, *Chicago Daily News,* reached Rumania together. Mowrer, however, encountered Red Army forces and was arrested as a spy. He managed to escape and was picked up about nine miles from the Rumanian border by Lehrbas, driving under a diplomatic flag with the departing U.S. ambassador in Warsaw, A. J. D. Biddle, Jr.

Other correspondents in Bucharest between 1939 and early 1941 were Ferdinand C. M. Jahn, UP, and Maurice Lovell, Reuters, who was expelled in November 1939. Karl J. Eskelund, a Dane, who had covered the Russo-Finnish War for the *New York Times,* was in Rumania for INS from late 1940 until early 1941, when he switched to the UP and was sent to Indo-China and then to Shanghai. John Scott, representing the *News-Chronicle* in Moscow, made a journey to Rumania in 1940 and another to the Middle East early in 1941, shortly after which he was

---

4 Allen was awarded the Pulitzer Prize for his coverage of the British fleet action in the Mediterranean in 1941. During his home leave in 1942 he learned to swim, before returning to the Mediterranean by mid-1942.

expelled from the Soviet Union. Beach Conger of the *New York Herald Tribune* was expelled from Germany in November 1939. He also was expelled from Hungary in August 1940 and went to Rumania.

Eugen Kovacs, correspondent for the *New York Times* in Bucharest since 1926, along with Alex Coler, a stringer for AP, and Liviu Artemie, a stringer for INS, were all three Rumanian Jews and had been ordered by the Bucharest government on September 30, 1940, to cease working for their foreign employers. In December, the government also acted to dissolve the Foreign Press Association in Bucharest on the grounds that "a majority of its members are foreigners and their attitude . . . is against the interests of the state."

These latter actions marked what Leland Stowe of the *Chicago Daily News* and Patrick Maitland of the London *Times* saw as growing German control in Rumania—what Stowe referred to as a "descent of the locusts." Maitland, along with Derek Patmore of Exchange Telegraph, later observed much the same thing in Belgrade, preliminary to the April 1941 invasion of Yugoslavia by the Wehrmacht. Stowe was joined in Bucharest in the autumn of 1940 by Edmund Stevens of the *Christian Science Monitor,* who had been with him in Norway. In Budapest since his expulsion from Berlin in June 1940, Stevens invited Stowe and Russell Hill of the *New York Herald Tribune* to drive with him in his motor car to Bulgaria and Greece.

Italy had attacked Greece at that time, and the conflict was reported not only by Stowe, Stevens, and Hill, but by Daniel DeLuce and James Wesley (Wes) Gallagher, AP, Sam Pope Brewer, *Chicago Tribune,* Cyrus L. Sulzberger, *New York Times,* David Walker, London *Daily Mirror,* Chester (Reginald William Winchester) Wilmot of the Australian Broadcasting Commission, and others.

From bases in Greece, the RAF undertook bombing missions against Italian targets. Both Aldridge of NANA and Agronsky of NBC were permitted to fly with them when the port of Brindisi was bombed in November 1940. On the next night, November 17–18, Yindrich of the UP and Ralph Barnes of the *New York Herald Tribune* flew in separate bombers attacking Valona and Durazzo in Albania, where Italian forces were established. The bomber in which Barnes flew for the Durazzo attack lost its way in rain and fog and crashed on a mountain side near Danilovgrad, Yugoslavia, just north of the Albanian border. All were killed and Barnes was the first U.S. correspondent to die under combat conditions during the war.[5]

---

5   The finest tribute to Barnes was written by Leland Stowe, who had known him through fifteen years of work in Europe. In these years Barnes earned the respect of all his colleagues and of officials with whom he came in contact in France, Italy, Russia, Germany, England and elsewhere. Utterly dedicated to conscientious reporting in every situation, his

Just as Hitler had supposed that, with the surrender of France in June 1940, Great Britain would be ready to make peace, so Italy felt that it would have a free hand to move from Libya and East Africa to almost any part of Africa, including Egypt and the Suez Canal. Italy had invaded Albania in April 1939 and moved into Greece in October 1940. The Greeks fought valiantly against larger Italian forces and drove them back into Albania by the end of November. Bitter winter weather in the mountains then slowed the fighting. Also in November 1940 British naval action destroyed about half the Italian fleet in the harbor at Taranto on the boot of Italy.

An Italian army, with Libya as a base, invaded Egypt in September 1940, penetrating more than sixty miles. Retreating British troops surprised the Italians in a December counterattack that threw the Fascist army back into Libya and forced its complete surrender in January 1941. At that time, other British forces in the Sudan and Kenya began a campaign against Eritrea and Italian East Africa (Ethiopia): Addis Ababa was taken in April and Emperor Haile Selassie returned from refuge in England in May.

These setbacks to Italian arms brought greater German participation in Italian affairs, and diverted German forces from other areas to bolster what had been Italian positions in Greece and Egypt. This German move began with the establishment of air bases in Sicily during the winter of 1940–41. The British position in the Mediterranean, including Malta, was threatened. German troops also were moved to Libya by way of Sicily under the command of Field Marshal Irwin Rommel, who then opened a desert blitzkrieg on March 31, 1941.

The British Eighth Army in Egypt, which also supported Greece against the Italians, was unable to resist the Rommel Panzer attack, as the tank maneuvers were called. The Eighth Army was driven back deep into Egypt by the end of April 1941, and was under German siege from June until November.

Germany also established control in southern Europe, which provided an avenue to its campaign in Libya and Egypt, and also for its

---

associates in Athens had affectionately dubbed him "The Field Marshal." Special honor was paid him by the RAF command, since he had won many friends and admirers in the bomber squadron both in Greece and in Egypt, where he had gone on missions with them. After the United States entered the war, a Liberty ship was named after Barnes. He also was remembered in a special radio broadcast in 1944. Like J. A. MacGahan and George Warrington Steevens of previous generations, he was seen as another brilliant young correspondent lost in mid-career. Dr. Paul Schmidt, active for the Nazi regime in dealing with the foreign press, in speaking after the German surrender with Marguerite Higgins, *New York Herald Tribune* correspondent, called Barnes "one of our bitterest critics, but nevertheless a remarkably fine man." See: Leland Stowe, *No Other Road to Freedom* (1941), ch. 11; Al Laney, *Paris Herald: The Incredible Newspaper* (1947), chs. 11, 21, 22.

prospective move into Soviet Russia. With the support of the Fascist-type Iron Guard in Rumania that country was under German control by November 1940. King Boris of Bulgaria made it possible for German troops to enter his country and Hungary as well, and thus to attack Yugoslavia and Greece in April 1941.

The German drive against Yugoslavia and Greece began April 6 and was concluded by May 31. Air superiority drove out British defensive forces in an evacuation comparable to that at Dunkirk the previous May. Young King Peter of Yugoslavia and George II of Greece found safety in England. The invasion included the German capture of the Greek island of Crete on May 20 in the first airborne invasion by parachutists, with glider planes carrying in additional troops. The British navy moved thousands of that country's troops out of Crete to Egypt.

The German occupation of Greece and Yugoslavia was extremely harsh, complicated by guerrilla activities within the country. One guerrilla group, known as the Chetniks, was headed by a regular army colonel, Dragoljub (Draza) Mihajlović, loyal to the monarchy. A Communist group, the Partisans, was headed by Josip Broz, more generally called "Tito," or Marshal Tito. Both groups fought the German occupation, but were in conflict with each other.

British military personnel had to be diverted from Egypt for action in Greece, Iraq, Syria, Lebanon, and Iran. In Iraq there was fighting with local elements seeking to force out British air bases established there by treaty during the 1930s. In Syria and Lebanon the contest was with French forces stationed there under terms of the 1920 mandate, but loyal to the Vichy government. Germany encouraged action against the British in both of these situations, including air attacks in Iraq. It was July 1941 before British control of the areas was assured. Meanwhile, there had been German infiltration into Iran during June-July 1941. British forces entered late in August, as did forces of the Soviet Union, by then at war with Germany since June. To assure the existence of a cooperative regime in Teheran, the abdication of pro-Nazi Reza Shah Pahlavi was forced, with his son, Mohammed Reza Pahlavi, made his successor.

Coverage of these events in 1940–41 by correspondents beyond those mentioned included Ronald Legge of the *Daily Telegraph;* W. F. Martin, *Daily Mail,* with the British Navy in the Mediterranean; Graham Stanford, *Daily Mail;* and Arthur Thorpe and Stanley Gardiner, Exchange Telegraph—all assigned to Gibraltar. Accreditation to the British fleet became far more general, and U.S. correspondents were among those favored. Attached to the fleet at various times were Preston L. Grover of AP; Edward H. (Harry) Crockett, AP and Wide World Photos; Grattan McGroarty, George Palmer, and Henry T. Gorrell, all of UP; Richard D. McMillan, BUP; Richard Mowrer, *Chicago Daily News;* Richard Busvine, *Chicago Times;* and Norman Smart, *Daily Express.* Busvine was aboard the aircraft carrier *Ark Royal,* which the Germans claimed three times in 1940 to have sunk and ultimately did sink in November 1941. Norman Smart sailed in four Malta convoys between May 1941 and September 1942. Two of his ships were sunk, once when the *Ark Royal* went down, with Thorpe of Extel also aboard at that time, and again when the cruiser *Cairo* was sunk.[6] George H. Johnstone of the *Melbourne Argus* was with ships in the Australian navy active in the Mediterranean in 1940–41.

The foreign press group in Greece and Yugoslavia and in the Egyptian-Libyan desert as late as 1943 included some of the correspondents already mentioned. They were Edward Kennedy, AP;[7] Alexander Graeme Clifford, *Daily Mail;* F. G. H. (Fred) Salusbury, *Daily Herald;* G. Gordon Young, Reuters; Arthur S. Merton, *Daily Telegraph;* and William J. Munday, *Sydney Morning Herald.*

Some of these men were in Greece and Yugoslavia two months later in April 1941 when Axis forces invaded. A complete stoppage on outgoing news dispatches was imposed for several hours in Berlin, Rome, Bucharest, and Sofia as the new campaign began. Joseph W. Grigg, Jr., of the Berlin UP staff was with German forces moving into Yugoslavia, and Reynolds Packard, UP, was with the Italians.

With the Greeks and British under attack in Athens, the foreign press group included Sulzberger, Stevens, DeLuce, Gallagher, Aldridge, and Walker. Others in Greece included Ben Ames, UP bureau chief in Athens; Gorrell and McMillan of BUP; J. Reilly O'Sullivan, AP; Betty Wasson, CBS; and Busvine of the *Chicago Times.* George Weller, former *New York Times* correspondent in the Balkans in 1932–36, returned to Greece from the U.S. for the *Chicago Daily News* in January 1941 to replace Stowe, then returning to the United States.

Correspondents in Yugoslavia at Belgrade included Hill, Maitland, and Brewer. Others were Basil Davidson and Peter Brown for Reuters; W. J. Makin, Reuters and the *Times;* Raymond Brock, the *New York Times;* Leon L. Kay, UP; Robert St.John, AP; Michael Chinigo and

---

6   Smart said that "I am known as the only correspondent who has been sunk twice without getting my feet wet on either occasion." He was taken off both ships before they went down. "I am inclined to agree with a remark Noel Monks . . . once made to me while strolling down Fleet Street," he added, "to the effect that there is no future in this business of war correspondence; it's too bloody dangerous." *World's Press News,* October 1, 1942, p. 12.

7   Dozens of Italian soldiers, mistaking Kennedy for a British officer, by reason of the uniform required for correspondents on that front, surrendered to him near Tobruk during the British counter-offensive of January 1941.

Desider Geleji, INS; John Ennals, *Daily Herald;* Terence Atherton, *Daily Mail;* Cecil Brown, recently expelled from Italy, CBS; and Leigh White, CBS and Overseas News Agency (ONA).

A number of these correspondents endured such hardships and risks that they were fortunate to have survived at all. Chinigo, INS, and Kay, UP, managed to get from Belgrade to Budapest, to file the first full reports of the initial German bombing of Belgrade; Brown, CBS, and Brewer, *Chicago Tribune,* also filed early accounts from Budapest. A number of the correspondents in Belgrade nearly lost their lives in the heavy bombing of that city.

Four correspondents participated in a desperate venture to get from Belgrade to Athens to file reports. Hill of the *New York Herald Tribune,* Atherton, *Daily Mail,* White, CBS, and St.John, AP, traded an automobile for a twenty-foot sardine boat. On April 16 they left Budva, Yugoslavia, without a compass and with very little gasoline or food. They took aboard a fisherman to guide the boat to Greece. Moving south along the Dalmatian coast, they were bombed and machine-gunned by a German plane and Atherton was wounded. Thanks to a U.S. flag spread on the little deck, they managed to pass as neutrals through much of the Italian fleet near Durazzo, Albania. They were nearly shipwrecked, and rowed through a stormy night after their gasoline was exhausted. Finally they put into the Greek island of Corfu, which was promptly bombed.

The men proceeded from Corfu aboard a small Greek ship, moving only at night, and arrived on the third day at Patras in Greece, which also was bombed soon after. They then boarded a Greek troop train, bound for Athens. When that train came under air attack, they took cover along the right of way. Both White and St.John were wounded, and they all were left behind when the train moved off, the dead and wounded abandoned. The correspondents hailed an RAF truck that took them into Argos, where they were bombed again. On this leg of the trip they lost all their possessions, and the fisherman who had been with them was killed.

Atherton, White, and St.John got medical attention at Argos; Hill alone had escaped injury. White was so seriously wounded that he was taken to Athens.[8] The others moved that night toward an evacuation port, since it was obvious that dispatches could not go out of Greece.

---

8   White remained in an Athens hospital for five months and underwent four operations. As a neutral, he then was permitted by the German occupation authorities to depart. He returned to New York by easy stages, flying from Lisbon. Hospitalized again in New York, he underwent further surgery.

St. John, upon reaching Alexandria, returned to New York by way of Capetown, where he interviewed survivors of the *Robin Moor.* The passengers and crew had been set adrift in lifeboats after that U.S. vessel was torpedoed in the South Atlantic by a German submarine on May 21, 1941.

They were halted frequently by British patrols, but eventually were taken aboard a British naval vessel that carried them to Alexandria. There they arrived May 3 after further bombings on the way, and only then could their reports go forward describing events that had transpired three weeks before.

In another misadventure, a group of British correspondents from among fourteen Anglo-American journalists in Yugoslavia had expected to be picked up by a Royal Navy destroyer in the Gulf of Kotor, near Dubrovnik, on April 17, along with members of the British Legation at Belgrade. The contact never was made, and the group was captured by Italian forces, taken to Durazzo and eventually to Chanciano, near Siena, Italy. Ray Brock of the *New York Times,* as a neutral among them, was sent on to Rome.

Other correspondents in Greece moved to Egypt. Edward Ward, of the *Chicago Times,* was evacuated with British troops. Ames and Gorrell of the UP, and McMillan of the BUP, went to Crete with the Greek government, and then to Egypt before Crete was lost. O'Sullivan of the AP reached Istanbul in a small sailboat. Busvine of the *Chicago Times* reached Cairo in the same manner. Among the last to leave Greece were DeLuce, AP, along with Cyrus L. Sulzberger of the *New York Times* and his Greek bride, Marina Tatiana Lada, whom he married in January 1942. They reached Smyrna (Ismir) in a small sponge-fishing boat.

Three U.S. correspondents who remained in Greece as neutrals while the Germans established their occupation of the country were taken under control by the occupation authorities and sent to Berlin. Then expelled, Weller of the *Chicago Daily News,* Wes Gallagher, AP, and Betty Wasson, CBS, went to Lisbon.

The end of the Balkan fighting, merging into the Egyptian-Libyan desert warfare, also marked the beginning of maneuvering in the Middle East during the heat of the summer in 1941. Among correspondents following this action in Iraq, Syria, Lebanon, and Iran were Aldridge of NANA, until he was injured and invalided home to Australia on leave; Wilmot, Australian Broadcasting Commission; Kennedy, AP; Agronsky, NBC; and Cecil Brown, CBS. Agronsky and Brown left the Middle East for Singapore.

Other correspondents, some of whom had been in Egypt, and others newly accredited to the British Middle East Command, included Australian-born Alan Moorehead, *Daily Express;* Ronald Matthews, *Daily Herald;* Leonard Mosley, *Daily Sketch* and the Allied Newspapers; C. D. R. Lumby, the *Times;* Martin Herlihy, Reuters; Arthur Merton, *Daily Telegraph;* Atherton, *Daily Mail,* recovered from his wounds; Richard Dimbleby, BBC; and John A. Hetherington, representing the *Melbourne Herald.*

U.S. correspondents included Alexander C. Sedgwick, *New York*

Times; Allan A. Michie, *Time* magazine; Merrill (Red) Mueller, INS, until he went to Singapore; Gorrell and Peters, UP; Robert Low, originally of *Liberty* magazine but also writing for UP; and Kenneth T. Downs, INS.

Downs and Low were in a party of fifteen ambushed by Vichy French forces near Damascus, Syria. Nine members of the group were killed, two were wounded, and Downs and Low were taken as prisoners to Beirut. There they were released as neutrals after representations by U.S. officials. Both then went to Turkey.[9]

U.S. Moves to Support Britain

The United States could not fail to feel the effects of the European war. The surrender of France and the position of Britain, still supported by the Commonwealth countries but subject to attacks from the air and by submarine, sympathetically moved millions of persons. President Roosevelt, who had entered the White House for his first term in 1933 at almost the same time that Hitler and the National Socialist government had taken office in Germany, was aware at least since 1935 of the threat inherent in that regime. Even so, a Neutrality Act had been passed by Congress in 1937 that tended to preclude any assistance by the United States to a belligerent in any war. That had been amended by November 1939, however, to permit the shipment of arms from the United States to belligerents on a cash-and-carry basis.

Following the French surrender in June 1940, Congress passed a National Defense Tax bill to finance a program of naval rearmament for the United States, and for the training of a large military force. This was further supported by the passage of a selective service measure, or a draft, to become effective October 29, 1940.

A special relationship was established between President Roosevelt and Prime Minister Churchill, and in September 1940 Roosevelt arranged for fifty supposedly "over-age" destroyers to be given to Great Britain for convoy use. These were in exchange for U.S. leases on British air and naval bases in Newfoundland and the West Indies. The U.S.

---

9   Downs received an official citation from the British Admiralty for "his zeal and skillful service" in April 1941. He was aboard an armed British merchant cruiser bound from Glasgow to Cairo when the ship caught fire and sank. German raiders were in the vicinity. Downs moved promptly to the bridge of the rescue ship and took over the signal system, while keeping a lookout against attacks.

After two months in Turkey, Downs went to India for INS. He was back in Cairo in November 1941, then representing the UP, but left early in 1942, after the Pearl Harbor attack. He became a major in the U.S. Army and was in North Africa in 1943.

Navy, within an interpretation of the nation's neutrality, provided qualified assistance to British ships in the Atlantic.

An Office of Production Management was set up in the United States by presidential action in December 1940. Its function was to coordinate production and delivery of material aid to Great Britain and other anti-Axis nations, making the United States "the great arsenal of democracy." Germany protested this as "moral aggression," but Roosevelt defended it, stressing what he termed an "Axis threat to the United States." A few days later, in his annual message to Congress, he proposed a lend-lease program. Voted by Congress in March 1941, this became a first step toward the provision of U.S.-produced arms and equipment to aid Great Britain and other allied nations.

Roosevelt began his third term as president that same month and presided over a nation becoming more deeply involved in the war while still technically neutral. In May the U.S. merchant ship *Robin Moor* was torpedoed off the Cape Verde Islands, but without loss of life. A few days later the British battleship *Hood* was sunk by the German battleship *Bismarck,* which was itself sunk three days later. In October two U.S. destroyers on convoy duty to Iceland were torpedoed, the *Kearny* and the *Reuben James,* with 100 men lost in the latter ship.

German and Italian consulates had been ordered closed in the United States in June, and U.S. consulates in Axis areas also were closed in responsive moves. By this time, British ships of war damaged in battle were being repaired in U.S. shipyards.

In April 1941 the United States arranged with the Danish government-in-exile to place Greenland under its protection, with naval and air base rights there. A comparable arrangement was made in July respecting Iceland, and U.S. troops were landed there. The U.S. Navy then began to protect British east-bound convoys as far as Iceland.

A group of London-based correspondents visited Iceland in September to observe actions taken there to counter the very serious Atlantic shipping losses being inflicted by German submarines. They were A. E. Watson of Reuters; Robert W. Cooper, the *Times;* Marsland Gander, *Daily Telegraph;* Geoffrey Edwards, *News-Chronicle;* Montague Lacey, *Daily Express;* A. B. Austin, *Daily Herald;* Barbara Ward, *Evening Standard;* Victor Lewis, *Daily Sketch;* Lord Donegall, *Sunday Dispatch;* Robin Duff, BBC; Drew Middleton, AP; Edward Worth, AP news photographer; Larry LeSueur, CBS; and F. A. Boville, Pathé News.

A comparable party had gone to Iceland from the United States in August. That group included Thomas Horgan of the AP; Philip Newsome, UP; Walter Kiernan, INS; Charles Hurd, *New York Times;* Joseph Driscoll, *New York Herald Tribune;* Frank G. Smothers, *Chicago Daily News;* Fletcher Pratt, *New York Post;* Thomas R. Henry, *Wash-*

ington Star and NANA; and Walter Karig, *Newark Evening News* and Cecil Brooks News Service of London.

Early in August 1941 Prime Minister Churchill sailed westward across the Atlantic in the new British battleship *H.M.S. Prince of Wales* for a conference with President Roosevelt aboard the U.S. cruiser *U.S.S. Augusta* in Placentia Bay, Newfoundland. From this meeting between August 9 and 12 there emerged the Atlantic Charter, an understanding in which both governments joined in a statement of peace aims, respecting the rights of other peoples and nations. Released August 14 in Washington and London, it was a statement in which the United States placed itself firmly alongside Great Britain in the war. Fifteen governments endorsed the Charter in September, nine of them in exile, but a grouping from which the United Nations was to grow.

Great secrecy and security surrounded the meeting. Churchill was accompanied by three writers: H. V. Morton of the *Daily Herald;* Howard Spring, formerly book critic of the *Evening Standard* and a novelist; and Paymaster Commander Ricci, a writer of sea stories under the name of "Bartimeus." Ricci was present as a representative of the Ministry of Information.

No writers or photographers were permitted to accompany Roosevelt, since it was his understanding that no publicity was to attach to the meeting. This caused some grumbling among members of the Washington press corps when the British writers later were permitted to produce accounts and photos of the rendezvous, as well as a story by J. Chetwynd Talbot of Reuters about a destroyer escort with which he traveled. Several Washington correspondents had intimations of such a meeting and had written something about the possibilities. These were Walter Farr, *Daily Mail* representative in Washington, Canadian-born Clifford A. Prevost, Washington correspondent for the *Detroit Free Press* and other Knight papers, and Bert Andrews, Washington correspondent for the *New York Herald Tribune.*

Changes naturally occurred in the 1940–41 period affecting the news personnel in the various capitals and countries. The entrance of Italy into the war in June 1940 meant that British correspondents left Rome, repatriated along with British diplomatic personnel and other citizens in an exchange for Italians in the same categories returning from Great Britain. With most of France then under German occupation, some former Paris correspondents went to the Vichy-controlled area of the country, once the Pétain government was set up there. Some French news personnel also were able to go to Algeria, Switzerland, England, or the United States, but others, perhaps already posted elsewhere, became "displaced persons." As German forces overran central and southern Europe later in 1940 and in 1941, some correspondents in other capitals were left equally displaced.

Between 1939 and 1941 additions and subtractions to the correspondent group in Rome included representatives of the periodical press and radio of the United States. Philip McKenzie was in Rome for the NBC in 1939, followed by Charles Lanius and David Colin. Charles B. Barbe represented the CBS, followed by Cecil Brown. Brown received the Sigma Delta Chi award for radio news broadcasts in 1940. He also wrote for INS, and Michael Chinigo was another in Italy for that agency. Peter Tompkins broadcast from Rome for the MBS. The weekly magazines, *Time* and *Life,* began to develop foreign representation in 1940, and M. Fillmore Calhoun and photographer Thomas D. McEvoy served both publications in Rome.

Correspondents in Rome suffered greater restraints because of the reverses of Italian military forces in their ventures in Albania, East Africa, and Egypt during 1939–41, and because of the subsequent movement into Italy of German forces. United States correspondents were affected beyond others by this change in the Fascist regime's temper, since it could not escape the notice of the Rome government that the people and media of the U.S. agreed with President Roosevelt's June 1940 statement that Italy had delivered a "stab in the back to France." Further, Italy's desire to control the French provinces of Nice and Savoy, Corsica, and Tunisia also offended public opinion in the United States and the United Kingdom.

The first correspondents to feel Fascist displeasure after June 1940 were Calhoun and McEvoy of *Time* and *Life,* both of whom were expelled. In September Thomas S. Treanor, a roving correspondent for the *Los Angeles Times* writing a series of reports on countries at war and then in Rome, was summoned to the Ministry of Popular Culture. There he was informed that, while no action was to be taken against him, his newspaper was banned from Italy. Unlikely as it was that many copies of the Los Angeles paper reached Italy, this proved to be an expression of the government's objection to an article the *Times* had published about Mussolini, one in a series about heads of government. Treanor had nothing to do with its writing or use, and was not aware of its publication.

A month later in October, Herbert L. Matthews, *New York Times* bureau chief in Rome since April 1939, and holder of the Italian war cross for valor in coverage of the Ethiopian war, was expelled because of a dispatch he had sent shortly before about a Mussolini-Hitler meeting at the Brenner Pass on the Italian-Austrian frontier. In his report, Matthews had commented that "the Axis is out to defeat President Roosevelt," then campaigning for re-election, with Wendell L. Willkie as the Republican party contestant. The Ministry of Popular Culture objected that the statement "tended to disturb relations between the two countries," and Matthews was given ten days to leave Italy. He went to Berne,

Switzerland, but some six weeks later was permitted to return to Rome and resume his post.

John T. Whitaker, *Chicago Daily News* correspondent in Rome since the expulsion of Richard Mowrer in May 1939, was the next U.S. correspondent affected. Like Matthews, he held the Italian war cross, and was a particular friend of Foreign Minister Ciano. The Ministry of Popular Culture early in 1941 requested the U.S. Embassy in Rome to persuade Whitaker to leave Italy voluntarily within ten days, "because of the number and importance of his contacts and [because] of the unfriendly attitude of his newspaper." When this very unusual and polite approach brought no result, he was told outright on February 26, 1941, that he must leave.

Whitaker was the third *Daily News* correspondent to be forced out of Italy in a period of twenty-seven months, and the Chicago paper decided not to replace him. For the first time since Edgar Ansel Mowrer had taken the Rome post in 1915, more than twenty-five years before, the *Chicago Daily News* was without a correspondent in Italy and the bureau was closed.

Saville R. Davis left Italy in the spring of 1941. He was successor to Cremona as Rome correspondent for the *Christian Science Monitor* in 1938, after a period during which he covered the Spanish Civil War. Davis chose to return to the United States so that he could write without censorship a series of articles about the situation in Italy. Whitaker did the same for the *Chicago Daily News* and its syndicate. Both men agreed that German control had been fixed firmly upon Italy.

With Davis's departure, Joseph C. Harsch came from the Washington bureau as *Monitor* correspondent in Rome, but he soon transferred to the Berlin bureau. He was replaced in Rome by Joseph R. Harrison from the Boston office. Harrison withdrew voluntarily before the end of 1941, leaving the *Monitor* without Rome coverage for the first time since the early 1920s.

After its declaration of war, the Italian government was reluctant to permit correspondents to move about the country with their former freedom. With heavier wartime censorship and other limitations on information, this contributed to reduced coverage and the voluntary departure of correspondents. As events worsened for the Fascist regime, the Italians themselves were deprived of information even beyond earlier limits. In February 1941, the people were warned that any person detected listening to foreign radio broadcasts would be subject to six months imprisonment and a fine of 10,000 lira. In June, all U.S. newspapers were excluded from the country, and in September this exclusion was extended to all non-Axis newspapers and periodicals.

Foreign news agency staffs were reduced through 1941. Among those departing was Thomas B. Morgan of the UP, perhaps on better terms with Mussolini than any other correspondent, in part because of his long service. He was also a specialist on Vatican affairs. Percival H. Winner of INS, in Italy from time to time since World War I, Charles H. Guptill, with the AP in Rome since 1935, and Michael Chinigo, another INS correspondent, also left. Allen Raymond of the *New York Herald Tribune,* one of the last special newspaper correspondents, departed in October. His paper became the third in the United States to end its Rome coverage.

Cecil Brown, representing both INS and CBS, was expelled in April 1941 for "continued hostile attitudes toward Fascism." By July, German control over broadcasting from Italy had become so direct and strong that the U.S. radio correspondents followed newspaper and agency representatives in departing. Rather than submit to the restrictive demands by then imposed, CBS withdrew Barbe, NBC withdrew Lanius, and MBS withdrew Tompkins.

In the United States, the Association of Foreign Press Correspondents, centering in New York and commonly meeting at the Lotos Club, had 113 active members in 1939 and fifty-four associate members. The outbreak of the European war in September introduced an element of tension into the organization. German correspondents, forbidden by the Nazi government to belong to "foreign organizations," soon withdrew. An article by Ernest A. Hepp of the German DNB agency, nevertheless appeared in the association's monthly mimeographed news-sheet, "The Foreign Press," of January 15, 1940. It was regarded by some members as "blatant German propaganda," and a number of those members, including officers of the association, resigned in protest, although most later returned. Italian members were out of the association by September 1941, and the organization itself was changed in October. The long and rather awkward title borne since its formation in 1917 was simplified to the Foreign Press Association (FPA). With Japanese members also formally dropped after the December 7 attack at Pearl Harbor, the active membership of January 1942 stood at seventy-seven, plus forty-four associate members.

The beginning of the war in Europe had brought a cautious closing of some doors in Washington, and certain security precautions were introduced. Even so, President Roosevelt continued his news conferences on schedule, and Stephen T. Early and Mrs. Roosevelt did the same at the White House. At the Department of State, Secretary Cordell Hull conducted conferences attended by ten to thirty correspondents of the domestic and foreign press. Michael McDermott and other staff assistants also met with media representatives.

At the cabinet level, correspondents met during this period with Secretary of War Henry L. Stimson, who had held that position in the Taft administration. Also meeting reporters was Frank Knox, publisher of the *Chicago Daily News* since 1931, who became secretary of the navy in a coalition cabinet in 1940. Others who did so in various positions at the White House or cabinet level included Henry A. Wallace, Harry Hopkins, Harold L. Ickes, and James A. Farley.

In Germany, after the surrender of France, a greater arrogance appeared both in the treatment of neutral news correspondents within the country, and in the use of the radio in the conduct of foreign propaganda. As early as March 1940, German papers responsive to official direction took exception to references in the Swiss press referring to Austria, Czechoslovakia, and Poland as countries "occupied" by Germany. This was interpreted in Berlin as an unfriendly expression of opinion. Switzerland was reminded, in a veiled threat, that it was a small country and would do well to curb such expressions.

A second incident occurred when Hitler addressed the Reichstag on July 10, reporting on the series of military successes that had by then so greatly extended German power over most of the European continent. The ninety-five minute speech was carried live by the U.S. radio networks, with running translations and interpretation. But Lewis Allen Weiss, general manager for the Don Lee Broadcasting System, a Pacific Coast affiliate of the MBS, took personal responsibility for cutting the speech off the air after the first ten minutes. In a statement broadcast at the time through station KHL, Los Angeles, Weiss explained that the Don Lee network did not consider the Hitler speech "in the public interest" or "in harmony with the attitude" of the United States government. He added that Hitler "should not be permitted to use our American facilities to justify his crimes against civilization itself."

Some objection was voiced in the United States against Weiss's action, arguing that he was in effect censoring material that the people had a right to hear. In Berlin, however, the reaction was prompt and uncompromising. Dr. Dietrich of the Propaganda Ministry notified Sigrid Schultz, *Chicago Tribune* correspondent and representative of the MBS, that he was suspending broadcasts by that network from Germany and from German-controlled areas of Europe, pending receipt of a "satisfactory" explanation of the incident.

Even though Berlin correspondents had been subject to no direct censorship, except for radio broadcasts, an army-directed censorship was made effective in the spring of 1940. Military censors in the post and telegraph office still did not cut material, however, without first consulting with the Propaganda Ministry, and cuts actually were rare. But dispatches were checked and a copy of every dispatch went into a dossier under the correspondent's name.

In October that year two orders affected the work of foreign correspondents in Germany. The first forbade transmission of military news between 11 P.M. and 6 A.M. The reason for this was that British RAF air raids on Germany had been growing in intensity, and the order was intended to prevent any prompt reporting of such attacks or their results. Even later, no reference was permitted to the time or effect of raids.

The second order issued the following day forbade speculation on German foreign policy. It noted that

> Germany is, of course, at present pursuing foreign policy. Wartime lends to this activity such weight and earnestness that any speculation about it designed to pry into its direction or character borders on political espionage. No such obvious and purposeful trial balloons, guesses and speculation will be tolerated in the future.

The Foreign Ministry warned further that "indiscretions" by correspondents would be handled under the regulations relating to military espionage. Literally applied, this could lead to execution.

The order was regarded by correspondents as political censorship. They believed it to have been inspired by widespread speculation earlier in the month relating to a conference between Hitler and Mussolini at the Brenner Pass. It also was made effective shortly before conferences due to bring Hitler together with Pierre Laval, Vichy France's vice-premier, on October 22, Francisco Franco of Spain on October 23, Marshal Pétain, Vichy chief of state, on October 24, and another meeting with Mussolini on October 28, this time in Florence. Later events indicated that the order was related especially to prospective German military moves into southern Europe in April 1941 and against the Soviet Union in June, all preceded by increased security to avoid knowledge reaching the press.

The intensive German air attacks on Great Britain in 1940 brought retaliatory RAF raids on Germany, with heavy bombing of Berlin and other cities. These attacks placed correspondents there in peril matching that of their colleagues in London. The general situation confronting correspondents in Germany by late 1940 was summarized by Sigrid Schultz, then on a visit to the United States. She said that

> In getting our stories out, censorship was a voluntary matter, but we knew if we sent something that had been declared taboo, we would be called on the carpet and banished from the country. On the destruction from air raids we had to follow the official communiqués. Matters are different with radio broadcasters. They are censored directly and you bargain with censors in trying to get your point over.[10]

_____

10   *Editor & Publisher* (March 22, 1941).

William L. Shirer, CBS correspondent back in the United States by early 1941, made the manner of this bargaining and its difficulties amply clear in his *Berlin Diary* published the same year. Edwin Hartrich, his assistant and successor, further explained the relationship between press or radio correspondents and the German government representatives when he left the country in 1941. He said:

> The German technique is simple. An American correspondent assigned to Germany is on his arrival subjected to the "buttering up" process. This means that he is given special treatment by officials of the Propaganda Ministry. He is taken on special trips, always provided with Ministry escorts. The Germans disregard the complaints registered by competitors of the new correspondent for this favoritism, being only concerned with winning the sympathy of the latest arrival.
>
> However, if the correspondent fails to "react favorably," if he continues to show an independent attitude, he is then dropped back into the corps of American correspondents to compete with them on equal terms. If he continues this independent and critical attitude, he is then pushed into the "dog-house gang," composed of those American correspondents who are considered "politically unreliable" by their German observers.
>
> The Germans also play favorites among the competing press association and radio correspondents. For instance, the AP bureau will be given a break on a story, leading the UP and INS to scramble to catch up with the "scoop." Then the process may be reversed, leaving the AP out on a limb to the advantage of the others. The same treatment carries through for the radio. . . . The radio correspondents will be played against the press and vice versa.
>
> The general idea of the Germans is to sow dissension among the American correspondents, and by this uneven treatment force all correspondents to make their private "deals" with the Propaganda Ministry and the Foreign Ministry. However, the American reporters are cognizant of this situation and with few exceptions have failed to allow themselves to be used in this fashion.[11]

A correspondent, American or otherwise, who displeased the German officials, not to the point of expelling him but to the point of remonstrance and trying to keep him "on the right track," might be subjected to a *kopfwaschen,* that is a "head-washing" or "friendly talking to by a representative of the government." The attempts to put correspondents on the "right track" sometimes went beyond mere "friendly talks." Some were offered inducements, such as private interviews with Hitler or other top officials, if they would change the tone of their reports. Some were offered outright money bribes. Of this method, Harsch, of the *Christian Science Monitor* and a CBS broadcaster back in the United States in the spring of 1941, wrote that

---

11 *Editor & Publisher* (February 1, 1941).

A government official once told me with amusement and candor the methods and rates of payment of some. The fact that Americans cannot be bought has baffled them and also won their respect. They have little respect for those they do buy.[12]

Harsch himself was excluded from all trips to the front lines during the fighting in the Low Countries and France in May of 1940. This is not to say that those correspondents who did report from those areas were subservient to the Nazi government's wishes. But, in Harsch's case, it was to punish him for his reporting of conditions in Denmark after the German invasion of that country in April. Such punishments, he said, were "worn as a badge of honor in the craft."

Another form of pressure was brought on the correspondents when Foreign Minister von Ribbentrop issued an order in 1940 that no U.S. correspondent was to be permitted to serve as president of the Foreign Press Association in Berlin. Italian and Japanese correspondents also were told by their embassies to oppose Frederick Oechsner of the UP, who had been nominated for the position. When the election occurred, Oechsner received every vote. A year later, with Oechsner a candidate for re-election to another term, the German government let it be known that if he was selected again as president of the organization, all privileges enjoyed by correspondents at the government-sponsored Auslands Klub would be cancelled, including their right to import food. To avoid any actual controversy, Oechsner withdrew his name from candidacy and a Swedish correspondent was elected.

U.S. correspondents in Berlin may have been treated more stiffly than most during 1940–41, partly because they were the largest national group and the most independent. Beyond that the Nazi government could not conceal its irritation at the obvious sympathy and support of the United States and its people for Great Britain and the Commonwealth through the provision of armaments, finance, and aid at sea.

Another cause of German ire directed at the United States, and vented on U.S. correspondents had arisen in March 1941 when a federal grand jury in Washington indicted Dr. Manfred Zapp and Guenther Tonn, managers of the German Transozean news service operating in New York since October 1938 as a propaganda agency. It was charged that Transozean had not registered with the U.S. Department of State as an agent of a foreign government, as required under the provisions of a Foreign Agents Registration Act passed by Congress in 1938.

Zapp had registered in January 1939 as manager of Transozean, but not as a writer for *Die Neue Woche,* a German-language weekly published in New York, nor as a representative of the Deutscher Verlag of

---

12   *Christian Science Monitor,* March 13, 1941.

Berlin, the former Ullstein Verlag taken over from its Jewish owners by the Nazi government and continued as a major publishing company. Tonn also was charged with failure to register as an agent of a foreign government. Both Zapp and Tonn were arrested in March 1941 and held for four and one-half hours at Ellis Island in New York harbor. They were released on $5,000 bail each, pending an appearance in court in August, and were instructed to remain in New York.

A direct response to the Zapp and Tonn arrests in New York came a few days later in Berlin and in France. In Berlin, Gestapo officers arrived early in the morning at the apartment shared by Richard C. Hottelet, UP bureau chief, and Joseph W. Grigg, Jr., also of the UP. Grigg was questioned and released after three hours. The apartment and the United Press office were thoroughly searched. Hottelet himself was imprisoned and held incommunicado from March to July, with frequent periods of questioning, accompanied by threats and personal indignities. In response to queries at government levels, German officials denied that Hottelet's arrest was related to the actions taken against Transocean or against Zapp and Tonn, or in any way a reprisal. Jay Allen, a correspondent in Vichy for NANA and formerly of the *Chicago Tribune,* was arrested in March and accused of crossing without permission into the German-occupied zone in France. He also was accused of "stealing documents . . . affecting the security of the French State," and was sentenced to four months in prison.

Whether or not the Hottelet and Allen arrests and imprisonments were related to the Zapp-Tonn indictments, their arrests were certainly coincidental in point of time. An agreement between Berlin and Washington arranged for the release and exchange of Zapp and Tonn for Hottelet and Allen.

Much later, in his book *High Tension* (1959), Hugh Baillie, president of the United Press when these episodes occurred, suggested that Hottelet's arrest may have been less related to the Zapp-Tonn arrests and intended instead to exercise a restraining influence on a United Press "team" assignment then in progress. Lyle Wilson, of the UP Washington staff, was visiting Germany, and Joe Alex Morris, UP foreign editor, was in the United Kingdom. Fresh on the scene, they were to view the war from both sides and only write after returning to the United States and comparing their impressions. Hottelet, Baillie speculated, may have been a "hostage" held in the hope that a moderate report might be produced.

However that may have been, the arrest and imprisonment of Hottelet and Allen was symptomatic of the worsening climate in which foreign reporters were obliged to work at that period in Germany and German-held areas. It served as a warning to them all.

The Transozean agency closed its New York office on July 19 by order of the U.S. government after Zapp and Tonn left the country. It had provided a service of reports going chiefly to German-language newspapers in the United States at a cost of $1 a month, payable to any German consulate. The agency had collected $3,045 in this way over a period of twenty-five months of operation. During that same period, Berlin had expended $164,625 to support the service. Transozean performed other functions as well. Eric T. Winberg, identified as a Swedish correspondent in New York, although not a member of the Foreign Press Association, testified at the August court hearing that one purpose of Transozean was to broadcast news to South America that might be "harmful to the United States." The agency had branch offices in Buenos Aires and Lima to handle the rebroadcast of programs. Those offices also were closed later in 1941 by the governments of Argentina and Peru.

German propaganda directed at Latin America by shortwave radio had become more aggressive after the surrender of France in June 1940. To counter the propaganda a new U.S. Council of National Defense ordered the replacement of the Division of Cultural Relations at the Department of State with an Office for the Coordination of Commercial and Cultural Relations Between the American Republics. In July 1941, the effort was strengthened with the creation of an Office of the Coordinator of Inter-American Affairs (CIAA) under the direction of Nelson A. Rockefeller. It was again modified in December 1941 to the Office of Inter-American Affairs (OIAA).

With the Transozean service made ineffective for propaganda purposes, Germany undertook to compensate for its loss by establishing dummy agencies under disguised German control. The first and most ambitious of these efforts involved the formation of Radio-Mundial, registered as a company in Lisbon on July 14, 1941. It was listed as having a capital of one million escudos (about $40,000), with 30 percent of the stock allegedly held in Switzerland, Sweden, and France. The director in Lisbon was a Dr. H. W. Lenz. The company sought to establish its operative headquarters in Switzerland, but the Swiss government denied it the right to do so. The headquarters then was set up in the tiny Republic of Andorra in the Pyrenees on the French-Spanish border. It was reported to have employed stringer correspondents in Lisbon, Madrid, Vichy, Geneva, Rome, Stockholm, Budapest, Bucharest, Ankara, Rio de Janeiro, and London.

The formation of the agency was officially announced with some style at a luncheon in Stockholm in September. There was no mention at any time of a German connection. Soon after the Stockholm announcement, however, the *World's Press News,* a London weekly publication for those in the newspaper, periodical, and advertising fields, asserted that Radio-Mundial was German-sponsored and had been formed to disseminate a disguised German propaganda service to Latin America and elsewhere. Dr. Lenz, was identified as a German agent. It also became known that the Lisbon office actually was directed by Dr. Manfred Zapp, recently of the Transozean office in New York. Thus exposed, Radio-Mundial apparently obtained only one client, a Sofia publication, and it went out of business in April 1942.

Almost immediately after the sponsorship of Radio-Mundial had been revealed, another agency appeared. In October 1941, a correspondent for an agency known as I.N.B.—presumably meaning International News Bureau—began to file reports from Stockholm directed to the daily *Pester Lloyd* of Budapest. The I.N.B. reports were clearly German-slanted and that agency soon faded away.

A Swiss Telegraph Bureau with offices in Zurich was equally unsuccessful. A Europa agency also was announced, again with headquarters in Stockholm, but it promptly vanished. Still another effort in Stockholm produced the Skaninaviska Telegram Buero (S.T.B. or Skantel). It attempted to arrange for reports from the established and respectable Swedish agency, Tidningarnas Telegrambyrå (TT), to buy broadcast time on the Swedish radio, and also to purchase Swedish-made A.E.G. wireless transmitters. Like the other efforts, this was exposed and failed. A Berlin service was set up to distribute articles written by foreign-born collaborators with the German Nazi government, of whom there were a number. Known as Korrespondenz und Artikel-Nachrichtendienst (KAN), it also was short-lived.

Somewhat as the difficulties of news coverage in Moscow in 1939–40 had brought the closing of newspaper bureaus there and the withdrawal of correspondents, so the difficulties of obtaining news in Berlin brought similar results in the spring and summer of 1941. There were comparable changes in Rome and Tokyo.

Harsch of the *Christian Science Monitor* returned to the United States in February 1941 so that he might write a series of uncensored articles appearing under the title "Inside the War." They also formed the substance of his book, *Pattern of Conquest,* published later in the year. In the same manner, the *Monitor* recalled Davis from Rome in March 1941 to produce a series of articles. Neither the Rome nor Berlin wartime posts were refilled for the *Monitor.*

The *New York Herald Tribune* closed its Berlin bureau in the spring of 1941, withdrawing Ed Haffel, who had been alone there since Barnes and Hill had been expelled in June 1940. The *Chicago Daily News,* having closed its Rome bureau in February, closed its Berlin bureau in June after some forty years of continuous operation. David M. Nichol, there since 1940, moved to Moscow. Carroll Binder, then foreign editor in Chicago, explained the Berlin closure by saying that it had become impossible to write or send independent or analytical dispatches. Stephen Laird, in Berlin for *Time* magazine, also was withdrawn and the office there closed after a brief period of operation. Pierre J. Huss, INS chief, left Germany, and Karl Von Wiegand, veteran of the Hearst service, had departed even earlier to report from the Far East, a new territory for him.

The *New York Times* coverage from Berlin was reduced by the departure of Percival Knauth and C. Brooks Peters, but the bureau remained staffed by Guido Enderis and George Axelsson. E. R. Noderer of the *Chicago Tribune,* who had replaced Sigrid Schultz in February 1941, also left and was replaced by Alex Small of the Paris bureau, before it was closed by the German occupation.

Edwin Hartrich, CBS correspondent since Shirer left Berlin in December 1940, was replaced early in 1941 by Howard K. Smith, who had arrived in Berlin for the United Press after service in London and Copenhagen. Max Jordan, NBC, was replaced by Warren Irvin, who was followed by Charles Lanius, formerly in Rome. He was succeeded by Alex Dreier, formerly of the AP. The departure of Sigrid Schultz, also representing MBS, brought John Paul Dickson into that radio assignment.

The general trend was away from Berlin in 1941, not only because of the news difficulties and the hazards of wartime bombing, but because poor living conditions and the general atmosphere contributed to what became known as the "Berlin blues." News agency and radio correspondents were regarded as the most essential among those remaining, providing such reports as they could. Some additional correspondents did arrive, however. Agency staffers of the U.S. press were Jack Fleischer, Walter Wilkie, Glenn M. Stadler, formerly in Paris, and Hugh Templeton Speck for the UP; and Jean A. Graffis, previously in Paris for Acme Newspictures.

London news representation changes were numerous during 1940–41. Sam Robertson was manager there for the Canadian Press. He was drowned in April 1941 when the ship in which he was returning from a period of leave in Canada was torpedoed off the Irish coast. He was succeeded as chief of the bureau by D. Ernest Burritt. Later in the year, Burritt was elected president of the Association of Overseas Empire Correspondents. Officers of that organization in 1941–42 also included W. T. Cranfield, *Toronto Evening Telegram;* A. W. Mitchell, New Zealand Press Association (NZPA); E. R. Mackie, *Statesman,* Calcutta; A. W. V. King, *Sydney Morning Herald;* N. F. Grant, *Cape Times,* Capetown; and L. W. Matters, *Hindu,* Madras. The Foreign Press Association of

London, dating from 1888 and with a general membership, was headed in 1941 by Gottfried J. Keller, correspondent for the *Basler Nachrichten*.

F. Raymond Daniell, chief of the *New York Times* London bureau, and Tania Long of the *New York Herald Tribune* bureau returned briefly to the U.S. to be married. William W. White transferred from the London AP bureau to the *New York Herald Tribune* bureau. Brydon Taves of the UP bureau was transferred to Cape Town, and William B. Dickinson and Robert Kelly of the New York staff joined the UP London bureau late in 1941.

The last correspondent of a neutral status to make a general circuit of the European continent prior to the entrance of the United States into the war probably was Henry J. Taylor, a business man and student of economics accredited to the NANA. He left New York October 4, 1941, and returned December 15 after a journey largely by commercial aircraft that took him to Lisbon, London, Edinburgh, Stockholm, and Helsinki, then to Stockholm again, to Berlin, Lyon, Vichy, Barcelona, Madrid, Gibraltar, Madrid, and Lisbon again, before going to London once more. From London, Taylor returned to Lisbon and then went south along the African coast to Natal, across the South Atlantic to Brazil, Trinidad, Bermuda, and to New York. He wrote of his observations and of his interviews with many heads of state.

In that first year after September 1939, the movement of correspondents reporting World War II had changed rapidly as events and government censors dictated. The entire war situation and relationships between nations had been greatly altered by the events of the Battle of Britain in 1940–41, and was further complicated by the German invasion of Russia. That latter event soon brought new demands upon the resources of correspondents and the news services.

The second half of the year 1941 brought World War II to its full geographical scope. It became a world war in the most literal sense. Germany, disregarding its nonaggression treaty of August 1939 attacked Soviet Russia on June 22.

Less than six months later Japan, the original aggressor of 1931, followed its decade of war in China by a coordinated December 7–8 attack at several points in Asia and the Pacific, including the British Crown Colony of Hong Kong, the Philippines and the United States Pacific naval base at Pearl Harbor, Hawaii.

The events changed the shape of the war and its impact on the world. The first brought Soviet Russia and Great Britain into an alliance against Germany and Italy. The second brought the United States and Great Britain into war against Japan and in support of China, and it also brought the United States into alliance with Great Britain and the Soviet Union against Germany and Italy.

In Berlin, before dawn on Sunday, June 22, propaganda minister Dr. Paul Joseph Goebbels read to the German people over the radio a proclamation by Adolf Hitler. After reciting a series of complaints against Soviet Russia, it announced that Germany had declared war on that country, and that the attack already was proceeding along a 2,000 mile line from Finland and the Baltic States in the north to the southern Ukraine on the Black Sea. Finland, part of whose territory had been seized by Russia in the brief 1939–40 war, made common cause with Germany in this move.

The first reports to reach the world of the German attack came from monitors listening to the Berlin radio. In London, the news reached the media offices there at 7 A.M. The Sunday papers were already printed, and the newspaper and news agency offices lightly staffed. The BBC, however, immediately broadcast the news. The AP, UP, and INS bureaus sent bulletins to New York. Messages also were relayed to Canada, Latin America, and other parts of the world. The AP message, for example, datelined "London, Sunday, June 22," stated routinely that "Adolf Hitler today ordered a march of the Nazi armies into Russia."

In New York at 11:26 P.M. Eastern Daylight time on Saturday, June 21, the Columbia Broadcasting System shortwave monitoring station had picked up a Berlin report stating that Goebbels was to issue a proclamation from Hitler at 5:30 A.M. Berlin time on Sunday (which was 11:30 P.M. New York time, still June 21). This was only four minutes after the first announcement, and the information was flashed on teleprinter circuits to New York newspaper offices and news agency headquarters. Goebbels did begin to speak at 11:30.

At 11:32 P.M. New York time, the CBS monitoring service reported that "Joseph Goebbels has mentioned Soviet Russia and the proclamation is criticizing Russia." At 12:05 A.M. (now June 22) the flash came that Germany had declared war on Russia. The New York Sunday morning papers had final morning editions on the presses, but promptly remade their front pages to report what was recognized as a great turning point in the war. The essential fact was supplemented almost immediately by added information and background material.[1] For papers in cities of the United States in time zones west of New York and the Atlantic coastal areas there were from one to three more hours to prepare the morning reports.

At the Soviet frontier, Jack Fleischer of the UP and some other correspondents were with the German armies. The position of correspondents both in Berlin and in Moscow underwent changes during the next few weeks. From Berlin, Alvin J. Steinkopf, AP, was permitted to accompany Nazi troops entering Smolensk in August, a city taken in the first great battle of the campaign intended to drive ahead to Moscow—a goal never attained.

Generally, however, the Wehrmacht did not provide opportunities for correspondents to visit the front, as it had earlier during the Polish campaign in 1939 and the French campaign of 1940. Instead, reports were provided as prepared by German correspondents, members of the *Pressekompagnie*. For the first time since the beginning of the war, or of the Nazi government in 1933, an acknowledged censorship was established in October 1941.

In July the Columbia Broadcasting System had been barred from making further broadcasts from Germany. Like the action against the MBS the year before, this ban was only temporary, and was attributed

---

1   For this writer, then working on the *New York Times* cable desk and helping to prepare the new edition, these were among the more memorable moments in years of desk experience.

to resentment in Berlin over a CBS network broadcast in the United States by Elmer Davis.[2]

On November 15, the German government imposed a ban on the three U.S. radio networks' Berlin correspondents—then Howard K. Smith, for CBS, Alex Dreier, NBC, and John Paul Dickson, MBS. They were informed by the Reichs-Rundfunkgesellschaft (German Radio Company), the government facility through which they broadcast, that they were no longer permitted to use those facilities because they had submitted "unjustified complaints" to their home offices without previously submitting those complaints to the company.

This was a face-saving action by the German company and government arising from a refusal by Dreier and Dickson to broadcast due to the great restrictions imposed, with Smith about to do the same. The New York offices of the three networks, informed by their correspondents of the situation under which it had become virtually impossible for them to function, announced that they were discontinuing broadcasts from Berlin, just as some newspapers had withdrawn their correspondents. The three radio correspondents were denied exit visas permitting them to leave Germany until their networks agreed to send replacements. Smith and Dreier left under that arrangement, with Paul Fischer taking over for NBC, Dickson remaining for MBS, and CBS temporarily unrepresented.

The possibility of U.S. correspondents accompanying German forces to the Russian front naturally vanished after December 11, 1941, when Germany and Italy declared war on the United States. From that time, U.S. correspondents in Germany were under arrest. Reports from Germany, when they were not derived from German publications and radio broadcasts, came from those few Swiss and Swedish correspondents remaining in the country, and reporting under great difficulties and restraints.

Upon going to war with Soviet Russia, Hitler was taking the risk of fighting on two or more fronts. His military authority seemed firmly established in the west. France had surrendered, and Hitler seemed to believe that Britain was finished. The campaign in Yugoslavia and Greece had completed Nazi control in the south of Europe by May 1941, and Rommel's Afrika Korps had backed British forces into Egypt. Hitler and his staff had planned a devastating *blitzkrieg,* with the expectation that two months would bring victory in Russia.

---

2   Davis had treated facetiously a shortwave broadcast from Berlin by Pelham Granville Wodehouse, a British author of humorous fiction. Captured by the Germans in their sweep along the French Channel coast in May 1940, Wodehouse had been induced to appear on radio in a nonpolitical talk. He then was interned in Germany for the remaining years of the war.

Germany professed to have been dissatisfied with Russia's performance under the provisions of the trade treaties of August 1939. Hitler also had been offended by Russia's unilateral action in seizing eastern Poland under the shadow of the German attack, and before Wehrmacht forces were able to reach that part of the country. There was offense taken also at Russian seizure of the three Baltic republics, a corner of Czechoslovakia, and the Rumanian provinces of Bukovina and Bessarabia in 1940 when Germany was engaged in the final assault on France.

Awareness of German irritation on these matters had led Ralph W. Barnes, then in Berlin for the *New York Herald Tribune,* to write in June 1940 that another year might see the two countries in open controversy. It was this sharp conclusion and its publication that resulted in the immediate expulsion of Barnes from Germany. Yet he was not alone in recognizing the possibility of a Nazi attack on the Soviet Union. Despite the Communazi pacts of August 1939, there was no reason to believe that Hitler was any less opposed to communism and a Communist neighbor than he had been before. Many also recognized that the surrender of France and the effectiveness of the air and sea war against Britain meant that Germany might safely turn its attention to the east.

In May 1941, Dr. Karl Bömer, director of the Foreign Press Section of the Propaganda Ministry, was arrested by the Gestapo for his indiscreet reference at a social function to the prospective Russian attack.[3] Through their own sources, the United States government and the British government learned of these preparations. There were rumors of such a move, and correspondents and diplomats in Berlin and Moscow discussed the possibility long before it became a reality. The reports of such prospective action were communicated to Soviet representatives in Washington and London for transmission to Moscow. Received seriously by some, Stalin and Foreign Commissar Molotov, although suspicious by nature, were unwilling to believe such an attack was coming.

The Wehrmacht invasion began on June 22 with armored units, tanks, and planes. Red Army defensive forces were driven back all along the line. Moscow was under air attack by October and the Soviet government moved some of its agencies and the diplomatic and press corps to Kuibyshev (the ancient Samara), 800 miles to the east.

By October the German armored columns had penetrated deep into Russia on a broad front. As the Red Army retreated, it adopted a "scorched earth" policy that left little for the Germans to use, whether food supplies, potable water, or buildings for shelter. There were no

---

3 Bömer, in an earlier conversation with this writer, had spoken frankly of the original Nazi seizure of Socialist and Communist newspapers of Berlin and had provided copies of them.

available railway facilities and highways were few and inadequate. For every mile gained, the German lines of communication and supply became that much longer and more difficult to maintain. The people of the Soviet Union did not welcome the Germans, much less rally to them as "liberators from Bolshevik slavery," as Berlin had half expected. Neither did the German invaders behave in such a way as to encourage them to do so. Indeed, guerrilla activities harassed the invaders.

German confidence in a quick victory began to vanish as their military forces were overwhelmed by the very size of the Russian countryside. Communiqués, formerly quite accurate and dependable so long as objectives were being attained, became exaggerated and misleading. Soviet communiqués were no more accurate. The only certainty was that losses of men and materiel on both sides were enormous. Then came the freezing winter of 1941–42. Well aware of the plight of the Napoleonic armies in Russia in the winter of 1812, the Germans had not expected their campaign to last so long and were unprepared for its rigors. Mechanized equipment failed, men suffered, and not until the spring of 1942 was the German army and air force able to renew its offensive.

In Moscow, by contrast to Berlin, the hostility with which the Soviet government had been treating foreign correspondents underwent a reversal as a result of the German attack upon the country. Because of the restrictions and frustrations to which they had been subjected, special correspondents had been leaving Russia since 1936. The German attack of 1941 meant that German, Italian, Finnish, Rumanian, and Hungarian correspondents were disaccredited and repatriated.

The whole foreign press representation remaining in Moscow numbered about twenty. A. T. Cholerton of the London *Daily Telegraph* was dean of the corps in terms of service in Moscow, and Henry Shapiro of the United Press was second. Henry C. Cassidy, AP, chief of the Paris bureau until the French surrender in June 1940, had been in Moscow since that period. Robert Magidoff was second man in the bureau, serving Exchange Telegraph (Extel) and NBC as well. Maurice Lovell represented Reuters.

Jean Champenois had represented the Agence Havas in Moscow, but with Havas ended because of the French surrender and the occupation of most of France, Champenois became correspondent for the Free French agency formed in London. This Agence L.E.F. was soon renamed the Agence Française Indépendante (AFI). Janet Weaver represented the London *Daily Worker,* the British Communist party paper, and later wrote also for a new Intercontinental Press, a propaganda service believed sponsored by the Cominform. Jesús Hernández, formerly a member of the Spanish Republican government, wrote for a group of South American papers. Three correspondents were in Moscow for the Japanese press. There was one Cuban correspondent, and seven other press representatives. Three of the latter had arrived in Moscow in May. One was novelist Erskine Caldwell representing *PM,* the new New York daily. Margaret Bourke-White, his wife, was a photographer for *Life* magazine, and had been in the Soviet Union on previous occasions. Caldwell wrote for *Life* on this visit and broadcast for CBS. A third visitor was Alice Leone-Moats, a writer for *Collier's Weekly.*

Once the German attack came, the Soviet government attitude toward foreign correspondents changed. They now were welcome, encountered no problems in obtaining visas to enter the country, received considerble assistance, and were accorded favored treatment. The invasion also had the effect of bringing the Soviet Union into close association with Great Britain in sharing the war effort. The former arms-length relationship changed, as it also did with the United States, especially after Pearl Harbor in December 1941. From the outset, the lend-lease arrangements between the United States and Great Britain were extended to provide a billion dollar credit to the Soviet Union. The relationship between Russian public officials and foreign media correspondents became almost intimate.

Cyrus L. Sulzberger of the *New York Times* was in Istanbul at the time of the German attack and one of the first of the new group of correspondents to reach Moscow. Wallace Carroll, in charge of the United Press administration in London, hastened to Moscow. Ralph Ingersoll, editor and publisher of *PM* of New York, was an early arrival and was granted the only wartime interview with Stalin. He was the first U.S. newsman to talk with Stalin since Roy Howard of the Scripps-Howard Newspapers had met with the premier in 1936. Ingersoll's interview was private and never was used for publication.

Alexander Werth, born in St. Petersburg, fluent in Russian, and experienced in Russia as a writer for the *Sunday Times,* returned to Moscow in July 1941. He returned to represent Reuters, at the special request of the British Foreign Office, and again wrote for the *Sunday Times.* Larry LeSueur, CBS, became the first radio correspondent to broadcast regularly from Moscow.

Philip Jordan arrived for the *News-Chronicle,* and his dispatches also appeared in the *Times* and the *Daily Express.* Vernon Bartlett wrote for the *News-Chronicle* and the BBC, and Charlotte Haldane for the *Daily Sketch* and the Allied Newspapers. Others arriving early included Archibald T. Steele of the *Chicago Daily News,* who was experienced in the Far East, and Dennis McEvoy of the *Chicago Times.* Walter Graebner, chief of the London office of *Time* and *Life,* reached Moscow in the spring of 1942. He returned to London some months later with many photos especially made for him or obtained through VOKS, the Soviet governmental society for cultural relations between the USSR and foreign countries.

Prime Minister Churchill was an early visitor to Russia after it became involved in the war. Foreign Secretary Anthony Eden, Sir Walter Monckton, and Lord Beaverbrook were other British leaders who reached Moscow. Harry Hopkins arrived as a representative of President Roosevelt, and W. Averell Harriman and Wendell L. Willkie were others. Quentin Reynolds flew from London as press attaché with a Beaverbrook-Harriman Mission in September 1941. He remained to write a number of articles for *Collier's Weekly* and reports for the *Daily Express.*

Willkie, unsuccessful as the Republican party candidate for the presidency in 1940, was designated by President Roosevelt as a special ambassador to make a world tour in the autumn of 1942 to meet with leaders of free and neutral countries. He was accompanied by Joseph Barnes, foreign editor of the *New York Herald Tribune* and former Moscow correspondent for that paper, and by John ("Mike") Cowles, copublisher of the *Des Moines Register and Tribune,* the *Minneapolis Star-Journal,* and *Look* magazine. Barnes and Cowles were present as representatives of the U.S. Office of War Information. In Moscow, all attended a meeting between Willkie and Stalin, along with Foreign Commissar Molotov.[4]

Although government information previously had been almost impossible to obtain through direct sources in Moscow, a Soviet Information Bureau (Sovinformbureau) was established within two or three days of the German attack in June 1941. Attached to the Foreign Commissariat, it was directed by Alexander Sergeevich Shcherbakov, a member of the Politburo and secretary of the Moscow District of the Communist party. He was rarely seen by correspondents, but Solomon A. Lozovsky, vice commissar of foreign affairs and assistant director of the bureau, acted as "official spokesman" at news conferences conducted twice each week, either at the Foreign Commissariat's Press Department or at the former Greek Legation. Vadim Kruskov was secretary-general of the Information Bureau.

Nikolai G. Palgunov, former Paris correspondent for Tass and former director of the Tass agency in Moscow, became chief of the Press Department. He attended the news conferences and was in general charge of the censorship until he was succeeded in 1943–44 by Apollon Petrov. Boris Mikhailov, formerly Paris correspondent of *Pravda* and editor of the French-language *Journal de Moscou,* became chief of the American section of the Press Department in 1942. A press room attached to the department served as a point to which correspondents

---

4 Neither Barnes nor Cowles made any public report on their experiences or observations. Willkie, upon his return, made a report to the president. He also made a significant radio report to the people of the United States, later published in brochure form under the title of *One World* (New York, 1943).

might turn in matters relating both to their professional and personal problems in Moscow.

Copies of war communiqués issued to the Tass agency from the time of the Russo-Finnish War and redistributed by Tass became available to foreign correspondents through the Press Department, along with any special wartime Orders of the Day.

Originally, there was one communiqué issued daily at about 3 A.M. This was 1 A.M. Greenwich Mean Time in London. However, with London on "double summer time" throughout the war years, it was actually 11 P.M. of the previous day's date. In New York it was 8 P.M. Eastern Standard Time of the previous day's date, or 7 P.M. when "daylight time" was in effect from April to October. Because the censors were not on duty in Moscow at 3 A.M., Radio Moscow had the first opportunity to report the news set forth in that communique'.

After the Nazi attack of June 1941, a second communiqué was issued each day at 11 A.M. This was 7 A.M. double summer time in London, still too late for use in the morning papers, but suitable for the early BBC news broadcasts. In New York it was 4 A.M. EST, or 3 A.M. "daylight time," and might be used in replates of the morning newspapers in the eastern time zone. There remained one to three hours more for time zones to the west, and full opportunity for broadcast use throughout the North American continent and the Western Hemisphere.

Communications facilities from Moscow also were improved. Radio-telegraphic transmission remained slow, even apart from censorship delays, but the war communiqués as broadcast by Radio Moscow moved promptly. Photographs were flown to London, beginning in July 1941, when airmail service became available. Shortwave broadcasts became possible by foreign radio correspondents in Moscow late that summer. Material that had taken eight weeks or more to move by sea between Moscow and New York soon could be delivered in New York in six weeks by way of the Far East in Soviet ships sailing between Vladivostok and San Francisco. This routing was slow but continued even after the United States became involved in the war in December 1941 because Russia was not at war with Japan until August 8, 1945, shortly before the Japanese surrender. Arrangements also were made whereby articles by Soviet correspondents at the war fronts became available promptly for use in the world press. By early 1944 radio-telephone service was available for the use of diplomatic and military personnel and for correspondents between Moscow and London or New York.

Even as conditions affecting the work of correspondents improved, they still performed under certain handicaps. A curfew required that people be off the streets in Moscow between midnight and 4 A.M. Accredited correspondents had passes, but their assistants—translators, secretaries, couriers, chauffeurs—did not. In theory, this meant that a correspondent had to be present himself to receive the 3 A.M. communiqué, translate it from the Russian, and prepare a story. Since censors were not on duty between 2 A.M. and 10 A.M., and since the 3 A.M. communiqué would be transmitted abroad by Tass and Radio Moscow seven or eight hours before a correspondent's report based on that same communiqué could clear the censorship for transmission, there was little point in his undertaking to do a special story on the 3 A.M. communiqué. If he did so, he would leave it for the attention of the censor at the fifth-floor walkup Press Department in the Foreign Commissariat. The correspondent could prepare a story earlier, have it reviewed by the censorship before 2 A.M. and taken to the communications office a mile away for night transmission, with the correspondent's day then ended.

The 11 A.M. communiqué gave a correspondent a better opportunity to write a story to meet a normal deadline in London or New York. Even though Moscow Radio also transmitted that communiqué promptly, and it was used by radio news broadcasters, the correspondent still could do a useful background story. If he also undertook to send a photo by radio and started the routine procedure at 7:30 A.M., for example, the picture might not reach London until 10 P.M. and New York even later, and therefore was not likely to be used until the second day after its dispatch.

Sources of information in Moscow remained limited, even with the addition of twice-weekly news conferences and greater assistance from the Press Department. There was still virtually no opportunity to see officials of the government, to move about the country, or go to areas where fighting was in progress. The exceptions were few.

One British correspondent in a period of several months submitted more than twenty requests to Palgunov, head of the Press Department, seeking interviews, opportunities to visit the front, and the like. Only one request was granted, and then thanks only to the intervention of the British ambassador. Some alternative interviews or visits were offered, but none bearing upon the major topic of interest—the war.

Correspondents wrote repeatedly to Stalin and other officials, requesting answers to questions or requesting interviews. Henry C. Cassidy of the AP wrote such letters on an average of twice a week for two years. He received two replies, one in October 1942 and another in November. In both cases, Stalin made his responses the occasion chiefly for stressing his desire to have the Allies establish a "second front" on the European continent to draw German pressure from the Russian front. Ralph Parker of the *New York Times* was the only other correspondent to receive a reply from Stalin, as he did in May 1943 in response to questions about prospective Soviet relations with Poland after the war.

For eye-witness reporting, correspondents were permitted to make eight trips to frontline areas between September 1941 and March 1943, but usually only after the fighting was ended, and where Soviet forces had been victorious. Conducted visits, the first, in September 1941, took a dozen correspondents in five cars to the Vyazma and Smolensk areas on the central front. The party included Cholerton, Shapiro, Cassidy, Carroll, Sulzberger, Werth, Steele, Jordan, Bartlett, Caldwell, Margaret Bourke-White, and Charlotte Haldane. Even though the areas supposedly had been recaptured from the Germans, they were bombed at Vyazma, never reached the firing line, and found that the Smolensk battle area had been cleaned up before they were permitted to see it.

Cassidy was in the Kalinin sector northwest of Moscow in June 1942. Leland Stowe of the *Chicago Daily News,* who arrived in Moscow in May 1942, went in October to the Rhzev front, in much the same sector. Henry Shapiro, UP, went to Leningrad in December 1942. Late in 1943 a group of correspondents was flown to Kharkov to report a trial of persons accused of atrocities, with every aid provided in matters of translations and transmissions. On that trip two censors and a conducting officer were killed when their car ran over a land mine.

Eye-witness accounts of another sort were produced by correspondents traveling aboard convoys carrying lend-lease materials to Murmansk under German air and submarine attack. Godfrey Winn, *Sunday Express,* and Robert Carse, *Saturday Evening Post,* were among those who wrote such accounts involving great peril and hardship. In a 1942 convoy, Winn was injured during a storm when his hand was jammed in a steel door.

With the German attack directed at Moscow in October 1941, and the capital under air bombardment, the Soviet government required the evacuation of foreign diplomats, correspondents, and certain agencies of the government, including the Foreign Commissariat. All went to Kuibyshev, 800 miles east on the Volga. The journey required five days by rail under difficult circumstances. Living conditions in Kuibyshev were even less satisfactory than in Moscow. The population of the temporary capital increased from about 450,000 to some 800,000. The Foreign Commissariat was in what had been a schoolhouse. The correspondents were quartered in what was loosely known as the Grand Hotel. The Soviet Information Bureau also was moved to Kuibyshev and the censorship necessarily moved there also.

For seven months, the correspondents were forced to remain in what Larry LeSueur, CBS, referred to as "a correspondent's purgatory." Not until May 1942 was the threat to Moscow sufficiently eased to permit a general return to the capital. The news conferences that had been meeting in Moscow from June to October of 1941 were suspended with the move to Kuibyshev and were not resumed until April 1944.

Stalin, Molotov, and most other Soviet leaders remained in Moscow. A variation in the correspondents' position occurred in mid-December, when some were permitted to fly to Moscow for a ten-day visit to report on the condition of the city after the failure of the Germans to take it in a concerted effort between November 16 and December 8, when a Russian counteroffensive turned the tide. Some of the correspondents on that visit attempted to reach the battle area but were forced back by a blizzard. A second group of correspondents flew to Moscow and remained from mid-January 1942 until late March.

The Moscow Radio broadcast the communiqués and war news throughout the October-to-May period. The correspondents in Kuibyshev had little to add, and what they could report was slow in reaching London or New York. Some took the opportunity during March-April to visit Iran, where Soviet and British forces had moved in to maintain and guard a supply line for the transportation of U.S. lend-lease supplies from the Persian Gulf overland to Russia. Mrs. Lea Schiavi Burdett, Italian-born wife of Winston Burdett, CBS, and representing *PM* in Teheran, was shot by Kurdish road guards north of Teheran and bled to death in the car in which she was riding.[5]

German forces were only 125 miles west of Moscow in May 1942, but a general return from Kuibyshev to the capital was permitted. From then until the end of the war in 1945, the correspondents operated in Moscow under a system that became well established, and was actually not greatly different from what it had been in the mid-1930s. The Soviet Information Bureau resumed its news conferences in April 1944, but they were rare and usually called on short notice. Meanwhile, the war communiqués and some information reached correspondents through the Press Department.

Germany had sustained such losses in Russia by 1942 as to bring deep disillusionment upon the nation, from the top Nazi leadership, through the military ranks, and the civilian population. The difficulties of that

---

5 Burdett was in India at the time. Mrs. Burdett had been an anti-Fascist Italian journalist when she met and married Burdett in Bucharest in the summer of 1940. He then was representing Transradio Press and began to serve as a stringer for CBS. They went to Belgrade in November, to Ankara in March 1941, to Teheran in November, and Burdett went to Ankara in March 1942 and on to India. Burdett is not to be confused with Wilfred Burchett, a correspondent for the London *Daily Worker* and other publications.

Burdett later took the view that his wife had been assassinated at the instigation of the Russians because she had learned that Yugoslav organizers were being trained in northern Iran to return to Yugoslavia to fight on the side of the Partisans, led by Marshal Tito, and to convert Yugoslavia into a Communist country. He believed Moscow did not want to risk the possibility that Mrs. Burdett might reveal this plan to British or U.S. journalists entering Iran at that time. See *U.S. News & World Report* (July 8, 1955), pp. 70–80.

campaign required the diversion of men and planes and other equipment to the Russian front. This prevented resumption of the air strikes against Britain. Meanwhile, the British RAF had increased its bomber squadrons and was raining destruction on Berlin and other German cities, on ports and industrial centers, and on German air fields and submarine centers in France. A third Axis offensive in the Libyan desert from January to August 1942 was effective within limits but not decisive, and it was costly to the Wehrmacht and Luftwaffe in terms of men and arms.

Through the winter and spring of 1942–43, the United States was moving into the war, and lend-lease supplies were flowing in growing volume to Britain and its forces in Egypt and Libya. For the USSR, tanks and planes and every other sort of wartime requirement was being delivered over the sea route to Murmansk, despite a great toll of men and ships through German submarine and air action. Supplies also moved over a tortuous land route from the Persian Gulf through Iran to Russia. This added strength to Soviet arms, while German strength was waning because shortages in gasoline supplies, for example, placed restrictions on the operations of planes, tanks, and other equipment.

This combination of circumstances enabled the Red Army and other Soviet military units to fight back at every point after the spring of 1942. The German advance was far from ended, however. The penetration of Soviet territory reached its greatest depth in the summer of 1943, more than 1,000 miles eastward from the point of the original invasion. It extended through the Ukraine and almost to the Caspian Sea in the south, and to the environs of Leningrad in the north. There, the city was besieged for seventeen months during 1942–43, with great peril and suffering among its people, but it never was taken. In the south, the historic battle for control of Stalingrad continued from August 22, 1942, until February 2, 1943, ending in a German defeat.

This German failure, at the point of greatest penetration within Russia, marked the beginning of a Soviet counteroffensive that ended in Berlin in May 1945. Germans retreating in the north left their associated Finnish military forces without direct contact and led to the conclusion by Finland of a separate peace with Russia and Great Britain in September 1944. It forced a roll back of German lines for some distance south from the Baltic, and a similar roll back in the south of Europe. This not only ended the siege of Leningrad, but ended the German occupation of Rostov, Vyasma, and other cities, and it involved German losses of more than 500,000 men killed, wounded, and captured in the 1943–44 winter campaign. By the summer of 1944 the Red Army was in Poland, and Rumania surrendered in August. Soviet troops were in Bulgaria and Yugoslavia by October, in Budapest in February 1945, and by then also fighting in Germany itself, where the final surrender came in May.[6]

The foreign media group in Soviet Russia naturally underwent changes during the war years. Wallace Carroll and Ralph Ingersoll were among those who left the country before the move to Kuibyshev. Others left during the seven months when that was the media center, including Sulzberger, Reynolds, Leone-Moats, Caldwell, and Bourke-White. Others arriving there were British-born Ralph Parker for the *New York Times* and the *Times* of London; Larry LeSueur, CBS; Walter Kerr, *New York Herald Tribune;* Eric McLoughlin, *Sydney Morning Herald;* Meyer S. Handler, UP, transferred from London; and Eddy Gilmore, AP, also previously in London. Robert Magidoff, who had represented the AP in Moscow, became correspondent for NBC.

The return of the diplomatic and media group to Moscow in May 1942 was followed by the arrival there of new or returning correspondents becoming numerous as the war proceeded. Leland Stowe, *Chicago Daily News,* returned to coverage of the war after an interval of recuperation, lecturing, and broadcasting in the United States. Edmund Stevens, *Christian Science Monitor,* in Moscow from 1934–40, also returned. Maurice Hindus, with prewar experience in Russia, returned as a magazine writer, and as a contributor to the *New York Herald Tribune.* Demaree Bess, a former Moscow correspondent for the *Monitor,* returned for the *Saturday Evening Post.* Paul Winterton, formerly in Moscow for the *News-Chronicle,* returned for that paper to replace Philip Jordan, who had been in Russia for the previous six months. Walter Graebner, London manager for *Time* and *Life,* was in Moscow from July to October 1942.

Other correspondents working in Moscow included Harold King, Reuters, replacing Maurice Lovell; Duncan Hooper, also for Reuters; Harrison E. Salisbury, United Press, coming from the London bureau; Daniel DeLuce and William McGaffin, both for the Associated Press; William W. Chaplin, James Brown, and Kendall Foss, all for the International News Service.

For the newspaper press, Ronald Matthews arrived for the London *Daily Herald;* Paul Holt and Alaric Jacob for the *Daily Express;* Iris Morley (Mrs. Alaric Jacob), the *Observer;* and Marjorie Shaw, *Daily Mirror.* Geoffrey Blunden represented the Australian Consolidated Press. For the U.S. media, arrivals included Ben Robertson, *PM,* and

---

6 The USSR later listed wartime battle deaths at 6,115,000 and wounded at 14,012,000. Comparable figures for Germany were 3,250,000 and 7,250,000; for China, 1,324,516 and 1,762,006; and Japan, 1,270,000 and 140,000. See *Information Please Almanac 1980,* p. 394.

David Nichol, *Chicago Daily News.* In 1944, Leigh White, recovered from wounds received in Greece in 1941 when with CBS, returned to the war in Russia for the *Daily News.* Edward Angly arrived for the *New York Herald Tribune,* Alexander Kendrick for the *Philadelphia Inquirer,* and John Gibbons for the Communist *Daily Worker* of New York and London.

John Hersey and Richard E. Lauterbach, representing both *Time* and *Life,* arrived in Moscow, and Craig Thompson, formerly in London for the *New York Times,* opened the first permanent Moscow bureau for *Time* magazine in 1945. Edgar Snow, greatly experienced in China, was in Moscow for the *Saturday Evening Post.* William W. White represented *Reader's Digest,* and Irina Skariatina Blakeslee, *Collier's Weekly.* Negley Farson, who had been in Russia during the 1917 revolution and later joined the *Chicago Daily News* staff, arrived to write for magazines. William T. Downs replaced LeSueur for CBS, and George Moorad also arrived later for CBS.

The foreign press group in Moscow during the winter of 1942–43 numbered about twenty-five, almost half of whom represented the U.S. press and radio. Nearly as many represented the British media. There was at least one Japanese correspondent, since Russia remained neutral in the Pacific war then in progress.

In June 1942 an Association of Anglo-American Correspondents in the USSR was formed, with about thirty-five correspondents then eligible for membership. Its first president was Henry Shapiro, UP, with Paul Holt, *Daily Express,* as secretary. The purpose of the association, as with similar organizations in other capitals, was to represent the correspondents in matters affecting their work and life in a foreign land. It gained formal recognition from the Soviet government in November 1942, the first such action by the Soviet regime.[7]

The Moscow correspondent's day, during the years from 1942 to 1945, began about 9 A.M. Nearly all press-radio representatives then gathered at the Press Department to be there when copies were delivered of the three leading dailies—*Pravda* (Truth), *Izvestia* (News), and *Krasnaya Zvezda* (Red Star), the army paper. The midday communiqué was distributed at about 11 A.M. Other newspapers appeared throughout the day, as did weekly or monthly publications. From these sources came most of the war news, since correspondents were so rarely permitted anywhere near the front, and never when action was in progress.

---

7   The presidency of the association alternated between U.S. and British correspondents. Alexander Werth, *Sunday Times,* followed Shapiro as president in 1943–44, and Eddy Gilmore, AP, was president in 1944–45, with Paul Winterton, *News-Chronicle,* vice-president, Duncan Hooper, Reuters, secretary, and Meyer S. Handler, UP, treasurer. Members of the executive committee in the latter year were Werth, Alaric Jacob, and John Gibbons.

In the afternoon, there might be a news conference at the U.S. Embassy, the British Embassy, or very occasionally elsewhere. In the evenings, the correspondents prepared their stories and would try to get them through the censorship before 2 A.M., when the censors went off duty until 10 A.M. If outside after midnight, when the curfew became effective they could expect to be stopped frequently on the street to show their passes.

Correspondents did not complain unduly about the censorship itself prior to 1944, although they might grumble about delays during the night hours, and about the problem of getting messages to the censorship and the communications offices on cold winter nights. Some engaged couriers to speed that delivery. The agency men who had drivers let them carry censored messages from the Press Department to the communications office before the midnight curfew forced the drivers off the streets.

Cassidy of the AP, when visiting in New York in 1943, said that the censorship, the strictest of any before the war, had become among the most liberal. He remarked:

> The censors watch for information which might aid or give comfort to the enemy, and also for any that might, in their opinion, be misleading or incorrect. But any article which seems to them a reasonable interpretation of the facts given in the Soviet press or communiqué, or witnessed at the front, is permitted to pass.[8]

He added that correspondents were presenting reports "as accurate as any that can be given from a great country at war." The stories, he conceded, "do not always tell the whole story, and the figures sometimes may be out of line, but, in general, what they say is true."

Paul Holt of the *Daily Express* in London on leave at about the same time also called the Soviet wartime censorship "reasonable." About two hours was required between the time a dispatch was handed to a censor and the time it was filed for transmission, he said.

Henry Shapiro in New York in 1944 added that censorship had eased to such a point that correspondents might even speculate on military developments and comment upon and analyze events with little more restraint than required by military security.[9] Ronald Matthews of the *Daily Herald,* in London at the time, qualified Shapiro's remark by noting that while "the whole story was all around you in Moscow," you could get perhaps a quarter of it, and then "only a fifth of the quarter would get past the censor."[10] He added that the Soviet Information Bu-

---

8   *New York Times,* March 8, 1943.

9   *Editor & Publisher* (March 4, 1944).

10   *World's Press News* (April 27, 1944).

reau was slow to provide information, and the Press Department, while pleasant, was not helpful. His estimate was that 80 percent of the news sent from Russia was of necessity gleaned from the Soviet press.

With the Germans retreating early in 1944, it was not surprising that correspondents had less trouble obtaining information in Moscow and moving it without serious censorship restrictions. Telephone service to London became available in February. A precensored script still was required before the connection was completed. Incoming press calls were permitted, but they were monitored, and messages had to be conveyed in Russian, French, or English.

The first news conference for correspondents since October 1941 took place in April 1944, and it was the most important ever held to that time. Foreign Commissar Molotov met correspondents to report that the Red Army, on strong counteroffensive since early 1943, had entered Rumania and cleared the Germans out of southern Russia. It was the first of several conferences addressed by Molotov himself.

Despite the successes of the Red Army, and the generally friendly treatment of all things Russian in the Anglo-American press, most correspondents felt that the censorship had grown stricter in the late spring of 1944, much as Matthews had said. There were the rare Molotov appearances, but nowhere to turn for information on even so simple a matter as the first name of a new appointee to an official position, or clarification of some statistical reference. Correspondents seldom were permitted to leave Moscow, except for a conducted tour about every two months to some airfield, a recaptured city, or some other place of supposed news interest.

Representatives of the Soviet press were almost the only reporters permitted near the actual fighting front, and it was upon their eyewitness accounts in Soviet newspapers and periodicals that the world press was obliged to depend. The best of those reports appeared in *Krasnaya Zvezda,* the official organ of the Commissariat of Defense, usually referred to as "the army paper." Although only a four-page tabloid, it was intended for the information of the armed forces, and its contents were regarded as entirely dependable.

With a small staff in Moscow, the *Krasnaya Zvezda* had about fifty reporters at the front, some known as writers of fiction or poetry, but all holding military rank. Those who became most widely known were Ilya Ehrenburg, chiefly because of his dispatches from Stalingrad, Konstantin Siminov, also writing from inside Stalingrad, and Boris Gorbatov and Yevgenii Petrov. Petrov was killed in a plane crash as he was being evacuated from Sevastopol just before that Crimean fortress fell. He was one of sixteen correspondents for the paper killed between June 1941 and the spring of 1944. In addition, some sixty photographers were killed in that period, some in the field for *Krasnaya Zvezda*. Many others were wounded.

Other staff reporters for the army paper included Nikolai Remisov, aviation editor and a fighter pilot, and Alexander Ogin, who took charge of a leaderless army unit surrounded by the Germans and led it safely through to rejoin its own lines. L. Loskutov, a staff photographer, spent a month with a guerrilla group behind the German lines. Still other reporters whose accounts formed the basis for news sent on to the rest of the world included Alexei Tolstoi, Mikhail Sholokhov, Alexander Poliakoff, Valentine Katayev, and Boris Yampolsky. The editor of the paper in the early period of the war was David Vadimov, who sometimes maintained his "office" in the field. Major General Nikolai Talinsky, a professor of military history, later assumed the editorship.

Tass agency war reporters, and those representing *Pravda* and *Izvestia*, also were at the front in competition with one another and with the *Krasnaya Zvezda* representatives. Soviet correspondents had their own troubles with censorship in the field and elsewhere. A correspondent serving both Tass and *Krasnaya Zvezda*, Colonel Sokolnikov, was accredited to the British Eighth Army in Libya early in 1943, and Michael Latvin-Sedoy was accredited to the western Allied Supreme Headquarters (SHAEF) in Paris in the last months of the war.

Stalin and the entire Soviet propaganda organization had been pressing for a second front in Europe at least since 1943, at which time Allied landings were made in Sicily and Italy. When landings were made in Normandy in June 1944, greater Soviet satisfaction was shown in the provision to correspondents of six conducted trips in only three weeks to combat areas in eastern Europe. The provision of such trips henceforth was keyed to the pace of Allied action in the west. When progress was slow in France, the news trips in the east ceased altogether. As the campaign picked up speed, the trips were resumed and increased in number.

Alexander Werth, then representing the *Sunday Times*, the *Daily Sketch*, and the BBC, and several other British and U.S. correspondents had a narrow escape while traveling together on an early trip in September 1943. They were visiting the Ukrainian front and the lead car in the convoy exploded a road mine near Bielgorod, killing or seriously wounding all passengers except the driver.

The first flight of U.S. bombers from African bases to Soviet airfields occurred in June 1943. The arrival was reported at first hand by Harrison Salisbury of the UP, and by Maurice Hindus representing the *New York Herald Tribune*. Even though this flight was related to efforts to knock out the Ploesti oil refineries in Rumania, then providing fuel for German planes and tanks, the Soviet Union placed limitations and close restraints on Allied flights to bases within the country. Similar official restraints lessened opportunities for correspondents to do original reporting in Russia, as the censorship seemed to become more restrictive in 1944–45, despite Soviet successes.

Matthews of the *Daily Herald* said in the spring of 1944 that the censorship permitted "only a fifth of the quarter" of all news to leave Moscow. Henry Cassidy of the AP and David Nichol[11] of the *Chicago Daily News* agreed in New York in the autumn of that year that the position of the correspondents involved growing frustrations. Not only were news sources restricted, but marked differences of opinion of what should be transmitted caused censorship difficulties. Some dispatches were delayed as much as two or three days before being forwarded. But such delay was not uncommon on other fronts at that stage of the war, and some news reports were held up for months.

There was a misunderstanding on the part of some Soviet officials, and occasionally a sense of injury, about what they regarded as references critical of the USSR in U.S. publications. The Soviet authorities, so Nichol explained,

> argue that they can't justifiably give the foreign press, for one of a variety of reasons, what they do not make public to their own people. What they don't admit is that Americans are interested in knowing more about the Russian people—what they have done, what they look like and how they think. They just can't understand the American press' demand for data about human beings.[12]

It was a sense of injury, so it was suggested, that induced David Zaslavsky to refer in *Pravda* in April 1944 to Hanson W. Baldwin, *New York Times* military and naval correspondent, as "admiral of the ink pool." Stalin himself was understandably irked by a United Press report out of London in February 1944 attributing to a "neutral diplomat" an account of an incident alleged to have occurred during the November 1943 Teheran conference of the Allied heads of state, Stalin, Churchill, and Roosevelt. During Churchill's sixty-ninth birthday party on November 30, the London report had said, Stalin hit Marshal Semyon T. Timoshenko on the head with a bottle. Protests conveyed to Harrison E. Salisbury, then acting chief of the UP bureau in Moscow, resulted in a

---

11 Eddy Gilmore succeeded Cassidy as chief of the AP bureau in Moscow, and Leigh White succeeded Nichol for the *Chicago Daily News.*

12 *Editor & Publisher* (October 14, 1944), p. 32. See also David M. Nichol, "A Bleak Assignment," *Quill* (March–April 1945), pp. 5, 17; Dwight Bentel, "Russians Feel Abused by U.S. Press—Cassidy," *Editor & Publisher* (August 12, 1944), p. 12; Henry C. Cassidy, "Important News," *Inter-Office* (AP house publication) (September 1944), pp. 8, 32.

"correction" from the United Press in New York and two formal apologies. [13]

The Soviet bureaucracy in 1941–42 was ready to modify its traditional restraints on correspondents and the press, for it was then under heavy German attack and needed all the friendship, understanding, and support it could get. By 1944, however, that readiness had vanished. Through lend-lease and delivery of materiel by sea and air, the Red Army and the general Soviet economy had been provided with the means to mount an effective defense and counteroffensive against German forces. Moscow's confidence in its own ultimate success was restored, especially in view of the strong Anglo–U.S.–Free French concentration of power which reduced German pressure. As one result, the Soviet Union was led to revert to its earlier policies, including censorship. The effect was noted by Nichol and Cassidy, but even more specifically by Alexander Kendrick of the *Philadelphia Inquirer*.

Formerly in the *Inquirer* Washington bureau and a Nieman fellow at Harvard, Kendrick arrived in Moscow in May 1944. Fluent in Russian, his opportunities to use it beyond reading the Soviet publications and government releases were almost nil. Soviet authorities refused to permit him to visit the front, to talk with officials or others, or to obtain news in any way except through the press and official handouts. Even then, his reports were not reaching his home office, nor were service messages reaching him in Moscow. The *Inquirer* recalled him in October 1944 after five months.

On his return to the United States, Kendrick said that correspondents then in Moscow were wasting their time, both because of the refusal of Soviet authorities to permit them to do any original reporting at the front or elsewhere, and because the censorship prevented the correspondent from doing anything much more than rewrite government releases and Soviet press material. He summarized his experience by saying:

> In their refusal to cooperate with us, the Russians take refuge in technicalities. They say, for example, that we war correspondents are accredited to the Soviet Foreign Office and not to the Red armies, therefore they decline to permit us to operate in the field within the zones of military activity. We write only what they choose to permit us to write.
>
> The truth is that the Russians are still very security-conscious. They are afraid of spies . . . and are not taking any chances. I was treated always with courtesy. Russians want our friendship and they mean to be friendly toward us. But they either do not know how to be friendly, or they are held back.

---

13   See Joe Alex Morris, *Deadline Every Minute, The Story of the United Press* (1957), pp. 268–69.

They have been through so much hardship and suffering, with so many changes of policy, and their reaction is to retreat within themselves, fending off all foreigners.

It is my opinion that close relations with our Russian allies will be impossible until many changes are made. There will have to be complete freedom of access to sources of information—otherwise it is impossible to interpret the Russians to the Americans and make them understandable to us.[14]

Kendrick, Nichol, Cassidy and others among the correspondents had many good things to say of the Russian people, but they were discouraged by the official obstacles hindering them as they tried to convey the human side of the news, along with a complete picture of a nation at war. The illogic of the rebuffs given them as friendly and admiring observers left them puzzled and somewhat hurt. Although they could not know it at the time, the correspondents in Moscow during 1944–45, the last year of the war, were only experiencing a foretaste of what was in store for those newsmen and newswomen who would undertake to report the news from Soviet Russia in postwar years.

---

14   *Editor & Publisher* (October 14, 1944), p. 32, and (December 23, 1944), p. 28.

United States and Japan, 1941–42   10

Japan's army supported by sea and air forces had consolidated its control of most of China by 1941. All of Manchuria had been converted into what the Chinese called the "puppet empire" of Manchukuo. Shanghai, Tientsin, Peiping, Nanking, Hankow, Canton, and other major cities were under Japanese domination. The foreign "settlements" in Shanghai, Tientsin, and Peiping, although still given nominal recognition, were blockaded. Japanese forces landed in 1938 at Bias Bay near Hong Kong posed a threat to that British colony. The French surrender in Europe in 1940 resulted in Japan gaining control of what had been French Indo-China.

The Chinese Nationalist government was forced out of Nanking in 1937 and established in its new capital, Chungking, by the end of 1938. The Chinese Communist regime based at Yenan had honored a 1936 private agreement with the Nationalist government to join in resisting the full-scale Japanese attack that came in 1937. Their combined forces were nevertheless defeated outside Shanghai that same year.

Shanghai continued to remain a major center for foreign correspondents after 1937. In advancing its own concept of a Greater East Asia Co-prosperity Sphere, Japan sought to discourage world recognition and aid to the Nationalist regime of China. It also undertook to forbid and prevent Chinese residents of Peiping and other places acting as staff or stringer correspondents for papers published in Shanghai's International Settlement or elsewhere, whether vernacular or in whatever other language. Alternative reports on the war in China came through Chungking, a new center to which leaders of the Anglo-American world in particular moved regularly, and through an augmented news coverage in Hong Kong.

When Japanese forces established control over Shanghai in November 1937, the last of the Chinese censors left the offices of the communications companies in the Settlement after six years. They were replaced early in 1938 by Japanese army censors, who supervised all incoming and outgoing traffic. The Japanese demanded that share of the revenue on outgoing traffic formerly paid to the Chinese government.

Except for the early period of the Japanese assault on Shanghai in August and September 1937, the International Settlement remained a relatively safe haven for neutral persons and correspondents. As the fighting moved away from the area in 1938, it became a kind of backwater, and yet one to which correspondents were confined because the Japanese declined to permit them to move out to the fighting fronts, even with Japanese units. A similar fragile independence was preserved in the foreign quarters or "settlements" in Tientsin and Peiping.

Neutral correspondents occasionally were taken on flights from Peiping over the areas under Japanese control. U.S. correspondents were able to get reports out as they had in the 1920s by way of the U.S. Navy radio station operating in Peiping, with the signals directed to the Navy station at Cavite, near Manila, and from there by regular commercial channels. Approximately 200 reporters for Japanese newspapers and the Domei news agency were in the field by 1938. The official Japanese contention was that they would provide all the information about the war needed by the world press.

To supplement those reports, Japanese military officials in Shanghai in 1938 began the practice of conducting three news conferences each week for correspondents. The military authorities also provided detailed instructions to the vernacular press, where it survived, indicating what might or might not appear and what must or must not be used.

The original concern of the Japanese censors in Shanghai reading reports by foreign correspondents bore chiefly upon what might seem "inimical to the operations of the Japanese armed forces." Actually, they interfered very little with the work of the correspondents for the foreign media. There was a feeling among those correspondents, however, that they had no right whatever to censor messages of neutral correspondents operating in an International Settlement, or to interfere in the conduct of newspapers published there under the ownership and direction of neutrals.

This feeling led to diplomatic intervention by the British consul-general in Shanghai when H. J. Timperley of the *Manchester Guardian* was summoned by the Japanese censor because of one of his dispatches. The U.S. consul-general also protested when an attempt was made in late December 1937 and again in the spring of 1938 to censor the U.S.-owned and edited *Shanghai Evening Post & Mercury*.

The Japanese did not at first attempt to halt publication of papers in the International Settlement, vernacular or otherwise. There the journalistic concentration was along the Avenue Edouard VII, the boundary street between the Settlement and the French Concession, an equally respected sanctuary. Located there were the offices of nine local dailies, several periodicals, the bureaus of twelve news agencies and newspapers of the world, and the studio of radio station XMHA, privately owned by U.S. businessman C. S. Harkson.

As Japanese control was established, a so-called Reformed Government of China was set up at Nanking in March 1940, headed by Wang Ching-wei, a close friend of the late Dr. Sun Yat-sen and a former vice-president of the Kuomintang. Wang had cast his lot with the Japanese. One of the Reformed Government undertakings was to establish at least forty vernacular newspapers in various provinces to present such material as the Japanese wished the people to read and believe. A vernacular *Central China Daily News* (the English version of its title) was established in Shanghai as the personal organ of Wang Ching-wei. Several others were made to resemble established and respected papers. They were designed to deceive readers into accepting them as legitimate. One was a fake version of *Shun Pao* of Shanghai, and was made the chief organ of the Japanese army in China. Others were false editions of *Ta Kung Pao* of Tientsin, the original of which had moved to Chungking, and *Yih Shih Pao*, also of Tientsin. A third Tientsin paper, *Yun Pao*, had been purchased by Japanese interests before 1937, and was published as the official paper of the Japanese army in northern China. *Sin Pao* was a new paper in Nanking. In Peiping, *Hsin Min Pao*, directed and edited by a Chinese collaborator with the Japanese, was a paper to which all shops in Peiping were required to subscribe.

To provide information to such newspapers, the Japanese set up two news agencies in occupied China. One was known in translation as the China News Agency, bearing the same identifying initials—CNA—as the official Kuomintang Central News Agency. The *Central China Daily News* pretended to be the Kuomintang party paper, the *Central Daily News* (Chung Yang Jih Pao). The real paper and agency operated in Chungking. The other Japanese agency was called the United Press of China News Agency, and sought to create the impression that it was related to the United Press of the United States. In the late spring of 1940, these two agencies were abolished in favor of a new one, the Central Press Service, with headquarters in Nanking. It was headed by Lin Pai-sheng, minister of information in the Reformed Government of Wang Ching-wei.

Neither foreign correspondents nor newspapers in Shanghai's International Settlement chose to pay full or respectful attention to the wishes and instructions of the Japanese military regime there. The result was that relations became strained in 1938 and violence escalated, concentrating particularly but not exclusively upon vernacular newspapers and those of their editors loyal to the Nationalist government.

Japanese control was established over general postal facilities, which were outside the International Settlement. This made it possible to interfere with the distribution of mail and newspapers, including papers published in the Settlement. This practice was countered by smuggling papers out through other channels. Chinese postal workers sometimes hid papers from Japanese inspectors, and then let them be distributed. Of course, such evasions could bring serious retribution.

Most of the Shanghai vernacular papers were produced in plants neither modern nor attractive and located in the Shantung Road area of the Settlement. About a dozen of them formed an Association of Chinese Newspapers of Shanghai to act jointly for their own protection and welfare. To support collective action, all journalists were eligible for membership in a Chinese Journalists Club. But neither of these associations afforded any protection against Japanese designs.

Chinese editors in the International Settlement were kidnapped even within its boundaries. Some never were heard of again; some died in captivity. In two or three instances, they were decapitated and their heads thrown into the streets of the Settlement, tags attached, as a warning to others against opposing the Japanese. Blacklists of U.S., British, and Chinese editors and correspondents were circulated, bearing threats of deportation or assassination.

From 1939, matters became more difficult. In February of that year death threats were received individually by nine British and U.S. correspondents, coming from a so-called "Society of Honorable and Righteous True Chinese." Newspaper editors were offered bribes; bombs were planted and exploded in the offices of several newspapers; and others were attacked with gunfire and grenades. Some journalists were shot in the streets, among them Chang Shih-hseuh (Samuel H. Chang), U.S.-educated general manager of *Ta Mei Wan Pao*, a vernacular affiliate of the *Shanghai Evening Post & Mercury*, of which Chang also was a director. The Shanghai Municipal Council under Japanese pressure notified the vernacular press late in the year of new regulations to be followed.

During 1940–41 the problems mounted. In July 1940 the Japanese published a list of eighty-seven "wanted" men living in the International Settlement. The list included L. Z. Yuan, news editor of the *Evening Post & Mercury,* Woo Kya-tang, assistant managing editor of the *China Press,* L. T. Soong, of that same paper, and C. H. Hoh, assistant editor of the *China Weekly Review.*

Written and telephoned threats and warnings intended to induce them to leave China voluntarily were conveyed by Wang Ching-wei's Reformed Government to seven British and U.S. newsmen. They were John B. Powell, editor and publisher of the *China Weekly Review;* Cornelius V. Starr, publisher of the *Evening Post & Mercury,* and an insurance company executive; Randall Gould, editor of the *Post & Mercury* and correspondent for the *Christian Science Monitor;* Carroll Alcott, then of the *China Press* and a news broadcaster and commentator over radio station XMHA; Harold P. (Hal) Mills, editor of *Hwai Mei Chen Pao* (Chinese-American Daily News); Norwood Francis Allman, former U.S. consular officer, then an attorney and member of the Shanghai Municipal Council who had become chief editor in 1938 of the true *Shun Pao,* one of the leading vernacular dailies; and J. A. E. Sanders-Bates, British director of *Ta Ying Yeh Pao* (Shanghai Evening News) and formerly correspondent in Manila for the *New York Herald Tribune.*

When the threats and warnings failed to persuade these men to leave China voluntarily, the Reformed Government ordered them to do so in the summer of 1940. They still did not leave and their lives were in greater danger. Perhaps none needed protection more than Alcott, whose radio broadcasts, heard throughout China and the Far East on both medium and shortwave, had a great following and particularly infuriated the Japanese.

Acheson Lucey of the *Evening Post & Mercury* had been the first XMHA news broadcaster in 1927. He was succeeded after a few weeks by Alcott, then recently arrived from Manila, where he had been a correspondent in the previous year for the *New York Herald Tribune.* In Shanghai, he was with the AP first, then with the *Evening Post,* which became the *Evening Post & Mercury* in 1931, and finally with the *China Press.* Because of the threats received, Alcott was at last persuaded in 1940 to wear an armored vest, to go armed, and to ride in an armored car, always accompanied by two armed men.

Threats also were sent in 1940 and 1941 to H. J. Timperley, *Manchester Guardian* correspondent, to Edgar Snow of the *New York Sun* and *Daily Herald,* and to M. C. (Henry) Ford, news editor of the *Evening Post & Mercury* and an INS correspondent. Hallett E. Abend of the *New York Times* was visited at his apartment in the Settlement and manhandled by two masked and armed Japanese terrorists, and the home of Kenneth Selby-Walker, manager for Reuters, was entered, but he was absent and nothing was disturbed. As a consequence of such threatening actions, many editors and correspondents, like Alcott, went armed and some were assigned bodyguards by the International Settlement police.

Three separate attempts were made to destroy the office and printing plant of *Ta Mei Wan Pao,* the *Post & Mercury* affiliate. Ten Chinese employees were killed on one occasion when a bomb exploded in the press room. Following the 1939 assassination of Chang, the paper's general manager, Chu Hsin-kung, the editor, also was killed. T. Y. Lee, the advertising manager, was assassinated in June 1941. Three other newspaper offices were attacked by gunfire. Sandbags were piled about most offices and other protective measures were taken. In Nanking, the Havas news agency office was destroyed by bombs. The violence was not completely one-sided. For example, in August 1941 the five-story building in Shanghai occupied by Wang Ching-wei's *Central China Daily News* was destroyed by fire.

Both as a matter of prudence and because news coverage in Shanghai had become almost impossible, some of those who had gained Japanese enmity left the city before December 1941, as others had left Tokyo. Alcott was among them. Timperley made his way to Chungking. Snow departed and later reached Moscow. Abend joined the *New York Times* bureau in Washington in April 1941, but left there in August to go to New Zealand, Australia, and the Dutch East Indies for the *Reader's Digest*. Gould returned to New York and was replaced by Frederick B. Opper in Shanghai as editor of the *Post & Mercury* and as *Monitor* correspondent.

As the news situation deteriorated in Shanghai after 1938, alternative reports on the war in China came through Hong Kong, where the press corps was enlarged, and through Chungking, the new Nationalist government capital. British officials in Hong Kong were careful to avoid giving offense to the Japanese lest they invade the colony. The vernacular press from 1937 was forbidden to use the word "enemy" with reference to Japan. The papers complied, but they did use a small cross where they might have used the banned word. Readers understood, and the Japanese protested the practice. The Hong Kong government also tried with moderate success to prevent the vernacular press from using other words and phrases, such as references to the "puppet regime" of Wang Ching-wei at Nanking, or to the "traitor Wang," and his "bogus regime," which were objectionable to the Japanese.

Hong Kong gained importance as a communications center free of censorship, and also as a point to and from which the Pan American Airways "China Clipper" Pacific flights moved after 1935 by way of Manila, Guam, Wake Island, Honolulu, and San Francisco. Flights by British Imperial Airways planes to and from London by way of India and Singapore were extended to Hong Kong in 1937. From 1938 the planes of the China National Aviation Corporation (CNAC) also flew into Hong Kong. This Sino-American company formed in 1929 also was able to maintain flights to and from Chungking until the seizure of Hong Kong by the Japanese in December 1941, when a Chungking-Calcutta service was substituted.

Among the first correspondents in Chungking after the Nationalist government established itself there in 1938 were F. Tillman Durdin of the *New York Times* and his wife, Peggy Armstrong Durdin; Hans Melchers of the German Transozean service; James Stewart, AP; George Wang and Robert P. (Pepper) Martin, UP; Thomas Ming-heng Chao, Reuters; Hugh Deane, the *Christian Science Monitor;* and Harold Isaacs, formerly of the *China Press,* who became Chungking correspondent for *Newsweek* magazine.

Dr. Hollington K. Tong, vice-minister of information in the Nationalist government since October 1937, worked particularly with foreign correspondents in Shanghai and Nanking at the special request of President Chiang Kai-shek, and continued to do so in Chungking. He also headed an International Department within a government Central Publicity Board.

The Nationalist government leaders were aware of a need to gain and maintain world interest, sympathy, and support in their struggle with Japan. They valued Tong's guidance on relations with the foreign media. The Foreign Ministry, through its Department of Intelligence and Publicity, provided accreditation to correspondents and was helpful in producing information. The department was headed at the outset by General Shu Shi-ming, minister of information.

Dr. Tong had broad responsibilities in exercising general supervision over the censorship of copy filed by correspondents for transmission. His position also embraced a propaganda function. He maintained a friendly and understanding relationship with all correspondents, helpful rather than restrictive. In charge of housing and feeding, he also did all that he could to make living and working conditions as satisfactory as possible for correspondents on what could only be regarded as an extremely difficult, uncomfortable, and dangerous assignment. Chungking was under frequent Japanese air attack and there were inescapable risks to all correspondents arriving or departing.

Tong arranged weekly news conferences conducted jointly by the International Department of the Central Publicity Board and by the Foreign Ministry's Department of Intelligence and Publicity. Military spokesmen usually were present to review the latest war developments, and representatives of government departments also participated. Meetings were arranged with Generalissimo Chiang Kai-shek and Madame Chiang. In flawless English, she and Dr. Tong acted as interpreters, since Chiang himself spoke only Chinese. Only a few correspondents were fluent in that language. Although expensive, the transmission of news from Chungking was reasonably satisfactory, using government radiotelegraphic facilities. Radio station KGOY also broadcast news and government messages, and its facilities were made available to radio correspondents for voice broadcasts.

The Chinese Central News Agency had its headquarters at Chung-

king, and the official *Central Daily News* (Chung Yang Jih Pao) was
published there. Although newsprint was not imported, a coarse version
was made locally from a straw base, and a number of small newspapers
appeared regularly on the crisp yellow paper. Among them was *Ta Kung
Pao,* formerly of Tientsin. Its press was dismantled there and carried to
Chungking where it was reassembled.

In his relations with correspondents, Dr. Tong had the advice and
assistance of William Henry Donald, formerly of the *Times* and advisor
to Chiang Kai-shek. He was aided also by Timperley of the *Manchester
Guardian,* formerly in Shanghai, and by Maurice Votaw, who had
headed the Department of Journalism at St. John's University in that
city. He had the assistance of Theodore H. (Ted) White, who had specialized in the language and history of China as a student at Harvard.
White arrived in China shortly before the full Japanese attack of 1937
began. He was recommended to Tong by John B. Powell, then correspondent for the *Chicago Tribune,* as well as publisher of his own *China
Weekly Review.*[1]

Tong also had the assistance of Melville Jacoby, a graduate in journalism at Stanford University and a former member of the *San Francisco Chronicle* staff, who had been studying at Lignan University in
Canton. Other assistants included Frank Martin, Jr., son of Professor
Frank Martin, then director of the University of Missouri School of
Journalism; Betty Graham, a native of Seattle; Warren Lee, a Chinese
school teacher with special knowledge of photography; H. S. Wong, a
newsreel cameraman; and James Shen, later director of China's information office in San Francisco. This group changed and was to become far larger. While a member of Tong's staff, White also became a
stringer in Chungking for the Associated Press and then for *Time* magazine. He moved to the staff of *Time* in 1939.[2] Jacoby also joined the
Time-Life staff in 1940 and left China for the Philippines. Betty Graham
became a stringer for the INS and NEA.

Aside from resident correspondents at Chungking, scores of writers,
correspondents, and news executives arrived as visitors, most of them
from the United States, but some from the United Kingdom. They trav-

---

1   Shortly after this, Powell was dismissed as *Tribune* correspondent, given to understand that Robert R. McCormick, the paper's publisher, had decided that "China is no
longer important as a source of news," that it soon was to be taken over by the Japanese and
its news better reported through Tokyo. There was speculation, however, as to whether the
Japanese consulate in Chicago, occupying space in the *Tribune* building, had complained
that Powell's dispatches were "anti-Japanese," and that McCormick had reacted to that.

2   See Theodore H. White, *In Search of History: A Personal Adventure* (1978), chps. 2–6;
and White with Annalee Jacoby, *Thunder Out of China* (1946).

eled usually by the Pan American Airways China Clipper between San Francisco and Hong Kong, and by CNAC flights to and from Chungking, at risk of Japanese intervention but with no actual incidents.

Visitors in Chungking for a few days and perhaps a week between 1939 and December 1941 included Christopher J. Chancellor, one of Reuters' general managers; Colin M. MacDonald, experienced Far Eastern correspondent for the *Times* of London; Henry R. Luce, publisher of *Time, Life,* and *Fortune,* who was born and brought up in China; his wife, Clare Booth Luce, former magazine editor, playwright, and a representative of *Life;* Leland Stowe, representing the *Chicago Daily News;* Roy W. Howard, director of the Scripps-Howard Newspapers; Royal Arch Gunnison of *Collier's Weekly,* NANA, and the Mutual Broadcasting System; Ralph M. Ingersoll, then editor of *PM,* a New York daily; novelist Erskine Caldwell writing for *PM;* and his wife, Margaret Bourke-White, photographer for *Life* and *Fortune.*

Other visitors in that two-year period included Robert Neville, foreign editor of *PM;* Vincent Sheean, NANA; Alice Leone-Moats, *Collier's Weekly;* Ernest Hemingway and Martha Gellhorn (Mrs. Hemingway), both writing for *Collier's;* Anna Louise Strong, *Moscow Daily News;* Carl Mydans, photographer for *Life,* and his wife, Shelley Smith Mydans; James R. Young, INS correspondent in Tokyo, who was able to cross and recross the lines as a neutral; Eric Sevareid, Columbia Broadcasting System, but also writing for the UP; James Shepley, *Time;* St. Clair McKelway, the *New Yorker* magazine; Robert Bryant, International News Photos photographer; and Joseph W. Alsop, Jr., formerly of the *New York Herald Tribune,* but then traveling on a U.S. government mission.

The number and status of the visitors to Chungking became a kind of index to world interest after 1939 in the spirit of the Chinese in the contest with the Japanese, and of concern over the possible relationship of that conflict to the war in progress in Europe. The autumn of 1941 brought a record number of visitors, and on November 7, Generalissimo Chiang Kai-shek gave a group interview to twenty-three visiting journalists. It was the first occasion of that sort in China, and 10,000 words of copy were transmitted, the heaviest press file for any one day to that time.

A month later, the Japanese attack at Pearl Harbor, Hong Kong, and elsewhere made the war in China and the war in Europe global. Among other changes, it introduced a new chapter in the position of correspondents at Chungking. The group increased in numbers, and new situations and problems arose. Hong Kong no longer was a transit point. It was replaced by air and road journeys by way of India and Burma, a tortuous backdoor route to China and Chungking.

In Japan, restraints upon foreign correspondents had been growing since 1937. With Japan's war against China taking new proportions from that time, the military dictatorship in Tokyo became uncompromising.

Anglo-American correspondents in Tokyo were working by 1939 in an atmosphere of hostility, arising because of a recognized sympathy with the Chinese position vis-a-vis Japan. There was no official censorship of what they might report, but two correspondents were arrested and held for several days in 1939, actions almost without precedent. In January 1940, James R. Young was arrested and held in jail for sixty-one days, where he was subjected to persistent and heckling interrogation.[3] He had been in Japan for ten years as a correspondent for International News Service, as a representative of King Features Service, and as business manager of the *Japan Advertiser*.

In July 1940, some weeks after Young was freed, James Melville Cox, widely experienced in Asia as a correspondent for Reuters, was arrested in Tokyo. Two days later, he was killed in a drop from a second-story window of the Tokyo police headquarters. Japanese officials asserted that he had jumped, but did not explain why. It was generally believed that Cox either was thrown out or, more likely, was driven to jump because of desperation caused by mistreatment or torture.

The Japanese style of terror had been observed at least as early as the massacre of civilians at Port Arthur during the Sino-Japanese War of 1894–95. The mass murder visited upon the Chinese people in the 1932 air attack on the Chapei district of Shanghai, and again in Nanking in 1937, had been followed by instances of senseless cruelty and violence to inoffensive civilians by Japanese officers and soldiers. There also had been the assassinations of two Japanese premiers in 1930 and 1932, and the murders in Tokyo during the "2.26 incident" in 1936.

Chinese and foreign newsmen had suffered under aspects of the terror in Shanghai and elsewhere. Archibald T. Steele, then representing the *New York Times* in China, and a Swiss correspondent, a Mr. Lindt, had encountered difficulties because of an interview obtained with a Chinese

---

3 Among other things, Young was regarded with suspicion because he possessed a membership pin bearing the Greek letters of Sigma Delta Chi, the U.S. professional journalism society. The police inquisitors could not understand why a professed U.S. citizen should belong to a Greek organization, and especially one in which no Greeks were represented.

H. E. Wildes, in *Social Currents in Japan* (1927), recounts a comparable inquiry in Japan in 1926 when members of the U.S. honorary scholarship society, Phi Beta Kappa, were subjected to a similar questioning. At the same period, Wildes reports, members of the Tokyo Rotary Club, a branch of Rotary International, were called upon by the police to prove that the organization was free of association with the Moscow-directed Communist International, or Comintern.

military leader, General Ma Chen-shan. A British freelance newsman, Lennox Simpson, was arrested by the Japanese in Manchukuo and died from "unknown causes." Frank Basil Riley, of the *Times,* had vanished earlier in Manchuria.

The Japanese press itself was unable to resist the pressure of the army group, but had retained a degree of independence until about 1939. Premier Konoye, for example, in making an important statement on national policy in December 1938 did so in a radio address and ignored the newspapers. A press response came promptly from the Mujuichi Nichi Kai (Twenty-first Club), an organization of Tokyo editors. Eight political editors, representing all seven leading Tokyo dailies and the Domei agency, addressed a manifesto to the premier. It protested that the Konoye government was high-handed in its treatment of the press and had oppressed some publications and brought undue pressure upon them. The manifesto called for a new policy of cooperation with the press, failing which the editors indicated they planned to boycott the Cabinet Board of Information (Naikaku Joho-kyoku), then recently established to disseminate government information and policy statements.

Within a month, and largely because of the manifesto, the Konoye government resigned. It was replaced in January 1939 by a new regime, with Baron Hiranuma as premier, but Konoye still a cabinet member. A stricter press policy was soon developed and enforced by the powerful Home Ministry and its related Metropolitan Police Board, by the procurators of the district and criminal courts, and by the ministries of war and navy.

By the end of 1939, some 600 newspapers and periodicals had been suppressed by the Metropolitan Police Board. Others had been required to enter into mergers. The size of newspapers also was reduced to save newsprint, much of which was imported, and to conserve foreign currency required to pay for such newsprint in overseas markets. The newsprint supply was brought further under government control in a rationing system, and allotments could be curtailed or denied altogether. Every newspaper was required to submit either galley proofs or page proofs in advance of publication for examination by censors. Japanese journalists were subject to arrest if the government found them "uncooperative." These measures, taken together, placed the Japanese press under full government control.

The treaties between Nazi Germany and the Soviet Union in August 1939 were as much a surprise to Japan as to other countries. The Hiranuma cabinet fell soon after and was followed by a government headed by General Nobuyuki Abe. There was a second change in January 1940, with Admiral Mitsumasa as premier, and a third in July, bringing the return of Prince Konoye.

Konoye consolidated the information bureaus then existing in the Ministries of War, Navy, Foreign Affairs, and in others, and merged them with the cabinet's Board of Information. In November 1940 that board became a central clearing point for information approved for release to the press and radio, domestic and foreign. Headed by Nobufumi Ito, a former ambassador to Poland, with Ko Ishii, former consul-general in New York and Chicago, as his assistant, and a staff of about one hundred, the board operated in a manner comparable to the ministries of propaganda then existing in Berlin and Rome, even though on a smaller scale. Ito attended cabinet meetings and was its official spokesman in providing information to the media. Conferences for foreign newsmen were conducted by Ko Ishii or his deputy, and later by Tomokazu Hori.

By late 1940, the people of Japan, including officials, were discouraged from having personal contacts with correspondents or other foreign residents. Correspondents were leaving Tokyo, as they were leaving Rome, Berlin, and Moscow, because of the growing problems of coverage. Smothers of the *Chicago Daily News* had left Japan in 1937. Chamberlin of the *Christian Science Monitor* left in 1939 and was not replaced. James R. Young of INS left after his ordeal in jail in 1940, and Wilfrid Fleisher, representing the *New York Herald Tribune,* also left that year but was replaced by Joseph Newman.

Fleisher's departure had special importance because of his family association with the *Japan Advertiser.* Just as the Japanese press was subjected to influences originating in the army-dominated government, so were the foreign-language papers in the country. In 1939 the *Japan Times* of Tokyo, even then a government organ serving as an arm of the Foreign Ministry, had purchased the British-owned *Japan Mail* and became the *Japan Times & Mail.* It also had purchased the *Japan Chronicle* of Kobe, but suspended the paper and the name did not survive. This left only the *Japan Advertiser* of Tokyo, the Fleisher paper, as a foreign-language daily in Japan.

B. W. Fleisher, as proprietor of the *Advertiser,* had been approached in 1939 by a German group in Japan with an offer to purchase the paper for $500,000. He believed that the Nazi government, seeking a voice in Japan, was behind the offer, and declined to sell. Early in 1940 he had an offer from British interests, but before any decision could be reached, Fleisher was informed by a representative of the Foreign Ministry, Toshi Goh, who also was president of the company publishing the *Japan Times & Mail,* that he would not be permitted to sell the *Advertiser* to any foreign interests. Goh indicated, however, that the Japanese government itself was prepared to buy the paper for $50,000. Fleisher declined to sell for such a sum, which would not even meet existing financial allowances required under Japanese law for those employees who would face dismissal if the paper ceased to appear, or if they became unemployed.

With Fleisher's refusal to sell, the *Japan Advertiser* became a target for government and police harassment. Its Japanese employees were intimidated, and Fleisher himself was in personal danger. None of his Japanese friends, however highly placed, dared to speak to him. At length, in the autumn of 1940, the government raised its offer for the paper to $100,000, and indicated that if that offer were refused it "would not be responsible for the consequences." Under this obvious threat, a forced sale was made on October 10, 1940, still at a fraction of the paper's value. Fleisher then returned to the United States late in November. The *Japan Times & Mail* moved its operation into the more modern *Japan Advertiser* plant. A *Japan Times & Advertiser* appeared, similar in typographical appearance to the *Advertiser*. It was produced by some members of the *Advertiser* staff and organization, some of the *Times*, and some of the *Mail*, but as a government propaganda sheet.

In another turn of the screw on the Japanese press, the Diet passed a cabinet-sponsored Defense Bill on February 28, 1941. It established penalties equally for Japanese or foreigners who might transgress existing regulations but allowed no right of appeal. The purpose of the bill was to prevent leakage of information, not only on military matters but also on political, diplomatic, economic, and financial subjects. Meetings attended by specified top-level government groups were in themselves classified as "state secrets," and were not to be mentioned. Under the bill, it also was an offense for any person with special knowledge of such "sensitive" matters to convey that knowledge to others, particularly foreigners.

The State Secrets Defense Law became effective May 10, 1941. State secrets included anything discussed in the proceedings of all Imperial conferences, in supreme council, cabinet meetings, or in any secret session of the Diet. This law induced the greatest caution on the part of all Japanese, including what they said in private conversation. To speak with foreigners became a risk, and correspondents were deprived of established friendships, as well as of news sources. The correspondent was placed in jeopardy by the new law in combination with the still effective Peace Preservation Law of 1925—the "Dangerous Thought Act." Almost anything reported could mean trouble, subject to interpretation as a "crime" of conveying information deemed "harmful to Japan." Yet to withhold relevant and important information meant failure of the correspondent to perform his function. It became a question whether a correspondent could work at all under such circumstances.

By early 1941, a new Board of Censorship was formally established in

Tokyo. This at least removed some of the earlier uncertainties and inconsistencies that had plagued correspondents. Another uncertainty was removed in March 1941 when Toshio Shiratori, "outspokesman" of the Foreign Ministry, told correspondents frankly that Japan's ultimate object was to drive the "white man" out of Asia. This was restated by General Hideki Tojo, who followed Konoye upon his resignation as premier in October 1941. Tojo declared in November that the influence of Great Britain and the United States must be removed from Asia.

In August 1941, with conditions almost impossible for the small remaining group of Anglo-American correspondents in Tokyo, Max Hill of the Associated Press, acting as spokesman, presented a petition to the Foreign Ministry through Ko Ishii of the Cabinet Board of Information. It requested that correspondents be told what censors cut from their dispatches so that the reports might at least be made coherent. It was requested, further, that correspondents be permitted to import food, clothing, medicines, and other items no longer normally available in Tokyo, that their business funds be released from control, and that they be issued gasoline ration cards such as were granted to members of the diplomatic corps and to German and Italian correspondents who had arrived in Tokyo.

None of these requests brought a favorable response. In September, it was further ruled that telephone conversations between Tokyo and Shanghai must be conducted only in Japanese or Chinese. In October, another ordinance provided for an intensified inspection of mail to and from foreign places. Any outgoing mail was to be submitted unsealed to the post office, with the name of the sender clearly indicated, and with stamps in the proper value clipped to it, but not affixed. Translations and explanations of the contents also might be demanded.

By that time, other correspondents had left Tokyo. Hugh Byas of the *New York Times* and the London *Times,* a veteran in Japan, had been replaced by Otto D. Tolischus for the New York paper and by Vera Redman for that of London. Joseph Dynan and Relman (Pat) Morin were recent arrivals for the AP; C. M. Crichton for Universal News Features; Raymond A. Cromley for the *Wall Street Journal;* Richard Tennelley for NBC; and W. R. Wills for CBS.

Joseph Newman of the *New York Herald Tribune* left in November when the paper decided to close its Tokyo bureau, as it also closed its bureaus in Moscow, Berlin, and Rome, "because censorship had made special correspondence unsatisfactory." Newman returned to the United States by way of Manila, from where he sailed December 4 and reached San Francisco safely, despite the Japanese attack at Honolulu on December 7.

Japan's invasion of Manchuria in 1931 offended the United States and other countries but, preoccupied with their own problems arising from the international economic depression, they made no effective protest. A year later, U.S. Ambassador Joseph C. Grew in Tokyo reported that expressions of disapproval in foreign nations concerning Japanese policy toward China had aroused animosity among military leaders in Japan, with the United States as a special target. By 1936, Grew could add reports of Japanese understandings with the Nazi government of Germany, and that Japanese officers were studying German military procedures. Japan's dissatisfaction with modifications in its naval strength based on treaties concluded between 1922 and 1936 was made evident.

From 1937, the major increase in Japanese aggression in China, along with Italian and German aggression in the western world, had brought some action both in Great Britain and in the United States toward restoration of a military defense that had been permitted to lapse since the end of World War I. More than that, Japan's air attacks on Shanghai in 1932 and again in 1937, and its attack on the U.S. gunboat *Panay* in the Yangtze, brought restrictions by the Roosevelt administration and the Congress on the sale to Japan of U.S. aircraft and instruments in 1938. Later an embargo was instituted on the shipment of scrap metal subject to conversion into weapons of war.

These points of controversy were seen by Ambassador Grew as justifying a warning to the State Department late in 1940 of a possible Japanese attack, perhaps in Indo-China. By January 1941, however, he had reason to suggest that there might even be a surprise attack on Pearl Harbor. This possibility was taken seriously by President Roosevelt and made known to U.S. military leaders. It also led to a long series of discussions in Washington between representatives of the U.S. government and those of the Japanese government.

Admiral Kichisaburo Nomura arrived as a new Japanese ambassador to the United States in February 1941. He appeared for a news conference following his arrival, but took shelter behind an interpreter. This he hardly needed to do, because he was a graduate of the U.S. Naval Academy. He also had been Japanese naval attaché in Washington during World War I, an aide during the Washington Naval Conference of 1921–22, had taken a training squadron of men and ships to Hawaii in 1929 and through the Panama Canal to east-coast ports of the United States. In 1932, he was in the United States on a "goodwill tour" to explain Japan's position in Manchuria. He also had been wounded in Shanghai in 1932 and had lost an eye. A man of six feet and 180 pounds, Nomura conferred chiefly with Secretary of State Cordell Hull and

Undersecretary Sumner Welles. President Roosevelt was kept constantly informed.

To assist Nomura, Saburo Kurusu arrived in Washington on November 17. In Japan's foreign service since 1910, he had been consul in Chicago in 1913–19 and had married a Chicago-born woman. Later, he was in various diplomatic assignments, including service in the Philippines, and as Japan's ambassador to Belgium (1937–39) and Germany (1939–40).

The "negotiations" between the two governments related largely to matters of trade and relations with the Philippines, soon scheduled to become independent. With its own private plans for creation of a Greater East Asia Co-prosperity Sphere, including China, Japan was unprepared to make compromises. Neither Nomura nor Kurusu were acquainted with the full Japanese schedule. They were instructed to insist, however, that any agreement with the U.S. government had to be completed by November 25. That date, as later revealed, was when the countdown for the Pearl Harbor attack began.

The Japanese attack at Pearl Harbor on Sunday morning, December 7, 1941, coordinated with attacks on Hong Kong, Shanghai, the Philippines, Guam and Wake Island, and the Dutch East Indies, brought the United States into a war already in progress in Asia since 1931 and in Europe since 1939. The United States and Great Britian immediately became wartime allies, both declaring war on Japan on December 8.

Minutes after the Japanese attack at Pearl Harbor, Roger Burns in Honolulu for the Associated Press had San Francisco on the telephone and gave a first report to Harold Turnblad, San Francisco bureau manager. Frank Tremaine in Honolulu for the United Press also reached the UP San Francisco bureau promptly and told the story to James Sullivan and Dan Bowerman, who heard bombing in the background. Commercial communications with the mainland were halted shortly after and for nearly three days public reports came only from sources in Washington.

From the White House, Stephen T. Early, President Roosevelt's press secretary, put through a "conference call" to the Washington bureaus of the three news agencies and gave them a prompt report by telephone of the bombing. The agency reports were immediately relayed by teleprinter networks and used by radio stations and radio networks to inform the nation on that Sunday morning. The news came at noon Pacific coast time, which was about 3 P.M. Eastern time, too late for any morning paper, and there were no afternoon papers published on Sundays.

The Japanese bombing was almost unchallenged despite the long advance warning of a possible attack on Pearl Harbor. About half the U.S.

Pacific fleet was moored at Pearl Harbor, and much of it was destroyed or put out of action by the early morning aerial action. The damage was so great and the U.S. defense both in the Hawaiian Islands and along the Pacific coast was so endangered that the tightest possible security and censorship was invoked to conceal the full measure of damage. It was months before the story was known to the public. Meanwhile, U.S. Naval censorship was controlling messages outbound from Hawaiian and U.S. shores. All Tokyo communications were halted, and Japanese naval forces cut the Pacific cable west of Midway Island.

Newsmen in Honolulu and Hong Kong were the first to find themselves serving as war correspondents in a new theater, and those in Manila were not far behind. Correspondents for the U.S. and British media in Shanghai and Tokyo were made ineffective almost immediately, and so also were U.S. correspondents in Berlin and Rome. Japanese correspondents in Washington and London, and German and Italian correspondents in Washington, were equally halted in their professional activities.

Radio correspondents in the Philippines provided some of the most vivid and informative reports during the first two days of the Pacific war. The reports were not encouraging because Japanese planes destroyed U.S. aircraft on the ground at Clark Field. Cavite, the U.S. naval base, and Manila were both captured by January 2. Until that time, a considerable group of journalists broadcast and reported from Manila, while hoping for the arrival of U.S. naval and air force units.

Thomas Worthin in Manila for CBS and H. Ford Wilkins of the *Manila Bulletin,* and a correspondent for the *New York Times,* broadcast their observations. Bertrand Silen and Don Bell broadcast for NBC, and Royal Arch ("Rags") Gunnison, on a journey through the Pacific areas and the Far East for *Collier's* and NANA, broadcast for MBS. After the first two hours on the first day these men were prevented from broadcasting for forty-eight hours. Their scripts, like press dispatches, required advance approval by censors at the headquarters of General Douglas MacArthur, former U.S. Army chief of staff and head of Philippine military forces since 1935. Major LeGrande A. Diller of the U.S. Army was press officer. Major Carlos P. Romulo, editor of the *Manila Bulletin,* was acting press officer for the Commonwealth of the Philippines.

Other newsmen in Manila at this time included Frank Hewlett, UP acting bureau chief in the absence of Richard C. Wilson, who was captured in Hong Kong when the Japanese attacked there, Bernard (Bert) Covit, Franz Weissblatt, Eric W. Friman, David Harvey, Robert Crabb, and George Teodoro, all of the United Press. The Associated

Press was represented by Ray P. Cronin, Jr., bureau chief, Russell Brines, and Clark Lee. Robert Robb was INS bureau chief, with Joseph Garrick as second man.

Melville Jacoby, who had been in Chungking shortly before, and Annalee Whitmore were in Manila for *Time* and *Life.* Carl Mydans was a photographer for both publications. Karl Von Wiegand, veteran Hearst correspondent usually in Berlin, happened to be in Manila on a Far Eastern journey with his associate, Lady Drummond-Hay. R. A. G. (Allan) Hammond and Curtis L. Hindson were present for Reuters; Jack W. Percival for the *Sydney Morning Herald;* Marc T. Greene, roving correspondent for the *Providence Journal* and the *Christian Science Monitor;* C.A.P. (Nat) Floyd of the *Manila Bulletin* and a stringer for the *New York Times;* and R. McCulloch Dick, British owner of the *Philippine Free Press,* also representing the *Times* of London. With them were Roy C. Bennett, manager and editor of the *Daily Bulletin,* and Theo Rogers, manager of the *Free Press.*

Corre-
spondents
in Custody

Within hours of the Pearl Harbor attack, representatives of the Federal Bureau of Investigation took into custody in the United States all German, Italian, and Japanese correspondents. As with members of the diplomatic corps representing those countries, they were kept under comfortable internment, with members of their families, until it was possible to make a formal exchange for U.S. diplomatic, consular, and media personnel.[4]

Time differences being what they were, the late Sunday and early Monday action affecting correspondents in the United States became known in Berlin shortly before six U.S. correspondents there went to the Propaganda Ministry for a Monday afternoon news conference. An official entered the room and interrupted proceedings to say that "Contrary to international practice, German correspondents have been arrested in the United States. I must now ask American correspondents to leave this room and proceed to their homes."

All U.S. correspondents remaining in Berlin, about twenty, were placed under house arrest. Following the declaration of war by Germany and Italy upon the United States on December 11, those U.S.

---

4 Leone Fumasoni-Biondi of Italy's Stefani agency in Washington resigned in April 1941 after nine years. Lacking sympathy with fascism, he ceased active news work, but remained in Washington, where in June he became a teacher of journalism at the Catholic University of America.

correspondents in Germany were moved to Bad Nauheim, about thirty miles north of Frankfurt-am-Main, and those in Italy were moved to Siena. The groups along with wives and children were brought together in Lisbon nineteen weeks later in June 1942 to be repatriated.

The U.S. correspondents arrested in Berlin included Louis P. Lochner, AP bureau chief; Alfred J. Steinkopf, Edwin A. Shanke, Ernest C. ("Tex") Fisher and Angus Thuermer, all of the AP; Frederick Oechsner, European manager, and Joseph W. Grigg, Jr., bureau chief for the UP; Jack Fleischer and Glenn M. Stadler, both of the UP, and Clinton Beach ("Pat") Conger of the Zurich UP bureau, younger son of the late Seymour Beach Conger, and brother of Beach Conger of the *New York Herald Tribune,* who was in Berlin on a visit. Others arrested then included Hugh Templeton Speck, INS bureau chief; Guido Enderis and George Axelsson of the *New York Times;* Alex Small, *Chicago Tribune;* Howard K. Smith, CBS; Paul Fischer, NBC; John Paul Dickson, MBS; and Jean A. Graffis, European manager for Acme Newspictures. Robert H. Best, a stringer for the UP in Vienna since the Nazi occupation in 1938, joined the group at Bad Nauheim.

Enderis who was ill, was not interned. Later, when he had recovered sufficiently, he was permitted by the Germans to go to Switzerland, where he died not long afterward.[5] Axelsson, a Swedish citizen but a *New York Times* correspondent, also remained in Berlin for a time, and then went to Stockholm for the paper. Rudolph Josten, a German citizen working for the AP bureau, remained in Berlin, in nominal charge of the office. Grigg, UP, and Shank, AP, arrived in Lisbon in June 1942, expecting to be repatriated, but were able to go instead to London to join their bureaus there. Small of the *Chicago Tribune* followed the same course, and then was assigned to Cairo for the paper. Best of the UP chose to remain in Berlin, where he broadcast for the Propaganda Ministry from 1942 to the end of the war.[6] Of the Siena group, Raymond Allen-Tuska, who was not a U.S. citizen, was permitted to go to Switzerland for the UP.

There were only nine U.S. correspondents in Rome when war was declared. They were Herbert L. Matthews and Camille M. Cianfarra,

---

5 Enderis was born and raised in Milwaukee, Wisconsin, and began his work as a newsman there. He joined the Associated Press staff and was assigned to Berlin before World War I. Upon the declaration of war between Germany and the United States in 1917, he remained in Berlin in charge of AP property, while reporting each day to the German police. A representative of the German Wolff agency in New York did the same for that agency. A report that Enderis was a Swiss citizen was inaccurate. See Desmond *Crisis and Conflict,* p. 229.

6 Arrested in Vienna in 1945 by U.S. military personnel, he was then returned to the United States. In Boston in 1948, he was sentenced to life for treason, and died in prison in 1952.

both of the *New York Times;* Reynolds Packard and his wife, Eleanor Packard; Livingston Pomeroy, and Raymond Allen-Tuska, all of the United Press; Richard G. Massock, Associated Press; David Colin, NBC; and Mrs. Paul Getty, a contributing correspondent to the *New York Herald Tribune.* Beach Conger of the UP Rome bureau, arrested in Berlin, was returned to Italy. Harold N. Denny of the *New York Times,* attached to British forces, and captured by the Italians while covering the desert war in Libya in December 1941 also was moved to Siena.

From 1942, the news of Germany and Italy reached the rest of the world through radio broadcasts from Berlin and Rome, through the DNB news agency, through German and Italian newspapers and periodicals reaching Switzerland and Portugal, and through those few remaining neutral Swiss and Swedish correspondents. They endured Allied air attacks growing in intensity, and had difficulties merely to live and eat, while also facing a censorship becoming stricter in proportion to the turn of events against the Axis.

Indicative of other problems confronting correspondents were two Berlin news conferences in October 1942 devoted almost entirely to verbal attacks by Dr. Schmidt upon Swiss and Swedish newspapers, their publishers, and their correspondents. The basis for the attacks was a statement by Sweden's foreign minister that the Swedish press would not permit itself to be influenced by foreign propaganda. It was clear that he was referring to propaganda from Nazi Germany. Schmidt took the line that "there is no room for editors who write against the New Europe."[7] He added a threat that such editors "will be given short shrift, perhaps, by finding them a new home in the steppes of Asia or, better, by extermination." In objecting to what he described as "unseemly polemics" against Germany, Schmidt asserted that "Germany must forbid meddling in her affairs," and named certain newspapers as carrying on "propaganda hostile to the Axis." He warned that "if one puts one's fingers into war machinery, one must not whimper if they are crushed."

This attack was not accepted without protest, even in the face of a German strength demonstrably effective and ruthless. The *Neue Zürcher Zeitung* in Switzerland replied editorially, saying that "terrorist propaganda will scarcely remove . . . the mistrust felt by small States toward the New Europe." The *National Zeitung* of Basle asserted that "the Swiss press will not allow itself to be moved . . . by any attempt at influencing it from its duty to support liberty, humanity and human dignity." In Sweden, the *Göteborgs Handelstidning* was equally out-

---

7 The "New Europe" was the German phrase for the world envisioned following the triumph of its forces, comparable to Japan's "Greater East Asia Co-prosperity Sphere."

spoken, its editorial statements reaching and heartening to the press and peoples of occupied countries.

Eleven correspondents were held in Japan from December 1941 until their delayed repatriation began in September 1943. Including their families, a total of twenty-six persons were interned. They were far less well treated than the Japanese correspondents and others interned in Great Britain and the United States pending exchange. The internment in the United States was in the luxurious Greenbriar Hotel at White Sulphur Springs, West Virginia.

Those in Japan were Otto D. Tolischus of the *New York Times;* Max Hill and Joseph Dynan, AP; Robert T. Bellaire, UP; Percy Whiteing, INS; Raymond A. Cromley, *Wall Street Journal;* Jack Bellinger, *Japan Times & Advertiser;* C. M. Crichton, Universal News Features; W. R. Wills, CBS; and Richard Tennelley, NBC. The eleventh was Relman (Pat) Morin, AP Tokyo bureau chief, who was in Japanese-held Saigon, French Indo-China, at the time of Pearl Harbor. He was seized by Japanese occupation forces and returned to Tokyo.

Tolischus was a victim of special mistreatment, perhaps in some part because he had been in disfavor in Nazi Germany prior to his expulsion there late in 1940 and reassignment to Tokyo. Word from Berlin may have shaped his treatment. Held in jail under conditions of great discomfort, rather than being properly interned, he was tortured and harangued to make him admit falsely to having been a spy and having sent reports deliberately intended to be harmful to Japan, contrary to the State Secrets Defense Law of May 1941.

Fully experienced in censorship as applied in Germany, Tolischus had accepted Japan's censorship. As a senior correspondent for a major newspaper, his was made a test case by Japanese authorities seeking to establish a basis for similar charges against other correspondents. The effort failed, since it was without foundation, and because Tolischus had the courage and fortitude to endure.[8]

In Tokyo, after Pearl Harbor, the few foreign correspondents remaining were mostly German, with some Italian, Swiss, and Swedish representatives or stringers. They were all under heavy censorship. Masayuko Tani became the spokesman at news conferences for the Cabinet Board of Information. All newspapers and services were brought under its control by late 1942. The board also operated a new organization, known in translation as the Public Opinion Patriotic Association. To this all news writers, radio broadcasters, critics, scholars, and research workers were

---

8   This writer had seen Tolischus off for Japan from San Francisco in 1940. Following his return to New York in 1943 and recuperation from his hardships, Tolischus became a member of the editorial board of the *New York Times.*

required to belong. The news of military operations ceased to reach the media through the board, but was announced through the Imperial Headquarters.

Early in 1943, the Japanese government also brought about the formation of an Association of Greater East Asia Journalists of Japan. Its membership included all newspapers, agencies, and periodicals published within"Greater East Asia," which included what had been French Indo-China. All Japanese journalists concerned with "East Asiatic" affairs were members also. The purpose of the association was to shape and influence the news about Japan published throughout Asian territory conquered and occupied by Japan, to advance Japan's international repute, and to consolidate its position in Asia.

From 1943, Japan's position deteriorated militarily, and the national information process deteriorated accordingly. Shortages of materials, including newsprint, had resulted in a licensing of newspapers by the end of 1941 and a reduction in their areas of distribution. Mergers and suspensions followed in 1942 and later. Where there had been 25 dailies in Tokyo alone in 1931, by 1945 only 5 appeared; where 1,215 dailies had existed in Japan in 1930, only 300 remained in 1940, and 76 in August 1945. Only 3 were permitted to circulate nationally, *Asahi* and the combined *Yomiuri-Hochi* of Tokyo, and *Mainichi* of Osaka. Eight known as "block" dailies were permitted to circulate regionally, but others only locally. Except for Tokyo, only one daily newspaper was permitted in each province. All remaining afternoon papers were suspended in March 1944, and in November all papers were limited to two pages, a single sheet printed on both sides.

The British Crown Colony of Hong Kong was attacked December 8, 1941, Tokyo time, although December 7 by western time, and finally captured on December 25. News reports continued to move out of the city until that final date.

Israel Epstein, UP, was killed by a shell explosion during the siege. F. P. Franklin of the *Daily Telegraph* was wounded and later captured. William A. O'Neill, Reuters' South China manager, was captured and interned until the end of the war. His wife, a volunteer nurse, was killed by the Japanese. Dorothy Jenner of the *Sydney Sun,* aboard a plane flying out of Hong Kong, was captured when the plane was forced down. Henry China of the London *Times* was missing.

With Hong Kong finally taken, other correspondents there were arrested and held. The group included George E. Baxter of UP, Victor F. Meisling, AP, and S. A. Gray, INS, all of whom had reported the Japanese attack on Nanking in 1937. Others were A. Patrick Perry of Reuters, George Giffen, Exchange Telegraph, and V. H. C. Jarrett of the

South China Morning Post, also representing the *New York Times.* Five other members of the *South China Morning Post* staff were seized: C. N. Dragon, K. D. Seyer, R. J. Cloake, J. R. Like, and Miss M. S. Bander. Some had served as stringers for agencies and papers. Four members of the *China Mail* staff also were held: W. J. Keates, editor, G. P. Burnett, R. A. E. Watson, and N. A. E. Mackay.

Richard C. Wilson, UP manager in Manila, in Hong Kong when the attack came, was captured there. Captured also was Joseph Alsop, Jr., formerly of the *New York Herald Tribune,* who had arrived in Hong Kong after a visit in Chungking on a mission for the U.S. government.

Those British and U.S. correspondents who remained in Japanese-occupied areas were seized, except for a few who managed to escape. Taken in Shanghai were John B. Powell, Harold P. Mills, M. C. Ford, and Norwood F. Allman, all on the earlier "warning" lists. Others were Frederick B. Opper, only recently arrived to replace Gould as editor of the *Evening Post & Mercury* and as correspondent for the *Christian Science Monitor;* George C. Bruce, also of the *Post & Mercury;* Robert V. Perkins, Universal News Service; James D. White, AP; Victor Keen, *New York Herald Tribune;* and Douglas Robertson, Canadian-born correspondent for the *New York Times,* replacing Abend. Taken in Tientsin were Henry G. W. Woodhead, long-time editor of the *Peking & Tientsin Times;* and Charles J. Fox, also long the publisher of the *North China Star.*

All newspaper plants in Shanghai's International Settlement were seized and sealed by the Japanese, as they were later in Hong Kong, Manila, and elsewhere. Editors of vernacular papers in Shanghai who did not manage to escape were imprisoned and some were executed. Some were offered inducements to continue their newspapers under a policy favorable to Japan, and three did so, but the papers bore no relation to their real or former ownership. They were the *Shanghai Evening Post & Mercury,*[9] *Shun Pao,* and the *Shanghai Times.* A fourth, the *Shanghai Shopping News* was continued by the Japanese, as was radio station XMHA.

Several media representatives escaped the Japanese net in Shanghai, Hong Kong, and elsewhere. Robert P. (Pepper) Martin, UP bureau chief in Shanghai, and William H. McDougall, also of the UP, left the city undetected and eventually reached Chungking. Karl Eskelund, a third

9 A New York edition of the *Evening Post & Mercury* was established by its owner, Cornelius V. Starr, and its former editor, Randall Gould, beginning January 1, 1943. A Chungking edition also was started in October 1943 and continued until June 1945.

UP staffer, and his wife, Paula, also reached Chungking. Both were Danish, and therefore neutral. Eskelund had reported the Red Army attack on Finland in 1939–40, shortly before arriving in Shanghai. Because Denmark was occupied by German forces, they were uncertain how their neutral status might be viewed by the Japanese, and chose to attempt the escape from Shanghai.

G. R. Graham-Barrow of Reuters in Mukden contrived to leave Japanese-held Manchuria (Manchukuo), and eventually reached London. In Bangkok, Darrell Berrigan, UP, and Harry A. Standish, *Sydney Morning Herald*, evaded the Japanese as they moved into Thailand. After a hazardous journey, they reached Rangoon, where Berrigan was hospitalized for a time to recover from the hardships he had experienced. Standish reached Singapore, where he continued to represent his paper and to write for NANA.

In Hong Kong, Colin M. MacDonald of the *Times* and Norman Soong of the *New York Times* hid from the Japanese when the city fell on Christmas Day. They escaped in January, even after the occupation of the city had been consolidated, and reached Chungking. H. J. Yappe and A. E. Gee of the *China Mail* also escaped to unoccupied China, as did three representatives of the British wartime Ministry of Information, D. M. MacDougall, C. E. Ross, and John A. Galvin, who had been assigned to Hong Kong.

News reports and shortwave radio broadcasts continued to emanate from Manila between December 8 and January 2, when the city was taken. There was no way for civilians to leave the Philippines and 4,000 American and British citizens were later rounded up by the Japanese and put in concentration camps, the largest of which was at Santo Tomás University in Manila. Nearly all were captives for three years until the arrival of U.S. military forces in February 1945. Press and radio correspondents and news photographers captured numbered more than thirty, some with wives and children.

Since Japanese correspondents were interned in Great Britain and the United States, most British and U.S. correspondents held by the Japanese were treated with some consideration. There were notable exceptions, as with Tolischus in Tokyo and Powell in Shanghai being brutally treated. But some were not even jailed, which was true for Douglas Robertson, *New York Times,* and James D. White, AP, both in Shanghai. Karl H. Von Wiegand of the Hearst news service, along with his companion and assistant, Lady Drummond-Hay, was given special treatment. A veteran correspondent then 68, Von Wiegand had lost the sight of one eye when a bomb exploded near the Manila Hotel on December 25. Arrested with others on January 2, he was taken to Shanghai in May so that he might receive better medical attention than was available in

Manila. There he and Lady Drummond-Hay lived in relative comfort at the Metropole Hotel.[10]

Since correspondents, like diplomats, were normally entitled to repatriation, those interned in Manila were informed during the summer of 1942 that any prepared to go from the Philippines to Shanghai by ship, risking a possible U.S. submarine attack en route, might do so, with expectation there of repatriation. Six who chose to do so were Gunnison, Mydans, and Cronin, accompanied by their wives, and Brines, Covit, and Greene. They arrived in Shanghai on September 21, 1942, after a grim nine-day voyage in a crowded and filthy Japanese troopship in slow convoy.

For a time, they were permitted to live at the Swiss-operated Palace Hotel, scarcely able to believe the comfort and good treatment, after months at Santo Tomás. They also were allowed considerable freedom of movement in the city, although obliged to wear identifying armbands and to suffer harassment. Brines attempted to escape, hoping to reach Chungking, but was captured and placed in the so-called Haipong Road Camp, where political prisoners were held.

On January 9, 1943, the Wang Ching-wei "Reformed" government of China, following the Japanese lead, declared war on the United States and Great Britain. All U.S. and British citizens not already interned then were placed in detention camps. Those correspondents transferred from Manila, except for Brines, were moved from the Palace Hotel to the Chapei Camp, and there were joined by Robertson, White, Von Wiegand, and Lady Drummond-Hay.

Seven months later, after several false hopes for the internees, the *Teia Maru,* the former French ship *Aramis* taken by the Japanese at Saigon, sailed on September 13 from Yokohama with seventy-eight Americans aboard, including those correspondents held in Japan. On September 19, correspondents held at Shanghai, along with diplomats, missionaries, and others to be repatriated to the United States and Canada, boarded the ship. Many still remained behind, but 1,500 made a month-long journey in the overcrowded, unsafe, and dirty *Teia Maru* to Goa in Portuguese India.

There, a day later, the spotless white Swedish liner *Gripsholm* arrived from New York on its second voyage of repatriation. It brought some 1,300 Japanese correspondents, diplomats, and citizens of Japan from the United States, South America, and South Africa. Most Latin Amer-

---

10   Von Wiegand, a newsman of more than thirty years experience, mostly in Germany, had many friends and admirers there and in Japan, including Yosuke Matsuoka, foreign minister prior to a cabinet reorganization the previous July. Von Wiegand also was credited in Tokyo for having written earlier in 1941 that the great threat to China was not Japan but communism.

ican nations having severed diplomatic relations with the Axis countries in January 1942, the *Gripsholm* had put in at Rio de Janeiro on the course to Goa, and at Port Elizabeth, South Africa, at war with Japan as a British Commonwealth country. The ship returned the same way and arrived in New York December 1, 1943.

The repatriation exchange at Goa was observed by correspondents from Bombay, New Delhi, and elsewhere, with emotional reunions between some who were old friends and colleagues. Among those reporting the exchange were F. Tillman Durdin of the *New York Times,* who had been in Chungking; Frank Hewlett and John R. Morris, UP; James Brown, INS; Archibald T. Steele, *Chicago Daily News;* Preston Grover, AP; and Charles Gardner of the *Sydney Morning Herald.*

John B. Powell, who had gained special Japanese disfavor because of unfavorable references made in his *China Weekly Review* of Shanghai, had been subjected to the worst treatment among all correspondents. His "internment" had amounted to two years of imprisonment. This included eight months of solitary confinement, without heat, proper cover, food, or care. It also involved persecution, humiliation, torture, and demands upon his physical stamina. Taken aboard the exchange ship, he was suffering from beri beri and gangrene, had lost all but the heels of both feet, and his normal weight of 160 pounds had dropped to seventy-five pounds. He was hospitalized for more than a year after his return to the United States, but never really recovered.[11]

Harold P. Mills, who had edited *Hwai Mei Chen Pao* of Shanghai, also was hospitalized for months after his return to the United States. Tolischus of the *New York Times,* mistreated in Tokyo, underwent long convalescence. Von Wiegand never returned to active work again; he died in Zurich in 1961 at eighty-six. George E. Baxter of the UP, one of the Hong Kong group, died in Florida in 1944 from the effects of hardships suffered during his internment.

Some repatriated correspondents returned to work, and a few even braved a return to areas where they were again at the risk of Japanese attack or capture. One was Frederick B. Opper, who went to Chungking to establish and conduct an edition of the *Evening Post & Mercury,* published there from late 1943 until June 1945.

Russell Brines, Royal Arch Gunnison, and Carl Mydans went out as war correspondents in 1944 to report the U.S. return to the Philippines. They landed at Leyte with forces commanded by General Douglas MacArthur, and accompanied them northward in the islands to reach Ma-

---

11   While still held by the Japanese in 1942, Powell and his *China Weekly Review* received an Honor Award for Distinguished Service from the University of Missouri, his alma mater. Powell died of a heart attack in 1947.

nila in February 1945. There Gunnison and Mydans were with the First U.S. Cavalry in the liberation of 3,700 persons still held at the Santo Tomás concentration camp where they and their wives had been interned from January to September 1942, and where many of their friends of that period remained, former correspondents and media representatives among them.[12]

The events of 1941, including warfare in North Africa, the German attack on Soviet Russia, and the Japanese attacks of December drawing the United States and Great Britain into the Asian war, combined to change the face of events. The Pearl Harbor attack brought immediate and far-reaching military response in the Pacific. The desert war in Libya and Egypt, in progress since September 1940, continued through 1941. Nineteen forty-two proved to be critical on the Pacific-Asian front, the Atlantic-African front, and the European-Soviet front.

---

12 As a close friend of Rags and Marjorie Gunnison, and a friend, also, of Marc Greene, this writer played a small role in gaining their repatriation and in supporting Gunnison's return to the Philippines.

Washington As a
Wartime News Center

Coverage of Washington news had increased and matured in the years between 1931 and 1941 both because of the grave economic dislocation affecting the nation and the world, and because the crisis and war situations had repercussions in the United States.

The Washington correspondent group was augmented during the decade by representation in the capital for developing radio networks, news magazines, and picture magazines, and by a greater emphasis on news pictures and film documentaries calling for the presence of more photographers. The significant topics requiring attention led to syndicated columnists, radio commentators, and analysts joining the news group. There were more correspondents for the media of other countries working as stringers as well as staff representatives in both Washington and New York.

Correspondents in Washington for the U.S. media had never been so numerous as in 1939, and there also were more there for the world press. The dean of the foreign press corps, Sir Willmott Lewis, one of the best informed and best liked of its members, had been in Washington for the *Times* of London since 1920. Hugh A. McClure Smith was second man for the *Times*. Alaric Jacob, representing Reuters, returned to Europe soon after the war began there, and was replaced in Washington by Frank Oliver, coming from China. Harold J. T. Horan, a U.S. citizen formerly in Paris for INS, represented the *Daily Express*. Herbert B. Elliston, then editor of the *Washington Post*, was a stringer for the *Observer*. J. C. Baube and Henry L. Sweinhart represented the Agence Havas. Kurt G. Sell was in Washington for the German DNB agency; Rudolf Mattfeldt for the *Frankfurter Zeitung;* George Barthelme for the *Köln Gazette;* Emil Opffer for *Politiken* of Copenhagen; Leone Fumasoni-Biondi for Stefani; Masuo Kato and Clarke H. Kawakami, a U.S. citizen, for Domei; Laurence Todd, a U.S. citizen, for Tass; Nelson A. Riley for *La Nación* of Buenos Aires; Edward Hadley, for the *Montreal Star* and *Toronto Evening Telegram;* and Arthur Webb from

1941 for the London *Daily Herald.* Some foreign papers never before represented in the United States had foreign coverage.

As usual, New York City was the favored center for foreign media representatives, but they made more frequent journeys to Washington during the war years. A. Bernard Moloney was in charge of a considerable New York staff for Reuters, including David Brown, A. G. Field, D. Kimpton Rogers, Douglas Rowley, and A. Frank Tinsley.

Louis Hinrichs, New York correspondent for the *Times* since 1922, remained throughout the war years. Douglas Williams of the *Daily Telegraph* was in England when the war in Europe began and did not return; the paper was represented by Alex H. Faulkner and by G. Campbell Dixon. Don Iddon represented the *Daily Mail,* with Alan Waters as an assistant. C. V. R. (Tommy) Thompson was correspondent for the *Daily Express,* assisted by William Hickey, but was replaced temporarily in the fall of 1941, when he was in London, by Charles Foley, the paper's foreign editor. Later, A. D. Skene Catling and Newell Rogers served the *Express* in New York. U.S.-born Dixie Tighe, working in the *Daily Express* bureau, became Mrs. Thompson.

Other British and Commonwealth correspondents in New York included Robert Waithman for the *News-Chronicle,* until moved to Washington in 1942. He was followed in New York by Gerard E. Neyroud, formerly representing the *Montreal Star* there. David H. Wills, who arrived in December 1940, had made a tour of the United States for the *News-Chronicle.* A. Wyn Williams was correspondent for the *Manchester Guardian,* and U.S.-born Bruce Bliven, then of the *New Republic,* also wrote for the paper. Veteran correspondent T. Walter Williams and John B. Walters wrote for the *Daily Mirror,* followed by Bromley Gray, Jr., and John Sampson, British-born, but earlier on the staff of the *New York American.* H. Hessell Tiltman served the *Daily Sketch* and *Sunday Graphic* in New York until the last year of the war, when he moved to Washington.

The *Evening Standard* was represented by F. G. Alletson Cook; the *Star* by Mrs. Doris B. Sheridan, followed by P. H. Powell. Frank MacDermont wrote for the *Sunday Times.* Harold Hutchinson represented the British United Press; Rader Winget and Ralph S. Morton, the Associated Press of Great Britain. Don Gilbert headed the Canadian Press bureau in New York, assisted in the first year of the war by D. Ernest Burritt, later in London. W. W. Davies, veteran New York correspondent, wrote for the *Sydney Morning Herald* and other newspapers in his native Australia, but also for *La Nación* of Buenos Aires. The Australian Associated Press was represented in New York by E. J. Richards, Frederick William Tonkon, and Walter Herbert Cummins. Arthur Richards and Leo Francis Armati wrote for the Associated Newspapers of

Australia, and J. B. Anderson and G. Warbecke for the Australian Newspaper Service.

The New York foreign press corps included Kenneth Durant and Harry Freeman for the Tass agency. Joseph Mannheim and Dr. R. Schwab wrote for the Agence Télégraphique Suisse, Guenther Reinhardt for *Der Bund* of Berne, Pers Person for *Svenska Dagbladet* of Stockholm, R. K. Lamborn and Einar Thulen for the *Stockholm Tidningen*, and Naboth Hedin for the Swedish-American News Service.

For the Latin American press, Carlos Davila conducted the Editors Press Service in New York, E. A. Franke wrote for *La Nación* of Buenos Aires, Alejandro Sux for *El Mundo* of Buenos Aires and for *Excelsior* of Mexico City, and Antonio Inglesias was correspondent for *El Universal* of Mexico City.

George Kao and Bruno Schwartz wrote from New York for the *China Press* of Shanghai until December 1941. Prior to that date, Sadao (Roy) Otake, U.S.-born and a graduate of New York University, and Chutzo Hagiwara, Doroh Teranishi, Chugo Koito, and Nagaharu Yasuo were in New York for the Domei agency of Japan. Hideo Kinosita, formerly in Lisbon, replaced Otake. *Asahi* of Tokyo was represented in New York by Shichishi Ito, Kyozo Mori, Giichi Imai, and Takatika Hosokawa.

A. Arib-Costa, a veteran correspondent in New York and a former president of the Association of Foreign Press Correspondents, wrote for *La Tribuna* of Rome. The German press was represented in New York by Ernest A. Hepp and E. Klaessig for DNB, Dr. Heinz Luedecke, for the *Berliner Börsen-Zeitung* and the *Kölnische Zeitung,* Paul Scheffer for the *Berliner Tageblatt,* and by Hans Ullendorf, stringer for several papers.

Among correspondents for the press of Denmark and Holland, until occupied by the Germans in 1940, Allen Jensen was in New York for the *Berlingske Tidende* of Copenhagen; Dr. G. J. M. Simons represented *De Telegraaf* of Amsterdam; Jan Houbolt wrote for a number of Dutch papers; Arnold Vas Dias represented the *Nieuwe Rotterdamse Courant;* and Simon Koster represented the ANP news agency. After the German occupation of the Netherlands, both Vas Dias and Koster switched to represent the Aneta agency of the Netherlands East Indies.

Until the surrender of France in June 1940, the Agence Havas was represented in New York by Guy Fritsch-Estrangin, André Péron, Albert Rocchia, J. H. Tobler, and Albert Grand. They tried to establish a new agency, Teleradio, after the surrender, but it failed. Other French correspondents in New York included Raymond Lange for *Le Petit Parisien,* Pierre Lamure for *Le Jour,* and John H. Simon for *l'Intransigeant.* Count Raoul de Roussy de Sales, who had represented *Paris-Soir,* became chancellor to the Free French (or Fighting French) delegation in New York, but died in 1942. Curt Riess (Steiner), who had fled Germany before the war and had become New York correspondent for *Paris-Soir,* switched after 1940 to represent the *Toronto Star* and to write for NEA.

The complexities of the New Deal program in the first year of the Roosevelt administration in 1933 led to the formation in Washington of a Division of Press Intelligence (DPI). Headed at the outset by Katherine M. Blackburn and later by Charlotte J. Hatton, its function was to provide a regular review of the national press with stress on its response to the New Deal. The DPI sampled the news and editorial content of 350 newspapers of the country, and issued a Daily Bulletin of 60 to 150 pages condensing material gleaned for distribution to members of Congress and to other officials. It also compiled a weekly abstract of magazine articles and editorials relating to public affairs. In 1935 the DPI became a division of a new National Emergency Council (NEC), with Charlotte Hatton still in charge.

The Division of Cultural Relations, established in the Department of State in 1938 to help counter Axis propaganda in Latin America, had gone through changes by 1942 to become the Office of Inter-American Affairs (OIAA). It was still within the State Department and directed by Nelson A. Rockefeller. Its radio listening posts became the Foreign Broadcasting Monitoring Service (FBMS) in March 1941 under the Federal Communications Commission, but was later renamed the Foreign Broadcast Intelligence Service (FBIS).

By 1939 the government had become so large and the need for information of such urgency that a new agency was created by President Roosevelt on July 1 of that year. This was the Office of Government Reports (OGR), an administrative unit of the Executive Office of the President. Directed by Lowell Mellett, former editor of the *Washington Daily News,* a Scripps-Howard newspaper, its purpose was to provide a central clearing house through which citizens, organizations, and state and local governmental divisions might transmit inquiries and complaints and receive advice and help in administrative matters.

With representatives in all states, the OGR also was to assist the president in dealing with special problems requiring an exchange of information between the federal government and state and local governments or private institutions; to collect and distribute information for members and committees of Congress, and for officials of executive departments and agencies; to keep the president and others in the government informed about the opinions, desires, and complaints of citizens and groups with respect to the work of federal agencies.

The OGR absorbed the DPI and added a United States Information

Service (USIS) headed by Harriet M. Root to provide a clearing center in Washington for inquiries concerning all branches of government. This service compiled a new *U.S. Government Manual,* a directory issued three times a year, with essential data about all government departments, divisions, and agencies, including addresses, phone numbers, and personnel.

Some expressions of alarm followed the establishment of the OGR, coming from those who professed to see in it a trend toward government propaganda and censorship such as was being used then in Italy, Germany, Russia, Japan, and elsewhere in a world already on the brink of war. The actual functions of the OGR were chiefly domestic, routine, and informational, and it had hardly been organized when the European war began.

President Roosevelt created two additional information agencies. The Office of Coordinator of Information (CIO) was established on July 11, 1941, "to collect and analyze all information and data which may bear upon national security; to correlate such information and data," and to make it available to the president and to certain departments and officials. The director of the CIO was William J. Donovan, an attorney and a military figure in World War I. Robert E. Sherwood, a Pulitzer prize-winning playwright, and Elmo Roper, a public opinion analyst, were assistants, and a distinguished group of educators served on a Research Board named in September. Sherwood also formed a Foreign Information Service (FIS) within the agency to undertake what amounted to an aggressive overseas propaganda program.

The second agency set up by the president was an Office of Facts and Figures (OFF) established October 7, 1941, to correlate information on defense and foreign policy matters such as might be put out by various departments, and to help prevent issuance of inaccurate or contradictory statements such as had embarrassed the government on several occasions. Defense agencies were directed to release to the OFF any nonsecret information, and the OFF might then make such information available to the media upon request. The head of the OFF was Archibald MacLeish, Pulitzer prize-winning poet and the librarian of Congress. Russell Davenport, editor of *Fortune,* became a member of the OFF staff.

The variety of agencies existing in Washington to provide current information become somewhat confusing by the end of 1941. Apart from the OIAA, OGR, CIO, and OFF, there also was a long-established Division of Current Information in the Department of State, a Public Information Bureau in the War Department, an Office of Public Relations in the Navy Department, and others, including the official *Congressional Directory* produced by the Government Printing Office for each session of Congress since 1809, and the *Statistical Abstract of the United States,* produced annually since 1879 by the Department of Commerce.

Not until the end of 1940, more than a year after the war began in Europe, was any special personal identification required by newsmen to enter buildings in Washington. Correspondents for the media of the United Kingdom, the British Commonwealth and the Axis countries, as well as of the United States and other countries neutral in the war were able to attend the presidential news conferences, conferences at the Department of State, and elsewhere.

Even before the Pearl Harbor attack of December 1941, however, considerable change had occurred in this casual arrangement. Joseph C. Harsch of the *Christian Science Monitor,* who left Washington in May 1939 to begin a two-year assignment in Rome and Berlin, observed this change in full perspective when he returned in May 1941. Not only had the capital changed in physical appearance, but in tempo, population, and personnel, he said, and also in the subjects of general news interest, while "the old freedom for a correspondent to move about had been very much curtailed."[1] In May 1939, he had written that a correspondent

> could go at will into any Government Department and knock on any door, [but] now to get into the White House, War Department or Navy Department he has to have a pass bearing his photograph just to get inside the door. The State Department is the only place concerned with national defense where it is possible to move about freely if one's face is known in the corridors.

Both U.S. and foreign correspondents in Washington turned increasingly to the White House, the Department of State, and the War and Navy departments for information after September 1939. The previous attendance of 100 to 150 correspondents at the president's twice-a-week news conferences grew larger. Where approximately fifteen reporters for the U.S. press and radio had been assigned to cover the White House regularly, and from five to ten news photographers, those totals increased. Steve Early, the president's press secretary, and William D. Hassett, his assistant, were available to news representatives on something close to a twenty-four-hour basis, and they added assistants of their own.

At the Department of State, a room assigned for the use of correspondents became more populated. Secretary of State Cordell Hull held

---

1   *Christian Science Monitor,* June 2, 1941.

a news conference each day, or Sumner B. Welles, under-secretary, substituted if Hull was absent. These conferences in 1938–39 drew twenty to twenty-five U.S. and foreign correspondents, including about ten regulars, and the numbers grew considerably after that time. Michael McDermott of the department's Division of Current Information, and Dorsey Fisher, his assistant, were available to correspondents at all other times, along with their own assistants.

At the War and Navy departments, officers of high rank were assigned to provide information and photos to the media. News conferences were conducted by Henry L. Stimson, secretary of war, and by Charles Edison, Frank Knox, and James V. Forrestal, serving successively as secretaries of the navy from 1940 until the end of the war.

Correspondents covered other departments of the government and such wartime agencies as were established. They also covered the Washington embassies of the warring countries, receiving information from the press attachés or at times from the ambassadors or others.

Beginning in March 1941, special passes placed further limitations on the earlier freedom of correspondents attending White House press conferences. Each pass carried not only the name, connection, signature, and photo of the correspondent, but his fingerprints as well. New cards in 1942 added the bearer's age, weight, and height. The White House Correspondents' Association was persuaded to assist in this closer control on attendance at the president's conferences.[2]

Until the United States entered the war in December 1941, Japanese, German, and Italian correspondents were members of the White House Correspondents' Association. They were free to attend the president's conferences although, by custom, foreign correspondents asked no questions. In July 1944 opportunities for resident or visiting foreign correspondents in Washington were broadened. New York-based members of the Foreign Press Association were given formal authorization when in Washington to attend any news conference in the capital and to ask questions, if they wished. Correspondents further gained the right at that time to priorities enabling them to travel more freely by air in a period when such transportation was limited. Groups had been taken on tours of the country as early as 1942 to visit war plants and military installations.

The last annual dinner of the White House Correspondents' Associa-

---

2 Any *bona fide* correspondent in the capital was eligible for membership in the White House Correspondents' Association, upon payment of a $1 fee. During the war, this group included some 400 correspondents, nearly 40 women among them. This was less than half the total membership in the general accrediting organization, the Press Galleries of the Congress of the United States. About half the membership of the White House Correspondents' Association normally attended President Roosevelt's conferences.

tion before the U.S. entered the war was in March 1941. Roosevelt, like other presidents before him, usually attended such dinners along with other distinguished guests and also was a speaker.[3] At the last dinner, in an address broadcast nationally, President Roosevelt said to the correspondents:

> For eight years you and I have been helping each other. I have been trying to keep you informed of the news of Washington, and of the nation, and of the world, from the point of view of the Presidency. You, more than you have realized, have been giving me a great deal of information about what the people of the country are thinking about and saying.
>
> In our press conferences, as at this dinner tonight, we include reporters representing papers and news agencies of many other lands. To most of them it is a matter of constant amazement that press conferences such as ours can exist in any nation in the world.
>
> That is especially true in those lands where freedoms do not exist—where the purposes of our democracy and the characteristics of our country and of our people have been seriously distorted.[4]

Provisions somewhat similar to those affecting entrance to the White House news conferences were applied after March 1941 to other Washington news sources. By 1943, forty separate passes, cards, badges, armbands, and automobile windshield stickers were required by those covering the news in Washington, and some thirty buildings could be entered only in the company of an armed guard.

As the need for personal identification for newsmen in Washington began late in 1940, the first move toward a wartime censorship soon followed. Navy Secretary Knox in January 1941 requested the U.S. press and radio, and, presumably, correspondents from other lands, to exercise a voluntary self-censorship on the use of navy news and general shipping news. When the Lend-Lease Bill was passed by Congress in March to help provide materials and munitions to democratic nations at war in return for goods and services, the need for such voluntary censorship was regarded as even more desirable, in part because the United States would become a repair base for British war vessels.

Secretary Knox on April 4 requested that the press, radio, and photo-

---

3 Presidents also attended dinners of the more exclusive Gridiron Club, established in 1885 and limited in membership to fifty Washington correspondents for U.S. newspapers and news agencies. There they spoke "off the record." They also attended quite regularly the annual dinners of the National Press Club, and sometimes of the Women's National Press Club. The wife of the president, by custom, attends the women's club dinner. Another Washington organization drawing distinguished visitors for its annual dinner is the Overseas Writers, with a membership consisting of U.S. correspondents at the capital with a record of service in other countries.

4 *Editor & Publisher* (March 22, 1941).

graphic agencies refrain from reporting, in any form, upon the arrival or departure of British ships, or about their presence in U.S. waters. Even though many persons—including Axis representatives and correspondents—might see such ships, or talk with members of their crews on shore leave, the secretary still proposed a policy of ignoring their presence.

This request met its first test later in April when the British battleship *H.M.S. Malaya* put into New York harbor for repairs of war damage. Secrecy was not observed. Reports and photographs of the arrival appeared in the press, whose spokesmen argued that because the ship sailed into port in full daylight, was observed by thousands, and its sailors on leave in and about New York talked freely, it would be absurd to pretend that the ship was not there. The resultant furor was such that the U.S. press and radio did manifest self-restraint about later ship arrivals. An exception occurred when the British aircraft carrier, *H.M.S. Illustrious,* heavily bombed by German planes in the Mediterranean in the summer of 1941, arrived at Norfolk, Virginia, for repairs. In this case, the British Information Service in New York, on the authority of the Ministry of Information in London, announced in August that Captain Lord Louis Mountbatten, a cousin of King George VI, had arrived to take command of the ship and supervise repairs.

In September, Secretary Knox joined with the British in enunciating a new policy, whereby it was permissible for the media to mention the presence of a ship, following announcement by the Navy Department. But no such mention was to be made until at least seven days after its arrival, with nothing added about the nature of the damage, the course followed in reaching the United States, the probable length of its stay, the date of departure, or reference to its future movements. U.S. newsmen might be given access to such ships, if agreeable to the British commanding officer, and subject to local regulations.

Almost immediately after announcement of these rules, the Navy Department released information about the presence in U.S. ports of twelve British war vessels. It was revealed that the aircraft carrier *H.M.S. Formidable* was at Norfolk, Virginia; the battleship *H.M.S. Warspite,* damaged off Crete, was in for repairs at Bremerton, Washington; the cruisers *Liverpool* and *Orion* were at Mare Island, California; the cruiser *Asturias,* at Newport News, Virginia; the cruiser *Dido,* at Brooklyn Navy Yard; the submarine *Pandora,* at Portsmouth, New Hampshire; two corvettes at Charleston, South Carolina; and a minesweeper at Baltimore, Maryland. A Free French destroyer, *Le Triomphant,* also put into San Diego in the summer of 1941. By October of that year, however, new British censorship regulations were put into effect in U.S. shipyards, and such reports ceased to appear.

An incident related to national security and press policy, if not precisely to censorship, occurred in December 1941 just prior to the U.S. entrance to the war. The *Chicago Tribune* published a copyrighted story outlining in some detail a reported government program for the creation of an expeditionary force of five million men, with an equal number in uniform to back them up. The plan was disclosed, the *Tribune* story asserted, on the basis of official documents.

The *Tribune* and its publisher, Robert R. McCormick, had been consistently in opposition to Roosevelt, the Democratic party, and the administration. This opposition extended to measures taken by the president since 1935 to alert the people of the United States to the threat inherent in the Nazi government of Germany; and to actions taken to support the British war effort, including the recent lend-lease legislation.

Washington officials neither denied nor confirmed the *Tribune* story about a planned expeditionary force. But the question was raised as to where the paper obtained its information, which would normally be classified secret, if true. It was suggested that an investigation on this point was probable, requested by the secretary of war and by the president himself. The propriety of publishing the story at all was questioned by some, viewed as intended to embarass the administration in a delicate period. Steve Early, the president's press secretary only said that, "It depends entirely on the decision of the publisher or the editor or the reporter whether, in printing it, it is patriotic or treason."[5]

The question Early raised became pertinent again in 1942 when the *Tribune* published a story about the defeat of Japanese naval forces west of Midway Island. The issue raised in 1941 had been of concern for some time to many in the Chicago area, especially with the *Tribune* then the only morning daily in the city since the suspension of the Hearst-owned *Chicago Herald-Examiner* in 1939. The anti-Roosevelt, anti-British policy of the *Tribune* induced Marshall Field, III, a member of the influential and wealthy Chicago merchandising family, to finance the establishment in 1941 of the *Chicago Sun* as a new morning daily with a more friendly attitude toward the administration and a more internationalist outlook.

The situation was reminiscent of World War I, when the *Tribune* also took a pro-German position until the United States broke diplomatic relations in 1917 with Germany, and only then changed its position. In 1941 the new *Chicago Sun* published its first edition on December 5, and the Japanese attack at Pearl Harbor occurred on December 7. From December 8 the *Tribune* policy was modified.

With the United States already training a draft army and also producing war supplies and equipment for its own use and for lend-lease delivery to Great Britain, several U.S. newsmen were taken on a twelve-day

---

5 *Editor & Publisher* (December 6, 1941).

air tour of defense plants in June 1941. The group included some who had returned from war coverage abroad and were able to observe preparations in the United States with special understanding. Among them were Stowe of the *Chicago Daily News;* Harsch of the *Monitor;* Tom Treanor, *Los Angeles Times;* Raymond Daniell, *New York Times;* William W. Chaplin, INS; Edwin Stout, AP; Dan Rogers, UP; Frank Kent, Jr., *Baltimore Sun;* Ralph McGill, *Atlanta Constitution;* and Ray Sprigle, *Pittsburgh Post-Gazette.*

Activities of the U.S. armed forces also were reported by news-radio representatives. Leon Kay, UP, who had reported the German move into Yugoslavia in April 1941, and later was to cover the desert war in Libya, wrote of maneuvers of the U.S. Third Army in Louisiana in the summer of 1941. With him were Charles P. Nutter, former AP chief in Paris; Robert Lee Sherrod, *Time* and *Life;* and Hanson Baldwin, *New York Times.* Richard C. Hottelet, UP, formerly in Berlin, covered maneuvers of the U.S. Second Army in Arkansas, along with Eric Sevareid, CBS, just returned from London. Later in 1941 several women correspondents covered Army maneuvers in South Carolina. Among them were Lee Carson, INS; Ruth Cowan, AP; Corinne Hardesty, UP; and Hazel Reavis of the *Red Cross Magazine,* who was formerly a correspondent in London and Paris for the AP, along with her husband, the late Smith Reavis.

The summer of 1941 brought the extension of the lend-lease provisions to the Soviet Union, following the German attack in June. It brought the Roosevelt-Churchill conference at Placentia Bay in Newfoundland in August, with the drafting of the Atlantic Charter. That summer also brought three German submarine attacks on U.S. ships in the Atlantic in September and October. U.S. news reporters and photographers also visited Iceland in August, arriving both from New York and London, to report the establishment of a U.S. naval base there.

The Pearl Harbor attack of December 1941 changed the censorship situation in the United States from its voluntary status to something stricter. The Espionage Act of 1918, a World War I measure never revoked, was announced as being in effect. Transgressions might bring severe penalties. News of casualties had to clear through military channels. Communications companies received orders to halt all cable, radio, and telephone traffic to or from Japan, Germany, Italy, and Finland, except for service messages to diplomatic and press-radio personnel, all of whom were immediately interned. The president signed an executive order authorizing a Defense Communications Board (DCB) to take over for operation or to close any radio or other communications facility. The DCB also became the Board of War Communications (BWC) under the Federal Communications Commission.

A Naval censorship was imposed on all news and other messages entering or leaving the United States. Shortwave broadcasts were placed under the supervision of William J. Donovan, formerly director of the COI but soon to head a new Office of Strategic Services (OSS). Rear Admiral Arthur J. Hepburn, director of public relations for the Navy Department, announced that news coverage might continue on a basis of voluntary censorship, backed by enforcement measures of the Espionage Act. This meant that certain categories of news were "restricted" or "classified." Specifically, information about troop and ship movements, or information that might be of possible aid to the enemy, was to be kept out of reports, and would be censored out if included. The same applied to references of weather conditions. J. Edgar Hoover, director of the Federal Bureau of Investigation (FBI), was appointed to coordinate and plan censorship of all news and communications until a permanent censorship organization could be set up.

President Roosevelt, at a news conference on December 10, assured the media representatives that full and frank reports on military and naval operations would be given out, although not authorized for use until they could be thoroughly checked, or assurance obtained that they would not give aid to the enemy.

The censorship situation was regularized with the formation on December 20, 1941, of an Office of Censorship (OC). It was placed under the direction of Byron Price, executive editor of the Associated Press, an AP staffer of twenty-nine years experience, of which twenty-two were in Washington. Theodore F. Koop, formerly of the AP Washington bureau, was named as assistant director and later as deputy director. The OC staff eventually numbered some 11,500 persons, and its budget for 1943 alone was $26,500,000.

Censorship plans previously worked out cooperatively by newsmen in a voluntary relationship with the Army, Navy, and Post Office departments and the Federal Communication Commission, and coordinated by Hoover and the FBI, were fused into a single plan. A Code of Wartime Practice for the press and radio was prepared with the advice and assistance of working members of both media and distributed in printed form in January 1942 for posting in offices. It was revised periodically during the war. Many of the former "voluntary" limitations were retained in the code, still with the use of such polite words as "asks" or "requests," rather than more imperative or mandatory usages. Repeated or serious departures from the code could bring official action through the Department of Justice. In practice, no such action ever was necessary.

Price had a Censorship Operating Board to advise and aid him. It consisted of a group of experienced editors of newspapers and magazines and radio newsmen on leave from their regular posts for rotating periods of service in Washington. A group of forty other editors in various parts of the country was named in April 1942 to observe the conduct of the censorship in their own areas, to help interpret the code, and to encourage compliance. Further, an Advisory Council was made up of officials representing the State, War, Navy, Treasury, Justice, Commerce, and Post Office departments, the FCC, Board of Economic Warfare, the OIAA, COI, and OGR, and several other divisions of government.

The Office of Censorship supervised not only the press and radio but mail and telegraph communications to and from the United States. This included dispatches by foreign correspondents in the country. They were not necessarily permitted to send reports on everything printed or broadcast even within the borders of the nation. As with the Ministry of Information in London, there were episodes during the first weeks of OC operations and later that certain correspondents found at fault, but procedures were generally smoothed out.

There was no direct censorship on domestic news publication or radio news boadcasts beyond the self-restraint under the terms of the code. Some information was withheld at the source by the armed forces or others possessing wartime security information. This extended to holding and delaying distribution on some reports from correspondents on the war fronts.

During World War I, the U.S. Committee on Public Information (CPI), directed by George Creel, handled both censorship and propaganda, but the World War II Office of Censorship was concerned with censorship only. The propaganda function was delegated to the Office of War Information (OWI), created by an executive order of the president on June 13, 1942.

The president's order provided for the consolidation within the OWI of the former Office of Government Reports (OGR), the Office of the Coordinator of Information (COI), the Office of Facts and Figures (OFF) and two or three smaller information agencies, such as the Foreign Information Service (FIS). The United States Information Service (USIS), formerly a part of the OGR, was detached and continued to perform a limited function. Some of the functions of the COI were transferred to the OSS, with Donovan as director of the new agency which assumed wartime espionage tasks. The OIAA remained under Rockefeller within the State Department. The FBIS and the BWC both continued to operate under the FCC. Close collaboration was maintained between all of these agencies, the White House, and the military.

The function of the Office of War Information was to coordinate information derived from the numerous sources in Washington, and to avoid conflicts in statements and releases while acting as both an information and a propaganda agency at home and abroad. Elmer Davis, its director, was a Washington-based news commentator and analyst for CBS prior to moving to the OWI, and was a former *New York Times* staff member and a magazine writer. Davis and his office worked closely with Byron Price of the Office of Censorship.

The OWI had both a domestic branch and an overseas branch, the first concerned with the dissemination of information relating to the war within the United States, the second with its dissemination in other countries. Every means and media was utilized to reach as many persons as possible with information about the United States at war and to advance the Allied cause. The personnel required to conduct what became an extensive operation was drawn largely from the information media. They totalled some 9,600 persons at the peak of activity of May 1945. The agency had a total budget of $132,500,000 for the three years and three months during which it operated.[6]

The domestic branch of the OWI was headed on a rotating basis by three experienced editors and publishers: Gardner Cowles, Jr., of the *Des Moines Register* and *Tribune,* the *Minneapolis Star-Journal* and *Tribune,* and *Look* magazine; E. Palmer Hoyt, editor and publisher of the *Portland Oregonian;* and George W. Healy, Jr., publisher of the *New Orleans Times-Picayune.* The total three-year budget for the domestic branch was about $12 million. A sharp budget cut in 1943 restricted the activities of that division of the agency.

The overseas branch was headed successively by Archibald Mac-Leish, former director of OFF; Robert Sherwood, formerly assistant to the director of the CIO and head of the FIS within that agency; and Edward W. Barrett, formerly executive editor of *Newsweek.* James B. Reston, formerly of the AP and *New York Times* bureaus in London, and then Wallace Carroll, formerly chief of the United Press operations in Europe, directed the important London bureau of the OWI set up in July 1942. Harold K. Guinzburg, owner of the Viking Press, New York, was chief of the Overseas Outpost Bureau, responsible for placing OWI representatives in Allied and neutral countries. There were twelve "outposts" in June 1942, with thirty-eight in twenty-three countries by the end of the war.

The broadcasting facilities of five companies that had been handling the dissemination of shortwave programs from the United States since

---

6 Of the staff, some 4,100 were citizens of countries other than the United States, including experienced correspondents and newsmen of countries overrun by the Axis. These totals in budget and personnel were roughly comparable to those of the British Ministry of Information, but considerably below those for the German Ministry of Propaganda and Public Enlightenment during the war period.

the late 1930s, including CBS and NBC, with ten transmitters, were taken over by the OWI in November 1942. News and other programs were beamed to Allied, enemy, occupied, and neutral countries throughout the world, eventually in about twenty-five languages, and to U.S. military forces abroad.

These programs, prepared at OWI offices in New York and in San Francisco, were broadcast in a service that became known as "The Voice of America" (VOA). Many journalists of occupied countries, who were working in the United States, contributed usefully to the writing and the voicing of VOA programs in a variety of languages. More than half were transmitted directly from the U.S.; others were relayed through London, where OWI operated an American Broadcasting Station in Europe (ABSIE). Close collaboration was maintained with the Psychological Warfare Branch (PWB) of the U.S. Army. Liaison also was maintained with its British equivalent, the Political Warfare Establishment (PWE), and with the BBC, in what amounted to a coordinated propaganda effort in support of the Allied military objective. Radio transmission eventually was arranged, from stations in Algiers, Bari, and Luxembourg. Radio programs directed to Asia originated chiefly in San Francisco, contesting with Japanese propaganda broadcasts. Programs for Latin America were conducted through the OIAA.

Top officials in the OWI, apart from those mentioned, included Milton S. Eisenhower, deputy director under Elmer Davis; Edgar Ansel Mowrer, formerly deputy director of the OFF and then also of the OWI until 1943, when he returned to news work; James P. Warburg, economist and a member of the planning board; Joseph Barnes, formerly of the *New York Herald Tribune,* and deputy director for Atlantic operations; Owen Lattimore, with extensive Far Eastern experience, deputy director for Pacific operations; George Backer, then publisher of the *New York Post*, head of the OWI policy division; Thurman L. (Barney) Barnard, executive director in Washington of the Overseas branch; Philip Hamblet, formerly in the OGR, and chief of the OWI London office; Louis B. Cowan, chief of the New York OWI office; and Ferdinand Kuhn, Jr., former chief of the London bureau of the *New York Times* and former assistant to the secretary of the treasury, was deputy director for OWI Information Policy, and later head of the British division in Washington dealing with the flow of news from the United States to Great Britain. Another division was headed by Alan Cranston, a 1936–38 correspondent for INS in Europe and Africa.

The Voice of America and the related overseas outpost and psychological warfare operations required more than 85 percent of all personnel and budget. The OWI provided photographs, magazine material, films and every other type of information that could be utilized to tell the story of the United States at war and contribute to victory.

Scores of experienced U.S. correspondents, editors, and writers shifted during the war years to work with the OWI, the Office of Censorship, and the OIAA. Others joined the military services and the OSS.

After the United States entered the war, and during the 1942–45 period, more foreign correspondents arrived in the country. Some went to Washington, and some who had been in New York also went to the capital. Foreign and domestic correspondents in Washington also left on war assignments. Even allowing for those changes, and for the departure of the Axis correspondents, the number of foreign representatives in the United States increased.

New York correspondents transferring to Washington included Robert Waithman, London *News-Chronicle;* Alan Waters, *Daily Mail* and *Sunday Dispatch;* H. Hessell Tiltman, *Daily Sketch* and Allied Newspapers; and A. Frank Tinsley, Reuters. Frank Oliver, in Washington for Reuters, switched to the *Times* staff in April 1942, and the agency named Kenneth Stonehouse in New York as chief correspondent to replace him and added John B. Leonard, Robert Reuben, Lloyd Burlingame, and David D. Newton. Paul Scott Rankine, who had been with the British Information Service and with the British Embassy in Washington, was added to the Reuters' bureau in the capital. Stonehouse remained in charge of Reuters coverage in the U.S. until June 1943, when he was killed in a plane crash at Lisbon when en route to London.

Other British and Commonwealth correspondents to arrive in the United States for service in Washington or New York included Walter Farr, Leonard O'C. Wibberley, and Robert Collier, all of the *Daily Mail;* Denys Smith, *Daily Telegraph;* Arthur Webb, *Daily Herald;* Richard Haestier, *Daily Express;* Philip Jordan, *News-Chronicle;* and Anthony H. Wigan, BBC. Canada received Washington reports from J. F. Sanderson and Clyde R. Blackburn, Canadian Press; R. T. Elson and R. T. Bowman, Southam Newspapers; Chester A. Bloom, Sr., *Winnipeg Free Press;* and Edward Hadley, *Montreal Star,* who also wrote for the *News-Chronicle.* The Australian press received reports from A. D. Rothman and Raymond Charles Maley of the *Sydney Morning Herald;* Sydney Randal Heymanson and Leander E. Fitzgerald, Australian Newspaper Service; and L. F. Armati, *Sydney Sun.*

The Tass bureau in Washington added five to its staff, Boris Kylov, Timofei Y. Remizov, S. S. Krafsur, Olive Chuba, and Beatrice Heiman. Walter Bosshard became correspondent for the *Neue Zürcher Zeitung;* Georges H. Martin, the *Basler Nachrichten;* Fernando Ortiz-Echague, *La Nación,* Buenos Aires; Else Ström, *Aftontidningen,* Stockholm; José M. Aladren, *El Alcazar,* Madrid; and A. H. Ghaffari, *Ettela'at,* Teheran. David C. H. Lu and Maurice Liu became representatives for the CNA of Nationalist China; Norman C. Cushman for the Dutch ANP agency in London exile; and Robert de Saint John for France-Afrique, a new Free French agency established at Algiers in 1943 and later made part of the Agence France-Presse (AFP) succeeding the Agence Havas.

Correspondents and the media in the United States accepted the limitations required to assure security in matters of troop and ship movements and travel by key individuals. One of the first such instances after Pearl Harbor related to the arrival in Washington on December 22, 1941, of Britain's Prime Minister Churchill after an eight-day crossing of the rough and submarine-infested Atlantic aboard the new British battleship *Duke of York*. Landing at Hampton Roads, Virginia, and flying to Washington as President Roosevelt's guest at the White House, Churchill was accompanied by Lord Beaverbrook, publisher of the *Daily Express* and a member of the British War Cabinet, and by Viscount Halifax, later British ambassador to the United States. Other war leaders were in the group, and a dozen or more correspondents representing the British and Commonwealth media. Some of the latter remained in Washington.

Once he had arrived in the United States, no restrictions were placed on news reports of Churchill's activities. He was present at a White House news conference on Tuesday, December 23, and answered some questions, even standing on a chair so that he might be better seen by the 200 reporters crowded into the president's office. He concluded the session by remarking that it was "just like the House of Commons." He also spoke from the White House balcony to those in the garden below, addressed Congress on the day after Christmas, and otherwise made his presence known. He went to Ottawa, addressed the Canadian Parliament on December 30, flew from Washington to Bermuda on January 14, addressed the Bermuda Assembly, and returned to England by air, so avoiding the submarine danger at sea.

Churchill attended a Quebec Conference in August 1943, along with Roosevelt and other leaders. Still another well publicized visit to Washington followed in September, with press and radio organizations as hosts at an off-the-record luncheon. There Churchill spoke for more than an hour and answered questions. In a ceremony at Harvard, he received an honorary degree. On this visit, Churchill had traveled under provisions of secrecy aboard the *Queen Mary* and sailed homeward aboard the battleship *Renown*.

Some other moves, by contrast, were unreported until they became history. This was the case, for example, when Soviet Foreign Minister Molotov visited Washington in June 1942. Hundreds of newsmen were aware of his presence, but the Office of Censorship requested secrecy. Only one paper, the *Philadelphia Daily News,* inadvertently made a reference to the visit in a local column.

The provisions of the censorship code restricted reference to the movements of the president, as commander-in-chief, and of other ranking officials of the government. Accordingly, President Roosevelt's visits to his home at Hyde Park, New York, and to Warm Springs, Georgia, went unreported during the war, at least until they had been completed. The one exception occurred during the 1944 presidential campaign, when his visits to various cities were heralded, and he rode in open cars over announced routes and made public addresses.

Apart from that, in the early autumn of 1942, President Roosevelt in a special train traveled about the country to visit factories, shipyards, and military installations. No word of the trip was published or broadcast until he was back in Washington. He had gone from the capital to Detroit, west to Seattle, south to San Diego, and back through the southwest to Washington. The press was informed of his journey, and representatives of the three news agencies traveled with him. He was seen by thousands, surprised because they had not been forewarned of his trip.

The president flew to Africa to attend a Casablanca conference in January 1943, meeting there with Churchill, General DeGaulle, and other leaders. He flew to Teheran and Cairo for conferences in November and December 1943 with Churchill, Stalin, and Chiang Kai-shek, and to the Yalta conference in February 1945, with Churchill and Stalin. The fact that Roosevelt made these three long journeys by air, under wartime conditions, prevented any large number of correspondents from accompanying him. The journey also went unreported until the safe return of all participants to their own capitals.

The practical solution, as with his trip about the United States in 1942, was to permit representatives of the three U.S. news agencies to fly in the president's party and make their reports available to all upon their return. Correspondents in the areas of the conferences were invited to be present, although obliged to operate under conditions of wartime secrecy, with their reports censored and held for delayed release. This worked reasonably well, except at Cairo and Teheran, where there was dissatisfaction and confusion over the handling of dispatches, resulting in a "leak" through Lisbon.

In his final report after the war on the activities of the Office of Censorship, Byron Price spoke of many "well-kept secrets"—matters known to the media, but unreported until officially released. These included details of the Pearl Harbor attack and the vast damage done to the U.S. Pacific fleet; the landings on western states of Japanese bomb-carrying windborne balloons, the story of radar, the preparations for the Normandy landings in June 1944, and, perhaps above all, the development of the atom bomb.[7]

---

7 The full damage at Pearl Harbor was described early to this writer, with sketches, by a correspondent returned to San Francisco. Later, in the U.S. Army and attached to Supreme Headquarters in London, he also had an advance view of the plans for the Normandy invasion.

There were, however, some slips and many complaints relating to censorship. Among the most serious probably was an exclusive story originated by the *Chicago Tribune* and signed by Stanley Johnston. The report was datelined Washington and published June 7, 1942, two days after the defeat by depleted U.S. naval forces of a strong Japanese navy and air force west of Midway Island. The story was published not only in the *Tribune* but also in the family-owned *New York Daily News* and *Washington Times-Herald,* and by four other papers using the syndicated *Tribune* service.

Johnston had been a *Tribune* correspondent aboard the U.S. Navy aircraft carrier *Lexington,* lost during the Battle of the Coral Sea in May 1942. He had been recommended for a citation for bravery in risking his life at that time to save other men. In Chicago as the news of the Midway engagement came to the *Tribune* in the news agency reports, he was given the task of preparing a special account based on those reports, enriched by his personal understanding of the naval situation and of naval strategy.

Included in Johnston's story was a statement that the United States Navy had advance knowledge that the Japanese were going to attack Midway and was prepared. He included a highly detailed listing of the Japanese ships involved in the action, and an outline of the Japanese battle plans. As authority, his story cited "reliable sources in the Naval Intelligence." It did not say, specifically, that the U.S. Navy had "broken" the Japanese communications cipher code. This was true, however, as Johnston knew, and an enemy agent might have been able to deduce that fact from his story.

The navy made a quiet investigation to determine the source or sources of Johnston's information. Early in August, U.S. Attorney General Francis Biddle announced that a Federal Grand Jury in Chicago would start an immediate inquiry into the publication "of confidential information concerning the Battle of Midway." The provisions of the Espionage Act gave authority for such an inquiry.

The Grand Jury met but a case charging the *Tribune* with revealing confidential information was dropped, with no indictment returned. After hearing testimony, the government's representative expressed doubt that willful intent to aid the enemy could be proved, as would be required under the Espionage Act. Navy officers called to testify also refused to explain why the story could have been useful to the enemy. Even though it was generally recognized and even stated that its usefulness was in the story's indication that the Japanese cipher was known to the U.S. Navy, Rear Admiral Frederick C. Sherman and six others apparently did not wish to confirm that fact by any formal statement.

An earlier case involving a censorship slip involved Walter Farr, correspondent for the *Daily Mail.* Farr went from Washington to the Pacific soon after Pearl Harbor and was accredited to the U.S. Navy. On March 6, 1942, the *Daily Mail* published one of his dispatches datelined "At Sea, Friday." The story was promptly relayed from London to New York by U.S. correspondents and the substance of it was reprinted in the United States.

Farr's story described "great convoys of ships carrying . . . a massive force . . . to build foundations for a great offense against the Japanese" in the Pacific and, at the same time, to help defend Australia. It reported the ships of the convoy as carrying thousands of airmen and infantry units.

Editors in the United States immediately demanded explanations as to the truth of the report involving troop movements, a forbidden subject, and also asked whether facts were being denied the U.S. press and public, while being made available to the British press. The navy finally reported that Farr's story had been filed from Honolulu, rather than from any ship "At Sea," and that it contained "no facts having any relationship whatsoever to new convoy operations . . . [and] no information previously unpublished by the American press."

The fact was, however, that a large convoy was bound for Australia at the time, as Farr said, and the story under censorship regulations should not have appeared anywhere. The navy censor who had passed Farr's dispatch in Honolulu was relieved of his duties, and Farr presently was deprived of his credentials as a war correspondent, although he was reaccredited later.

Other instances in which U.S. censorship regulations were transgressed during the war years were surprisingly few and unintentional.

One of the first acts of war to touch North American shores directly, apart from nearby submarine activity, was the seizure of two tiny French islands, St. Pierre and Miquelon, off Newfoundland on the approach to the Gulf of St. Lawrence. This occurred on Christmas Eve 1941, when French naval units under Vice Admiral Emile Muselier acted in accordance with a request by General DeGaulle in London. DeGaullists in Canada wanted the matter to be reported as it took place. Edwin L. James, managing editor of the *New York Times*, given advance information through a Canadian source, consulted with John Wheeler, general manager of the North American Newspaper Alliance. They arranged to have Ira Wolfert, NANA staff writer, fly to Montreal, proceed to Halifax, and go aboard a Free French corvette. He was able to report the peaceful occupation of the islands on behalf of the Free French. Robert Martin of Paramount News made films of the event.

Following Pearl Harbor, the question of priorities arose. Japanese pressure made the war in the Pacific immediately urgent. The battle in the North African desert, the submarine campaign in the Atlantic, and the defense of Russia—all required attention at the same time, as did the effort toward restoration of independence in Europe and China.

PART III
Battle Joined

———————————————————————

With the extension of the war to the Pacific on December 7, 1941, the press-radio organization moved correspondents to the area or out of it. Information service between Honolulu and San Francisco was resumed December 11, operating under U.S. Navy censorship. Pearl Harbor remained throughout the war as the major U.S. Pacific naval base and a center for Pacific war news.

Tom Yarbrough of the AP and formerly in London, who was bound for Manila, arrived in Honolulu by ship at the very time the Japanese attack on Pearl Harbor was in progress on December 7. He remained for a time, and then was assigned to Australia. Francis L. McCarthy, UP, also in Honolulu en route to Manila, went instead to Australia. Wallace Carroll, UP manager in London and then European manager, who had made a long journey from London to Soviet Russia and across Siberia to Vladivostok, was at sea aboard a ship bound from Manila to Honolulu and San Francisco as the Pearl Harbor attack occurred. He arrived safely in Honolulu after the bombing. Joseph Newman of the *New York Herald Tribune,* who had only recently gone from Tokyo to Manila, had left there December 4 aboard a ship bound also for Honolulu and San Francisco and also arrived safely.

Joseph C. Harsch, *Christian Science Monitor* correspondent with recent European war experience, was in Honolulu as the attack came. Alan Campbell, Acme Newspictures photographer, obtained pictures during and after the attack, and about sixty were passed by the censors. Other photographers in Honolulu had varied successes in getting their pictures past the censors. Among them were Richard Haller, INP, Langdon V. (Don) Senick, Fox Movietone News, David Walden, Paramount Newsreel, and Al Ross, Pathé Newsreel.[1]

The Japanese success at Pearl Harbor was such that its naval and air

---

1   The damage done to the U.S. Pacific Fleet units concentrated at Pearl Harbor was so severe and extensive that it was concealed by the censorship for many months in its details, providing time for the reassignment of ships.

units were able to remain in the central Pacific. Olen Clements, AP, transmitted an eyewitness account of a bombing of Wake Island on Christmas Eve, 1941—a story pooled to all U.S. papers. Joseph F. McDonald, Jr., a construction engineer and UP stringer on Wake Island, was erroneously reported to have been the first U.S. correspondent killed in the Pacific war, said to have been hit during a Japanese air attack on December 22. Son of Joseph F. McDonald, Sr., editor of the *Nevada State Journal* in Reno, he was captured when the island was taken just after Christmas, and not liberated until September 1945.

From Manila, the news moved by cable, radiotelegraph, and short-wave radio until the Japanese established control there on January 2, 1942.[2] From Hong Kong, prior to its capture on Christmas Day 1941, George E. Baxter, UP, and S. A. Gray, INS, managed to get reports out by wireless to Chungking or Manila. Guam, lacking an effective defense, was invaded December 10. From Rangoon, Burma, the advance of Japanese forces, first through Thailand and then into Burma itself was reported by Leland Stowe of the *Chicago Daily News,* and later by Daniel DeLuce, AP. The Japanese moved against Malaya on December 7–8. From the Middle East, Cecil Brown, representing *Newsweek* and the CBS, arrived in Singapore. Merrill (Red) Mueller, INS, and Martin Agronsky, NBC, arrived there by air. Mueller had been with the British Eighth Army in Libya and Agronsky had been in Ankara. O'Dowd Gallagher of the *Daily Express* was assigned to Singapore for some time before the Pearl Harbor attack.

Others in Singapore as the Pacific war began included James Henry, Reuters manager; Lawrence Impie, *Daily Mail;* C. Yates McDaniel, AP; Harold Guard, British-born and formerly in the British navy, and Stanley Jones, both of the UP; Stanley A. Wykes, INS; and Frank E. Noel, news photographer for Wide World Photos, which had become an AP subsidiary. F. Tillman Durdin was in Singapore as chief Far Eastern correspondent for the *New York Times;* David White, editor of the *Singapore Free Press,* was acting as stringer for the *Times* of London, but Ian Morrison, born in China, educated at Cambridge, and experienced both in Japan and China, was appointed as correspondent for the *Times* in Singapore in December 1941. Ronald Matthews arrived for the *Daily Herald.* Harry A. Standish, *Sydney Morning Herald,* who had escaped from Bangkok, wrote from Singapore for NANA as well as for his paper.

---

2   See chapter 10 for more detail. The National Headliners' Club of the United States, made a series of awards in June 1942 for war coverage during the previous twelve months. For reports from the Philippines, such awards were made to Royal Arch Gunnison for a "series of outstanding radio reports" for the MBS; to Frank Hewlett, UP; and to Bert Silen, Don Bell, and Ted Wallace, NBC, for "eyewitness accounts of the bombing of Manila." Bell was later reported to have been bayonetted to death by Japanese soldiers.

One of the most dramatic reports of the Pacific war was an eye-witness account of the sinking of the British battleships *Repulse* and *Prince of Wales* in a Japanese torpedo bomber attack on December 10, 1941, in the South China Sea fifty miles from the Malaya coast and 150 miles north of Singapore. The ships had sailed from Singapore with a destroyer escort on the night of December 8 to try to intercept any convoys that might be carrying reinforcements to Japanese units already in Thailand and Malaya. As it turned out, the two powerful ships were themselves lost, and 600 British sailors and Marines were killed or drowned.[3]

Aboard the *Repulse* were Cecil Brown of CBS and *Newsweek* and O'Dowd Gallagher of the *Daily Express*. They went over the side when the battleship began to sink and were picked out of the water two hours later by British destroyers, which rescued some 2,000 men. Their exclusive and deeply moving accounts were promptly transmitted and widely published, and Brown received a National Headliners' Club award for his CBS broadcast report of the sinking.

Brown was barred shortly after from continued news activities in Singapore, not because of his *Repulse* stories but because his coverage of the worsening situation in Singapore and Malaya was regarded as "detrimental to public morale." This meant his reports were too frank in revealing circumstances that were to bring about the loss of Malaya and capture of the supposedly impregnable British naval base by mid-February 1942. Brown went to Batavia (now Djakarta), to Australia, and then returned to the United States, where he became chiefly concerned with radio news broadcasting and commentary.

Meanwhile, reports were coming from many of those correspondents already mentioned as present in the Philippines. The Japanese had made a landing in the Lingayen Gulf area in the north of the main island of Luzon on December 22. Japanese planes flying from aircraft carriers had caught planes on the ground at Clark and Nichols fields near Manila and put half of the U.S. Pacific air force out of action. Planes also bombed the U.S. naval base at Cavite, near Manila, where more ships were lost.

Manila itself was captured on January 2. United States and British civilians were placed in concentration camps. Some were held at Fort Santiago and then sent to Santo Tomás University near Manila. Correspondents were at Santo Tomás, including those later moved to

---

3   The *Repulse* had carried King George VI and Queen Elizabeth on their visit to Canada and the United States in the summer of 1939. The newly completed *Prince of Wales* had taken Prime Minister Churchill across the Atlantic in August 1941, just four months earlier, for his conference with President Roosevelt in Newfoundland waters. The destruction of the U.S. naval vessels at Pearl Harbor about forty-eight hours before had left the two British battleships as the only other Allied capital ships in the Pacific.

Shanghai and repatriated. After the seizure of Manila, such island defenses as remained were concentrated on the Bataan Peninsula, across Manila Bay to the west, on Corregidor Island, a rocky and strongly defended point just off the tip of that peninsula, and some forces on the large island of Mindanao at the extreme south of the Philippines island group.

Combined U.S. and Filipino military forces were under the command of General Douglas MacArthur, retired after a long career in the U.S. Army but serving since 1935 as a field marshal and advisor to a Philippine army being readied for the day when the islands were due to become an independent republic in 1945. MacArthur centered his command at Corregidor.

Some correspondents on leaving Manila had gone to Corregidor with MacArthur. These were Frank Hewlett and Franz Weissblatt, UP; Clark Lee, AP; Dean Schedler, *Manila Bulletin* and AP; Curtis L. Hindson, Reuters; C. A. P. (Nat) Floyd, *New York Times* and London *Daily Herald;* Melville Jacoby, *Time* and *Life;* and Annalee Whitmore, a *Time* and *Life* writer, who was to become Mrs. Jacoby during the campaign.

A lack of manpower, armament, and air support doomed the Philippines, although Japan required five months, rather than the anticipated two months to gain control, and then was to be plagued by Filipino guerrilla opposition through the years of occupation. On orders from Washington, General MacArthur left Corregidor March 11. With a small group, he made a rough and hazardous journey in four PT mosquito boats to Mindanoa and by plane from there to Australia to set up a new Southwest Pacific U.S. Army headquarters at Brisbane. His arrival was made known March 19.

Among those accompanying MacArthur to Australia were several correspondents: Clark Lee, AP; Jacoby and his bride for *Time* and *Life;* Hindson, Reuters; Floyd, *New York Times* and *Daily Herald;* and Hewlett, UP, and Schedler, AP, both arriving later. In the party, also, was Carlos Romulo, editor and publisher of the *Manila Herald,* who also held rank as a colonel on MacArthur's staff.[4] With MacArthur's departure from the Philippines, General Jonathan Wainwright assumed command. The Bataan defense position fell in April, followed by the so-called "death march" of prisoners taken by the Japanese. Franz Weissblatt, UP, was wounded and was among the captives. Corregidor surrendered on May 6.

The Japanese campaign had forged ahead in other areas, and by May most of Burma was under control, including Rangoon, Mandalay, and

---

4 Romulo shared the Pulitzer Prize award of 1942, recognized for his writing in the *Herald* during 1941.

the "Burma Road" leading into China from the west. All of Malaya had been brought under control by the end of January 1942. An attack directed at Singapore from the land side, rather than from the sea, attained complete success by mid-February.

A considerable number of correspondents had gathered in the East Indies before the group fleeing Singapore arrived. The direction of the Japanese drive was obvious, and some newsmen were at Batavia, the capital of the island of Java, or at Malacca, Medan, or Palembang, on the island of Sumatra. These islands offered no more permanence to correspondents than Singapore. Japanese forces, supported by air and sea power, established control of the major portion of the great island archipelago by the end of February 1942, excepting only parts of New Guinea and Borneo. In June, Japanese forces struck in the north Pacific as well, with landings on the U.S. islands of Attu and Kiska, in the Aleutian chain adjacent to Alaska. These various moves threatened Alaska in the north and India, China, Australia, and New Zealand in the south. All therefore became points of Allied military concentration and defense, along with Hawaii.

Correspondents who had been in Singapore in December 1941 were joined by others before the mid-February capitulation. Among them were E. R. (Al) Noderer, *Chicago Tribune;* George Weller, *Chicago Daily News* and *Daily Telegraph;* Henry W. Keyes, *Daily Express;* Gilbert Mant, Reuters; and Stanley Gardiner, Exchange Telegraph. Concern in Australia and New Zealand over the Japanese moves was reflected by the presence in Singapore of Ray Maley, Australian Associated Press; Geoffrey Tebbutt, *Melbourne Herald,* also writing for NANA; William Knox, *Sydney Mirror;* Douglas Wilkie, *Sydney Sun,* also writing for the *Times* and NANA; Thomas Fairhall, *Sydney Telegraph;* and Colin Fraser, *Melbourne Sun-Pictorial.*

Harold Guard, UP, was wounded in the leg by shell fragments during fighting in the Singapore area on July 31 and was moved to Batavia and later to Australia. Frank E. Noel, Wide World–AP Photos, upon leaving Malaya was hurt when the ship in which he was traveling was torpedoed and sank in the Indian Ocean. He saved his cameras. A photo he took while at sea in a lifeboat, showing an East Indian sailor pleading for drinking water was awarded the Pulitzer Prize for news photography.

In the Netherlands East Indies (N.E.I.), the UP had John McCutcheon (Jack) Raleigh,[5] the AP had H. Haydon, and the INS had J. P. Kosak. Dixon Brown and W. T. Knox were there for the *News-*

---

5 Raleigh, a nephew of John T. McCutcheon, *Chicago Tribune* cartoonist and correspondent in wars between 1898 and 1918, went as a *Tribune* correspondent to Germany in 1939. He was in Poland, Italy, and Mexico writing also for the *Daily Mail* and later joined the CBS.

Chronicle, Sydney Albright for NBC, and Elizabeth Wayne for MBS. The N.E.I. news agency, Aneta, was directed from Batavia by Dr. H. A. Colijn. He was in daily telephone connection with the agency's New York bureau, headed by Arnold Vas Dias, at a time when Holland itself was under German occupation.

Other correspondents in Java and Sumatra were William H. McDougall, UP, who had escaped from Shanghai in December; John R. Morris, Far Eastern manager for UP; F. Tillman Durdin, who had been in Singapore for the *New York Times;* C. Yates McDaniel, AP, one of the last to leave Singapore; Witt Hancock, also for the AP; Kenneth Selby-Walker, Reuters; Jack Findon, *Daily Express;* John D. Bouwer, Aneta and the *News-Chronicle;* Edward Greennock, also of the *News-Chronicle;* William Dunn, CBS; Frank J. Cuhel, MBS; Charles Buttrose, *Sydney Morning Herald;* Allen Raymond, *New York Herald Tribune;* and H. R. Knickerbocker, foreign editor of the recently established *Chicago Sun.*

As the Japanese completed their seizure of the East Indies, Europeans were placed in concentration camps comparable to those at Santo Tomás in the Philippines. The correspondents left as best they could to avoid internment. Morris, Durdin, and others went to India. Some went to Ceylon, but most traveled to Australia. Wykes of INS and Extel was captured by the Japanese at Batavia. Hancock of AP, Mac-Dougall, UP, Selby-Walker, Reuters, and Findon, *Daily Express,* remained until the first days of March, when the Japanese were very near. Hancock and McDougall left by ship for Ceylon on March 4. The ship was bombed at sea three days later and sank. Hancock was drowned, but McDougall was picked up and spent the following three years in a Japanese civilian internment camp at Palembang in Sumatra. Selby-Walker and Findon were listed as "missing," and never heard from after Selby-Walker's farewell dispatch of March 6.

The first thought of the people and government of the United States, following the Japanese attacks of December 7–8 was to strike back. In this they were joined by the people of the British Commonwealth. For such action in the Pacific, the Hawaiian Islands remained the obvious base from which to make the first move. Considering the rapid advance of Japanese forces in southeast Asia, Malaya, the Philippines, and the East Indies, the second obvious move was to halt that advance before Australia and New Zealand felt its force, and to make Australia, in particular, a base in the South Pacific area. India and China were further points in Asia from which to stage an Allied counteroffensive, while defenses in Alaska also required bolstering.

Despite the great naval losses at Pearl Harbor and Cavite, and air force losses at Manila, all occurring in December 1941, and the setbacks in Malaya, Singapore, and the East Indies, U.S. naval and air and ground forces began to strike sooner than might have been expected. Troops were moved in convoy to Australia and New Zealand beginning in March, and MacArthur set up a Southwest Pacific headquarters at Brisbane at that time. United States planes under the command of Brigadier General James H. Doolittle took off from the aircraft carrier *U.S.S. Hornet,* 800 miles from Japan, and bombed Tokyo, Yokohama, and Nagasaki on April 18, 1942. In May the Japanese fleet suffered losses inflicted chiefly by U.S. carrier-based planes in the Battle of the Coral Sea, southeast of New Guinea, between the Australian coast and the Solomon Islands. Losses to the U.S. also were serious, but less so than Japan's. Japanese naval forces suffered an even heavier blow in the Battle of Midway early in June.

The first of many amphibious landings occurred in August, when U.S. Marines went ashore at Guadalcanal and Tulagi Islands in the Solomons to begin a long and bitter battle for control of those key spots on the sea route between the United States and Australia. The landings themselves were made without opposition, but violent fighting soon developed at sea, in the air, and on the islands. Near the end of November 1942, U.S. Army forces replaced Marines at Guadalcanal. By February 1943 most of the several thousand Japanese troops committed there had been eliminated. Meanwhile, Allied forces landed in New Guinea and conducted raids on islands occupied by the Japanese. These forays were costly and it was not until later in 1943 that territory other than Guadalcanal began to be retaken.

The attack at Pearl Harbor had hardly occurred when the media began to shift correspondents already in the field and to augment coverage by new appointments. Within a matter of days, scores of newsmen were arriving in San Francisco to obtain transportation to Honolulu and beyond, even as British newsmen were being flown to Singapore.

Among the first to move out from San Francisco was Ralph B. Jordan, former West Coast manager for INS, who had returned to that agency after a period in public relations in Hollywood. He was sent to Honolulu and then to Australia. James L. Kilgallen, INS, went to Honolulu and later was at sea with the navy. William F. Tyree, UP, in the Honolulu bureau on Pearl Harbor day and accredited to the navy, was an observer at the Battle of Midway in June. Frank Smothers and Robert J. Casey were both experienced correspondents for the *Chicago Daily News.* Casey was accredited to the navy and Jonathan (Jack) Rice went out as an AP news photographer.

Others who left San Francisco were Foster Hailey, *New York Times;* Alfred D. Brick, Fox Movietone News, accredited to the navy; H. R.

Knickerbocker, chief of the foreign service of the *Chicago Sun,* who went to Honolulu and on to Batavia and then to Australia; Edward Angly, *Chicago Sun,* but formerly of the *New York Herald Tribune* staff in Europe, who went to Honolulu and later to Australia; and Harry Lang, another *Chicago Sun* correspondent.

The group of correspondents traveling from San Francisco in the first days of the Pacific war also included Wendell Webb, AP; Edwin E. Dowell, UP, former bureau manager at Salem, Oregon, who flew to Honolulu; Joe James Custer, also UP, accredited to the navy; and Robert Bryant, INP photographer. Walter Farr, *Daily Mail,* formerly in Washington, was the only British newsman to go to Honolulu at that early period. Stanley Johnston, *Chicago Tribune,* was aboard the U.S. aircraft carrier *Lexington* when it was sunk during the Battle of the Coral Sea in May. Keith Wheeler, *Chicago Times,* accredited to the navy, was with a task force that went to Alaska in the summer of 1942 to contest the Japanese landings in the Aleutians. He received the Sigma Delta Chi award for foreign correspondence for the year. Bernard J. McQuaid, *Chicago Daily News,* also went to Alaska with the navy.

As early as January 8, 1942, a month after Pearl Harbor, the U.S. War Department announced the accreditation of 115 correspondents in the Pacific area. All correspondents accredited to U.S. forces were required to wear officers' uniforms, minus insignia of rank, but with a green brassard on the left arm designating the wearer as a "War Correspondent." This later was modified to permit a less conspicuous pocket or shoulder patch. The correspondents were attached to the headquarters of a field force commander, with privileges of accommodations, transportation, and mess facilities comparable to those of an officer. They had a simulated rank of captain in the event of capture, to assure treatment accorded officers taken prisoner. Government communications facilities were made available where necessary or permissible, but all dispatches were subject to censorship as prescribed for the zone in which the correspondent was operating.

As distinct from an "accredited" correspondent, there was a category of "visiting" correspondent, required to wear the brassard, but not necessarily the regulation uniform. They came with special permission, limited to a fixed itinerary and ordinarily accompanied by a conducting officer. Publishers of newspapers or magazines were among these visitors.

Special provisions were made for news photographers and newsreel cameramen whereby their photos or films were available to all in a pooling arrangement. International News Photos, AP News Photos, Acme Newspictures, and *Life* magazine entered into this agreement in February 1942, and it was extended to include all other services. In other respects, the photographers were under the same regulations as press-radio correspondents, including censorship.[6] The radio correspondents later worked out a pooling arrangement of their own whereby, if necessary because of limited radio transmission facilities, one correspondent might serve as a "neutral voice" to be carried by any or all networks.

Another group of enlisted "combat correspondents"—fighting men comparable to those with Japanese, Chinese, German, and Soviet forces—accompanied U.S. Marine Corps units into action, both as writers and photographers. After participating in or observing action and hopefully surviving, they would write their news accounts or would have their photos or motion pictures processed, censored, released, and distributed by the Navy Department. These men all went through regular Marine training. Most had been engaged in journalistic activities prior to entering the service as volunteers. Three reported the Guadalcanal-Tulagi landings in August 1942, and on September 1 forty-eight additional Marine combat correspondents were ready to join units in the Pacific.

General MacArthur arrived in Australia from the Philippines on March 15, 1942, accompanied by his family and staff officers. In Melbourne, his first headquarters, he found Lieutenant Colonel Lloyd (Larry) Lehrbas, former AP correspondent, serving as press officer there and at the permanent headquarters in Brisbane.[7] MacArthur established himself at Brisbane, both at the request of the Australian government and on orders from President Roosevelt, to command all land, sea, and air forces east of Singapore in the southwest Pacific, including the Philippines, even though under Japanese occupation. Other important headquarters were set up in New Zealand, the New Hebrides, and New Caledonia.

Thousands of U.S. Marines and units of the army had arrived in Australia in convoys by March, and others followed in preparation for a counteroffensive against the Japanese. Scores of correspondents also gathered there. Many represented media in the United States and traveled in the troop convoys or flew there. Others represented British media, coming by way of India, or were evacuees from Malaya, Singapore,

---

6 Amos Puck Chun, a photographer for the *Honolulu Star-Bulletin*, and of Chinese heritage, is reported to have become the only Chinese to be accredited as a U.S. war correspondent during World War II.

7 Lehrbas, although only forty-three at the time, had been an officer in World War I. As a newsman, he had known MacArthur as chief of staff in Washington in 1933. Later, he had been a correspondent in China and Europe, and had been in Warsaw for the AP when the German attack began there in September 1939. Following Pearl Harbor, he was commissioned as a lieutenant colonel in the U.S. Army, and assigned to MacArthur's headquarters.

and the N.E.I. Still others represented the media of Australia and New Zealand.

All were accredited to the new headquarters at Brisbane. There General MacArthur on March 23 held the first of his limited number of news conferences, with more than fifty U.S., British, and Australian correspondents attending. His second conference on July 19 drew more than a hundred. Both were off the record. The headquarters maintained a sharp censorship, and the official Australian censorship itself was one of the most severe in any country.

Among correspondents early on the scene in Australia were Brydon C. Taves, who had set up a UP bureau in Melbourne in February 1942, and C. Yates McDaniel, who set up an AP bureau there about March 1 after his arrival from Singapore and Batavia. Patrick Robinson, who opened an INS bureau, had been a soldier in MacArthur's Rainbow Division in France during World War I.

Other early arrivals among U.S. correspondents were Harsch of the *Christian Science Monitor;* Knickerbocker and Angly, *Chicago Sun;* Carleton (Bill) Kent, *Chicago Times;* Byron ("Barney") Darnton, *New York Times;* Lewis Sebring, Jr., *New York Herald Tribune;* Jack Turcott, *New York Daily News;* Lee Sherrod, *Time* magazine; John Lardner, *Newsweek* and the NANA; William B. Courtney, *Collier's;* Vernon A. (Vern) Haugland, AP; and Lee Van Atta, INS, then under twenty years of age, the youngest correspondent in the field and perhaps in the war.

In Australia at this period also were a number of correspondents with previous experience in the war in China, Europe, or the Pacific. For U.S. media, they included Clark Lee, AP; Melville Jacoby, *Time* and *Life;* Annalee Whitmore Jacoby, accredited to *Liberty* magazine; and C.A.P. (Nat) Floyd, *New York Times* and *Daily Herald,* all of whom had reached Australia from the Philippines. Others were Harold Guard, UP; E. R. (Al) Noderer, *Chicago Tribune;* Merrill ("Red") Mueller, INS; George Weller, *Chicago Daily News* and *Daily Telegraph;* Allen Raymond, *New York Herald Tribune;* Sydney Albright and Martin Agronsky, NBC; John McCutcheon Raleigh, formerly UP, and William Dunn, both CBS; and Frank J. Cuhel, MBS.

Among British and Commonwealth correspondents with comparable experience were Ronald Matthews, *Daily Herald;* Henry W. Keyes, *Daily Express;* Ian Morrison, the *Times;* Dixon Brown, the *News-Chronicle;* and Thomas Fairhall, *Sydney Telegraph.* Others were Australian-born Noel Monks, the *Daily Mail;* Chester Wilmot, representing the Australian Broadcasting Commission and experienced in war coverage in Libya, Greece, and Syria; Richard Greenlees and David Georgeson, also representing the *Daily Mail;* Patrick Maitland, *News-*

Chronicle, who had represented the *Times* in the Balkans campaign in 1941; George Taylor, also of the *News-Chronicle;* Walter E. Lucas, Alan Burbury, and Bruce Niven, all of the *Daily Express;* Martin Moore, *Daily Telegraph;* and William Courtnaye, the *Daily Sketch* and Allied Newspapers. Writing for Australian papers were Harold J. Summers, *Sydney Morning Herald;* Norman Stockton, *Sydney Sun;* William Mattingley, *Melbourne Herald;* and Beth Thwaites, the weekly *Truth.*

Joining U.S. correspondents in Australia during the early period were Tom Yarbrough, AP, formerly in London and Honolulu; Don Caswell, UP; Ralph B. Jordan, INS; Theodore H. White, *Time,* formerly in Chungking, and soon to return there; Hanson W. Baldwin, military and naval correspondent for the *New York Times;* Robert J. Doyle, *Milwaukee Journal;* and William M. (Bill) Henry, *Los Angeles Times* and CBS. Francis L. McCarthy, UP, was assigned to cover Canberra, the capital. A number of newsreel cameramen and news photographers foregathered in Australia, among them Norman Alley, formerly in China; Jonathan Rice and Edward Widdis, AP Photos; Wallace Kirkland and George Strock, *Life;* Frank Prist, Jr., Acme Newspictures; Robert Bryant and Joseph A. Dearing, INP; Martin Barnett, Paramount Newsreel; and Earle Crotchett, Universal Newsreel.

Between March 1942, when MacArthur arrived, and June, there was a considerable shifting of correspondents in Australia. There were new arrivals, but others who had come to observe the first activities in the area left on other assignments. Some who had come from the United States returned there, at least temporarily, including Knickerbocker, Harsch, Lardner, Angly, and Jordan. Raymond also returned to resign from the *New York Herald Tribune.* Floyd, who had been in the Philippines, returned to join the army. Melville Jacoby of *Time* and *Life,* which he had represented in Chungking in 1940 and later served in the Philippines, and Brigadier General H. H. George, a veteran of Corregidor, were killed in an airplane accident during take-off from an airfield near Darwin on April 27, 1942.[8]

Jonathan Rice, AP Photos, left Australia in time to go aboard a U.S. Navy escort vessel accompanying the aircraft carrier *Hornet* bearing the planes that bombed Japan in April. Accredited to the navy in the same expedition were Keith Wheeler, *Chicago Times;* Joe James Custer, UP;

---

8 Jacoby's brief career was memorialized at his alma mater in the annual Melville Jacoby Fellowship at Stanford University for a graduate student in journalism specializing in problems of the Far East.

Mrs. Jacoby later went to Chungking, where she worked in Dr. Tong's International Department of the government, and also represented *Time* again. In this, she was associated with Theodore H. White, *Time* correspondent, and they collaborated on a book, *Thunder Out of China* (1946).

Richard Tregaskis, INS; and E. Astley Hawkins, Reuters. Rice and Wheeler also were present when a task force under Admiral William F. Halsey, Jr., shelled the Japanese-held Gilbert and Marshall Islands. Robert Landry, *Life,* also was on that assignment. Rice was present, again, during the major Battle of Midway, along with William F. Tyree and Robert P. ("Pepper") Martin, both of the UP. Accreditation to ships in the Pacific, necessary even for correspondents traveling to Australia, fell within the jurisdiction of Admiral Chester W. Nimitz, commander of the U.S. Pacific Fleet, and commander-in-chief of the Pacific areas (CINCPAC) not under MacArthur's authority in the southwest.

The first effective counter-strokes against the Japanese in the Pacific, those at the battles of the Coral Sea in May 1942 and Midway in June, were followed in the southwest Pacific in July and August. Landings then in New Guinea were intended to establish bases for further moves in the islands. They were followed by a combined naval, air, and ground force operation in August to establish positions at Guadalcanal and Tulagi in the Solomon Islands northeast of Australia and east of New Guinea. Six months of bitter fighting followed, especially in Guadalcanal.

Many of the correspondents in Australia reported both actions, while others accredited to the navy observed sea and air campaigns. Vernon A. (Vern) Haugland of the Associated Press took off from Australia in an army bomber on August 7, 1942, to fly to New Guinea to report the fighting then several weeks advanced. The plane was caught in a severe tropical storm, ran out of gasoline, and Haugland and five members of the crew parachuted 13,000 feet into the New Guinea jungle. The party became separated. Four crew members reached Port Moresby in from eight to twenty days. The copilot, Lieutenant James A. Michael, was never found. Haugland spent forty-three days wandering in the jungle, inadequately clothed, soaked by rains, mostly without food, cold at night, and ill with malaria much of the time. Late in September, he was found by missionaries in a native village, delirious, and near death. He was taken to Port Moresby, where he received hospital care and recovered. After a period of convalescence in Australia, he was back in New Guinea as a correspondent in 1943.[9]

While in New Guinea in October 1942 to report action there, Byron Darnton of the *New York Times,* with that paper since 1934, was killed when another U.S. plane mistakenly attacked the plane in which he was a passenger.[10] Edward Widdis, AP Photos, narrowly escaped death in

---

9   A Silver Star for valor was conferred upon Haugland by General MacArthur in the Port Moresby hospital on October 3, 1942. A brochure, *43 Days,* chiefly Haugland's diary kept during his wanderings, was published in a limited edition by Montana State University, his alma mater.

10   Darnton was awarded a Purple Heart, posthumously, in 1945.

New Guinea somewhat earlier when a fragment of a Japanese bomb knocked his camera from his hands. Ian Morrison, the *Times,* and Thomas Fairhall, *Sydney Telegraph,* both suffered wounds. William Boni, AP, was injured in December when thrown from a jeep.

Other correspondents in New Guinea during 1942–43 included many already noted as having been in Australia: Durdin, *New York Times;* Sebring, *New York Herald Tribune;* Kent, *Chicago Times;* Sherrod, *Time;* Van Atta, INS; Guard, UP; Noderer, *Chicago Tribune;* Weller, *Chicago Daily News;* Wilmot, Australian Broadcasting Commission; Strock, *Life;* and Dearing, INP. Later arrivals included Dean Schedler, AP; Patrick Robinson, INS; Robert Cromie, *Chicago Tribune;* John Graham Dowling, *Chicago Sun;* Osmar E. White, *Daily Express;* Barry Young and Hayden Lennard, both of the *Sydney Daily Mirror;* and George H. Johnstone, *Melbourne Argus,* also representing *Time* and *Life* and known for his reporting of desert fighting in North Africa. Two visitors to the battle area were Frank H. Bartholomew, United Press vice-president and manager of the agency's western division in San Francisco, and Barry Faris, INS editor-in-chief, based in New York.

On the very day that Haugland and his companions had parachuted into the New Guinea jungle in August 1942, U.S. Marines made amphibious landings at Guadalcanal and Tulagi. From then until February 9, 1943, there was almost constant fighting between the Japanese and U.S. Marine and army units on the islands. The frequent nightly Japanese air attacks and naval activity were ended in the closing weeks of 1942.

Members of the newly formed Marine combat correspondent group made eye-witness reports of the landings and of subsequent action. The first report came from Lieutenant L. Herbert Merillat, a former Rhodes scholar and a press analyst and adviser to the secretary of the treasury. The second report came from Sergeant James W. Hurlbut, formerly of the *Washington Post* circulation department staff, and of radio station WJSY, Washington. A third report was from Sergeant Edwin J. Burman.

Among press-radio correspondents who went ashore at Guadalcanal during the second wave or soon after were Robert P. ("Pepper") Martin, UP; Richard Tregaskis, INS; Francis L. McCarthy, UP; Sherman (Monty) Montrose, NEA-Acme Newspictures; Ralph Morse, *Life* photographer; and John Graham Dowling, *Chicago Sun.* Others arriving later to report the Guadalcanal-Tulagi conflict included Tom Yarbrough, J. Norman Lodge, and William Hipple, all of the AP; William F. Tyree, UP; Robert Brumby, INS; E. Astley Hawkins, Reuters; Durdin and Foster Hailey, both of the *New York Times;* Cromie, *Chicago Tribune;* and Kent, *Chicago Times.* Still others were Gordon Walker, *Christian Science Monitor;* John Hersey, *Time* and *Life;* Henry W.

(Harry) Keyes, *Daily Express;* Jonathan Rice and Frank Filan, AP Photos; Allan Jackson, INP photographer; and J. A. Brockhurst, News of the Day newsreel cameraman.

Tregaskis, Martin, and Marine Sergeant Hurlbut shared a tent during the months on the island and posted a sign outside designating it as the "Guadalcanal Press Club." This set a precedent followed with appropriate adaptations by correspondents participating in later landings in the Pacific. Martin was the last of the three to leave "Guadal" permanently in March 1943, although he had been relieved temporarily in September-November 1942 by Francis L. McCarthy. A number of correspondents remained on the island for periods of five or six months, including Tregaskis, Martin, and Montrose.[11] Other correspondents went to Guadalcanal in later months to report conditions on the basis of brief visits. One who did so was Mark Hellinger of the *New York Mirror*.

Correspondents with the navy also covered the action off the Solomon Islands. Ralph Morse of *Life,* who had made photos of the August 7 landing at Guadalcanal, lost them when the ship was sunk two days later. Joe James Custer, UP, aboard the cruiser *Astoria* at the time of the landing, was struck by Japanese shell fragments and lost the sight of his left eye. He was awarded the Purple Heart in 1944. Jack Singer, INS, aboard the aircraft carrier *Wasp,* was killed when that ship was torpedoed and sunk during the Solomons battle on September 15. He received the Purple Heart, posthumously. Officers of the ship finished Singer's story of the ship's action, with a full account of the sinking. It was released with a Pearl Harbor dateline on October 27.

Charles H. McMurtry, AP, aboard an aircraft carrier in the Solomons battle of Santa Cruz on October 26 was seriously burned when a Japanese bomber crashed into the ship's signal bridge, spewing flaming gasoline.[12] Ira Wolfert, NANA, reported the fifth battle of the Solomons late in 1942. He was flying over the *President Coolidge,* former Pacific liner converted to use as a troop transport, when it hit a floating mine and sank, but with only four men lost. Wolfert was awarded a Pulitzer Prize for his reports of the Solomons battle. Hanson Baldwin of the *New York Times* also received a Pulitzer award for a series of articles based on his tour of the Solomon Islands area in 1942.

Apart from the Southwest Pacific headquarters in Australia and the Pacific command in Honolulu, a third headquarters was established on

---

11 Tregaskis produced a book, *Guadalcanal Diary* (1943), which was a best seller and the basis for a motion picture. He received the George R. Holmes Award in 1942 and the INS Medal of Honor for Heroic Devotion to Duty, 1942–43.

12 After his recovery, McMurtry became chief of the AP bureau in Honolulu, in charge of coverage of the Pacific area under the Pearl Harbor command of Admiral Nimitz. He was awarded the Purple Heart in May 1945.

January 15, 1942 at Kandy in Ceylon. Known as the Southeast Asia Command (SEAC), its concern was with the China-Burma-India (CBI) theater, and with its authority extending for the time to Malaya, the Netherlands East Indies, and the approaches to Australia. British General Sir Archibald P. Wavell, formerly in Egypt, was in command. In 1943, he was replaced by Admiral Lord Louis Mountbatten, who remained until the end of the war.

In the Burma campaign of early 1942 much of the area was lost to the Japanese by May. It was reported by Leland Stowe, *Chicago Daily News,* one of the first correspondents to arrive, coming from Chungking; by Darrell Berrigan, UP, recovered in Rangoon from illness following his escape from Bangkok ahead of the advancing Japanese; O'Dowd Gallagher, *Daily Express,* after his rescue from the *Repulse* sinking; and by some who had escaped from the Malaya and Singapore areas lost in February.

Others in Burma included Richard Busvine, *Chicago Times;* T. E. A. (Tim) Healy, London *Daily Mirror;* Victor Thompson, *Daily Herald;* Norman Tresham, *Daily Mail;* Philip Jordan and Roderick Macdonald, both of the *News-Chronicle;* William J. Munday, also of the *News-Chronicle* and the *Sydney Morning Herald;* L. Marsland Gander and Martin Moore, *Daily Telegraph;* James Lonsdale Hodson, *Sunday Times* and the Allied Newspapers; Cedric Salter and Wilfred Burchett,[13] both serving the *Daily Express;* Jack Belden, *Time;* John D. Bouwer, Aneta and the *News-Chronicle,* who had escaped from the N.E.I.; and Gordon Waterfield, Reuters. Bouwer and Waterfield were wounded.

Some of the correspondents who had been in Singapore, Malaya, the N.E.I., and Burma escaped to India as the Japanese advanced. Mention has been made in this respect of Durdin, *New York Times;* John R. Morris, UP;[14] and Frank E. Noel, AP Photos. Among those arriving in India from Burma were Busvine, Jordan, Bouwer, and Hodson. Others in India in 1942 included Herbert L. Matthews, *New York Times,* who had covered the war in Ethiopia and the Spanish Civil War; Preston L. Grover, AP; Archibald T. Steele, *Chicago Daily News;* Stuart Emeny, *News-Chronicle;* Stanley Gardiner, Exchange Telegraph; and Raymond Clapper, Scripps-Howard Newspapers syndicated columnist out of Washington. India became an important point for "flying the hump" over the Himalayas on the journey to and from Chungking after flights by way of Hong Kong ended in December 1941.

By the spring of 1943, the war in Europe and Asia was at its general

---

13 He was erroneously bylined as "Peter" Burchett for a time while on his first assignment as a war correspondent.

14 Morris received an "Honor Award for Distinguished Journalism" in 1943 from the University of Missouri, his alma mater.

turning point, even though that was not yet clearly apparent. Until the late autumn of 1942, the Axis partners had had almost uninterrupted success. The Wehrmacht was to make further advances in Russia, but would be rolled far back before the end of 1943. The German submarine weapon had been blunted in the Atlantic. The Luftwaffe was doing less damage, while German cities were receiving return payment for the damage inflicted earlier in Britain. The British Eighth Army was making a decisive drive in Libya and an Allied landing in Algeria in November 1942 drove eastward to meet the westward move of the Eighth Army in Tunisia that would drive Axis forces out of Africa in May 1943 and bring an Italian surrender by September.

In the same period, the Japanese advance in the Pacific and in Asia was halted. United States positions had been established in New Guinea and the Solomons by the end of 1942, and Australia and New Zealand were secure from direct attack.

A new phase in the Pacific war began during the spring of 1943. The fighting was bitter, centering chiefly in the southwest Pacific as U.S. forces attempted further to dislodge Japanese elements while preparing also for the long push aimed at Japan itself. The U.S. naval and air power, so badly crippled in the first attacks of 1941, had been greatly restored. The counteroffensive began in earnest in June 1943, with attacks directed at New Georgia Island, still in the Solomons, on Lae and Salamaua in September, Rabaul in October, and Bougainville, New Britain, Tarawa, and Makin in November. By early 1944, U.S. and Anzak (Australia–New Zealand) forces had established themselves in solid positions to make advances during 1944. Meanwhile, the Japanese were driven out or withdrew from the Aleutian Islands in May 1943, thus removing the threat to Alaska.

The correspondents in the Pacific and elsewhere necessarily depended upon the armed services for transportation, billeting, food, supplies, medical care, and for basic information and communications facilities. Censorship took place either in the field, aboard ships, or at one of the headquarters. Copy to be cleared through navy headquarters at Pearl Harbor arrived by ship and plane. Censorship there was highly organized, as it was also in San Francisco. From the Southeast Asia area in Brisbane, British copy also cleared through London.

General MacArthur held his third news conference at Brisbane on March 17, 1943, a year after his arrival in Australia from the Philippines. This was his first conference since July 19, 1942. Like the other two, it was mostly off the record, but it continued for two hours and included a review of the war situation, followed by numerous questions, which MacArthur answered frankly.

The pattern of the Pacific war was generally established by mid-1943.

Under the general direction of Colonel LeGrande A. Diller, press relations chief for MacArthur, and under Colonel Lloyd Lehrbas at MacArthur's advanced headquarters at Milne Bay, on the eastern tip of New Guinea, every arrangement was made to inform correspondents, to enable them to observe actions, and to handle their copy speedily so that it might be passed through censorship and transmitted to its destination. Courier planes from New Guinea were dispatched to carry copy to points in Australia where telegraphic and radiotelegraphic facilities were fully operative.

Correspondents were accredited in 1943 to one of three U.S. headquarters: U.S. Navy headquarters, under Admiral Nimitz at Honolulu; U.S.–British Commonwealth headquarters for the southwest Pacific at Brisbane, under General MacArthur; or the Southwest Pacific naval headquarters (COMSOPAC), under Admiral William P. Halsey, Jr., at Noumea, New Caledonia, established in March 1943. There Captain Ray Thurber, formerly head of navy public relations in Washington, conducted daily news conferences and provided assistance to correspondents. A fourth headquarters was the CBI southeast Asia command (SEAC) under Admiral Lord Mountbatten at Kandy in Ceylon. A fifth provided accreditation to the Chinese government and an allied U.S. headquarters at Chungking. Some correspondents moved from one command to another, or were accredited to two or more.

The first major operation in the Allied counteroffensive against the Japanese in the Pacific and Asia was an amphibious landing at New Georgia Island in the Solomons on June 30, 1943. A score of correspondents accompanied the military forces. They were selected by lot from among a group of forty or fifty U.S. press-radio representatives, eight or ten British correspondents, and Australian–New Zealand correspondents based at MacArthur's headquarters at Brisbane or Milne Bay.

Marine raiders landed behind Japanese lines before the main offensive. They were accompanied by Walter Farr, *Daily Mail;* Clay Gowran, *Chicago Tribune;* and Gordon Walker, *Christian Science Monitor.* When the main assault occurred, places in the landing craft were occupied by Vern Haugland, AP; William C. Wilson, UP; Art Cohn, INS; Curtis L. Hindson, Reuters; Pendil Raynor, *Brisbane Telegraph;* Mervyn Weston, *Sydney Morning Herald;* Technical Sergeant David G. Richardson, combat correspondent for *Yank,* a U.S. Army publication; Martin Barnett, Paramount Newsreel cameraman; and Frank Bagnall, newsreel cameraman for the Australian Department of Information.

Correspondents with the U.S. naval forces involved in the New Georgia operation included Hal O'Flaherty, active as a correspondent before and during World War I, and former foreign editor and managing editor of the *Chicago Daily News.* For two years since Pearl Harbor, he had been in Washington as special assistant with the rank of Lieutenant Commander to Rear Admiral A. J. Hepburn, director of U.S. Navy public relations. O'Flaherty left Washington and gave up both his military rank and his managing editorship of the paper to return voluntarily to active war coverage.

Others with the naval forces at New Georgia Island included Cromie, *Chicago Tribune;* Dowling, *Chicago Sun;* David Wittels, *Philadelphia Record;* Dixon Brown, London *News-Chronicle;* Norman Brown, photographer for the Australian Department of Information; Harry Summers, representing Australian morning newspapers; Frank Prist, Jr., Acme Newspictures; and Alan Jackson, INP photographer. Jackson was aboard the cruiser *U.S.S. Helena,* sunk in the Battle of Kula Gulf on July 6, but survived. Other correspondents reporting the New Georgia operations in the days following the first assault included John Purcell, *Life;* Edward Wallace, NBC; Frank Smith, *Chicago Sun;* and Peter Hemery, Australian Broadcasting Commission.

In subsequent or coordinating actions, Carl Thusgaard, Danish-born Acme Newspictures photographer, was among those killed in July 1943 when a bomber in which he was flying to record an attack on Madang, off the north coast of New Guinea, was shot down by nine Japanese Zeros. He became the thirteenth correspondent for the U.S. media known to have lost his life while engaged in war coverage, the fifth known fatality to that time in the Pacific area, and the first accredited war photographer to die.

William F. Boni, AP, was one of nine men wounded in an attack in July on a landing barge in Nassau Bay, New Guinea. He was hit by shell fragments but survived, and was the first correspondent in the southwest Pacific to receive the Purple Heart, although others wounded earlier received the same decoration belatedly.

When a combined operations encirclement of Japanese troops occurred in September in the Lae-Salamaua area on the New Guinea coast, a press camp was set up at Milne Bay. A wireless transmitter was moved in from Australia to handle reports by some thirty correspondents. Censorship officers were present, headed by Captain Jerry T. Baulch, formerly of the AP. Some of the group had covered the New Georgia action, but others joined in the campaign.

Among those with land and naval forces were Cromie, *Chicago Tribune;* O'Flaherty, *Chicago Daily News;* Technical Sergeant Richardson, *Yank;* Hemery, Australian Broadcasting Commission; Barnett, Paramount Newsreel; and Summers, representing Australian morning newspapers. Richardson was wounded at Lae, and later was awarded the Legion of Merit. Other correspondents involved were Guard, UP; Morrison, the *Times;* Olen Clements, AP; Myron Davis, *Life;* William Carty and Harold Dick, photographers for the Australian Department of Information; Geoffrey Hutton, Allan Jones, Allan Dawes, and Barry Young, all representing Australian newspapers.

The first Pacific use of paratroopers occurred in the Lae-Salamaua campaign. Eight correspondents accompanied them: Frank Smith, *Chicago Sun;* Raynor, *Brisbane Telegraph;* William Courtnaye, *Daily Sketch* and Allied Newspapers; Jack Turcott, *New York Daily News;* Mervyn Weston, *Sydney Morning Herald;* William Marien, Australian Broadcasting Commission; and Earle Crotchett, Universal Newsreel cameraman. With them went Roy Driver of the Australian Department of Information.

To write eye-witness stories of the landings, as seen from the air, Edward Widdis, AP photographer, was in General MacArthur's personal plane. Others flying in bombers included Haugland, AP, Van Atta, INS, and George Thomas Folster, NBC. Other correspondents participating in the Lae-Salamaua operations included Boni, Schedler, and McDaniel, all of the AP; Taves, UP; Frank Robertson, INS; James Henry, Reuters; and Robert J. Doyle, representing the *Milwaukee Journal* and the *Detroit News.*

Frank Kluckhohn, *New York Times,* who was most recently in North Africa, replaced Durdin in the Southwest Pacific for that paper. Durdin moved to India. Charles Rawlings was present for the *Saturday Evening Post.* Hayden Lennard, Fred Simpson, and Dudley Leggett represented the Australian Broadcasting Commission. Hugh Dash, H. S. Mischael, Geoffrey Reading, Axel Olson, Fred Petrerson, Harry Williams, and James Vines were present for Australian news groups or individual newspapers.

Among correspondents remaining in Brisbane in this September 1943 period were Dixon Brown of the *News-Chronicle* and Edward Wallace of NBC, both of whom had covered the New Georgia operation in June. Others were Lewis Sebring, Jr., *New York Herald Tribune;* William Dunn, CBS; Stanley Quinn, MBS; Nelson Braidwood, *Daily Telegraph;* Mrs. Lorraine Stumm, London *Daily Mirror;* Walter E. Lucas, *Daily Express* and *Christian Science Monitor;* and Mrs. W. E. (Leonore) Lucas, Overseas News Agency (ONA) of New York. M. K. Slosberg was in New Zealand for NBC. These correspondents had occasion to report a visit to Australia and New Zealand by Mrs. Franklin D. Roosevelt.

Correspondents who had covered the New Georgia operation on June 30 had filed 374 messages within the first twelve hours, totalling some 45,700 words—the largest file for any single day up to that time in the Southwest Pacific. During the first twenty-four hours of the Lae-Salamaua action of September 6–7, the file totaled 85,000 words, declined on the second day, and leveled off at about 20,000 words daily for the middle and latter part of September.

The naval and air attacks moved north, with a concerted attack October 12 on the Japanese base at the port of Rabaul, New Britain. The raid involved the first use of fighter-escort planes in the Pacific to protect the bombers and resulted in heavy enemy losses. Kluckhohn of the *New York Times,* who observed from one of the bombers, called it "the greatest blow yet struck anywhere in the Pacific." William C. Wilson, UP, aboard another bomber, had a narrow escape, when the plane was attacked by several Zeros and forced to make a crash landing. Other correspondents on the mission included Boni of the AP, recovered from wounds received in July; Cromie, *Chicago Tribune;* Smith, *Chicago Sun;* Van Atta, INS; and Hemery and Lennard of the Australian Broadcasting Commission.

Allied landings followed at Bougainville, still in the Solomons, on October 31, then in the Gilbert Islands, considerably north, in November, and in the Marshall Islands in February 1944, taking U.S. forces on a course ever nearer to Japan itself.

General MacArthur held a brief news conference on November 3, two days after the attack on Bougainville. Among correspondents who had covered that operation were George E. Jones, UP, who was about to earn the nickname of "First Wave Jones" through participation in a series of landings; Frank Tremaine, James E. Lowery, and Francis L. McCarthy, all of the UP; Rembert (Jimmy) James and Fred E. Hampson, AP; Patrick Robinson, INS; Gordon Walker, *Christian Science Monitor;* and Keith Palmer, a New Zealander representing both the *Melbourne Herald* and *Newsweek.* Palmer was killed when a Japanese bomb exploded nearby. James of the AP was wounded at the same time. He was later awarded both a Purple Heart and a Silver Star.

Following up the Rabaul attack, U.S. forces returned in November to the island of New Britain, where they established a beachhead and won full control before the end of December. Robert Eunson, AP, and Ralph Teatsorth, UP, waded ashore in the first wave. Other correspondents reporting the action included "First Wave" Jones and Wilson, UP; Boni, Schedler, McDaniel, Murlin Spencer, and Asahel ("Ace") Bush, all of the AP; Van Atta, INS; Hemery, formerly of the Australian Broadcasting Commission but transferred to INS; Cromie, *Chicago Tribune;* Kluckhohn, *New York Times;* and Turcott, *New York Daily News.* Others were Howard M. Norton, *Baltimore Sun;* Cletus (Clete) Roberts, Blue Network (NBC); Thomas L. Shafer, NEA-Acme Newspictures; and Gary Sheahan, an artist for the *Chicago Tribune.*

Two correspondents were killed when the plane in which they intended to watch a Marine landing on New Britain, crashed during a take-off in New Guinea. These were Pendil Raynor of the *Brisbane Telegraph* and Brydon C. Taves, UP manager in Australia. Taves was previously in London for the agency during the 1940 blitz, and was a participant in Lae-Salamaua operation in September.

The major central Pacific operation in the Gilbert Islands began November 22, 1943, with navy and marine forces concentrating on Japanese positions at Tarawa and Makin islands. Whereas the other island attacks had stemmed from Australia and New Guinea under MacArthur's command, the Gilbert Islands attack was directed from the Pacific headquarters of Admiral Nimitz at Pearl Harbor. Commander William Waldo Drake, formerly of the *Los Angeles Times* and a member of Nimitz's headquarters staff, arranged for the accommodation of twenty-seven correspondents accompanying the task force and for handling their copy, all of which had to be sent by plane or ship to Pearl Harbor for censorship and transmission. In addition, about thirty-five Marine Corps combat correspondents and photographers covered the landings. Appropriate to the size of the operation itself, more correspondents were involved than for any previous move in the Pacific.

Japanese resistance in the islands was largely overcome in the first three days, but involved some of the bloodiest fighting of the war, especially in the landing at Tarawa and the capture of the island. One of the most vivid eye-witness accounts of that landing came from Technical Sergeant James G. (Jim) Lucas, combat correspondent with the Second Marine Division and formerly of the *Tulsa Tribune*.[15] Combat correspondent Lieutenant Ernest Matthews, Jr., formerly a *Dallas Morning News* reporter, was killed. First Lieutenant John N. Popham, formerly of the *New York Times,* and First Lieutenant Earl J. Wilson, formerly of the *Washington Post,* both Marine Corps public relations officers, helped direct marine combat correspondents and photographers. A Marine Corps photographer was killed in the landing and an artist was wounded.

Some correspondents who had been at Guadalcanal in 1942, and others who had covered action in the southwest Pacific, also reported the Gilbert Islands attack. Among those who went ashore with the marines at Tarawa were Keith Wheeler, *Chicago Times;* Harold ("Smitty" or "Hal") Smith, *Chicago Tribune;* Robert Sherrod, *Time;* Henry W. Keyes, *Daily Express;* Horace D. ("Doc") Quigg and Richard W. Johnston, both of UP.[16] William Hipple, AP, and Frank Filan, AP photographer;[17] and Langdon V. ("Don") Senick, Fox Movietone News cameraman.

---

15 Lucas was awarded a Bronze Star in April 1944, and also was recognized by the Headliners' Club with a prize for the best combat reporting of 1943.

16 Johnston received a citation from Major General Julian C. Smith, commander of the 2nd Marine Division, commending him for "bravery and efficient service under extraordinary conditions of combat." The citation was presented to Johnston by Admiral Nimitz.

17 Filan was awarded the Pulitzer Prize for newspaper photography in 1944 for his photograph of the previous year entitled "Tarawa Island." Filan, in the first assault, in

Other correspondents covering the Tarawa and Makin actions included Bernard J. McQuaid, *Chicago Daily News;* John R. Henry and Richard V. Haller, INS; Wendell ("Leif") Erickson, William L. Worden and Eugene Burns, all of the AP; Clarence Hamm, AP Photos; Charles Arnot, UP; and Archer Thomas, *Melbourne Sun News-Pictorial.* Raymond Coll, Jr., was present for the *Honolulu Advertiser,* while Robert Trumbull, former city editor of that paper, was representing the *New York Times.* John D. Beaufort represented the *Christian Science Monitor,* Frank Morris, *Collier's,* and John Floreo, was a photographer for *Life.* Corporal Larry McManus represented *Yank,* and Sergeant John Bushemi was a photographer for that army publication. W. Eugene Smith was a photographer for the Ziff-Davis Publications, New York, Gilbert Bundy an artist for the King Features Syndicate, and Kerr Eby an artist for the Association of American Artists.

Handling the story from Pearl Harbor and Honolulu were Joseph Driscoll, *New York Herald Tribune;* George F. Horne, *New York Times;* William F. Tyree and Malcolm R. ("Mac") Johnson of UP; Charles H. McMurtry, AP; Clinton Greene, INS, who had been in North Africa and Sicily for that agency before moving to the Pacific; Bernard Clayton, *Time* and *Life;* Webley Edwards, CBS; and James Wahl, NBC.

Events on the periphery of the Pacific also were important during 1943 and received news attention. Accompanying the U.S. naval and air expedition in the late spring of 1943 to the Aleutian Islands, which the Japanese abandoned by May, were Keith Wheeler, *Chicago Times;* Sherman Montrose, NEA-Acme Newspictures, who broke a leg;[18] Frank H. Bartholomew, UP vice-president in charge of the Pacific area, with Russell Annabel and James A. McLean, both also of the UP; Eugene Burns and William L. Worden, AP; Clarence Hamm, AP Photos; Howard Handleman, INS; Foster Hailey, *New York Times;* Robert Sherrod, *Time;* and Charles Perryman, News of the Day newsreel cameraman.

Morley Cassidy of the *Philadelphia Bulletin* went to Alaska in June to do a series of articles, while John Tresilian, *New York Daily News* photographer, made a series of photos there shortly before. William Gilman, NANA, and Wilson Foster, NBC, were others in Alaska in 1943.

---

turning to help a Marine who had been shot, lost his cameras in the heavy surf. On the third day, he was able to borrow a camera and made the prize-winning photo.

18   Montrose, hospitalized for a month, won a special citation from the secretary of war for maintaining order among green troops landing at Attu in 1942. The explosion of a phosphorus shell nearby led some soldiers to believe the Japanese were loosing a poison gas attack. They were prepared to return to their landing craft when Montrose boomed that it was not gas and turned them back to the attack.

Panama and the Canal Zone provided a strategic gateway to and from the Pacific and were strongly defended. Although not consistently covered for news, correspondents visiting the area included Vaughn Bryant, AP; Nat Barrows, *Chicago Daily News;* Richard Armstrong, INS; Fred Parker, INP photographer; and Peter Brennan, NBC.

The China-Burma-India theater saw hard campaigning during 1943. Troops fought Japanese in the jungle and fought nature to keep supplies flowing to China by air over the "hump," after the Burma Road was closed off in mid-1942. Correspondents moved to and from Chungking by way of India and Burma.

Correspondents covering the Burma front in 1943 included Martin Herlihy, Reuters; Alaric Jacob, formerly in Cairo for Reuters, who moved to the *Daily Express* early in 1942; Stuart Wallis Emeny, *News-Chronicle,* formerly in Egypt and the Middle East for that paper, and a correspondent there during the Italo-Ethiopian War; Graham Stanford, *Daily Mail,* formerly at Gibraltar; Jack Potter, *Daily Sketch* and Allied Newspapers; and Preston L. Grover, Thoburn H. ("Toby") Wiant, Frank L. Martin, Jr., H. R. Stimson, and Clyde A. Farnsworth, all represented AP, some formerly in Chungking; Frank Hewlett, Darrell Berrigan, Albert Ravenholt and Walter Briggs, all for the UP; Eric Sevareid, represented both CBS and UP; and Robert Bryant was an INP photographer.

Sevareid's visit to Burma was unscheduled and occurred when he was on a flight from India to Chungking. The plane's engine failed and, along with other passengers, he parachuted into the jungle. They emerged to safety only after a long and difficult trek. Walter Briggs, UP, was wounded early in the year while with British forces in the front lines.

In India, giving attention to affairs in New Delhi and to the Burma campaign, there were Alan Humphreys, Reuters, formerly in North Africa; Wilfred Burchett and Ian Fitchett, *Daily Express;* Martin Moore and Frank Moraes, Indian journalist stationed in Bombay, both for the *Daily Telegraph;* and Stanley Wills, formerly at Allied Force headquarters in Algiers, and Victor Thompson, formerly in Cairo, both for the *Daily Herald.* Ian Lang represented the *Sunday Times* and the Kemsley Newspapers. Herbert L. Matthews wrote for the *New York Times* until replaced later in the year by F. Tillman Durdin, who returned to India from the Southwest Pacific. John R. Morris was in India as Far Eastern representative of the UP. On the way to India to paint war scenes, Lucien Adolph Labaudt, French-born artist for *Life,* was killed December 13, 1943, along with eleven others, when their plane crashed in Assam, near the India-Burma border.

The shifting of some correspondents to new areas during the winter of 1942–43 continued as 1943 passed into 1944. Some U.S. representatives who had been in the Pacific for months returned to the mainland, at least temporarily. Among them were Robert Cromie, *Chicago Tribune;* Francis L. McCarthy, UP; Arthur Burgess, AP; James G. (Jim) Lucas, promoted to Master Technical Sergeant as a combat correspondent in the Marine Corps; and several other combat correspondents and photographers who had reported the Gilbert Islands operations.

At the same time, others took new assignments in the Pacific. William Dickinson succeeded Brydon Taves as UP manager for the Pacific, with headquarters at Honolulu rather than Brisbane. Taves was killed in December at New Britain. Daniel F. McGuire also arrived in the Pacific theater for the UP. Elmont Waite reached the Pacific for the AP, balancing the resignation of William Hipple, who became a correspondent for *Newsweek*. Leonard E. Welch arrived as a correspondent for the Cowles papers, the *Des Moines Register* and *Tribune* and the *Minneapolis Star and Tribune*. In the spring of 1944, the Honolulu group was joined by Peggy Hull. She was one of the very few women correspondents in Pacific and Asian war coverage, and wrote for the *Cleveland Plain Dealer* and the NANA.[19]

---

19   Peggy Hull had represented the NEA on the Mexican border in 1916, at the time of the U.S. punitive expedition into that country. She had been in France in 1917–18 and had accompanied the American Army Expeditionary Force in Siberia in 1919–20, after which she had worked in China for a time as a correspondent. Then Mrs. Henrietta Eleanor Goodnough Kinley, she used "Peggy Hull" as her pseudonym. In 1932 she returned to China to cover the Chinese-Japanese conflict in Manchuria and Shanghai, representing the *Chicago Tribune* and *New York Daily News* organization. She was remarried in 1933 to Harvey V. Deuell, editorial executive of the *Daily News*. His death occurred in 1939.

Great Britain and her Commonwealth associates stood alone against German and Italian attacks from June 1940 until late 1942. Soviet Russia, invaded by the Wehrmacht in June 1941, became an ally but remained concerned with her own defense. The same was true of the United States, brought into the war as an ally in December 1941.

Soviet resistance to the German invasion was greater than Berlin had anticipated. This reduced the pressure upon Britain, while the U.S. alliance provided lend-lease aid and support at sea. It was November 1942 before the United States was able to mount a counteroffensive in North Africa to help divert pressure on the British army in Egypt, and not until 1943 was the USSR capable of a strong counteroffensive against the Nazis in Europe. During this time, limited British resources had to be stretched to provide support for Russia and to defend newly threatened areas in East Asia and the Pacific under Japanese attack. To make matters worse, German submarines took enormous toll of shipping throughout the Atlantic and Caribbean, from the shores of the Western Hemisphere to Great Britain, to Soviet Russia, and to the entrance to the Mediterranean at Gibraltar.

The U.S. Navy had instituted a wartime Atlantic patrol in 1939–40, and it was greatly strengthened after Pearl Harbor in a close association with the British navy. Two U.S. correspondents bound from New York to South Africa happened to be in the Egyptian motorship *Zamzam,* which was sunk by a German raider in the South Atlantic in April 1941 and the passengers taken aboard the raider. Correspondents David Scherman, *Life* photographer, and Charles J. V. Murphy, *Fortune,* were flown back to New York in June. Scherman brought four rolls of exposed film he had managed to smuggle through German control, although his cameras and 104 other rolls of film were confiscated. Murphy wrote the full story of the sinking of the *Zamzam,* and Scherman's photos were available for publication.

The U.S. Navy had undertaken to protect the Danish territories of

Iceland and Greenland after Germany occupied Denmark in May 1940. The navy increased its efforts after April 1941. In May, the British navy sank the German battleship *Bismarck,* but Britain lost its own battle-cruiser, *Hood.* Every means was sought to counter German submarines and land-based planes attacking Allied ships in the Atlantic. Not until 1943 was the threat substantially reduced, but even then the Battle of the Atlantic actually continued until the end of the war in Europe.

The German battleship *Tirpitz* was put out of action in September 1943 by British midget submarines in Norway's Aalten Fjord where that great ship was sheltered. It then was bombed several times while undergoing repairs, and finally was sunk by RAF bombers in November 1944. Another German battleship, the *Scharnhorst,* had been sunk in November 1943, reducing the threat particularly to convoys bound for Murmansk.

British and U.S. correspondents were aboard vessels of both navies operating in the Atlantic, the Mediterranean, and the Pacific. Arthur Oakshott, Reuters, was with Arctic convoys to Soviet Russia in 1942 and 1943. Walter Cronkite, UP, was the only newsman aboard the U.S. naval transport *Wakefield,* burned and sunk in the North Atlantic early in 1942. Clinton Beach (Pat) Conger, with the UP staff in London since repatriation after his arrest in Berlin in December 1941, was named in October 1942 as the first U.S. correspondent accredited to the British Home Fleet, which previously accredited only Reuters correspondents. His dispatches were shared with the AP and INS. In February 1943, he was replaced by Alfred Edward Wall, AP, followed in July by John Edgerton Lee, INS, and by Leo S. Disher, Jr., UP, in January 1944. Disher had recovered from wounds suffered in the Allied North African landings of November 1942.

Martin Sheridan, *Boston Globe,* was assigned to a U.S. Coast Guard cutter on Greenland patrol in 1944. He also wrote a series of articles on Greenland itself. Thomas R. Henry, *Washington Star,* reported U.S. naval activities both in the North and South Atlantic.[1]

Aside from traveling aboard ships in convoy, or ships depending on their speed and evasive action to escape submarine dangers while running alone, some correspondents made special voyages with commando groups raiding enemy-held territory.

Perhaps the first British commando action occurred in September 1941 when a raid was made on the German-held island of Spitzbergen in

---

1   A German submarine shelled the Dutch island of Aruba, a source of oil, off the coast of Venezuela, on the night of February 19, 1942. One shell passed through a building where five U.S. correspondents were sleeping. They were Nat A. Barrows, *Chicago Daily News;* Frank Smith, *Chicago Tribune;* Chandler Diehl, AP; J. Rufus Hardy, *New York Times;* and Walter Davenport, *Collier's.*

the Arctic, adjacent to Norway. Ross Munro of the Canadian Press accompanied the force. His story was cleared through the British Ministry of Information and made available to the entire press, along with photographs.

A secret semi-commando action by Free French representatives in Canada occurred late in December 1941, when the small Vichy French islands of St. Pierre and Miquelon, just off the south coast of Newfoundland, were seized in a peaceful and unopposed occupation. In a plebiscite the residents indicated their solidarity with the Free French under DeGaulle.

At about the same time, British commando forces landed on December 27, 1941, at Vaagso, in German-occupied Norway. They were accompanied by Ralph Walling, Reuters, and by British army and War Office photographers, who made some remarkable pictures of the raid. Among them were Jack Ramsden, formerly of Movietone News, and Lieutenant A. G. Malindine, formerly with the *Daily Mirror, Picture Post,* and *Illustrated.*

Earlier visits to Iceland by correspondents from New York and London were followed by visits to the U.S. Army base established there to supplement the navy. The base was visited early in 1942 by Phillip H. Ault, UP; Leo Branham, AP; William Wade, INS; and Bjorn Bjornson, NBC.

A British paratroop raid on Bruneval on the French coast in February 1942 was covered for the world press by Alan Humphreys, Reuters; L. A. Puttnam, official War Office photographer; and J. Edmonds, Gaumont British newsreel cameraman. A British naval raid directed against German installations at the French port of St. Nazaire in late March 1942 put a dry dock out of operation. This action was covered by Edward J. (Ted) Gilling and Gordon Holman, both of Exchange Telegraph (Extel). John Allan May, formerly of the London bureau of the *Christian Science Monitor,* participated in the raid as an officer in the Royal Navy. A British commando raid on Boulogne during June 1942 was covered by Ronald Maillard ("Ronny") Stead of the *Christian Science Monitor* London bureau.

These 1942 raids on Bruneval, St. Nazaire, and Boulogne were preliminary to a heavy cross-channel attack on the night of August 18, 1942, directed at German positions in and near the port of Dieppe. More than 10,000 British and Canadian commando forces took part in the action, plus some Fighting French and a battalion of U.S. Rangers. Known as Operation Jubilee, and under the command of Admiral Lord Louis Mountbatten, it had support and assistance from the Royal Navy and from the RAF, with 1,000 planes in the air. The objective was to test German defenses along the French coast, to destroy certain installations, and to capture prisoners for questioning. The landings were made, and a nine-hour battle followed on a ten-mile shore front. The operation was a success, but at considerable cost in men and materiel, including tanks that had been landed but were deliberately destroyed at the time of withdrawal.

This expedition was both dramatic and significant and referred to as an "invasion rehearsal." It was covered by twenty-two correspondents. Ross Munro, Canadian Press, produced a classic of combat reporting on the action by Canadian forces penetrating more than three miles inland. Drew Middleton, AP, represented the Association of American Correspondents in London, with a "pool" account. G. L. (Larry) Meier represented INS; Quentin Reynolds, *Collier's* and the *Daily Express;* Alan Humphreys, Reuters; Robert Bowman, the Canadian Broadcasting Corporation; John MacVane, NBC; Wallace (Mac) Reyburn, New Zealand-born London correspondent, and Fred Griffin, the *Montreal Star*. British-born Gault MacGowan, a captain of Indian cavalry during World War I, represented the *New York Sun;* Frank Gillard, BBC; A. B. Gilliard, air correspondent and war commentator, and A. B. Austin, the *Daily Herald;* and W. T. Cranfield, the *Toronto Evening Telegram.*

Munro, Reyburn, and Meier went ashore at Dieppe with troops in the first wave. Reyburn was wounded by shrapnel while in the landing barge, and Meier was cut in the face and chest by shrapnel.[2] Brigadier W. W. Southam, one of the officers on the raid, and vice-president of the Southam Newspapers in Canada, was captured. Major Clifford Wallace, press relations officer for the Canadian forces, and former managing editor of the *Toronto Globe and Mail,* was in charge of the newsmen participating in the landing.

Vichy and Unoccupied France

Under the terms of its surrender to Germany in June 1940, France was permitted to maintain a government and a so-called "free zone" in the south of France, unoccupied by German forces. It extended roughly from the Spanish border in the west, about as far north as Tours, running slightly southeastward to the Swiss border near Geneva, and then south to the Italian border.

Germany exercised the right of an occupying power in all of France

---

2   Meier was returned to the United States for hospitalization, and later awarded the Purple Heart. After recovery, he joined the staff of *Look* magazine.

north of that line, by far the larger part of the country, and southward along the Atlantic coast to the Spanish border. The authority of the German government and its administrative arm in Paris could be extended to the Free Zone, under the armistice agreement, but the fiction of an independent government was maintained until November 1942, when the German occupation was extended to the area. The Free Zone was administered until that time by Marshal Henri-Philippe Pétain, one of France's great military figures of World War I, ambassador to Spain in 1939–40, and successor to Paul Reynaud as premier just before the surrender in June.

The new government was established July 2 at Vichy, a resort city of 25,000 population, but soon to become a greatly overcrowded place of 110,000. As chief of state, Marshal Pétain had his headquarters at the Hotel du Parc. Pierre Laval, who had been premier in 1931–32 and in 1935–36, and had served in a number of cabinets, became vice-premier until December 1940, when he was succeeded by Pierre Etienne Flandin, also with cabinet experience. Laval returned to the vice-premiership in April 1942, and Pétain appointed him his successor as premier of France in November of that year. Laval then converted his near-dictatorship since April into a rule directed by the German occupation authorities.

The Vichy government had undertaken to exercise control over France's colonies and mandated areas, over a small military force at home, and over elements of the French navy, wherever located. This was not wholly successful, but it was sufficiently so prior to November 1942 to give meaning to the Vichy regime. Apart from the pressure from Germany, Japan as an Axis member gained an almost enforced Vichy assent to make French Indo-China a military base to be used against China in 1940 and, after December 1941, a base for the Japanese campaign in southeast Asia and the Pacific.

Vichy also was under British pressure to prevent German military power from gaining control over the French mideastern mandated areas of Lebanon and Syria. Of even more immediate concern to the British was the control of French naval vessels. Many were in Toulon, Oran, Dakar, and other ports. When the French naval commanders felt compelled to abide by orders of the Vichy government rather than yielding their ships to the British or scuttling them, the British responded at Oran by firing upon the ships.

France's General Charles DeGaulle formed a government-in-exile in England and later a provisional government in Algiers. He was able also to rally a Free French, or Fighting French military force. With the British, he attempted to establish control where possible, but loyalties were greatly mixed. The effort failed at Oran and at Dakar, in French West Africa, but succeeded in the islands of St. Pierre and Miquelon, off

Newfoundland, and was notably successful in the general Allied landing in North Africa in November 1942.

The actions at Oran, Dakar, and Alexandria in 1940 virtually forced the Vichy regime to yield to Axis demands for a more positive collaboration. This included the use of French air bases and those French enlisted men remaining in North Africa and in Syria to support Axis designs. Vichy planes bombed Gibraltar, as one result.

Even as the French government left Paris in June 1940, moving first to Tours, then to Bordeaux, to Clermont-Ferrand, and finally to Vichy, it was accompanied by French and foreign press-radio representatives. At Tours on June 13, Vice-Minister Laval of the Council of Ministers assumed control of all information services, and retained that control through December. Even afterward as vice-premier and particularly as chief of government, he continued to exert influence on the press and its contents. Laval himself owned *Le Moniteur,* of Clermont-Ferrand and soon gained control of *Le Lyon Républicaine* of Lyon.

Clermont-Ferrand and Lyon, like Vichy, were within the unoccupied Free Zone in 1940–42. Dailies in that area of France also included such other major newspapers as *Le Progrès de Lyon, Le Petit Marseillais, La Depêche de Toulouse, Le Petit Niçois* of Nice, and *Le Petite Gironde* of Bordeaux.

Some dailies formerly published in Paris undertook to establish themselves in cities in the unoccupied zone. This was difficult, and few succeeded. Among those appearing for a time were, *Paris-Soir, Le Petit Parisien, L'Oeuvre, Le Journal, l'Action Française, Le Journal des Débats, Le Jour-l'Echo de Paris, Le Figaro,* and a version of *Le Temps,* published as *Le Nouveaux Temps.*[3]

During the first ten days of the French government's presence in Vichy in 1940, the only foreign correspondents in the new center were U.S. media representatives, most of whom had followed the government on its moves from Paris. These correspondents included John Lloyd, Lloyd Lehrbas, and L. M. Nevin, all for the AP; Ralph Heinzen and Percy Noël, UP; Percy Philip, Lansing Warren, Daniel Brigham, and Gaston H. Archambault, *New York Times;* Paul Ghali, *Chicago Daily News;* John Elliott, *New York Herald Tribune;* David Darrah, *Chicago Tribune;* Arno Dosch-Fleurot, *Christian Science Monitor;* Paul Archinard, NBC; Charles Michaelis, Benjamin Branjon, and James King, AP-Wide World Photos. King later represented Transradio Press as well.

---

3 Dailies that continued to appear in Paris under the German occupation were denied the right to publish after the war, judged to have become collaborationist because they had been permitted to exist.

Diplomatic representatives of other countries also appeared in Vichy. This was a further reason to extend regular news coverage, and a reason for the French newspaper press to resume, even under difficulties. Other correspondents then also moving to Vichy included Robert Okin, AP bureau chief, with Roy Porter, Taylor Henry, and Mel Most as staffers; Kenneth T. Downs and Herbert G. King, UP; Jay Allen, NANA; Philip Whitcomb, *Baltimore Sun;* and Thérèse Bonney, photographer and writer for *Collier's.* Roger Vaucher, a Swiss newsman, some Italian journalists, and a number representing DNB and German newspapers also were in Vichy.

Official information offices were opened by the French Ministry of Information at the Hotel de la Paix. U.S. correspondents had a press room on the floor below. Correspondents could obtain some information from the ministry, and three news conferences were held each day, one for representatives of the French press, one for German and Italian correspondents, and a third for correspondents of other countries.

Instructions were given at the daily conference on what the French press and radio might report and in what manner. Known as "steering notes," these instructions came until December from Laval's office. To assure variety of treatment, they were marked "not to be published in this form." As in Italy and Germany, where the same effort for variety was made, caution induced editors to hold so closely to the approved line that there was great similarity. In the circumstances, the press was dull, circulations shrank, and some papers ceased to exist, partly for that reason.

Some news did not appear because of censorship, with German officers among the censors. The first censor for foreign correspondents' dispatches was a priest, the Reverend Pierre David, but he soon had a considerable group of assistants. There was much complaint concerning the rulings of individual censors. At the outset, only German war communiqués could be used; later Italian and even British communiqués might be used, but with some risk. Laval early told representatives of the French press that "from now on, you will all have to obey orders. If you don't, you will suffer the consequences. I will not stand for any opposition. You might as well make up your minds to it." Most French journalists resented the restrictions, disliked Laval, and were instrumental in having him removed in December 1940 as vice-premier, so ending temporarily his control of information. Even so, the degree of freedom accorded the French media remained almost nil, the foreign press was under censorship, and Laval returned in April 1942 with even greater power.

Flandin, who succeeded Laval as vice-premier and also as minister of foreign affairs, directed the information services in the intervening

1940–42 period. No opposition press was permitted in the Free Zone. Editorial articles, traditional in the French press, were largely abandoned except as they might deal with collaborationist themes, such as "moral and economic reorientation" of individuals or a "return to the soil." Swiss newspapers reached some parts of the Free Zone, eagerly sought and read even at triple the cost of the zone papers, because they were more informative, but they were blocked off after October 1942.

The position of the papers in the Free Zone might have been still more difficult had it not been for the influence of Marshal Pétain. Flandin also informed correspondents in February 1941 that they need no longer submit copy for advance censorship. But they were warned that any indiscretion would subject them to possible expulsion. This type of responsibility censorship did not continue for long. No correspondent was expelled, but four U.S. media representatives did have encounters with the authorities.

John Elliott of the *New York Herald Tribune* was under suspicion for ten days and denied all communications rights, presumably because he had suggested in a dispatch that France was seeking another Jeanne d'Arc to drive out Nazi collaborators. Another correspondent was barred from Vichy for three days because he objected to the posting of a large lithograph of Pétain in the U.S. correspondents' newsroom. Pétain himself learned of this, took personal offense, and only the intercession of the U.S. Embassy saved the correspondent from expulsion. The lithograph remained. A third correspondent also narrowly escaped expulsion because of a dispatch reporting the death of French Marshal General Charles Léon Clement Huntziger, who had headed the French delegation signing armistice terms with the Germans and the Italians in June 1940. The dispatch suggested that Huntziger had been responsible for the German breakthrough in the Sedan area in May 1940.

The most serious situation affecting the correspondents concerned Jay Cooke Allen of NANA and earlier of the *Chicago Tribune*. He had been in Vichy, where he talked with Pétain and with General Maxim Weygand, commander of what remained of French military forces. He also had been in French North Africa. In January 1941, along with Kenneth Downs, INS, Allen crossed the line between the Free Zone into the occupied zone of France. Neither had a pass authorizing them to do so, but they reached Paris and remained there undetected for a week. Downs then returned to Vichy by the same route, but soon left officially for Lisbon, proceeded to England, and then went to the Middle East. Allen remained in the occupied zone until March. On his return to Vichy, he was apprehended and sentenced to four months in prison for crossing the line without authorization. Two weeks to a month would have been more normal for such an offense, but the Vichy government also charged that he had stolen documents "affecting the security of the French State." Allen had, in fact, bought photostatic copies of police reports on DeGaullist and Communist activities in France from a Hungarian journalist, paying the equivalent of about twelve dollars. The Hungarian journalist also was jailed.

Allen was held for a time in a military prison at Chalon-sur-Saône, and then transferred to another military prison at Dijon. Both were in the occupied zone and Allen said later that he was able to get much more information about German-occupied France, particularly at Dijon, than he could have obtained anywhere else because prisoners were brought there from various parts of the country, and also from Belgium and Holland. In July 1941, Allen was released and returned to the United States, along with Richard Hottellet, UP, who had been arrested in Berlin in March 1941 and held in prisons there. Hotellet had done nothing to warrant arrest, but both men were exchanged for the directors of the German Transozean news service in New York, Dr. Manfred Zapp and Guenther Tonn. They were arrested there in March for failure to register with the Department of State as agents of a foreign government.

Legal permission to cross the line between the Vichy free zone and occupied France was virtually impossible to obtain, which explained the Allen-Downs evasion, and there were restrictions on travel even in the Free Zone itself. It was difficult also to obtain direct contact with responsible officials of the Vichy government. Almost the only exception was an exclusive interview with Laval obtained in May 1941 by Ralph Heinzen, UP bureau head, who had known Laval for a decade.

The Vichy censorship forbade any reference to Pétain personally, except as relating to his activities as chief of state. Nothing was to be sent that might be interpreted as endangering the safety of the state, or that bore upon Vichy's relations with the German government or its occupation authorities, much less anything even remotely critical of the occupation itself. The Vichy restrictions were complicated by the fact that they actually represented a double censorship, one from the Vichy-French point of view, the other from the German occupation administration viewpoint.

Until Press Wireless was able to obtain the right to set up a transmitter in the Vichy area, dispatches were sent to the United States by slow and indirect relays, or were telephoned from Vichy to Berne, and dispatched from Switzerland by radiotelegraph. With the exception of a very few Swiss and Swedish correspondents in Vichy, reports reaching the world from that area possessing any objectivity came from the U.S. correspondents.

Since the United States was not at war with Vichy France, even after

December 1941, correspondents for the U.S. media were able to remain. The German occupation administration in France, citing what it called "tendentious reports," brought pressure on the Pétain government to have them expelled. This was not done, but the government did exclude four U.S. correspondents from covering trials conducted at Riom, near Vichy, in February 1942, by which the French sought to assess responsibility for the nation's military collapse in 1940. The trials were suspended before any conclusions were reached. The four correspondents barred were Heinzen, UP; Paul Ghali, *Chicago Daily News;* Mel Most, AP; and James King, AP-Wide World Photos and Transradio Press. Four others were admitted, however: Herbert G. King, UP; Lansing Warren and Gaston H. Archambault, *New York Times;* and Paul Archinard, NBC. The Vichy government also yielded to German pressure in September 1942 by warning U.S. correspondents that they would be liable to expulsion for sending "mendacious messages."

The difficulties of coverage had increased since the summer of 1941. The effectiveness of the Free French, or Fighting French, under General DeGaulle exercised increasing influence from that time. The authority of the Vichy government also was contested by British military forces in Syria and Lebanon, in the Canadian and West Indies areas, and in French North Africa. Vichy's authority collapsed completely in French Morocco and Algeria after the Allied landings there in November 1942. On November 11, three days after the landings, the German occupation of France was extended to include the Free Zone.

Nine U.S. correspondents still remaining in Vichy were arrested and interned. They were Ralph Heinzen and Herbert King of the UP; James King, of AP-Wide World Photos; Mel Most, Taylor Henry and Philip Whitcomb, all of the AP; Lansing Warren, *New York Times;* David Darrah, *Chicago Tribune;* and Arno Dosch-Fleurot, *Christian Science Monitor.*[4] These men, some with wives and families, were taken to Bad Nauheim, Germany where Berlin correspondents had been interned from December 1941 until June 1942. The Vichy group was held there for sixteen months, until repatriated in April 1944. Whatever news of occupied France reached the world after November 1942 and until liberation came either through official German sources or from the French underground.

The French government was moved by the Nazis from Vichy to Garmisch, Germany, with Marshal Pétain and most members established there. A French government committee also was established at Belfort,

---

4 Sisley Huddleston, Paris correspondent for the *Christian Science Monitor* from 1924, had become increasingly an apologist during the 1930s for the Fascist dictators in Europe, and he came to a parting of the ways with the *Monitor* in 1939. He remained in France and was in the Free Zone after 1940. Huddleston broadcast in support of the Pétain government and the Nazis. See Erwin D. Canham, *Commitment to Freedom* (1958), pp. 212–15.

France, near the borders both of Germany and Switzerland. Headed by Fernand de Brinon, its object was to facilitate German administration in France.[5]

After the armistice, news originating in Paris and occupied France began to reach the world, directly or indirectly, through the German official news agency, DNB, by way of Berlin. Newspapers in occupied France also began to receive service from DNB, but soon also through new agencies set up in France under German superivision.

All existing French news services were suspended when the German army entered Paris. The Agence Havas, with its offices and radio transmitting equipment, was seized. Its advertising division was continued separately under the Havas name. The news function was carried on at first through an office in Lyon in the Free Zone. The service was directed to the press in unoccupied France, but distributed also by shortwave radio to former Havas subscribers in Latin America, Switzerland, Spain, and Portugal. It was obliged to accept German guidance, which made its propaganda content so obvious that it had no acceptance, and was soon suspended. This ended the Havas name in the news field.

The former Havas agency was reorganized in a manner not publicly announced until June 1, 1941, in a report from Vichy. The change involved a stock-splitting arrangement where the total number of shares was increased to 162 million, and the value of each share reduced to 250 francs. Of the total, 438,000 shares were reserved to the French state at Vichy and taken over at par value. Although the advertising service retained the Havas name, the news service was assigned to a new Vichy-based agency, the Service Officiel de Nouvelles (Official News Service). This was supplanted almost immediately, under a decree of December 20, 1940, by an Office Française d'Information (OFI).

Made operative January 27, 1941, the OFI was the official agency of

---

5   In March 1945, Marshal Pétain left Germany in what was interpreted by some as "an escape" and went to neutral Switzerland. By that time, France was liberated and Germany was within two months of surrender. The Swiss government turned Pétain over to the new DeGaulle government of France in April 1945, and he was tried during July-August. An original charge of treason and a sentence of death was reduced, on a jury recommendation of clemency, to intelligence with the enemy and life imprisonment. Pétain died in 1951, aged ninety-five.

Pierre Laval had gone to Spain. After the German surrender, he flew to Austria and surrendered to the U.S. Army, which turned him over to French authorities on August 1, 1945. He was executed for treason in October 1945. DeBrinon also was executed for treason on April 15, 1947.

the Vichy government. It collected and distributed news in the Free Zone, supplemented by news provided by DNB, Stefani, and Domei, the three Axis agencies. Charles Houssaye, general manager of the old Agence Havas, had resigned and retired. Henri Mourchet was director-general of the OFI, replaced later by Jean Fontenoy, formerly Havas correspondent in Shanghai and Moscow.

A second new agency built on the Havas foundation was called Havas-Telemondial, with headquarters at Clermont-Ferrand in the Free Zone. It was intended to preserve and maintain the identity of the Havas world news service for distribution in Latin America and elsewhere. The name of Havas-Teleradio also was used. An office in New York was headed by Guy Fritsch-Estrangin, former head of the Havas bureau there, and a Washington office was in charge of U.S.-born Henry L. Sweinhart, former Havas correspondent there, and also a former president of the National Press Club. Both men were obliged to respond to assertions that the agency was serving as an outlet for the German DNB and Transozean services. Since this was basically true, the Telemondial/Teleradio agency operated under a handicap. The Vichy regime expended 14,300,000 francs to maintain the service during its first and only year, 1941–42, as contrasted to a net profit of 3,000,000 francs earned by the Agence Havas in 1939, its last full and normal year of existence.[6]

Apart from the efforts made in France to maintain the Havas organization in some form, French journalists abroad or who escaped when the surrender occurred quickly recognized the need for a wartime news service that would provide a reflection of the true France.

The Agence Havas had sponsored the formation in 1935 of the Agencia Noticiosa Telegrafica Americana (ANTA), based in Mexico City and subsidized in part by the Mexican government. Reuters, also represented in Mexico City, tried to keep ANTA going in 1940, but it expired in 1943. As Reuters had helped the Agence Havas survive a stormy period in its history seventy years before, after the Franco-Prussian War, so it attempted in 1940 to bolster the Havas position in Latin America. But the circumstances were quite different, with the three U.S. agencies—UP, AP, and INS—well established in that part of the world by 1940 and already rivalling Havas there in providing world news to the press and radio.

Representatives of the Agence Havas in London were more successful

---

6 The Telemondial/Teleradio loss was due in part to the financial problems of Havas reorganization, combined with the absence of recorded revenue from the advertising division, the totally abnormal business conditions in France, and the failure to hold clients for the service outside the country. It also was partly a "bookkeeping" loss, with nothing to compensate for the funds made available to the prewar Agence Havas by the French government subsidy on various pretexts and through various ministries.

in collaborating with General DeGaulle and the Free French organization to restore a French service of information. Pierre Maillaud, who had been in charge of the Havas bureau in London, and Albert Grand, who had been second man in the New York bureau, joined in the late summer of 1940 to form a new agency in London. It was known as the Agence L.E.F.—the initials standing for the slogan of the First French Republic, *liberté, egalité, fraternité*. It was intended to provide an independent service directed to foreign countries of news and comment representing the Free French group and keeping alive the sense of France as a great and inevitably resurgent nation.

Maillaud arranged a joint working agreement by which the Reuters agency would contribute service for use by the Agence L.E.F. The British Ministry of Information also extended facilities for transmission and diffusion of the service.[7] French journalists free of the Nazi grip, including many who had been with Havas, agreed to work for the new agency. Special efforts were made again to continue what had been the Havas service to Latin America, with a relay from London through New York, where M. Grand returned to take charge. There he prepared a news file, augmented by 4,000 words provided daily by Reuters from London. Christopher J. Chancellor, then inspector-general for Reuters just returning from a survey in Latin America, was prepared to recommend to his board that the Reuters organization take over all the Havas facilities there and make them available to the Agence L.E.F. for an "unslanted" Anglo-French news service.

Actually, this plan was never used, and the Agence L.E.F. was reorganized within six months, becoming known on January 29, 1941, as the Agence Française Indépendante (AFI), with headquarters in London. It was still headed by Maillaud, with Grand in New York, and staffed chiefly by Havas men. Among the directors was Pierre Comert, formerly in charge of the press department in the French Ministry of Foreign Affairs, and prior to that director of the Information Section in the League of Nations Secretariat, after service before World War I as Berlin correspondent for *Le Temps*. Another director was Jean Massip, former London correspondent for *Le Petit Parisien* and chief of a Free French Information Bureau in London. He returned to occupied France as editor of the Paris wartime underground paper, *Libération*. Jean Baube, formerly in London and Washington for Havas, returned to

---

7   While in London during the war, M. Maillaud made frequent broadcasts to the people of France over the facilities of the BBC. To protect members of his family in France against German retribution, he used the name of "Pierre Bourdan." Returning to France at the time of the liberation of Paris in 1944, he found he had become widely known under that *nom de guerre*. The result was that he continued to use it. He served as minister of information in the French cabinet in 1947–48.

London in October 1941 to help handle press relations for the agency.

The new AFI organization developed reasonably well. André Géraud (Pertinax), formerly of *l'Echo de Paris* and *l'Europe Nouvelle,* who escaped from France in 1940, became its Washington correspondent. The AFI was moderately active in Mexico and South America, where its service was distributed through the Reuters organization. Its service went by radio from London to Free French areas in Africa, and to Syria and Lebanon after the defeat of the Vichy forces there during the summer of 1941, and to Egypt and to certain parts of Asia. It also provided service to the Anatolian Agency (AA) of neutral Turkey for distribution in that country, and it concluded an arrangement with the Tass agency for an exchange of news.

Meanwhile, an underground Free French news agency had been established under another name at Algiers in French North Africa. Known as the Agence France-Afrique (AFA), it had been organized in 1940 through the efforts of Paul Louis Bret, an associate of Maillaud's in the London bureau of Havas. Bret was in Algiers again in 1941. After the Allied landings in North Africa in November 1942, AFA was able to operate openly to serve the North African press with news independent of Vichy or German influence, and in alliance with AFI in London and with Reuters.

Formation of AFP

The French Committee of National Liberation in London gave consideration to the reestablishment of the press after the liberation of France. General DeGaulle insisted that there should be only one news agency, and that it should be subject to his orders, at least during the period of liberation. He could not control the existing AFI or AFA, but they did not oppose him in any way. Subject to his wish, however, the two were combined in December 1943 and, although legal formalities had not been completed, they began to function as one after January 1, 1944. Maillaud and Bret were directors, joined by Fernand Moulier, also of AFI, and by Gérard Jouve, director of Radio Brazzaville in French Equatorial Africa, which had allied itself with the Free French.

The name originally proposed for the new agency was La Presse Française Associeé. This later was changed to l'Agence Française de la Presse (AFP), subsequently further abbreviated to Agence Française de Presse and, in October 1944 after the liberation of Paris, to the Agence France-Presse, always without change of the initials AFP. It has remained the Agence France-Presse (AFP), the real successor of the Agence Havas.

Within a month after the announcement of the merger under the four-man directorship, a further high-level decision, actually by DeGaulle, led to an order from the French Committee that the new AFP should be directed by Gérard Jouve, with Bret as administrative director, Maillaud as chief of the London office, and Moulier as his assistant. This proposed arrangement did not satisfy the latter three. They had not wholly approved the merger plan, fearing too much concentration in one organization, and possible government control, such as the Committee on National Liberation had seemed disposed to favor. This, and their own relegation to subordinate positions in the purposed organization, led them along with eight others to submit their resignations to Henri Bonnet, commissioner of information for the committee.

Despite the protests of the dissident members, the new AFP was formed officially in London on July 1, 1944, with Jouve as director. Moulier and Maillaud soon resumed their association with the agency. Moulier was in charge of the London bureau and director of foreign bureaus. Maillaud went as a war correspondent for the agency to France, where Allied troops had landed in June. Bret became London correspondent for a Paris newspaper of the underground military organization, *Le Parisien Libéré,* and continued as its London representative after the liberation of Paris made it possible to publish the paper openly as a daily.

For several days after the Allied landings in French North Africa on November 8, 1942, the Havas-Telemondial/Teleradio agency was denied recognition in North America. Its Washington and New York representatives were barred from official news conferences until their status could be explored. Several days later their rights were restored, and the agency was offered the cooperation of the U.S. Office of War Information in providing news from North Africa. This was an empty gesture, because the German occupation of France had been extended at that period to include the Free Zone. The OFI was moved to Paris and the Telemondial/Teleradio agency lost meaning and faded from the scene.

As the OFI was moved from Vichy to Paris late in 1942, several minor executives and reporters within the agency began secretly to provide to the underground press in Paris information withheld from the controlled press. This group was discovered and broken up. A second group within the OFI formed what they called the Agence d'Information de la France Libre (AIFL), also a clandestine operation distributing information not given official dissemination, and adding information obtained from the group's own foreign radio monitoring efforts. The copy, in mimeographed form, was conveyed by couriers to underground papers. This group also was broken up, with some of its members executed. Survivors, persisting, formed a third group known as the Agence d'Information et de Documentation (AID). This became the most elaborate underground news service, providing daily and weekly reports, plus documents, and also false identity papers for resistance workers. A radio monitoring service was maintained, and telegraph operators also picked up reports from Reuters, the AP, and UP. The AID group operated until the liberation of Paris in August 1944, when it also seized control of the OFI offices—actually the former Havas headquarters—and prepared them so that the new Agence France-Presse (AFP) was able to move in and go to work immediately, even though it was October before the Havas assets and offices were taken over officially.

By that time, AFP correspondents were established not only in London and Algiers, but in Washington, Moscow, Stockholm, Berne, Geneva, and Ankara. The agency had exchange arrangements with Reuters and Tass. Within a very short time, it had 650 correspondents, staff, and stringers, throughout France, and was to add more. Communications still were not well organized in the war situation, and service often was slow and rates high.

Some editors viewed the AFP as a possible government propaganda agency, but it continued and won its place. There was difficulty at the administrative level, however. M. Jouve, the first director, was soon replaced by Léon Rollin, a former Havas news executive and director of its foreign service from 1924–39. He had remained in France throughout the occupation, and was held for a time in a German concentration camp, but was released as not dangerous to the occupation. Soon after, he succeeded Roger Massip as editor of *Libération,* one of the most effective and popular of the underground papers.[8]

A French provisional government established in Paris acted in October 1944 to suspend six small specialized information agencies. One was the Agence Fournier, dating from 1879, specializing in political and financial information, largely for provincial dailies. Another was the Agence Inter-France, a war-born agency in which Pierre Laval had an interest. Four others dealt in economic and literary information. All had received subsidies from the Vichy Ministry of Information from 1940 to 1942, but were regarded as collaborationist.

Rollin was forced out as director of the AFP at the same period in October 1944, under pressure from Communist elements. He was succeeded by Martial Bourgeon, with the Agence Havas for some twenty

---

8 Established in Paris early in 1941, an edition of *Libération* also was published in the Free Zone from July 1941 until November 1942. Its operations then centered in Paris, with an office in a small hotel on the Boulevard Raspail, next door to German Gestapo headquarters. It used presses located in various places, however. It had correspondents throughout France, received information from abroad, and had the support of the Free French in London. Published weekly, its estimated circulation was as high as 145,000, with distribution managed at constant hazard by the resistance group.

years, a political and diplomatic correspondent with special experience in Canada and South America, and more recently active in the underground press organization. Bourgeon served as director of the agency until April 1945, followed by François Crucy until the spring of 1946. Maurice Nègre, director from 1946 until June 1947, headed Havas bureaus before the war in Warsaw, Budapest, and Bucharest, and was a leader in the resistance movement. By then, Pierre Millaud under his *nom de querre* as Pierre Bourdan was minister of information, and he summoned Paul Louis Bret from London to become the sixth director of the AFP.

Neutral News Centers

The main news centers in Europe in 1942 continued to be London, Berlin, Rome, and Moscow. Neutral correspondents, chiefly Swiss and Swedish, remained almost alone among foreign media representatives in Berlin and Rome after December 1941. U.S. correspondents remained in Vichy, however, until November 1942, when the Free Zone was occupied by the Nazis.

Among other countries that preserved their neutrality in the European area after January 1942, the Irish Free State (Eire) had limited news importance. Spain and Portugal, Switzerland, Sweden, and Turkey served as listening posts and communications points.

As some British and U.S. correspondents in Asia avoided capture by the Japanese in December 1941, so did a few in Europe. Ralph Forte and a younger brother, Aldo, were in Rome for the UP in the early war years. Ralph went to Zurich and Madrid in 1940–41. Aldo soon took direction of the UP bureau in Berne, but soon risked a return to northern Italy in 1944 to estimate the attitude of the people there following the Allied landing in the south of France.

Guido Enderis, in Berlin for the *New York Times*, was ill when other U.S. correspondents there were interned. He was permitted to go to Switzerland, somewhat as he also had enjoyed special treatment from the German authorities during World War I, when he had been in Berlin for the AP. George Axelsson of the *New York Times*, a Swedish citizen, was able to leave Berlin for Stockholm.

Switzerland's neutrality was important as a clearing point for dispatches telephoned from Rome and central Europe, and from Vichy, Athens, and Istanbul. Other U.S. correspondents in Switzerland included Ludwig Popper, UP, John Evans, in Berne since March 1941, and Charles Foltz, Robert Parker, Thomas F. Hawkins, and Frank Bruno, all for the AP. Daniel Brigham and Gaston H. Archambault, both formerly in Paris, and Ira H. Parsons were in a new *New York Times* bureau in Berne. Paul Archinard, NBC, Charles Barbe, CBS, and Howard K. Smith moved from Berlin and Rome to Berne. Bert Wyler represented the Overseas News Agency (ONA). David M. Nichol, formerly in Berlin for the *Chicago Daily News,* was in Berne from June 1941 to January 1942, when he was succeeded by Paul Ghali, formerly in Paris and Vichy.

British or U.S. correspondents in Switzerland could send and receive messages by radio, but were effectively trapped there, with German forces completely surrounding Swiss territory. Nichol and Barbe did manage to cross southern France to Spain and reach Lisbon before the cordon became completely effective, while Ghali moved from Vichy to Berne. Nichol returned to the United States by air from Lisbon in January 1942 and described Berne as then the only place where it was possible to get any important central European news. Even so, such news had to pass through an unprecedented Swiss military censorship intended to protect that country against trouble with any of the belligerents because of what might be dispatched or published within its borders.

There were Axis correspondents in Switzerland, as well as Allied correspondents. The Swiss press retained a freedom greater than any other on the European continent during the war years, unless it was the Swedish press. Papers of both countries were attacked by German authorities, and their correspondents in Berlin were under pressure. After Allied landings in France had cleared the approaches to Switzerland late in 1944 correspondents were able to move with greater freedom. Charles Foley, foreign editor of the *Daily Express,* was a visitor early in 1945, and so was Cedric Salter, formerly in Burma and Turkey for the same paper and for the *Chicago Sun* as well.

Lisbon was a sort of escape hatch from Europe throughout the war years, and a transit point for correspondents and others flying in commercial aircraft to and from the continent. German aircraft also flew to Lisbon. All belligerents had diplomatic representatives there, not to mention spies. Daily papers and periodicals from the warring countries were available and carefully gathered for transmission and examination everywhere else.

Two U.S. correspondents were killed at Lisbon when the Pan American "Yankee Clipper" carrying them to new assignments crashed when landing February 22, 1943. They were Ben Robertson, Jr., *New York Herald Tribune,* and Frank J. Cuhel, MBS. Robertson, who had worked for the *Herald Tribune* and for the AP, had joined *PM* in 1940. He represented that paper in London during the 1940 blitz and was later in Moscow, the Middle East, and India, where he also represented the

Chicago Sun. He had just rejoined the *Herald Tribune* and was en route to London. Cuhel had been in the export business in Java when the Japanese attacked there in February 1942. He was named MBS representative in the East Indies and reported the action there. He then broadcast from Australia for a time, and was on the way to North Africa for the network when he was killed.

Two other victims of an air disaster near Lisbon in June 1943 were Kenneth Stonehouse, chief of Reuters' Washington bureau, and the actor Leslie Howard, both en route to London. Their plane, taking off from Lisbon, was shot down by the German air force in the belief that Prime Minister Churchill was aboard, returning from a wartime conference in North Africa.

Most Allied news agencies and papers depended upon local stringers for coverage in Portugal, although staff correspondents occasionally spent some time in Lisbon. Douglas Brown of Reuters; Henry Buckley, *Daily Express;* Hugh Muir, *Daily Mail;* Adolfo V. da Rosa, UP; J. Wes Gallagher, AP; and Joseph D. Ravotto, UP, formerly in Madrid, were among those who wrote from Lisbon at various periods.

By tradition, news from Spain was more thoroughly reported than from Portugal. Foreign correspondents were chiefly in Madrid and Barcelona. The fact that German and Italian support had helped General Francisco Franco and the Falangists win control during the civil war of 1936–39 provided reason to assume that Spain, although officially neutral, was sympathetic to the Axis and might be aiding it in a variety of ways. Spanish territory on both sides of Gibraltar and on both sides of the Strait of Gibraltar, along with movements of Spanish fishing fleets, allowed for constant observation of Allied shipping and convoys and made the British position at Gibraltar itself less than comfortable.

During the war years in Madrid, U.S. correspondents present at various times included John Lloyd and Charles S. Foltz, Jr., for the AP; John D. Ravotto and Ralph Forte, UP; Thomas J. Hamilton, *New York Times;* and stringers and visitors. One visitor was A. L. Bradford, then director of the United Press foreign services. In Madrid in November 1944, he obtained the first interview with General Franco.[9] Harold Cardozo of the *Daily Mail,* was one of the British correspondents in Madrid.

9　One U.S. correspondent in Spain and Portugal in 1944 was Alice Leone-Moats, who also had been in China and Soviet Russia as a writer for *Collier's* in 1940–42. This adventurous and talented New Yorker flew to Lisbon, entered Spain, crossed the Pyrenees on foot into German-occupied France in the spring of 1944, posed as a French woman, managed to get to Paris, and there talked with Germans in the occupation administration as well as with French citizens. Then she retraced her course to Lisbon, where she wrote an eye-witness report of France under the occupation. It was published and syndicated in the *New York Herald Tribune* shortly before D-Day.

Concentrations of correspondents for the media of Allied and Axis countries alike occurred in such other neutral cities as Istanbul, Ankara, and Stockholm. These were strategic spots because of possible military moves in the vicinity, and because they were also centers of real or supposed espionage. While there was less drama in the work of correspondents there than on the more active war fronts, they performed an important function, because they were close enough to Germany and to occupied countries to be able to glean a certain amount of information from travelers, and diplomats, and from publications. The Swedish press in particular was able to maintain a coverage in Berlin. Conditions of life were neither so difficult nor dangerous as in areas more directly engaged in the war, but wartime shortages and abnormalities existed everywhere on the continent.

The British press had maintained coverage in Turkey for nearly a century, and attention there was intensified during the war years. Coverage was provided not only by resident staff correspondents, but by scores of journalists moving to and from the war fronts in Egypt, the Middle East, India, Burma, China, and the Pacific. Among others, these included Constantin (Tino) Mavroudi, a former member of the Turkish diplomatic corps and dean of the correspondents in Istanbul, representing the *Times;* James Holburn, also of the *Times;* Cedric Salter, *Daily Express,* and the *Chicago Sun;* Derek Patmore, *News-Chronicle,* and the *Christian Science Monitor;* Reuben H. Markham, another *Monitor* staffer with long experience in the Balkans; L. Marland Gander, *Daily Telegraph;* Noel Monks and Edwin Tetlow, *Daily Mail;* and Gordon Young, R. F. Rowland, and Robert Bigio, all of Reuters.

Representatives of the U.S. media in Turkey at various times included Cyrus L. Sulzberger, *New York Times;* Ray Brock, of the same paper, in Turkey and the Middle East throughout the war; and Percy Knauth, formerly in Berlin for that paper, but in Ankara for *Time* magazine. Others were Daniel DeLuce, Dana Adams Schmidt, Paul K. Lee, and John Wallis, all of the AP; Hugo Templeton Speck, UP, expelled in December 1940 and who went then to Sofia; Eleanor Packard, also for UP; Kenneth T. Downs, INS; Frank O'Brien, also for INS and for the *Daily Herald,* who was ordered out of Turkey in 1940, but returned in 1943 for the AP; Robert Low, *Liberty* magazine; Sam Pope Brewer, *Chicago Tribune* and MBS; Carleton (Bill) Kent, *Chicago Times;* and Farnsworth Fowle and Winston Burdett, both of CBS. Eric G. E. R. Gedye, formerly in Vienna, Prague, and Moscow, for the *Daily Telegraph* or the *New York Times,* was in Turkey throughout the war, but on a British government assignment rather than as a correspondent. A number of German correspondents also were in Turkey.

During the war, Stockholm drew more than a hundred correspondents from nearly a score of countries. Many used the Grand Hotel as a kind of headquarters, making for a rather tense atmosphere. Axis correspondents there outnumbered Allied media representatives by about two to one. But all rubbed elbows in the corridors and restaurants, and the capital was a center of intrigue and espionage. The Swedish Foreign Ministry provided facilities for correspondents, and the various embassies and legations disseminated information through their press attachés, and by other means. Tipsters were active, but correspondents had to beware of "planted" information and propaganda. Communication between Stockholm and London or Berlin was reasonably fast for news transmission, but slow on private telegrams and mail. The U.S. correspondents arranged for a special air courier service to mitigate this latter problem.

Stockholm correspondents, like those in Switzerland, by interviewing arriving travelers were able to learn quite promptly of air raids and their effectiveness in Germany and to maintain some sort of check on morale within the Reich. Correspondents for the Swedish and Swiss media had remained in Berlin and elsewhere in Germany, despite dangers and hardships. In the last months of the war, with the cooperation of the Danish underground, Swedish and Allied correspondents crossed from Sweden to Denmark and visited Copenhagen. Among those risking this journey were Gordon Young and Yves du Guerny, both then of the *Daily Express;* Charles Shaw, CBS; Dublin-born Ossian Goulding, *Daily Telegraph;* Cyril Marshall, Exchange Telegraph; Ralph Hewins *Daily Mail,* and Peter Herschend, Danish member of the *Daily Mail* bureau in Stockholm; and Baumgarten, Reuters.

Other Allied representatives in Stockholm at various times during the war included George Axelsson, a Swedish citizen who had represented the *New York Times* in Paris and Berlin, and who was reassigned to Stockholm after December 1941; R. O. G. Urch, the *Times* of London, formerly in Riga for two decades for that paper; Stephen Charing and E. D. Masterman, former Stockholm correspondent for *Le Petit Parisien,* and Edmond Demaitre, all three representing the *Daily Express;* Wallace King, *Daily Herald;* Denis Weaver, *News-Chronicle,* also writing for the *Chicago Times;* and William J. Munday, *Daily Telegraph,* following service in North Africa. Constance Smith was in Stockholm for Reuters in 1942, but joined the British Legation press staff there and was replaced by Bernard Valery. Formerly correspondent in Norway and Finland for *Paris Soir,* Valery wrote for the *New York Times* as well. In 1943 Thomas Harris also became a Reuters correspondent in Stockholm.

Other correspondents in Stockholm included Elmer Peterson, formerly in Warsaw; Edwin A. Shanke, formerly in Berlin; John H. Colburn and Robert H. Sturdevant, all for the AP. Peterson later became

Stockholm representative for NBC. David Anderson followed him for
NBC, succeeded in turn by Bjorn Bjornson, formerly in Iceland. Representation for the UP in Stockholm was provided by Jack Fleischer,
formerly in Berlin, and by Frederick Laudon and Herbert Uexkuell.
Sten Hedman of *Dagens Nyheter,* Stockholm, was a stringer for INS.
Roger Simon wrote for the *New York Herald Tribune,* and Karl Frahm
for the Overseas News Agency.

By special invitation of the Swedish government, Stockholm was visited in June 1943 by Charles E. Gratke, then foreign editor of the *Christian Science Monitor;* Raymond Clapper, syndicated Washington columnist; Blair Bolles, *Washington Star;* Marquis W. Childs, Washington correspondent for the *St. Louis Post-Dispatch,* and a writer of a
syndicated column from the capital, as well as author of a well-received
study of the Swedish economy, *Sweden—The Middle Way* (1939); and
Nat A. Barrows, *Chicago Daily News,* who remained in Sweden for a
time. Other visitors in 1944 included John Scott, *Time,* and Eliot Elisofon, *Life* photographer. Correspondents for Tass in Stockholm included Alexander Pavlov and Michel Kossow. Among Axis correspondents were Helmuth Lindemann, Transozean; Count Knyphausen,
Hamburger Fremdenblatt; Dr. Boettiger, *Völkischer Beobachter;* and
Shin-ichiro Watanabe of Domei.

Areas more remote from the fighting fronts understandably had a
limited coverage by the world media, but were by no means ignored.
Arnaldo Cortesi, forced to leave Rome early in 1939 as correspondent
there for the *New York Times,* represented that paper in Mexico City
and then in Buenos Aires until he was able to return to Rome in 1945.
Joseph Newman, *New York Herald Tribune,* who returned from Japan
just before Pearl Harbor, and Allen Haden, *Chicago Daily News,* were
among others in Buenos Aires.

Percy Philip, a British citizen and former Paris correspondent for the
New York Times, moved to Ottawa following the French surrender in
June 1940, and represented the paper at the Canadian capital through
the remaining war period. Fred L. Strozier, AP, was in Havana. Puerto
Rico was covered by Joseph Dynan, AP, Peter McKnight, INS, and
Harwood Hull, Jr., NBC. U.S. correspondents in the Union of South
Africa included Henry P. McNulty, UP, and Jack Joffe, INS, both at
Johannesburg; Henry Duthie, INS, in Cape Town; and Herbert Hux-
ham, INS, at Durban. Jack Iams, NBC, was in the Belgian Congo.

With most fighting ended by 1943 in Egypt, North Africa, and the
Middle East, correspondents did not cease to cover the news in those
areas. Ray Brock of the *New York Times* was constantly on the move
from his base in Istanbul. George Tucker, Stephen Barber, and Clyde A.
Farnsworth, all of AP, were among others who visited the Middle East

during 1943–45. W. P. Saphire was in the area for INS; Eliav Simon, UP, and Arthur Kay, NANA, were in Jerusalem and Palestine; Dana Adams Schmidt, Leon Kay, and George Palmer, all of UP, were in Cairo and Alexandria.

Some correspondents of the Allies and neutrals moved to the active war fronts, or had been there. The net result was a substantial coverage of international events, supported by a monitoring of radio broadcasts and an exchange between news agencies. In contrast, the people of Axis countries and of Axis-occupied countries were subjected to heavy doses of propaganda. With their media also under strict censorship, they were less informed than the people of Allied or neutral countries. Even in Allied countries, and in many others, newsprint was in short supply because of transport and foreign exchange problems. This tended to reduce the size and the number of publications, which cut the space available for reports, whether related to the war or to general affairs.

Changes at Reuters

With the surrender of France in 1940, the British Reuters agency ceased to have any correspondents on the European continent except in Switzerland, Sweden, Spain, and Portugal. To compensate in some measure for the consequent reduction in the flow of information, Reuters organized a three-man team of experienced correspondents in London to evaluate the political news received from whatever sources. Fergus Ferguson, with a half-century as correspondent for the agency in the Middle East and Geneva, directed the efforts of the team. With him were Sir John Pollock, a new member of Reuters who was abroad for years with the *Times,* the *Morning Post,* the *Daily Mail,* and the *Daily Express;* and Guy Bettany, in Warsaw for the agency when the war began in 1939.

Reuters itself underwent a fundamental change after February 1941. At that time, Sir Roderick Jones, chairman and director since 1915, resigned. Samuel Storey, former chairman of the Press Association (PA), director of the Portsmouth and Sunderland Newspapers, a member of the board of directors of Reuters since 1935, and also a member of Parliament, assumed temporary direction of the agency.

Certain internal tensions had arisen in recent years within the Reuters organization. To counter a hostile Axis propaganda campaign, the agency had been persuaded by the British government to accept a grant in 1938–39 to make a larger service of British news available around the world. Sir Roderick had been in sympathy with this action and its purpose. Some of the younger directors in Reuters, however, and especially those associated with the Press Association, holding substantial stock ownership in Reuters since 1925, were disturbed lest acceptance of the government grant be viewed as giving an official status to the agency. The issue became increasingly sharp in 1940 when Reuters also was drawn into a wartime arrangement with the Ministry of Information that made it subject to government policy. Further, Reuters was put to considerable expense, and the effort was questioned, when it undertook to enter Latin America in strength in 1940 to replace the Agence Havas, a casualty of France's surrender to Germany.

The combined influence of these developments brought Sir Roderick's resignation at sixty-three. He also sold his remaining 1,000 shares of stock in Reuters to the Press Association. Since all other shares had been sold to the Press Association in 1925, this gave PA full ownership of Reuters. The Newspaper Proprietors' Association (NPA) had not then been prepared to share in the management of Reuters, although invited to do so, but the members of that organization active in 1941 felt differently. An agreement on a full partnership arrangement was reached on October 17, 1941, whereby the NPA would join with the PA in equal ownership of Reuters.

The NPA was an organization of London metropolitan newspaper publishers. Since some of them also had provincial newspapers sharing in the ownership of the cooperative Press Association, these so-called "press lords" already controlled about twenty-five per cent of the existing Reuters stock through their representation in the Press Association. The Reuters–PA agencies also owned jointly and occupied the same headquarters building at 85 Fleet Street, completed just before the outbreak of the war on the site of the Bryant Byron House, former PA headquarters. In these circumstances, some concern was expressed in Parliament lest the contemplated partnership arrangement should have the effect of giving actual control of Reuters to the big London publishers, rather than to the British press as a whole.

An alternative proposal was advanced in the House of Commons for the nationalization of Reuters, a plan to place the agency under government control. That suggestion was rejected on behalf of the government, with Brendan Bracken, wartime minister of information, speaking against it. It also was opposed by many others on the ground that it would seem to make Reuters an official government agency. After a spirited debate, the House approved the agreement already approved by the Reuters board of directors and by the NPA and PA separately whereby the latter two organizations would share equally in the ownership of Reuters. This partnership was formally announced in London on October 31, 1941.

A so-called Reuters Trust was set up stating the principles governing the new ownership. The parties to the Trust agreement—the Press Association and the Newspaper Proprietors' Association—gave assurances on five points intended to safeguard the objectivity and national loyalty of the service:

1. That Reuters shall at no time pass into the hands of any one interest, group, or faction.
2. That its integrity, independence, and freedom from bias shall at all times be fully preserved.
3. That its business shall be so administered that it shall supply an unbiased and reliable news service to British, Dominion, Colonial, foreign and other overseas newspapers and agencies with which it has or may hereafter have contracts.
4. That it shall pay due regard to the many interests it serves in addition to those of the press.[10]
5. That no effort shall be spared to expand, develop, and adapt the business of Reuters in order to maintain in every event its position as a leading world news agency.

Three trustees were named from each of the two associated organizations, PA and NPA, and it was specified that an independent chairman should be appointed by the lord chief justice. Sir Lynden Macassey, a lawyer, was appointed as the first chairman. The Trust also was made irrevocable for a minimum period of twenty-one years (until 1962), and it was not to be amended or dissolved thereafter except with the approval of the lord chief justice.

The agreement meant that Reuters was the property of the British newspapers, London and provincial, independent of any governmental or outside influence or control. It was to operate as a nonprofit cooperative undertaking, rather than as a private and commercial venture, as previously, and was protected against policy control or alteration rooted in any possible open or secret transfer of stock control.

Thus the basic concept advanced by Sir Roderick Jones in 1925 to

---

10   This had reference to Reuters' service to business and radio, among other things. The BBC had become Reuters' largest single customer. The "Reuterian" service of commercial information and market quotations sent by wireless to many parts of the world, and particularly to Europe, Africa, the Middle East, and Far East for nearly ten years prior to 1939, was matched by a subsidiary company, Commercial Telegraph Bureau (Comtelburo), distributing commerical and financial information by wireless to clients in Latin America and elsewhere in the world. This latter company was handicapped in its operations during the war because so many markets were closed and world trade was disrupted. Even in 1945, the company showed a net profit of £5,000. Reuters also accepted fees to compensate it for the distribution of company or corporate reports that would not normally be carried in full as news, or distributed to every portion of the world. It had an arrangement, further, with the Exchange Telegraph Company (Extel) for the distribution of financial and commercial information to subscribers in London. Reuters and Press Association after 1945 established and owned jointly the P.A.–Reuter Photos and P.A.–Reuter Features, formerly known as Atlas Despatches.

protect the independence and integrity of Reuters was at last realized. In the change, Reuters took on a resemblance both to the Press Association, as it had existed since its formation in 1868, and to the Associated Press of the United States, since its reorganization in 1892. Both were nonprofit cooperative agencies owned by their member newspapers.[11]

With the completion of the negotiations and the formation of the Reuters Trust, Samuel Storey, who had opposed the partnership while favoring a trust arranged by the government, left the chairmanship of the company.

The administration of the agency business continued, as it had since February 1941, under the joint general-managership of Christopher J. Chancellor and William J. Moloney, both with extensive executive experience at home and abroad. At the same time, Walton A. Cole, night editor of the Press Association, became joint editor of Reuters, along with Moloney.

One of the first actions of the new management in 1941 was to free Reuters of the arrangement with the British Ministry of Information by which it received special financial grants for world dissemination of approved or selected news reports. The Reuters board regarded that as a disguised subsidy, and wanted to end it as tending to support such assumptions as might exist that Reuters was an official agency and one engaged also in disseminating propaganda.

This latter action, based on principle, cost the agency revenue. Reuters' old power exercised through the Ring Combination had ebbed

---

11   The reorganization of Reuters in 1941 as a nonprofit cooperative agency wholly owned by the British press did not immediately put an end to occasional assertions that it was in some degree associated with the British government in an official or semiofficial capacity. Even though this never had been true beyond certain special, temporary, and acknowledged relationships, it continued to receive expression. In 1944, James L. Fly, then chairman of the U.S. Federal Communications Commission, told a House of Representatives committee that Reuters received preferential treatment from the British government in transmission rates. Later, he corrected this statement, based on a misunderstanding, but the original comment had been publicized.

A more serious reference was made in 1945 in a "working paper" provided for the U.S. Department of State by Dr. Arthur W. MacMahon of Columbia University and publicly made available through general distribution and sale. The MacMahon *Memorandum* gave the impression that Reuters occupied at least semiofficial status, received special privileges and financial aid from the British government, slanted its news reports to favor British interests, and provided a service for almost nothing to Latin America as a form of British propaganda.

Early copies of this report, available to Reuters, were strongly protested. Although Dr. MacMahon's references to the agency were incidental to the main theme of his report, the public release of the document was delayed a week so that Reuters might have time to prepare a statement for simultaneous release in rebuttal of statements it called "libelous and utterly untrue." That reply, when it came, was convincing, but the text of the MacMahon *Memorandum* was unchanged and has remained in the public domain as a source of misunderstanding.

away since that association ceased to exist in 1934. Reuters had lost its monopoly position in Japan after 1923 and Japanese aggression in the Far East resulted in further loss of clients. Its subsidiaries in South Africa and India underwent changes giving them independent status. It failed in its attempt to replace the Agence Havas in Latin America after June 1940. It also felt competition in the United Kingdom itself from the Associated Press and the British United Press.

Chancellor and Moloney were obliged to take energetic action to maintain the Reuters service from 1941. For financial reasons, with the war in progress, it was forced to advance its subscription rates considerably for newspapers in the United Kingdom, and for the BBC as well. Moloney retired in 1944, after thirty-six years with the agency, and Cole became editor. Chancellor became managing director, the fourth head of the agency since its establishment in 1851. He had been engaged by Sir Roderick Jones a year or two after he left Cambridge, had been sent to Shanghai about eighteen months later in 1931 to act as general manager for the agency in the Far East, and had returned to London in 1939 to take up administrative responsibilities there.

From 1941, Chancellor recognized that a world news organization needed to be based in London or New York because of the greater freedom existing in those centers and the availability of communications. He advanced the working relationship with the Press Association for an improved coverage of news in the United Kingdom and for the organization of photo and feature services. He also took steps to establish a more friendly relationship with the Associated Press than had existed for some time prior to 1941.

Early in May 1944 a new high-speed beam wireless transmission of news began between London and New York, with war reports received in New York, Washington, or Chicago as promptly as in a London newspaper office. They were used under the Reuters' logo, rather than being incorporated into the Associated Press service as prior to 1934. Nearly 2,000 miles of telegraph wires also were leased in the United States to speed delivery of the service to teleprinters at radio stations and newspaper offices. Early in 1945, a further arrangement was made whereby the Chicago Tribune–New York Daily News Syndicate became exclusive sales agent for the Reuters service west of the Mississippi and south of the Ohio River.

Reuters also signed a contract in July 1944 with the Swedish cooperative news agency, Tidningarnas Telegrambyrå. It was the first agreement with any European news agency since the beginning of the European war in 1939 or since the reorganization of Reuters in 1941. As in the United States, it meant that the service would be used in Sweden with credit to Reuters, rather than merely being incorporated in the TT service, as had been the practice under Ring Combination contract usage prior to 1934. A similar arrangement was made a few months later with the Canadian Press. As Allied forces advanced in Europe from 1943 through 1945, Reuters bureaus were reopened in Rome, Paris, Brussels, and other capitals. Reuters dispatches were used in the press of those cities and countries, by the new French AFP agency, and by the national agencies of Turkey and Portugal for distribution within their countries.

By the end of 1945, with the war concluded, Reuters was employing a full-time staff of nearly 2,000 persons—the greatest number in the history of the agency. Revenue had doubled between 1941 and 1945, and so had expenses, with the result that Reuters completed 1945 with a deficit of £19,000. The report of the Board of Directors was optimistic, however. The policy, the board reported, was "to develop and expand Reuters as rapidly as is physically possible."

Media representation on the news fronts during World War II was greater than ever before. Even though the media of China, Poland, Norway, Denmark, Holland, Belgium, and France were unable to operate normally, and the movement of correspondents was blocked between nations at war, the actual number of correspondents and the vigor of the media in belligerent and neutral countries more than compensated for the other losses. Radio alone, as a new medium, accounted for some of the increase in activity, more periodicals were represented, as was the medium of photography. The greatest coverage was provided by the media of the United Kingdom and Commonwealth countries, and by the media of the United States.

The United Kingdom was represented in the coverage and dissemination of news by Reuters, the Press Association, the Exchange Telegraph, the BBC, the London and the provincial newspaper press, and certain periodicals, feature and photo syndicates, and newsreels. The London press representation included the *Times*, the *Daily Telegraph*, the *News-Chronicle*, the *Daily Express*, the *Sunday Express* and the *Evening Standard;* the *Daily Mail* and the *Sunday Dispatch;* the *Daily Herald;* the *Sunday Times;* the Sunday *Observer* and *News of the World*. The *Daily Mirror* and its *Sunday Pictorial* were somewhat active in war coverage, and so was the tabloid *Daily Sketch*, with other Kemsley-owned provincial papers. The *Manchester Guardian* led, as usual, among provincial papers, but Manchester Sunday papers, and the dailies in Plymouth, Leeds, and several other cities had limited wartime representation.

The British Commonwealth press was represented by the Canadian Press news agency and newspapers and some periodicals, by agencies and newspapers and periodicals in Australia and New Zealand, and by some in the Union of South Africa and India.

The United States was represented by the Associated Press, the United Press, and the International News Service, plus the three radio networks, NBC, CBS, and MBS. The representation also included a considerable number of periodicals, including the weekly news magazines, *Time* and *Newsweek,* magazines such as *Life* and *Fortune;* and many feature and photo syndicates and newsreels. As in the United Kingdom, the established daily newspaper services continued. These included those special services of the *New York Times,* the *New York Herald Tribune,* the *Chicago Daily News,* the *Chicago Tribune,* the *Christian Science Monitor,* and the *New York Sun.* The *New York Daily News,* the *Baltimore Sun,* and the *Los Angeles Times* became somewhat active during the war, as did a number of other dailies not normally represented outside the country. The *Chicago Times,* an afternoon tabloid, became active in international and war coverage from 1938. A New York afternoon tabloid established in 1940, *PM,* and the *Chicago Sun,* established as a morning daily in 1941, both entered into war coverage.

North Africa and Desert War, 1941–43 14

Following the French surrender in June 1940, Germany had almost an entirely free hand on the European continent. Italy, on entering the war as a partner in the Rome–Berlin Axis in June, not only sought to capitalize on France's helpless position, but undertook campaigns of its own in the Balkans, in the Mediterranean, in East Africa, and in Libya, looking toward Egypt. None of the Italian campaigns was successful. British assistance given to Greece to resist the Italian invasion by way of Albania, drove Italian forces back into Albania by November 1940. In that same month, about half of Italy's battle fleet was destroyed in Taranto harbor by British air and navy action.

Italy had a considerable concentration of troops in Libya, a North African territory wrested from Turkish control in the Italian campaign of 1911–12. Its forces also were in Ethiopia and Somaliland, both annexed by Italy following the campaign of 1935–36. From Libya, Italy planned a campaign to control Egypt, the Nile, and the Suez Canal. Great Britain had held a dominant position in that area for decades, even though Egypt was under its own monarchial government. With Britain standing alone in the war after June of 1940, and expected to be occupied with its own defense, Italy anticipated no great difficulty in a desert campaign coordinated with air and naval forces.

The Italian drive eastward from the Libyan frontier began September 13, 1940. General Sir Archibald Wavell of the British Middle East Command based in Egypt, and Admiral Sir Andrew Cunningham, commander of the British Mediterranean naval forces, prepared for the possibility of such an action. Divisions were moved in from Australia, New Zealand, and India, by way of the Red Sea, rather than sending convoys through the narrow waist of the Mediterranean, or on a long voyage around Africa. These forces became the nucleus of the British Eighth Army.

On December 6, British mechanized forces in Egypt began a counter-offensive against the Italians, who had penetrated some sixty miles into

Egypt. They were driven back quickly into Libya, which was bordered by only one good highway of a thousand miles along the Mediterranean coast from Tripoli, near the Tunisian frontier in the west, to Alexandria and Cairo in the east. In January 1941, the British attack was resumed with air and naval support, and the Italian army was crushed, with thousands made prisoners of war and vast amounts of materiel lost. Italian war vessels in the eastern Mediterranean were put out of action in March 1941. Italy also was driven out of Ethiopia by British forces moving from the Sudan, West Africa, and Aden, and Emperor Haile Selassie was returned to his throne in Addis Ababa in May.

These Italian setbacks brought German forces to Italy's assistance. German air bases established in Sicily in 1941 threatened British ships in the Mediterranean and its island base of Malta. A German drive in the Balkans in March-April 1941 in support of the Italians in Greece, was extended to Libya.

Field Marshal Erwin Rommel, commander of the German Afrika Korps, originally in Sicily, opened a desert *blitzkrieg* against the British in Libya on March 31, 1941. His Panzer tank divisions and planes drove the British Eighth Army back by the end of April. British forces were diverted from Egypt at that period to counter German moves in Yugoslavia and Greece, and they also faced the first airborne invasion in history as German parachutists and troop-carrying planes and gliders captured the island of Crete on May 20.

British military forces were further diverted by the East African campaign in Ethiopia, and by German-sponsored conflicts in the League-mandated areas of Iraq, Syria, and Lebanon, as well as in Iran. In Iraq local elements were encouraged and aided by Germany to try to force the British out of air bases established near Baghdad by treaty in the 1930s. In Syria and Lebanon the contest was with French forces stationed there under terms of the 1920 mandate, but taking instructions from the Vichy government under German control. The fighting continued from May to July 1941. By then, British control was established, at least temporarily. German infiltration into Iran in June-July led British troops to enter that country in August. They were joined by troops from the adjacent Soviet Union, with which Germany by then was at war. The Shah Riza Shah, viewed as pro-German, was forced to abdicate in September and was succeeded by his son, Muhammed Riza Pahlavi.

On the desert front in Africa action was at a relative standstill between April and November 1941, when the heat was intense. Not only were the British occupied in the Balkans and the Middle East, but Germany also was busy there and preoccupied even more with its attack on the Soviet Union, which had begun in June and required a concentration of men, equipment, and supplies. There was the further concern in London about Japan's intentions in Asia, including its move into French Indo-China with the assent of Vichy, and its use as a military base. General Wavell was sent from the Middle East Command to India. General Sir Claude Auchinleck, succeeding Wavell in Cairo, required some time to familiarize himself with that command and its problems.

A second British counteroffensive against the Axis in the Egyptian-Libyan desert began under Auchinleck in November, and Tobruk, key-point in Libya, was reached by the end of the month. Rommel opened a new Axis offensive in January 1942, which carried the Afrika Korps deep into Egypt by the end of August, to within sixty miles of Alexandria. There the advance was halted at the so-called El Alamein Line, a defensive position prepared by Auchinleck and manned not only by British and Commonwealth forces, but also by Free French elements.

This was a campaign of maneuver in the desert. The Germans had the advantage of a shorter supply line, provided by air and by ship from Greek ports across the Mediterranean to Benghazi and Tripoli. By contrast, British supplies had to move thousands of miles around Africa and through the Red Sea, or across the Pacific from the United States. The German drive by August 1942 was itself at the end of a long supply line, had lost impetus, and was subject to new and serious harassment by British air bombardment. Early in September, Rommel pulled back to restore his forces. Auchinleck by then had turned over command of the Eighth Army to General Sir Bernard (later Field Marshal Viscount) Montgomery.

Montgomery commanded a third British counteroffensive between October 1942 and April 1943 that was to drive both the Germans and the Italians out of Egypt and Libya. This campaign was coordinated in its final stages with another from the west by British, U.S., and Free French (now "Fighting French") forces under the command of General Dwight D. Eisenhower, following Allied North African landings (Operation Torch) in French Morocco and Algeria in November 1942. These forces moved eastward and joined the British Eighth Army in Tunisia. Together, they drove the Axis forces out of Africa in May 1943.

British naval landings also occurred in Madagascar in May 1942, followed by occupation of that Vichy-French island in the Indian Ocean off the African coast. French West Africa, including Dakar, had joined the Allies at the time of the Operation Torch landings farther north in November. Those landings caused the Germans to extend promptly their occupation in France to include the Vichy area, but not before that portion of the French fleet remaining at Toulon had been scuttled by its officers and crew.

A kind of capstone was put on the African phase of the war by three high-level conferences. The first was a ten-day conference at Casablanca in January 1943, attended by President Roosevelt, Prime Minister Churchill, and General DeGaulle, representing the Fighting French. The second was a conference at Cairo in November-December 1943, resuming in January 1944, with a conference at Teheran in the intervening days. The Cairo meetings brought together Roosevelt, Churchill, and China's Generalissimo Chiang Kai-shek. The Teheran conference brought together Roosevelt, Churchill, and Marshal Stalin, along with the new Shah of Iran. Major decisions were made on each occasion, but the conferences were conducted with a secrecy more remarkable for the fact that each head of state was accompanied by a large staff of political and military advisers.

Correspondents attached to the British navy in the Mediterranean in 1940–41, included Alexander Massey (Jock) Anderson, heading the Reuters bureau in Alexandria. Laurence Edmund (Larry) Allen of the Associated Press was also in Alexandria. Others accredited to the British navy were Ronald Legge, *Daily Telegraph;* W. F. Martin, *Daily Mail;* Grattan McGroarty, George Palmer, Henry T. Gorrell, and Jan H. Yindrich, all of the United Press; Richard D. McMillan, BUP; Richard Mowrer, *Chicago Daily News;* Richard Busvine, *Chicago Times;* Arthur Thorpe, Exchange Telegraph; and Norman Smart, *Daily Express.*[1] George H. Johnstone of the *Melbourne Argus* was with Australian war vessels.

As the British forces formed up in Egypt in 1940 to resist the anticipated Italian attack from Libya that began in September, a group of correspondents was accredited to the British Expeditionary Force under General Wavell's Middle East Command. Although Swedish and other correspondents sought accreditation then and later to report the desert warfare, such accreditation always was limited to British, Commonwealth, and U.S. media representatives.

Among the U.S. group at the outset was Ralph W. Barnes, *New York Herald Tribune,* most recently in that paper's Berlin and London bureaus. He was killed while flying with the RAF on the night of November 17–18, 1940. Others at that time included Yindrich, UP; McMillan, BUP; Edward Kennedy, AP; G. Gordon Young, Reuters; Joseph Levy, *New York Times;* James Aldridge, NANA; Martin Agronsky, NBC; Alexander Graeme Clifford, *Daily Mail;* F. G. H. (Fred) Salusbury, *Daily Herald;* Arthur S. Merton, *Daily Telegraph;* William J.

---

1 Smart sailed on four Malta convoys between May 1941 and September 1942 and was sunk twice. He later said that "I am known as the only correspondent who has been sunk twice without getting my feet wet on either occasion." He was taken off both ships, one the *Ark Royal,* before they went down. *World's Press News* (October 1, 1942), p. 12.

Munday, *Sydney Morning Herald;* and Chester (Reginald William Winchester) Wilmot, Australian Broadcasting Commission.

Arriving a bit later were Christopher Buckley, *Daily Telegraph;* Gorrell, UP, and Ben Ames, former UP chief in Athens; Alan Moorehead, *Daily Express;* Ronald Matthews, *Daily Herald;* Terence Atherton, *Daily Mail;* Leonard Mosley, *Daily Sketch* and the Allied Newspapers; C. D. R. Lumby, the *Times;* Martin Herlihy, Reuters; Richard Dimbleby, BBC; John A. Hetherington, *Melbourne Herald;* Alexander C. Sedgwick, *New York Times;* Kenneth T. Downs, INS, Harold Peters and Robert Low, both UP; Merrill (Red) Mueller, INS; and Allan A. Michie, *Time* magazine.

Downs and Low were in a party of fifteen that went from Cairo to Syria and there were ambushed late in 1941 by Vichy French forces near Damascus. Nine members of the group were killed, two wounded, and Downs and Low were taken as prisoners to Beirut. They were released as neutrals after representations in their behalf by U.S. officials.

The resumption of the British desert campaign from November 1941 to January 1942 was followed promptly by a Rommel counteroffensive between that time and August, driving east to El Alamein. Many of the same correspondents for the Allied media were again active. General Wavell had transferred to India in 1941, as had a number of the correspondents. There were still other changes among them as General Auchinleck was replaced by Montgomery in September 1942.

The large group accredited to the British Eighth Army[2] from 1941, some for short periods and others right through to the end of the North African campaigns in May 1943, included Moorehead, *Daily Express;* Atherton and Clifford, *Daily Mail;* James Holburn, the *Times;* Merton, Buckley, and Richard Capell, *Daily Telegraph;* Clifford Webb, *Daily Herald;* James Lonsdale Hodson and Aubrey Hammond, *Daily Sketch* and Allied Newspapers; William Forrest, David Woodward, and Norman Clark, all of the *News-Chronicle;* Alaric Jacob, Desmond Tighe, and A. Patrick Crosse, all of Reuters; André Glarner and P. S. Taylor, Exchange Telegraph; and Edward H. H. Ward, Roylston Morley, and D. Aitkin, all of BBC.

For the Commonwealth media, correspondents in Egypt included Munday and Guy Harriott, *Sydney Morning Herald;* Johnstone, *Melbourne Argus;* Hetherington, *Melbourne Herald,* the *Sydney Sun,* and NANA; Ronald Monson, Australian Consolidated Press; David Friedman, briefly, and Carel Birkby, both of the South African Press Association; J. C. Lamprecht, South African Broadcasting Company; E. A.

---

2   John Gunther asked an officer in 1943 why the British force in Egypt had been designated as the "Eighth Army." The reply was, "Oh, that's easy. So the enemy would think we really had seven others."

Hinds, South African Cine-Photo newsreel; and Matthew H. Halton, *Toronto Daily Press.*

U.S. media representatives included Eric Bigeo, Cairo bureau chief, Grover, Kennedy, Yarbrough, and Godfrey H. P. Anderson, all for the Associated Press; J. Walter Collins, Cairo bureau chief; Virgil Pinkley, in charge of general coverage; Gorrell, Yindrich, Low, Brydon C. Taves, Leon Kay, and Dana Adams Schmidt, all for the United Press; Kenneth T. Downs, formerly of INS, but switched to the UP; McMillan, BUP; W. P. Saphire, Cairo bureau chief, and Merrill Mueller, INS; Levy and Harold N. Denny, *New York Times;* Russell Hill, *New York Herald Tribune;* Richard Mowrer, *Chicago Daily News;* Sam Pope Brewer, *Chicago Tribune;* Richard Busvine, *Chicago Times;* Harry Zinder, *Time;* and Quentin Reynolds, *Collier's* and the *Daily Express.* Taves of the UP left Cairo to set up a bureau at Melbourne in 1942. Mueller, INS, also went to the Pacific, as did Yarbrough and Grover of the AP, and Johnston of the *Melbourne Argus.*

British correspondents in Egypt had a version of the sharing or "pooling" system, comparable to that which had existed in France in 1940. Such an arrangement existed between the *Daily Herald* and the *Daily Mail,* the *News-Chronicle* and the *Daily Express,* the *Daily Telegraph* and the *Sydney Morning Herald.* The system of exchanging dispatches also existed between the UP and the BUP.

Jan H. Yindrich of the UP had covered the Eighth Army as it was driven back by the Afrika Korps between February and April 1941. He was caught in besieged Tobruk and forced to remain there until the port was relieved in November 1941 by a new British offensive under General Auchinleck. That relief came in the otherwise generally ineffective British counteroffensive of November 1941 to January 1942.

E. A. Hinds, South African Cine-Photo cameraman, was killed in the Battle of Sidi Rezegh in that period while photographing approaching German tanks. Four correspondents also were captured late in November. They were: Harold N. Denny, *New York Times;* Edward H. H. Ward, BBC; Godfrey H. P. Anderson, a British subject representing the AP; and J. C. Lamprecht, South African Broadcasting Company. Captured with them were two representatives of the South African Bureau of Information, Conrad Norton and Uys Krige. Patrick Crosse, Reuters, also was captured in January 1942. All were taken to Italy as prisoners of war, and some later were transferred to prisoner of war camps in Germany.[3]

The third Axis offensive in the desert, between January and August

---

3 Denny, as a neutral correspondent, was being held in Italy when the December 1941 Pearl Harbor attack occurred, so transforming him into an enemy correspondent. He was moved to a Berlin prison, but was returned to Italy some time later. There he was held until

1942, drove the British Eighth Army back to the El Alamein line. The advance had been slowed by June, but was nearly disastrous to the British position. The correspondents shared the dismal lot of the troops in the long retreat, and suffered equally from the blistering summer heat of the desert. About 100 correspondents and photographers were actively engaged, plus thirty to forty army photographers. Censorship and communications facilities were centralized in Cairo, and radio transmission of photos had been possible from there since mid-1942.

Between August and October, the British conducted a commando raid on the German-held port of Tobruk, with George Palmer, UP, and Larry Allen, AP, aboard ships of the Royal Navy. Palmer returned safely to Alexandria. Allen, however, was aboard the British destroyer *Sikh,* carrying dynamite for demolition. It was one of two destroyers sunk in Tobruk harbor, close to shore, and Allen was captured. The U.S. by then was in the war, and Allen spent twenty months as a prisoner in Italy and in Germany. He was released in May 1944 in an exchange of sick and wounded prisoners, in which he was included as a noncombatant civilian newsman.

Other correspondents had left the Eighth Army by October 1942, but newcomers included Ralph Walling and Eric Lloyd-Williams, Reuters; André Glarner, Exchange Telegraph; Leonard Mosley, *Daily Sketch* and the Kemsley Allied Newspapers; Harry L. Percy, UP; Edmund Stevens, *Christian Science Monitor;* Chester Morrison, *Chicago Sun;* Jack Lait, INS; and Croswell Bowen, *Collier's* photographer.

The great and final British counterattack began October 25, 1942, under the command of Field Marshal Montgomery. From El Alamein, correspondents moved with a revitalized and reequipped Eighth Army west some 1,300 miles from Egypt through Libya along the familiar coastal road and into Tunisia. Among about twenty-five correspondents, some were veterans of that desert campaign, and included Edward Kennedy, AP; Christopher Buckley, *Daily Telegraph;* Alaric Jacob, *Daily Express,* but formerly of Reuters; William Forrest, *News-Chronicle;* John A. Hetherington, *Melbourne Herald* and *Sydney Sun;* Harry Zinder, *Time* magazine; Alexander C. Sedgwick, *New York Times;* and George Lait, INS, also acting for the *Daily Express.*

Newer to the desert scene were L. G. Crawley and Denis Martin, Reuters; Edwin Tetlow, *Daily Mail;* Don Whitehead, AP; E. A. (Ned)

---

repatriated to the United States in June 1942 along with other U.S. correspondents who had been in Berlin and Rome when the United States entered the war against the Axis.

Anderson, Ward, and Crosse were held as prisoners of war in Germany until March 1945, when the U.S. First Army overran a prisoner-of-war camp for officers near Limburg. The three were sent back to regimental headquarters as the first step toward a return to the free world.

Russell, UP; Farnsworth Fowle, INS; Edward Howe, of a recently formed Arab News Agency (ANA) of Cairo; and Fred Bayliss, Paramount newsreel cameraman. Claire Hollingsworth, a woman correspondent was in Cairo for the Allied Newspapers. DeWitt Mackenzie, experienced AP correspondent serving as a war analyst in New York, flew to London and Cairo, where he interviewed Montgomery, and then went on to India and China during a three-months journey to interview war leaders.

Some of the correspondents became casualties. Bayliss, of Paramount newsreel, was wounded by shell fire. Zinder of *Time* was injured in a plane takeoff at Cairo and was replaced by Jack Belden, formerly in China and Burma. Jack Lait, INS, previously wounded in London in 1941, Sedgwick of the *New York Times,* and Hammond of the *Daily Sketch* and Allied Newspapers, all received superficial wounds from mortar fire.

While the campaign was in progress along the Libyan coastal area, British and U.S. air and naval forces maintained constant pressure on Italian and German ships and installations throughout the Mediterranean. Bombing attacks on the Greek coast disrupted the German supply lines to Libya in October 1942, and German positions on Crete were attacked by planes in January 1943.

On these occasions, Gorrell, UP, flew with a U.S. bomber group and in January 1943 was awarded the U.S. Medal for "extreme gallantry in conduct under fire" in the course of the Navarino Bay attack on the Greek coast. The Crete attack was observed by Kennedy, AP; Fowle, INS; and L. G. Crawley, Reuters. Desert operations were observed by Tighe, Reuters; Tetlow, *Daily Mail;* Palmer, UP; James A. Cooper and John Redfern, *Daily Express;* and Weston Haynes, AP Photos.

Correspondents with the British navy supporting the desert operations faced dangers matching those on the land. Edward H. (Harry) Crockett, AP and Wide World Photos, who had suffered injuries during German bombing raids in the desert in June 1942, was fatally wounded in February 1943 when aboard the British minelayer *Welshman,* torpedoed in the Mediterranean. He was picked out of the water four hours later, died aboard the rescuing destroyer, and was buried at sea. Bernard Gray, representing the *Sydney Morning Herald* and the *Daily Mirror,* also was lost at sea in May. Norman Thorpe, Reuters, narrowly escaped drowning when the British aircraft carrier *Eagle* was torpedoed; he was rescued by a destroyer.

As the Eighth Army lines lengthened with the advance westward in the spring of 1943, and after it had made contact with the U.S. Second Army Corps entering Tunisia from the west, the handling of correspondents' dispatches presented a problem. All had to be sent to Cairo by courier plane, rather than by radio, which would have introduced security considerations. This meant delays, especially if weather conditions interfered with flying. The fact that censorship took place in Cairo rather than in the forward line meant further delay until changed. In April, Alan P. Sinclair became director of MOI news services in Cairo to assist press representatives there and in the Middle East.

A solution to the problem of the censorship and forwarding of press dispatches was sought in 1943 when the desert campaign drew near its close, with the juncture of British and United States forces in Tunisia. The decision was worked out from London and through the visit of J. H. (Jack) Brebner, on behalf of the British Ministry of Information. In London, Brebner, controller of press and publications at the General Post Office prior to 1939, had become assistant director of the News Department, and organizer of that department in the British Ministry of Information. By February 1940 he was director of the News Division of the Press and Censorship Bureau, headed by Sir Walter Monckton, former legal adviser to Edward VIII. Brebner assigned a special room in the bureau for use by members of the Foreign Press Association. Alfred Duff Cooper, former secretary of state for war, returning from a visit to the United States in May 1940 was appointed as the third minister of information, succeeding Sir John Reith, himself previously director of the BBC.

In September 1940, Sir Frederick Whyte was succeeded as head of what had become known as the "American Division" of the MOI by Douglas Williams, formerly New York correspondent for the *Daily Telegraph*. Geoffrey Crowther, editor of the *Economist*, was adviser to the division. René MacColl, formerly of the *Daily Telegraph* and with earlier experience on the staff of the *Baltimore Sun*, became head of the Press and Radio Division of the British Press Service (British Information Services, or BIS), in New York. Members of the American Division of the MOI in London included Guy Innes, formerly with the Australian Press Association; Charles Hargrove, formerly of the *Wall Street Journal*; and Frank Darvall, formerly with the English Speaking Union, as deputy director. R. J. H. Shaw, formerly of the *Times*, and Hewitt Myring, formerly in the AP London bureau, both were sent to the United States. Brendan Bracken, in public relations and early in the MOI, was detached to serve as parliamentary private secretary to Prime Minister Churchill, but returned to the MOI in July 1941 to succeed Duff Cooper as the fourth minister of information.

The first great amphibious wartime landing in the west occurred on the night of November 7–8, 1942. Known as Operation Torch, U.S. and British forces went ashore against Vichy French resistance along a 1,300-mile Atlantic and Mediterranean front at a number of points in French Morocco and Algeria. They were transported, landed, and given gunnery support by units of the U.S. Navy and the British Royal Navy, and air cover by U.S. Army and Navy flyers and by Royal Air Force planes, which brought inland landing fields and garrisons under control. The operation was commanded by Lieutenant General Dwight D. Eisenhower of the U.S. Army.

This operation had been planned by the joint military staffs of the United States and the United Kingdom on the basis of July agreements between Roosevelt and Churchill. It included by November an understanding with Admiral Jean-François Darlan, previously in Algiers as commander-in-chief of the French fleet under Vichy control, and with responsibility for French interests in North Africa. On November 12 he ordered all French forces there to cease resistance to the Allies, and elements of the French fleet in Toulon were ordered to sail for North Africa. Since Toulon already was surrounded by German forces and was at the mercy of German planes, this was not possible, and the French ships remaining in the port were scuttled by their crews.

Admiral Darlan proclaimed himself high commissioner for French North Africa and West Africa, formed an Imperial Council and took the title of chief of state for North and West Africa. He named General Henri-Honoré Giraud as commander-in-chief of French forces in North Africa, and those forces turned from early resistance at Casablanca and Oran in July 1940 to support of the Allies in 1942. Darlan, a controversial figure from the outset, was assassinated on December 24, and Giraud became high commissioner of North Africa. The Free French under DeGaulle had been unwilling to recognize Darlan, and accepted Giraud only reluctantly and temporarily. Complicating matters further, DeGaulle resented not being informed of the proposed invasion of French North Africa until almost the very eve of the event.

The logistics of the North African attack and landing were complex. Some 850 ships had to be loaded with men and equipment to sail both from British and U.S. ports to rendezvous and reach their assigned positions on a close schedule. All had to be done with such secrecy as to avoid destroying the value of surprise, while also facing the uncertainties of weather and submarine action.

The landings were made according to plan, and the port of Algiers was taken on November 9, the second day. Allied Force Headquarters (AFHQ) was established there. Except for brief French opposition at

Casablanca, the Allied forces were able to advance eastward to stand within a dozen miles of Tunis by November 25. The plan was for the invading forces to make contact with the British Eighth Army by then on the Tunisian border.

Rommel and his Afrika Korps had been driven back from Libya, but was reenforced in Tunisia by other German and Italian forces arriving by ship and plane from Sicily and the south of Italy. The Allied drive on Tunisia was blocked and in some cases reversed by December 1. Sharp fighting and air action made Tunisia a battle zone from late November until May 1943. The U.S. Army forces were obliged to retreat at the Kasserine Pass in Tunisia in February by a heavy German tank attack.

By March 1943, Allied air power had turned the tide, and Allied forces advanced from both east and west to establish contact on April 7 and to break the power of the German and Italian armies in Tunisia on May 12. Caught in a pocket, thousands were made prisoners, while others left African shores and crossed the Mediterranean as best they could. Rommel had been recalled to Germany. General D. J. von Arnim, who had shared in the German maneuvers since November, was captured. Tunis and the French naval base at Bizerte fell on May 7, and the African fighting was at an end.

The military situation in French North Africa, although suddenly at a crisis point in February, had seemed secure in January, two months after the landing. Prime Minister Churchill, President Roosevelt, General DeGaulle, and other principals held a high-level conference at Casablanca between January 14 and 24. Secrecy marked the meeting, which was not reported until the leaders had returned home or reached areas safe from German attack. It was a conference, however, that decided upon the next move, an invasion of Sicily and Italy, and a demand for "unconditional surrender" by the Axis partners.

One aspect in the logistics of the North African landings was arrangement for some correspondents to accompany the convoys, and for others to arrive later. Most in the first group went from London, departing with no more knowledge than the troops they accompanied.

The organization of the correspondents was handled by U.S. Brigadier General Robert A. McClure, public relations officer for General Eisenhower. He was assisted by Major Joseph B. Phillips, formerly of the *New York Herald Tribune* and *Newsweek,* and by Lieutenant Colonel John Victor MacCormack, of the British army. Those correspondents who joined in the landings at Casablanca, Oran, and Algiers were accompanied by officers assigned to them. Once headquarters had been established at Algiers, press headquarters also was set up at the Maison Agricole, some distance from AFHQ, located in a former luxury hotel

high on the hill above the city. Most correspondents were billeted at the
Hotel Aletti, in the lower part of the city.

Some twenty-six U.S. and British correspondents and six photographers were involved in the landings on November 8. These men and
others who followed within the first fortnight included eight for the
United Press: Clinton Beach (Pat) Conger, E. A. (Ned) Russell, C. R.
(Chris) Cunningham, Leo S. (Bill) Disher, Jr., Walter Cronkite, John
Parris, Walter Logan, and Phillip H. Ault, who also wrote for the London *News-Chronicle.* The Associated Press group included William B.
King, J. Wes Gallagher, Harold V. (Hal) Boyle, John A. Moroso III, Lee
Noland ("Boots") Norgaard, and Russell C. Landstrom. Those representing the International News Service were Lowell Bennett, Robert G.
Nixon, John R. Henry, Graham Hovey, Thomas C. Watson, John E.
Lee, and John W. Jarrell. The Reuters staffers were Alan Humphreys,
Charles Wighton, and David Brown. Ernie Pyle of the Scripps-Howard
Newspaper Alliance, who had been in Northern Ireland with the first
U.S. troops to cross the Atlantic, arrived in May to begin war
correspondence.

Special correspondents for newspapers included Philip Jordan and
Guy Ramsey for the *News-Chronicle;* Philip S. Ure, the *Times;* Ronald
Maillard Stead, *Christian Science Monitor;* Frank L. Kluckhohn and
Drew E. Middleton, *New York Times,* both formerly of the AP; William
H. Stoneman, *Chicago Daily News;* John Hall Thompson, *Chicago
Tribune;* H. R. Knickerbocker, *Chicago Sun;* William W. White, *New
York Herald Tribune;* and Gault MacGowan, *New York Sun.*

The radio, magazine, and photo group included Charles Collingwood, CBS; John MacVane, NBC; M. C. Donovan, BBC; Merrill
("Red") Mueller, formerly of INS, and Albert H. Newman, both for
Newsweek; William Lang, *Time;* Lincoln K. Barnett, *Time* and *Life;*
Eliot Elisofon and J. R. Eyerman, *Life* photographers; Harrison B. Roberts, AP–Wide World Photos; Samuel Schulman and Samuel Goldstein, both of International News Photos (INP); Charles Corte and Joseph Boyle, Acme Newspictures; Jack Barnett, Fox Movietone News;
Howard M. Winner, Pathé News; and Irving Smith, Universal Newsreel.

The landings were contested by the Vichy French naval forces, and
correspondents did not escape injuries. Disher of the UP, assigned to the
U.S. Coast Guard cutter *Walney,* broke an ankle aboard ship before the
invasion began. With his leg in a cast, he got about on crutches and
remained at his observation post as the ship moved into Oran harbor.
He received eight wounds from shrapnel and bullets, plus fifteen "superficial" scratches. When it became necessary to abandon ship, he swam
ashore, despite his heavy leg cast and wounds. Once ashore, and advanc-

ing with troops, he received three other bullet wounds. Later, he dictated a story of the landing, and was awarded a Purple Heart.

Moroso of the AP suffered a concussion when a shell struck his ship, a light cruiser, off Fedhala, French Morocco. Goldstein, INP, lost everything except his cameras when his ship was torpedoed at the time of the landing. Walter Logan, UP, with assault troops at that time, received a knee wound during the bombing of Safi.

Five other correspondents were in the landing: Harold (Hal) Boyle, AP; John W. Jarrell, INS; David Brown, Reuters; Samuel ("Sammy") Schulman, INP photographer; and Irving Smith, Universal Newsreel cameraman. Three correspondents also flew with paratroopers who captured an airfield near the Algerian-Tunisian border. They were John H. Thompson, *Chicago Tribune,* who had qualified by three earlier practice jumps and dropped with them; Lowell Bennett, INS; and Kluckhohn, of the *New York Times.* Robert G. Nixon, INS, flew with Brigadier General James H. (Jimmy) Doolittle and Brigadier General Alfred M. Gruenther on a reconnaisance flight from Oran to Casablanca on November 14.

The correspondents were assigned in four groups to accompany the U.S. First Army in North Africa. Each group had its conducting officers. Some were with Field Headquarters, originally at Oran, but later at Algiers. Others were with forces in the east, some with a central task force, and still others with the Twelfth Air Force. Many were under fire.

One of the early stories of importance, aside from the news of the landing and fighting, was an Allied agreement with French Admiral Darlan for him to order the Vichy forces to cease their resistance and cast their lot with the Allies. Gallagher of the AP obtained an exclusive interview at Algiers in which Darlan responded to a written questionnaire, and also disclaimed selfish motives in his change of allegiance. Marcel Sauvage, a French journalist, obtained the last interview with Darlan before his assassination on December 24, and M. C. Donovan, BBC, was first to report the assassination.

Communications facilities were limited at the outset of the North African operation, with most stories pooled by correspondents. No more than 200 words a day could be dispatched by any one newsman in the early period. Dissatisfaction with communiqués, problems of censorship, delays of as much as fifteen days in the release of dispatches, and confusion in announcements originating with the MOI in London and the OWI in Washington all became subjects of controversy during the first weeks.

Pierre Maillaud, who had been in charge of the London bureau of the Agence Havas and headed the London-formed Free French agency, originally the Agence L.E.F. but known since January 1941 as the

Agence Française Indépendante (AFI), flew to Algiers in January 1943. His purpose was to study the situation and to relate the AFI activities to those of an underground agency, the Agence France-Afrique (AFA) formed in Algiers in 1940–41 by Maillaud's London associate, Paul Louis Bret. The AFI and AFA became one on January 1, 1944, called L'Agence Française de la Presse (AFP). This was simplified in October to the Agence France-Presse (AFP), and it took the place vacated by the Agence Havas.

Some of the correspondents who had agreed to leave London in late October 1942 to go on the North African expedition without knowing their destination, returned to London in December or in January 1943. Among them were Disher and Moroso, both convalescent; Henry and Jarrell of INS, about to return to the Pacific and CBI theaters where they had been previously; Parris and Cronkite, UP; Watson and Bennett, INS; Goldstein, INP; Knickerbocker, *Chicago Sun;* and Barnett, *Life.*

Other correspondents arrived in Algiers. One was Henry T. Gorrell, UP, who had been with the British Eighth Army in Libya. Almost immediately, he flew with a U.S. bomber group attacking Italian naval units at Naples. Joseph Morton, AP, was the only reporter aboard the French battleship *Richelieu,* at last released on Darlan's orders and sailing from Dakar to New York. John M. Mecklin, UP, sailed in a French cruiser accompanying the battleship.

A number of correspondents seeking to reach Algiers after Allied headquarters had been established there were routed by way of West Africa. They were sometimes forced to spend considerable waiting periods, often at Dakar, for lack of available sea or air transportation. Edgar T. Rouzeau of the *Pittsburgh Courier,* the first Negro correspondent accredited by the U.S. War Department, was one who went by way of West Africa in May 1942. He was later in Egypt, the Middle East and India. Others traveling via West Africa and Gibraltar were David Woodward, *News-Chronicle;* Graham Stanford, *Daily Mail;* Desmond Tighe and John Nixon, Reuters; Henry Buckley, *Daily Express;* John MacDowell, *Daily Sketch* and Allied Newspapers; and Roderick Macdonald, *Sydney Morning Herald.*

Several women correspondents arrived in North Africa. Margaret Bourke-White, *Life* photographer, flew on a bombing mission over Tunis late in January 1943.[4] Ruth Cowan, AP, and Inez Robb, INS, ar-

---

4 Bourke-White (then Mrs. Erskine Caldwell), formerly in Russia, had been assigned by *Life* in 1942 to cover the U.S. Army Air Force in England. In December 1942, she started for North Africa aboard a troopship. The ship was torpedoed en route, and she arrived in North Africa aboard a British destroyer that had picked up survivors after eight hours in

rived in January from the United States with the first members of the Women's Army Auxiliary Corps (WAAC)—later the Women's Army Corps (WAC)—assigned overseas as part of the headquarters staff in Algiers. Virginia Cowles was in North Africa for the *Chicago Sun* and the London *Sunday Times.*

President Roosevelt's 10,000 mile roundtrip flight to the Casablanca Conference of January 14–24, 1943, was unprecedented. On the return journey, he visited U.S. Negro troops in Liberia and stopped in Rio de Janeiro to meet with Getulio Vargas, president of Brazil, which had declared war on the Axis in August 1942. While at Casablanca, he entertained the Sultan of French Morocco, and reviewed U.S. troops at Rabat, eighty-five miles northeast of Casablanca. Prime Minister Churchill also flew from London to Casablanca, and General DeGaulle followed. General Giraud, successor to Darlan as commander of the French forces in North Africa supporting the Allies, was among military and civilian leaders present from the U.S., the British Commonwealth, and Free France.

The press conference at the Casablanca meeting was marked by special precautions. Arrangements were handled by Lieutenant Colonel Joseph B. Phillips, public relations officer for Eisenhower at AFHQ. All he could tell correspondents in advance was that there was to be an important story that would keep them out of Algiers for a few days and for which, if they were interested, the Army would provide transportation. Only one representative from any one agency, newspaper, or other medium was authorized to attend.

All of the chief correspondents at Algiers accepted the invitation, and twenty-four press-radio representatives and fifteen photographers were flown to Casablanca on January 21 and 22. They still had no knowledge as to why they were there, and were directed to remove brassards and insignia identifying them as war correspondents, lest so large a gathering should imperil security by advertising to possible Axis agents that some major event was in prospect. They were then kept occupied with various conducted trips in the general area.

Not until January 24, the last day of the conference, were the correspondents taken as a group to a well-guarded seaside suburban area, Aufa, where the principals had been living and working at a large hotel surrounded by villas. There they were ushered into the presence of Churchill, Roosevelt, DeGaulle, and Giraud, for a news conference. The correspondents were required to turn over their stories to Lieutenant Colonel Phillips for censorship. With another officer, he took all of the dispatches, totalling some 75,000 words, and flew to Gibraltar and then

---

lifeboats. Kay Summersby, Irish woman driver for General Eisenhower, was another of the group. Bourke-White returned to the U.S. by air in February 1943.

to London. Only after the principals had returned home, or were in safe areas, were the stories transmitted and released for use on January 27.

The correspondents who went from Algiers to Casablanca for this historic conference included fifteen in one particular plane: Gallagher, AP; Nixon, INS; Brown, Reuters; Middleton, *New York Times;* C. R. Cunningham, UP; William W. White, *New York Herald Tribune;* James Wellard, *Chicago Times;* G. Ward Price, *Daily Mail;* Alan Moorehead, *Daily Express;* Philip Jordan, *News-Chronicle;* John D'Arcy Dawson, *Daily Sketch* and Allied Newspapers; Harrison B. Roberts, AP–World Wide Photos; McVane, NBC; Collingwood, CBS; and Edouard Baudry, Canadian Broadcasting Corporation. The plane became lost in bad weather, strayed into air space above Spanish Morocco, and was subjected to anti-aircraft fire. Baudry of the CBC was wounded. Moorehead and Dawson tried to give him aid, but Baudry died in an ambulance taking him from the Casablanca airfield to a hospital.

Three other correspondents present at the January 24 news conference had not been in the Algiers group, but had appeared in Casablanca independently while the meetings were in progress. They were Walter Logan, UP; Sammy Schulman, INP photographer; and Ollie Stewart, of the *Baltimore Afro-American,* a Negro weekly. Logan sensed that some big story was brewing. His persistent inquiries gained him a summons to the Army G-2 (intelligence) headquarters, where he was warned that if he approached a certain villa he would be shot. He was, however, permitted to accompany the presidential party on January 21, when President Roosevelt reviewed U.S. troops at Rabat. Logan therefore was the first correspondent to learn of Roosevelt's presence in Africa. Corporal Ralph Martin, a reporter for the U.S. Army newspaper, *Stars and Stripes,* also was present as Roosevelt reviewed the troops. Their stories were released with the others on January 27, pooled for use by all services and papers.[5]

Between January and April 1943, as the Eighth Army forces under Field Marshal Montgomery drove west from Libya, the First Army forces moved east to squeeze Axis forces in the Tunisian pocket. Algiers became the important news center in that part of the world, replacing Cairo, and U.S. Brigadier General McClure in February set up a Department of Information and Censorship, known colloquially as INC, attached to AFHQ. It aided correspondents in every legitimate way,

---

5   Frank Kluckhohn, *New York Times,* was in Casablanca shortly before the conference met. He learned that President Roosevelt was arriving. Assuming that the president would fly by way of the South Atlantic, as he did, and would make Dakar his first stop in Africa, Kluckhohn managed to get to that port. He was there when Roosevelt landed in Liberia, several hundred miles south, and flew on directly to Casablanca, without stopping in Dakar. Kluckhohn became involved in a controversy over censorship in March 1943 and, as a disciplinary action, was ordered by General Eisenhower to remain away from the front for ten days.

made conducting officers and transportation available, distributed communiqués, and offered daily briefings on the progress of the war in that area. These briefing sessions were conducted by U.S. Lieutenant Colonel Phillips[6] or by British Colonel John Victor ("Little Mac") MacCormack. The briefing room also was a workroom for correspondents, who provided their own typewriters. Censorship and communications facilities were on the same floor.

A limitation of 200 words of copy per day from any one correspondent for transmission in the early weeks of the North African campaign had become 2,000 words by the spring of 1943, although no more than 300 words could be sent at the urgent rate. Delays of from two to five days or more between the time a dispatch was filed and the time of its arrival in London or New York were corrected much sooner. It became the practice to make transmissions of about two hours each twice daily, at noon and at midnight. Beams carrying voice transmission would be directed on a given day, first to the United States and then to the United Kingdom, with the order reversed the next day. British correspondents were so outnumbered by U.S. correspondents, and handicapped also by time zone pressure, that their dispatches often were flown to Gibraltar and transmitted from there to London. There also were special British Army and R.A.F. wireless circuits from Algiers to London, with relay to the U.S. from there. A U.S. Signal Corps circuit between Algiers and Washington was made available without charge for limited use by U.S. correspondents, but the growing volume of official traffic soon brought this to an end for press use.

The Mackay Commercial Cables system was prepared to handle press copy between Algiers and New York at five cents a word, but final agreement on that arrangement was delayed by the French administration of Posts, Telephone, and Telegraph (P.T.T.), which cited prewar contractual agreements at a ten-to-eleven cent rate. Meanwhile, Press Wireless also introduced a three-cent Algiers-New York rate, somewhat slower on delivery but widely used for all except the most urgent reports because of the low rate. Press communications from Algiers never were wholly satisfactory. Protests by British correspondents and editors to the War Office in London brought little improvement. Some British correspondents found they achieved better results by filing messages and photos from Algiers to New York and back to London.

One element that complicated coverage and communication was the sheer growth in numbers of correspondents in North Africa. The twenty-six who had landed with Allied forces in November 1942 had

---

6   The Legion of Merit was conferred on Phillips by Major General Walter Bedell Smith, Eisenhower's deputy chief of staff, in the autumn of 1943, in recognition of his work in organizing press coverage at Algiers and Casablanca.

increased by May 1943 to something between 131 and 200. They included several who had been with the British Eighth Army from El Alamein to Tunisia, as well as others who had joined the group in French North Africa.

Correspondents with the U.S. First Army, in the field far from the Algiers headquarters, were assisted in their work by an Advanced Echelon of AFHQ under the command of Major John D. LeVien. Seven public relations officers and sixteen enlisted men arranged for food, lodging, and transportation for about thirty-five correspondents as the action approached its conclusion in Tunisia. They had a mobile press camp ten to twenty miles behind the lines of combat, with contact maintained through officers at the command posts. Morning and evening orientation conferences provided correspondents with the background on existing military situations, largely off the record, but useful in writing. On the basis of these presentations, correspondents also could select points of vantage from which they might observe action.

A dozen jeeps took correspondents with conducting officers on trips averaging fifty to one hundred miles daily. They would return to the press camp for the evening conference and write their stories—not more than 450 words—to be ready by a 9 P.M. deadline for transmission over a field teleprinter to AFHQ. There the copy would be censored and the stories sent along to the home offices. Other stories of greater length could be prepared for transport the following morning by air courier to AFHQ. Photographs, newsreel films, and voice recordings taped in a sound truck moving with the Advanced Echelon also went to Algiers and AFHQ by courier plane.

The winter campaign in North Africa, closing in from east and west on Tunisia, was a grim and difficult operation. The German and Italian forces used their tanks and planes skillfully, but the Allied armies made actual contact in central Tunisia on April 7. This was reported by E. A. (Ned) Russell, UP; Donald F. Whitehead, AP; George Lait, INS; and Alexander G. Sedgwick, *New York Times,* all with the British Eighth Army. Reports also were prepared by Harold V. (Hal) Boyle and Lee Noland Norgaard, AP; Phillip H. Ault, UP; Michael Chinigo, INS; and Frank Kluckhohn, *New York Times,* all with the U.S. First Army.

A month later, on May 7, 1943, when Allied forces entered Tunis itself and the port of Bizerte, the German and Italian military resistance in all of North Africa was at an end. On May 12, AFHQ announced that "organized resistance, except for isolated pockets of the enemy, has ceased." On May 13 it was reported that "No Axis forces remain in North Africa who are not prisoners in our hands." British Colonel MacCormack read these and other communiqués to correspondents in Algiers, who immediately reported the news to the world.

Among the reports from North Africa none were read in the United

States with more attention than those by Ernie Pyle of the Scripps-Howard Newspaper Alliance. His copy was distributed through the United Features Syndicate. He was in the field with U.S. Army units almost constantly from January to May. He wrote of the enlisted men and officers as individuals, by name, conveying a sense of the lives and personalities of those doing the fighting, with their hardships and humors, tragedies and triumphs.[7] Hal Boyle, AP, for another, demonstrated a talent for capturing the human qualities of both civilians and soldiers at war. As an artist and cartoonist, in *Stars and Stripes,* Bill Mauldin also made "GI Joe" a person.

Correspondents shared the risks of the North African campaigns with the troops. William H. Stoneman, *Chicago Daily News,* ambushed in the Ousseltia sector of Tunisia in January, was wounded and later awarded the Purple Heart. Charles (Chuck) Corte, Acme Newspictures, hospitalized for shell shock in January, was wounded at Kasserine Pass in February, and received the Purple Heart. Ivan H. (Cy) Peterman, *Philadelphia Inquirer,* was injured in a jeep accident while under fire at El Guettar in March. Merrill Mueller, *Newsweek* and formerly INS, previously wounded during the London blitz in 1941, was wounded again in March 1943 while with the Eighth Army near the Mareth Line in Tunisia. Both Peterman and Mueller were awarded Purple Hearts in June by U.S. Major General Walter Bedell Smith.

George Lait, INS, wounded in London in 1941, was wounded again near Mersa Matruh, as were Alexander C. Sedgwick, *New York Times,* and Aubrey Hammond, *Daily Sketch* and Allied Newspapers. William Forrest, *News-Chronicle,* was struck in the head by bomb splinters while with the Eighth Army in pursuit of Rommel. Gault MacGowan, *New York Sun,* was wounded in Tunisia in April while with Sengalese troops; later he was awarded a Croix de Guerre as well as a Purple Heart. Michael Chinigo, INS, suffered two wounds. J. Wes Gallagher, AP, was injured in Bizerte on May 8 when a jeep in which he was riding overturned, pinning him underneath. George W. Tucker, AP, was injured in a plane crash in Algiers, and was flown to the United States for surgical treatment.

Frank J. Cuhel, MBS, en route to North Africa, was killed at Lisbon in February 1943 when his plane crashed. Frederick C. Painton, *Reader's Digest,* survived when his ship was torpedoed and sunk on the way to North Africa. Other correspondents had narrow escapes, among

---

7 A Pulitzer Prize went to Ernest Taylor Pyle in 1944, based largely on his 1943 reports from North Africa, Sicily, and Italy. Pyle also received the Raymond Clapper Memorial Award for 1943 correspondence, and the Sigma Delta Chi award for war correspondence (human interest) in 1944.

them Ernie Pyle, SHNA; Lee Noland Norgaard, AP; Graham Hovey, INS; and Howard K. Winner, Pathé newsreel cameraman.

Correspondents in North Africa at some period with the British Eighth Army or the U.S. First Army between 1941 and 1943, some already mentioned, included Daniel DeLuce, Stephen Barber, Frank J. O'Brien, Paul Kern Lee, and Clyde A. Farnsworth, all for the AP; and Herbert White and Weston Haynes, both for AP–Wide World Photos. For the UP, there were Dana Adams Schmidt, Donald G. Coe, Leon Kay, George Palmer, Eleanor Packard, and Reynolds Packard, one of a group of correspondents to fly in U.S. bombers in May 1943 in a heavy raid on Palermo, Sicily. For the INS, there were Pierre J. Huss, of long experience in Berlin; Clinton H. Greene, and W. P. Saphire. For Reuters there were Eric Lloyd Williams, Denis Martin, Leonard Crawley, and James H. Nicholson. There were Edward J. Gilling and André Glarner for Exchange Telegraph, and Colonel Sokolnikov, for the Tass agency, also writing for *Krasnaya Zvezda* of Moscow.

Special correspondents for U.S. newspapers in North Africa included Cyrus L. Sulzberger, Hanson Baldwin, Ray Brock, and Grant Parr, all for the *New York Times;* Russell Hill, John O'Reilly, and Homer W. Bigart, *New York Herald Tribune;* Joseph G. Harrison, Edmund Stevens, and Derek Patmore, *Christian Science Monitor;* Richard Mowrer, *Chicago Daily News;* Burnet Hershey, *New York Post;* Kenneth Crawford, *PM,* New York; Carleton (Bill) Kent, formerly in the Southwest Pacific, and Claire Hollingsworth, formerly in Cairo for the Allied Newspapers, both writing for the *Chicago Times;* Seymour (Sy) Korman and Sam Pope Brewer, both for the *Chicago Tribune;* Chester Morrison, *Chicago Sun;* and Thomas R. Henry, *Washington Star* and NANA, and also formerly in the Far East. (He should not be confused with John R. Henry of the AP).

The British and Dominions' newspaper press, among others had Geoffrey Hoare and Gerald Morgan in North Africa for the *Times;* E. A. Montague, *Manchester Guardian,* also writing for the *Times;* Ronald Legge, Christopher Buckley, Richard Capell, and William J. Munday, all for the *Daily Telegraph;* Norman Clark, *News-Chronicle;* John Redfern, Gordon Young, Norman Smart, Eric Grey, and Lawrence Wilkinson, *Daily Express;* Alexander Graeme Clifford and Paul Bewsher, *Daily Mail;* Alexander Berry Austin, F. G. H. Salusbury, and Clifford Webb, *Daily Herald;* Evan Williams, Arthur D. Divine (writing under the name of David Rame), and Aubrey Hammond, *Daily Sketch* and Allied Newspapers of the Kemsley group; B. Archer Brooks and T. E. A. Healy, *Daily Mirror;* William J. Munday and Roderick MacDonald, formerly in India and Burma, both for the *Sydney Morning Herald;* Keith Hooper, *Truth,* a Sydney weekly paper; Ronald Monson, H. D.

Brass, J. O. Lodge, and J. Jaris, all for the Australian press and the government Information Department.

The radio, periodical, and photo group of correspondents included some representatives still unmentioned, among them a number for the BBC: Robert Dunnett, Howard Marshall, Godfrey Talbot, Frank Gilliard, and New Zealand-born E. G. Webber. Charles Collingwood[8] represented CBS; Winston Burdett and Farnsworth Fowle, formerly of INS, both broadcast for CBS. Elmer Petersen broadcast for NBC, as did Merrill Mueller, *Newsweek,* and Grant Parr, of the *New York Times.* Arthur E. Mann represented MBS, for which both John H. Thompson and Sam Pope Brewer of the *Chicago Tribune* also broadcast.

The Henry R. Luce publications, *Time, Life,* and *Fortune,* had added wartime, overseas representatives. Although normally in London, Charles T. Wertenbaker, Walter Graebner, and Noel Busch also were in the North African area, and James Aldridge and Harry Zinder, formerly in Egypt and the Middle East, also got to French West Africa. Jack Belden, formerly in China and Burma, was in North Africa, as were Fletcher Martin, an artist for *Life,* and Robert Landry, a photographer.

For other magazines, Demaree Bess and Edgar Snow represented the *Saturday Evening Post* in North Africa. Donald S. Grant represented *Look,* with Robert Hansen as a photographer. Frederic Sondern, Jr., then wrote for the *Reader's Digest;* Gordon Gaskill for the *American Magazine;* A. J. (Abbot Joseph) Liebling and George Sessions Perry, for the *New Yorker;* and Robert Capa, a photographer for *Collier's.* Carol L. Johnson was in the area as an artist for NEA. Terry Ashwood represented Pathé Newsreel; Michael J. Ackerman, Acme Newspictures; Norman Fisher, Fox Movietone News; and Ian Struther, Fred Bayliss, and Douglas Hardy, Paramount Newsreel.

With the end of the North African campaign in May 1943 an important period of the war was ended. Along with the changes that had occurred in the Pacific area, it could be said that the Allied position, internationally, was stronger; that of the Axis, weaker. Most correspondents left North Africa, going chiefly to the United States or to the United Kingdom.

All news agencies and most major newspapers and periodicals and radio groups kept representatives in Algiers, however, to cover AFHQ, which remained there, the center of the European Theater of Operations (ETO). It also was the place from which to report the activities of the French Committee of National Liberation, set up at Algiers early in June 1943, with a provisional consultative assembly at the time bearing a tie to the Fighting French organization based in London, with General DeGaulle as its spokesman.

---

8 Collingwood received the Peabody Award in 1943 for his broadcasts in 1942–43 from North Africa.

The war had gone favorably for Japan from 1931 in Asia, and for the Axis from 1939 through most of 1942 elsewhere. By the middle of that year, however, the Allies, while still greatly on the defensive, were sufficiently organized to begin an effective counterattack. The Japanese were set back at the Battle of the Coral Sea in May 1942, at Midway Island in June, and at Guadalcanal and elsewhere in the southwest Pacific after November and on into 1943.

Germany was being heavily bombed by British and U.S. planes by late 1942, and its submarine threat was reduced by 1943. The Allied landing in French North Africa and the joint British and U.S. campaigns against the Axis positions there between October 1942 and May 1943 forced both German and Italian forces out of Africa. In those same months, the Soviet Red Army and air force, aided by lend-lease supplies and materiel and benefitted by the winter cold, were able to check and reverse the German invasion of 1941–42.

By mid-1943, the Allies were on the move. The interval was brief between the end of the North African campaign and the beginning of the Allied assault on what Prime Minister Churchill had called "the soft under-belly of Europe." Even as the Tunisian campaign was ending on May 12, Churchill arrived in Washington for the so-called Trident Conference. A plan to move into Sicily had been approved at the Casablanca Conference in January, and designated as "Operation Husky." The two-week Washington conference covered every aspect of the war, but confirmed the campaign to capture Sicily, coordinated with an attack on the mainland of Italy itself. Churchill, accompanied by General George C. Marshall, U.S. chief of staff, then flew to Algiers by way of Newfoundland and Gibraltar to discuss plans with General Eisenhower and other military personnel there. Churchill returned to London by air early in June.[1]

---

1   It was at this time that a German fighter plane flying from a French base shot down a Pan American commercial plane just leaving Lisbon for London, in the belief that it was carrying Churchill. Among the thirteen passengers and crew lost were Kenneth Stonehouse, Reuters Washington chief, and Leslie Howard, actor of stage and screen.

Combined air and naval attacks were made by the Allies in June 1943 on islands standing between Africa and Sicily, enemy air bases from which Malta had been bombed, and presenting a threat to the planned Sicily operation. These attacks, with bloodless landings, occurred at Pantelleria, Lampedusa, and Linosa.

Landings in Sicily followed early on July 10, preceded by a week of heavy air attacks. First use was made of a newly developed amphibious truck, a DUKW (referred to as "duck-boats"), to put men and supplies ashore, and also of two new types of vessels, an LCI (Landing Craft Infantry) to move men, and an LST (Landing Ship Tank), to permit tanks or other heavy equipment to roll directly ashore from an open bow.

Twelve German and Italian divisions contested the Sicily landings, which were made under adverse weather conditions, with a rough sea, and accompanied by certain mishaps, particularly in the landing of glider troops. With more than thirteen Anglo-American divisions, strong air superiority and naval gunfire, the landings were successful, aided also by German miscalculations as to the points of attack. There was also the element of surprise that the attempt should be made at all in bad weather. Major airfields were captured, troops and tanks were brought ashore and, although resistance was heavy, the island of Sicily was all but lost to the Axis by late July and was firmly in Allied control by August 17.

The seizure of Sicily was an added blow to Italy's position in the war. Its other reverses since 1940 in the Balkans, the Mediterranean, East Africa, and North Africa had shaken general confidence in the government. On July 24, the Fascist Grand Council, meeting in Rome, voted in effect to form a new national government, with command of the armed forces to be restored to the king. This was a personal affront to Mussolini, who also was unaware that plans already existed to remove him from the leadership he had occupied in the Fascist party and in the Italian government since 1922. On July 25, after a meeting with King Victor Emmanuel, Mussolini was arrested as he left the royal villa, and Marshal Pietro Badoglio, conqueror of Ethiopia in 1935–36, became head of a new cabinet under the king. The Rome radio announced that Mussolini had been forced to resign as premier; he was taken two days later to the island of Ponza in the Tyrrenean Sea.

The reaction in Germany was that the Fascist party had been "stunned," as Hitler said, by the sequence of events, but could be revived to continue the war. Mussolini was moved by the new Badoglio government from Ponza to La Maddalena, another small island off the coast of Sicily, and then in August to a mountain resort, the Gran Sasso

Hotel, at Lake Bracciano, in central Italy, where he was under a light guard. On the morning of September 12 some ninety German parachutists landed by gliders near the hotel and rescued Mussolini without difficulty and without casualities. He was taken to Munich in a light plane for a meeting with Hitler. Again with German support, a skeleton Italian Fascist government was set up under Mussolini at Salò on the shores of Lake Como in Northern Italy.

Meanwhile, the Badoglio government, undertook to function in Rome. Cautious indirect negotiations were commenced in August, chiefly through Lisbon and Madrid, toward an Italian armistice with the Allies. This led to Italy's surrender on September 3, 1943. An armistice was signed in an olive grove near Siracusa (Syracuse), Sicily, by General Castellano, representing the Italian government, and General Walter Bedell Smith representing Eisenhower for the Allied nations. Churchill was at that time again in Washington, following a so-called Quadrant Conference of August in Quebec. The Italian surrender was announced to the world on September 8.

The Italians feared that announcement would bring a German occupation of Rome, since Wehrmacht troops were present in force both in northern and southern Italy. The report of the armistice broadcast late on September 8 was indeed followed during the night by deployment of German troops about Rome. General Badoglio, with senior officials of his government, the king, and members of the royal family, went to the War Ministry building. Early in the morning of September 9, they slipped out of Rome and drove eastward in a convoy to the port of Pescara on the Adriatic, and were taken then southward by corvette to Brindisi, on the heel of Italy. From there, and in Bari to the north, the Badoglio government functioned.

Elements of the Italian fleet also had left Genoa and Spezia in the north, as well as Taranto in the south, on the night of September 8 to surrender to the Allies at Malta on September 10. Meanwhile, some fighting had occurred in Rome between German forces and units of the Italian army or bands of Partisans supporting the Allies. A truce was signed September 11 under which Nazi forces were able to move freely in Rome. On October 13, the royal Italian government at Brindisi declared war on Germany and assumed status as a "cobelligerent" with the Allies.

The change that came upon Italy in July was reflected in the Italian press. Senator Manlio Morgagni, president and general director of the official Agenzia Stefani and a friend of Mussolini, committed suicide. He was replaced at Stefani by Dr. Roberto Suster, its editor-in-chief, and the agency's Berlin correspondent during the first two years of the war.

The office of Mussolini's Milan daily, *Il Popolo d'Italia,* was attacked by anti-Fascists or Partisans. Vito Mussolini, nephew of Il Duce and the paper's director, along with Mario Appelius, political and military editorial columnist, withstood a week's siege before being driven out by tear gas.[2] The editorship of Italy's leading paper, *Il Corriere della Sera,* also of Milan, was returned to Ettore Janni, its pre-Fascist editor who had suffered as a Jew because of the government's acceptance after about 1938 of the Nazi anti-Semitic line.

Count Galeazzo Ciano, Mussolini's son-in-law and former foreign minister, saw his newspaper, *Il Telegrafo* of Leghorn, suspended. Giovanni Ansaldo, its editor, was placed by the Germans in a concentration camp, where he was executed before the end of 1943 on a charge of spreading anti-German propaganda from the camp. Ciano himself, along with Marshal Emilio de Bono, one of Mussolini's earliest associates, went to Germany, where they were placed under house arrest in Munich. Both had voted against Mussolini in the Fascist Grand Council meeting of July 24, and in January 1944 both were shot as traitors with Mussolini's approval.

In Cremona, *Il Regime Fascista,* owned and edited by Roberto Farinacci, former secretary of the Fascist party and a life member of the Grand Council, was suspended. One of the most pro-German of all Fascist leaders, Farinacci's relations with General Badoglio were not good. More than a year later, in December 1944, he was killed by Partisans.

The editors of all newspapers in Rome, as well as in some other cities, were changed during the summer of 1943. Virginio Gayda, editor of *Il Giornale d'Italia,* a direct spokesman for Mussolini and probably the most widely quoted Fascist journalist, was replaced by Alberto Bergamini, who had founded the paper in 1901 and edited it until forced out by the Fascists in 1924. Gayda was killed some weeks later in a bombing attack. Allesandro Pavolini, former minister of popular culture and manager of *Il Messaggero,* and Francesco Malgero, the acting editor, were replaced by Xipio Perrone, a non-Fascist and a former editor. In Turin, *La Stampa,* another leading paper, came under new direction. In Naples, *Il Mattino,* was edited by Paolo Scarfoglio, son of the founder, Eduardo Scarfoglio, who had been forced out by the Fascists.

Other significant changes were made in the existing press structure. One of the old liberal papers, *Il Mondo* of Rome, suppressed in 1926, reappeared, produced by Ivanoe Bonomi, former editor and Italian premier in 1920. It was printed from the presses of the suspended *Il Tevere,* founded in Rome as a Fascist paper in 1926. Bonomi himself became premier in the new Badoglio government.

---

2   Both men escaped at the time. Appelius soon was reported captured by the Partisans. He was arrested by Allied forces in Rome in June 1944 and died there in December 1946.

The liberal wave that brought these changes in the Italian press did not last long, but the changes were not reversed. Badoglio's government put a restraint on freedom of expression lest it arouse the wrath of the Germans still in Italy and still regarding Italy as an ally until the September 8th announcement of surrender ended any such belief, to say nothing of the October 13 declaration of war on Germany by the new Brindisi administration. In these new circumstances, a wartime censorship was reimposed on the press of Italy.

General Eisenhower told correspondents at a news conference summoned at AFHQ in Algiers in June 1943 that an attack would be directed against Sicily within a month. He gave some details, and said that the Allies might be "riding for a bloody nose," but thought the island could be taken. Sternly, he warned the correspondents not to write or even talk about the plan until after D-Day. That he spoke to them so openly indicated the excellent relationship existing between the Allied media and the command.

At least two British political correspondents, among many to arrive in Algiers before the July 9 invasion date, were denied cooperation by AFHQ. These were Barclay Barr, of the *Daily Sketch* and Allied Newspapers, and Claud Cockburn, editor of a London weekly, *This Week,* and also a writer under the name of "Frank Pitcairn" for the *Daily Worker* of London, the British Communist party paper. Both men had intended to write about the involved and delicate relationship between General DeGaulle, heading the Free French in London, and General Giraud, commanding the French forces in North Africa. They had no military accreditation from the British War Office, however, and were denied such accreditation by AFHQ. Cockburn, in fact, was ordered out of North Africa. Both men returned to London where they later asserted that "everybody in Algiers" knew of the plan to invade Sicily two weeks before it occurred.

A number of other correspondents without military accreditation also were ordered out of the North African area, or were denied facilities by AFHQ and left Algiers after brief visits. Official British figures in July showed 78 correspondents accredited to AFHQ. Of these, 20 were for U.S. news agencies and 18 for U.S. newspapers and other media; 18 also were for British news agencies and 12 for British newspapers and other media. Two correspondents were allowed for a newspaper, six for a news agency.

Figures released in Washington in September, after the Sicily action was over and fighting centered in the south of Italy, showed that AFHQ by then was providing facilities for more than 125 media representatives. A typical day was said to involve service to or contact with 68 U.S.

representatives, 36 British, 20 Canadians, two French, and three from other countries. In October, a newsman returning to London reported that there were about 100 U.S. media representatives in Algiers, compared to only 20 for the British, and this without reference to those in Sicily or Italy. Newsmen then in Algiers were obliged to find their own quarters. Most tried to get into the Aletti Hotel, crowded and run-down though it was. They were permitted to eat at an officers' mess, however; were provided with transportation, so far as possible; could buy supplies at army post exchanges (PX), and could use military communications facilities without cost when necessary to supplement commercial service.

About a dozen correspondents went into Sicily with the first assault wave on the night of July 9–10. One was John Hall Thompson, *Chicago Tribune,* who jumped with U.S. paratroopers, as he also had done in North Africa. This time, he cracked a rib and wrenched a knee in landing, and later was awarded the Purple Heart. Another was Clark Lee, who had been in the Philippines and the Solomon Islands for the AP but who switched to INS in May 1943, and who went into Sicily with an amphibious task force, pushing ahead to Vittoria. There, along with a half dozen soldiers, he narrowly escaped capture by Germans in two armored cars. Ross Munro of the Canadian Press entered Sicily with Canadian forces and produced the first eye-witness account of the operation, transmitted by way of Malta and London.

Merrill Mueller, *Newsweek* and INS, a veteran of nearly every front, Asian and European, was in the Sicily landing. Jack Belden, *Time* and *Life,* and a veteran of the China and Southeast Asia campaigns, also was with an amphibious force landing at Gela. Desmond Tighe, Reuters, who had been in North Africa, landed in Sicily with Scottish troops of the Eighth Army, swimming ashore through German machine gun and rifle fire.

Roderick MacDonald, *Sydney Morning Herald* and *News-Chronicle,* experienced in Burma, China, and North Africa, actually was the first correspondent in Sicily. He landed with glider troops under heavy anti-aircraft fire. Many of the soldiers were wounded or lost at sea because some of the gliders were released too soon by towing aircraft. MacDonald himself was captured by Italian troops, but escaped after fourteen hours and was in Tunis on July 16, ready for another move.

The first blood among correspondents in the Sicily operation was shed by Michael Chinigo, INS. Twice injured in Tunisia, he landed in the first assault. During the later advance on Palermo with U.S. troops, his arm was gashed by a shell burst and his wrist was broken. He went on, nevertheless, giving aid to more seriously wounded men, and questioning prisoners. Later, he was awarded the Silver Star for "gallantry in action." Richard McMillan of the BUP and UP who was long active in prewar Europe and a veteran of the North African campaigns, was also in the landing in Sicily, where he was wounded in the face and hands by a powder blast.

Other correspondents engaged in the Sicily operation, some of them veterans of earlier moves, included John Moroso III, AP; John M. Mecklin, UP; Ivan H. (Cy) Peterman, *Philadelphia Inquirer;* and Ronald Maillard Stead, *Christian Science Monitor.* New figures were among those aboard the flagship directing the U.S. amphibious attack at Scoglitti, including Reginald Ingraham, *Time* and *Life,* formerly in Washington for the AP; George Sessions Perry, *Saturday Evening Post;* Alan Humphreys, Reuters; and Clinton Greene, INS. All were under the guidance of navy Lieutenant John Mason Brown, formerly dramatic critic of the *New York Evening Post* and the *New York World Telegram,* who was task force officer aboard the ship.

Others in the field included Richard Tregaskis, INS, with earlier experience at Guadalcanal; Ernie Pyle, Scripps-Howard Newspaper Alliance and already a familiar name because of his reports from North Africa; John Gunther, an experienced "name" correspondent back in service for NANA and the NBC Blue Network; Edward J. (Ted) Gilling, Exchange Telegraph and BBC; and H. R. Knickerbocker, *Chicago Sun,* who was back from the Pacific. Still others included William Forrest, *News-Chronicle;* Christopher Buckley, *Daily Telegraph;* Richard Mowrer, *Chicago Daily News;* John O'Reilly, *New York Herald Tribune;* and E. A. Montague, *Manchester Guardian.* Robert Dunnett represented the BBC. Experienced correspondents for the UP included Dana Adams Schmidt, Christopher R. Cunningham, Ned Russell, and George Palmer. Those for the AP included Don Whitehead, Hal Boyle, Paul Kern Lee, and Lee Noland Norgaard.

Special coverage of Canadian troop activity in Sicily was provided by William Stewart, Louis Hunter, and Maurice Desjardins, all of the Canadian Press (CP), with Desjardins writing especially for the French-language press of the country. Others in the field included Richard L. Sandburn of the Southam Newspapers; Lionel Shapiro, *Montreal Gazette;* Peter Sturzberg, Canadian Broadcasting Corporation; and William A. Wilson, BUP. A group of Canadian correspondents had remained in North Africa during the landings, but proceeded to Sicily later. They were Fred Griffin, *Toronto Star* and New Zealand-born Wallace Reyburn, *Montreal Star,* both of whom had participated in the Dieppe raid out of England into France in August 1942; Sholto Watt, *Montreal Star,* and formerly of the *Daily Telegraph;* Ralph Allen, *Toronto Globe and Mail;* Bert Wemp, *Toronto Evening Telegram;* J. A. M. Cook, Sifton Newspapers; Andrew Cowan, Canadian Broadcasting Corporation; and J. R. Chambers and Robert Vermillion, BUP.

The active Anglo–U.S. group in Sicily also included Ian Hunter and

James H. Nicholson, Reuters; James A. Cooper, *Daily Express;* Donn Sutton, editor of NEA service; Frederick C. Painton, *Reader's Digest;* and four correspondents for the U.S. Army newspaper, *Stars and Stripes,* Sergeants Jack Foisie, Philip Stern, and Ralph Martin, and Lieutenant James Burchard.

Photo correspondents included Herbert White, AP Photos, representing the Wartime Still Photographic Pool; Samuel Schulman and Walter Bordas, INP; Charles Corte, Michael Ackerman, and Charles Seawood, all of Acme Newspictures; George Rodger, Robert Landry, and J. R. Evemen, all of *Life;* Robert Capa, *Collier's;* Norman Alley, Paramount Newsreel; Irving Smith, Universal Newsreel; Jack Barnett, Movietone News; and Philip John Turner, Gaumont-British Newsreel.

Communications arrangements had been greatly improved at Algiers since the North African and Tunisian campaign. Copy moved promptly by Mackay radio, with 1,400,000 words sent to New York during the first thirteen days of the Sicily campaign. London was equally well served. There were delays, however, in getting copy from Sicily to Algiers. Courier planes were not as available as had been anticipated. The result was that some correspondents found it easier to return to Algiers themselves to get their copy to the censors and on its way. Among those who did so were Thompson of the *Chicago Tribune* and MBS; Merrill (Red) Mueller of *Newsweek* and NBC; Clinton Greene, INS; and Roderick MacDonald, *Sydney Morning Herald* and London *News-Chronicle.*

Most of the early copy from the U.S. Army sector in Sicily cleared through an army office set up at Gela on the south coast under Major John Hutchinson, formerly of the *Memphis Commercial Appeal,* and Captain Peter D. Aldred, formerly of the AP, both of whom were transferred from AFHQ. Joseph B. Phillips, now a colonel, remained at AFHQ, where the pool plan for handling copy during the first week was directed by Lieutenant Colonel Albert L. Warner, formerly a Washington correspondent for the *New York Herald Tribune.* Captain T. L. Laister of the British army, formerly of the *Daily Herald,* was in charge of the copy room at AFHQ concerned with expediting transmission of stories after they passed the censorship.

In the eastern part of Sicily, the Eighth Army set up its own air courier system by which correspondents with the British and Canadian forces might have their reports flown to Malta to be transmitted from there to London and on to New York and Canada. The dispatches, carried in red bags, received special and generally satisfactory attention.

In Algiers, as the Sicily campaign was in progress, key men remained to administer news agency bureaus, to cover AFHQ itself, and to check other news sources in North Africa. Among them were Hugh Baillie, president of the United Press, who arrived from New York and went on to Sicily; Virgil Pinkley, UP bureau chief; and Reynolds Packard, also of UP. For the AP there were Edward Kennedy, bureau chief; Daniel DeLuce, Relman (Pat) Morin, repatriated and reactivated after his internment in Japan; and Joseph Morton, and Lee Norgaard, returned from Sicily. For INS, there were Pierre Huss, bureau chief, and Graham Hovey. Alan Humphreys represented Reuters, but most British coverage was at Malta after July. For the newspaper press, Drew Middleton remained at AFHQ for the *New York Times,*[3] Homer Bigart for the *New York Herald Tribune,* and Helen Kirkpatrick for the *Chicago Daily News,* sent from London to replace William H. Stoneman, on leave in the United States.

A. D. Divine of the *Daily Sketch* and *Sunday Times* was one of the few British correspondents remaining at AFHQ in this period. Facilities and military accreditation had been denied Martin Herlihy, formerly Middle East manager for Reuters; Henry Stone, *News-Chronicle;* and E. B. F. Wareing, *Daily Telegraph.* For the magazine press, Demaree Bess of the *Saturday Evening Post,* who had covered the Tunisian campaign, received full cooperation at AFHQ in writing even of delicate political issues, such as those relating to French relations with the U.S. and British military and diplomatic branches.

The last weeks of the military campaign in Sicily in August 1943 were reported by a large group of correspondents, including most of those who had gone in during July, plus others arriving from Algiers. Among this latter group were John Hersey, *Time;* Quentin Reynolds, *Collier's;* Alfred H. Newman, *Newsweek;* Homer Bigart, *New York Herald Tribune;* Herbert L. Matthews, *New York Times;* and both Farnsworth Fowle and John Charles Daly of CBS.

In addition to reporting the final action, when Messina was taken on August 16–17, some of the correspondents reported the beginnings of Allied Military Government (AMG) in Sicily, with headquarters in Palermo.[4] Early members of the military government organization, both British and American, were brought together at Tizi-Ouzou, about seventy-five miles southeast of Algiers, for early transfer to Sicily and Italy. Thus the first AMG headquarters in Palermo was manned by many specialists in uniform, including newsmen, this writer among them.[5] They were to move later to Naples, London, and elsewhere.

---

3   Middleton received the Headliners' Club award in 1943 for his war reports.

4   One who did so was John Hersey, *Time,* who later produced a brief novel, *A Bell for Adano* (1944), presenting the plight of a U.S. "town Major" in charge of military government in a Sicilian town. It was made into a play, produced in New York in 1944, with Frederic March in the leading role, and later appeared as a motion picture.

5   Other former newsmen attached to the AMG headquarters at Palermo included Captain Charles C. Poore, formerly of the *New York Times;* Captain Coleman A. Harwell, *Nashville Tenneseean;* Major James C. Hanrahan, *Des Moines Register and Tribune* and

One story that developed in Sicily in August 1943 but was unreported then concerned an incident in which U.S. Lieutenant General George Patton, commander of the U.S. Seventh Army, slapped and berated a private recuperating in the 93rd Evacuation Hospital, suffering from what was described as "battle fatigue." The full disclosure of the incident, although suppressed for months, resulted in a reprimand for Patton from General Eisenhower, with a requirement that he apologize publicly to all concerned for his treatment of the soldier. Patton was further penalized by being kept out of action until after the invasion of Normandy began nearly a year later.

Correspondents remaining in Sicily or Algiers were prepared for the Allied move against the Italian mainland. This came on September 3, the very day the reconstituted Italian government signed surrender terms with the Allies. That surrender also came just after the conclusion of the Quebec (Quadrant) Conference of August 1943, where plans for the Italian campaign had been among the subjects discussed.

The Campaign in Italy

Allied landings in Italy occurred at two points. In Operation Baytown, the British Eighth Army under Field Marshal Montgomery crossed the Strait of Messina from Sicily before dawn September 3 to land on the toe of the Italian boot. The forces were well established by nightfall, having met little opposition. Between then and September 30, reenforced units of the Eighth Army spread northward toward Salerno, with air and sea support, while others moved eastward to capture Brindisi, Bari, and airfields at Foggia. There a strong German counterattack slowed the British for about a week, but a new landing in the German rear on the Adriatic coast relieved the situation.

The second major landing, Operation Avalanche, was at Salerno on September 9, with Naples the objective of the U.S. Fifth Army and the British 10th Corps under the command of U.S. General Mark Clark. Because of stiff German resistance, the beachhead was not secure until September 15. Naples was entered on October 2, and the Volturno River to the north was crossed in mid-October. By November 1, these combined operations brought the southern quarter of the Italian boot under Allied control. The cobelligerent Italian government under General Badoglio drove the Germans from Sardinia on September 19, and the ci-

Scripps-Howard Radio; Captain Thomas P. Headon, *New York Sun;* Captain Daniel J. Mahoney, *New York Herald Tribune;* and Major Douglas W. Meservy, NBC.

vilian population of the adjacent French island of Corsica seized control there, despite the presence of Italian Fascist troops.

In November, the Allied advance in Italy was blocked by weather conditions and the establishment of German forces in mountain positions spanning the peninsula in what was called the Gustav Line. Fighting was bitter and casualties high through the winter of 1943–44. An attempt to break the deadlock and to flank the Gustav Line was made by an Allied amphibious force seeking to establish a beachhead on the Tyrrhenian seacoast at Anzio and Nettuno on January 22, 1944. This Operation Shingle met strong German resistance, which prevented a breakout from what became a pocket where Allied forces were pinned down for nearly five months.

Those correspondents who had moved across the Strait of Messina on September 3 with the British Eighth Army, to which the Canadian First Division was attached, included Edward J. (Ted) Gilling, Exchange Telegraph (Extel); Daniel DeLuce, AP; William Wilson, BUP; Ross Munro, William Stewart, and Maurice Desjardins, all of the Canadian Press (CP); Matt Halton, Canadian Broadcasting Corporation (CBC); Gregory Clark, *Toronto Star;* Sholto Watt, *Montreal Star;* and Ralph Allen, *Toronto Globe & Mail.* Following very soon were Eric Lloyd Williams, Reuters; Christopher Buckley, *Daily Telegraph;* Alan Moorehead, *Daily Express;* and Ronald Monson, representing both the *Express* and Australian newspapers.

Other correspondents aboard naval units based at Malta but soon in Italy were Desmond Tighe and Ion Monro, Reuters; Philip Ure, the *Times;* William Forrest, *News-Chronicle;* Noel Monks, *Daily Mail;* James A. Cooper, *Daily Express;* A. W. Helliwell, *Daily Herald;* Paul Kern Lee, AP; Alfred Wagg, representing *Collier's* and the NBC, and others.

A British airborne attack on the Italian naval base at Taranto on September 9 was supported by a commando force to push toward Bari against German opposition. David Driscoll, news director for MBS out of New York, was with the commandos and struggled ashore with some seventy-five pounds of recording equipment to try to capture the sounds of battle. D. H. J. Hardy of Paramount Newsreel also was in the landing.

The landing at Salerno, also on September 9, was covered by a larger group. Hal Boyle, Don Whitehead, and Pat Morin were present for the AP; Reynolds Packard, UP; Quentin Reynolds, *Collier's;* Jack Belden *Time* and *Life,* and Robert Capa, photographer now also with *Life;* Alfred H. Newman, *Newsweek;* Herbert Matthews, *New York Times;* John O'Reilly, *New York Herald Tribune;* William H. Stoneman, *Chicago Daily News;* and Mark Watson, *Baltimore Sun.* Henry T. Gorrell of the UP was aboard a British cruiser acting as flagship, with aircraft carrier support, and Ivan H. (Cy) Peterman of the *Philadelphia Inquirer* was aboard the *U.S.S. Savannah.*

As the beachhead fight was in progress other correspondents arrived, including Stewart Sale, Reuters; Basil H. T. Gingell, Exchange Telegraph; Ronald Maillard Stead, *Christian Science Monitor;* Alexander Berry Austin, *Daily Herald;* William J. Munday, *Sydney Morning Herald,* also representing the *News-Chronicle;* and John Steinbeck, novelist, writing for the *New York Herald Tribune.* Heavy though the battle was at Salerno, the sole casualty among the correspondents was Jack Belden, *Time* and *Life,* who was shot in the leg.

Other correspondents arrived in Italy to report the advance on Naples, which was entered October 2. These included Homer Bigart, *New York Herald Tribune;* James Wellard, *Chicago Times;* Seymour (Sy) Korman, *Chicago Tribune;* Edgar T. Rouzeau, *Pittsburgh Courier;* Richard Tregaskis and Clark Lee, both of INS; William Lang, *Time;* Frank Gillard, BBC; and Farnsworth Fowle, CBS.

In the push toward Naples, three British correspondents were killed and a fourth was wounded at Scafati on September 28 by a shell fired from a German half-track. Those killed were Sale, Reuters; Austin, *Daily Herald;* and Munday, Sydney *Morning Herald* and the London *News-Chronicle.* Both Austin and Munday had long experience by then in war coverage on several fronts. It was the most tragic episode affecting the press corps since a similar loss near Teruel during the Spanish Civil War in 1938. Gingell of Extel, standing nearby, was wounded. Several other correspondents in the group escaped because they saw the German vehicle approaching and took shelter in time. They were Gillard, BBC; Fowle, CBS; Korman, *Chicago Tribune;* Rouzeau, *Pittsburgh Courier;* Matthews, *New York Times;* and Morin, AP.

This occurrence brought an order from AFHQ to correspondents directing them to refrain from going ahead of combat troops, as these correspondents had done, perhaps inadvertently. Daniel DeLuce of the AP was one of a number of correspondents who had forged ahead of the British Eighth Army a few days earlier to make the first contact with advance elements of the U.S. Fifth Army moving inland after the Salerno landing. In October 1943, DeLuce also made a hazardous journey in a fishing boat across the Adriatic to Yugoslavia. He had been one of the last correspondents out of that country ahead of the Germans in 1941. Now one of the first to return, he remained four days, reached the Tito Partisan headquarters in a little mountain town, and returned to Italy with the first eye-witness account of the Partisan guerrilla activities against German occupation forces.

Another daring exploit was carried out by Boston-born Aldo Forte, chief of the UP bureau in Berne, who was formerly in Rome. Disguised as a mountain-climber, he crossed from Switzerland into German-held northern Italy on September 13. Forte remained for four days, talked with Italians and returned with reports of conditions in the country, of the attitude of the people following the surrender of the Badoglio government, and of the Allied move into the toe of Italy.

Richard Tregaskis, INS, and several other U.S. and British correspondents entered Naples on October 1 ahead of troops. In the months following the capture of that city, as troops moved northward to the area of the Volturno River, correspondents followed. Among them were Michael Chinigo, INS, recovered from wounds received in Sicily; Helen Kirkpatrick, *Chicago Daily News,* en route to London after a period at AFHQ in Algiers; Ernie Pyle, Scripps-Howard Newspaper Alliance (SHNA), returned from a visit to the United States; and Jonathan (Jack) Rice, AP Photos, and Sherman Montrose, NEA-Acme Newspictures, both with experience in the Pacific theater. Cecil Sprigge, Reuters, and former Rome correspondent for that agency returned to Italy. Gordon Waterfield, also of Reuters, returned to the European Theater of Operations (ETO) after assignments in India and Turkey. Others arriving in Naples included photographer Margaret Bourke-White, *Life;* Bert Brandt and Charles Seawood, NEA-Acme Newspictures; Barry Faris, INS editor-in-chief, visiting the war fronts; J. Wes Gallagher, AP; Robert Vermillion, UP and BUP; George Hicks, Blue Network (NBC); Don Hollenbeck, NBC; Thomas R. Henry, *Washington Star* and NANA; and Frank Gervasi, *Collier's.*

Some of the correspondents moved north to report the fighting along the Gustav Line. Richard Tregaskis, INS, among this group, was seriously wounded near Venafro on November 22, 1943. Shell fragments striking him in the head caused him to lose his power of speech and movement for several weeks. He was returned to the United States for treatment at Walter Reed Hospital, Washington, D.C., where a metal plate was inserted to replace a portion of his skull. He was awarded a Purple Heart in June 1944, and was able to return later to active service.

The landings at Anzio, in Operation Shingle, one hundred miles north of Naples and some forty miles south of Rome, was made January 22 and covered by fourteen correspondents. Among them were James H. Nicholson, Reuters; Norman Clark, *News-Chronicle;* Vaughan Thomas, BBC; W. J. Barr, representing Australian newspapers and much of the combined British press; H. T. Gingell, Exchange Telegraph, recovered from wounds received near Naples in September and also representing the combined British press; Don Whitehead, AP; Reynolds Packard, UP; Clark Lee, INS; Stoneman, *Chicago Daily News;* Stead, *Christian Science Monitor;* Lang, *Time;* and Capa, *Life* photographer.

Ernie Pyle, SHNA, arrived in the Anzio-Nettuno area in March 1944 and remained for some weeks. Others to arrive between February and the break-out at the end of May included DeLuce, AP;[6] George W. Tucker, also of AP; Vermillion, UP; Chinigo, INS; Bigart, *New York Herald Tribune;* Carleton (Bill) Kent, *Chicago Sun,* and Eric Sevareid, CBS, both of whom had been in the Pacific and Burma-China areas; A. C. Sedgwick, *New York Times;* William Strand, *Chicago Tribune;* Wick Fowler, *Dallas Morning News;* John Vandercook, NBC; and George Aarons, *Yank.*

Considering the difficulties and dangers of the Anzio operation, it is surprising that no correspondent was killed there. Five were hurt, however, in a March 16 bombing that destroyed their quarters at Nettuno. These were Pyle, Tucker, Strand, Fowler, and Aarons. Chinigo, already wounded three times, and holder not only of the Purple Heart but also of the Silver Star for "gallantry in action" in Sicily, was injured once again at Anzio in a jeep collision of February 17 when returning from a night patrol; he suffered a split kneecap and a dislocated arm.

As the winter stalemate set in along the Gustav Line, some correspondents in Italy turned to political subjects relating, among other things, to the position of the prospective Italian government in the postwar world. Philip Ure of the London *Times,* and Herbert L. Matthews of the *New York Times,* interviewed Marshal Badoglio, premier in the provisional government. Lee, INS, and DeLuce, AP, found and interviewed Count Carlo Sforza, Italian foreign minister of pre-Fascist times, and an exile from Italy. He had returned from the United States to Naples, where with Allied support he was prepared to take a part in a new government. Cecil Sprigge, formerly Rome correspondent for the *Manchester Guardian* but with Reuters since 1943, who was well acquainted with Italian political figures, interviewed a number of them in the context of their possible contributions to later government policies.

A so-called Allied Mediterranean Council (AMC) toured the Mediterranean basin early in January 1944 to consider postwar policies to be advanced by the Allies. The small group of high-level representatives included Andrei Vishinsky of the Soviet government as the dominating member, Harold Macmillan as the British representative, and others from the United States and Fighting France. In Italy several days with staff assistants, the group conducted interviews in Naples, Sorrento, and

6   While at Anzio, Pyle and DeLuce received notification that they had been awarded Pulitzer Prizes for war reporting in 1943. Pyle also received the National Headliners' Club award in 1943 and 1944; Sigma Delta Chi awards in 1943 and 1944; and the first Raymond Clapper Memorial Award.

elsewhere with Badoglio, Sforza, Senator Benedetto Croce, and other prospective postwar leaders.[7]

With Sicily and southern Italy secured by the Allies from November, news of the war relating to the Mediterranean area came mostly from Palermo and Naples. One exception related to the Dodocanese Islands in the eastern Mediterranean. Held by Italy since 1912, the co-belligerency of the Italian government with the Allies made it likely that these islands would fall to Allied control, affording useful air fields and naval bases, as some did. But the Germans had established control there as far as they could in October, while the Allies were too much occupied with the Italian invasion to save the islands or even to salvage ships and equipment there. Several thousand men were rescued, however, including L. Marsland Gander of the *Daily Telegraph,* the only correspondent to reach the area.

In December 1943, General Eisenhower relinquished his command at Algiers and went to London to prepare for the cross-channel landing in France, Operation Overlord, which had been agreed upon for the spring of 1944. Field Marshal Montgomery, General Patton, and others also went from the Mediterranean to London. General Sir Henry Maitland, who had been British commander in the Middle East, succeeded Eisenhower at AFHQ in Algiers, but was soon succeeded in turn by Field Marshal Sir Henry R. L. G. Alexander.

An advanced Allied Force Headquarters was established at Caserta, north of Naples. Both Foggia, as a center for the Allied air force, and Bari as a center for the Italian government under Badoglio became points of activity and of concern to correspondents. The Allied forces in Italy were joined by French Moroccan troops, a Polish corps, a Brazilian division, and a Greek brigade, all of whom were to participate in the 1944 campaign.

Correspondents reporting from Italy also joined with others in Cairo in watching events as best they could in German-occupied Greece and Yugoslavia. The Germans in Yugoslavia were opposed by resistance groups under General Drazha Mihailovich, a member of the monarchial government, who had been friendly with the Axis.[8] A leader of a Communist Partisan group, Josip Broz, became known as Marshal Tito. He conducted a persistent guerrilla campaign against the occupying Germans from 1943, and had the support of the Allied governments, including the Soviet Union, from 1944. At risk, DeLuce and other correspon-

---

7   This writer, then a major in AMG, U.S. Army, working with members of the British 10th Corps, handled arrangements for the visit of this group.

8   Mihailovich was captured after the war, tried for collaboration with the Nazi occupation forces, and was executed July 17, 1946.

dents managed to enter Yugoslavia by way of Italy after 1943 to interview Tito.

The coverage of the sequence of events in Italy between September 1943 and May-June 1944 brought scores of correspondents to the scene for the U.S. and British media. Many were veterans of previous campaigns. The changes at AFHQ in later 1943 also affected correspondents in the Mediterranean. New men accredited in Algiers included Ronald Legge, *Daily Telegraph;* Alexander H. Uhl, foreign editor of *PM,* New York; Harold Callender, long in Paris and London for the *New York Times;* and Henry Griffin, AP Photos. The billet and mess for correspondents was established at the Hotel Regina, although the Aletti Hotel continued as an alternative center.

British correspondents who briefly visited air bases in the Mediterranean included Stanley W. Burch, Reuters; Cyril Ray, *Manchester Guardian;* Colin Bednall, *Daily Mail;* Howard Williams *Daily Telegraph;* Charles Bray, *Daily Herald;* Arthur Narrcott, the *Times;* Ronald S. Walker, *News-Chronicle;* and Victor Lewis, *Daily Sketch* and Allied Newspapers. With the British navy in the Mediterranean during the winter period were L. Marsland Gander, *Daily Telegraph;* and J. H. Magee, *Picture Post.* John F. Chester replaced William McGaffin as AP bureau chief in Cairo. Victor M. Bienstock, Overseas News Agency, also was in Cairo.

Much of the copy going to London and New York from AFHQ beginning in the latter part of 1943 was transmitted by "voice cast"—the news reports were read over the air and recorded at the destination. This method became available originally in December 1942 through U.S. Army Public Relations to help break the logjam in transmission then existing. Between December 1942 and October 1943 nearly 2,225,000 words were handled by voice cast, and from October 1943 more than 10,000 words a day were being transmitted in this manner. Two-thirds of the total went to New York, with the UP leading in use of the method, followed by AP and Reuters. Apart from the agencies, twenty-eight British and U.S. newspapers, magazines, and syndicates also used the voice cast, led by the *Chicago Daily News* and the *New York Times.*

On the Italian front during the winter of 1943–44, the group of accredited correspondents included Cyrus L. Sulzberger, *New York Times,* alternating with Turner Catledge, who had rejoined the *Times* staff after a period as editor of the *Chicago Sun;* Allen Raymond, formerly in the Southwest Pacific for the *New York Herald Tribune,* but now representing the *Saturday Evening Post;* Gordon Gammack, *Des Moines Register and Tribune;* Walter E. Lucas, *Daily Express,* formerly in the Pacific; Alexander Graeme Clifford, *Daily Mail;* and Alan Moorehead,

Daily Express;[9] John Redfern, also of the *Daily Express;* Christopher D. R. Lumby, the *Times;* Cyril Bewley, *Sunday Times* and the Kemsley Newspapers; Cyril Ray, *Manchester Guardian* and the BBC;[10] Godfrey Talbot, Dennis Johnson, and Reginald Beckwith, all of BBC; L. Marsland Gander, *Daily Telegraph;* Leonard Oswald Mosley, *Daily Sketch* and Allied Newspapers; Astley Hawkins, David Brown, and F. Reynolds Jones, all of Reuters.

Others of the correspondents for the U.S. media accredited to AFHQ in 1944 included H. R. Knickerbocker, *Chicago Sun;* Ralph Howard, NBC; John Charles Daly, CBS; Fillmore Calhoun, *Time;* John Lardner, *Newsweek;* Edward Kennedy, Kenneth L. Dixon, and Lee Noland Norgaard, all of AP; Walter Logan, Clinton B. (Pat) Conger, Christopher R. Cunningham, and James E. Roper, all of UP; Byron Evans, *Yank;* and Sergeants Milton Lehman, Jack Foisie, and Max Montgomery, all of the *Stars and Stripes.*

Early in 1944, a number of correspondents left Italy either to return home or to go to other assignments, whether in Europe or the Pacific. Among those departing were Ernie Pyle, SHNA;[11] Gorrell and Cunningham, UP; Hal Boyle, AP; Clark Lee, INS; George Hicks, NBC Blue Network; and Robert Capa, *Life* photographer. Clifford of the *Daily Mail* was replaced in Italy by Edwin Tetlow, and Mosley of the *Daily Sketch* by Sydney Sterck.

Correspondents going and coming between Italy and other areas in the Mediterranean until the end of the European war in May 1945 continued to be accredited to AFHQ. The headquarters was moved permanently from Algiers to Caserta in the spring of 1944. The French provisional government remained at Algiers until September 1944, when it was moved to Paris, liberated the previous month. Ivanoe Bonomi succeeded Badoglio in January 1944 as premier of the Italian government at Bari and Brindisi.

---

9 Clifford and Moorehead were "mentioned in dispatches" in April for "gallant and distinguished services in Italy." This was the second occasion on which these two received such special mention.

10 Ray was "mentioned in dispatches" for action during the Canadian army attack at Ortona at Christmas 1943.

11 In 1945, *The Story of G.I. Joe,* a United Artists motion picture, was released in the spring. It was a reenactment of incidents that Ernie Pyle had reported, and in some of which he had participated, along with U.S. infantrymen, in North Africa, Sicily, and Italy. The part of Ernie Pyle was played by Burgess Meredith. Pyle returned to the United States in August 1944, and was in Hollywood when parts of the film were being made. George Lait, INS, played a small part. Boyle and Don Whitehead, AP, and Cunningham, UP, were technical advisers.

Important Allied Conferences late in 1943 took place in Cairo November 23–26, in Teheran November 27 through December 1, and again in Cairo December 2–7.

The first Cairo meeting, referred to as Operation Sextant, was at the Mena House, a luxury hotel near the Pyramids at Giza, south of the city. It brought together Prime Minister Churchill, President Roosevelt, and Generalissimo Chiang Kai-shek of Nationalist China. Mme. Chiang Kai-shek also attended. The purpose was to present to Chiang Kai-shek and members of his delegation the plan of operations for the war in Southeast Asia as agreed upon by Anglo–U.S. government and military leaders at the Quebec (Quadrant) conference of August. Admiral Lord Louis Mountbatten and his staff were present, representing the India-Burma command, as was General Joseph W. Stilwell, U.S. commander in the CBI theater.

Churchill and Roosevelt, with staff assistants, flew from Cairo to Teheran on November 27 for that conference, referred to as Operation Eureka. They met with Marshal Stalin and his group. There was no fixed agenda, but the entire war situation was reviewed, with discussions continuing until December 1. The Soviet government had been bringing pressure upon the western allies to establish a "second front" in Europe to relieve the German military pressure upon Russia. Churchill had called the Italian campaign a "third front," possessing the same value, pointing out that it occupied twenty German divisions, plus ten or twenty more in the Mediterranean and Balkan areas. There was an agreement at Teheran, nevertheless, on plans for the invasion of France in a cross-channel campaign, Operation Overlord, to begin in June 1944, and clearly forming a "second front."

Back in Cairo on December 2, Churchill and Roosevelt held further conversations. The conference, without a code name, continued until December 7, when Roosevelt returned to Washington, and Churchill later returned to London.

Some seventy-five correspondents were gathered in Cairo in advance of the Sextant conference, permitted only to know that a meeting of importance was in prospect there. Among them were Geoffrey Hoare, the *Times;* W. J. Makin and Geoffrey Imeson, Reuters; Noel Monks, *Daily Mail;* Philip Jordan, *News-Chronicle;* Peter Duffield, *Evening Standard* and *Melbourne Herald;* Henry T. Gorrell, UP; William McGaffin, Charles Grumich, and John F. Chester, all for the AP; Cyrus L. Sulzberger, *New York Times;* Joseph G. Harrison, *Christian Science Monitor;* Gault MacGowan, *New York Sun;* Donald MacKenzie, *New York Daily News;* John Fleming, *Newsweek;* and Grant Parr, switched from the *New York Times* to NBC. Also present, having been in Cairo since August, were Chester Morrison, *Chicago Sun;* Frank Gervasi, *Collier's;* and Fred Sondern, *Reader's Digest.*

The correspondents, anticipating an opportunity to report something significant, were deeply disappointed and irritated by a curtain of secrecy drawn around the meeting at the Mena House. There and in forty-three villas nearby, the participants in the conference and their staff aides lived under heavy guard. The correspondents did not get near the scene of the conference, and they were given no opportunity to see, much less interview any of the principals. They were prevented from sending any information whatever until the conferences were concluded, both at Cairo and Teheran, and until the principals had returned home. As a matter of guarding the safety of the leading personalities, this was understandable, but the correspondents still had nothing upon which to base even delayed dispatches except unrevealing official communiqués and such details and anecdotes as they were able to gather by talking with hotel staff members and others.

The correspondents' annoyance at what they regarded as a fiasco at Cairo was directed particularly at a representative assigned there by the British MOI. Curteis F. M. Ryan, a former treasury official with no understanding of press and communications matters, was accused of adding to security difficulties, of asking for unrealistic release dates on stories, and of displaying an attitude devoid of helpfulness. Representatives of the U.S. Office of War Information, also present, shared in the correspondents' displeasure. The OWI as well as the MOI both presented what Monks of the *Daily Mail* described as "the most abominable tripe" at 10 A.M. and 6 P.M. news conferences each day. The only photos were made by official photographers.

The final blow for the correspondents was that the first accounts of the Cairo conference to reach the world came, not from Cairo, but through the Lisbon bureau of the Reuters agency, and then more than thirty-two hours before the reports from Cairo itself were to have been given simultaneous release in London and Washington. Because Lisbon was a neutral capital, and under no censorship restrictions, the news went from there to Reuters clients in neutral countries, where it was picked up by Berlin and broadcast from Germany with propaganda overtones. Even then, neither London nor Washington was ready to admit that there had been a conference in Cairo. Further, when the release time came in Cairo, there was a serious jam in outgoing transmission of reports. Correspondents in Cairo protested both to Brenden Bracken, British minister of information, and to Elmer Davis, director of the U.S. Office of War Information. Their protests were supported by directors of news agencies and newspapers, but the harm had been done.

It was revealed later that the Lisbon "leak" had occurred because

Thomas Ming-heng Chao, Reuters correspondent in Chungking, and a graduate both of the University of Missouri and Columbia University schools of journalism, had stopped in Cairo en route by air from Chungking to London, accompanying a Chinese delegation. He had learned that the Cairo conference was in progress. Since he was not there in his capacity as a correspondent, he was under no obligation to observe a release date. His information was limited, but when he reached Lisbon on his flight, he told Douglas Brown, then Lisbon correspondent for Reuters, of the Cairo meeting. Brown prepared and dispatched a story on the subject in what Reuters later called a spirit of "spontaneous journalistic enterprise."

The situation at the Teheran conference was no better for the correspondents than it was in Cairo. Correspondents were denied facilities to proceed to the Teheran meeting on the grounds that transportation was lacking, and perhaps accommodations. When three of them contracted to hire a French plane to take them to Teheran, they were denied the right to leave Cairo.

Lloyd Stratton, assistant general manager of the Associated Press and president of the Associated Press of Great Britain, had been in Cairo on agency business, but not as a correspondent. Noticing that the USSR was not represented in Cairo, he deduced or learned that a second meeting would be held in Teheran, and flew there before a restriction was imposed on such travel. John Phillips, *Life* photographer, also flew to Teheran early. John Wallis, Reuters, and Oskar Guth, a former Czech newsman representing UP, were in the Iran capital on permanent assignment. Edward Angly, *Chicago Sun*, who had been in the southwest Pacific for that paper, happened to be in Teheran awaiting plane transportation to Moscow on a new assignment. He and Stratton were obliged to go to Cairo after the Teheran conference, however, to file reports which were held along with all others for delayed transmission. Wallis, although remaining in Teheran, also had to clear his copy through the Cairo censorship, again with delayed transmission.

Representatives of the Tass agency were present at Teheran, and also representatives of the MOI and OWI. Before any reference to the conference was made available through Cairo, London, or Washington, the Tass agency released the news through Moscow that the conference was in progress. It had met at Teheran on the insistance of Stalin and contrary to the wishes of Roosevelt. The release of the news by Tass came as an ill-timed breach of security affecting the travel arrangements of the British and U.S. leaders and their staff associates. It also brought further grumbling from the gagged representatives of the Anglo–U.S. media.

When Churchill and Roosevelt returned to Cairo and held the second meeting there, Soviet and Turkish representatives joining them were

André Vishinsky of the Foreign Commissariat and President Ismet Inönü. The same closed situation on information confronted the correspondents as before. Most of them were forced to live in Cairo itself, ten miles from the meeting place at El Giza. Commiserating with one another on the terrace at Shepheard's Hotel, overlooking the Nile, they referred to the Cairo meetings as the "Sphinx Conference" and conferred upon Ryan of the MOI, in absentia, an unofficial special order of knighthood, the Order of Barren Mena, by which he also was to be styled as "Lord Mena."

Churchill, who had been unwell throughout the period of the Cairo and Teheran conferences, and whose departure from Cairo was delayed for that reason, held an off-the-record news conference at the British embassy after Roosevelt and other principals had left, as had most U.S. correspondents. Although he permitted no questions, this timing was viewed by the U.S. media as a further flaw in the Cairo-Teheran meetings. Roosevelt, responding to their objections in Washington, proposed that in future no war information having a security aspect should be issued in advance on a hold-for-release basis, but should be released only when it might also be available for immediate publication. This could not bind other governments but as it happened no comparable situation arose again during the period of the war.

Return to Rome, 1944

When the Allied offensive in Italy was about to resume in the spring of 1944, Lieutenant General Sir Oliver Leese, who had been with Field Marshal Montgomery in Egypt, Libya, and Tunisia, and had succeeded to his command in Italy, briefed members of the British Eighth Army facing the German Gustav Line. The force included Canadian units as well as those from the United Kingdom. General Mark W. Clark briefed the U.S. Fifth Army, divided between the Gustav Line and Anzio sector.

The new offensive began on the night of May 11. It was successful in capturing the heights at Monte Cassino, an ancient monastery and a German defensive keystone. It had survived a devastating attack in February, but was reduced to rubble by air strikes and artillery fire. With that particular obstacle removed on May 18, the Allied forces pushed northward. Those in the Anzio sector drove toward Cisterna, where contact was established on May 25 with the forces advancing in the center. A concerted drive followed, with the last German line south of Rome penetrated on May 31.

Early in the Sicily campaign, on July 19, 1943, but with the move into

the heart of Italy in prospect, a group of seven U.S. and British correspondents went as observers when about 500 planes flew from bases in
North Africa and Sicily for a daylight reconnaissance and bombing raid
on the Rome airfields and railroad marshalling yards. The object also
was to interfere with the movement of German troops and supplies for
use in Sicily and southern Italy. It was, however, the first bombing raid
upon Rome, and was planned carefully to avoid damage to the Vatican
or other areas beyond those targeted.

The correspondents on that Rome flight of 1943 included Raymond
Clapper, Washington syndicated columnist on a visit to North Africa,[12]
Herbert L. Matthews, *New York Times,* former Rome correspondent of
that paper who had recently arrived in Algiers after a period in India;
Thomas L. Treanor, *Los Angeles Times,* and Richard McMillan, UP
and BUP, both of whom had reported from Italy before 1941; Richard Tregaskis, INS; James H. Nicholson, Reuters; Joseph Morton, AP;
Sergeant Milton Lehman, *Stars and Stripes;* and Sergeant M. H. Montgomery, U.S. Army Air Force photographer. Matthews later broadcast
the story of the raid to radio listeners in Italy, speaking in Italian from
Algiers. Matthews and Sergeant Lehman were to be among the first
correspondents to enter Rome in 1944.

The German resistance below Rome broke on June 2, 1944, and Allied forces reached the heart of the city on June 4. Correspondents were
in Naples, Caserta, and Foggia, in the Anzio sector, and with the Eighth
Army when the drive on Monte Cassino began in May, and they followed the action through to Rome. The advance continued northward,
and reached Florence on August 12. Strong German defenses were encountered beyond the city along a so-called Gothic Line across the last
relatively narrow part of the Italian peninsula from Leghorn, in the
west, to Ancona, on the Adriatic in the east.

The active correspondent group at the outset of the 1944 compaign
included some already mentioned as remaining in Italy; some who
returned after a period out of the theater, and some newcomers. The
experienced group included Eleanor Packard, UP, who had been in
Turkey; Reynolds Packard, UP; Joseph Morton, AP, and Graham Hovey, INS, who had been in Algiers; Sy Korman, *Chicago Tribune;* Frederick C. Painton, *Reader's Digest;* Henry Buckley, Reuters; Samuel
Goldstein, INP; Charles Seawood, NEA-Acme Newspictures; and Roderick MacDonald, *Sydney Morning Herald* and *News-Chronicle.*

Newcomers included James L. Kilgallen, experienced INS correspondent, who had been in the Pacific, and then became INS chief in

---

12 Clapper never lived to learn of Rome's liberation in June 1944. He was killed that
January in a plane crash over Eniwetok while reporting the war in the Pacific.

Naples. The Hearst organization and INS was further represented by William Randolph Hearst, Jr., himself, by Frank Conniff, *New York Journal-American* and INS; Burris Jenkins, Jr., *New York Journal-American* cartoonist and sketch artist; and Rita Hume, INS.

Others included Milton Bracker, *New York Times;* Russell Hill, experienced correspondent for the *New York Herald Tribune;* Carl Mydans, *Life* photographer, repatriated to New York in December after his capture by the Japanese in Manila in January 1942; Edward Laning, *Life* artist; Lynn Heinzerling and Stephen Barber, AP; Edd Johnson, *Chicago Sun;* Edward P. Morgan, *Chicago Daily News* and *New York Post;* Frederick Faust, *Harper's* magazine; Winston Burdett, CBS; John Talbot, Reuters; and Graham Beamish, *Sunday Times* and Kemsley Newspapers.

The Allied advances of May-August 1944 were conducted against heavy German opposition, and casualties occurred among the news corps as among the troops. Frederick Faust, writing for *Harper's* magazine, was killed by German mortar fire only about thirty minutes after the Allied offensive began on May 11. Known for his fiction, he published under the name of Max Brand and was author of a popular "Dr. Kildare" series of motion picture stories. Roderick MacDonald, representing the *Sydney Morning Herald* and the *News-Chronicle,* who had been in action in Burma, China, North Africa, and Sicily, where he was captured during the first assault but escaped, was killed in a land mine explosion on May 18. Cyril Bewley of the *Sunday Times* and the Kemsley papers was killed in the same blast. Henry Buckley, Reuters, and Edward Laning, *Life* artist, were injured.

Among the first correspondents to enter Rome on June 4 was Daniel DeLuce, AP, who sent the first story by any U.S. correspondent bearing a Rome dateline since December 1941. Reynolds Packard, UP, carried a key to the Rome UP office that he had been obliged to abandon on December 8, 1941, and which he now reopened to resume his post as bureau manager. Edward Kennedy, AP, a member of that agency's Rome staff in December 1941, was prepared to reopen the bureau, of which Richard Massock a former Rome chief, took charge. Cecil Sprigge, Reuters, reopened that agency's office, which had been closed in June 1940 as Italy entered the war.

Others entering Rome included Herbert L. Matthews, *New York Times,* a former Rome bureau chief for that paper; Milton Bracker, also *New York Times;* Eleanor Packard, UP, who had served there with her husband prior to December 1941; James E. Roper, also UP; Kenneth L. Dixon and George W. Tucker, both of the AP; James L. Kilgallen, INS chief; Frank Conniff, Graham Hovey, Rita Hume, and Michael Chinigo, recovered from his jeep accident of February, all representing INS;

Burris Jenkins, Jr., *New York Journal-American* artist; Homer Bigart and John Chabot Smith, both of the *New York Herald Tribune,* with Smith reopening the paper's bureau; Stead, *Christian Science Monitor;* Morgan, *Chicago Daily News* and *New York Post;* Carey Longmire, also *New York Post;* Daniel Lang, *New Yorker* magazine; Painton, *Reader's Digest;* Sergeant Lehman, *Stars and Stripes;* Fred Rosen, *Yank;* Mydans, *Life* photographer; Sevareid, Fowle, and Burdett, all of CBS; and Allan Michie, *Reader's Digest.*

The problem of communications was constantly in the minds of correspondents during the move toward Rome. Mobile transmitters were available at points set by the army so that copy could be relayed to Naples for transmission from there to New York by RCA Communications, and rebroadcast from there to London. Direct service for copy and for voice broadcast was established from Rome to New York and from Rome to London after June 11. Military press headquarters was established in Rome at a foreign press building (Stampa Estera), where Colonel Kenneth Clark, Fifth Army public relations officer, and Major Henry Erlich, his assistant, set up offices.

Correspondents in Rome occupied themselves at first by producing eye-witness reports of the move into the city and the reactions of the populace. They obtained interviews in Vatican City, including an informal conference with Pope Pius XII.

The Allied capture of Rome brought a number of correspondents to the city for special coverage, although some remained as war reporters. Among them were Anne O'Hare McCormick, *New York Times,* Pulitzer Prize winner of 1937, in part for her perceptive reports on Italy at that period; Alexander H. Uhl, *PM,* arriving from Algiers and Bari; William Boss and Douglas Howe, Canadian Press; Pat Frank and Victor Bienstock, coming from Cairo for the Overseas News Agency; John Jordan, *Norfolk Journal and Guide,* a Negro paper of Norfolk, Va.; and John Osborne, *Time.*

As the fighting moved north of Rome several other correspondents joined the Allied group. Aldo Forte, UP, manager of the agency bureau in Berne since December 1941, returned to his previous post in Rome. Terence Southwell-Keely, previously in the Southwest Pacific for the *Sydney Morning Herald,* became a representative of that paper and of the *News-Chronicle,* and was a replacement in Italy for Roderick MacDonald killed in May. Graham Beamish, New Zealand-born, represented the *Sunday Times* as a replacement for Cyril Bewley, also killed. John F. Chester, AP, came from Cairo to Italy, and French-born Paul Ghali, *Chicago Daily News,* was in the area.

At least three correspondents were injured in the July-August campaign to reach Florence. Beamish, so recently arrived for the *Sunday*

Times and having served previously in North Africa, suffered a broken leg. Roper, UP, sustained injuries to his eyes when the jeep in which he was riding was dive-bombed. He was awarded a Purple Heart. Eleanor Packard, UP, in returning from the front, was hurt near Leghorn in another jeep accident when her vehicle swerved sharply to avoid collision. She also was nearly taken by Italian Partisans in Volterra, mistaken for a German spy.

Seventeen correspondents covered a combined naval and ground-force operation resulting in the capture during June of the German-held island of Elba, just off the Tuscany shore in the Tyrrhenian Sea. The action was brief, but marked by heavy fighting during which correspondents were in grave danger. This was especially so for Conniff, INS; Barber, AP; and Lucas, *Daily Express.* Other correspondents engaged included A.C. (Chan) Sedgwick, *New York Times;* Conger, UP; Frank Jones, Reuters; Maurice Fagence, *Daily Herald;* Chester Morrison, NBC; Norman Fisher, Fox Movietone News; R. W. V. Parker, Exchange Telegraph; and Sergeant Len Smith and Lieutenant William Brinkley, USN, both for *Stars and Stripes.*

While these advances proceeded in Italy, the Red Army momentum of 1944 carried it westward into Rumania, Bulgaria, Hungary and what had been Austria. To avoid being pinched off, German forces occupying Crete, Greece, and Yugoslavia withdrew by the autumn of 1944. Allied landings took place in Greece early in October, but internal conflicts in progress there since 1943 led to a civil war after the German withdrawal, with Communist elements in conflict with royalists. The royalists supported the return of King George II, who had left the country in April 1941 when an armistice was signed between Greece and the German invaders. The issue was not settled until September 1946 when the king returned to the throne.

Operation Dragoon: France, 1944

The Allied push northward in Italy, halted at the Gustav Line in the autumn of 1943, was halted again at the Gothic Line above Florence in the autumn of 1944. This was in part because of the German defensive position there, but more particularly because any appreciable advance would have required more forces to cover the broad extent of northern Italian territory spreading out between the Yugoslav and French frontiers, just when available troops were viewed as more urgently required in France.

There Allied forces had landed in Normandy on June 6, 1944, two days after the occupation of Rome. Operation Overlord had almost overshadowed the triumph in Rome. Paris had been liberated on August 25, shortly after Florence was liberated in Italy. German forces in France were being driven eastward toward the border of their own country. To assist and expedite their expulsion from France, points in liberated Italy became bases for new Allied amphibious operations, and for the diversion of forces in Operation Anvil, soon retitled Operation Dragoon, for the invasion of France from the South.

The U.S. Seventh Army, previously active in North Africa and Sicily and now under Lieutenant General Alexander M. Patch, drew ten U.S. and French divisions from the Italian front for this landing in France, even before the capture of Florence. Other forces were brought from North Africa, strong naval and air support was added, and partisan groups in France gave aid to the operation. Landings were made west of Nice on the French Riviera on August 15, 1944. With mechanized forces, the troops moved northward up the Rhone River valley and on September 15 established contact with General Patton's Third Army northeast of Dijon. The combined forces then joined in a direct assault on Germany.

Coverage of this operation was provided by correspondents who had been in Italy, and some who continued to report from there. In the first period the dispatches cleared through Rome, forwarded to London and New York by commercial communications companies.

Reynolds Packard, UP, was in charge of a four-man staff covering the landing in France. The other three were Robert Vermillion, who jumped with paratroopers, Pat Conger, and Dana Adams Schmidt. Handling their reports in Rome were Eleanor Packard and James E. Roper, then recovering from his July injury. For the AP, the invasion staff included Kenneth Dixon, George W. Tucker, Sid Feder, and Joseph Dynan, who came from Algiers with Free French troops participating in the operation. Henry Griffin represented AP Photos and the Wartime Picture Pool. Edward Kennedy remained in Rome in charge of the AP bureau, with Lee Noland Norgaard as an assistant. The INS invasion team included Graham Hovey, Frank Conniff, and Larry Newman, with Michael Chinigo at air headquarters, Rita Hume in Corsica, a departure point, and James Kilgallen in Rome. Harold King, Reuters, who had represented the agency in France for fifteen years prior to 1940, supervised that agency's coverage.

Others engaged in the operation included Richard Mowrer, *Chicago Daily News,* who jumped with paratroopers; Matthews of the *New York Times,* and Bigart of the *Herald Tribune,* both of whom represented the Combined American Press, with their reports widely distributed; Carleton (Bill) Kent, of the *Chicago Times;* Ronald Maillard Stead, *Christian Science Monitor;* Carey Longmire, *New York Post;* and Edd

Johnson, *Chicago Sun.* There also were Guy Norman, the *Times* of London; L. Marsland Gander, *Daily Telegraph;* André Glarner, Exchange Telegraph (Extel); and Vaughan Thomas, BBC; Newbold Noyes, Jr., *Washington Star;* Frank Gervasi, *Collier's;* Carl Mydans, *Life;* Frederick C. Painton, *Reader's Digest;* and Eric Sevareid and Winston Burdett for CBS.

At Algiers, Harold Callender, *New York Times,* and Sonia Tomara, *New York Herald Tribune,* both with rich prewar experience in Paris and elsewhere in Europe, were able to produce reports supplementing the news of the landings. Correspondents for the French media accompanied forces moved from Algiers. Fernand Pistor, who had represented the French radio at Algiers, was killed in the fighting at Marseille, the only casualty among those correspondents.

Edd Johnson, *Chicago Sun,* received a special citation for giving aid to wounded men while under fire during the Seventh Army advance up the Rhone River valley. He gained another distinction by riding into Grenoble in a tram and being received by a cheering throng as the first Allied liberator of that university town. Dana Schmidt on September 7 became the first newsman to reach Vichy, with assistance from the French underground forces aiding the Allies. In November, he produced the first detailed reports on the collapse of the Vichy government under Pétain, who had been forced to leave France and live in Germany under a Nazi threat to shoot one hundred French hostages if he refused.

Some correspondents remained in Italy during the landings, but later managed to get to southern France at intervals. In late August, Edward Kennedy, AP, and four other Rome correspondents obtained a jeep and driver and made a wide loop through western France to Paris, by then liberated. They passed safely between two German military columns on the way, obtained considerable information about sections of the country through which they passed, and made the first connection between northern and southern France. What they did was contrary to regulations, and they were suspended for two days, denied the right to file copy from France, and then were sent back to Rome. Kennedy had arrived in Paris with a smashed thumb, the result of a jeep accident en route.

Rome traditionally had been an observation post for diplomats and newsmen from which to watch the course of affairs in Italy and all of southern Europe. The war had interfered with this opportunity, obscuring and distorting the perspective. Prospects for a return to earlier conditions began to reappear, however, in the spring of 1944.

Almost coincidentally with the resumption of the Allied offensive in May of that year, six correspondents turned their attention from the assault on the Gustav Line to cross the Adriatic to Yugoslavia, as Daniel DeLuce, AP, had done in the previous October, and also to look beyond to Bulgaria, Greece, Hungary, and Rumania. The first of the six to do so was Joseph Morton, AP, who obtained an interview with Tito in May 1944 and then returned to Italy. There his account was held up by Allied censors for twenty days because of political elements. These related to a high-level controversy as to whether the Allies should recognize General Mihailovich, leader of the royalist-oriented Chetnik group in German-occupied Yugoslavia, or the opposing Partisans headed by Tito (Josip Broz). Consideration also was given to the relations of both groups to Soviet Russia, long interested in the Slavic heritage in that part of the world, and especially so with the Germans retreating from an advancing Red Army.

Sergeant Walter Bernstein of *Yank* went to Yugoslavia, also in May, and obtained an interview with Tito. Some of his accounts appeared in the *New Yorker* magazine. A few weeks later, John Talbot of Reuters, representing the combined British and U.S. press, arrived in Yugoslavia from Italy. So did Serbian-born Stoyan Pribichevich of *Time* and *Life,* with two photographers, Slade and Fowler. They made contact with Tito and observed Partisan activities. All four of these men were captured, however, by German paratroopers in a surprise descent on the town of Drvar, about sixty miles due north of the port of Split. Pribichevich managed to escape,[13] but the others were held. Talbot was taken to Germany as a prisoner of war, and only gained his release in the final Allied advance into Germany in April 1945.

During July 1944, Sulzberger of the *New York Times* contrived to have a series of written questions conveyed to General Mihailovich. Although the contest between Chetniks and Partisans had been resolved in June, with Tito winning Allied favor, Mihailovich replied, and his views, as presented in the *New York Times* of August 6, were widely quoted.

Joseph G. Harrison of the *Christian Science Monitor* was able to spend about a month in Yugoslavia early in 1944, and then move to Greece prior to returning to Italy. Eleanor Packard, UP, went from Rome to Belgrade, the Yugoslav capital, in November 1944 at a time when the city had come under Red Army occupation. Stories passed by Allied censors there made clear the strong Soviet and Communist influence on the Yugoslav government under Marshal Tito, a Moscow-trained Communist. As a result, Mrs. Packard was expelled.[14]   The

---

13   Winston Churchill's son, Major Randolph Churchill, then at Tito's Bosnian headquarters with the British 8th Corps, told Pribichevich, "you have the biggest story of the war! In fact, since my father's escape from the Boers, no one has had such a story to tell." This was a reference to Winston Churchill's escape from captivity during the South African or Boer War of 1899–1902, when he was serving as a correspondent for the London *Morning Post*. See R. W. Desmond, *The Information Process* (1978), pp. 410–11.

14   Her precise offense was to count and mention the number of photos of Stalin and Tito displayed, and the absence of any of Churchill or Roosevelt.

first Allied newsman to enter Bulgaria after Soviet military advances had forced the German withdrawal in 1944 was Leon Kay, UP, who was well received in Sofia. Joseph Morton, AP, having interviewed Tito in May, was the first correspondent to reach Rumania in September 1944, after Bucharest had been freed of German control and brought under Red Army occupation. In "cloak-and-dagger" circumstances, he was able to interview King Michael, and then return to Yugoslavia and Italy. In December, Morton returned to Rumania with seventeen U.S. and British military men and won the release of Allied airmen captured by the Germans earlier in the bombing of the Ploesti oilfields and refineries there.

Morton chose to remain in Rumania, but nothing more was heard from him. In March 1945, it was learned that he had been captured in Slovakia by Germans on December 26, 1944, and had been taken to a concentration camp at Mauthausen, near Linz, Austria. After the German surrender in May 1945, it was further learned that Morton had been executed by the Germans on the previous January 24. He was one of thirteen American and British captives executed and then cremated. All except Morton were members of the U.S. Office of Strategic Services (OSS).

Still another southern European operation involving correspondents, some of whom had been based in Italy, was the Allied landing in Greece during October 1944. As the Germans withdrew from that area and from Yugoslavia, correspondents who arrived included Roper, UP, and Gander, *Daily Telegraph,* both of whom had reported the landing in southern France; Lucas, *Daily Express;* and Southwell-Keely, *Sydney Morning Herald* and *News-Chronicle.* Others were Joseph G. Harrison, *Christian Science Monitor,* also writing for the *News-Chronicle* and for the Sunday *Observer;* Edwin Tetlow, *Daily Mail;* and Milton Bracker, *New York Times.* Marcel W. Fodor, formerly Balkans correspondent in Vienna for the *Manchester Guardian* and the *Chicago Daily News,* arrived to represent the *Chicago Sun;* George Weller, *Chicago Daily News;* Clay Gowran, *Chicago Tribune;* Rex Ingraham, *Time* magazine; Peter Lessing, Reuters; and Emery Pearce, *Daily Herald.*

Constantine Poulos, an American of Greek parentage, had been director in New York of the OWI foreign language division overseas broadcasts by the Voice of America (VOA). He went to Cairo as a correspondent for the Overseas News Agency (ONA), and arrived in Athens in mid-August 1944. Poulos lived with Greek guerrillas for two months before liberation occurred in September-October 1944, and then remained in Athens as the only Greek-speaking correspondent representing ONA.

In Italy, the Allied advance against the Germans remaining above the Gothic Line resumed in January 1945. The final assault began in April and the German force, along with the remnant of the Italian Fascist army, surrendered May 2, six days before the surrender at Reims that ended the war in Europe.

Apart from the military action and the capture of such cities as Genoa, Bologna, Venice, and Milan, and the general collapse of the Wehrmacht, a major event of the last days in Italy was the capture of Mussolini on April 27 by Italian Partisans at Dongo, on the shore of Lake Como. He was in a motor convoy with his mistress, Clara Petacci, and a group of associates in what was left of the Fascist government. They were bound for what they hoped would be a safe haven in Switzerland. Lieutenant Colonel Valerio of the Partisan force, acting under the terms of a decree of a "North Italian Committee of National Liberation," directed against "those responsible for the catastrophe into which Italy has been led," summarily shot and killed Mussolini and his mistress on the day after their capture. Their bodies were taken to the Piazzale Loreto in Milan where a group of Partisans recently had been publicly executed. The bodies were hung by the heels outside a gasoline service station and later were buried in an unmarked grave. In 1957, Mussolini's body was exhumed and placed in a family vault.

The relative inactivity of the war in Italy after August 1944, contrasted to the great activity in France and the Pacific, had resulted in the departure of perhaps half of the correspondents who had been present earlier in the year. When the campaign began again in northern Italy in the spring of 1945 the relatively few correspondents included Rex Ingraham, for *Time* and *Life;* James P. Roper, UP; John Chabot Smith, *New York Herald Tribune;* Howard Norton, *Baltimore Sun;* Gene Rae, *Il Progresso-Americano,* an Italian-language daily of New York; Helen Hiett, the Religious News Service, New York; and Louis Vernay-Ramondy, of the recently formed Agence France-Presse (AFP), successor to the former Agence Havas of France.

A different group of correspondents was able to report the killing of Mussolini and Signorina Petacci. These were Christopher D. R. Lumby, of the London *Times,* and Stephen Barber, moved from the AP to the *News-Chronicle,* who were the first to reach Milan. Early to arrive, also, were Milton Bracker, *New York Times;* Joseph G. Harrison, *Christian Science Monitor;* and Richard Mowrer, *Chicago Daily News.* These three saw the bodies on display, as did Paul Ghali, also of the *Chicago Daily News,* who was present when the bodies were hung and then went to Switzerland to report the story. Thus ended the Fascist dictatorship of Mussolini and the war in Italy.

PART IV
Into the Atomic Age

The Last Wartime Year in Europe, 1944–45

16

At the beginning of 1942, those nations forming the Rome-Berlin-Tokyo Axis seemed in a dominant position in the warring world. Germany, under Hitler, had confidence that its power would result in the creation of a "New Europe" through which it could control the "heartland" of the world, as conceived by geopoliticists. At the same time, Japan was advancing claims to direct what it called the Greater East Asia Co-Prosperity Sphere. Italy, less successful in battle, remained nevertheless as an Axis partner.

The Allied countries, at a serious disadvantage, still did not lack for courage, resources, imagination, and determination. Their leaders never permitted themselves to contemplate anything other than ultimate victory. Priorities had to be set, however, for measures both defensive and counteroffensive in various parts of the globe. In this, the first order of importance was given to the defeat of Germany and Italy. The defeat of Japan in the Pacific and in Asia then would follow.

Among the Allies, Stalin and the Soviet Union urged a second front in the west to keep the German and Italian forces occupied, and so to relieve the pressure on Russia itself. The Anglo-American campaign in Africa, Sicily, and Italy from 1941–45 was not a second front, as viewed from Moscow. What was desired was a frontal attack on Germany or on German positions on the European continent.

At the Quadrant Conference in Quebec in August 1943, Allied leaders agreed that a major attack would be directed at the Normandy coast of France in an all-out effort to dislodge the German hold on that country and to push on to victory in Europe. It was to be a joint British and U.S. campaign, with Free French elements participating, supported by the Maquis, or resistance group, within France. The tentative date was set for May 1944, and the invasion was designated "Operation Overlord."

General Eisenhower, who had commanded the North African, Sicilian, and Italian actions of 1942–43 from AFHQ in Algiers, and Field Marshal Bernard L. Montgomery, who had led the British Eighth Army to victory from Egypt to Tunisia, as well as in Sicily and Italy, were among those who moved to London during the winter of 1943–44 to prepare for the new campaign. Again, Eisenhower was named to direct the operation from the new Supreme Headquarters, Allied Expeditionary Force (SHAEF). Originally based in St. James's Square, with major branches in Grosvenor Square, it was moved in the spring of 1944 to Bushy Park, south of London, near Hampton Court.

Because of the expectation that such an attack on Germany would be undertaken from the United Kingdom, and because of the wartime decisions centering there, the U.S. media continued to be well represented in London.

The RAF had made its first daylight attack on Berlin in late January 1942. A saturation raid on Cologne had occurred in March, with 1,000 aircraft flying from British bases. Subsequent British attacks were directed at a dozen German cities, most of them in night flights. The U.S. Eighth Air Force was activated in the spring of 1942. Its base was in England, but it did not fly any mission until August. Meanwhile, most U.S. aircraft were going to the Pacific and to the North African theaters. A U.S. Ninth Strategic Bombing Command had been set up in Egypt to aid in the Rumanian (Ploesti), North African, Sicilian, and Italian campaigns. Its base was transferred to Britain in September 1943, and its planes flew missions against targets in France and Germany.

The first U.S. ground force installations were established in Northern Ireland late in 1942. Dixie Tighe, INS, arrived in the United Kingdom in October, the first woman to be accredited for war reporting overseas with U.S. forces.[1] She covered the Irish encampment, the U.S. Eighth Air Force base, and accompanied Eleanor Roosevelt on a tour of the British Isles. In mid-February 1943, Tighe flew with the British coastal command on a thirteen-hour operational mission into the Atlantic and off the coast of Spain.

One of the first big stories of 1943 for the British press and for U.S. correspondents in London was a heavy night air attack on the heart of Berlin on January 16. Seven correspondents flew as observers in RAF Liberator bombers. It was the first major air action out of Britain in which correspondents had been permitted to participate. The seven were Stewart Sale, Reuters; Louis Hunter, Canadian Press; Richard Dimbleby, BBC; Keith Hooper, *Daily Express* and *Sydney Daily Mirror;* James (Jamie) MacDonald, *New York Times;* Stanley Richardson, NBC; and Australian-born Colin Bednall, *Daily Mail.* Bednall had replaced Arthur R. Narracott of the *Times,* who was grounded at the airfield by RAF medical authorities because of ear trouble. All produced

---

1   Dixie Tighe was an experienced newspaperwoman, then the wife of C. V. R. Thompson, New York correspondent for the *Daily Express.* She had worked in that paper's New York bureau. Formerly with the *New York Post,* she covered ship news and met Thompson in the course of that work.

memorable stories, including Narracott, who described the atmosphere at the field as planes departed and returned—or failed to return.

The German Luftwaffe had not been particularly active over the British Isles for almost two years, having been occupied in the Soviet Union and eastern Europe. The RAF attack of January 16 on Berlin was followed on January 27 by the first U.S. Eighth Air Force attack on German targets, with press participation, and the air war against Germany grew from that period.

A group of eight U.S. correspondents completed a week of special training with the Eighth Air Force in February to prepare them to accompany bombers flying on missions at high altitudes. They were Robert P. Post, *New York Times;* Gladwin Hill, AP; Walter Cronkite, UP; William Wade, INS; Homer Bigart, *New York Herald Tribune;* Paul Manning, MBS; Sergeant Denton Scott, *Yank;* and Private Andrew Rooney, *Stars and Stripes.*

These men, unofficially referred to as "the Writing 69th," were obliged to pass physical examinations, to learn how to perform while wearing oxygen masks and while flying at altitudes in which subzero temperatures were inevitable even in the plane, how to sling and use a parachute, how to conduct themselves in the event of a "ditching" at sea, and how to accustom themselves to flying as the pilot might take evasive action by diving, climbing steeply, and weaving to prevent antiaircraft gunners or pursuing fighter planes from getting an accurate "fix" on the bomber.

This group had scarcely completed the training program when all except Manning, who was ill, flew on a February 26, 1943, daylight raid on Wilhelmshaven. The B-17 Fortress in which Post of the *New York Times* was an observer was shot down near Oldenburg. His death was confirmed from Berlin in August. Post's death resulted in a message from Edwin L. James, managing editor of the *New York Times,* advising correspondents for that paper not to make combat flights over enemy territory. He regarded the risks as unwarranted. Some other news executives agreed with James. While not forbidding correspondents to fly, they made it clear that an option existed, with the decision left to the individual. Some did fly later in British and U.S. planes, but perhaps fewer than might have done so except for James' advice.

Colin Bednall, *Daily Mail,* who had been in another bomber on the same raid in which Post was killed, went in a U.S. B-17 Flying Fortress raid on St. Nazaire in April. Earle Poorbaugh, INS, replacing Wade on the agency's air assignment, received the special Eighth Air Force training. A number of photographers also went on combat missions, among them David Scherman, *Life;* Joseph Dearing, *Collier's;* James E. Ewins, Gaumont British newsreel; and Eric Barrow, Universal Newsreel.

Another situation involving London correspondents as observers on combat missions occurred December 2, 1943, when four flew with the RAF on a large-scale night bombing of Berlin. They were Lowell Bennett, INS; Edward R. Murrow, CBS; A. W. V. King, *Sydney Morning Herald;* and Norman Stockton, *Sydney Sun,* formerly a correspondent in China, Hong Kong, and New Guinea. A fifth participant was Captain N. Ordhal Grieg, a Norwegian author and war reporter, who had arrived in the United Kingdom in June 1940 after British forces retired from Norway.

Stockton and Grieg failed to return from the mission, and Grieg's death was confirmed in February 1944. The aircraft in which Bennett was an observer was hit by shells fired by a German interceptor plane while on the bomb run over Berlin. It burst into flames and all aboard, Bennett included, bailed out at a four-mile altitude.

A letter from Bennett written from a German prisoner-of-war camp, dated December 11, was addressed to the INS office in London. It was delivered to the agency's New York office on January 21. Two days later a second letter was delivered in New York. Dated December 23 and smuggled out of Germany, it was Bennett's full and dramatic account of how the bomber had been destroyed on the night of December 2. The letter recounted how he had parachuted and survived, almost miraculously, after landing half-conscious in a lake, being rescued and cared for by people of the village nearby, not far from Berlin, and then taken in charge by the military and placed in the prisoner-of-war camp.The second letter revealed that Bennett had escaped from the camp during a transfer of prisoners from one truck to another, and that he was free as he wrote. However, a third letter to reach New York was dated March 8 from another prisoner-of-war camp. Upon his release in May 1945, after the German surrender, it became known that he had been recaptured and held at Stalag Luft No. 1, at Barth, in Pomerania.[2]

Bednall of the *Daily Mail,* having failed to gain a place as an observer on the December 2 Berlin raid along with Bennett and the others, did

---

2   Lowell Bennett had led an unusually adventurous life. He had gone from the United States to Australia in 1939, aged 20, and joined the Royal Australian Air Force, but was obliged to resign when his U.S. citizenship was revealed. He proceeded to England and joined an International Brigade organized by Kermit Roosevelt to fight for Finland in the Russo-Finnish War. That war ended before he reached the front. Next he went to Paris and joined the French Foreign Legion, but withdrew when he learned that U.S. citizens, as neutrals, were not permitted to serve in combat units. He then joined the American Volunteer Ambulance Corps and drove on the Saar front in May-June 1940. He was captured by the Germans just before the French surrendered and was held in a concentration camp for five months. After his release, he reached England by way of Madrid and Lisbon. In London, he joined the Free French Army and served as an ambulance driver during the London blitz of late 1940, and later as a parachutist until his U.S. citizenship was revealed, when he was forced to withdraw. In July 1941, he joined the INS bureau in London. In the spring of 1943 he covered the fighting in Tunisia, after which he returned to England to report RAF and U.S. Army Air Force actions.

accompany an RAF attack on targets at Leipzig on the following night. It was his third trip over Germany, a record at the time for correspondents. Among others to fly on missions was Wilson C. ("Collie") Small, UP, who went over France and Belgium late in May 1944 to observe an attack on German defenses.

The tides of war brought changes in the number of correspondents in London at any one time. The very considerable group present during 1939–41 declined somewhat in 1942, especially as many went to North Africa late in the year. It was estimated that only about fifty U.S. media representatives remained in London at that time. The succession of events through 1943 in Tunisia, Sicily, and Italy drew more correspondents to that area, with many passing through London.

The British press itself was well staffed, and the Free French had establishments both in London and Algiers. The Commonwealth countries, notably Canada and Australia, sent more correspondents to London. The size of the U.S. media representation there seemed to be regarded as an index by which to measure the general preparations for an Allied invasion of the European continent. By August 1943 the *World's Press News* of London had raised a March estimate of 120 to 160 correspondents in the United Kingdom for the three major U.S. news agencies, 23 newspapers, 15 magazines, four radio networks, and several syndicates and special services.

Some of the arriving correspondents were visitors, remaining only briefly. Others were returning to London from the Sicilian and Italian area during the winter of 1943–44, some for rest or reassignment, and some to await the expected cross-channel invasion of France. Among the visitors were Marquis W. Childs, *St. Louis Post-Dispatch* correspondent in Washington and a syndicated columnist; Raymond Clapper, also a syndicated Washington correspondent; Charles Gratke, foreign editor and former Berlin and London correspondent for the *Christian Science Monitor;* and Blair Bolles, *Washington Star.* These four flew to Stockholm, the leading neutral capital, and returned to London en route to the United States. Scott Newhall, Sunday editor of the *San Francisco Chronicle,* journeyed from San Francisco to England aboard a British aircraft carrier, following its repair in the United States.

The novelist John Steinbeck, representing the *New York Herald Tribune,* passed through London early in 1943 en route to Sicily and later coverage of the Salerno landing. Grove H. Patterson, editor of the *Toledo Blade,* and Freda Kirchway of the *Nation* were visitors in London. Ernest Hemingway arrived for *Collier's;* he was injured in an automobile accident that hospitalized him for a week. S. J. Woolf, artist-biographer for the *New York Times,* arrived on an assignment from NEA to do a series of sketch-interviews with Allied military leaders. André

Laguerre, press director to the French Committee of National Liberation in Algiers, was another London visitor.

Arrivals also included some correspondents who had been actively engaged on other fronts. These included Beattie, UP, and Yarbrough, AP, both of whom had been in London during the 1940 blitz; Matt Halton, senior war correspondent for the Canadian Broadcasting Corporation, and also with the Eighth Army in Libya and Tunisia; Gallagher, AP, recovered from injuries in Tunisia; Hal Boyle, AP, back from the Mediterranean area; John MacVane, NBC, formerly in Algiers; and William A. S. Douglas, *Chicago Sun*, who had reported part of the Spanish Civil War and the beginning of the war in France and England.

Still other experienced men, perhaps remaining only briefly, included Knickerbocker, *Chicago Sun;* Richard G. Massock, AP, former Rome bureau chief, interned from December 1941 until his repatriation; Edward P. Morgan, *Chicago Daily News,* formerly in Mexico City for the UP, but soon reassigned from London to Italy; Walter Rundle, UP, formerly in Chungking; Robert Vermillion, UP, later in Italy;[3] Henry Ivor Williams, *Sydney Morning Herald,* who had covered the war in New Guinea; Fred Parker, INP photographer who had covered Panama for several years; Maurice Lancaster and Robert Navarro, motion picture cameramen, who had filmed earlier aspects of the war and returned to London for the "March of Time."

The London press corps was augmented by Frederic Sondern, Jr., for *Reader's Digest;* Robert Richards, Ed Murray, and Wilson C. ("Collie") Small, all for UP; John W. Willicombe, INS; Edward Lockett, *Time* and *Life;* John Morris, *Life;* John F. Chester, AP, former Washington correspondent and Boston bureau chief and later in Cairo and Italy; Abraham I. Goldberg, Judson O'Quinn, E. K. Butler and Wilmot W. Hercher, all also of the AP; and Wright Bryan, associate editor and managing editor of the *Atlanta Journal.*

The group of women correspondents in London, already included Mary Welsh, of *Time* and *Life;* Helen Kirkpatrick, *Chicago Daily News,* for a time at AFHQ, in Algiers; Dixie Tighe, INS; and Tatiana (Tania) Long (Mrs. F. Raymond Daniell), *New York Times.* The group was increased by the arrival of Marjorie (Dot) Avery for the *Detroit Free Press* and other newspapers then owned by John S. Knight in Akron and Miami; Kathleen Harriman, *Newsweek,* daughter of Averell Harriman; Dudley Ann Harmon, UP; Lee Miller, *Vogue;* Doris Fleeson

---

3 Vermillion had a remarkable escape in London during August 1943 when a German two-ton "blockbuster," dropped in an earlier air raid, exploded belatedly within 300 yards of where he stood. The irregularity of the terrain deflected the blast sufficiently to give protection to him and to others nearby.

(Mrs. John O'Donnell),[4] *Woman's Home Companion;* Betty Gaskill (Mrs. Gordon Gaskill), *Liberty;* and Rosette Hargrove (Mrs. Charles Hargrove), NEA. In addition, Iris Carpenter, London *Daily Herald,* became the first British woman correspondent accredited to the U.S. Army. Mary V.P. ("Mollie") McGee, Australian-born writer for the *Montreal Herald* and representative of the *Toronto Globe and Mail* at the Ministry of Information in London, also was accredited to the U.S. forces early in 1944.

Certain changes took place in the direction of the London bureaus for U.S. media. James B. ("Scotty") Reston, former London correspondent for the AP and then the *New York Times,* served briefly in that paper's Washington bureau, but returned to London in August 1943 to replace F. Raymond Daniell as bureau chief, while Daniell took an extended home leave, accompanied by his wife, Tania Long Daniell. John Martin Mecklin, formerly in the UP London bureau, joined the *Chicago Sun* bureau there as assistant to Frederick Kuh. William L. Shirer, CBS, and former Berlin correspondent, replaced Edward R. Murrow as London bureau chief during a period of home leave for Murrow. Elmer W. Peterson, NBC, formerly with the AP and most recently in Stockholm for the radio network, replaced Morgan Beatty in London when Beatty also took a period of home leave. As John MacVane came to London from Algiers for NBC, Don Hollenbeck left London to replace him at AFHQ and in the Mediterranean area. Alan Randal, Canadian Press, became chief of the London bureau when D. Ernest Burritt was transferred to New York as chief of that bureau. Lionel Shapiro, in London for the *Montreal Gazette,* was named a roving correspondent for *MacLean's Magazine.*

Among news executives visiting London in 1943 and early 1944, chiefly to participate in conferences concerned with coverage of the anticipated invasion of France, were Gillis Purcell, assistant general manager of the Canadian Press; Hugh Baillie, president of the United Press; Lloyd Stratton, secretary and assistant general manager of the Associated Press, and Alan J. Gould, also an assistant general manager of the AP, in charge of news and pictures; and Roy W. Howard of the Scripps-Howard Newspapers.

In line with the special training program given correspondents as flight observers with the U.S. Eighth Air Force in 1943 a comparable "invasion school" for correspondents accompanying ground forces was started at a U.S. Army base in England early in May 1943. The first class was attended by twenty-five newsmen who were given instruction in

4   John O'Donnell was with the *New York Daily News* as a Washington columnist; Gordon Gaskill was London representative of the *American Magazine*; and Charles Hargrove was in London for the *Wall Street Journal.*

map-reading, aircraft recognition, first aid, and other matters. Training for combat photography was given by the U.S. Ninth Air Force Bomber Command, by then transferred from North Africa to England. Reuters also sought to prepare its own correspondents by asking some of its staffers who had covered combat action to share what they had learned with others. Among those acting as instructors were Alan Humphreys, who had been at Dieppe and with the Royal Navy in North African landings during the Tunisian campaign, and Denis Martin, who was with the British Eighth Army during its advance from El Alamein to Tunis.

*Operation
Overlord*

Operation Overlord, the Allied campaign intended to defeat Germany, had been in the planning stage since the Casablanca Conference of January 1943, with final approval at the Quadrant or Quebec Conference of August 1943. By that time, the North African victory had been attained, the Sicilian campaign was in progress, the Italian surrender was near, and so was the invasion of Italy. By January 1944, the Allies were firmly established in Italy. From AFHQ, General Eisenhower transferred to London to the new Supreme Headquarters, Allied Expeditionary Force (SHAEF), to direct the joint cross-channel operation originally scheduled for May, but actually begun early on the morning of June 6, 1944, the long-awaited D-Day.

A Publicity and Psychological Warfare division (P&PW) of SHAEF was formed, under the direction of Brigadier General Robert A. McClure, who had been General Eisenhower's chief public relations officer at AFHQ. With P&PW arrangement, Eisenhower conducted his first London news conference in mid-January at the Grosvenor Square headquarters of SHAEF.

In April 1944, a division of functions was made whereby the P&PW became two separate organizations. General McClure took charge of an existing Psychological Warfare Branch (PWB), while Brigadier General Thomas Jefferson Davis of the regular U.S. Army and of the general staff became director of a Public Relations Branch (PRB). The PRB responsibility was to provide "the best possible facilities for full coverage of every phase of the forthcoming operations." Established in the headquarters of the British Ministry of Information, the PRB set general policies for the accreditation of war correspondents, their assignment to particular units, and the handling of their copy. It also supervised arrangements to help arriving correspondents find billets in

London, obtain ration cards, and adjust themselves to living in wartime England.

The staff of PRB included Colonel R. Ernest Dupuy, a member of the general staff, a former West Point faculty member, and one who had experience in the accreditation of correspondents to the AEF in France during World War I. British representatives were Brigadier William A. S. Turner of the War Office, and Air Commodore Lionel F. Heald. British Lieutenant Colonel H. C. Chappell was executive officer. U.S. Colonel Joseph B. Phillips, former assistant to General McClure at AFHQ, and formerly with the *New York Herald Tribune,* was placed in charge of communications, and British Lieutenant Colonel George Warden was in charge of censorship.

The Public Relations Branch had seven subdivisions concerned with liaison and news dissemination. It had its representatives not only at the MOI, in the Bloomsbury area of London, but at Grosvenor Square, referred to colloquially as "Eisenhower Platz" because of the location there and nearby of the U.S. Embassy and many offices used by U.S. wartime agencies, as well as at SHAEF in St. James's Square.

Within the seven divisions, Barry Bingham, publisher of the *Louisville Courier-Journal*, a lieutenant commander, was in charge of media liaison with the U.S. Navy. British Major S. R. Pawley of the *Daily Telegraph* was in charge of liaison with the British army. U.S. Lieutenant Colonel Thor M. Smith of the *San Francisco Call-Bulletin* was in charge of liaison with the U.S. Army and Air Force. Major Fred M. Payne, a Canadian officer formerly with the *Toronto Star,* was in charge of liaison with the Canadian forces. British Wing Commander T. S. Sprigg, a former air correspondent for the *Daily Herald* and for the *Evening News*, and once editor of the magazine *Airways*, was in charge of liaison with the RAF. British Commander E. C. Tufnell was in charge of liaison with the Royal Navy. Formerly of the *Buffalo Courier-Express,* U.S. Major Burrows Matthews was in charge of a PRB News Section.

Among others concerned with general information and accreditation were Colonel David Sarnoff, former president of the Radio Corporation of America, who was assistant to Colonel Phillips in the Communications Section. George Lyon was London representative of the U.S. Office of War Information. J. H. Brebner then was chief of the British MOI News Division. John S. Knight, publisher of the *Akron Beacon-Journal, Detroit Free Press,* and *Miami Herald,* was London representative of the U.S. Office of Censorship.[5] Rear Admiral George Thomas

---

5   While in London in 1944, Knight was first vice-president of the American Society of Newspaper Editors (ASNE). Wilbur Forrest, *New York Herald Tribune,* who had been a correspondent in France during World War I and later, was second vice-president.

was chief British censor in the MOI, and Francis Williams, former editor of the *Daily Herald,* was MOI controller of news and censorship.

Plans for news coverage of the prospective operations on the continent were discussed in advance with representatives of the Association of American Correspondents in London, the Overseas Empire Correspondents' Association, the Empire Press Union, the Newspaper Proprietors' Association, and the American Society of Newspaper Editors.

Methods were worked out for communications between France and London. This required attention to the handling of news copy, radio broadcasts, news pictures and newsreels, censorship, the release of communiqués, and every other contingency and requirement it was possible to imagine in advance of actual invasion. It included provision for a Press Information Room at the MOI building in London, complete with a huge wall war map and a reference library containing periodicals, background materials, photos, and every sort of volume likely to be useful to correspondents. It was agreed that two communiqués would be issued daily, at 11 A.M. and 11:30 P.M., with a simultaneous release through the OWI in Washington. Special bulletins might also be released at any time.

The prerequisite for accreditation of a British correspondent for overseas service was to be a license issued in London by the War Office, the Admiralty, or the Air Ministry. For a U.S. correspondent, a license was to be issued by the War or Navy Department in Washington with an endorsement stamp from SHAEF, plus an "overseas" visa before the correspondent could properly land in France. SHAEF was to determine how many correspondents could be accredited to the armed forces. The order of priorities was to begin with the large international news agencies, followed by radio networks, large newspapers with syndicates, newspapers with regional or national distribution, news magazines, other newspapers or magazines, photo services and syndicates, and general syndicates.

Once overseas with ground forces, a correspondent was expected to remain for a minimum of three months, but might be permitted to move from one unit or formation to another. Naval correspondents were not permitted ashore except by special permission, or if they held a proper visa. Special visits to the front might be permitted, provided the Command was willing, in which case the three months' rule could be waived.

It was estimated that, with the number of correspondents increasing, about 169 accredited to SHAEF would remain in London during the early stages of the invasion. They were to have full access to the Press Information Room. Censorship arrangements would continue as before, but with more censors on duty to handle the anticipated volume of copy. Until information was flowing freely, copy and photos were to be pooled and distributed to all media through the MOI. That intended for Canada and the United States was to go through the London division of the OWI. Fast communications routes were made available for the transmission of "hard" news, moved in short takes.

Correspondents accredited to SHAEF, it was agreed, would look to its Public Relations Branch for news. At the hours for release of the twice-daily war communiqués an officer attached to the PRB would enlarge upon the subject matter at a briefing session. In addition, an extra briefing session was to meet at 5:30 P.M. each day to provide general information, some of which might be used, but rarely with attribution to the source. This system had been developed at AFHQ in Algiers during 1942–43 and had worked well.

Other sources of news in London during the war, beyond the MOI, included the Ministry of Economic Warfare and the Foreign Office, as by tradition. Through the U.S. Office of War Information, established in 1942, with a London office also then open, considerable matter relating to U.S. war activities was made available to the British press, the Commonwealth press, and the neutral press, channeled through the MOI.

The Ministry of Economic Warfare provided information on occurrences within Germany and the occupied countries of Europe, as based upon intelligence reports. The press division of the Foreign Office conducted daily news conferences. The British Air Ministry also conducted a fortnightly conference at which war correspondents were able to obtain background information. Frequent opportunities were extended to correspondents by British or U.S. military commands by which they were able to obtain information and, at times, to observe special maneuvers. The U.S. Embassy was an important news source. Correspondents also kept in touch with the Free French headquarters in London. Most governments-in-exile located there had their own information divisions and press attachés.

The 160 U.S. correspondents estimated to have been in London in August 1943 had risen to 196 in February 1944, and 59 other British and Commonwealth media representatives were accredited to U.S. forces by then in the United Kingdom. Of the 255 total, 43 were photographers. By March the total had reached 306. The largest representation was that of the AP, with 35 correspondents. By May the figure was nearing 400. When the invasion actually occurred in June, the MOI in London controlling censorship handled copy and photos from 558 accredited correspondents. Many were with units engaged in the assault on the French coast, but most were still in the United Kingdom, covering SHAEF and other London sources, air bases, and military installations.

By advance agreement, anything produced by a correspondent during the first period of the invasion was to be pooled, that is made available to all appropriate media and outlets, distributed through the MOI after censorship in the field, or at the MOI or both. Copy, films, and recordings from the invasion beachheads were to be moved by means of portable transmitters, by aircraft, and by boat. Brought across the Channel, the copy would be transmitted to London over leased printer circuits. Films or recordings would be carried by motorcycle or automobile couriers.

Copy reaching the MOI traffic control room, after clearance by censorship and treatment by the pooling desk in the PRB branch of SHAEF, was to go to the press in London and the United Kingdom and to the BBC for use. Cables and radiotelegraph circuits operated by Cable & Wireless, Ltd., were to be used to move copy to points in the British Empire and Commonwealth. Transatlantic channels to the United States included cable and wireless circuits, with the U.S. Army Signal Corps providing channels for overflow traffic. Radio networks were to have special telephones. News agencies and some newspapers had their own leased radiotelegraph and telephone circuits. Press Wireless, Inc., had its own circuit. Five additional transatlantic communications channels were available for use on peak days, when more than a half million words of copy were expected to be filed. Circuits for voicecasts and transmission of photos were arranged.

The urgency of the Allied move across the Channel was underlined by a resumption of German air attacks on London and other areas of southern England during the late winter and spring of 1943–44. This "little blitz," was in contrast to the heavy attacks of 1940–41. It was followed in June 1944 by "flying bombs," or V-1 rockets aimed at London by the Germans from launching sites in France, Belgium, and Holland. Until these sites were entirely overrun by Allied invasion forces in September, about 8,000 bombs were directed at London. About 2,400 got through defenses, and more than 6,000 persons were killed and about 18,000 injured. A longer-range German-based rocket, referred to as a V-2, was more threatening and was used from September 1944 until the end of the European war in May 1945. About 200 a month were aimed at London. By November the German launching points were forced back beyond reach of British shores, but Belgian and French points were within range. Hits in or near Antwerp, Brussels, and Liége were fatal to 3,470 Belgian civilians and 682 Allied servicemen.

As D-Day approached the buildup of men and equipment had been going on for nearly a year in England and other parts of the United Kingdom. Since March 1944, the entire French coastal area had been subjected to intense air bombardment to destroy both offensive and defensive German installations.

Among some 550 correspondents in and near London waiting to report the invasion when it occurred, there were scores who by then had gained experience in other landings or campaigns throughout the world in a dozen years preceding.

For the Associated Press, J. Wes Gallagher was to head the invasion staff, as he had done in the North African landings in November 1942. Because of injuries in Tunisia, however, he remained in London, coordinating staff action from there. With him was Robert E. Bunnelle, chief of the London bureau and president of the Association of American Correspondents in London. Also remaining in London for the time being were Hal Boyle, a veteran of Africa, Sicily, and Italy, and Tom Yarbrough, experienced in the London blitz, the Pacific, and Italy.

Scheduled to go in with the first wave for the AP were Donald F. (Don) Whitehead, who had covered the African and Italian campaigns; John A. Moroso, III, with experience both in the Mediterranean and the Pacific; Jonathan B. (Jack) Rice, AP photographer with Pacific and African experience; and James F. King and Gladwin A. Hill, both of whom had been in Italy. Wilmot W. Hercher and Henry Jameson were to cover the air phase for the AP from bases in England, and Lewis Hawkins and Ernest A. Agnew, the naval phase, with Agnew assigned to the British Home Fleet. William S. White, a former war editor in the AP New York headquarters, and Roger Greene, with similar experience, were to be in the landings. E. K. Butler was to head the AP Photos staff, with Rice, Edward S. Worth, Peter Carroll, Joseph J. Wurzel, Harry L. Harris, and Horace Cort as members.

Backing up this Associated Press staff in London, and prepared to move to France later were Abraham I. Goldberg, who had been in Italy; Ruth Cowan, who had been in North Africa; and Howard Cowan, Edward Ball, Oscar E. Werner, Richard Kasischke, Henry B. Jameson, Henry W. Bagley, Austin Bealmear, Franklin F. Banker, Russell C. Landstrom, Judson C. Quinn, Howell E. Dodd, James M. Long, Pugh C. Moore, Neville E. Nordness, Bryon Rollins, Alexander Singleton, Blake Sullivan, and George B. Irvin.

For the United Press, with the second largest staff, Virgil Pinkley, experienced as a war correspondent and general European manager for the agency, headed the staff organization. Joseph W. Grigg, Jr., was in charge of the London bureau, assisted by Clifford L. Day, long in the bureau and head of the special war bureau in Amsterdam between 1939 and the time of the German invasion of Holland in May 1940. The main stories written in London were to be produced by Grigg or by Edward W. Beattie, Jr., who had extensive experience; or by Phil Ault or John A. Parris, both veterans of the African and Italian campaigns; or by Robert C. Dowson, Bruce W. Munn, J. Edward Murray, or John F. Frankish.

Richard D. McMillan, long representative of the BUP as well as the

UP, and who had reported the war in Egypt and Libya, the Middle East, Tunisia, Sicily, and Italy, was to accompany British forces landing in France. Henry T. Gorrell and James C. McGlincy, both veterans of the Mediterranean and Italian campaigns, were to go in with U.S. assault forces. Edward V. Roberts, UP, was to represent all three U.S. news agencies at General Eisenhower's field headquarters. Leo S. (Bill) Disher, Jr., wounded in the North African landings and correspondent with the British Home Fleet, and Samuel D. Hales and William R. Higginbotham were all UP representatives to be attached to the naval forces. Assigned to report the war in the air for the agency were Walter Cronkite, Wilson C. ("Collie") Small, H. Tosti Russell, Dougald Werner, Robert Richards, and Dudley Ann Harmon, representing among themselves broad experience in coverage of war and peace.

Other UP staffers in London, also standing in reserve, included Robert C. ("Pepper") Martin, greatly experienced in the Pacific, Robert Musel, Charles T. Hallinan, Charles Bernard, Frank Breese, George B. Chandler, Donald G. Sweeney, Everett L. Vilander and Joan Twelftree.

For the International News Service J. Kingsbury Smith, general European manager, was in charge of the war staff. Charles A. Smith, London bureau chief, and Thomas C. Watson were to supervise the handling of copy coming from correspondents in the field. Charles Smith, also directing International News Photos in London, was to direct INP photographers and head the picture pool.

Clark Lee and Pierre Huss, experienced correspondents, headed the INS invasion staff. Richard Tregaskis was recovered from wounds received in Italy. John Edgerton Lee and William W. Wade, both with previous war experience, and Joseph W. Willicombe, Jr., and Louis Azreal, formerly of the *Baltimore News-Post,* also were to go to the fighting front. Accredited as INP photographers were Hugh Broderick, Sol Senne Gottlieb, and William Whippy Jones. After the beachheads were established it was planned that two women correspondents, Dixie Tighe and Lee Carson, would go to France for INS. Jack W. Jarrell, an experienced war reporter, was in reserve. Robert Considine and Thurston Macauley also were expected to arrive in London.

Other U.S. services and syndicates prepared for coverage included the North American Newspaper Alliance (NANA), with Ira Wolfert, L. S. B. Shapiro, and H. J. J. Sargint as representatives. The Newspaper Enterprise Association (NEA), had Thomas Wolf, S. J. Woolf, an artist, and Rosette Hargrove. The Scripps-Howard Newspaper Alliance was represented by Ernest Taylor (Ernie) Pyle and William Philip Simms, whose experience dated from World War I. Paul H. Manning, MBS, was also accredited for the McNaught Syndicate, and William Hickman Pickens for Transradio Press Service.

U.S. daily newspapers with syndicated reports were well prepared. For the *New York Times,* with the largest staff, Edwin L. James was in New York as managing editor. F. Raymond Daniell, returned from home leave, was in charge in London. Staff members in readiness included Daniell's wife, Tania Long Daniell; Harold N. Denny, in Egypt and Libya before his capture in November 1941 and repatriation in 1942; Drew Middleton, formerly of the AP, and with experience in North Africa; Hanson W. Baldwin, military and naval correspondent, with experience in the Pacific; James (Jamie) MacDonald, Eugene Currivan, and Frederick P. Graham.

The *New York Herald Tribune* coverage was directed by Geoffrey Parsons, Jr., head of the London bureau. His staff included Edmund Allen (Ned) Russell, until 1944 with the UP in London, but also a war correspondent for the agency in North Africa, Sicily, and Italy; John D. ("Tex") O'Reilly; Eric Hawkins, managing editor of the Paris edition of the paper until the German occupation in 1940; Joseph Barnes, former foreign editor and European correspondent; Joseph Francis Driscoll, Jack M. Tait, Richard L. Tobin, and John Durston.

The *Chicago Daily News* service was headed in London by Helen Kirkpatrick, with William H. Stoneman, Robert J. Casey, and Bernard John McQuaid, all with experience in war coverage. The *Chicago Tribune* coverage was in general charge of Larry Rue in London, with John Hall Thompson, E. R. (Al) Noderer, and Robert A. Cromie as members of an experienced war staff.

Among U.S. dailies represented in the corps, but not syndicating their reports, the *Christian Science Monitor* service in London was headed by Mallory Browne, with Mrs. Barbara Browne, J. Emlyn Williams, Peter Lyne, and Richard L. Strout, formerly of the Washington bureau, among staff members. The *Chicago Times* had James Wellard and Bruce Grant waiting in London, and the *Chicago Sun* had Frederick Kuh as bureau chief; H. R. Knickerbocker, editor of the foreign service, William J. Humphreys, John M. Mecklin, and W. A. S. Douglas, all with war experience.

Still other U.S. newspaper representatives standing ready were Gault MacGowan, who had covered aspects of the war for the *New York Sun,* backed by Wilfred Charles Heinz and Mrs. Judy Barden. Thomas R. Henry, *Washington Evening Star,* also formerly in North Africa, Sicily, and Italy, was backed by Walter R. McCallum. The *Baltimore Sun* had Mark S. Watson and Lee A. McCardell as experienced war correspondents, backed by Thomas M. O'Neill and Holbrook Bradley. Ivan H. (Cy) Peterman, in North Africa, Sicily, and Italy for the *Philadelphia Inquirer,* was another poised in London. So also were the experienced Melvin K. Whiteleather, formerly of the AP, but now serving the *Phila-*

delphia Evening Bulletin, and Gordon Gammack for the *Des Moines Register and Tribune.*

Newcomers to the war front, waiting in London, were Marcel Wallenstein and Duke Shoop, *Kansas City Star;* Marjorie (Dot) Avery, *Detroit Free Press;* Howard J. Whitman, *New York Daily News;* Sam Adkins, *Louisville Courier-Journal;* Wright Bryan, *Atlanta Journal;* Carlyle H. Holt, *Boston Daily Globe;* Gilbert Hammond, *Boston Herald* and *Traveler;* Warren Kennet, *Newark Evening News;* Peter D. Whitney, *San Francisco Chronicle;* Frank Plachy, *New York Journal of Commerce;* William R. Dixon, Jr., *Pittsburgh Courier,* and Edward N. Toles, *Chicago Defender,* both representing Negro newspapers; and Herbert A. Finnegan, *Boston American;* and Ernest L. Byfield, *Chicago Herald-Examiner,* each for Hearst papers.

The U.S. periodical press representation was led, numerically, by those correspondents for *Time, Life,* and *Fortune,* three Henry R. Luce publications. This group included Charles C. Wertenbacker, in Europe as the war began, but soon foreign editor in New York during much of the time. Jack Belden, with experience in China, the Pacific, Malta, Sicily, and Italy; Mary Welsh (Mrs. Noel Monks) and J. J. Sherry Mangan, both in Paris as the occupation began; William White, Wilmot T. Ragsdale, Dennis Scanlan, William Walton, and Joseph M. Jones all waiting in London. Photographers accredited to the group included Robert Capa, with war experience during the Spanish Civil War, and in China, North Africa, Sicily, and Italy; Robert T. Landry, who had been in the Pacific, Egypt, Libya, Tunisia, and Sicily; Robert Morse, who had been at Guadalcanal; Frank L. Scherschel, who had been in the Pacific and on Arctic convoys; George I. Rodger, who had been in the Middle East and Burma; and David E. Scherman, John R. Morris, and Byron Thomas.

Other U.S. magazines represented included *Newsweek,* with Joseph F. Evans, Jr., in charge in London, backed by Alfred H. Newman, experienced in war coverage, Kenneth G. Crawford, Robert Littell, Mary B. Palmer, and Frederic E. Sondern, Jr. Allan A. Michie wrote for *Reader's Digest.* The *Saturday Evening Post* had Demaree Bess, widely experienced in coverage during war and peace, and Robert J. Garland as a photographer.

Collier's had William B. Courtney, Joseph A. Dearing, photographer, Ernest Hemingway as a special writer and others. The *American Magazine,* also of the Crowell-Collier group, had Gordon Gaskill, who had been in Italy, and Clarence M. Woodbury; and the *Woman's Home Companion,* of the same group, had Doris Fleeson (Mrs. John O'Donnell). The *New Yorker* was represented by A. J. (Joe) Liebling; *Look* by Donald S. Grant; *Cosmopolitan* by Albert Q. Maisel; *Liberty* by Erika

Mann; *This Week,* a Sunday supplement with many papers, by Arthur C. Bartlett; and the *Infantry Journal* by William F. Shadel.

The two U.S. army service publications, the daily *Stars and Stripes* and the weekly *Yank,* were prepared to send correspondents into France. Omitting designations of rank, for *Stars and Stripes* the group based in London included Andrew A. Rooney, with prior experience; Bruce Bairnsfather, British artist of World War I; David Breger, Russell Jones, Thomas H. Bernard, Howard Braeutigam, Philip Bucknell, Bryce W. Burke, Joseph B. Fleming, Harry A. Harchar, Gaylord K. Hodenfeld, Oram C. Hutton, Charles F. Kiley, Ray Lee, Ensley M. Llewellyn, Earl Mazo, Benjamin F. Price, Park Senigo, Sidney Shapiro, Curtis D. Swan, Arthur W. White, Edward H. Whitman, Richard E. Wilbur, and John C. Wilkinson.

For *Yank,* the group included Denton Scott, Charles Brand, Jack Coggins, Joseph Cunningham, William Davidson, Thomas Fleming, Benjamin Frazier, Durbin Horder, Saul Levitt, Louis McFadden, Peter Paris, Walter Peters, John Preston, and Sanderson Vanderbilt.

U.S. radio network representation included men of extended experience. The National Broadcasting Company (NBC) staff had Stanley D. Richardson, John MacVane, Merrill Mueller, formerly of INS, Milton Anderson, William W. Chaerline, Edwin L. Haaker, Francis C. McCall, and George Y. Wheeler. For the Blue Network,[6] staff members in London then included Thomas B. Grandin, George F. Hicks, Herbert M. Clark, Frank A. Russel and Arthur S. Feldman.

The Columbia Broadcasting System (CBS) London representation included Edward R. Murrow and Mrs. Janet Murrow, Charles Collingwood, Richard C. Hottelet, Larry LeSueur, and William R. Downs. The Mutual Broadcasting System (MBS) personnel included John S. Steele, Arthur E. Mann, and George Laurence (Larry) Meier.

The photo syndicate and service representation, beyond the several individuals already noted, included Acme Newspictures, with Bertram G. Brandt, experienced in the Pacific, and Andrew Lopez. For Wide World Photos there were Albert E. Crefield and Cecil A. C. Phillips; for Movietone News, Robert H. Blain; RKO Radio Pictures, Edward C. Buddy; News of the Day newsreel, John A. Brockhurst and Jack Lieb; Universal Newsreel, Thomas A. Priestly; and Pathé newsreel, Neil Sullivan, Frank A. Bassill, William Chambers, Cyril F. Danvers-Walker, R. K. L. Gordon, John J. Heddon, Harry Reynolds, and John L. V. Woodwiss.

---

6 The NBC had been divided in January 1927 with some stations in the network forming the Blue Network. In 1942, it was sold by NBC and operated independently until 1945, when it became the American Broadcasting Company (ABC).

In addition to all of the above, for the U.S. media Cecil Brooks was prepared to provide special coverage through his Cecil Brooks News Service of London. Other coverage was available through the Robert M. McBride Publishing Company of New York, with David C. Cooke in London. Cashel Button represented United Writers. Freelance writers accredited included Alfred Wagg, formerly of UP, Lawrence Beall Smith, Clark B. Fay, Frank E. Beresford, William J. Donoghue, Stanley F. Grammer, Ronald S. Hewitt, Bernard L. Jacoy, Kimone Marengo, and George Jiri Mucha.

The British media understandably were well prepared also for coverage. The Reuters agency was organized in depth in London in close association with the Press Association. The correspondents for Reuters included Stanley W. Burch, Alan Humphreys, and Denis Martin, all greatly experienced in war, William S. Stringer, Doon Campbell, John Remsen Wilhelm, Robert Reuben, and Mrs. Rene De Vere Billingham. The Press Association had Frank A. King, E. E. Sandford Louis, and L. V. Wulf. In addition, Exchange Telegraph (Extel) had Edward J. (Ted) Gilling, experienced in North Africa, Sicily, and Italy, and R. W. V. Parker.

British newspaper representation had Arthur R. Narracott, with war experience, and Eric E. Phillips for the *Times.* The *Daily Telegraph* had George Fyfe and Cornelius John Ryan; the *Daily Express,* Montague Lacey, Alexander Boath, and Basil D. Cardew; the *Sunday Express,* Edward J. Hart; the *Daily Mail,* the experienced Colin B. Bednall and William Hall; and the *Sunday Dispatch* had the Marquess of Donegall.

Other British papers also had correspondents, many already experienced in war. For the *News-Chronicle* there were Ronald S. Walker and S. L. Olon; the *Daily Herald* had Charles Bray and Iris Carpenter; the *Daily Sketch* and Allied Newspapers, John D'Arcy Dawson, Victor Lewis, and William McC. Mulligan; the *Sunday Times* and the Kemsley Newspapers, Peter G. Masefield, Leonard Oswald Mosley, and William C. Granger; the *Daily Mirror,* Ian H. Fyfe; the *News of the World,* Norman Rae and Ward Smith; and the *People,* Herald Kersh.

The London afternoon papers had Philip Grune and Mrs. Betty Knox for the *Evening Standard;* John Logan Barclay-Barr for the *Evening News;* and Charles W. Ingham for the *Star.* The Westminster Press, including the London *Financial Times* and a group of provincial papers, was represented by Frederick M. Inwood, Alfred C. Ricketts, and Alfred E. Shaw. David Woodward represented the *Manchester Guardian,* William G. Willis the *Yorkshire Post* of Leeds; and Henry P. Twyford the *Western Morning News* of Plymouth.

For the British periodical press, Charles E. Turner was an artist for the *Illustrated London News;* Maurice Edelman was with *Picture Post;*

Frank W. Creacal with *Current Affairs;* and Carl A. Ollsen was attached to *Illustrated,* with James Jarache and Reuben Saidman as photographers for that publication.

The British Broadcasting Corporation (BBC) invasion staff, directed by Howard Marshall, included Robert F. Dunnett, Richard Dimbleby, Robin B. Duff, Robert W. Reid, and Chester Wilmot.

The photo group, beyond those mentioned earlier, included Herbert P. Andrews for Planet News; Frederick J. Ramage for Keystone Press Agency; John L. Ramsden for British Movietone News; Arthur W. Farmer, Donald L. Read, and L. H. Cave-Chinn for British Paramount News; and Harold J. Morley for Gaumont British newsreel.

British Commonwealth media representation in London just prior to the invasion included Ronald Clark, Frank Fisher, and Paul Eve for the British United Press (BUP), which had become an affiliate of the United Press. The Canadian Press (CP) representatives included Alan Dandal as London bureau chief; William Stewart, an experienced war correspondent, and Margaret Francis. Matthew Halton was senior correspondent for the Canadian Broadcasting Corporation (CBC) and Mary V. P. ("Mollie") McGee represented the *Toronto Globe and Mail.*

The Australian Consolidated Press was represented by Anne Matheson. The Truth Newspapers of Australia were represented by Frederick E. Baume, Mark Gallard, and Lady Margaret Stewart; the *Brisbane Telegraph* by René H. M. Tait; and the *Sydney Morning Herald* by Harry A. Standish.

Several representatives of news agencies and newspapers of other countries were accredited. The Agence Française Indépendante (AFI), a Free French or Fighting French news agency based in London, with a branch since 1942 in Algiers, had Pierre Gosset and André J. Rabache in London, and Fernand Moulier in Algiers. It was reorganized in 1944 as the Agence France-Presse (AFP). The Polish government-in-exile in the British capital had military elements with the Allies. It was represented by a Polish Forces News Bureau in London, headed by Lucyna Anna Tomaszewska.

Neutral countries, as a rule, were not permitted to have correspondents accredited to SHAEF. For security reasons, this applied on D-Day and after. At least three neutral correspondents, however, occupied special positions in London with favored access to information. They were Hans W. Egli of the *Neue Zürcher Zeitung,* Zurich; Nils D. Biklund, *Dagens Nyheter,* Stockholm; and Mrs. Helvig R. M. MacFarlane, *Göteborgs Posten,* Gothenburg.

Such listings of accredited correspondents in London on the eve of D-Day, long as they are, still do not include all media representatives or individual writers then in the British capital. Even apart from the neutrals denied accreditation, there were scores who did not seek such accreditation to SHAEF or to units of the armed forces because they had no wish to act as war correspondents. There were many who were needed and who wanted to work in London in a conventional fashion, providing media coverage for those many aspects of the news and human activities not related to the war.

The Allied plan was to invade the Continent in May 1944, but that original date for Operation Overlord was advanced to June 5. When that day arrived the English Channel was too choppy and a twenty-four-hour postponement was ordered. Even on the following morning the Channel was rough, but further delay was judged unwise, considering tides, weather forecasts, and the possibility that vital information might reach the Germans.[1]

Everything was in readiness for a move of massive Allied forces across the channel from English shores to those of France, in Normandy. German installations on the French coast had been under almost unceasing Allied air attack for two weeks. The bombing had been even more intensive since June 2, but spread broadly enough to avoid giving the Germans any clear idea where the actual landings might occur.

At thirty minutes after midnight on the morning of Tuesday, June 6, planes and gliders of the U.S. 82nd and 101st Airborne Divisions were aloft with paratroopers to be carried over the Cotentin Peninsula of France. They jumped in the dark to drop near Cherbourg. Meanwhile, an invasion fleet of 4,000 vessels was maneuvering in the Channel off the Normandy coast. At 5:30 A.M. a withering bombardment of that coast began, with planes and naval guns combining to reduce defenses in areas where U.S., British, and Canadian troops in landing craft were to go ashore at H-hour, set for 6:30 A.M.[2]

1   A false report of an Allied landing in France had been transmitted from London to New York on June 3 over AP facilities. This occurred because a girl operating a teleprinter punched a strip of practice tape and neglected to tear it off before proceeding with the regular transmission. The message therefore went through. It was killed two minutes later, but not before the report had been broadcast over some radio stations in the United States.

2   When the actual invasion began, the first news report came from the German radio and was only confirmed from Allied sources about three hours later. In London, correspondents remaining there and accredited to SHAEF had been summoned by telephone at 6:15 A.M. to report at the Ministry of Information. There they were informed that the invasion had started, were given time to prepare their stories or broadcasts, which were necessarily limited as to detail. At 9:32 A.M. London time the news was officially released to the world

U.S. forces were landed on the Normandy coast east of the Carentan Estuary and established positions on what were designated as Utah and Omaha beaches. British and Canadian forces landed farther east at points designated as Sword, Juno, and Gold beaches. The German Wehrmacht was not surprised by the landings, but had not judged the date or places accurately. Despite the advance bombardments, fierce resistance was delivered by shore batteries and ground troops, resulting in heavy casualties. The Allied command of the sea and the air enabled the invading forces to get ashore, however, and to stay there.

On the second day, British and Canadian troops captured Bayeaux, five miles inland, the first liberated city in France. By June 14 the invasion forces were well inland, with all beaches secured to permit the arrival of more men and supplies.

The hedgerow country of Normandy provided ground cover but was difficult fighting territory. By the end of July, however, U.S. forces were out of that area and were able to advance more rapidly. Cherbourg had been taken by the end of June, Caen by July 9, and St. Lô on July 19. All of these were key objectives. By early August some units had passed Avranches, at the base of the Cotentin Peninsula, and Rennes, farther south, and had swung west to take the Brittany Peninsula. Other units deployed eastward toward Paris.

Alarm and discontent rising in Germany, because of the successful Soviet Russian counterattack that had carried the Red Army to the approaches to Warsaw since August 1943, was advanced by the Allied landing in France. A German desire for peace, extending to the military, was manifested in an effort on June 20, 1944, to kill Hitler. He had a miraculous escape when a bomb was exploded in his headquarters, although his hearing was permanently impaired. Some 3,500 persons were executed in reprisal including Nazi party and military leaders.

French resistance elements were active against the German occupation forces in many areas, especially from the time of the invasion. They assisted significantly in the liberation of Paris on August 25, and Fighting French forces led a great parade down the Champs d'Elysees, followed by U.S. troops. A few days later, British and Canadian forces captured Rouen and Amiens, and soon Le Havre and other Channel ports as far east as Ostend and Dunkirk, where the great evacuation of 1940 had occurred. Meanwhile, in the south of France, U.S. forces landed on August 16 in Operation Dragoon to begin the advance up the Rhone Valley to establish a meeting with the U.S. Third Army near Dijon in September.

---

from that Allied headquarters, beginning with the first communiqué from SHAEF. Allowing for time differences, that flash reached New York at about 4:32 A.M., at 1:32 A.M. in San Francisco, and similarly in Canadian time zones. In Latin American areas the news arrived at from 6:32 A.M. to 2:32 A.M.

This entire operation was under the supreme command of General Eisenhower. British Admiral Sir Bertram Ramsay commanded the joint naval forces engaged, and Air Chief Marshal Sir Trafford Leigh-Mallory directed the air arm, British and U.S. alike. Field Marshal Sir Bernard L. Montgomery commanded the 21st Army Group of British and Canadian troops in landings on the Channel coast in the area close to Caen and Bayeaux. Lieutenant General Omar W. Bradley and Major General J. Lawton Collins commanded the U.S. 12th Army Group, including the First Army and air-borne divisions assaulting the western sections of the Channel coast at the Utah and Omaha beaches and the Cherbourg Peninsula.

Later, the U.S. Third Army, commanded by Lieutenant General George S. Patton, Jr., poured over the beaches into France, headed a Brittany assault, and then turned eastward toward Paris and beyond. There, in the drive east into Germany, it joined with the 21st Army Group, the 12th Army Group, the First Army, and the U.S. Seventh Army under Lieutenant General Alexander M. Patch moving up from the Mediterranean coastal landing.

The Allied buildup of men and armor in France was rapid, and German forces were driven back, with thousands of prisoners taken. By early September both British and U.S. elements were in Belgium and Holland, where bitter fighting occurred. They crossed the German border on September 11. Aachen, on the German-Belgian border, was taken by the U.S. First Army on October 12. A. U.S. Ninth Army under Lieutenant General W. H. Simpson added new strength in September and October. By the end of November, the Allied armies were solidly established from the Channel and the North Sea to the Swiss border and the Mediterranean coast and had crossed the German frontier.

German opposition stiffened, and in December a counterattack was made in the Ardennes in Belgium. The so-called "Battle of the Bulge" caused Allied reverses there and in Alsace and Lorraine, but by January 1945 these had been erased. On March 5, U.S. and Canadian forces were on the west bank of the Rhine River. Cologne, Bonn, and Coblenz were entered on that day. The Germans blew up every Rhine bridge between Bonn and Cologne, except one at Remagen. Elements of the U.S. Ninth Armored Division forced a passage over that bridge on March 7. The U.S. First Army crossed the Rhine at that point, while the Third and Seventh Army forces pushed eastward below the Remagen area. By April, Allied forces were in the Ruhr area, main center of German industry and war production, and deep into Germany.

The collapse of Germany neared as the Allies moved in from the west and the Soviet Red Army forces moved in from the east. The long siege of Leningrad had ended in January 1944. Finland, fighting with the Germans, surrendered to the Russians and to the British in September

1944. Although it received no Soviet aid and was crushed by the Germans, the underground in Poland helped the Red Army, which overran Warsaw in January 1945. German forces already had been forced out of Bulgaria and Rumania, had withdrawn from Greece and Yugoslavia and then from Hungary, all indefensible against the advancing Red Army. By February 1945, its units were near Berlin and in April entered Vienna.

By that time U.S. forces were well into Germany and in Czechoslovakia, and French and British troops also were within the borders of the Third Reich. Soviet and U.S. army patrols made contact at the Elbe River, near Dresden, on April 25. British and Soviet elements met May 2 at Wiemar and Lübeck. Red Army forces still were besieging Berlin, which also was under devastating U.S. and British air attack.

On May 1 German Admiral Karl Doenitz announced the death of Adolf Hitler, who had shot himself the previous day in a concrete air raid shelter beneath the Reich Chancellory on the Wilhelmstrasse in Berlin. Eva Braun, his mistress, whom he had married shortly before, took poison and died with him. Joseph Goebbels and his wife, also in the shelter, poisoned their children and took their own lives. Admiral Doenitz became head of the German state after the death of Hitler.

On May 2, Berlin surrendered to the Red Army, and the German army on the Italian front also surrendered. On May 4, the German army retreated from Denmark and Holland, and all German submarines were ordered by Doenitz to return to port. French forces driving through southern Germany just above the Swiss border turned south into Austria and made contact on May 4 with U.S. Fifth Army elements that had moved north following the German surrender on the Italian front. This juncture united all Allied armies on the western front.

The first indirect German negotiations looking toward a surrender had started in February 1945 when Gestapo chief Heinrich Himmler had arranged to meet with Count Bernadotte, head of the Swedish Red Cross. They met again in April in Berlin and solid negotiations began. On May 3, a German delegation visited Field Marshal Montgomery's headquarters under a flag of truce to seek a surrender agreement. On the day following, all German forces in northwest Germany, Holland, Denmark, and adjacent areas surrendered to the British.

The same delegation that had visited Montgomery appeared at General Eisenhower's advance headquarters at Reims on May 5 and 6 to discuss terms, which were given as "unconditional surrender." Early in the morning of May 7, the act of surrender was signed at Reims, with hostilities to end at midnight May 8. The act of surrender was ratified and finally concluded in Berlin on May 9, under Soviet and Red Army arrangements. Pockets of German resistance, notably on the Brittany

Peninsula, ended, Norway was freed, and the German submarines were surrendered.

With Hitler and Goebbels, who might have became chancellor under the terms of Hitler's will, both dead, Admiral Karl Doenitz became head of a provisional government, effective for about three weeks, during which time the full German surrender took place. Doenitz then was among others taken into custody by the Allies, some of whom were brought to trial later at Nuremberg for "war crimes." Among them, Heinrich Himmler and Hermann Goering, who had been Hitler's deputy and also a possible successor, killed themselves by taking poison.

Preparation for coverage by the media of the Normandy invasion of June 6, 1944, and the campaign to follow was as carefully planned as the military operation itself. The media had selected and assigned staff members, accreditation had been arranged, and SHAEF and the MOI had worked out the procedures described earlier.

On May 31, those correspondents who were to participate in the invasion itself received instructions from the Public Relations Branch of SHAEF in London, and later were addressed by General Eisenhower. Soon they vanished from the city under conditions of the greatest secrecy, and reported at designated airfields, ports, and points of troop concentration in southern England. Some twenty-eight U.S. correspondents and about an equal number of British and Commonwealth media representatives took part in this initial stage of the operation.

When D-Day came some correspondents flew with the air force. Ivan H. (Cy) Peterman, *Philadelphia Inquirer,* was in the lead plane in the formation spearheading a bombing attack preceding the landing shortly after midnight of paratroopers on the Cotentin Peninsula to capture Cherbourg. He became the first newsman over the French coast. Ward Smith of the *News of the World* also was over the peninsula, at 1:40 A.M. with the first wave of U.S. airborne troops. He returned to London and gave the first radio report of the invasion over the BBC facilities at 7:15 P.M. Frank J. Scherschel, *Life* photographer formerly in the Pacific, was in a plane that bombed the French invasion coast four minutes before the 6:30 A.M. H-Hour, when the first landing barges were to put troops on the beaches.

Three correspondents jumped with paratroopers near Cherbourg before 1 A.M. They were Philip Bucknell, *Stars and Stripes,* Robert Reuben, Reuters, and Leonard Oswald Mosley, *Daily Sketch* and other

Kemsley newspapers. Others went in with glider troops, landing behind the German lines. They were Marshall Yarrow, Reuters; Howard Cowan, AP; Chester Wilmot, BBC; David Woodward, *Manchester Guardian;* Ian Fyfe, *Daily Mirror;* Stanley Frank, *New York Post;* William Walton, *Time* and *Life;* and Wright Bryan, *Atlanta Journal.* Bryan returned to England in time to make an evening broadcast the same day to the United States over NBC and CBS stations.

Other correspondents who flew over the invasion coast as observers on that first day were Gault MacGowan, *New York Sun,* also representing the London *Star;* Montague Taylor, Reuters; Wilson C. ("Collie") Small, UP; Howell Dodd, AP features artist; Gladwin Hill, *New York Times;* Charles Gray, *Daily Herald;* William Randolph Hearst, Jr., Hearst Newspapers; Richard Hottelet, CBS; and Larry Meier, MBS.

Correspondents also were with the invasion fleet. Some remained aboard ship and others went ashore after the first assault on the first or second day. George Hicks, Blue Network, in Admiral Alan Goodrich Kirk's U.S. flagship during the channel crossing and the landing, described the scene for radio listeners to the accompaniment of gunfire, sounds of German planes overhead, bombs exploding, and background voices. His recording was broadcast later over U.S. networks and internationally by the Voice of America.

Others with the invasion fleet were Hanson W. Baldwin, *New York Times,* an Annapolis graduate, also aboard the U.S. flagship; Desmond Tighe, Reuters; Edward D. Ball, John A. Moroso III, Tom Yarbrough, and Lewis Hawkins, all of the AP; Jonathan (Jack) Rice, AP Photos; Robert C. Miller, Samuel D. Hales, and W. R. Higginbotham, all of UP; John Edgerton Lee and Pierre Huss, both of INS; Sol Sonnee Gottlieb, INP photographers; Ira Wolfert, NANA; Thomas H. Wolf, NEA; W. H. Hartin and Reginald Eason, *Daily Mail;* W. A. Crumley, *Daily Express;* Gordon Holman, *Evening Standard;* Eric Greenwood, photographer for the *Times;* Richard Lee Strout, *Christian Science Monitor;* William C. Heinz, *New York Sun;* Wilmot T. Ragsdale and British-born Dennis Scanlan, both for *Time;* Ralph Morse and David Scherman, *Life* photographers; Cecil Carnes, *Saturday Evening Post;* Joseph A. Dearing, *Collier's* photographer; William Schadel, CBS; and Edward Candy, Gaumont British News newsreel cameraman.

Correspondents on the beaches in the first hours included Doon Campbell, one of twelve D-Day Reuters correspondents, and the first to land. Others in the beach landings were William Stringer and John Wilhelm, both U.S.-born and also for Reuters; Ross Munro, Canadian Press; Howard Marshall, director of war coverage for BBC; Arthur A. Thorpe and Edward J. (Ted) Gilling, both for Exchange Telegraph; Don Whitehead, Henry B. Jameson, and Roger Greene, all of AP; Richard D. McMillan, BUP, and Henry T. Gorrell, UP; Clark Lee, William Wade, and Jack W. Jarrell, all of INS.

On the beach for U.S. newspapers were John Hall Thompson, *Chicago Tribune;* John O'Reilly and Joseph Driscoll, *New York Herald Tribune;* William H. Stoneman, *Chicago Daily News;* Mallory Browne, *Christian Science Monitor;* Tom Treanor, *Los Angeles Times;* and Holbrook Bradley, *Baltimore Sun.* Still others were Charles C. Wertenbacker, *Time* and *Life;* Robert Capa and Robert Landry, *Life* photographers; Kenneth G. Crawford, *Newsweek;* Gordon Gaskill, *American Magazine;* Bert Brandt, Acme Newspictures; and J. F. Gemmell, British Paramount News newsreel cameraman.

Within a day or two of the landings, the number of correspondents in the beachhead areas increased. Some who had been observing the action from ships of the fleet arrived on French soil, joined by some who had been with the air force or who came from England aboard vessels bearing additional troops.

These early arrivals included Baldwin, of the *New York Times;* Lee and Huss, of INS, and also Joseph Willicombe, Jr., of that agency; Lewis Hawkins, AP; Dougald Werner, UP; Henry Buckley, Robert Reuben and Charles Lynch, all of Reuters; and L. S. B. Shapiro, NANA.

Others were Ernie Pyle, of the Scripps-Howard Newspaper Alliance; Paul Holt, Alan Moorehead, Montague Lacey, and Alan Wood, all of the *Daily Express;* James Wellard, *Chicago Times,* also writing for the *Daily Express;* Ronald Matthews and Clifford Webb, *Daily Herald;* Ronald Walker, William Forrest, Norman Clark, Fred Griffin, and Michael Moynihan, *News-Chronicle;* Noel Monks and John Hall, *Daily Mail;* Leslie Randall and Philip Grune, *Evening Standard;* Jack Tait, *New York Herald Tribune;* Ralph Allan, *Toronto Globe;* and James W. Lee, Jewish Telegraph Agency.

Still others included A. J. Liebling, *New Yorker* magazine; Stanley Richardson and John MacVane, NBC; William Downs and Larry LeSueur, CBS; Thomas B. Grandin, Blue Network, who was formerly of CBS and had been director of the U.S. Foreign Broadcast Intelligence Service (FBIS) under the FCC in 1942–43; and Matthew Halton, Canadian Broadcasting Corporation.

Some of these men were with U.S. forces, others with British or Canadian. By June 9, D-Day-plus-3, there were twenty-six U.S. correspondents in Normandy. British staffers were somewhat fewer because the London War Office was less generous with landing visas.

Remaining in England during the first days of the invasion, but covering its progress from General Eisenhower's advanced command post on the Channel coast, were Merrill Mueller, NBC, Edward Roberts, AP, Stanley Burch, Reuters, and Robert Barr, BBC, all serving the combined Allied press and public. Others at ports or air bases were Geoffrey Parsons, Jr., Richard L. Tobin, and E. A. (Ned) Russell, all of the *New York Herald Tribune;* Drew Middleton and James MacDonald, *New York Times;* Donald MacKenzie and Howard Whitman, *New York Daily News;* Helen Kirkpatrick, *Chicago Daily News,* also representing the *New York Post;* Colin Bednall and Courtenay Edwards, *Daily Mail;* Murray Edwards, *Daily Herald;* Norman Smart, *Daily Express;* James Stewart, *Evening Standard;* Judy Barden, *New York Sun;* Virginia Irwin, *St. Louis Post-Dispatch;* Mary Welsh, *Time;* David Anderson, NBC; Hal Boyle, William Smith White, Ruth Cowan, and Neville E. ("Ned") Nordness, all of the AP; and Bruce W. Munn, Robert Richards, and Dudley Ann Harmon, UP.

In London, at the same time, covering SHAEF or writing other invasion matter for the U.S. media were Edward W. Beattie, Jr., Walter Cronkite, Philip H. Ault, and James C. McGlincy, all of the UP; Robert Bunnelle, J. Wesley Gallagher, John A. Parris, Jr., Austin Bealmear, and Richard Kasischke, all of the AP; J. Kingsbury Smith, Thomas C. Watson, and Joseph Thomas, INS; Raymond Daniell, Tania Long Daniell, Harold N. Denny, John MacCormac, Gene Currivan, David Anderson, E. C. Daniel, and Frederick Graham, all of the *New York Times;* Joseph Barnes, *New York Herald Tribune;* Frederick Kuh, *Chicago Sun;* Dorris Lorelle Hearst, *New York Journal-American;* and Edward R. Murrow, CBS.

Casualties among correspondents engaged in covering the invasion were inevitable. Staff Sergeant Peter M. Paris, writer, artist, and photographer for *Yank,* was killed in the landing. Ian Fyfe, *Daily Mirror,* landed under fire in a glider on the Cherbourg Peninsula on the early morning of D-Day and was reported missing in action. David Woodward, *Manchester Guardian,* in a similar glider landing, suffered a broken wrist and face lacerations from flying splinters. Philip Bucknell, *Stars and Stripes,* parachuted onto the Cherbourg Peninsula and broke a leg.

Gordon Gaskill, *American Magazine,* was wounded by shrapnel and bullets in the first assault. Joseph A. Dearing, *Collier's* photographer, had his wrist shattered by machine-gun fire from a German plane. Henry B. Jameson, AP, aboard a landing craft, was put out of action when knocked down by a shellburst. His knee was sprained, a shoulder wrenched, and then a leg was creased by falling flak. Robert C. Miller, UP, was aboard a ship torpedoed and sunk during the D-Day landing; he was picked up after two hours in the Channel and taken back to England, but returned to the beachhead almost immediately.

A second fatality occurred on June 11 when Arthur A. Thorpe of the British Exchange Telegraph (Extel) agency, accredited to the Royal

Navy, was killed by enemy fire while aboard a small craft in the Channel. Richard D. McMillan, BUP, received a shrapnel wound in the back during the assault on Cherbourg, but continued his work; he returned to England soon after for treatment, but was in France again within a few days. Don Whitehead, AP, received a knee injury. James W. Lee, Jewish Telegraph Agency, was captured by the Germans. Alan Moorehead, *Daily Express,* was arrested by a British forward platoon on suspicion of being a spy, but was soon identified and released.

A number of correspondents narrowly escaped on the night of June 14 when an anti-personnel bomb was dropped by a German plane outside a chateau in a forward area of Normandy, apparently in the belief that it was occupied by high-ranking Allied officers, as it had been by Germans during the occupation. Joseph Willicombe, Jr., INS, broke a heel when he jumped from the flaming building, and was obliged to return to England. Other correspondents who lost most of their clothing and equipment were Ross Munro and William Stewart, Canadian Press, Halton of the CBC, Ralph Allen, *Toronto Globe,* Charles Lynch, Reuters, and L. S. B. Shapiro, NANA.

The correspondents in London were not working under conditions without peril because the German V-1 "buzz-bomb" rockets, robot bombs or "doodlebugs," so-called, were falling in the capital during this period. Robert Musel, UP, was among the first to be shaken by the explosion of one of these devices as early as March 1944. Frederick Kuh, *Chicago Sun,* was cut by glass splinters in such an explosion in July. Joseph Cerutti, *Chicago Tribune,* had a narrow escape; and Virgil Pinkley, UP, was blown across the room when one exploded nearby.

The arrangements made before the invasion to assure smooth handling of dispatches did not proceed as satisfactorily as had been hoped. Those correspondents able to make a first-day report on the landings did so either by personal good fortune or by returning to London to write, as some had done seventy-four years before at the time of the Franco-Prussian War.

This method was used by correspondents who flew over the beaches in RAF and U.S. Air Force planes, by some news photographers such as Bert Brandt of Acme Newspictures, by Howard Marshall of the BBC, Marshall Yarrow of Reuters, who also went on the air for the Canadian Broadcasting Corporation, and by Ward Smith of *News of the World,* who also spoke over BBC facilities.

The first report from a beachhead correspondent came from Ross Munro, Canadian Press, who also had been the first to report the landing in Sicily less than a year before. Despite jokes about carrier pigeons, one of the first messages was in fact brought by a pigeon released by Montague Taylor, Reuters, with the fleet some distance off the beaches.

Doon Campbell, also of Reuters, sent a D-Day account from the beach itself by pigeon.

During the first week, there were delays of as much as four or five days in the transmission of copy from Normandy. The pooling system, expected to continue for a fortnight, was suspended after five days, except for the four correspondents at General Eisenhower's headquarters, because it was not working well and also was no longer regarded as necessary. In London, communiqués were issued twice daily, as planned, and accredited correspondents were briefed at 11 A.M. and 5 P.M. at conferences in Chancellor's Hall in the Ministry of Information. Nonaccredited correspondents and those of neutral countries were able to attend separate conferences at 12:15 P.M. and 6:15 P.M.

There were complaints from British sources about a virtual absence of British photographers and newsreel cameramen in the first-day operations, about delay in sending newsmen to Normandy, and about the treatment accorded them when they did arrive. Dissatisfaction with public relations policies, personnel, and communications in the British 21st Army Group under Montgomery resulted in the departure of all correspondents from that headquarters in July because they felt they were wasting their time.

Despite delays and complaints, British Cable & Wireless during the first seven days of the invasion forwarded press messages originating both in London and in Normandy totalling more than a million words, and directed them to the United States, Canada, India, South Africa, Australia, and New Zealand, plus 296 photos sent electronically. A total of 400,000 words handled on D-Day alone was doubled on a later day in the first week. Wordage to the United States was highest, as handled by C&W, with that to Australia second in volume.

Many additional thousands of words were sent by other communications channels to Allied and neutral countries, and still more thousands by shortwave radio voicecasts for rebroadcast over medium wave transmitters. At the end of three weeks, the copy and radio scripts passed through the censorships at the beachheads and in London totalled nearly 6,000,000 words, plus 32,242 photos and 284,900 feet of motion picture film.

Communications from Normandy improved after the first week. An advance command post was set up during the third week, including a press section in charge of U.S. Lieutenant Colonel Thor M. Smith, with direct connections to SHAEF in London. The four representatives of the Allied media at General Eisenhower's command post in England moved to Normandy at that time. British and U.S. photographic sections also were represented there.

Press Wireless set up a mobile transmitter in the Cherbourg area on

June 12, D-Day-plus-six, and made it possible to get press messages from there to New York within twenty minutes, while also affording facilities for voice broadcasts. Henry T. Gorrell, UP, sent the first dispatch. Known as Station PX, it was used by British and U.S. correspondents, who sent dispatches to London by way of New York, still at a saving in time. The Press Wireless mobile transmitter remained available to correspondents during the later move across France and into Belgium and Germany. A second Press Wireless mobile transmitter was added in January 1945. Known as Station PV, it was of great advantage in assuring prompt and economical handling of reports.

The BBC had its own mobile transmitters, the first of which went into operation near Bayeux during the second week of the invasion. Known as MCO, it was used not only by BBC reporters for broadcasts to the United Kingdom, but by Canadian and U.S. radio reporters and others. Pierre Lefèvre, a BBC correspondent, used it to speak in French to the people of France by way of London. Later in the campaign, a transmitter designed to be carried in a suitcase was used. One that had been dropped by an RAF plane much earlier for the use of the Belgian underground was used at least once by Chester Wilmot, BBC correspondent, after Brussels had been liberated by British forces on September 3, 1944. A second more powerful BBC mobile transmitter, known as MCN, was put into operation that same month.

Telephone transmission for press use became possible from Caen in northwestern France to London in mid-July and, as the campaign progressed successfully, the general communications situation stabilized and improved.

A new listing of correspondents accredited to SHAEF was made a week after D-Day. Basically the same as the May list, the total edged up slightly to 558, with others continuing to arrive in London and usually seeking accreditation. About fifty correspondents were in the beachhead areas of France in mid-June, and some felt that was too many, considering the limited terrain held and the limited facilities.[3] A U.S. War Department order of July 11 halted the movement of more correspondents from the United States to London. This restriction soon ended, however, because the pressure was eased with the breakout from the invasion beaches in July, and because some correspondents left France and also left the United Kingdom for new assignments.

Among correspondents to arrive in England in June and July were Taylor Henry, AP; Alexander H. Uhl, *PM;* Arthur Peters, Blue Net-

---

3   When a U.S. agency sought accreditation for "one more" a SHAEF official suggested that perhaps there were enough. "But," the agency man protested, "this is the biggest thing since the Crucifixion!"

work; John A. Fairfax, *Sydney Morning Herald;* and Robert J. Doyle, *Milwaukee Journal.* The latter two had been reporting the war in the Pacific. Others were John McG. Carlisle, *Detroit News;* Lawrence W. Youngman, *Omaha World-Herald;* John M. O'Connel, Jr., *Bangor Daily News* of Maine; Elizabeth May Craig, Washington correspondent for the Guy P. Gannett Newspapers, also of Maine; Eric Baume, European editor for the *Truth* weekly newspapers of Australia, returning from home leave; and Paul Gallico, *Cosmopolitan Magazine.*[4]

Correspondents who moved across the Channel in June and July included William Stewart, Canadian Press; Christopher Buckley, *Daily Telegraph;* Knickerbocker, *Chicago Sun;* Casey, *Chicago Daily News;* Denny and MacDonald, *New York Times;* Russell, *New York Herald Tribune;* Boyle, AP; Harold L. (Harry) Harris, AP Photos; James C. McGlincy, UP; Ronald Clark, BUP; and Melvin K. Whiteleather, *Philadelphia Bulletin.* Lloyd Stratton, assistant general manager of the AP, arrived in London in mid-July and went to Normandy, along with Robert Bunnelle, London bureau chief, and J. Wes Gallagher, chief of the AP invasion staff. Their purpose was to gather information as a basis for planning further coverage of the campaign.

At the end of June, a group of women correspondents flew to the beachhead. They remained about three hours, primarily watching casualties being put aboard planes for return to England. They were Dixie Tighe, INS; Helen Kirkpatrick, *Chicago Daily News;* Iris Carpenter, *Daily Herald;* Mollie McGee, *Toronto Globe and Mail;* Judy Barden, *New York Sun;* and Virginia Cowles, *Sunday Times.* Early in July, after WAC units had arrived in Normandy, Barden returned to France, along with Dudley Ann Harmon, UP, Barbara Wace, AP, and Marjorie Avery, *Detroit Free Press.*

Correspondents in the beachhead area in June formed a so-called Beachhead Correspondents' Committee to deal with matters of communication, censorship, transportation, billets, and relations with army public relations officers. John Hall Thompson, *Chicago Tribune,* was chairman and also represented the interests of correspondents for U.S. newspapers; Montague Lacey, *Daily Express,* represented the British press; Don Whitehead, AP, news agencies; Herbert Clark, Blue Network, radio; Harold L. Harris, AP Photos, cameramen; and A. J. Liebling, the *New Yorker,* magazine correspondents.

Other correspondents to move to France in July included three who had been in the invasion fleet or in the air on D-Day: Baldwin, *New*

---

4   Gallico, formerly of the *New York Daily News,* had been in England in 1940 at the time of the Dunkirk evacuation. His short story written soon after, "The Snow Goose," became something of a classic.

York Times; Treanor, *Los Angeles Times;* and William Randolph Hearst, Jr., *New York Journal-American* and all Hearst papers. Richard Tregaskis, INS, was back on active duty after recovery from wounds suffered in Italy in November 1943. Robert Cromie, *Chicago Tribune,* who had been in the Pacific, also arrived in France.

Still others, most with extensive war experience, were: Gladwin Hill, Frederick Graham, and Gene Currivan, all of the *New York Times;* Henry Tosti Russell, UP; Edward D. Ball and William Smith White, both of AP; G. B. Irvin and Horace Cort, AP Photos; William Wade, INS; Sol Sonnee Gottlieb and Hugh Broderick, INP photographers; John M. Mecklin, *Chicago Sun;* William Humphreys, *Chicago Sun* and *Daily Express;* Seaghan Maynes, Reuters; Robin B. Duff, BBC; Cornelius Ryan, *Daily Telegraph;* Austin Hatton, *Evening News;* Lee A. McCardell, *Baltimore Sun;* Donald MacKenzie, *New York Daily News;* and John Groth, artist for *Parade* magazine. One of the few correspondents in France at this time, other than U.S., British, or Canadian, was D. F. Krominov of the Tass agency.

Late June brought the capture of the port of Cherbourg, stubbornly defended by German forces. From heights overlooking the city and its approaches and later from inside the city, the action was observed by a group of correspondents, including John ("Tex") O'Reilly, *New York Herald Tribune;* Thomas R. Henry, *Washington Star;* H. R. Knickerbocker, *Chicago Sun;* William Stringer, Reuters; Clark Lee, INS; Don Whitehead, AP;[5] Henry T. Gorrell, UP; Peter Carroll, AP; Harold L. Harris, AP Photos; William H. Stoneman, *Chicago Daily News;* Bert Brandt, Acme Newspictures; Charles C. Wertenbacker, *Time* and *Life;* and Robert Landry and Robert Capa, *Time* and *Life* photographers.[6]

Correspondents moved into the front areas with the combat troops. Bede Irvin, AP Photos, was killed near St. Lô late in July when a bomb from a U.S. B-26 Marauder plane fell short and exploded among advanced U.S. infantry units. Lee McCardell of the *Baltimore Sun,* with

---

5   After entering Cherbourg, Knickerbocker, Stringer, Lee, and Whitehead reached the Hotel Atlantique as fighting continued outside. Later, while watching from windows on an upper floor, a German officer and four enlisted men entered the room. Correspondents were obliged to go unarmed, but Knickerbocker, with long experience in Vienna and Berlin, speaking to them in German, learned that they were surrendering.

6   Following the surrender of all German forces in Cherbourg, German Lieutenant General Karl von Schlieben and Rear Admiral Walther Hennecke emerged under guard from the headquarters of the U.S. Ninth Division, commanded by Major General Manton S. Eddy.

Capa and other photographers took pictures of the captive Germans. General von Schlieben grumbled, but was informed by General Eddy that the U.S. press was free, and that the photographers were privileged to make pictures. Von Schlieben remarked that he was bored with the whole idea of a free press. Capa, Hungarian-born and multilingual, responded in German, saying, "And I am bored with photographing defeated generals."

Irvin, escaped injury. In another action, on the approach to Lessay, three correspondents dove from their jeep into a ditch to escape a German mortar barrage. They were Edward D. Ball, AP, driving; Pierre Huss, INS; and Sol Gottlieb, INP, who was slightly hurt.

Near Roncey, Gorrell, UP, and Thompson, *Chicago Tribune,* accepted the surrender of seventeen Germans, searched them for weapons and sent them on the way to prisoner-of-war cages. McCardell and two infantry corporals took thirty-five prisoners near Grimesnil. Six correspondents "captured" the town of Périers, normally a place of 10,000 population. These men were Cromie, *Chicago Tribune;* Mecklin, *Chicago Sun;* Maynes, Reuters; Duff, BBC; MacKenzie, *New York Daily News;* and Broderick, INP. Cornelius Ryan, *Daily Telegraph,* and two other correspondents, also "captured" the famed town of St. Michel, at the base of the Brittany Peninsula.

By early August 1944, events were moving so rapidly on the French front, and over such an area, that it became difficult for operational staffs in the field and at SHAEF to produce two daily communiqués. In London, only one was issued, and that at 11 A.M. This was an advantage for afternoon papers in the United Kingdom and in the United States and Canada, but left the morning papers without fresh news based on the former 5 P.M. communiqué. Two news conferences continued to be held at SHAEF, however, with the hours changed to 10:30 A.M. and 10:30 P.M. These produced information for morning papers as well as for afternoon papers.

Procedures had become sufficiently established to make it clear that two kinds of information were being presented to the public relative to the campaigns in France and in the Pacific. First, there were the on-the-spot and eye-witness accounts by correspondents in the field. Second, there were background accounts and explanations of general strategy. Each type supplemented the other and provided a good general understanding of the progress of the war.

As the campaign in France gained greater scope through September, the correspondent group was further augmented. Most of the new arrivals were experienced in war coverage. Alexander Graeme Clifford, *Daily Mail,* had been in France in 1939–40 and later in Egypt, Libya, and Italy. Thomas H. Wolf, NEA, had been in the invasion fleet. Others arriving in France included Edward R. Murrow and Charles Collingwood, CBS; Ira Wolfert, NANA; Edd Johnson, *Chicago Sun;* Sonia Tomara, *New York Herald Tribune;* John M. Carlisle, Jr., *Detroit News;* John F. Chester and Neville E. (Ned) Nordness, both of AP; Thurston Macauley, INS; Peter D. Whitney, *San Francisco Chronicle;* Ernest Hemingway, *Collier's;* and Hugh Baillie, president of the United Press, returned once again to the war zone.

Others to arrive in France were John D'Arcy Dawson, Victor Lewis, and William Makin, all of the *Daily Sketch* and Allied (or Kemsley) Newspapers; Peter Lawless, *Daily Telegraph;* Blair Moody, also of the *Detroit News;* David MacNicoll, Australian Consolidated Press; Stuart Macpherson, Basil Thornton, Cyril Ray, Stanley Maxted, and Guy Byam, all of BBC; Edward Connolly, Exchange Telegraph (Extel); Jack J. Smythe, Reuters; Rosette Hargrove, NEA; Lee Carson and Robert C. Wilson, AP; Daniel Grossi and British-born Edward Worth, both of AP Photos.

Still others reaching France were Paul Manning, MBS; Jack Tait and Stanley Woodward, *New York Herald Tribune;* Richard J. H. Johnston, *New York Times;* William H. Stringer, *Christian Science Monitor;*[7] Bruce Grant, *Chicago Times;* Morley Cassidy, *Philadelphia Bulletin;* Holbrook Bradley, *Baltimore Sun;* Duke Shoop, *Kansas City Star;* Charles G. Shaw, *McKeesport News* (Pennsylvania) and CBS; and Bud Kane, *Stars and Stripes.* Further, there were William J. Kinmond, *Toronto Star;* H. D. Ziman, *Daily Telegraph;* William Troughton, *Daily Express;* George McCarthy, *Daily Mirror;* S. L. Solon, *News-Chronicle;* the Marquess of Donegall, London *Sunday Dispatch;* Harold W. Kulick, *Popular Science Monthly;* S. R. G. Bonnett and A. S. Prentice, Gaumont British Newsreel cameraman; Kenneth Gordon, Pathé Newsreel; and D. G. Monick, French AFI news agency.

The correspondents continued to share the risks confronting the troops. Two French correspondents were captured at Rennes early in August. Gene Currivan, *New York Times,* Joseph Driscoll, *New York Herald Tribune,* and David MacNicoll, Australian Consolidated Press, narrowly escaped capture at Le Mans on August 10. They had reached a part of the city not yet evacuated by German forces, and evaded a German patrol when a French woman guided them to safety. Ernie Pyle, Scripps-Howard Newspaper Alliance, and Edward Worth, AP Photos, caught in heavy German air attacks, were fortunate in escaping injury.

Colin Bednall, *Daily Mail* air correspondent, summoned from London to participate in a special RAF emergency flight of 700 bombers ordered to help bottle up tens of thousands of German troops in the so-called Falaise pocket southwest of Caen, had no time to change into uniform. He flew the mission in civilian clothing, earning the strange distinction, as he said, of "going into battle in a grey flannel suit," with the risk of being shot as a spy if his plane had been forced down behind German lines.[8]

---

7 Not to be confused with William S. Stringer of Reuters.
8 Bednall was named as assistant editor of the *Daily Mail* early in September. His place as air correspondent for the paper was assigned to Courtenay Edwards.

Richard Tregaskis, INS, flew in a cub spotter plane over Argentan. The plane's gasoline tank was machine-gunned and a stream of bullets also came within a foot of the correspondent's head. Having been so seriously wounded in Italy, Tregaskis landed safely on this occasion. Some correspondents were less fortunate.

Tom Treanor, *Los Angeles Times* and NBC, who had landed on D-Day and had been in Normandy and Brittany, died August 20 from multiple injuries received the previous day when the jeep in which he was riding in an area northwest of Paris was crushed by a U.S. Army tank. Charles G. Shaw, *McKeesport News* and CBS, injured in the same collision, was hospitalized in England. Sol Gottlieb, INP, received a leg injury in the accident, his second brush with death.

William Stringer, Texas-born correspondent for Reuters, who also had landed on D-Day and was the first correspondent to enter Cherbourg, was killed by a German shell on August 17 while riding in a jeep on the approaches to Paris. Riding with him, Andrew Lopez, Acme Newspictures, and the driver, Private Lawrence Sabin, were wounded by shrapnel. The two hid in a woods for thirty-six hours without food, as German troops moved nearby. When they tried to get back to the U.S. lines in the dark, Private Sabin was mistaken for a German by a French resistance fighter and fatally shot. Lopez later was awarded the Purple Heart.

Three correspondents riding in a jeep near Chartres on August 15, with a French civilian acting as a guide, were in an area they believed to have been cleared of Germans. Two German armored cars emerged from a side road, however, and fired upon them. Paul Holt, *Daily Express,* driver of the jeep, and the French civilian, broke away and managed to escape. Of the other two correspondents, William Makin, *Daily Sketch* and Kemsley Newspapers, was shot in the stomach, and Gault MacGowan, *New York Sun,* was taken prisoner. Both were driven fifty miles to Chalons-sur-Marne, where Makin was cared for by a German doctor. When the Germans evacuated the place soon after, he was left behind. Quite remarkably, Makin was found by Holt and moved again to a hospital in the Chartres area where he died.

MacGowan's experience, following his capture, was unusual. Upon his arrival at Chalons-sur-Marne with Makin, he was placed in the temporary custody of a group of German war correspondents of the *Pressekompanie.* They treated him well, but eventually delivered him to a prisoner-of-war camp on the line of the German retreat. From there he was started on a journey eastward aboard a train, en route to Germany. At 2 A.M., after six hours in the slow-moving train, and as the guards drowsed, MacGowan opened the compartment door and jumped from the car, fell and then ran, with bullets flying about him. Still in France, he was fortunate in reaching a group of Maquis, or French resistance forces. Once he had established his identity, they hid him until U.S. forces had advanced to the area early in September. Interviewed for the *World's Press News* after his return to England, that publication described British-born MacGowan as the only "British correspondent" ever known to have escaped after capture, with the exception of Winston Churchill in his escape from the Boers during the South African War in 1899.

Other correspondents injured during August included Holbrook Bradley, *Baltimore Sun,* who was wounded, and Samuel D. Hales, UP, who received a wrenched back in another of the numerous jeep accidents and was returned to England for care.

The liberation of French cities by Allied troops after four years of occupation produced highly emotional responses in the French people and members of the armed forces themselves. This began at Bayeaux, liberated by the British on June 7, and was repeated elsewhere.

Understandably, the liberation of Paris was to be a particularly emotional occasion. In prospect of that event, correspondents had gathered in mid-August 1944 at Rambouillet, thirty miles southwest of Paris. They were prepared to move in by way of Versailles with troops of the Fighting French, the French 2nd Armored Division under General Jacques Leclerc leading the march, and followed by the U.S. 2nd Armored Division. Street fighting was still in progress in Paris. Resistance fighters of the French Forces of the Interior (FFI), battled with Germans for several days before the liberation. The FFI occupied public buildings to guard them as the Allied troops moved into the city, and they guarded what was to be the ceremonial line of march.

The U.S. First and Third armies under Lieutenant Generals Courtney H. Hodges and George S. Patton, Jr., moved around the city, pushing eastward to establish contact by early September with the U.S. Seventh Army under Lieutenant General Alexander M. Patch, moving north from the Mediterranean landing of mid-August. They also joined with the British-Canadian forces under Field Marshal Montgomery, and with other U.S. forces moving southward from the Channel coast. A continuous front was formed east of Paris from the North Sea and the Dutch border along the French frontier to Switzerland and south to the Italian frontier and the Mediterranean.

On August 25, French and U.S. armies entered Paris in full battle array to march down the Champs d'Elysées from the Arc de Triomphe to the Place de la Concorde. About a hundred French, British, and U.S. correspondents moved into Paris with the troops and immediately thereafter. Peter Carroll of AP Photos made one of the great pictures of the war, showing U.S. troops marching in a vast flood, filling the width of the broad avenue, with the Arc in the background.[9]

In one of the rare happy events of the war years, "the people of Paris stood along the sides of the streets," Clark Lee of INS wrote later, "and poured their hearts out to us. The women looked at us with the innocent ardor of young girls greeting their sweethearts." Ernie Pyle called it "the loveliest, brightest story of our time."

What was in effect the recapture of Paris was reported first by Don Whitehead of the AP. From Rambouillet, he joined the French forces under General Leclerc, entering Paris ahead of all others, and returned to Rambouillet at noon to write an eyewitness account of the taking of the city. This was published in London and New York three or four hours before any other accounts were available.

Six correspondents entering Paris reached the headquarters of the French radio and were offered the opportunity to broadcast. Four of them were radio correspondents: Howard Marshall and Robin B. Duff, both of BBC; Larry LeSueur, CBS; and Paul Manning, MBS. No censors were available in Paris, nor would they be for sixteen hours afterward, as it developed. With stories to tell, the four took advantage of the offer to use the French radio. This was contrary to SHAEF regulations, and the correspondents were required to return to London under suspension for sixty days—a penalty that was halved some three weeks later.[10]

Other correspondents entering Paris with the troops included Seaghan Maynes, Reuters, and James C. McGlincy, UP, both of whom had been with the four radio correspondents at the French station. They also were ordered out of France, even though innocent of broadcasting. Still others were Robert Reubens, Reuters; Harry Harris, Daniel Grossi, and E. K. Butler, AP Photos; Robert C. Miller, Richard McMillan, and Dudley Ann Harmon, UP; Lee Carson, INS; and Hal Boyle, AP.[11]

With the liberation of Paris, correspondents and photographers had

---

9   Like Joseph Rosenthal's 1945 photo of Marines raising the U.S. flag over Mt. Suribachi on Iwo Jima, Carroll's photo also was used after the war on a U.S. postage stamp.

10   Four correspondents had been penalized earlier in August in another case. Accredited to the U.S. Ninth Air Force, they had been ordered from France, charged with paying too much attention in their reports to general aspects of the war and too little to the Ninth Air Force. They were McCardell, *Baltimore Sun;* Frank, *New York Post;* Gammack, *Des Moines Register and Tribune;* and John Groth, *Parade* magazine. The expulsion was protested and heard in Washington. The public relations officer for the Ninth Air Force, who had issued the order, was replaced. By that time the correspondents had been reassigned.

11   Boyle, survivor of many hazards in the months since the North African invasion of November 1942, was struck by a motorcycle while covering the Champs d'Elysées parade. He was hospitalized for three days because of torn ligaments in his back.

opportunities to produce pleasant stories and pictures as a welcome change from the grimness of war. But there were dramatic ones as well, some very much related to the war. Stories reporting the arrival of General DeGaulle in Paris from Algiers a few days after the liberation provided examples. During the day, he journeyed to Notre Dame Cathedral, and the throng gathered there in the square to greet the leader of the Fighting French and head of the provisional government was fired upon from nearby rooftops.

With Paris becoming a capital again, and with France still a battlefield, press headquarters was established appropriately at the Hotel Scribe, in the street of that name near the opera house. The advanced Public Relations Branch of SHAEF and the censorship were established there, and correspondents reported upon arrival. Most were also billeted in the hotel, where an army mess was set up in the basement.

Among the first to become established at the Scribe were Raymond Daniell, *New York Times* London bureau chief; William C. Heinz, *New York Sun;* and Gault MacGowan, also of the *Sun,* returned after his escape from the Germans. He wore borrowed French civilian clothing provided by the French Forces of the Interior because of his acceptance by the Maquis after his escape. As such, and from FFI positions, he had watched the U.S. attack on Chalons-sur-Marne, where he himself had been held for a time.

Apart from those news agency correspondents noted as having entered Paris with the troops at the time of the city's liberation, newspaper correspondents arriving at that time, or soon after, included Alexander Graeme Clifford, Noel Monks, Courtenay Edwards, and John Hall, all of the *Daily Mail;* Austin Hatton of the London *Evening News;* Alan Moorehead and Paul Holt, *Daily Express;* Peter Lawless, *Daily Telegraph;* Robert J. Casey and Helen Kirkpatrick, *Chicago Daily News;* William H. Stringer, *Christian Science Monitor;* Stanley Frank, *New York Post;* Jack Tait, *New York Herald Tribune;* and Frederick Graham, *New York Times.* There also were Gordon Gaskill, *American Magazine;* Ira Wolfert, NANA; Charles Collingwood, CBS; Frank L. Scherschel, *Life* photographer; Charles Hacker, Acme Newspictures; S. R. G. Bonnett and A. S. Prentice, Gaumont British Newsreel cameramen; and Kenneth Gordon, Pathé newsreel cameraman.

News agencies and newspapers with offices in Paris prior to France's surrender in 1940 undertook to reopen those offices. Eric Hawkins, who had been editor of the *New York Herald Tribune* European edition in Paris, returned from London in September. Geoffrey Parsons, Jr., chief of the London staff of the parent paper in New York, also arrived. Together they reopened the Herald Tribune building in the Rue de Berri, off the Champs d'Elysées, and presided once more over the publication there of the European edition of the paper. As correspondent for the New York paper, Tait also moved into his office there. From the same presses came the U.S. Army *Stars and Stripes* edition for France.

The *Daily Mail* of London reestablished the *Continental Daily Mail* through the efforts of Hugh Muir, its former director, and others. Earlier token editions had been produced by Noel Monks, Courtenay Edwards, John Hall, and Austin Hatton, the paper's war correspondents in Paris. These and other newspaper offices had not suffered serious damage during the 1940–44 period of occupation. Former French employees reappeared to work and were able to produce some typewriters and other equipment or materials that they had hidden or safeguarded.

Correspondents in Paris did have difficulties with communications, however, during the first days after liberation. The Press Wireless mobile transmitter was with the U.S. First Army beyond Paris. Mackay Radio had a transmitter with the U.S. Third Army headquarters, also outside Paris. Matters improved in September, however, with the reopening in Paris of a Cable and Wireless circuit to London, a Paris–New York circuit operated by the Mackay Radio & Telegraph Co., and a direct Paris–New York radiotelegraph channel by RCA Communications.

In the first days, copy had to be in the hands of censors at the Hotel Scribe by 6 A.M. and later at 8 P.M. to be ready for handling by a system of army couriers in jeeps. They took the copy to transmitting stations, but were required to be off the highways by nightfall. Dispatches destined for London were carried by courier planes. There were failures in all of these arrangements, but the problems did not last long, nor prevent a record volume of news being dispatched from Paris.

Cable & Wireless reported in September 1944 that nearly 24 million words of press matter had been transmitted from London to all parts of the world over the British Imperial telecommunications system between June 6 and September 4, the first three months after D-Day. Of that total, nearly 9 million words went to the British Dominions and India. Australia received nearly 3.5 million words, South Africa, 1.48 million; Canada and Newfoundland, 1.24 million; New Zealand and the Pacific Islands, 553,000 words. More than 3.84 million went to the United States, nearly 1.24 million to the Soviet Union, and 1.246 million to Central and South America.

The Surrender at Reims, 1945 18

There was a shifting of correspondents in France during September 1944. A number engaged throughout the intense three months of campaigning in Normandy and the liberation of Paris were in need of rest and recuperation in the United Kingdom or the United States. But some also went on to new assignments.

Leaving France for home visits were John A. Moroso, III, AP, who had been in the invasion fleet on D-Day, and William Wade and Jack W. Jarrell, INS, both in the D-Day landings. Others seeking a change of scene were Lewis V. Hunter, Canadian Press; Duke Shoop, *Kansas City Star;* and James C. McGlincy and Dudley Ann Harmon, UP. J. Kingsbury Smith, chief of the INS war staff in London, was on a brief visit to New York in August. Clark Lee, INS, and Ernie Pyle, SHNA, left Paris early in September to return to the United States on the way to the Pacific theater of war.

Even as some correspondents left France, so many others sought to reach Paris from London that SHAEF found difficulty transporting them and housing them. Among those who arrived, or returned after an absence, were Stoneman, *Chicago Daily News,* Peterman, *Philadelphia Inquirer,* and Gaskill, *American Magazine,* all of whom had participated in D-Day coverage; Harold Callender, *New York Times,* with experience in Paris since the 1920s; Gerald Barry and Stanley Barron, *News-Chronicle;* John Redfern and Basil Cardew, *Daily Express;* W. A. S. Douglas, *Chicago Sun;* Alistaire Forbes and Phyllis Davis, *Daily Mail;* and Mary Munton, *Daily Telegraph.*

Ernest Hemingway, *Collier's,* and Mary Welsh, *Time,* both familiar with prewar Paris, had met in London and now set up at the Hotel Ritz in Paris, while their former spouses, Martha Gellhorn, also writing for *Collier's,* and Noel Monks of the *Daily Mail,* were enduring the hazards of other news fronts. Hemingway and Welsh were not married until after the war. Hemingway's first wife, the former Hadley Richardson, became Paul Scott Mowrer's second wife in 1933, two years before he himself left the post as Paris correspondent to become editor of the *Chicago Daily News.*

Other correspondents in Paris in the fall of 1944 included Bruce Grant, *Chicago Times,* and his son, artist-reporter Gordon Grant, first in Italy and then in London and in France for the *Tampa Tribune.* They formed a father-son combination covering the war, matching Paul Scott Mowrer and his son Richard Mowrer. Also in Paris were Leslie Hotine, BBC; James McDowell and Dr. Catherine Calvin, *Daily Sketch* and Kemsley Newspapers; Ori Ottley, *PM;* Ned Calmer, CBS; Alton Smalley, *St. Paul Pioneer Press* and *Dispatch;* Hilde Marchant, *Daily Mirror;* the Misses P. Deakin, M. Allen, E. Irons, and E. Riddell, representing respectively the *Times, Daily Herald,* and *Evening Standard,* all of London, and *Truth* of Australia. Carl Ollsen and James Jarache were in France for the *Illustrated,* and E. K. Butler of AP Photos representing the still picture pool. A reviving coverage by journalists of other countries was foreshadowed by the presence in Paris of three representatives of the Agence Belga of Brussels, André Cauvin, Robert A. Francotte, and M. G. Levy.

Correspondents in Paris covered SHAEF and also the new French Provisional Government there, headed by General DeGaulle, but the greater number remained with the armies. Their activities continued without reference to what was transpiring in Paris. Fighting went on west of Paris, in a last-ditch German stand on the Brittany Peninsula, but the more dramatic military action was in the east, toward Germany itself.

A group of U.S. and British correspondents arrived in Brittany on September 2 to report a battle underway at the port of Brest. Richard J. H. Johnston, *New York Times,* was wounded by shrapnel less than two hours after his arrival and was returned to England. Edward V. Roberts, UP, also wounded by shrapnel was cared for in a field hospital and was able to file dispatches from there. Both men received Purple Heart decorations. Roy Porter, NBC, formerly with the AP reporting the war in Poland, the Low Countries, and France, and later in the Far East, landed at St. Nazaire with a U.S. Army Air Force officer. In the fluid situation existing, the two men received the surrender of no less than 27,000 German troops and "liberated" six French towns.

While driving to cover the surrender of 20,000 Germans near the Loire River southwest of Paris on September 13, three U.S. correspondents drove into a trap and were themselves captured after their jeep was fired upon. They were Edward W. Beattie, Jr., UP, John M. Mecklin, *Chicago Sun,* and Wright Bryan, *Atlanta Journal.* Bryan was shot in the leg and the bullet was removed by a German army doctor. Separated, the three were started on the way to Germany as prisoners. On the following day, a U.S. attack in the area where Mecklin was being moved eastward resulted in his guards releasing him, and he returned to press headquarters on September 19. Beattie, who had covered important stories in Europe and the Far East since 1933, and Bryan, who had obtained one of the first eye-witness accounts of the D-Day invasion, were taken to Germany as prisoners of war.[1]

Harold W. Kulick, correspondent and photographer for *Popular Science Monthly,* was killed early in September when a U.S. bomber in which he had flown on a mission over France crashed when landing at an airfield near London. John F. Chester, AP, and Edward Connolly, Exchange Telegraph, were injured in a jeep accident in northern France; Chester's ankle was broken.

The U.S. Third Army under General Patton moved so rapidly eastward from Paris during August–September that correspondents found difficulty in keeping up. They sometimes had to ride 300 miles a day in a twelve to eighteen-hour effort to reach the front, gather information, and then return to the communications point. Patton himself briefed them at times. They were required to accept special security and censorship regulations, however, so that the Germans might be kept as much in the dark as possible about the movement of the forces and their intentions.

The Allied sweep overran areas that had figured in World War I, including the Argonne Forest, Verdun, and Chaumont. The latter had been General Pershing's AEF headquarters in 1918. Pierre Huss, INS, was first with published reports of the arrival in the Argonne and of the first action at Verdun. During the bombardment of Verdun, Robert C. Miller, UP, was severely wounded in the left arm by shrapnel and spent two years in hospitals. J. A. Bockhurst, a newsreel cameraman, crawled to Miller under fire and put a tourniquet on his arm.

In the north of France, Frank Fisher and Walter Cronkite, both UP, accompanied British forces in the recapture of Dunkirk and the thrust into Belgium. Fisher had reported the BEF evacuation from that French city and the beaches in 1940. Accompanying U.S. First Army troops, also in the north, were Don Whitehead and Kenneth L. Dixon, AP; Robert Richards, UP; Roelif Loveland, *Cleveland Plain Dealer;* and

---

1   Bryan was moved to Oflag 64, a prisoner-of-war camp near Posen in Poland, where Larry Allen, AP, also had been held from the time of his capture in Libya in 1942 and until his release in May 1944 as a non-combatant civilian newsman in an exchange of sick and wounded prisoners. Bryan was freed late in January 1945 as the Red Army approached the camp area and all prisoners were started walking toward Germany. Bryan walked to Paris, where he arrived in April. Beattie, after a period in a Moorsburg prison camp was transferred to a Luckenwalde prison camp. When Red Army forces took that camp late in April, he was liberated.

Peter Carroll and Harry Harris, both of AP Photos. These were the first Allied correspondents into Belgium. They arrived at Abbeville on September 2, with Carroll and Harris riding atop a tank. Henry T. Gorrell, UP, was the first correspondent into Germany, riding in the lead jeep in a column entering Roetgen on September 11. Whereas Whitehead and his colleague had been received by cheering and weeping Belgians, Gorrell observed only sullen faces among the German civilians. Also in Roetgen, Robert Reuben of Reuters sent the first dispatch from Germany on September 15.

Correspondents accompanying forces of the British Second Army and the Canadian First Army pushing into northern Belgium and Holland included Alan Moorehead, *Daily Express;* Doon Campbell, Reuters; Alexander Graeme Clifford, *Daily Mail;* Christopher Buckley, *Daily Telegraph;* John D'Arcy-Dawson and Leonard Oswald Mosley, both of the *Daily Sketch* and Kemsley Newspapers; Mallory Browne, *Christian Science Monitor;* William J. Kinmond, *Toronto Star;* and Sholto Watt, *Montreal Star.* Kinmond was captured while driving his jeep from Ghent to Antwerp, heading straight into an enemy position. Watt suffered three broken ribs in a jeep mishap near Brussels.

Allied airborne landings near Arnhem, Holland, during September were reported by a pool of six correspondents parachuting with the troops or landing in gliders. They were Alan Wood, *Daily Express;* Stanley Woodward, *New York Herald Tribune;* Cyril Ray, BBC and MBS; Stanley Maxted and Guy Byam, both of BBC; and J. J. (Jack) Smythe, Reuters. The objective of the operation was to drive a wedge into German defense positions, while forming a juncture with other Allied forces also landing sixty miles behind the German line. The operation encountered heavy opposition, with the Allied forces in the Arnhem area surrounded and isolated for several days. Another airborne operation near Nijmegen on the Rhine River frontier between Holland and Germany captured the Rhine bridge at that point. This allowed the besieged forces near Arnhem to slip out of the encirclement and cross the Rhine under bombardment.

Jack Smythe of Reuters was captured during this interval.[2] The other correspondents escaped. Byam of the BBC swam the Rhine to avoid machine-gun fire directed at the bridge. Maxted was stunned by a mortar bomb blast and was out of action for some hours.

Correspondents who followed up the Arnhem air drop and, in some cases, reported the Nijmegen action, included Ward Smith of the Lon-

---

2   Smythe was held a prisoner of war in Germany until April 1945, when he was freed in an Allied advance. The war in the Pacific ended before his arrival there for Reuters via the United States.

don *News of the World* and BBC. He became one of those to escape the Arnhem pocket. Upon returning to England in March 1945, he stood for Parliament in the general election of July as a Liberal party candidate for Bexley in Kent. Others in the action in Holland included William F. Boni, AP; Walter Cronkite, UP; William C. Heinz, *New York Sun;* Victor Lewis, air correspondent for the *Daily Sketch* and other Kemsley papers; Jack Eston, *Daily Herald* photographer; William Warhurst, photographer for the *Times;* Ian Struther, Paramount News newsreel cameraman; Sidney Bonnett, Gaumont News cameraman; Kenneth Gordon, Pathé newsreel cameraman; Douglas Amaron, Canadian Press; Edward R. Murrow, CBS; and Basil Thornton, BBC.

Thornton went into the Nijmegen operation in a glider and was able to return to London in time to broadcast a report over the BBC that same night. Boni had been born and raised in the Netherlands and was able to talk with the people and produce an especially effective report. The action also was covered from the airfield in western England from which the planes departed and to which some returned. Representation there produced reports by Leo S. Disher, UP and BUP, William R. Downs, CBS, and Michael Moynihan of the *News-Chronicle.*

The speed of the Allied advance in eastern France, Belgium, and Holland between September 1944 and the end of that year kept the correspondents moving and introduced special problems of coverage. One related to delays in the handling of copy, much of which was transmitted to London by RAF Signals. Censors could not operate in the advance field positions, however, because they were no better informed than the correspondents. Their caution, in the circumstances, introduced delays and differences of opinion as to what might be passed.

In Brussels and other places accommodations were inadequate for the very considerable number of correspondents present. The British system of attaching a conducting officer to assist each correspondent also broke down because the correspondents outnumbered available conducting officers by about three to one. Most correspondents had sufficient battlefront experience by the time the troops reached Belgium so that they were able to operate independently, with younger conducting officers less battle-wise than some of the correspondents.

No correspondents were armed, aside from the enlisted combat correspondents, since it would make them liable to execution, if captured. An exception occurred, however, when the British Second Army entered Germany by way of Holland in September. On the assumption that German civilians would be hostile, the correspondents at their own request were provided with tommy-guns or Sten guns. As events shaped up, they never needed the weapons, never used them, and soon ceased to carry them.

The advance in the northeast went "so fast that we can hardly believe it ourselves," wrote Clifford of the *Daily Mail.* "You can travel all day and never catch up with the front." Alan Moorehead, *Daily Express,* compared the scene to "one of Waterloo or Borodino—except, of course, the kind of wreckage is different." He wrote:

> There is a profusion of everything—field-glasses and typewriters, pistols and small arms by the hundreds, cases of wine, truckloads of food and medical stores, a vast mass of leather harness. Every car is full of clothing. . . . If you want a car you walk up and take your pick—anything from a baby tourer or a Volkswagen to a 10-ton half-track. I have just selected a Volkswagen to take me back to my billet. The back seat is piled up with the belongings of the man who now lies dead by the front wheels.[3]

Christopher Buckley, *Daily Telegraph,* complained later in September that:

> There are far too many correspondents out in France. It would have been better to use the pool system more extensively, while at the same time allowing the main papers one correspondent each. As it is, briefing officers who would normally give correspondents an "off the record" picture of the battle, are met by about 50 correspondents in all and, seeing such a great number as this, and so many strange faces, they are reticent to give out more than a formal and official statement.[4]

Correspondents with the British and Canadian forces seemed to voice more complaints than those with the U.S. forces. Censorship tended to be tighter with the U.S. armies, but briefings appear to have been generally somewhat better: there were no complications with reference to conducting officers, and communications facilities were satisfactory. Two Press Wireless mobile transmitters were in the forward areas, and Mackay Radio technicians also showed courage and initiative in keeping channels open and positions conveniently located for the use of correspondents so that press messages and even radio broadcasts moved from France to New York in a matter of minutes.

In London staff adjustments were made in the latter months of 1944. J. Kingsbury Smith, INS, returned from a period in the United States to resume direction of that agency's European service. James W. Grigg, Jr., became manager of the UP bureau, joined by Boyd Lewis. Further additions to the U.S. press corps there included Holbrook Bradley, *Baltimore Sun,* returning from France, where he had been wounded in August; Edward P. Morgan, *Chicago Daily News,* back from an assign-

---

3 *World's Press News,* September 7, 1944.
4 *World's Press News,* September 28, 1944.

ment in Spain; Demaree Bess and Arch Whitehouse, both of the *Saturday Evening Post;* Charles Chamberlin, AP; James Sloan, *Chicago Tribune;* George Backer, then publisher of the *New York Post;* Dennis Scanlan, *Time* and *Life;* Henry Wolfe of the *This Week* Sunday supplement with the *New York Herald Tribune* and many other newspapers; and Samuel Adkins, *Louisville Courier-Journal.*

A number of U.S. correspondents in London began to broadcast in German to Germany in September over the facilities of a station then operated in England by the U.S. Office of War Information under the name of ABSIE (American Broadcasting Station In Europe).

The transfer of correspondents from London to Paris took on considerable proportions after October 10, 1944, when those accredited to SHAEF at its MOI Public Relations Branch headquarters were moved to Paris aboard special planes. The formal establishment of the Public Relations Branch headquarters at the Hotel Scribe at that time meant that nearly all elements of SHAEF were in France.

Some lack of accommodations in Paris, and limitations still existing in communications, led SHAEF to propose certain temporary limitations on the accreditation of correspondents, with two to each news agency, one for each newspaper, and one for certain other media. Those not acting as war correspondents also were asked to leave Paris. This and other proposed restrictions brought protests from British and U.S. sources. It was argued that correspondents of long prewar experience were being excluded from Paris at a time when they could be most useful in interpreting actions of the French provisional government, as well as reporting on the war situation itself. The billeting and communications problems in fact were resolved very soon so that political reporters as well as war correspondents were able to live and work in Paris, and no more was heard of any limitation on numbers.

In late October and early November scores of correspondents, even some newly assigned, moved eastward through France, Belgium, and Holland into Germany. They were with the U.S. First, Third, and Seventh and Ninth armies, and the British Second and the Canadian First armies, and the French First Army. The German city of Aachen on the Belgian border was captured on October 12 by the U.S. First Army after a bitter battle, and mopping up operations continued for another week. By then Allied forces had reached the Rhine near Strasbourg.

Hugh Baillie, president of the United Press, and Bert Brandt, Acme Newspictures, were severely shaken up in a jeep accident while returning from a visit to First Army units in the Aachen area late in September. Baillie went through the windshield, and only his steel helmet saved him from probable serious injury or death.

Two correspondents returning from Aachen to press headquarters on October 19 were in another jeep disaster when the car touched off the explosion of a string of anti-vehicular Teller mines on the road. David Lardner of the *New Yorker* magazine and son of Ring Lardner, who had reported for the *Chicago Tribune,* died of multiple injuries. On his first war assignment, he had written only one story. The driver of the jeep, Private Edward Litwin, also was killed. Russell Hill, *New York Herald Tribune,* suffered a broken arm and cuts and bruises. Richard Tregaskis of INS, already a survivor of wounds, had been with them but decided to remain in Aachen and so escaped.

A leading German correspondent and member of the Pressekompanie, Lieutenant Kurt Pauli, tried to break out of Aachen, then under U.S. control, on the night of October 18. He later was reported as missing in action.

Correspondents involved in the actions during this period also included Ira Wolfert and Lionel Shapiro, NANA. Wolfert left the combat zone before the end of October to return to the United States for a period of rest following long experience on many fronts. He chose to travel by ship because, he said, "I've gotten allergic to airplanes." He returned because he had become "bored" with war. "A person gets bored with being afraid," he said. "Fear is a simple emotion that fills your whole mind. It gets monotonous." Wolfert paid tribute to correspondents. If they wished, he observed, they could expand communiqués from headquarters and interview survivors of actions and never go near the front. But their faithfulness actually carried them into the thick of things, he said, moving them into the field, enduring hardships day after day, facing dangers, and showing devotion to their tasks.[5]

Other correspondents who left France included Sol Sonnee Gottlieb, INP photographer, who needed further treatment for injuries received in the August jeep accident that had cost Tom Treanor his life. Robert Vermillion, UP, who had moved from the south of France northward to the Belfort Gap with the U.S. Seventh Army, went to Greece with Reynolds Packard to reestablish UP coverage there. Frank J. Scherschel and Robert Landry, *Life* photographers, and E. K. Butler, AP Photos, also left France in October.

Sherman Montrose, NEA-Acme Newspictures, arrived from Italy to replace Butler as U.S. Still Photo Pool representative. Henry Griffin, AP Photos, and Fred Ramage and Alan Jackson, both INP photographers, also arrived to maintain photo coverage.

Other correspondents engaged in France in October included J. Emlyn Williams, *Christian Science Monitor;* John Prince, the *Times;* Peter Lawless, *Daily Telegraph;* David Anderson and Clifton Daniel, *New York Times;* Lewis Gannett, *New York Herald Tribune;* Ross Munro,

---

5 *Editor & Publisher,* October 21, 1944.

Canadian Press; Seagham Maynes, Reuters; Frank Conniff and Lee Carson, INS; Don Whitehead and William S. White, AP; Henry T. Gorrell, Boyd Lewis, and Jack Frankish, all for UP; William Wilson, BUP; David Darrah, *Chicago Tribune;* Graham Miller, *New York Daily News;* Allen Kent, *Toronto Telegram;* Ralph Allen, *Toronto Globe and Mail;* John Clare, *Toronto Star;* Catherine Coyne, *Boston Herald;* Marjorie (Dot) Avery, *Detroit Free Press;* Roelif Loveland, *Cleveland Plain Dealer;* Mark Watson, *Baltimore Sun;*[6] and Carl Giles, illustrator, *Daily Express.*[7]

With Allied forces at the Rhine by late November, many of the correspondents remained with the troops. These included Tregaskis, Carson, and Conniff, INS, plus Pierre J. Huss, John Egerton Lee, Graham Hovey, and Larry Newman of that agency. They included Montrose, NEA-Acme; Whitehead and White, of the AP, plus Thoburn H. (Toby) Wiant, formerly in China. Edward Kennedy directed the AP staff from the bureau in the Scribe Hotel, Paris. AP staff members included J. Wes Gallagher, Hal Boyle, George Tucker, Robert Wilson, Wade Werner, William F. Boni, Ned Nordness, Ruth Cowan, Franklin Banker, Lewis Hawkins, and Kenneth L. Dixon. The UP had Gorrell, Lewis and Frankish with troops, plus Clinton B. (Pat) Conger, Virgil Pinkley, Wilson C. ("Collie") Small, Robert Richards, Ned Roberts, Ronald Clark, and Richard McMillan, BUP.

With the advancing Allied armies Gannett represented the *New York Herald Tribune;* James Holburn, the London *Times;* Noel Monks, the *Daily Mail;* Stanley Bishop, *Daily Herald;* Philip Jordan, *News-Chronicle;* Peter Duffield, *Evening Standard;* Philip Wynter, Australian News Syndicate; Ronald Maillard Stead, the *Christian Science Monitor;* Frederick Graham, *New York Times;* William H. Stoneman, *Chicago Daily News;* John Mecklin, *Chicago Sun;* Bruce Grant, *Chicago Times;* Gordon Grant, his son, *Tampa Tribune;* Hugh Schuck, *New York Daily News;* Louis Azreal, *Baltimore News-Post;* Louis Wallenstein, *Kansas City Star;* Carlyle Hill, *Boston Globe;* Alton Smalley,

---

6   Mark Watson was awarded the Pulitzer Prize in 1945 for international telegraphic reporting in 1944. One of his reports figuring in that award appears in *A Treasury of Great Reporting,* L. L. Snyder and R. B. Morris, eds., pp. 657–59. Watson had been a war correspondent for the *Chicago Tribune* in World War I.

7   The *Daily Express* asserted that Giles was the first political cartoonist to be accredited as a war correspondent. This may have been true for the period of World War II, although Bill Mauldin and George Baker of the U.S. Army became known as cartoonists during the war. In World War I, Captain Bruce Bairnsfather gained repute as a cartoonist, with his work appearing in the London *Bystander* and receiving syndication abroad. John T. McCutcheon, a political cartoonist of the *Chicago Record* and later of the *Chicago Tribune,* was a correspondent during the Spanish-American War, the South African (Boer) War, the Russo-Japanese War, and World War I.

St. Paul Pioneer Press and Dispatch; and Ernest Hemingway, *Collier's.* Conger, UP, and Montrose, NEA-Acme photographer, with the French First Army, were reputedly the first correspondents to reach the Rhine. Conniff, INS, with the forces pushing toward the river, was wounded by a mortar explosion, and later awarded the Purple Heart.

An expectation by late November 1944 that winter mud and cold might halt the swift Allied advance, including that of the Red Army in the east, and that lengthy preparations might be necessary before any concerted spring drive could carry Allied forces into the Reich itself, may have persuaded U.S. correspondents, in particular, that the winter of 1944 was the time to return to the United States for a period of recuperation. Among those who did so, after having been in the field for months, were John H. Thompson, *Chicago Tribune,* departing in October; Cyrus L. Sulzberger, *New York Times,* who had been in Cairo; Carleton (Bill) Kent, *Chicago Sun;* Robert J. Casey, *Chicago Daily News;* Herb Graffis, *Chicago Times;* Pat Frank, *New York Post* and Overseas News Agency, who had been in Italy; John M. Carlisle, *Detroit News;* Robert J. Doyle, *Milwaukee Journal;* Gordon Gammack, *Des Moines Register and Tribune;* Lawrence Youngman, *Omaha World Herald;* and Roelif Loveland, *Cleveland Plain Dealer.*

News agency correspondents returning to the U.S. included Don Whitehead, AP; Charles Seawood and Henry Griffin, AP Photos; Henry T. Gorrell, UP; Bert Brandt and Andy Lopez, Acme Newspictures; and Pierre J. Huss and Dixie Tighe, INS. Richard Tobin, *New York Herald Tribune,* injured in a London blackout accident also departed. Ross Munro, Canadian Press, returned to Canada. Sholto Watt, *Montreal Star,* who had suffered broken ribs when his jeep collided with an army truck near Brussels, returned to Montreal in December.

Other correspondents were returning to the European theater at the same time. Ann Stringer, widow of Texas-born William Stringer, who was killed near Paris in August while representing Reuters, arrived in London for the UP. Robert Musel, John McDermott, Corinne Hardesty, and Malcolm Muir, Jr., also joined or rejoined the UP staff. Chris R. Cunningham, a veteran of the North African, Sicilian, and Italian campaigns, returned to the UP staff, after completing a period in Hollywood as technical adviser for the motion picture, "The Story of G.I. Joe," based on Ernie Pyle's reports of areas and events also familiar to Cunningham.

Louis P. Lochner, AP, chief of the Berlin bureau at the time of Pearl Harbor and repatriated to the United States in 1942, joined the agency staff in France. Gault MacGowan, *New York Sun,* returned after three months in the United Kingdom. George Hicks, Blue Network, who had participated in the D-Day invasion, also returned, as also did Martha Gellhorn (Mrs. Ernest Hemingway) for *Collier's,* and Neil Sullivan, Pathé News cameraman. New arrivals included James Shepley, for *Time* magazine; German-born Curt Riess for NEA;[8] and Mrs. Elizabeth B. M. Phillips for the *Baltimore Afro-American,* as the first accredited Negro woman correspondent.

German elements under Field Marshal Karl Gerd Von Rundstedt opened a counter-offensive against the Allies in December 1944. Referred to later as "the Battle of the Bulge," in the Ardennes area of Belgium, it centered around Bastogne and continued through the Christmas period.

Press headquarters in the area of the attack had to be moved promptly to a more secure position. The correspondent group included Gallagher and Boyle[9] of the AP, both of whom had been at the Kasserine Pass in North Africa during the U.S. Army reversal there late in 1942, and Denny of the *New York Times,* who had been in British reversals in Libya and Egypt in 1941. These three were virtually the only correspondents present possessing any experience in the coverage of forces on the defensive. The only correspondent in Bastogne itself, the chief target of German attack, was Fred MacKenzie of the *Buffalo Evening News.*

Other correspondents in the Ardennes during the critical battle period included John H. Thompson, *Chicago Tribune,* just returned from home leave; William Strand, also of the *Tribune;* George Hicks, Blue Network, and Neil Sullivan, Pathé News cameraman, both also recently returned from periods of leave; John Wilhelm, U.S.-born, Reuters; Noel Monks, *Daily Mail;* Gene Currivan, *New York Times;* Lewis Gannett, *New York Herald Tribune;* William H. Stringer and Ronald Maillard Stead, *Christian Science Monitor;* Morley Cassidy, *Philadelphia Bulletin;* Ivan H. (Cy) Peterman, *Philadelphia Inquirer;* Jack Belden, *Life;* and Meyer Levin, Overseas News Agency. In addition to Gallagher and Boyle, the AP was represented in this action by William B. Boni, Tom Yarbrough, Lewis Hawkins, Kenneth L. Dixon, and Edward D. Ball. The UP was represented by "Collie" Small, John McDermott, recently arrived, and John Frankish.

Casualties in the Ardennes and elsewhere in France during December included Frankish, who was killed when four German planes dive-bombed a Belgian village on December 23. He was said to have been the

---

8   Riess edited *They Were There* (1944), a collection of articles by U.S. war correspondents. He contributed a long and useful essay "On Correspondents" and a who's who of correspondents.

9   Boyle was awarded the Pulitzer Prize in 1945 for his reports written in 1944, including those on the Battle of the Bulge.

twenty-eighth U.S. correspondent to die in the war, and the thirteenth in 1944. Denny of the *New York Times,* Hicks of the Blue Network, and Sullivan of Pathé News were slightly wounded in the same attack.

William Hanford of Press Wireless, who was attached to the mobile Station PX since it was placed in operation on the Normandy beach in June, was wounded in December while operating the transmitter close to the front with the U.S. First Army. He later was awarded the Purple Heart. Martha Gellhorn, recently returned from a period of leave, suffered broken ribs and bruises in an automobile accident. Frank Conniff, INS, recovered from wounds received during November from a mortar shell explosion, was hurt again in a jeep accident in Belgium and ordered out of action.

There were complaints in Paris during December from Allied and neutral correspondents about inadequate facilities at SHAEF and the briefing sessions. Lack of information there and in the field at the time of the German counterblow in the Ardennes brought especially strong protests from such respected correspondents as Drew Middleton, *New York Times;* James McGlincy, UP; and Joseph F. Evans, Jr., *Newsweek.* In the matter of briefing, the SHAEF rule was that the positions of the Allied and German armies would be made public through one daily communiqué only, and even then the positions would be described as of twenty-four to forty-eight hours preceding to avoid giving the Germans information of any possible value.

Noel Monks, *Daily Mail* front-line correspondent, called the Scribe Hotel "the Madhouse of Europe." In this, he had reference to the SHAEF Public Relations and press headquarters located there. This harsh designation was rejected, however, by a number of correspondents directly accredited to SHAEF: Evans of *Newsweek;* Robert W. Cooper, the *Times;* J. R. L. Anderson, *Manchester Guardian;* John ("Tex") O'Reilly, *New York Herald Tribune;* and Colin Bingham, *Sydney Morning Herald.* SHAEF also was defended in its information function by Sir James Grigg, British war minister, speaking in the House of Commons early in January 1945. Even so, Stephen T. Early, press secretary for President Roosevelt, went to Paris in February 1945 in part to investigate SHAEF public relations practices. His report was completed in March and submitted to Major General A. D. Searles of the U.S. War Department. It was not made public.

With the invasion year of 1944 near its close, Cable & Wireless announced in London that press matter originating in Europe and transmitted over its facilities in the six months between June 6 (D-Day) and December 5 had totalled 46,500,000 words and the transmission of 8,950 photographs. This did not include matter transmitted directly from France to the United States or elsewhere, or transmitted by Press Wireless or other carrying agents.

In February 1945, SHAEF announced that more than 100 million words had been written by correspondents in the European Theater of Operations (ETO) since D-Day, with only about 1.5 per cent lost through censorship. In addition, SHAEF counted about 1,500,000 photos and three million feet of motion picture film as having passed through the censorship.[10]

The procedure followed by correspondents in covering a war so unlike any in the past, even in Europe, and so unlike any peacetime situation, was described early in 1945 by Alexander H. Uhl, foreign editor of *PM,* New York. His prewar experience as an AP correspondent in European capitals and as a war correspondent gave Uhl a perspective reflected in a long descriptive article.[11] He said, in part:

> Correspondents don't just "cover the war." There is a regular echelon that compares more or less with the structure of the Army itself. Let's begin with the man in the field.
>
> In the first place, he is accredited to some particular army, and he can't hop from one army to another without having the authority to do so.
>
> This army has a public relations office and a headquarters. Sometimes this headquarters is a hotel located in a convenient city. Often it is in the field, as one to which I was attached in Italy. It was pitched in a grove of oak trees and was about 40 miles behind the lines.
>
> We lived in tents, ate at the regular army mess, took showers in the shower tent, and sometimes saw movies out in the open sitting on the grass and fighting mosquitoes as best we could.
>
> We wrote our dispatches in a big central tent and they were sent back to Rome by courier for transmission to the U.S.A. Frequently armies have portable radio transmitters which are used instead of couriers.
>
> Each morning a regular procession of jeeps containing as a rule two correspondents not in direct competition, would leave camp for the front. For the most part, each jeep was off about its own business—the correspondents selecting whatever part of the front they thought might be of most interest that day.
>
> Farther up toward the front and usually well within enemy artillery range, you would come to divisional headquarters and pop in to see the public relations officer who would fill you in on what was happening on his divisional front and might be worth seeing.
>
> From him the correspondent would filter down toward regimental headquarters, battalion headquarters and company headquarters—which means that by this time the correspondent is right up where he has to keep an eye out for snipers. Most of the time the front is reasonably quiet and the correspondent can drift around, talking with the men and getting their stories.
>
> For the most part, the men who are covering well up at the front are chiefly

10   *World's Press News,* December 21, 1944; February 15, 1945.

11   Alexander H. Uhl, "How Foreign Correspondents Gather the News," *PM,* January 12, 1945, p. 6.

interested in human interest stories, while some of them are specialists in locality stories. This means that the man's chief job, if he is from Buffalo, let's say, is to find Buffalo GIs and get their stories. Correspondents get known for their special interests, and it is common for GIs to tip them off on their specialties.

The picture changes radically when there is action. For then the chief job of the correspondent is to get to some observation post where he can see what is going on. . . .

Then when the day's observations are over, the correspondent has to high-tail it back to where he can get to communications, for the best story in the world means nothing unless he can get it back to his paper, and fast.

It is from these correspondents, for the most part, that you get the stories of action, talks with GIs, the eyewitness accounts, and sometimes the little item in the paper, "Another Correspondent Killed."

But in back of these correspondents are other groups whose jobs are not less important but far less spectacular. In Paris right now there are perhaps a hundred correspondents who rarely ever see the battlefields. They work mostly for press associations and big newspapers that have large staffs in the field.

It is they who must keep the picture in proportion, who must combine the news from two, or three, or four armies.

They work closely with headquarters, public relations offices and briefing offices. The briefing room is about as close as the outsider can get to coming into contact with Army operations.

On the walls of the briefing room are listed the locations of all our divisions, the enemy divisions, the observed movement of enemy troops, the broad picture, sometimes involving millions of men. Only accredited correspondents are ever admitted. It is the job of these correspondents to take all this mass of information and rewrite it into a useable newspaper story, discarding the minor details and sharpening up the broad picture. . . . They are looking for "leads" in the material that is handed them. And for the most part they are looking for good leads. . . . —that is, good news instead of bad.

The weakness in this setup is that day after day these men must find something on which a headline can be built. If it is a dull day they are quite likely to pick out some obscure development, which in the rush of daily journalism gets virtually as much attention as some really big story.

This headline-hunting zeal is one of the things that account for the distorted picture of the war that we frequently get. It would take a correspondent of iron courage to tell his readers frankly: "Nothing important happened . . . today." . . .

And somewhere back home another rewrite man sits, poring over the mass of copy that flows to his desk, and comes up with a new rewrite that frequently leads the paper. Here again the man writing the main story is still farther from the scene of action.

Actually, of course, there are other correspondents who are not in such fixed assignments. They write special articles for their papers or magazines, and they are quite likely to wander from one army to another. They are mostly taken care of by a facilities officer attached to army headquarters, who will arrange trips for them to the field that may vary from one day to a couple of weeks.

They can't just pop in on any PRO headquarters. Those headquarters down the line are equipped to handle only so many men, and unless they can take care of these roving correspondents they just notify them that the situation is "frozen" for the moment, and that they will have to wait for a vacancy to occur. As a rule these correspondents make their headquarters in Paris.

Paris press headquarters is at a hotel [Hotel Scribe] which has been taken over by the Army. Here you will find most of the American, British and even French correspondents living together just as they would in any other hotel in the world, eating at a regular mess in the hotel, and working directly with the censorship and communications officers who are also housed with them.

There is a considerable amount of competition among PROs in the lower echelons for the attention of correspondents. . . .

Then finally there is the correspondent whose job it is to cover politics. These correspondents turn up mostly when we get to big cities like Rome and Paris. The Army doesn't quite know what to do about them. There was quite a to-do about them in Paris for a while when some of the army PROs felt that they really were not war correspondents. Actually, of course, the Army insists that they be accredited just as everybody else is, that they conform to army regulations, go through censorship, etc. It finally was decided that as long as the Army maintained authority and control over them, it would have to accept the responsibility for them also.

The poor political reporter, despite the fact that he is an orphan, can't always get his politics in Paris or London. In this war, political reporting goes right up to the front lines. And if you are going to follow military governments, for example, you very soon find yourself going into towns with military officers—which frequently means going into one end of a town while the Germans are scurrying out of the other. . . .

By mid-January 1945 the German break-through in the Belgian "bulge" had been repaired by the Allies, with Wehrmacht forces driven back beyond their own so-called Siegfried Line by early February. The U.S. First and Third Armies established a juncture to restore that front. Correspondents with the First Army included Chris R. Cunningham, UP; Hal Boyle and Tom Yarbrough, AP; Lee Carson, INS; John H. Thompson, *Chicago Tribune;* Jack Bell, *Chicago Daily News;* John Florea, *Life* photographer; and Meyer Levin, Overseas News Agency. With the Third Army there were John Prince, the *Times;* Seaghan Maynes, Reuters; Cornelius Ryan, *Daily Telegraph;* Norman Clark, *News-Chronicle;* Edward Murray, UP; and Byron Rollins, AP Photos. Others reporting the action included Carlyle Holt, *Boston Globe;* Harold Siepman, Acme Newspictures; Gaston Madru, News of the Day newsreel cameraman; and Thomas Priestly, Universal Newsreel cameraman.

In February, Canadian and U.S. troops approached the Rhine in the Cologne area. The U.S. Ninth Army established a front on the Roer River near Jülich and was joined by elements of the First Army to make a crossing of that river and push toward Munich and Cologne, which was taken early in March. The west bank of the Rhine was held in the Remagen area, spanned at that point by the Ludendorff Railway Bridge. German opposition was overcome and five U.S. divisions were put across the bridge and spread out east of the river. Farther south, the Third Army under Patton overcame the German Fifth Panzer forces to capture Bad Godesberg and Bonn by March 10. French and British forces joined in the advance all along the western front. Meanwhile, the Red Army had been advancing from the east, with some forces within 100 miles of Berlin by February.

Alton Smalley, *St. Paul Dispatch and Pioneer Press,* was wounded while with the U.S. Ninth Army at West Jülich when a fragment of a German mortar shell struck his elbow. Then, in driving from the front to obtain treatment, his jeep collided with another during the blackout and fog of early dawn and Smalley suffered an additional compound fracture of his arm. He was hospitalized until July and later awarded a Purple Heart.

Max Lerner, *PM,* came close to capture or death while with the Ninth Army late in February. His jeep, along with two other army vehicles, drove into a group of German soldiers on a road north of Webberg. The driver, Private Richard Fanning, drove the jeep out in reverse while lying on the floor to avoid German shots. Chris Cunningham, UP, also had a narrow escape when two rockets hit the side of a building from which he was watching a night action near the Roer River. Ann Stringer, UP, became one of the few women correspondents to observe front line infantry action when she and James C. McGlincy, also UP, visited forward positions at Jülich, near Cologne, late in February.[12]

Lucyna Tomaszewska, a woman correspondent with the Polish Forces Press Bureau of London, was severely injured in February when the jeep in which she was riding was blown up by a German anti-tank mine in the Alsace sector. Guy Byam, BBC, an observer aboard a U.S. B-17 Flying Fortress during a daylight raid against Berlin on February 3, was listed as missing when the bomber vanished over the North Sea on its return flight.

Other reporters covering these operations, sometimes at enormous risks, included Ivan H. (Cy) Peterman, *Philadelphia Inquirer,* and John

---

12   Both were reprimanded by SHAEF for being so near actual combat. McGlincy was disaccredited in March for violation of SHAEF regulations forbidding correspondents to carry arms.

H. Thompson, *Chicago Tribune,* both among the first to enter Cologne. Sigrid Schultz, a former Berlin correspondent for the *Chicago Tribune* and still affiliated with the paper, was with the Ninth Army for *McCall's* magazine. Hank Wales, *Chicago Tribune* correspondent in Paris from 1919 to 1933, was also back in service for the paper. Ann Stringer, UP, was in Bonn.

Peter D. Lawless, *Daily Telegraph,* struck in the stomach and legs by shell splinters when he was attempting to cross the Remagen Bridge on March 10, died fifteen minutes later. He was the sixteenth British correspondent killed in the war.[13] Walter Farr, *Daily Mail,* and William Troughton, *Daily Express,* who were near him, were slightly injured.

Other correspondents reporting the Rhine crossings in March, and the subsequent advances deeper into Germany, included Frederick Kuh, *Chicago Sun;* John Hall, *Daily Mail;* Gladwin Hill, *New York Times;* Volney D. Hurd, *Christian Science Monitor;* Hal Boyle, William Frye, and Thoburn H. (Toby) Wiant, AP; Chris Cunningham and John B. McDermott, UP; Harry Austin, *Sydney Morning Herald;* Andrew Rooney, *Stars and Stripes;* and William R. Downs, CBS. Edward D. Ball, AP, was the first correspondent to cross the Rhine with General Patton's Third Army, and the only correspondent to do so for some twelve hours. He complained that his copy had been brutally censored.

Correspondents with the 21st Army Group, the British and Canadian armies commanded by Field Marshal Montgomery, had the most rugged experiences. Seaghan Maynes, Reuters, parachuted with British troops landing beyond the Rhine, while Doon Campbell, also of Reuters, went in with U.S. glider troops. Robert C. Wilson, AP, flying aboard a troop carrier plane, was forced to parachute when the plane was hit and caught fire.

Maynes, Campbell, and Wilson made their landings behind German lines. Maynes had his typewriter blown off his back as he dropped. He landed near a German machine-gun position but dodged behind a tree. A captain of British parachute troops who had landed close by, equipped with a Sten gun, shouted orders to other paratroopers whose presence was purely imaginary at the moment. From the shelter of his tree, Maynes also shouted a "hands up" order in German. The trick worked, and five German machine gunners came out and surrendered, supposing themselves outnumbered and surrounded. Wilson, of the AP,

---

13   Lawless, fifty-five, had been *Daily Telegraph* correspondent with the RAF in France during the first year of the war. After the fall of France in 1940 he became a captain in the British Army Intelligence Corps, but was released in 1944 to rejoin the *Daily Telegraph* as a special correspondent. He had served in World War I, and was awarded the Military Cross. An international Rugby player, he had been a sports correspondent for the *Morning Post* until it was merged with the *Daily Telegraph* in 1937.

by contrast, attached himself to a group of thirty-one British soldiers who had landed by glider. They all took cover in a house, soon attacked by German tanks. Only six of the soldiers, along with Wilson, got back to the Allied lines.

Robert Capa, *Life* photographer, also jumped with the 17th U.S. Airborne Division troops, and made pictures during the drop. Charles B. Lynch, Reuters, covered the British Second Army attack. Alan Wood, formerly of the *Daily Express,* but transferred to Exchange Telegraph, suffered a leg injury and was hospitalized. Geoffrey Charles Bocca, *Daily Express,* and Corporal Robert Krell, *Yank,* covering the 21st Army Group crossing of the Rhine on March 21, were reported missing.

A record volume of copy was filed from the British and Canadian sector and a record number of photos also reached London, including official Air Ministry pictures showing the Rhine crossing in progress. Richard McMillan, BUP, was the first correspondent to get a report to London from the Second Army front. Clinton B. (Pat) Conger, UP, was first with reports from the U.S. Ninth Army sector, but his copy went to New York and was relayed from there back to London

Louis P. Lochner, AP, of long prewar experience in Germany, was with U.S. troops pushing into that country in March. The first of several stories he produced, with the advantage of his intimate acquaintance with the country and its people, was a belated circumstantial account of the attempt of July 1944 by disillusioned members of the Wehrmacht and of the Nazi party to kill Adolf Hitler.

The events of January–March 1945 in Europe pointed toward the end of the war in that theater. From February 4 to 11 President Roosevelt, Prime Minister Churchill, and Premier Stalin met in another conference at Yalta on the Crimean Peninsula. It was known as the Argonaut conference in the code used for security purposes. Churchill had been in Moscow in October 1944 for a meeting with Stalin, but there were agreements to be made about the general conduct of the war in Asia and the Pacific, as well as in Europe; about political problems relating to Poland and other countries adjacent to the Soviet Union; about relations with China, France, Czechoslovakia, and Yugoslavia; and about other postwar settlements. The results of the conference were not very satisfactory then or later.

The pace of the war, however, was reflected at SHAEF. The Hotel Scribe was crowded, with more than 150 correspondents living there, plus SHAEF Public Relations officers and censors. To protect their own interests, correspondents accredited to SHAEF in October had formed an Allied Press Committee. The need for such a committee had seemed clear to some early in 1945. Scarcely a dozen telephones were available to correspondents in the hotel, for example, and those did not work well. The army had proposed that the number of correspondents be reduced. Tensions rose as the season approached for renewal of the Allied campaign in the spring, and increasing political considerations complicated the reporting task.

Members of the Allied Press Committee were John O'Reilly, *New York Herald Tribune,* representing U.S. dailies; William Forrest, *News-Chronicle,* for British dailies; Edward Kennedy, AP, for U.S. news agencies; John MacVane, NBC, for U.S. radio; Thomas Cadett, BBC, for British radio; Colin Bingham, *Sydney Morning Herald,* for the British Commonwealth press; and John Evans, Jr., *Newsweek,* for magazines. André Laguerre, with long prewar experience in Paris for Exchange Telegraph, was honorary chairman.

Among other correspondents at SHAEF early in 1945 were Robert W. Cooper, the *Times;* J. R. L. Anderson, *Manchester Guardian;* George Slocombe, a correspondent of World War I experience, and Clifford Webb, both for the *Daily Herald;* Rupert Downing, *News of the World;* Charles Wertenbaker, *Time* magazine; Drew Middleton, *New York Times;* Mallory Browne and William H. Stringer, both of the *Christian Science Monitor;* Wade Werner, Joseph Dynan, and Austin Bealmear, all of the AP.

Outside of Paris, correspondents began to reopen news bureaus for the agencies and larger newspapers, foreshadowing a return to normal press activities in postwar Europe. For example, Walter Cronkite was named manager for the United Press in the Low Countries, with instructions to open a permanent bureau in Amsterdam.

What had been one daily briefing session at SHAEF, became three. They met at 10 A.M., 3 P.M., and 10 P.M., with the day's communiqué released at the third of the sessions. There were map-illustrated explanations of such developments as the military command was prepared to reveal, and question-and-answer periods. Military leaders themselves appeared at some sessions, including General Eisenhower occasionally.

In March 1945, the war was going so badly for the Germans on all fronts that secret inquiries looking toward a truce or an armistice were made on behalf of Germany through the British Embassy in Stockholm. By that time, a million German prisoners had been taken in Europe since D-Day, and nearly four million of the Allied forces were on the line. Correspondents attached to the Allied armies totalled nearly 300, with press billets in camps filled in anticipation of the spring move toward the hoped-for victory. They were with the U.S. First Army (45), the U.S. Third Army (35 and 13 roaming); the U.S. Ninth Army (12); the British Second Army (38); the Canadian First Army (37 and 17 roaming); the U.S. Seventh Army (15); the French First Army (22); and 25 air correspondents.

Moving rapidly, the war gave Allied correspondents the same problem they had in the previous summer and autumn, that of keeping pace
with the advancing troops. The press camp often was left in the rear as
the front lines were pushed far ahead even in one day. Equipment was
left at the press camp, where briefings took place, where censors functioned and communications facilities were available, and where meals
and billets were to be found. This obliged correspondents to drive many
miles to reach the front lines and return. The journeys were wearisome
and also dangerous, as was made clear by the many jeep mishaps. One
further example occurred April 29 when William Frye, AP, and Doon
Campbell, Reuters, both with the British Second Army in Germany
covering the Elbe river crossing, were severely injured on the return trip
when their jeep was crushed between a truck and a tree.

Having returned to the press camp after a long day, correspondents
had little zest or energy left to write their accounts, which might be held
up by the censorship. Correspondents at SHAEF in Paris, meanwhile,
wrote what the front-line correspondents called "second-hand" stories
that often received major display or use in the media. Such problems
confronting correspondents in the field were recognized by SHAEF,
and in some areas transportation from the press camp to the forward line
was made available by special aircraft, carrying jeeps as well as men, and
returning copy to the communications point.

Some correspondents left the war zone[14] and others arrived, but by
April those in the front-line areas were producing numerous stories that
took precedence over those written from Paris. Some were military in
substance, but others related to dramatic and heart-moving revelations
of abuses found to have been centering in concentration camps overrun
by troops, centers maintained by the Nazi regime for those deemed in
opposition and for Jews taken in Germany and other countries during
the war years and subjected to mass executions.

Ilya Ehrenburg of *Izvestia* in Moscow, a correspondent with Red
Army forces, had provided the earliest indication of what the German
horror camps were like in reports written for his newspaper as early as
August 1944. These accounts were reprinted in *PM*, in other newspapers
in the United States, and in other countries. The Red Army moved
through areas where some of the death camps were located—camps
where some six million Jews were killed in what was later referred to as
the Holocaust.

With U.S. troops advancing into Germany from the west during April

---

14   One who left temporarily was John O'Reilly, at SHAEF for the *New York Herald
Tribune*. In March, he went to the United States aboard a hospital plane, and wrote three
articles on how U.S. wounded were being flown home for treatment and care. He returned
later to France.

1945, reports came from the Buchenwald concentration camp near Weimar, and from others at Belsen, Erla, Nordhausen, and later from the Hockert munitions plant in Leipzig, Auschwitz, Ohrdruf, and Dachau, the first one established. At such places correspondents found men and women who were hardly more than emaciated and misshapen walking skeletons. They found naked corpses stacked like cordwood or tossed into open trenches, and they found gas chambers and crematoria for the mass executions.

The first reports on these horrors in the areas entered from the west came from Marguerite Higgins, a young, multi-lingual correspondent for the *New York Herald Tribune,* who had arrived in Paris in February 1945 and was attached to the U.S. Third Army in Germany. She and Sergeant Peter Furst, *Stars and Stripes,* and Percival Knauth, *Time* magazine, reached the Buchenwald camp a few hours after it had been liberated.

Gene Currivan, *New York Times,* and Patrick Gordon-Walker, BBC, also produced early reports on the Buchenwald and Belsen camps. Morley Cassidy, *Philadelphia Evening Bulletin,* wrote one of the most perceptive accounts of the German political prison camps and torture centers, one both published and broadcast. [15]

Plans had been under consideration at SHAEF for press coverage of an anticipated Allied entrance into Berlin, including an elaborate communications arrangement. William R. Downs, CBS, was reported ready to parachute into the city as a representative of U.S. radio networks. All such plans were made inoperative, however, when Red Army units reached the environs of Berlin late in April and brought the city under full control on May 2 at a time when the western Allies, by high-level decision, had refrained from moving so far east.

The first press message from Berlin came from Roman Karmen, a Soviet correspondent and photographer, who rode into the city on April

---

15   At General Eisenhower's request, a congressional delegation of twelve, and a group of seventeen U.S. editors and publishers were flown to Europe to inspect the German camps. They were to report their observations and to make them known to the UNCIO delegates in San Francisco later in April.

A corresponding British delegation visited the camps. General Patton of the U.S. Third Army also forced citizens of nearby Weimar to walk through the Buchenwald camp to see what the Nazis had done.

Among the U.S. group of visiting editors and publishers were Julius Ochs Adler, *New York Times;* Joseph Pulitzer, Jr., *St. Louis Post-Dispatch;*E. Z. Dimitman, *Chicago Sun;* Norman Chandler, *Los Angeles Times;* L. K. Nicholson, *New Orleans Times-Picayune;* Ben McKelway, *Washington Star;* Malcolm Bingay, *Detroit Free Press;* Glenn Neville, *New York Mirror;* Gideon Seymour, *Minneapolis Star-Journal;* M. E. Walker, *Houston Chronicle;* Walker Stone, Scripps-Howard Newspaper Alliance; Duke Shoop, former war correspondent and then Washington correspondent, *Kansas City Star;* Ben Hibbs, *Saturday Evening Post;* William L. Chenery, *Collier's;* Beverly Smith, *American Magazine;* Stanley High, *Reader's Digest;* and William L. Nichols, *This Week.*

24 in a T.34 tank forming part of Marshal Georgi Konstantinovich Zhukov's armored force. Karmen's dispatch, sent to Moscow, was relayed to London and the rest of the world by the UP bureau in Moscow. Subsequent reports from Berlin also cleared through Moscow.

German-born Curt Riess (Steiner), NEA, had risked a journey into Germany during the winter of 1944–45 and came out with a series of stories held for publication in April throwing light on conditions in the country. In April, also, Thomas Twitty, *New York Herald Tribune,* was able to report the discovery at Bromskirchen of a train loaded with V-2 rockets such as had been fired on London until the Germans had been driven back beyond range. Correspondents also were able to report the discovery in a salt mine at Merkers of stores of gold and of art treasures, some taken by German leaders from France and other occupied countries.

Red Army and U.S. patrols met at Torgau on the Elbe river on April 25, and British and Soviet forces met at Wismar and Lübeck on May 2. Harold Siepman, Acme Newspictures, Andrew Tully, *Boston Traveler,* Virginia Irwin, *St. Louis Post-Dispatch,* and Ann Stringer, UP, were present at the Torgau meeting. The first news report of the British-Soviet contact came from Henry Shapiro, UP correspondent and bureau chief in Moscow.

Andrew Tully and Virginia Irwin set out from Torgau on April 27 for Berlin. Their jeep, driven by Sergeant John Wilson, flew a small improvised U.S. flag. Transported across the Elbe on a raft, the vehicle was driven over roads crowded with Red Army troops, who greeted the passing correspondents with great enthusiasm. They reached Berlin in less than eight hours and returned with the first eye-witness account by any western correspondents of the capital in ruins and under Red Army control. Their journey had been unauthorized, however, and their stories were held up by the censorship until May 8, the day of the war's end in Europe. SHAEF disaccredited them for having gone "off limits."

Clifford Webb, *Daily Herald,* John Hall, *Daily Mail,* and Sam White, Australian Consolidated Press, also went "off limits" to visit Nuremberg. They had been with a U.S. Third Army armored column supposedly headed for Czechoslovakia. When they found that was not, in fact, the destination, they detoured to Nuremberg, then recently taken by the U.S. Seventh Army, and filed stories. Since they were accredited to the Third Army, this was technically out of their territory and Seymour (Sy) Korman, *Chicago Tribune,* president of the Correspondents Committee for the Seventh Army, objected. Webb and Hall were admonished and withdrew their stories. White, who insisted that his story should be sent, was placed under two months' suspension.

Thomas E. Downes, London *Evening News,* who flew over Berlin with a British pilot, also was placed under a month's suspension. Technical Sergeant Ernest Leiser, *Stars and Stripes,* and Sergeant Mack Morriss, *Yank,* made trips to Berlin, and both lost their SHAEF credentials.[16]

With interest in conditions in Berlin still high, Seymour Freiden, *New York Herald Tribune,* and John Groth, *Parade* and the *American Legion Magazine,* left the units to which they were accredited as correspondents and, with willing Red Army cooperation, proceeded to Berlin and returned with eye-witness accounts. They also were disaccredited and ordered to return to the United States. Protests from their publications and also from the SHAEF correspondent group in Paris brought modifications which allowed them to keep their accreditations, but they were ordered to the United Kingdom and placed under suspension for a month.

German rear-guard fighting in April was responsible for the death of Gaston Madru, News of the Day newsreel cameraman, who was killed by a sniper in Leipzig. Another fatality occurred when Clifford W. Speer, Canadian Broadcasting Corporation, was so badly hurt when his mobile broadcasting van collided with an army truck that he died in a London hospital on May 12.

As the Allied armies advanced, they not only overran concentration camps, but prisoner-of-war camps, where correspondents sometimes found colleagues who had been captured earlier. Among correspondents who thus regained their freedom in April and May 1945 were Godfrey H. P. Anderson, British-born AP correspondent, Edward H. H. Ward, BBC, and Patrick Crosse, Reuters, all of whom were captured in Libya in 1941 and 1942; Lowell Bennett, INS, captured in 1943 when he was forced to parachute into Germany; John Talbot, Reuters, captured in Yugoslavia in 1944; Wright Bryan, *Atlanta Journal,* and Edward W. Beattie, Jr., UP, both captured in France in September 1944; and Jack Smythe, Reuters, captured at that same time in Holland.

Newsmen of another stripe, apprehended in Europe at the end of the war or later, included two former correspondents who had served the Axis as radio propagandists. These were Robert Best, formerly in Vienna for the UP, and Donald Day, long in Riga for the *Chicago Tribune.* Other propagandists taken included U.S.-born William Joyce, known to British radio listeners during the war as "Lord Haw-Haw," and John Amery, son of L. S. Amery, British secretary for India and *Times* correspondent during the South African War. Among U.S. propagandists, also, were Edward Delany, broadcasting from Berlin as

---

16 All of these efforts by correspondents to reach Berlin, contrary to regulations, were reminiscent of similar efforts after the World War I armistice in 1918.

"E. D. Ward," and Douglas Chandler, broadcasting as "Paul Revere." Fred Kaltenback, Otto Koischwitz, Jane Anderson, and Florence Drexel were arrested in Vienna. Arrested in Genoa at this period also was Ezra Pound, American poet. All were considered guilty of treason. Joyce was hanged in London on January 3, 1946, and Best died in jail in Boston.

Other correspondents engaged in reporting the Allied push into Germany in the last days included John O'Reilly, *New York Herald Tribune,* then returned from his brief journey to the United States; Russell Hill, also of the *Herald Tribune;* William C. Heinz, *New York Sun;* William Walton, *Time;* George Rodger, *Life;* Fred Ramage, INP photographer; and Selkirk Patton and George Reid Millar, both of the *Daily Express.*

The April 12 to May 9 period of 1945 was climactic and one of the biggest news weeks of history. It brought the death on April 12 of President Roosevelt, who was succeeded by Harry Truman. Adolf Hitler killed himself in the bunker beneath the Reich Chancellery in Berlin on May 1. On the same date, Joseph Goebbels, Nazi minister of propaganda and public enlightenment, and his wife and children also died of poison. Mussolini had been shot on April 28 by Italian Partisans.

Heinrich Himmler, Gestapo chief, who was arrested by the British on May 22, also poisoned himself and died the next day. Marshal Goering and a score of other Nazi leaders were arrested and brought to trial for war crimes in 1946 at Nuremburg, where Goering poisoned himself.

The first week of May brought the end of German resistance on the Italian front, Red Army seizure of Berlin, suspension of German propaganda broadcasts, and the collapse of the Wehrmacht on the western front. The German unconditional surrender came on May 7, with an armistice signed on that date. May 8 was proclaimed as V-E Day (Victory-in-Europe Day), and there was a ratification of the surrender in Berlin on May 9 between representatives of Germany and the Soviet Union.

Two premature reports of German surrender had reached the world, both originating in the United States. The first came on March 27, when Gil Martyn, Blue Network radio commentator in Los Angeles, misinterpreted an INS bulletin and announced on the air that President Roosevelt and his cabinet were in session "preparing for word of victory in Europe," and that members of the diplomatic corps in Washington had been asked "to remain close to their posts." Both INS and the Blue Network sought to clarify the situation immediately, but a flurry of excitement was aroused nonetheless.

The second premature report came on April 28 from San Francisco, where the United Nations Conference on International Organization

(UNCIO) was in session. Paul Scott Rankine of Reuters' bureau in Washington, who was covering the meeting, filed a dispatch to London at 1 A.M. reporting that "it was authoritatively stated in official circles tonight that a message from Himmler guaranteeing German unconditional surrender to Britain and the United States, but not to Russia, had been conveyed to the British and United States governments." Then at 4:55 P.M. of the same day, April 28, the Associated Press sent out a bulletin from San Francisco reporting that "Germany has surrendered to the Allied governments unconditionally, and announcement is expected momentarily, it was stated by a high American official today."

The "high official" proved to be Senator Tom Connally, chairman of the Senate Foreign Relations Committee, and vice-chairman of the U.S. delegation to the UNCIO conference. In the belief that it was true, Senator Connally had given this information to Jack Bell, AP Washington correspondent, then in San Francisco for the UN Conference. The story went out, with the qualified attribution. Not forgetting the "false armistice" report of 1918 at the end of World War I, the AP queried both President Truman in Washington and General Eisenhower in France. Both were reported as denying knowledge of any such imminent surrender. Connally still insisted that the announcement might come very soon. Preliminary negotiations for surrender were, in fact, going on. But the final signature did not come for another ten days, effective at midnight of May 7–8.

The German surrender and the manner of its reporting by the media was marked by complexities and circumstances to be felt for months and even years after the date. Negotiations for surrender had been started, tentatively, in February 1945, and seriously in April, with Heinrich Himmler of the German Gestapo taking the initiative through meetings with Sweden's Count Bernadotte, head of the Swedish Red Cross, and then with meetings between Bernadotte and the British and U.S. diplomatic envoys in neutral Stockholm. Marshal Stalin was informed of the negotiations from the outset.

With surrender imminent, General Eisenhower at SHAEF was faced with the problem of obtaining that capitulation as promptly as possible so that fighting might end and lives be spared, while also providing for a ceremony in which the Red Army High Command might participate to assure a simultaneous conclusion on all fronts. To this end, Eisenhower reached an agreement by which he might accept the German surrender, effective on the western and eastern fronts alike, but with the formal announcement delayed until the Russian military had held its own separate and formal meeting with the Germans for a second signature of terms. The situation was delicate because of a disposition to be on guard against possible German trickery, and because of suspicion in Moscow that Germany might be seeking to split the wartime Allies by making a separate peace with those in the west.

These latter circumstances led General Eisenhower to prefer that the first surrender ceremony should be conducted by military representatives only, with no others present. This would have excluded media representatives as well as political or civilian figures.

The media representatives at SHAEF in Paris were aware that a surrender might be near, and made it clear that they wished to witness any such ceremony. Brigadier General Frank A. ("Honk") Allen, Jr., director of the Public Relations Division at SHAEF, was sympathetic to those wishes and made "earnest representations" to General Eisenhower, assuring him that if the media representatives were permitted to attend "no newspaperman would release any information concerning the proceedings until authorized to do so by me."

On this understanding, Eisenhower approved an arrangement whereby General Allen might invite a pool of seventeen newsmen to witness the ceremony at which German military representatives were to sign the unconditional surrender demanded by the Allies.

The seventeen media representatives (ultimately twenty-one) selected by General Allen included Edward Kennedy, chief of the AP staff at SHAEF; Boyd Lewis, UP; James L. Kilgallen, INS; H. C. Montague, Reuters; Margaret Ecker (Mrs. Margaret Ecker Francis), Canadian Press; Jean E. Lagrange, Agence France Presse; Michael Litvin-Sedoy, Tass;[17] and André Glarner, Exchange Telegraph. Glarner chose not to accompany the group, however, and was replaced by Price Day, *Baltimore Sun,* with the expectation that Day would write for Extel as well as for his own paper; in the end he wrote only for his paper.

The other nine members of the group included Staff Sergeant Charles Kiley, *Stars and Stripes;* Sergeant Ross Parry, *Maple Leaf,* a Canadian army publication; and Omar E. White, Australian Press. The newspaper and periodical press were no further represented. The radio medium, however, was represented by Charles Collingwood, CBS; William W. Chaplin, NBC; Herbert E. M. Clark, Blue Network; Paul Manning, MBS; Thomas Cadett, BBC; and Gerald Clark, Canadian Broadcasting Corporation.

Since it was obvious that only a relatively small number of correspondents could be accommodated as witnesses of the ceremony, it was believed that those representatives of news agencies and radio would assure the greatest and fairest coverage. Four photo correspondents were

---

17   Litvin-Sedoy, never seen before at SHAEF, was a member of a Soviet delegation in Paris, rather than a correspondent. He did not file a report on the Reims ceremony, nor was the ceremony ever mentioned in the Soviet press.

added to the group, however, with their pictures to be pooled. They were Ralph Morse, *Life,* representing the U.S. Still Picture Pool; Fred S. Skinner, the British Still Picture Pool; Roni Read, the British Newsreel Pool; and Yves Naintre, the U.S. Newsreel Pool.

This group of twenty-one was alerted on Sunday morning, May 6, with members told that they had been selected to cover "an important story" out of Paris, and to be ready to leave on short notice. They suspected the nature of the story and followed instructions, which included saying nothing to others about the prospective assignment.

When word came through to SHAEF later on Sunday that Colonel General Gustav Jodl, chief of staff of the German army, was on the way to the meeting place at Reims, the advance headquarters for SHAEF, the correspondents also were started by bus to Orly Field, near Paris. They flew to Reims, arriving about 5 P.M., some ten minutes after Jodl had reached the same airfield. Military personnel with the party, both British and U.S. from the Public Relations Branch of SHAEF, included General Allen; Colonel Thor M. Smith, press liaison officer for General Eisenhower at SHAEF; U.S. Navy Captain Harry Butcher, former CBS radio executive and an aide to Eisenhower; Lieutenant Colonel Burrows Matthews; Colonel George Warden; Lieutenant Colonel S. R. Pawley; Lieutenant Colonel Richard Merrick; Group Captain G. W. Houghton; Lieutenant Colonel Reed Jordan; and Captain Don Davis. These, plus radio technicians and service photographers, brought the total in the party to forty-seven persons.

Aboard the plane, General Allen spoke to the group, raising his voice to be heard over the sound of the engines. "Gentlemen, we are going on a mission to cover the signing of the peace," he informed them. "This group has been chosen to represent the press of the world." But, he added, "This story is off the record until the respective heads of the Allied governments announce the fact to the world. I therefore pledge each and every one of you on your honor not to communicate the results of this conference or the fact of its existence until it is released by SHAEF." He added, with emphasis, that it was to be regarded as "top secret."

From the Reims airfield, the group was driven into the city to the Ecole Professionelle, a large three-story red brick structure built around a courtyard and situated several hundred yards from the Reims cathedral, partially destroyed by artillery fire during World War I. The city and the cathedral were referred to then and later as "Rheims." The building in which the peace was to be signed was in no sense a "little red schoolhouse," as later described in some stories, but a substantial specialized industrial school.

In a room on the ground floor, correspondents were given an account of events and negotiations preliminary to the surrender conference, even then beginning on the floor above. There Lieutenant General Walter B. ("Beedle") Smith, chief of staff to General Eisenhower, represented him. Lieutenant General Sir Frederick Morgan of the British army, and Eisenhower's deputy chief of staff, Major General Ivan Susloparov of the Soviet Red Army, and General François Sevez of the French forces, were among Allied representatives at the table. Facing them and speaking for the new German government headed by Admiral Doenitz, who had succeeded Hitler as head of the state, were General Jodl, Colonel Fritz Poleck, and Admiral Hans Georg von Friedeburg.

Correspondents had plenty of time to write background stories on the basis of what they already knew, what they had been told, and what they were able to observe. The Germans had requested a forty-eight hour extension of time preliminary to accepting the unconditional surrender terms presented to them. This request was denied, but Jodl was permitted to send a coded message to Admiral Doenitz asking permission to sign the surrender terms. Not until 2 A.M. of Monday, May 7, was the reply received granting that permission.

In the hours intervening, the correspondents, in addition to preparing their copy, waited like everybody else. There had, however, been a leak of information in Paris with reference to the event transpiring at Reims and by midnight or sooner a dozen or more other correspondents had arrived in the city and found the school building. They were not admitted, but were waiting outside in no very good temper. Nor was their temper improved when military police forced all but five to leave the immediate area.

At length, those media representatives in the party that had flown from Paris with General Allen were taken upstairs at 2:15 A.M. and admitted to the map room to witness the signing of the surrender documents. They took positions behind a chalk line on the floor. Shortly after 2:30 A.M. General "Beedle" Smith entered and checked arrangements. The other Allied officers then entered, with the Germans coming last. In five minutes the ceremony was over, with General Jodl and then General Smith signing the document at 2:41 A.M. with Generals Susloparov and Sevez signed as witnesses. The surrender provided that all hostilities in Europe should end at midnight on Tuesday, May 8.

General Allen told the correspondents that the release time on their accounts had been set for 3 P.M. on May 8, but he hoped to have the time advanced. By 6 A.M. on Monday, May 7, less than four hours after the surrender ceremony, the official group of correspondents was back at the Reims airfield, and by about 7:30 A.M. the short flight put them in Paris. There they filed the dispatches prepared at Reims and on the plane for transmission in the order filed, but only when SHAEF finally gave the word to release them. Boyd Lewis, UP, Kilgallen, INS, and Kennedy, AP, were the first three to file, and in that order.

A news conference was called at SHAEF, in Paris, at 10 A.M. of Monday, May 7, for correspondents not at the Reims ceremony. Many were annoyed by what seemed to them an arbitrary selection of those who did go, but they were given a complete account of all that transpired. Their own accounts were filed for later release.

By 11:30 A.M. on that morning, there was reason to believe that the surrender stories certainly would not be released before 3 P.M. on Tuesday, May 8, at the earliest, with no advance in that time such as General Allen had suggested as possible. Indeed, there was reason to believe that the release might not come until sometime on Wednesday, May 9. The delay was indicated because the Soviet government wanted its own surrender ceremony in Berlin on that day, and wanted the announcement held until that time. In short, the decision as to the time of release had been taken out of SHAEF's hands, and was to be determined by the heads of government, notably that of the Soviet Union.

The news of the surrender actually was out, however. The only radio transmitter operating in Germany at the time was at Flensburg on the Danish border. It was the voice of the Doenitz government. At 2:03 P.M. of Monday, May 7, about twelve hours after the Reims signature, Count Ludwig Schwerin von Krosigk, foreign minister in the new government, officially announced the German surrender in a broadcast to the world. German forces, including submarines at sea, were directed to end all resistance to the Allies. This announcement was followed by a report from radio stations in neutral Sweden, based on the Flensburg broadcast, that the surrender had been signed. The Reuters agency reported the Swedish broadcast, and so did the AP, UP, and INS. Radio stations, in turn, broadcast these news agency reports in Great Britain, the United States, and in other countries.

The Flensburg broadcast was not sufficient, however, nor the sequence of announcements and broadcasts immediately following, to induce the Russians, or presumably Marshal Stalin himself, to modify the desire to have the announcement of the German surrender come from Berlin, by way of Moscow, on May 9.

There then arose a situation that was to figure in the history of journalism, and which touched off a controversy of many months' duration. Correspondents at SHAEF, in Paris, were both infuriated and frustrated by the prospect of at least a delay of thirty-six hours in releasing the reports of the Reims surrender. They saw no justification in the Soviet wish to hold back the announcement, although the group that had gone to Reims had agreed to wait until SHAEF gave the official release.

Edward Kennedy, head of the AP staff at SHAEF, and one of those at

Reims, saw no element of military security in the story. He took the view that another day's delay in release of the news the world had awaited so eagerly was based on political considerations without proper validity. He also felt that further delay in announcing the surrender might cost lives among the fighting forces, for lack of knowledge that the peace had been signed.

Kennedy reasoned that the Flensburg radio broadcast could not have occurred without the approval of SHAEF. Even if not, it had been released by Germany, a participant in the ceremony, and broadcasts had followed in Sweden, repeated in turn by the BBC, all networks in the United States, as well as stations in other countries. These broadcasts also had been noted in the press. King George VI was reported to have sent a message of congratulation to General Eisenhower, and General DeGaulle was reported preparing to proclaim May 8 as V-E Day in France.

Convinced in these circumstances that the news of the surrender should be delayed no longer, Kennedy late on May 7 went to Lieutenant Colonel Richard Merrick, one of the Reims party and chief censor for U.S. press representatives at SHAEF. He showed him the text of the Flensburg broadcast and said that since SHAEF had released the news of the surrender through the Germans, he no longer felt bound by the pledge of secrecy exacted from the group of correspondents on the flight to Reims. Relman (Pat) Morin, also of AP, was with Kennedy at this meeting, during which he told Colonel Merrick he intended to send the story. Merrick responded by inviting Kennedy to "go ahead and try to get it out; it's impossible," and added a "do as you please."

Kennedy returned to the AP bureau in the Hotel Scribe and talked the matter over with Morton P. Gudebrod of the AP staff. He was aware that, even after the formal release of the stories prepared by the Reims group, some 10,000 words of copy prepared by Lewis, of the UP, and Kilgallen, of INS, having been filed earlier, would presumably be transmitted before his own. Competition between the agencies, each valuing priority in its reports, was a very real consideration.

Kennedy wrote a new brief story on the surrender ceremony, and then asked Gudebrod to call the AP bureau in London on the telephone from the Hotel Scribe AP bureau. The process was to ask for "Paris Military" and then "Military London." Gudebrod obtained that promptly, and next requested "Civilian London." That operator was given the telephone number of the AP bureau in London, Central 1515. With almost no delay, Gudebrod had Russell Landstrom and then Lewis Hawkins of the AP London bureau on the phone.

The fact that the connection was made so easily and so promptly was somewhat surprising. The connection was bad, but Kennedy spoke to

Hawkins and then dictated the story he had just prepared to a woman traffic operator in the London bureau. Because of fading on the line, words and phrases had to be repeated and names laboriously spelled out. After 300 words had been dispatched in this fashion, the connection failed entirely in the midst of a brief statement made at Reims by General Jodl.

The London AP bureau flashed Kennedy's report to New York. Because it was a story originating outside the United Kingdom, the British censors passed it automatically. It was received in New York at 9:38 P.M., eastern war time, of Monday, May 7. It was by then early Tuesday morning in London and Paris. Out of caution, the New York bureau waited about ten minutes after the by-lined Kennedy story began to arrive. When no correction or kill followed, it was released and went to all parts of the United States, Canada, and Mexico. Radio broadcasts followed, morning newspaper accounts were prepared, and the story also was flashed back to London and Paris. The news was reported to the rest of the world not only by the AP but also through the OWI-Voice of America broadcasts. Victory celebrations began in all Allied countries except the Soviet Union on the basis of the Kennedy story so far carried exclusively by the AP, although preceded by the Flensburg broadcast and the citations following.

Kennedy's action in reporting the surrender caused General Allen to suspend accreditation for the entire AP staff in Paris, pending investigation. The suspension was extended a few minutes later to all AP correspondents on the western front, and to Robert Bunnelle, chief of the London bureau, and all members of that bureau—although there was a four-hour delay in its application there because of failure to convey the suspension order to all censors. Seven hours later, after an investigation, the suspension orders were lifted on the AP and all of its correspondents except Kennedy and Gudebrod.

About an hour and one-half after the release of Kennedy's report in New York, an announcement also came from SHAEF in the form of a voicecast. It stated that "SHAEF nowhere has made any official statement concerning the complete surrender of all German armed forces in Europe, and no statement to that effect is authorized."

The first satisfaction felt by the AP at having an early and exclusive account of the end of the war in Europe became tinged with worry when no verification came from SHAEF or any fully recognized Allied source. There was real concern following the SHAEF statement. It was inevitable that the false report from San Francisco on April 28 should be remembered and, the so-called World War I "false armistice" of November 7, 1918, reported by the United Press on the basis of a dispatch from France by Roy W. Howard, then president of the UP.

Once the Kennedy story had received world attention, however, there no longer was reason to hold other stories at SHAEF, and all were released Tuesday morning, May 8. This at least ended the worry in the AP headquarters.

Of the correspondents accredited to SHAEF, however, fifty-four were irritated at having been technically beaten on the news because they faithfully observed General Allen's release agreement. They signed a letter late on May 8 protesting to General Eisenhower not only against Kennedy's action but against the lifting of the suspension on the Associated Press itself.[18]

Correspondents in Paris were hardly less irritated at SHAEF itself because of the selection of those permitted to go to Reims, by the treatment of others who had hastened there, by the refusal of SHAEF to approve correspondents going to Berlin, and the disaccreditation of eleven who had done so.

There also was an immediate issue relating to the presence of Paris-based correspondents at the Russian-managed surrender ceremony of May 9 in Berlin. The Russians did not invite any correspondents from Paris, but General Allen asked that they be included as members of the SHAEF delegation, and this was approved. Perhaps to placate the Paris group, whose Anglo-American Press Committee had protested the selection of those at the Reims ceremony, General Allen invited them to select eight of their number to attend the Berlin ceremony. Those selected to attend were Harold King, Reuters; Joseph W. Grigg, UP; Fernand Moulier, Agence France Presse (AFP); John O'Reilly, *New York Herald Tribune;* Clifford Webb, *Daily Herald;* Thomas Cadett, BBC; Howard K. Smith, CBS; and Matt Halton, Canadian Broadcasting Corporation (CBC), also representing the Commonwealth media. They witnessed signatures by Field Marshal Keitel for Germany, Marshal Zhukov for the Soviet Union, and British Air Chief Tedder as Eisenhower's representative.

It was significant that no representative of the AP attended the Berlin ceremony. Nor was the Kennedy affair at an end. General Allen, in a statement actually drafted by General Eisenhower, asserted that Kennedy's transmission of the surrender story made it appear that SHAEF had broken an understanding with the Russians. There was a

18   Rather naturally, no AP correspondents signed the letter. But neither did many others. Those who did sign included seven who flew to Reims with Kennedy. These were Lewis, UP; Kilgallen, INS; Legrange, AFP; Chaplin, NBC; Manning, MBS; Clark, Blue Network; and Day, *Baltimore Sun.*

The total list, the letter, and other details appear in the *New York Times,* May 9, May 10, and May 14, 1945; *Editor & Publisher,* May 12 and May 19, 1945; and *World's Press News,* May 17, 1945.

concern, the statement said, lest any premature or unauthorized announcement might result in a breakdown in the "entire chain of negotiations, involving an agreed upon later meeting between the German, Russian, and Allied High Commands," and so prolong the war.

SHAEF did not feel it had final authority to release the Reims surrender story, it was further explained, without formal authorization from the heads of the Allied governments, Churchill, Truman, and Stalin. Nor was there complete confidence that German forces actually would cease fighting. The statement concluded by saying that the incident raised "a question of the most serious import to all representatives of the Press in this theater. This question is the extent to which the Allied Command can, in any future case, permit pressmen advance access to news of the most secret character on the same basis that has always applied in the past."

The correspondents at SHAEF responded to this by proposing a resolution declaring that they no longer had the slightest confidence in the Public Relations Division of SHAEF or in General Allen, as its director. No such resolution ever was adopted, however, and General Eisenhower conferred the Legion of Merit upon Allen in a personal presentation on May 28.

Unauthorized though it had been by SHAEF, Edward Kennedy's report of the surrender forced the hands of the leaders of the Allied governments. Some four hours after the AP report had reached the world on May 7–8, the Ministry of Information in London announced that Prime Minister Churchill would make a formal proclamation in London on May 8, naming that as V-E Day, and that King George VI would speak later. It was further announced that President Truman in Washington, and General DeGaulle in Paris, also would broadcast victory messages on May 8.[19] It was after these announcements that the stories being held for release by SHAEF, giving details of the Reims surrender ceremony, were transmitted for use.

SHAEF completed its investigation promptly of Kennedy's action and his method of transmitting the news of the surrender without official authorization or clearance. He might have been subjected to court martial proceedings. The final disposition of the case in Paris came a week after the incident, with both Kennedy and Gudebrod disaccredited and ordered to leave for the United States by May 17. Gudebrod,

---

19   Russ Munro, Canadian Press, in a pool set up with thirteen fellow correspondents on April 3 at Canadian First Army headquarters in Europe, had guessed May 8 as the V-E date, and so won a portable typewriter with an engraved plate. Lieutenant General Patch, commander of the U.S. Seventh Army, entered a similar pool with correspondents covering that army in March. He picked May 9 as the date, and was entitled to $5 for coming closest to the actual date.

stricken with pneumonia, was allowed an appropriate delay in his departure.

Kennedy had been with the AP since 1932, had been in the Washington bureau, and was assigned to the Paris bureau in 1935. He covered periods of the Spanish Civil War, went to Istanbul and, after the European war began in 1939, he was with British forces as a correspondent in the Middle East, Egypt, Greece, and Libya, and with the Royal Navy in the Mediterranean. With the end of the North African campaign in Tunisia in May 1943, he covered the Sicily campaign and then the campaign in Italy. He transferred to Paris after the liberation of that capital in August 1944, and became head of the AP bureau there.

When the Kennedy surrender story was distributed by the AP late on May 7, 1945, the agency referred to it as "one of the greatest [news beats] in history." Then came the announcement from SHAEF that the report had been unauthorized, and that Kennedy had broken his pledge to observe SHAEF regulations in its release. Kennedy himself never ceased to insist that his action was justified, considering the Flensburg broadcast and other circumstances. Opinion among editors and other newsmen was divided as to the propriety of that action.

Some of his associates at SHAEF, in their written protest to General Allen had called Kennedy's action "the most unethical double-cross" in news history, and some called him a "disgrace to his profession." Others, however, praised him for "the greatest public service of the war." One of his defenders was Roy W. Howard, president of the Scripps-Howard Newspapers in 1945, but still retaining memories of how he and the United Press, of which he then was president, had been pilloried in 1918 for his own premature, but defensible armistice report.

Kent Cooper, as general manager of the AP in New York, reserved judgment in the first days. The scales had been tilted against Kennedy in the agency administration before he left Paris, however, by a statement issued by Robert McLean, editor of the *Philadelphia Bulletin,* and president of the Associated Press. McLean's statement said that the AP "profoundly regrets" the distribution of Kennedy's report, contrary to SHAEF's authorization, and cited the record of the AP in manifesting a "high sense of responsibility as to the integrity and authenticity of the news and the observance of obligations voluntarily assumed."

Kennedy left Paris in mid-May, sailing aboard a slow ship bound for Trinidad. He arrived in New York on June 4. There he found himself in an anomalous position. Because of McLean's statement, the AP could not return him to work, but neither could it disavow him. He reported to the AP office, but was given no assignment; indeed, Cooper gave him to understand that, largely because he had announced that he would "do it again" in comparable circumstances, he could no longer work for the

AP. Gudebrod, after his return, resumed work in the New York bureau. Kennedy, however, was officially "on vacation" and received his salary regularly until November. Then he discovered that $4,982.20 had been deposited in his bank account by the AP. This he assumed to be his severance pay, but the AP did not tell him, officially or otherwise, that he was no longer a member of the staff. He was, however, off the payroll from that time. The AP, responding to questions, no longer described him as "on vacation," but replied with a "no comment."

Kennedy received various offers of employment. As a matter of personal satisfaction, however, he wanted first to justify his action in releasing the surrender story and to regain his accreditation as a correspondent. With his Washington connections, he was able to enlist the assistance in the spring of 1946 of two senators, H. Styles Bridges of New Hampshire, and Sheridan Downey of California. Senator Downey put four documents into the *Congressional Record* of July 22 in support of Kennedy's position.

First, was a statement signed by Lieutenant General Bedell Smith, deputy to General Eisenhower and signator of the Reims surrender document, in which he affirmed that

> Ludwig Schwerin von Krosigk did officially announce the unconditional surrender in a broadcast to the German people and to the world from Flensburg. This announcement was made pursuant to orders from Supreme Headquarters that the German troops were to be informed by every possible means of the surrender and directed to cease resistance.

This substantiated Kennedy's belief and contention that the Flensburg broadcast would not have been made except with the knowledge and approval of SHAEF and, indeed, upon its "order," so justifying his own report, since the pledge asked of correspondents by General Allen had been that they hold back their stories until the respective heads of the Allied governments announce the fact of surrender "*or . . . until it is released by SHAEF.*"

Second, was a U.S. War Department statement establishing the time of the Flensburg announcement as having been one hour and fifty-four minutes before Kennedy's story appeared on the wires.

Third, was the text of the Flensburg announcement.

Fourth, was a statement by Relman Morin, AP, that he had been present when Kennedy told the chief U.S. censor at SHAEF, Lieutenant Colonel Richard Merrick, that since the story had been released through the Flensburg broadcast, he intended to send the dispatch.

This latter was by way of contradicting a statement cabled by General Eisenhower to Kent Cooper at the time of the original controversy, and sent through War Department channels, in which Kennedy was said to have admitted a deliberate violation of SHAEF regulations and a breach of confidence. This Kennedy always had denied.

Coincidentally with his presentation of these documents, Senator Downey announced that General Eisenhower himself, persuaded that the story of the surrender had in fact been released through Flensburg with SHAEF authorization before Kennedy's story went out, had "removed any bar which might prevent Mr. Kennedy from working with the War Department and the Army in his profession as a writer." Senator Downey added that, while General Eisenhower's action did not rescind the SHAEF decision in the particular case, a decision still defended by the War Department, "it restores to Mr. Kennedy the opportunity of resuming, without prejudice, his work as a military correspondent should he desire to do so in the future."

Kennedy had not wished to accept any other post until he had gained his clearance on this matter. In receiving that clearance in July 1946, with World War II ten months over, reaccreditation as a war correspondent was irrelevant. Kennedy then became managing editor of the *Santa Barbara News-Press* in California. In October 1949 he moved to Monterey, California, as associate editor and assistant publisher of the *Monterey Peninsula-Herald.* He also was to have the satisfaction of a generally favorable summary of the case by Kent Cooper in his book, *The Right to Know,* published in 1956, eight years after his own retirement as AP general manager. In it Cooper belatedly expressed the view that the real issue in the surrender story was an essentially political censorship that held up the release of news to which all peoples were rightfully entitled.

British censors reported just after V-E Day that more than 900 million words of copy had been dispatched from London to all parts of the world during the course of the European war from 1939 to 1945. Byron Price, director of the U.S. Office of Censorship, estimated that some 400 million words had been dispatched from the United States to the rest of the world since December 1941.

Other estimates indicated that war news received by the three major U.S. news agencies from 1939 to 1945 had totaled some 270 million words. Press Wireless had handled 16 million words through its mobile stations alone in France and the Philippines between June 13, 1944, and May 8, 1945. It was conservatively estimated that between 600 and 800 correspondents for the U.S. media alone had been on the various fronts, and that there had been 149 casualties among them. To this group could be added other hundreds of correspondents representing both the Allied and Axis powers, and neutrals as well, with their casualties.

As V-E Day came, the war with Japan was still in progress, of course, and censorship continued in all Allied areas. This included restriction on references to the transfer of units, ships, weapons, or even individuals to the Pacific and Asian area. Some elements were moving from Europe in that direction as early as the Spring of 1944, even before D-Day in Normandy. After V-E Day that move was expected to grow.

There was no need to try to keep from the Japanese the intent to move Allied forces to the Far East, and full publicity also accompanied the return of some elements of the U.S. First Army to the United States within a month after V-E Day. With these seasoned troops there also returned a group of correspondents accredited to that army. Among them were Hal Boyle, AP; Chris R. Cunningham, UP; Lee Carson, INS; Robert Reuben, Reuters; John H. Thompson, *Chicago Tribune;* Harold N. Denny, *New York Times;* William C. Heinz, *New York Sun;* Iris Carpenter, *Boston Globe;* John Florea, *Life;* George Hicks, Blue Network; and Tom Priestly, Universal Newsreel cameraman. With them were Virginia Irwin, *St. Louis Post-Dispatch,* and Andrew Tully, *Boston Traveler,* both disaccredited by SHAEF because of their unauthorized trip to Berlin in April.

Other correspondents returning to the United States almost immediately after V-E Day were Ivan H. (Cy) Peterman, *Philadelphia Inquirer;* Edward W. Beattie, Jr., and Robert Richards, both UP; Ruth Cowan, AP; Larry Newman, Frank Conniff, and Lowell Bennett, all INS; and Robert Cromie, *Chicago Tribune.* Cromie soon went to the Pacific theater, while Bennett returned to Europe after a home leave and rest following his long period in a German prisoner-of-war camp. Others arriving or returning to the Continent included Jack Bell, *Chicago Daily News,* and Edgar Snow, *Saturday Evening Post,* both moving from London to Vienna in June 1945.

All correspondents in Paris continued to be attached to SHAEF and subject to its regulations. They were given to understand in May that Berlin and Vienna remained off limits to British and U.S. correspondents. Those cities were in a military zone then open only to those accredited to Moscow, and anything produced there was subject to Soviet censorship.

In early June 1945, however, five U.S. and five British correspondents accompanied General Eisenhower and Field Marshal Montgomery to Berlin with an Allied Control Commission (ACC) to establish a quadrapartite administration of that city. Control was divided between British, U.S., Soviet, and French forces and administrators. The same arrangement was in prospect for Vienna.

None of the restrictions pleased correspondents based in Paris. They first had entered Berlin in April and May and were disaccredited by SHAEF for doing so, or even for flying over the city. While eight had gone as members of the SHAEF delegation to witness the surrender ceremony of May 9 in Berlin, A. I. Goldberg of the AP had been at U.S. Seventh Army headquarters in Germany on that same day and had reported that Reich Marshal Hermann Goering had been flown in "soon after a lunch of chicken and peas." General Dahlquist, of the 36th U.S. Infantry Division was also reported to have arrived soon after and, following greetings and a handshake, to have dismissed an interpreter and talked with Goering in German. This report brought repercussions. A few days later the Seventh Army headquarters denied that there had been "handshakes or chicken dinners" for Goering. General Eisenhower warned senior officers "for reported friendly treatment of captured Nazi bigshots," and SHAEF put a ban on news conferences with captured German leaders.

This edict did not apply to Dr. Kurt Schuschnigg, former Austrian chancellor, released from a German concentration camp by U.S. Army forces in their final advance. He was found at Capri by Ann Stringer, UP, and interviewed there. Captured German leaders were interviewed officially and extensively by Allied interrogators preparing material for prospective war crimes trials against them. Later, however, when there was no longer risk that such cases might be prejudiced by premature or unofficial meetings, the ban on press interviews was ended and a number took place.

In Yugoslavia, as early as February 1945, Marshal Tito had ended an earlier ban on reporters. Landrum Bolling of the Overseas News Agency, who reached Belgrade at that time, was able to move about Yugoslavia and later Austria, Czechoslovakia, and Hungary as well. He talked with such leaders and other persons of interest as he was able to find before returning to the United States in September. His experience was an exception.

It was August before Vienna was declared open to newsmen. Even then, John Phillips and Tom Durrance, of *Time* and *Life,* and Maurice Fagence, of the *Daily Herald,* were arrested at that time by Russian military police. Fagence had been out after a curfew then in effect. Phillips and Durrance had been making photographs, and film was taken from Phillips' camera. These three were detained for several hours and then released with apologies. Phillips was promised that his film would be returned after development and censorship.

Raymond Daniell, *New York Times,* reported in May that "almost every inch of territory held by the Russians" is closed to American correspondents, and SHAEF was reported to be doing nothing to correct the situation for "fear of offending Russia." Lawrence Fairhall, New Zealand-born correspondent for the Kemsley newspapers, put it more sharply when he said, "I think we have had enough nonsense from our

Russian Allies. We are not allowed in Vienna or Prague or Budapest. It's time something was done about it." Another correspondent called it "kowtowing to the Russians."

Although the censorship policy at SHAEF was modified, a highly elastic provision remained after V-E Day authorizing removal from copy of matter that censors might interpret as "unauthorized, inaccurate, or false reports, misleading statements and rumors, or reports likely to injure the morale of Allied forces (or nations)."

Within a month, also, there began to be a separation at SHAEF between those correspondents concerned with war subjects or military matters and others concentrating on the reactivation of political and diplomatic developments in France and in Europe. A number of prewar Paris correspondents left the Hotel Scribe to reopen their former offices. The picture pool ended after more than three years. Direct press telephone service was resumed between Paris and London for the first time since 1939, and new radiotelegraphic circuits were opened in August between New York, Berlin, and Vienna.

Louis Lochner, prewar head of the Berlin AP bureau, was back there in June, but was seriously injured in another of those jeep accidents when a Red Army truck crashed into his vehicle and drove off without halting. He was in a U.S. military hospital for several weeks with a concussion and other injuries.

General Eisenhower returned to Washington late in June. In July the SHAEF headquarters was moved from Paris to Frankfurt-am-Main, Germany, with the Public Relations Division at Wiesbaden, a few miles away. A rear echelon office remained at the Hotel Scribe. But SHAEF went out of existence on July 14, with France under its own government again and a new form of military government introduced in Germany.

Correspondents were in Berlin and Frankfurt in July, as well as in other cities of western Germany, and they were in Berlin to cover the nearby Potsdam Conference from July 17 to August 2. It was December 1945 before western correspondents were permitted to visit the Soviet zone of Germany, when a group was taken on a 700-mile, eight-day conducted tour. Russell Hill of the *New York Herald Tribune,* a former Berlin correspondent for that paper, was one of the group.

Postwar settlements had been discussed by the western allies at a second Quebec Conference in September 1944 and at Yalta in February 1945. Just two months later, on April 12, President Roosevelt died, and Harry Truman succeeded to that office. The United Nations Conference on International Organization met in San Francisco later in that month to formulate a charter for a postwar organization to preserve the peace. On May 8–9 the war in Europe ended.

In the United Kingdom, Prime Minister Churchill on May 23 dissolved the war cabinet and called for a general election, scheduled for July 26. Meanwhile, attending the "Terminal Conference" at Potsdam with Marshal Stalin and President Truman, Churchill invited Clement Attlee, Labour party leader, to accompany him as his deputy. Churchill saw a great need for understandings to be reached at Potsdam.

At Yalta, President Roosevelt had indicated that U.S. troops could not remain in occupation in Europe for more than two years, and that peace treaties should be concluded within that period. To Churchill, this suggested that Great Britain might be expected to bear a heavier burden in the occupation. Although agreements had been reached between the Allies at Yalta and later relating to zones of occupation, Churchill had observed what he regarded as a "changed demeanour" on the part of Soviet Russia. These changes he noted in "constant breaches of the understandings reached at Yalta" and in what he called a Russian "dart for Denmark, happily frustrated by General Montgomery's timely action, the encroachments in Austria, and Marshal Tito's menacing pressure at Trieste"—all creating "an entirely different situation from that in which the zones of occupation had been prescribed" at Quebec and reaffirmed at Yalta.[20]

In the midst of the Potsdam Conference the general election in the United Kingdom resulted in Labour party candidates winning control of Parliament and displacing Prime Minister Churchill and his Conservative party majority. Clement Attlee was invited by George VI to form a new government and Attlee then returned to the Potsdam Conference as prime minister. A notable feature of the Potsdam Conference was that President Truman and, in the last days, Prime Minister Attlee were both new faces at the conference table where Joseph Stalin had sat since earlier in the war.

---

20   Winston S. Churchill, *Triumph and Tragedy* (1953), pp. 601–02 and passim.

The End of the War in Asia
and the Pacific

19

The Allied counteroffensive against the Axis made great advances in the Pacific during 1943, as well as in Europe. U.S. and British naval and air power, along with U.S., Australian, New Zealand, Indian, and other Commonwealth land forces had placed the Allies in a strong position by early 1944. They were spread through India, Burma, and parts of China, and in the Solomon, Gilbert, and Marshall islands, moving ever closer to Japan itself.

The major Japanese naval base at Truk in the Caroline Islands, and the islands of Kwajalein and Eniwetok and Bikini to the northwest were taken in February 1944. In April and May Allied forces went ashore at Hollandia and Biak, and British naval elements joined in attacks on Japanese positions in the Dutch East Indies. By August 1944 positions had been secured in the Marianas—at Saipan, Tinian, Guam, and elsewhere—permitting direct air attacks on targets in Japan. Other islands provided bases for the return to the Philippines, as MacArthur had promised when he left Corregidor in 1942.

From MacArthur's advanced headquarters on New Guinea, action to recover the Philippines was begun in April 1944. In June, Japanese naval and air forces suffered serious losses in the Battle of the Philippine Sea, and in September air attacks began in strength against the Japanese airfields in the Philippines. On October 2 a landing was made at Leyte on Samar in the central island group. A Japanese naval force opposing the landing was severely mauled, effectively ending Japan's power at sea. Heavy fighting continued, but U.S. forces also landed on the large northern island of Luzon in January 1945 and entered Manila on February 7. Civilian prisoners held at nearby Santo Tomás since 1942, and military prisoners, including survivors of the Bataan "death march," were freed, and by July 1945 the Philippines were rid of Japanese occupation.

In the China-Burma-India (CBI) theater, where Admiral Lord Louis Mountbatten was in command, with U.S. Major General Albert C. Wedemeyer as deputy chief of staff, the real strike-back began in May

1944. A Chinese expeditionary force under U.S. General Joseph W. Stilwell crossed the Salween River in Burma to attack the Japanese in a campaign that reopened the Burma Road by January 1945 in the first successful Chinese offensive. At the same time, British Brigadier General Orde C. Wingate and his so-called "Wingate's Raiders" blocked Japanese advances, relieved the pressure on China, and saved areas of Burma from capture, often through the use of commando tactics. U.S. Brigadier General Frank D. Merrill organized "Merrill's Marauders," and fought in Burma and elsewhere. British and Indian troops captured the last important Japanese naval and air base in Burma in January 1945, Indian troops recaptured Mandalay in March, and British paratroopers regained control of Rangoon in May.

General Stilwell had differences with Mountbatten, and particularly with Generalissimo Chiang Kai-shek, and was recalled to Washington in October 1944. Major General Wedemeyer took command of U.S. forces in China, and British General Oliver W. H. Leese, formerly with the Eighth Army in Italy, took over some of Stilwell's forces in Burma.

Japanese elements in China made new advances in the summer and autumn of 1944 and caused serious difficulties for U.S. air bases in that area. A Chinese counteroffensive in December relieved that pressure somewhat, and the U.S. Fourteenth Air Force with better planes and under the command of General Claire L. Chennault was able to operate effectively against the Japanese in China and in Japan itself. New supplies also began to flow into China over the reopened Burma Road and over a new Ledo or Stilwell Road from India, sufficiently completed in January 1945 to be useful.

Correspondents reporting the war in Asia and the Pacific for the Allies were accredited to some one of four or five headquarters, occasionally to two or more, or moved from one command to another. They necessarily depended upon the armed forces for transportation, billeting, food, supplies, and communications facilities, with payment made to the appropriate governments by their media. Censorship took place either in the field, aboard ships, or at one of the headquarters. Much of the war news cleared through Honolulu or, more specifically, the navy base at Pearl Harbor, and in such volume that the U.S. Navy censorship there was important and greatly staffed. The same was true for the navy headquarters in San Francisco. From the Southeast Asia area, the British censorship cleared through Kandy, Ceylon, and London.

Fast communications were vital, and the facilities improved as all persons concerned gained experience. The manner in which war reports from the Pacific were handled as directed to the media in the United States and to the rest of the world took four forms. The same system applied to dispatches handled through London.

One form was that of communiqués prepared on the basis of official reports to Pacific fleet headquarters and released from Pearl Harbor. The second form was a news account written by representatives of news agencies and newspapers permanently in Honolulu. The account was based on the official communiqué augmented by background matter received from correspondents and possibly from a briefing officer at the base. Both factual and interpretative, these stories were given prompt review by the censorship and normally received quick transmission.

The third form of report was written from the scene of action by a pool correspondent. This was an arrangement dating from the time of the Kwajalein attack early in 1944 by which one correspondent was designated by each of the four major news agencies, AP, UP, INS, and Reuters. Lots then were drawn to see which of them would write the day's story to be used by all four agencies and to have priority in transmission.

This method was a means of conserving and making the best use of the time during which radio transmitting facilities would be occupied in handling press matter. The pool correspondent could write an 800-word report, have it censored aboard the force commander's flagship and transmitted over the ship's radio to Pearl Harbor. Already censored, it then could be relayed directly to San Francisco. There the report would be reviewed again by naval censorship before being released. This account, written from the scene, was expected to reach newspapers and radio stations very soon after the communiqué itself, but probably following the second account prepared by the pool in Honolulu. Radio correspondents, voicing broadcasts, sometimes used this same pool arrangement where transmission facilities were limited, or the time for their use was restricted.

The fourth type of story was that written by individual correspondents for news agencies, newspapers, magazines, or syndicates at the scene of action, but apart from any pool arrangement. Their accounts might go by courier plane to Pearl Harbor for censorship and transmission—a process requiring anywhere from thirty-six hours to eight days—or the correspondent might send up to 300 words daily, censored aboard the flagship and forwarded by courier plane when possible. That might mean a flight of hundreds of miles to a navy radio station in the advanced area, where it would be transmitted to the United States at three cents a word, but with a censorship check at San Francisco. This also took time and the subject matter of this fourth story type obviously could not be spot news.

Photographers and newsreel cameramen could send their undeveloped films by courier plane to Pearl Harbor. There the films were processed and reviewed by the censorship. This, again, took time. Radio photo transmission became possible from the South Pacific late in 1943.

A complicating factor affecting the pool correspondents and detracting from the timeliness of their reports was a requirement that the correspondent's story should in no case depart from the essential substance of the latest communiqué. Since the communiqué was written at Pearl Harbor, it was not available to the pool correspondent at a forward position until eighteen to twenty-four hours later. Until then, technically, he could not properly write or dispatch an account of the action described. This meant that contrary to theory the pool correspondent's report rarely if ever reached newspapers or radio stations until long after the same news had been reported both in the original communiqué and in the story prepared in Honolulu by a writer far from the scene of the action.

Dissatisfaction with such delays and affecting stories of the fourth variety, brought a meeting of media representatives in New York in October 1944. By that time Guam had been recaptured. Admiral Nimitz established a forward headquarters there in January 1945, and navy censorship handled press dispatches from the island, along with their transmission, which solved some of the problems. Press Wireless operated mobile transmitters attached to army units in France and received authority to do the same in the Pacific. On November 14, 1944, about a month after the Philippines operation began, a Press Wireless 400-watt mobile unit was in operation at Leyte. Known as Station PZ it handled press copy promptly and at a minimum cost of three cents a word to Los Angeles, plus a cent and one-half from Los Angeles to New York. Direct radio voice transmission over Prewi facilities from the Philippines also began on December 23, 1944, to help speed the news.

A group of twenty-two correspondents organized a Pacific War Correspondents Association (PWCA) in Honolulu early in 1944. Its objectives were to maintain liaison between correspondents and the Nimitz CINCPAC headquarters, to try to iron out problems of censorship and news transmission, and to seek better news briefing and improved facilities for travel and news gathering. All accredited correspondents in the Pacific were invited to membership. The chairman of the PWCA administrative committee was Robert Trumbull of the *New York Times.* Richard Haller, INS bureau chief in Honolulu, was vice-chairman, and Murray Befeler, AP Photos and photographic pool chief, was secretary-treasurer. Webley Edwards, CBS, was a member of the administrative committee, representing radio correspondents.

Other correspondents active in the organization of the PWCA and in its membership included Keith Wheeler, *Chicago Times;* Henry Keyes, *Daily Express;* George F. Horne, *New York Times;* John D. Beaufort, *Christian Science Monitor;* Harold P. (Hal) Smith, *Chicago Tribune;* Lasalle Gilman, *Honolulu Advertiser;* Frank Morris, *Collier's;* John Bishop, *Saturday Evening Post;* Nicholas F. Loundagin, *Newsweek;*

William Hipple, AP and then *Newsweek;* William L. Worden, Wendell ("Lief") Erickson, and Charles H. McMurtry, all of AP; Clarence Hamm and Ernest H. King, AP Photos; William F. Tyree and Horace D. ("Doc") Quigg, UP; and Clinton Greene, INS.

The Pacific campaigns and those in the CBI theater in 1944 reflected mounting Allied strength, presaging the victory that was to come in 1945. The largest correspondent group to be engaged in any Pacific action up to that time joined in February 1944 to report the U.S. Navy–Marine attack on the Marshall Islands in the central Pacific, with landings at Kwajalein, Wotje, Namur, Eniwetok, and elsewhere. Some forty correspondents were involved, their status improved in ways that had been proposed by the PWCA. They held simulated rank as lieutenant commanders aboard ships, had good working quarters and mess facilities, and received better briefings. Navy and marine officers with news experience were assigned to aid correspondents and authorized to discuss operations more freely than in the past. Courier planes were directed to speed press copy and films to Pearl Harbor, using envelopes marked with conspicuous blue seals. This, of course, did not prevent copy being lost or delayed, even when not held for a period of time by censorship for security reasons.

Some correspondents tried to gain assignments to aircraft carriers, which not only provided the major striking force in many of the operations but sometimes made it possible for a correspondent to get his copy off more promptly by handing it to a pilot about to fly to a shore station. Both navy Captain William Waldo Drake of Pacific Fleet headquarters and marine Lieutenant John Popham in battle areas aided correspondents as they had done before.

The correspondents in the Marshall Islands campaign included veterans of earlier assaults and landings. Among them were Trumbull, Wheeler, Smith, Worden, Erickson, and Quigg, all active in the PWCA; George E. ("First Wave") Jones, Richard W. Johnston, Malcolm R. ("Mac") Johnson, and Charles Arnot, all of the UP; Eugene Burns, Alva N. (Al) Dopking, and Paul Beam of the AP; John R. Henry, Howard Handleman, and Philip G. Reed of INS; Hal O'Flaherty, *Chicago Daily News;* Sergeant Merle Miller, *Yank;* and Staff Sergeant John A. Bushemi, *Yank* photographer. Others were William Henry Chickering, *Time,* and Percy Finch, Reuters, both new to the Pacific theater, and Raymond Clapper of the Scripps-Howard Newspapers, writer of a syndicated Washington column. He had been in southeast Asia in 1942 and also in North Africa.

Ten marine combat correspondents were engaged in the Marshalls operation. Also helpful to correspondents were several former newsmen on active duty as officers. Among them were Captain Lou Ruppel, former managing editor of the *Chicago Times,* former editor of *Collier's,* and vice-president of the Crowell-Collier Publishing Company; Captain William P. McCahill, former AP night editor in Milwaukee; Major Lewis B. Rock, publisher in Ohio of the *Dayton Journal-Herald;* Second Lieutenant Gerald A. Hoeck, formerly assistant bureau chief for INS in Seattle; and Lieutenant Robert Hewett, formerly with the AP in Chicago.

Raymond Clapper, well liked and highly respected for his news work in Washington, was killed while flying in a carrier-based plane involved in a mid-air collision over Eniwetok, the sixteenth death among U.S. correspondents. Staff Sergeant Bushemi of *Yank* was killed on Eniwetok itself a few days later. Captain Drake, navy public relations officer, was slightly wounded. Jones and Johnson of the UP and Smith and O'Flaherty of the two Chicago newspapers had narrow escapes during the same action.

The Marshalls operation was scarcely over, when the U.S. Navy sent a task force to strike at the important Japanese naval base at Truk in the Caroline Islands. Two experienced correspondents who had had the rare opportunity to visit security-bound Truk as guests of the Japanese government before the war were able to contribute background stories. They were Junius B. Wood, who had been with the *Chicago Daily News* at the time of his visit in 1923, and Willard D. Price, who wrote for the *New York Herald Tribune* in 1934. Neither man was present in the Pacific at the time of the war.

George E. ("First Wave") Jones, UP, and Robert Trumbull, *New York Times,* went on bombing raids over Truk. Norman Bell, AP, had been the first correspondent to fly with U.S. Navy bombers attacking the Caroline Islands in January 1944, and he was aboard a navy destroyer forming part of the task force approaching close enough a few weeks later to shell land installations. An attack on the Japanese-held Admiralty Islands, north of Papua, was covered by William B. Dickinson, UP, and Thomas L. Shafer, NEA-Acme Newspictures.

In the Southwest Pacific some action continued in the Solomons group. One episode indicating that Japanese strength remained formidable occurred in March-April in the so-called Second Battle of Bougainville. A sharp Japanese attack on U.S. positions in Empress Augusta Bay brought nearly a score of correspondents to the scene with naval units. Among them were McMurtry, AP, and Frank Filan, AP Photos; Quigg, UP; Handleman, INS; O'Flaherty, *Chicago Daily News;* Smith, *Chicago Tribune;* Wheeler, *Chicago Times;* Lawrence E. Welch, Cowles newspapers of Des Moines and Minneapolis; Robert W. Martin, *Time;* Dil Ferris, Robert Greenhalgh, and Barrett McGurn, all of *Yank.* McGurn was painfully wounded when a mortar shell burst near him.

One of the first major advances along the northern coast of New Guinea, and the first positive move toward the recovery of the Philippines, occurred in April 1944 in landings at Hollandia and other points. Some of the same correspondents who had covered the Empress of Augusta Bay action were among the larger group reporting this move. Others included Murlin Spencer, Spencer Davis, Asahel ("Ace") Bush, Robert Eunson, and C. Yates McDaniel for the AP; Ernest H. King and Joseph John (Joe) Rosenthal, AP Photos; and AP correspondents William L. Worden and Alva N. Dopking covered the landings from separate aircraft carriers. Olen Clements was aboard a plane, and Fred E. Hampson was aboard the attacking force flagship. Other correspondents included William C. Wilson, UP; Frank Robertson and Lee Van Atta, INS, with Van Atta in a plane; Jack Lait, INS, who went ashore with troops; and Robert Shaplen, *Time.*

One move nearer the Philippines came in May with a landing at Biak. A difficult operation, it also was reported by some of the correspondents who had observed the action at Augusta Bay and Hollandia. Spencer Davis, AP, remained at Biak longer than most, and was able to provide an eye-witness report of a strong Japanese counterattack. Don Caswell, UP, and Frank Prist, Jr., NEA-Acme Newspictures photographer, went ashore with the first wave in a Sansapor beach landing that marked the final clean-up of Japanese positions in New Guinea. In a supporting British naval action at Sabang in the East Indies during July 1944, A. E. Aubury, a Gaumont-British newsreel cameraman, received wounds that were fatal.

Further ground was gained in the approach to the Philippines in a difficult U.S. Marine and army occupation of Peleliu and Anguar islands in the Palau group during September and October 1944. Damien Parer, Paramount News cameraman, was killed by machine gun fire on Peleliu, and Master Technical Sergeant Donald A. Hallman, Sr., a marine combat correspondent formerly with the *New York Daily News,* lost a leg. Joseph Rosenthal, AP Photos, and Stanley Troutman, NEA-Acme Newspictures cameraman, were on Peleliu. Rosenthal and Paige Abbott, INP photographer, were with the army's 81st Division when it invaded Anguar Island.

Bases had been established during 1944 in the Solomon, Gilbert, Marshall, and Caroline islands, and from them U.S. Navy and carrier-based planes gave support to marine and navy landings in June and July at Saipan, Tinian, and Guam, in the Marianas. Nearly a hundred correspondents covered this notably heavy attack occurring in the Pacific at the same period as the Normandy invasion in France.

Communications during the landings were better than for any previous operation of its kind. Copy was dispatched from flagships directing the attack, with censorship also centering there, so that approved reports could flow directly into San Francisco through an instantaneous semi-automatic high-speed relay at Pearl Harbor. Some 76,000 words were sent from Saipan alone, which was secured by July 10, although mopping-up operations continued.

James G. (Jim) Lucas, a marine combat correspondent active earlier at Tarawa, was back in the Pacific theater after a period of home leave. Now a second lieutenant, he was one of many marine correspondents covering the new campaign. Five were killed, including four Marine Corps photographers, and three others were wounded during the first ten days.

Stories pooled to the entire press were written in that period by Alva N. Dopking, AP; Charles P. Arnot, UP; John R. Henry, INS; and Percy Finch, Reuters.[1] Other correspondents present included William L. Worden, AP; Clarence Hamm and Joseph Rosenthal, AP Photos; Richard W. Johnston, Malcolm R. ("Mac") Johnson and Daniel F. McGuire, all for UP; Howard Handleman and Philip Reed, INS; Robert Trumbull, *New York Times;* Frank Kelley, *New York Herald Tribune,* who had been in London through the blitz; Keith Wheeler, *Chicago Times;*[2] John Beaufort, *Christian Science Monitor;* Wilfred Burchett, *Daily Express;* Guy Harriott, *Sydney Morning Herald;* John Brennan, *Sydney Sun;* and Denis Warner representing a group of Australian afternoon papers.

At the time the landings were under way in the Marianas, U.S. naval forces spearheaded an attack on Japan's Matsuwa Island, 900 miles north of Tokyo and much closer than that to the northern island of Hokkaido, and the city of Sapporo. On June 15, 1944, the first bombing of Japan occurred, aside from the exceptional attack of 1942. U.S. Army Air Force B-29 Superfortresses of the Twentieth Bomber Command,

---

1   Finch, a British citizen, had been in China for some twenty years with the *North China Daily News* (Shanghai), and as a representative of the London *Daily Mail.* His wife, Barbara Finch, Iowa-born and a graduate in journalism at Stanford University, also had worked as a journalist in Japan and China. Married in Shanghai, they were taken into custody by the Japanese after Pearl Harbor, and repatriated in the summer of 1942. In London, Finch worked on the *Daily Herald* cable desk until 1943, when Reuters sent him to report the Pacific war. Barbara Finch was assigned to Honolulu early in 1944 to direct the Reuters bureau there.

2   Wheeler, in a letter to his paper, the *Chicago Times,* written from Saipan on July 9, 1944, complained that the action was inadequately treated by the U.S. press, and that editors failed to recognize its importance or to communicate its importance to readers. He ascribed this to competition for space by other important news developments of the time, notably those in Normandy, and to delays in transmission of the Saipan stories. Wheeler also felt that the edge had been taken off reports written from Saipan by stories prepared in Honolulu on the basis of official communiqués, and which were over-imaginative and inaccurate because the writers had not actually been present. These assertions became the basis for a controversy over the reliability of war reports from the Pacific area, particularly those originating in Honolulu.

flying from bases in western China near Chungking, made Yawata on the southern island of Kyushu the main target.

The Matsuwa assault was reported, among others, by Russell Annabel, UP. Nine correspondents and three photographers were aboard Superfortresses in the bombing of Japan. These were Thoburn H. (Toby) Wiant, AP, F. Tillman Durdin, *New York Times,* Clay Gowran, *Chicago Tribune,* Frank Cancellare, Acme Newspictures, and Robert Bryant, INP photographer, all formerly in South Pacific action. Others were Harry Zinder, *Time,* formerly in Libya and the Middle East; Roy Porter, NBC, and formerly AP; James Stewart, CBS; Bernard Hoffman, *Life* photographer; Lou Stoneman, *Yank;* Walter G. Rundle, in Chungking for the UP for some time; and William T. Shenkel, *Newsweek*. At the bomber base itself reports were prepared by Brooks Atkinson, *New York Times;* Clyde A. Farnsworth, AP; and James E. Brown, INS.

The plane in which Rundle was flying was forced to turn back because of mechanical difficulties. Four other planes failed to return after the raid. Shenkel, an observer aboard one of them, was killed with all members of the crew in a crash near Yawata.

Earlier U.S. Army Air Force missions had flown from bases in China to attack Japanese positions there and in Burma. Sonia Tomara, *New York Herald Tribune,* made such a flight in the summer of 1943. Theodore H. (Ted) White, *Time* and *Life* correspondent at Chungking, and Toby Wiant, AP, had gone on raids directed at Hong Kong, the Hainan Islands, Lashio, and other points. Both were awarded Air Medals in 1944. White made other flights to join both the Nationalist and Communist Chinese forces in the field, and to join Generals Stilwell, Chennault, and others. He also accompanied China-born Henry R. Luce, publisher of *Time* and *Life,* on Luce's return visit to China for ten days early in 1941 and in his conferences with Generalissimo and Mme. Chiang Kai-shek.

John Hlavacek, UP, was cited by General Chennault in 1944 for gallantry in aiding the evacuation of Hengyang airfield at a time when Japanese planes were approaching. John J. Andrew, also UP, who went as an observer on a B-29 mission on November 5, 1944, was killed when the plane was lost.

The capture of Saipan, Tinian, and Guam in August 1944 provided new airfields from which heavy bombers, accompanied by fighter escorts, were able to extend U.S. action in the far western Pacific, and to bombard targets in Japan, while also providing cover for the return of U.S. forces to the Philippines, beginning in September. The Twenty-first Bomber Command based on Saipan, together with the Twentieth Bomber Command, in China and India, increased their bombing attacks early in 1945 on Tokyo and other Japanese cities, and on Japanese-held cities throughout southeast Asia.

Early in 1945 several correspondents flew from Saipan as observers on at least one B-29 Superfortress attack on Tokyo. They were Clark Lee, INS, formerly of the AP who was at Corregidor; William Hipple, *Newsweek,* also formerly of the AP; Robert P. ("Pepper") Martin, of *Time* and *Life* and formerly of the UP; Malcolm R. ("Mac") Johnson, UP; Ted Leimert, CBS; William Reed, *Yank;* and Denis Warner, writer for Australian newspapers.

Other correspondents, active in the CBI theater in 1944, included Alan Humphreys, Reuters; A. E. Watson and S. H. Sinha, both of Exchange Telegraph; George Palmer, British United Press, formerly in the Mediterranean-Egyptian area; John R. Morris, Far East manager for the UP; and Frank Hewlett, also UP. He later returned to the Pacific area, where he had been before transferring to India. Harold Guard, Darrell Berrigan, Albert Ravenholt, Walter F. Logan, and George Wang were other UP men in the CBI theater.

The Associated Press had Preston L. Grover, Frank L. Martin, Jr., and Eugene Burns, formerly in the Pacific, reporting from the CBI area. Others there were Stanley Wills, *Daily Herald,* who had been at AFHQ in Algiers before going to India and Burma in 1943; Alex Small, *Chicago Tribune,* formerly in Europe; Stuart Wallis Emeny, *News-Chronicle;* Graham Stanford, *Daily Mail;* Ian Fitchett and O'Donovan Bailey, both of the *Daily Express;* Martin Moore and Ronald Legge, both of the *Daily Telegraph;* and Allington Kennard and John Nixon, representing the BBC.

Technical Sergeant David Richardson, *Yank* correspondent in a number of Pacific actions, was assigned to General Stilwell's headquarters in Burma after recovering from wounds received at Lae, New Guinea. George H. Johnstone, *Melbourne Argus,* arrived in India after covering action for fifteen months in and around New Guinea and later went on to China. Geoffrey Tebbutt represented the *Melbourne Herald.* Philip Wynter, who had written for the *Sydney Daily Telegraph,* moved to the European theater in mid-1944. He was replaced in the CBI by David McKie.

Correspondents attached to the Southeast Asia Command (SEAC) headquarters at Kandy, Ceylon, sometimes complained of boredom and of problems with censorship and communications. Where it might have taken ten days for a news dispatch to reach London from the earlier headquarters in Burma in 1942, that time lag had been reduced to a matter of hours by the end of 1944. Stanford of the *Daily Mail* reported an arrangement whereby copy written in the field would be carried by jeep to an airfield, flown to a base near headquarters, received there by a public relations officer from SEAC, carried to censorship, relayed to a radio transmission point, and so forwarded to London.

Many of the CBI correspondents in the Burma area were in the field, or went out as observers during air and naval actions. Emeny of the *News-Chronicle,* and Wills of the *Daily Herald,* were both killed in Burma on March 24, 1944, when the plane in which they were traveling crashed and burned on a mountainside.

By the end of 1944 a number of the CBI correspondents had returned to Australia, New Zealand, Great Britain, or the United States for home leave or recuperation. Others moved to a different war front, and changes occurred in the Pacific media representation. Among those returning from the CBI to the United States were Morris, Logan, and Hlavacek, all of UP, and Grover, Burns, and Wiant of the AP. Wynter of the *Sydney Daily Telegraph* moved to the European theater, and Hewlett of the UP to the Pacific. Rundle, UP, and Atkinson, *New York Times,* both returned from China to the United States.

From the Pacific, Captain William Waldo Drake, chief of naval public relations, who was wounded at Eniwetok, was transferred to Washington as deputy director of the Office of War Information. Hal O'Flaherty, *Chicago Daily News,* a victim of malaria, returned to serve as Washington correspondent for his paper. Other U.S. correspondents returning home in the summer of 1944 included Keith Wheeler, *Chicago Times;* Harold P. Smith, *Chicago Tribune;* Gary Sheahan, *Chicago Tribune* artist; William C. Wilson and Don Caswell, UP; Wendell ("Leif") Erickson, Robert Eunson, and William L. Worden, all of AP; Clarence Hamm, AP Photos; John R. Henry, INS; and Clete Roberts of the Blue Network. One key man in the handling of Pacific war news during 1943–45, but who never left San Francisco, was Norman Montellier in the UP bureau there.

Return to the Philippines, 1944–45

Preparations for the Philippines campaign had been under way virtually from the time General MacArthur established his headquarters in Australia in March 1942. Upon leaving Corregidor, shortly before, MacArthur had vowed he "would return," and in October 1944 did so. Many of the military operations in the southwest Pacific under his direction, particularly from the spring of 1944, had been to establish secure bases for the return to the Philippines and to insure the defeat of Japan.

D-Day in the final campaign for the Philippines was October 20, when landings were made on the island of Leyte, centrally located in the

Philippine group, in a combined air, naval, and ground force operation. The landing was followed by a three-day decisive naval battle, the Second Battle of the Philippine Sea, or Leyte Gulf, with U.S. ships under Admirals Halsey, Sprague, Kinkaid, Mitscher, and Oldendorf. The outcome ended Japanese sea power. Fighting on land and in the air continued, however, until June 1945 before Manila, the main island of Luzon, and other parts of the Philippines were freed of Japanese occupation.

About fifty U.S. correspondents were with the army and the fleet, the largest number to cover any Pacific operation. Their numbers were increased by the presence of British and Australian press-radio representatives and others for the U.S. Office of War Information. Included were veterans of other campaigns, among them three seized by the Japanese in Manila in January 1942 and held for nearly two years before repatriation. There were two others who had been with MacArthur at Corregidor and Bataan. There were some who had reported the Battle of Britain, the Libyan desert campaign, the African landings of November 1942, and the invasion of Normandy.

From the cruiser *Nashville* of the invasion fleet, General MacArthur waded ashore at Leyte in a symbolic gesture dramatizing his return. He was accompanied by Colonel LeGrande A. Diller, Colonel Lloyd Lehrbas, Brigadier General Carlos P. Romulo, who had directed newspapers and radio stations in the Philippines, and by others who had been at Bataan and Corregidor.

Correspondents for the U.S. media included fourteen representatives of the Associated Press alone, led by C. Yates McDaniel. This group included Dean Schedler, who had been at Corregidor in 1941–42; Wendell ("Lief") Erickson, returned from home leave, Asahel ("Ace") Bush, Rembert ("Jimmy") James, Murlin Spencer, Spencer Davis, Alva N. Dopking, Fred E. Hampson, James Hutcheson, Elmont Waite, Richard C. Bergholz, Morrie Landsberg, Frank Filan of AP Photos, and others.

The United Press group included Frank Hewlett, who also had been with MacArthur on Corregidor; Francis L. McCarthy, Charles P. Arnot, William B. Dickinson, Ralph Teatsorth, and Lisle Shoemaker. For the International News Service, Lee Van Atta and George Lait, who had been in North Africa, were present, with Paige Abbott, INP photographer.

The U.S. newspaper special correspondents included Harold P. ("Hal") Smith and Arthur Veysey, *Chicago Tribune;* Jack Turcott, *New York Daily News;* Frank Smith, *Chicago Times;* John Graham Dowling, *Chicago Sun;* Frank Kelley and Homer Bigart, both of whom had been in the European theater, *New York Herald Tribune;* Gordon Walker, *Christian Science Monitor;* John B. Terry, *Chicago Daily*

News; Lindsay Parrott, *New York Times;* Stanley Gunn, *Fort Worth Star Telegram* and *Houston Chronicle;* and Martin Sheridan, *Boston Globe.*

Photo services and newsreels were represented by Frank Prist, Jr., and Thomas L. Shafer, Acme Newspictures; Langdon V. (Don) Senick, Fox Movietone News; and Earle Crotchett and Irving Smith, Universal Newsreel.

The U.S. periodical press correspondents included Royal Arch ("Rags") Gunnison, for *Collier's* and also for NANA and MBS, and Carl Mydans, *Life* photographer. Both had been held at Santo Tomás University internment camp, along with their wives, after capture in Manila in January 1942. They had later been moved to Shanghai and were repatriated in December 1943. In returning to the Philippines as correspondents in 1944 they were risking recapture by the Japanese. William Henry Chickering and John Walker were present for *Time,* and Robert Shaplen represented *Newsweek.*

Radio correspondents included George Thomas Folster and Fleetwood Lawton, NBC; William Dunn, CBS; Clete Roberts and Art Feldman, Blue Network; and Gunnison for MBS.

Correspondents for the British and Commonwealth press included U.S.-born John Leonard, Reuters; Nelson Braidwood, *Daily Telegraph;* John Brennan, *Sydney Bulletin;* Blaine Fielder, *Sydney Morning Herald;* and Cliff Bottomley, Australian Department of Information.

Aboard Vice-Admiral Marc A. Mitscher's flagship *Lexington* during the Second Battle of the Philippine Sea near Leyte from October 24 to 27, George E. ("First Wave") Jones, UP, observed the action against strong Japanese naval units opposing the U.S. return to the islands. Admiral Halsey's flag secretary, Lieutenant Commander Harold Stassen, a former governor of Minnesota, obliged Jones by carrying a copy of his pool report of the victory on a return flight to Guam. From there it was transmitted to provide a first and exclusive publication.

The mobile Press Wireless transmitter, known as Station PZ, was put in operation at Leyte on November 14, less than a month after the landing. Following censorship, copy was transmitted direct to Los Angeles. The first dispatch sent was written by Frank Hewlett, UP. Voice transmission over the Prewi circuit began on December 23, with William Dunn, CBS, as the first radio correspondent to speak. Picked up in Los Angeles, his report was rebroadcast over the CBS network.

Correspondents were in constant danger in the Philippines from Japanese bombing and from snipers, as well as other hazards shared with the military forces. On October 25, five days after the original landing, Asahel ("Ace") Bush, AP, was killed in Tacloban as a result of a dawn air attack during which a Japanese bomb landed about fifty feet from a flimsy house in which several correspondents were sleeping. Stanley Gunn, *Fort Worth Star-Telegram* and *Houston Chronicle,* and John B. Terry, *Chicago Daily News,* were seriously wounded and died later. Cletus (Clete) Roberts, Blue Network, also was wounded, but recovered.[3]

This was the most disastrous single incident affecting correspondents in the Pacific war. It had been matched near Naples on September 28, 1943, when three British correspondents were killed and one was wounded, and precisely matched near Teruel in 1938 during the Spanish Civil War.

The Tacloban casualties might have been even more tragic because four other correspondents were sleeping in the same house, and a fifth nearby. About forty other correspondents, in a second house about fifty yards away, were rocked by the explosion, but escaped injury. Less than three weeks later, Frank Prist, Jr., Acme Newspictures, a veteran of the Pacific campaign and due to return to the United States, was killed on November 13 by a sniper. Lindesay Parrott, *New York Times,* was wounded and later awarded the Purple Heart.

On December 15, 1944, General MacArthur landed a second invasion force on Mindoro Island south of Manila, and another at Lingayen Gulf in northern Luzon on January 9, 1945. The latter was the point where the Japanese invasion of the Philippines had begun in December 1941. About sixty correspondents reported the Lingayen Gulf landings. They moved with the invasion force in three ships, two of them equipped with communications facilities. Under Japanese air attack before the landing, William Henry Chickering, *Time,* was killed on January 6. In other action, John Graham Dowling, *Chicago Sun,* was injured in making a parachute landing at Aparri on Luzon with the 11th Airborne Division. Later, he was awarded paratrooper wings. The push from Lingayen Gulf southward to Manila included the overrunning of Japanese military prisons and camps and the liberation of U.S. military and civilian personnel. Francis L. McCarthy, UP, found his brother and his sister in the Los Banos camp.

Correspondents who had been in the Philippines in 1941 pushed with special eagerness toward Manila. These included Royal Arch ("Rags") Gunnison, *Collier's,* NANA, and MBS, and Carl Mydans, *Life,* both of whom had been in the Leyte landing, as well as Russell Brines, AP, who had been in the Lingayen landing. All three had been prisoners at Santo

---

3 Bush, graduated from Amherst in 1933, and a Phi Beta Kappa, had been with the AP since 1939. He had at least two previous narrow escapes from death in the Pacific. Gunn was a 1937 University of Texas graduate in journalism. Terry, born in the Philippines, had been a Washington correspondent for the *Honolulu Star-Bulletin,* a Nieman Fellow at Harvard in 1943–44, and had joined the *Daily News* staff for service in the Pacific in August 1944, when Hal O'Flaherty returned to the United States. Clete Roberts later was awarded the Purple Heart.

Tomás. The correspondent group also included Dean Schedler, AP; Frank Hewlett, UP; and Clark Lee, INS, formerly of AP. Lee had been with Brines in the Lingayen landing, and they had been with MacArthur at Corregidor.

Gunnison and Mydans were with the First U.S. Cavalry, a tank outfit in the new army, when it liberated in February the 3,700 men, women, and children held at Santo Tomás. Gunnison and Mydans had been able to leave Santo Tomás with their wives in 1942. Brines found his wife and daughter in the camp, and Frank Hewlett, UP, also found his wife, Virginia Hewlett, who had been serving as a nurse during the three years that had elapsed since she had been seized in Manila.

In an emotional reunion, correspondents also found at Santo Tomás R. A. G. Hammond, Reuters; Jack Percival, *Sydney Morning Herald,* and his wife and child, who had been born there; H. Ford Wilkins, CBS and *New York Times;* Robert Crabb, David Harvey, and Robert Robb, INS; Roy C. Bennett, *Manila Daily Bulletin;* H. McCullough-Dick and Theo Rogers, *Philippine Free Press;* and Bert Silen, NBC.[4]

One of the happy revelations from Santo Tomás was that Don Bell, part-time stringer for NBC, had not been bayonetted to death, as had been reported in 1942. Just before Manila fell he had gone to Heacock's Department Store, where he was publicity director, and was arrested under his real name of Clarence Beliel. Although the Japanese looked for him under his radio pseudonym of "Don Bell," they gave up the search, assuming that "Bell" actually had been killed after they learned of reports to that effect in U.S. publications. Those in the Santo Tomás camp who knew the truth said nothing.[5]

The day after Santo Tomás was liberated, U.S. forces also took Bilibid prison in the southern section of Manila. There Horace D. ("Doc") Quigg, UP, found Franz Weissblatt, UP correspondent who had been wounded and captured on the Bataan Peninsula in 1942. He was the only correspondent attached to the group at Corregidor who did not get away. Badly treated by the Japanese, Weissblatt was lodged for three years in the prison. His wife, Vivian Weissblatt, was in the Santo Tomás camp, but neither knew of the other's status. After liberation they were flown to New York, where Weissblatt received proper medical care. He was awarded the Purple Heart in July 1945.

---

4   Silen made a broadcast to the United States after his liberation, introducing his remarks with the words, "As I was saying when I was so rudely interrupted over three years and a month ago. . . ."

5   After liberation, Bell joined the Mutual Broadcasting System staff. While flying over the China coast soon after, his plane was shot down by Japanese, but made a safe landing in the occupied area of China. He managed to evade capture, reached Chungking on foot, and was in New York in May 1945.

Other correspondents reporting the Luzon landing and the liberation of Manila, some of them previously at Leyte, included George E. ("First Wave") Jones, who switched from the United Press to the *New York Times* to cover the Lingayen landing. The group also included the AP staff members, McDaniel, Dopking, Davis, Hampson, Bergholz, and Filan; Dickinson, Teatsorth and William C. Wilson, for the UP; Van Atta for INS, backed by Howard Handleman and Frank Robertson; and John Leonard for Reuters. Others were Kelley of the *New York Herald Tribune;* Smith, *Chicago Sun;* Veysey and Walter Simmons, *Chicago Tribune;* Walker, *Christian Science Monitor;* John M. Carlisle, *Detroit News;* Nixon Denton, *Cincinnati Times-Star;* Thomas L. Shafer, NEA and Acme Newspictures; Corporals Roger Wrenn and Joseph Stefanelli, *Yank;* William Gray, *Time;* Robert Burns, Australian Information Department; Patrick Flaherty, NBC; and William Dunn, CBS.

Arrangements had been made for a communications vessel, the *Apache,* once used by William McKinley as a presidential yacht, to be moored in Lingayen Gulf, with a transmission line fed out from the ship as the military advance occurred on land in the direction of Manila. Although the line was cut frequently, Lieutenant Colonel Abel A. Schechter, formerly NBC news director in New York, made it possible for correspondents to get their dispatches out with a minimum of delay. He also gave radio correspondents an opportunity to get their broadcasts through. When Press Wireless, Inc., established a mobile transmitter on Luzon, as it had previously done on Leyte, the *Apache* no longer was required.

Although the advance southward from Lingayen Gulf was quite rapid and was matched by advances from the south toward Manila, Japanese resistance was stubborn. One of the grim episodes was a shelling of Santo Tomás after its liberation, resulting in death or injury for many of those who had only just regained a measure of freedom after their long internment. On July 5, 1945, however, General MacArthur was able to announce that the Philippine Islands had been liberated and were fully under U.S. control.

The toll of correspondents in the Pacific and Philippines action and in the CBI during 1944–45 was large. Observers whose experience in the African and European theaters gave them a basis for comparison were unanimous in regarding the Pacific-CBI area as more hazardous and more difficult. Although the European war was at an end in May 1945, it was believed that the Japanese resistance would prolong the battle and cost perhaps a million lives.

Admiral Nimitz, commander-in-chief for the Pacific, moved his U.S. Navy headquarters from Pearl Harbor to Guam in January 1945, at the same time that the new Ledo Road supply route from India into China was opened as an alternative to the Burma Road. The key Burmese cities of Myitkyina and Mandalay were recaptured also after a long campaign in which British, Australian, New Zealand, Indian, U.S., and Chinese forces participated. By May 1945 the port of Rangoon was retaken and the Japanese were being driven back into Thailand. In the same period, Japanese troops still in the Solomons, New Guinea, Borneo, the Dutch East Indies, and Truk were being mopped up.

In mid-February 1945, a U.S. naval force, including aircraft carriers, sailed close enough to Japan to send 1,200 planes to bomb Tokyo. From Saipan, Tinian, and Guam heavy U.S. bombers with fighter escorts bombarded Iwo Jima, only about 750 miles from Tokyo.

The landing of the U.S. Fourth Marine Division on Iwo Jima on February 19 was somewhat comparable in strategic importance to the Allied crossing of the Rhine in March 1945. By late March, after twenty-six days of bloody fighting, the island was captured and became a more advanced base for air attacks on the Japanese home islands. Careful arrangements had been made for the transmission of news copy and photographs from Iwo Jima, and a new record for Pacific communications was established when photos of action there were in San Francisco within seventeen and one-half hours of the first assault.

On the morning of February 23 a marine patrol reached the height of Mount Suribachi and raised a small flag. Several hours later another marine group raised a larger U.S. flag at the same spot. A photograph of this second flag-raising made by Joseph Rosenthal, AP Photos, became one of the most widely-reproduced and dramatic pictures of the war. Variously compared to "The Spirit of '76" and other paintings, the unposed Iwo Jima photograph became a subject presented in various forms.[6]

Correspondents on Iwo Jima included Keith Wheeler, *Chicago Times,* a veteran of Pacific war coverage returned from a period of recuperation in the United States. He was seriously wounded on the second day when a bullet cut an artery in his throat and smashed his jaw. John Lardner, representing *Newsweek,* NANA, and the *New Yorker* magazine, was painfully injured.[7]

---

6   These included statues, a U.S. postage stamp, and others. Services honoring the 60,000 marines who took the island, after many casualties, were held at Iwo Jima in February 1947. Joe Rosenthal, then on the photo staff of the *San Francisco Chronicle,* returned for the ceremony.

7   He was one of four Lardner brothers, sons of Ring Lardner (1885–1933). James was killed in Spain during the civil war, a volunteer in the Lincoln Brigade with the Republican forces. David, writing for the *New Yorker,* was killed in a land mine explosion near Aachen in October 1944.

Alvin S. McCoy, *Kansas City Star,* was aboard the carrier *U.S.S. Franklin* when it was hit by a diving Japanese kamikaze plane on March 19. He produced notable stories on the successful effort to save the ship. Bonnie Wiley, AP, the first woman correspondent to accompany an island invasion force, observed the action from aboard a hospital ship. Morris Landsberg, AP, was with the flagship of the fleet. Lisle Shoemaker, UP; Thomas Morrow, *Chicago Tribune;* Don Donaghey, *Philadelphia Evening Bulletin;* and Paige Abbott, INP photographer, were among others reporting the battle for Iwo Jima. Marine combat correspondents in the action included John Barberio, who was killed; First Lieutenant James G. Lucas; Technical Sergeants W. Keyes Beech, David Dempsey, and Alvin W. Josephy, Jr.; and Captain Raymond Henri.

Of changes which occurred in the Pacific correspondent group in the early months of 1945, one was the February arrival of Ernie Pyle, the Scripps-Howard Newspaper Alliance correspondent whose columns from North Africa, Italy, and elsewhere telling the story of the war in terms of the enlisted men had won him fame and affection. His reporting also had become the subject of a major motion picture. Jerry Thorp, *Chicago Daily News,* arrived to replace John B. Terry, who had died of wounds received at Tacloban in Leyte. Paul F. Cranston, *Philadelphia Evening Bulletin,* was another new arrival. Charles P. Gorry, AP Photos photographer, in the Pacific for some months, was cited for heroism in January 1945 because of his special assistance when a ship was on fire at sea. Robert L. Sherrod, experienced *Time* correspondent, was at the new Guam headquarters and prepared to go out on new landings. John Cashman, after a navy career in which he lost an arm when a gun misfired aboard ship in the Atlantic during May 1942, had joined the INS staff in New York in October of that year and was sent to Guam in March 1945.

Unconditional Surrender, 1945

The next full-scale landing after Iwo Jima was at Okinawa in the Ryukyus, part of the Japanese islands group. On April 1, U.S. Marines and army units made an amphibious landing there. Okinawa was in effect part of Japan and defended savagely by land and sea forces and by kamikaze or suicide plane attacks. The battle continued for nearly three months, with casualties heavy on Okinawa and adjacent islands, until Japanese resistance collapsed on June 21.

This difficult campaign was reported by about forty correspondents. Among them were Ernie Pyle; McCoy, Gorry, Sherrod, and Cashman, moving from Guam; George E. Jones and William H. Lawrence, *New York Times;* Mac R. Johnson, formerly of the UP, and Homer Bigart, both of the *New York Herald Tribune;* William McGaffin, *Chicago Daily News;* Harold P. Smith, *Chicago Tribune;* John D. Beaufort, *Christian Science Monitor;* Gordon Cobbledick, *Cleveland Plain Dealer;* John Leonard, Reuters; Russell Annabel, Evans G. Valens, and Edward Thomas, all of UP; Vern Haugland, Alva N. Dopking, Robert E. Geiger, and James Lindsley, all of AP; John R. Henry and George McWilliams, INS; and W. Eugene Smith, *Life* photographer. As the campaign moved across the island, Frank H. Bartholomew, UP vice-president, was the first newsman in Naha, the capital of the island.

Ernie Pyle, after having escaped death or injury during earlier campaigns in Africa and Europe was killed by Japanese machine-gun fire on the little island of Ie Shima, west of Okinawa, on April 18, 1945. By one estimate, he was the thirtieth U.S. correspondent killed in the war.[8]

Cashman, INS, having lost an arm while serving in the navy, was killed in a plane crash at Okinawa on July 31. W. Eugene Smith,[9] *Life* photographer, was seriously wounded there on May 22, and Evans G. Valens, UP, was wounded during the June fighting.

The U.S. Eighth Air Force had been transferred from Europe after the German surrender in May 1945, and was based on Okinawa in July under the command of Lieutenant General James H. Doolittle, who had led the first air attack against Tokyo on April 18, 1942. By July 1945 Japan was under almost constant day and night air attack. The bombardment had started in May and was part of what had become the conventional pattern preliminary to an amphibious landing. A suicidal resistance to a landing on the main Japanese islands was anticipated, and heavy casualties had to be expected.

With such concentration on Japan, and with Guam as the new center of command in the Pacific, Pearl Harbor, Brisbane, and Kandy were left somewhat in shadow, except as communications points. About 125 correspondents were accredited to the Guam headquarters in April 1945, representing media in the United Kingdom, Canada, Australia, the United States, and China. Most of them were with ships at sea or with troops on an island.

---

8   The day before Pyle was killed he cabled his sorrow upon learning of the fatal heart attack suffered on March 31 on the Guam airstrip by Frederick C. Painton, correspondent for *Reader's Digest.* He also added his gratitude that Painton had not had "to go through the unnatural terror of dying on the battlefield." Pyle and Painton had been together for months in the ETO and Painton had been Pyle's biographer.

9   There were three Smiths who were veterans of many Pacific campaigns between 1942–45. W. Eugene Smith, *Life,* was known in the press corps as "Wonderful Smith." Harold P., *Chicago Tribune,* was known as "Hal," and also as "Packrat Smith." Irving H., Universal Newsreel cameraman, was referred to affectionately as "Horrible Smith." All these nicknames were derived from their initials.

Frank Tremaine, UP, was more permanently at Guam directing coverage of the Pacific for that agency. He had participated in the liberation of Manila in February. After about three months, he went to Honolulu to relieve William F. Tyree. Replacing Tremaine at Apia on Guam was Richard W. Johnston. Lloyd Tuplin, UP, after several months in the forward area, also went to Honolulu, while Ernest (Ernie) Hoberecht, representing the UP, left Hawaii for the Philippines.

For the Associated Press, Morrie Landberg, Wendell ("Leif") Erickson, Robert Geiger, and others were in Guam. Max Desfor was sent there from the Washington staff to act as photo pool coordinator for the Central Pacific, replacing Ernest King, AP Photos, who returned to New York.

Robert Trumbull, *New York Times,* who had been at Guam and in forward areas, returned to Honolulu in May to relieve Clinton Greene, who had switched to the *Times* from INS and returned to the mainland. Later, Trumbull returned to the Pacific aboard the British battleship *King George V.* Bruce Rae became *New York Times* bureau chief at Guam, with George E. Jones and Warren Moscow working with him.

Meanwhile, in the Philippines, Spencer Davis, AP, was in charge of the reopened agency bureau in Manila, aided by James Halsema and Frank Filan, AP Photos photographer. In the mopping up campaign in the Philippines, Jerry Thorp, *Chicago Daily News,* and John Graham Dowling, *Chicago Sun,* participated in paratroop operations at Aparri on Luzon during June. Dowling suffered injuries to both ankles in making a landing. He was awarded paratrooper wings. Thorp was cited for bravery by the commander of the U.S. Eleventh Airborne Division. Russell Brines, Dean Schedler, Fred E. Hampson, and James Hutcheson, all of AP, also were active in reporting the conclusion of military action in the Philippines. Lindesay Parrott, *New York Times,* was at General MacArthur's headquarters during that period. Joseph Laitin, formerly of the *Brooklyn Eagle* and in Washington for the UP, became chief of the Reuters bureau in Manila in July.

Military operations were in progress also in other areas to secure Allied positions. Correspondents with ground, air, and naval units engaged in these hazardous tasks. Two were killed July 3 by Japanese machine-gun fire at Balikpapan on the north coast of Borneo. They were John Elliott of the Australian Broadcasting Commission, and William Smith of the Australian Department of Information.

Kyle Palmer, *Los Angeles Times,* spent some months at sea with U.S. Navy Task Force 58 under Vice-Admiral Marc A. Mitscher, but returned to Los Angeles in May. William H. Lawrence, *New York Times,* remained at Okinawa. Lee Van Atta, INS, who had served in the Pacific throughout the war and had flown as an observer on 111 combat missions, was named an honorary member of the U.S. Fifth Air Force on July 22, 1945, his twenty-fourth birthday, in recognition of "his unique position and extremely conscientious and consistent coverage of Army air forces in this theater." Other U.S. correspondents with long service in the Pacific returned to the mainland in the early months of 1945. Among them was C. Yates McDaniel, AP, who was named foreign editor in the agency's San Francisco bureau in May and assigned to coordinate the work of about forty AP correspondents in the Pacific. John Leonard, Reuters, but a U.S. citizen, and Francis L. McCarthy, UP, were others who returned.

The end of the war in Europe in May 1945 brought a movement toward the Pacific by some correspondents who had been in the other theater. They included Harold V. (Hal) Boyle, AP, and Jack Smythe, Reuters, who was captured in Holland in September 1944 but released in April 1945 after seven months in a German prisoner-of-war camp.

A number of editors and publishers in the United States visited the Pacific in the first months of 1945 as guests of the navy, with officers assigned to conduct them. Among these visitors and and observers were Arthur Hays Sulzberger and Julius Ochs Adler, *New York Times;* Ogden Reid, *New York Herald Tribune;* Roy W. Howard, Scripps-Howard Newspapers; Joseph M. Patterson, *New York Daily News;* Frank W. Taylor, *Chicago Sun;* John S. Knight, of the Knight Newspapers, by then including the *Chicago Daily News;* John Cowles, of the Cowles Newspapers of Des Moines and Minneapolis; J. David Stern, *Philadelphia Record* and *Camden News-Post;* W. C. Shepherd, *Denver Post;* P. L. Jackson, *Portland Journal,* Oregon; William R. Matthews, Tucson *Arizona Daily Star* and *Citizen;* E. M. (Ted) Dealey, *Dallas Morning News;* and Frank Ahlgren, *Memphis Commercial Appeal.* One British news executive included was Colin Bednall, assistant editor and former war correspondent for the London *Daily Mail.*

In the CBI and the Southeast Asia Command, the reopening of the Burma Road into China early in 1945, after two and one-half years under Japanese control, was reported by some fifty-six media representatives accompanying the first convoy moving over the road in twenty-six jeeps and four trucks. The recapture of Mandalay by the Fourteenth Army also had been well reported by a press group occupying a jungle encampment about thirty miles from that city.

The continuing perils of the Burma campaign were demonstrated when William E. West, Exchange Telegraph, was killed fifty miles north of Rangoon in May 1945. He had been with a tank squadron near the village of Pegu and was driving back to the press camp in a jeep with Richard Sharp, BBC, when he was shot through the heart by a Japanese sniper.

George Weller, *Chicago Daily News,* who had qualified to jump with U.S. paratroopers while in Australia in 1942, did jump in Burma in June 1945 with a group of U.S. and Burmese guerrillas—the so-called Jing-paw Raiders. The landing intentionally was made behind Japanese lines, where Weller avoided capture and returned with a story to tell.

Other correspondents in the Burma area in the last months of the war, many of them veterans, included Ian Morrison, the *Times;* Sam Jackett, D. O'Beirne, and N. Rajamani, all of Reuters; Ian Lang and Brian Reynolds, Kemsley Newspapers; Arthur W. (Tony) Helliwell, *Daily Herald;* Stuart Gelder, *News-Chronicle;* Clive Graham, *Daily Express;* Alfred Wagg, *Daily Mail;* Richard Sharp and Douglas Cleverdon, BBC; George H. Johnstone, *Melbourne Argus;* Thomas Goodman, *Sydney Morning Herald;* H. Plumridge, Associated Press of Australia; Hayden Lennard, Australian Broadcasting Corporation; Alex Tozer, Movietone News; G. B. Oswald, Universal Newsreel; Reuben Saidman, *Illustrated London News,* photographer; Daniel Lee, *Ta Kung Pao,* Chungking; Eddie Tseng, Central News Agency of China; George Alexanderson, Chinese Ministry of Information; and George Kinnear, *Nairobi Times,* Kenya.

Still others in Burma at some period in the late months of the war were F. Tillman Durdin, *New York Times;* Mrs. Peggy Durdin representing *Time* and *Life;* Theodore H. White, *Time;* Harold (Hal) Isaacs, *Newsweek;* Frank L. Martin, Jr., AP; James Brown, INS; MacQueen Wright, UP; Technical Sergeant David Richardson, *Yank;* Frank Cancellare, Acme Newspictures; and John Graham Dowling, *Chicago Sun.*

Those correspondents in the CBI at this period had the assistance of a particularly able group of public relations officers. Former newsmen themselves, they provided good briefings on operations. The transmission time of copy to London also improved, especially after the recapture of Rangoon in May, thus eliminating a previous relay by way of Calcutta. A special group of correspondents and editors was flown from the United States to the CBI theater in June to tell the story of the Air Transport Command and what it was able to do in flying war materials and men over the Himalayas—the "hump" between India and China—during the long period when the land routes were closed.

Among those who made this journey were Hallett E. Abend, NANA, a former *New York Times* correspondent in China; Edward A. Lahey, *Chicago Daily News;* Harry Grayson, NEA; Robert Considine, INS; Harry Flannery, CBS; William Howland, *Time;* Bruce Gould, editor of the *Ladies Home Journal;* and five women correspondents: Elsie McCormick, *Readers's Digest;* Greta Palmer, *Woman's Home Companion;* Mary Day Winn, *This Week;* Pauline Frederick, Western Newspaper Union, Chicago; and Evelyn Eaton, G. P. Putnam Sons, publishers, New York.

Beginning in May 1945 the Japanese home islands were subjected to increasingly regular heavy attacks from the advanced positions held by U.S. ships and planes in preparation for an amphibious landing and a drive for victory. Correspondents flying as observers in these attacks included Clark Lee, INS; William Hipple, *Newsweek;* Malcolm R. Johnson, UP; Robert C. Martin, *Time* and *Life;* Ted Leimert, CBS; William Reed, *Yank;* and Denis Warner, Australian papers. Richard W. Johnston, UP, was aboard the U.S. battleship *Iowa,* Admiral Halsey's flagship of the U.S. Third Fleet, directing both shelling and air bombing of Japanese production centers. In July, William F. Tyree, UP, also was an observer in a bomber flying over Japan and Korea.

For an all-out attack on Japan, to be directed at the southernmost island of Kyushu in the fall of 1945, Operation Olympic was in preparation. It was to be commanded jointly by General MacArthur and Admiral Nimitz. Japanese resistance on the beaches and beyond was expected to be of such persistence as to require a further Operation Coronet in the spring of 1946.

There was, however, an alternative plan well advanced and known to only a few persons directly connected with it.

The concept of an unprecedented power to be derived from what was described in simple terms as "splitting the atom" had long been a subject of scientific speculation and experimentation. Its application to warfare was included in the speculation. The theory was represented in a mathematical equation produced in the 1920s by Albert Einstein, then a professor of physics and a mathematician at the University of Berlin. It reflected an advance toward an understanding of the possibility of atomic (or nuclear) fission, and of its potential.

Einstein left Germany in 1932, joined the Institute for Advanced Study at Princeton University in 1933, and became a U.S. citizen in 1940. Meanwhile, the European war had started, understanding of nuclear fission had advanced, and there was reason to believe that the Nazi government was supporting research to develop atomic weapons. Research also was proceeding elsewhere, and some saw a race developing for atomic power that could possibly place a mastery of the world in the hands of the winner of that race.

Aware of the hazard that rested in the prospect of a Nazi victory in the race, Einstein appealed to President Roosevelt to support a program of defensive research in the United States. After the Japanese attack at Pearl Harbor, the president created in December 1941 a United States Office of Scientific Research and Development to study nuclear power and possibly develop an atomic weapon to be used in the Allied war effort.

The research and experimentation developed in great secrecy within what was known as the Manhattan Engineering District. This "Manhattan Project," as it became known, was a joint U.S.-British-Canadian undertaking directed by U.S. General Leslie R. Groves. The actual work was done at the University of California, Berkeley;[10] at the University of Chicago; at Oak Ridge, Tennessee; at Hanford, Washington; and at Los Alamos, New Mexico. The scientific leaders included Ernest O. Lawrence, J. Robert Oppenheimer, Harold Urey, James B. Conant, Vannevar Bush, Neils Bohr, Enrico Fermi, and Lise Meitner, all of whom had worked in nuclear research, the last three in Europe.

Harry Truman, who became president in April 1945 upon the death of Franklin Roosevelt, had not been told of the experimentation until then. The project was so well advanced that the first atomic bomb was detonated near Alamogordo, New Mexico, on July 16. President Truman was attending the Potsdam Conference near Berlin with other Allied leaders, where the continuance of the war with Japan was discussed, among other concerns.

In private conversations at Potsdam, Truman informed Churchill and Stalin of the impressive report from Alamogordo. The conference agreed that the bomb should be used against Japan unless Tokyo agreed to an unconditional surrender, such as had been accepted by the German Nazi government.

On July 21 a radio appeal was made to Japan to surrender or face total destruction, but no mention was made of the atom bomb or of its test. Japanese radio broadcasts on July 25, and diplomatic messages through Stockholm and Berne, sought terms less severe than unconditional surrender. An ultimatum was then issued by the Allied Powers on July 27, but its terms were formally rejected by Japan on July 29. The attacks on Japan by air and sea increased in the days immediately following, with a new variety of fire bomb used in low-level B-29 attacks that burned much of Tokyo. Still no surrender was in prospect.

Early on August 6 the first atomic bomb was dropped on the port of Hiroshima, a city of about 350,000, from a B-29 Superfortress moving unescorted over the city. The devastation and casualties resulting were unprecedented in the history of warfare. By later estimates, 130,000 were killed, injured, or missing, and 90 percent of the city was destroyed. Still Japan did not surrender. President Truman, in returning to the United States from the Potsdam Conference aboard the cruiser *Augusta*, announced the attack on Hiroshima and the fateful introduction to the world of the "atomic age." On August 8, Soviet Russia declared war on Japan, as it had agreed to do at the Yalta Conference in February.

On August 9, a second atomic bomb was dropped, this time on the

---

10   The Department of Journalism at Berkeley, of which this writer then was chairman, was moved out of its building to make way for engineers working on the Manhattan Project with Lawrence, Oppenheimer, and Urey, leaders in the study of nuclear physics. Later they moved to Los Alamos, New Mexico.

port of Nagasaki on the island of Kyushu. About 75,000 persons were killed or wounded, and one-third of the city of 250,000 was destroyed. The Japanese Supreme War Council, which had met early that day, was summoned again by Emperor Hirohito after he learned of the Nagasaki bombing. Most Japanese officials by then were persuaded that the Potsdam demand for an unconditional surrender must be met, and on August 10 Japan agreed to surrender, provided the emperor remained as head of state. The Allies agreed, on the understanding that the emperor take orders from the occupation authorities. Japan accepted this final provision on August 14 through its envoys in neutral Sweden and Switzerland.

The official Japanese news agency, Domei, broadcast the government's acceptance as a means to provide assurance that no more atomic bombs would be dropped. Emperor Hirohito in a recorded statement was heard over the radio by the Japanese people on August 15 ordering the end of hostilities. Surrender had not been universally expected in Japan, and many committed hara-kiri. August 14 and 15 thus brought the end of the war in Asia and the Pacific and of World War II.

The formal Japanese surrender ceremonies took place aboard the battleship *U.S.S. Missouri* in Tokyo Bay on September 2, 1945. General MacArthur signed the surrender documents for the Allies. Foreign Minister Mamoru Shigemitsu and General Yoshijiro Umegu, chief of the imperial staff, signed for Japan. Admirals Nimitz and Halsey were among many others present. Also attending the ceremony was General Jonathan M. Wainwright, successor to MacArthur as commander at Corregidor in 1942. Wainwright was captured there by the Japanese and taken to Mukden as a prisoner of war, from where he was flown to Tokyo to attend the surrender on the express order of General MacArthur.

Much of the story of the last days of the war in the Pacific and of the breathtaking implications of the atomic bomb that foreshadowed the new "atomic age" came from Washington, London, and other cities, rather than from the battle zone. It was a subject largely in the realm of science writers and political correspondents.

The attention given to science by the newspaper and magazine press had grown greatly since the 1920s. Qualified writers were attached to the staffs of quality dailies, news agencies, and some periodicals. One such writer, William L. Laurence, educated at Harvard, Boston University, and Besançon, in France, had been a writer on education and science for the *New York Times* since 1930, and was a Pulitzer Prize winner in 1937. In 1939 and 1940 he wrote two significant reports of research on uranium fission as a potential source of power and as an explosive force. These reports appeared in the *New York Times* and in the *Saturday Evening Post*.

In April 1945, General Groves, head of the secret Manhattan Project, asked the *Times* to lend Laurence to the project as its historian. From his headquarters at Oak Ridge, Tennessee, Laurence visited all the centers where work was in progress, and only wrote of what he observed for the private records and not for publication. On July 12, he went to Alamogordo to witness the first test of a bomb on July 16 that nobody could be sure would explode, or with what possible devastation if it did.

After a brief visit to New York, where he could only tell his wife that he was going to London, he actually flew late in July to Tinian Island in the Pacific. The first atom bomb was prepared there, and Laurence watched it being put together and loaded into a B-29, the *Enola Gay.* Turner Catledge, assistant managing editor of the *New York Times,* went to Washington in response to a cautious message from General Groves. Waldemar Kaempffert, previously long engaged as a science writer for the paper, but retired, was recalled to New York from a vacation in Canada.

The news of the Hiroshima bombing on August 6 reached the *New York Times* about noon, and the paper of August 7, a Tuesday, gave ten pages of a thirty-eight page edition to the story in detail. Much of it was written by Laurence, or rewritten from material he had prepared and which was closely guarded until ready for release. The news agencies reported the story, much of it as derived from the *Times*. Other papers and periodicals of the United States and of the world did the same, and so did radio news broadcasters. All media added their own comments.

On August 9, Laurence himself was permitted to occupy a place in the B-29 which left Tinian early that morning to drop the second atomic bomb on Nagasaki. This was a story he was able to write in full descriptive detail, but still not for publication. That story, as published, was written for the *New York Times,* as it happened, by William H. Lawrence. He became known as "Political Bill" within the office, with William L. Laurence known as "Atomic Bill." Political Bill, formerly in the Washington bureau, was a war correspondent at the Guam headquarters in August 1945. Atomic Bill received a second Pulitzer Prize in 1946, as well as many other honors for his work as an historian of the beginning of the atomic age.[11]

It was August 14 before Japan accepted the surrender terms, and the emperor's broadcast to the people came the day after, which became "VJ Day." Actually, a false report of Japan's acceptance of the terms was sent as a "flash" over the United Press domestic wire system in the United States at 9:34 P.M. EST on Sunday, August 12. It was "killed" two minutes later, but the interval was long enough for the UP report to

11   See Meyer Berger, *The Story of The New York Times, 1851–1951* (1951), ch. 43.

be broadcast over the MBS radio network, setting off premature celebrations even as far away as Sydney, Australia. Hugh Baillie, president of the UP, promptly offered $5,000 reward for apprehension of the person who sent the false flash. Its origin was traced to an unattended teleprinter machine in a southern city, possibly Nashville, Tennessee. The mystery never was solved, or if solved the explanation never was made known publicly.

With Japan's acceptance of the terms, a delegation from Tokyo arrived in Manila on August 19 to confer with General MacArthur and to receive his instructions. The group returned to Japan the following day. On August 27, the U.S. Third Fleet under Admiral Halsey moved into Sagami Bay, adjacent to Tokyo Bay. On August 28 Army Air Force specialists landed at Atsugi airfield, about twenty miles from Tokyo, to prepare for the arrival of transport planes bearing occupation troops. Navy units also moved into Tokyo Bay. Early on the morning of August 30 paratroopers of the U.S. Eleventh Airborne Division accompanied by correspondents landed at Atsugi airfield where they greeted General MacArthur when he flew in later in the day. He established temporary headquarters at Yokohama, eighteen miles south of Tokyo and the port for that capital city. On the same day and through September 2, occupation troops arrived in Japan in great numbers and fanned out through the area south of Tokyo.

Correspondents participating in the August 30 landing in Japan were issued weapons. This was contrary to previous practice, but was based on what commanding officers regarded as a "calculated risk" of an ambush. The people of Japan, however, and all elements of the military, honored Emperor Hirohito's broadcast and kept the peace.

Two correspondents who landed at Atsugi, Gordon Walker, *Christian Science Monitor,* and Frank Robertson, INS, went to Yokohama, where U.S. troops had arrived. There they joined Japanese civilians and some soldiers aboard a train to Tokyo, where they were the first Americans to arrive. Wilfred Burchett of the *Daily Express* was the first to reach Hiroshima and to write a story handled for him by Domei, datelined September 6. Four U.S. correspondents arrived there on that day, Homer Bigart, *New York Herald Tribune,* "Political Bill" Lawrence, *New York Times,* Haugland, AP, and McGlincy, UP. Other correspondents arriving early in Japan commandeered automobiles or used whatever means of transportation they could. Some went to Tokyo, even though it was "off limits" until September 9. Where possible, they established themselves at the Imperial Hotel, a favored prewar gathering place for correspondents.

The formal surrender ceremony of September 2 on the deck of the *Missouri* was witnessed by representatives of the United States, Great Britain, China, Australia, New Zealand, Holland, the Soviet Union, Canada and France. Among them were more than 300 media representatives. Every accredited correspondent who wanted to be present on that occasion was enabled to be there, even if it meant flying from Guam, Manila, Honolulu, Brisbane, Noumea, or Kandy. The Japanese media were represented by Masuo Kato of the Domei agency.

Active coverage by so large a group would have been superfluous. Instead, about fifteen U.S. and British press and radio correspondents and photographers were selected to provide pool coverage. Photographs were transmitted by navy communications specialists over equipment aboard the battleship *U.S.S. Iowa,* also in Tokyo Bay.

On the following day, September 3, the first of the occupation, three correspondents who had followed General MacArthur's campaign from Australia to Japan were his luncheon guests at the Yokohama headquarters. They were Lee Van Atta, INS, Don Caswell, UP, and William Dunn, CBS. The headquarters were moved very soon from Yokohama to Tokyo, where the modern Dai Ichi building was the operations center for the Supreme Command of the Allied Powers (SCAP). MacArthur lived at the former U.S. Embassy, miraculously undamaged.

Other correspondents in Japan during the first week of the occupation included William L. ("Atomic Bill") Laurence as well as William H. ("Political Bill") Lawrence, both of the *New York Times;* Harold P. ("Packrat") Smith, *Chicago Tribune;* William McGaffin, *Chicago Daily News;* Theodore H. White, *Time;* David Brown, Reuters; Thomas L. Shafer, Acme Newspictures; Richard W. Johnston, UP; Morris ("Morrie") Landsberg, AP; Howard Handleman, Julian Hartt, and Clark Lee, all of INS, and Robert Brumby, MBS, but formerly of INS. Lee and Brumby in Japan helped locate and capture a wanted German, Joseph Alfred Meisinger, known as "the Butcher of Warsaw" because of his cruelty to Jews and others in that city during the early period of the Nazi occupation.

Among correspondents active in Japan as the occupation began were Hugh Baillie, president of the United Press, and Frank L. Kluckhohn, *New York Times.* Both were successful in interviewing Emperor Hirohito through interpreters before the end of September. Baillie also interviewed General MacArthur and later, in China, he interviewed Generalissimo Chiang Kai-shek, again through an interpreter.

Others establishing themselves in Tokyo were Keith Wheeler, *Chicago Times,* sufficiently recovered from wounds received in Iwo Jima in February; K. Samiloff, Tass, released from a Japanese internment camp; Hal Boyle, AP, arriving from the United States after long service in Europe; Frank Bartholomew, UP vice-president and news executive; Hazel Hertzog, UP, first woman correspondent in postwar Japan; and Norman Soong, Central News Agency of China.

The correspondents present also included Murlin Spencer, Spencer Davis, Kenneth Dixon, Alva N. Dopking, Richard O'Malley and Hamilton Faron, all of AP, and Charles P. Gorry, AP Photos. Others were John R. Henry and Elgar Brown, INS; William F. Tyree, Ernest Hoberecht, Russell Annabel, Ralph Teatsorth, William B. Dickinson, Mac R. Johnson, Richard Harris, and Hugh Crumpler, all of UP; George E. ("First Wave") Jones, *New York Times;* Cornelius Ryan, *Daily Telegraph;* David Boguslav, *Chicago Sun;* Robert P. ("Pepper") Martin, *New York Post,* formerly of the UP and *Time/Life;* John M. Carlisle, *Detroit News;* Arthur S. Deter, *Collier's* and CBS; Sergeant Dale Kramer and George Burns, *Yank;* and Harry Brundidge, *Cosmopolitan* magazine.

The work of the correspondents centered in Tokyo after September 9, and censorship was directed from there. This was regarded as desirable and even necessary in Japan, even though the war was over. Censorship extended to the Japanese Domei news agency service, to Radio Tokyo and other radio stations, to all newspapers permitted to appear, and to Allied correspondents.

Those correspondents were so enmeshed in army red tape as the occupation began that the Domei agency was able to provide some news reports ahead of any other service, not only within Japan but by radio to the world. This brought protests from western newsmen and, since Domei also was taking some liberties, General MacArthur suspended it for eighteen hours on September 15. Later, he deprived it of monopoly privileges in Japan. The result was that Domei ceased to function on October 31. Supplanting it was the Kyodo Tsushin-sha, or Kyodo News Service (Kyodo), formed as a cooperative nonprofit general news agency owned by the reorganized Japanese press and, later, in company with the Japan Broadcasting Company. A second agency formed late in 1945 was Jiji Tsushin-sha, or Jiji Press, Ltd., (JP). It was owned by its own staff members and specialized in business, financial, and commercial information. These agencies, like the Japanese press itself, underwent changes in the months and years following.

One of the first major news stories out of Japan after the occupation began was the attempted suicide of General Hideki Tojo, premier since October 1941. Frank H. Bartholomew, UP, and Toichiro Takamatsu, *Mainichi,* were in the garden beside Tojo's suburban home on September 11 seeking an interview when Tojo fired a shot into his chest. They helped force a way into the house and into his study. Tojo was taken to a military hospital and recovered, but later was tried and convicted of war crimes and hanged in December 1948.

Some correspondents left Japan during September 1945. New arrivals included Russell Brines, AP, who reestablished that agency's bureau in Tokyo. Frank Tremaine arrived from Honolulu to do the same for the UP. Kenneth McCaleb, INS, set up that agency's bureau in Yoko-hama, pending the availability of suitable quarters in Tokyo.

Other arrivals were Donald Starr, *Chicago Tribune;* Robert Coch-rane, *Baltimore Sun;* and Robert Reuben, Reuters. Glenn Babb, foreign editor in New York but of long prior experience in China and Japan, came to Tokyo for the AP. Miles W. (Peg) Vaughn, former far eastern manager of UP returned in that same capacity. Robert Bellaire, bureau manager for the UP in Tokyo in December 1941, also returned as rep-resentative for *Collier's* and the American Broadcasting Company (ABC), as the former Blue Network was renamed in the summer of 1945. Frank Morris also arrived for *Collier's.* Bellaire was killed in a jeep accident in Tokyo late in September, only a week after his arrival. Mor-ris, riding with him, was injured.

Correspondents established a Tokyo Correspondents' Club on Oc-tober 15, 1945, to represent the group in its relations with SCAP, General MacArthur's headquarters. Such an organization was needed to speak for the newsmen on matters of censorship, which was heavy on outgoing dispatches and a subject of frequent complaint, on billeting, food supplies, medical care, transportation, and other essentials. The need for the Correspondents' Club was further indicated by an an-nouncement from SCAP on October 12 calling for a sharp reduction in the number of correspondents in Japan. An official listing then showed 102 Allied correspondents in Tokyo, including 75 for U.S. media. Brig-adier General LeGrande A. Diller, chief public relations officer for General MacArthur, ruled that this total should be reduced to 76, in-cluding 49 U.S. representatives.

Because of protests from the United States as well as from the Tokyo Correspondents' Club, General MacArthur rescinded Diller's order be-fore its effective date. He did approve an alternative arrangement on October 25, however, disaccrediting all correspondents attached to the armed forces. Since there no longer was a war in progress, there were no longer "war correspondents," it was reasoned. Those correspondents in Japan were to revert to civilian status on that date, get out of uniform, and shift for themselves in matters of billets and rations. Their media would have to pay the costs of moving them about or returning them home, even though they still would be dependent on military transport, and would be subject to travel priorities. Those remaining in Japan would require passports and special military permits.

Although some allowances were made, almost of necessity, in matters of rations, this change, along with the end of the picture pool in the Pacific on November 7, concluded the official war period for news re-porting in the Pacific and in Asia. Since the end of the war in Europe had come several months before, the same general conversion already had taken place there, or was in the process. Just as news coverage was being resumed in Japan, so it was being resumed in China and elsewhere in the world. Archibald T. Steele, long experienced in China, returned there to represent the *New York Herald Tribune*. F. Tillman Durdin, *New York Times*, returned to Shanghai, and Richard J. H. Johnston, also of the *Times*, entered Korea with U.S. occupation troops.

Thus the end of World War II and the reporting of the conflict set the stage throughout the world, especially so in those areas where the fighting had raged most violently, for the reporting of the aftermath of the war and the events transpiring in the middle years of the century.

Coverage of World War II:
A Recapitulation

20

Having begun in 1931 when Japan attacked Manchuria, World War II had been in progress for fourteen years when the last shot was fired in 1945. More than 60 nations ultimately were engaged as combatants and more than 75 million persons were in uniform, including large contingents of women. Battle deaths exceeded 15 million, with 25 million or more wounded and missing, and another 10 million more dead from other causes. Beyond that, scores of millions of civilians were killed during military operations, were deliberately put to death, maimed or wounded, made homeless and penniless, or stateless. The costs of the war were estimated to be more than a trillion dollars, plus property damage exceeding $230 billion. By any standard, it was the biggest and most tragic war in the history of the world.

It was a war reported by more men and women representing more media of information than any other, and one that had available more technical aids for coverage and communication. The number of correspondents never has been tallied, but certainly totalled several thousands for Allied, Axis, and neutral countries, including combat correspondents with Japanese, German, Soviet, and U.S. fighting units.

With so many countries involved in the war, international reports during the 1931–45 period tended to be concerned very largely with the events and issues of the conflict, even though not all correspondents were on the war fronts. Numerous as that group was, more news personnel retained civilian status and went about their more routine tasks, some in cities under attack but most inevitably in cities and capitals far removed from centers of conflict.

Apart from stringer correspondents and clerical personnel, it has been estimated that the U.S. press-radio organization of the mid-1930s had about 300 staff correspondents outside the boundaries of the country. This was a considerable advance over any previous total, and during the war the number grew to exceed 2,600. Of these, U.S. War Department listings indicate that 1,800 were accredited to the army and 800 to the navy. In addition, there were other U.S. media correspondents abroad not seeking military accreditation. The total of 2,600 were not all engaged at the same time, and one estimate indicates that no more than 800 were active in the theaters of war at any one period.

In Europe during 1944–45, SHAEF accredited 1,338 correspondents. These included British, French, U.S. and some neutral representatives. Something less than 1,000 ever were with fighting units in France and far fewer even than that at any one time. The total in the South Pacific, Central Pacific, and CBI theaters was smaller than that in the North African and European theaters, and the number in Soviet Russia was relatively small.

Because the United States had three news agencies, three radio networks, and several periodicals—all active in reporting the war—in addition to about ten daily newspapers with foreign coverage, it was not surprising that there were more U.S. correspondents covering the war than for any other country. Even so, the media of the United Kingdom and of the British Commonwealth were extensively represented. So also was Nazi Germany within its own areas of action, as were the media of Italy, Japan, and the Soviet Union, all within the same limitations. Such neutral countries as Switzerland and Sweden were represented modestly, but France was forced by the Nazi occupation to restrict its coverage, along with Norway, Denmark, the Netherlands, Belgium, and Finland.

As the war years began, the correspondent group included men who had reported World War I, and wars before that, plus many who had become active during the 1920s and 1930s. A considerable number of these men continued in service through 1945, although some turned their experience to account in governmental positions, usually relating to the information process. Some entered the armed forces, and others assumed executive roles with the media. The need for more personnel to cover the wide-ranging events of the times and to provide for the increased requirements of periodicals and radio brought scores into international reporting. They included more women than ever had been in that field before.

The printed media in most countries had been dependent for paper before the war largely or entirely upon imports—chiefly from Canada, Newfoundland, Finland, Norway, and Sweden. This traffic was halted in some cases by the events of the war. Where it was not halted, it usually was sharply reduced by a compelling need on the part of the nations at war to use available shipping space and available foreign exchange credits for munitions, military equipment, and essential foodstuffs. There was also a considerable conversion of cellulose, the basic woody substance from which newsprint and other paper is made, to the manufacture of explosives. In these circumstances, it was necessary to distribute the limited supplies of newsprint under a government-administered rationing system in most countries. This had the effect of reducing the permissible size or the possible size of newspapers and periodicals and the total number of copies that could be printed. Some governments used the rationing system to control the press and, under war conditions, newsprint distribution was difficult in some countries.

The number of newspapers was reduced as a result of paper shortages in wartime Germany and Japan and in Axis-occupied countries. The size and circulations were restricted in Soviet Russia and other lands. Neutral countries were no less affected than others, and even those in Latin America were obliged to ration their newsprint imports.

The British press, vigorous as it had been, was seriously affected. With a vast amount of vital information to convey, the papers lacked the space to do it full justice. Neither was there space to present advertising messages in anything like normal volume. Because they were smaller in size, the publications required less manpower to produce them, mechanically as well as editorially. Manpower was diverted to other wartime purposes, and those remaining active in the press organization were forced to cope on some occasions with bomb damage to buildings and equipment. Repairs and part replacements also were difficult in a time when men and supplies for such purposes were limited.

British correspondents, reporters, and editors learned to accommodate themselves to wartime editorial limitations by making better use of available news space. The size of body type and headlines was reduced to permit the use of more text on a page, and some material was rewritten in condensed form or omitted entirely. The white space in the "gutters," or center margins, was utilized for publication of such things as radio logs. Reporters learned to write with greater economy of words, and some professed to believe that the enforced brevity of style actually was beneficial.

The press in the United States had relatively undiminished supplies of newsprint available from domestic mills and from Canada and Newfoundland, and newspapers and magazines were little affected by limitations on space. Correspondents, reporters, and editors were concerned, however, with finding the means to make the vast flow of information comprehensible. They also had to compensate so far as possible for the real or imaginary effect of wartime censorships and propaganda campaigns.

Press practice in the United States had been modified in the 1930s by the acceptance of factual interpretation as a legitimate style of news writing. The virtues of objectivity were preserved in the presentation of background news. The editorial columnist, syndicated or not, came into being during this same period. Added devices used for news presentation through the war years included the "undated lead" in which two or more reports, usually from news agencies, were drawn together and rewritten to provide a more comprehensive and unified account, the "sidebar," a story presented adjacent to a major account to provide background or personality references or colorful aspects relating to the major subject, and "boxed" background material, for quick reference.

Casualties Among Correspondents

The correspondents in World War II faced greater personal risks than their predecessors in earlier wars. Because of air and submarine attacks, they could not escape danger even in places removed from what might technically be described as the war fronts. So long as they were with the men and ships and planes engaged in the fighting, they were in equal peril.

Archibald Forbes, a noted correspondent for the London *Daily News* in wars of the nineteenth century and a former soldier, observed that "the war correspondent may as well stay at home with his mother unless he has hardened his heart to take his full share of the risks of the battlefield." Yet Forbes would have been quick to agree that it is part of the war correspondent's job to stay alive, since dead or wounded he could produce no reports.

In speaking to this point, Joe James Custer, UP, who lost an eye while with the U.S. Navy during the Guadalcanal landings on August 1942, suggested that if the correspondent was in fact to stay alive he also needed to be toughened to endure hardships and to meet the physical demands upon him somewhat as the soldiers and sailors were prepared in their weeks of basic training. As it was, Custer commented, correspondents tended to train on "beer and cigarettes," and usually were in poor condition to cope with combat situations. Nearly every correspondent in the Southwest Pacific, he said, "has had malaria, dysentery and feet and leg sores. . . . It's a hard physical grind, working 24 hours a day, with a nap only now and then." He recommended "courses like the Marines get to toughen up . . . to learn hand-to-hand combat and the tricks of war. A correspondent is a non-combatant, but if he's surrounded by the enemy . . . he'll be a dead duck."

The same could have been said of correspondents in North Africa, Sicily, and Italy. Enough was learned there to result in some training being given to a few correspondents in England prior to the invasion of Normandy in June 1944. It was not marine training, but it was intended to help them survive.

Casualties among correspondents became of special concern in 1943–44 as they rose somewhat in proportion to the pace of military action, both in the European and Pacific theaters. Although precise totals were not available at the time, one estimate for the period from September 1939 to the spring of 1943 cited a casualty rate of 15 to 20 percent among U.S. correspondents in Europe, as contrasted to 5 percent among members of the U.S. armed forces since December 1941.

A survey by *World's Press News* of London completed in March 1943 counted 23 British, British Commonwealth, and U.S. correspondents killed up to that time, with seven more reported missing, many wounded, and others captured and interned. Some of those already had been repatriated, but nine were held as prisoners of war. Of the 23 killed, 12 were named by *Editor & Publisher* of New York as U.S. correspondents, with 3 more listed as missing, 60 as wounded or otherwise injured, 19 as captured and still held, 7 others as captured and released, 10 interned and still held, 40 others repatriated after internment, and 50 hospitalized abroad as ill.

The U.S. Office of War Information produced a report soon after in April 1943 stating that more than 600 U.S. correspondents had been accredited to military theaters since Pearl Harbor, with 400 on active war fronts. *Editor & Publisher* amended that in May by holding that 475 to 500 press-radio-photo representatives for U.S. media had been covering the war on all fronts since 1939.

For whatever value it may have had, the *New York Times* carried life and accident insurance policies for its correspondents. The policies did not cover them if death or injury occurred while they were on flights over enemy territory. If it were known in advance that such a flight was to be made, special coverage could be obtained at an added premium cost of $1,250. Lloyd's of London offered life insurance to cover correspondents assigned to the invasion forces being organized to move into France in 1944, so William H. Stoneman of the *Chicago Daily News* reported. The actuarial estimate was that a correspondent accompanying a second-wave assault had better than 97 chances in 100 to return alive, Stoneman learned, and Lloyd's was quoting a rate of £15 (about $60) for £500 ($2,000) of insurance, good for six months. A schedule of payments also was offered for various injuries. So far as known, these offerings were ignored by the media.

Whether because of the emphasis early in 1943 on the high casualty rate among correspondents or for other reasons, U.S. Admiral Halsey, commander-in-chief in the South Pacific, ordered that civilians in that area be denied air transport, with only rare exceptions. This required that correspondents, classified as civilians, use means of transport other than by air. General MacArthur issued a comparable order applying to correspondents accredited to army ground forces in his command.

These rulings were put almost immediately to a test by correspondents who had been accustomed to flying as an essential to coverage of the news. Three of the most experienced, Vern Haugland, AP, Harold Guard, UP, and Lee Van Atta, INS, made a flight over Lae and Salamaua in the New Guinea area. Under the new rulings, they were disciplined by an order of expulsion. This was protested in an appeal to Admiral Nimitz at Pearl Harbor, commander-in-chief of all naval forces in the Pacific. He rescinded the Halsey order, which also placed the MacArthur order in question. Nimitz also assigned naval Lieutenant Frank Rounds, formerly of the *United States News,* to facilitate air transport in the Pacific for correspondents and photographers, of whom sixty-eight were even then working out of Honolulu.

During the war, the work of correspondents was praised by military and civilian leaders in all belligerent countries. United States correspondents wounded in the course of their work were awarded the Purple Heart, and some received other decorations for gallantry. In a related form of recognition, British correspondents were "mentioned" or "cited in dispatches." It was announced in Washington in the autumn of 1943 that each U.S. correspondent killed up to that time was to be commemorated by having a Liberty Ship carry his name. Webb Miller of the UP was the first to be so recognized.

When the war was over, theater ribbons were awarded in 1946 to 519 U.S. correspondents by the War Department. Thirty-six correspondents also received decorations at that time, including the Silver Star, Bronze Star, Air Medal, and special commendations. A new Medal of Freedom was bestowed upon a score of correspondents by General Eisenhower in a ceremony at the National Press Club in Washington in November 1947.

A new count in 1948 indicated that 49 U.S. and 18 British newsmen had lost their lives while reporting the war from 1939–45. Many others were wounded. But these figures did not include correspondents of both countries killed or wounded in war coverage between 1931–39 in China, Ethiopia, and Spain.

Figures released by SHAEF in June 1945 indicated a casualty rate of 4 to 5 percent among Allied correspondents covering the European campaign from Normandy to Germany in 1944–45, compared to 19 percent among the Allied fighting forces. This was almost a precise reversal of the estimate previously cited for the 1941–43 period, which was a 15 to 20 percent correspondents' casualty rate, as against 5 percent for U.S. forces.

A memorial to U.S. correspondents who died during the war was unveiled at the Pentagon in Washington in September 1948. The memorial arch designed and constructed in 1896 by George Alfred Townsend on the Antietam National Battlefield site in Maryland to commemorate 151 Civil War correspondents was rededicated in October 1946, with the names of World War II and Spanish-American War correspondents added. The Overseas Press Club of America, formed in 1939, also honored those U.S. correspondents who lost their lives in World War II when the club dedicated its new home in New York City in 1955.

Facts and figures are not available, but it is known that there were heavy casualties among Soviet media representatives with the Red Army in 1941–45. Figures for Axis media casualties also are lacking, but they were at least as numerous as for the Allies. Decorations also went to correspondents of other countries, Allied, Axis, and neutral, and memorials were erected and tributes paid both during and after the war.

Whether with reference to casualties or more particularly to describing and evaluating the work of correspondents during the war, the years since have produced a spate of books by correspondents themselves and by others. Of those taking the broad view of the wars of the 1931–45 period, three are outstanding. These are *The First Casualty* (1975) by Australian-born Philip Knightley, *Foreign Correspondence* (1964) by John Hohenberg, and *Reporting the Wars* (1957) by Joseph J. Mathews. Both of the latter authors are university professors. A fourth book of value is *They Were There* (1944), edited by Curt Riess.

The United Nations

Just as during the Great War of 1914–18, hopes grew during World War II that repetition of a third such disaster might be avoided through the formation of a permanent supra-national organization providing for the peaceable settlement of differences between peoples. Obviously, it would need to be more effective than the League of Nations had been.

In their meetings of August 1941 aboard ship off the Newfoundland coast, Prime Minister Churchill and President Roosevelt had drafted what became known as the "Atlantic Charter" stating principles and policies looking toward a better postwar world. The fifth of eight points expressed a desire for "the fullest collaboration between all nations" and the last added the belief that "all of the nations of the world, for realistic as well as spiritual reasons, must come to the abandonment of the use of force."

With twenty-six nations in alliance against the Axis on January 1, 1942, a "United Nations Declaration" was signed at Washington on that day by representatives of all those nations. The term "United Nations" had been suggested originally by President Roosevelt. A United Nations conference on food and agriculture met at Hot Springs, Virginia, during May and June 1943 and established a Food and Agriculture Organization (FAO) of the United Nations. It proposed to assume the functions of the International Institute of Agriculture, an advisory and informational agency formed in 1905 by fifty-five nations and based in Rome. In 1924 that agency had gained a relationship to the League of Nations.

A conference of foreign ministers in Moscow in October 1943 produced a Moscow Declaration. Signed by representatives of the USSR, the U.S., Great Britain, and China, it recognized "the necessity of establishing at the earliest practicable date a general international organization, based on the principle of the sovereign equality of all peace-loving states, and open to membership by all such states, large and small, for the maintenance of international peace and security."

In the month following, a United Nations Relief and Rehabilitation Administration (UNRRA) was formed by forty-four nations in Washington. Its purpose was to assist persons in war-devastated areas of Europe and Asia in need of care and rehabilitation. That need already was urgent and the member nations contributed $4 billion between March 1944 and December 1945, plus food and supplies. Most of this aid was provided by the United States.

The firm establishment of the United Nations Organization began at the Bretton Woods Conference in New Hampshire in July 1944. There a United Nations Monetary and Financial Conference was attended by the representatives of forty-four nations. Even more important was the August to October Dumbarton Oaks Conference near Washington, D.C. The Bretton Woods meeting established an International Monetary Fund (IMF) of $8.8 billion, 25 percent contributed by the United States government, to be used to stabilize national currencies and to advance world trade in the postwar period. It also set up an International Bank for Reconstruction and Development, with a capitalization of $9.1 billion, of which about 35 percent was to come from the United States, to extend loans to nations requiring rehabilitation. The Dumbarton Oaks Conference was attended only by representatives of the United States, Great Britain, the Soviet Union, and China. They discussed plans for that permanent postwar international organization proposed both in the Atlantic Charter and the Moscow Declaration.

The result was a "Dumbarton Oaks Plan" to be submitted as a basis for discussion at a United Nations Conference on International Organization, scheduled for San Francisco in April 1945.

The San Francisco Conference was agreed upon at the Yalta Conference of February 1945. Its objective was to draft a charter for the United Nations. A Committee of Jurists representing forty-four nations meeting in Washington in April prepared a draft statute for an International Court of Justice. This carried forward the concept of the Permanent Court of International Arbitration existing at The Hague since 1899, and more specifically the functions of the League-sponsored Permanent Court of International Justice, sometimes referred to as the "World Court," also at The Hague from 1922 until it became a victim of the war.

A United Nations Association was formed following the Dumbarton Oaks Conference of August to October 1944. With representatives and offices in the major Allied countries, which were prospective members of the United Nations (UN), the association publicized the concept of the organization and sponsored further discussion among those interested in international affairs. Out of this came further proposals and amendments to the Dumbarton Oaks Plan for consideration at San Francisco.

The United Nations Conference on International Organization (UNCIO) met in San Francisco from April 25 to June 25, 1945, to draft and approve a charter to make the United Nations organization a reality. It brought together representatives of fifty governments with their considerable delegations. It also brought to San Francisco from many countries some 2,636 accredited correspondents for news agencies, newspapers, magazines, and radio, with photographers and motion picture cameramen included in the total. Although this was the most thoroughly covered conference in history, with the greatest concentration of media representatives, it was undoubtedly the most *over*-covered conference or event. Even so, some correspondents were denied accreditation.

The conferences at Bretton Woods and Dumbarton Oaks had not been hospitable to the media. For the San Francisco Conference, however, Edward J. Stettinius, Jr., U.S. secretary of state and general chairman, announced an open-door policy. The conference, he said, would "be conducted with the greatest possible consideration for the widespread interest of the world in its deliberations. Plenary meetings and meetings of the principal commissions of the conference will be open to press and radio news correspondents and photographers and, insofar as facilities permit, to the general public."

For a number of weeks before the conference opened, three members of the U.S. Department of State's information staff were in San Francisco making preparations for the press-radio coverage. They were Lincoln White, William D. Wright, and Lyle Schmitter. The Palace Hotel was made the headquarters for the newsmen. Working space and assistance for them was to be provided at the War Memorial Opera House, where the main sessions of the conference were to take place. The San Francisco Press Club also invited visiting newsmen to use the club as a center and to take advantage of added work facilities made available there. Despite all these preparations, there were some failures in the smooth operation due in part to the presence of so many correspondents, who outnumbered the delegates six to one.

Two special trains brought about 400 correspondents across the country from New York and Washington. Others contended with the difficulties of wartime transportation and arrived by regular trains and planes and even by ship. The Washington press corps and the New York newspapers and those news agencies and radio networks based there were heavily represented, while many other U.S. newspapers, periodicals, and the Office of War Information added to the total. There were press and radio representatives from the United Kingdom, France, the U.S.S.R., China, Canada, Australia, New Zealand, India, South Africa, Turkey, Greece, the Philippines, Egypt, Poland, Czechoslovakia, Holland, Belgium, countries of the Middle East and Latin America, Switzerland, Sweden, and Spain, and from others as well.

The British delegation was headed by Foreign Secretary Anthony Eden and proved extremely helpful to correspondents. Francis Williams, public information officer of the Ministry of Information and a former editor of the *Daily Herald,* was highly cooperative and had a staff of about ten assistants who made themselves available to the media. Eden held a useful news conference on May 9.

For the United States, Michael J. McDermott, an experienced press officer of the Department of State, with Lincoln White and other assistants, provided background information, and Secretary Stettinius conducted news conferences.

Foreign Commissar Vyacheslav M. Molotov led the Soviet delegation and after an early reluctance became helpful. Establishing a precedent for Soviet officials in such circumstances, Molotov held three news conferences, each more satisfactory than the previous one, so far as news results were concerned.

The vast number of correspondents present sent out some six million words of copy by telegraph during the two months of the conference, and more was sent by airmail. Other millions of words were broadcast. During the first three weeks, the average volume dispatched by wire was 190,000 words daily, with the high point April 26, the day of Molotov's first conference, when 266,500 words were moved. The daily average tapered to about 60,000 words toward the end, when the cream of the news had been skimmed and many correspondents had departed.

Of the more than 2,600 accredited correspondents, one estimate was that perhaps 200 were qualified by experience and background to cover a conference of that sort. Many others were there because it seemed the place to be. Among them were some Hollywood and nightclub columnists. One of their number, Earl Wilson, a syndicated columnist for the *New York Post,* infuriated serious correspondents at Molotov's first news conference when he asked the Soviet foreign commissar how to pronounce "vodka," and asked whether it could be consumed without fear of internal injury. Molotov was so irritated by the frivolous question that he broke off the conference.

With little solid news to report on most days, the tendency was for correspondents to write sidebar stories on the personalities of conference delegates and to reach otherwise into the bottom of the barrel for subjects. The conference was of obvious importance, however, and among the multitude of correspondents were many of the best.

Apart from the regular communications channels open to the media representatives, the U.S. Office of War Information was prepared to carry the news of the meetings to the world. It used the radio facilities of the Voice of America and had its own staff of fourteen news, radio, film, and language specialists on hand from New York and Washington, and fourteen from the San Francisco office. Heading this group was Arthur Sweetser, deputy director of the domestic branch of the OWI and former head of the Information Section of the League of Nations.

Some of the senior correspondents found the San Francisco gathering reminiscent of League sessions, not only because of Sweetser's presence, but because of the general gathering of government leaders, some of whom had been at the Geneva meetings, and because of the presence of other correspondents who also had been at Geneva. Among these were Clarence Streit, formerly of the *New York Times* but in San Francisco for the *St. Louis Star-Times,* and Edwin L. James, managing editor of the *New York Times,* but formerly at posts in Paris and London and often in Geneva. Others were Wilbur Forrest, assistant to the publisher of the *New York Herald Tribune* but former Paris correspondent and an attendant at Geneva meetings, and Erwin D. Canham, executive editor of the *Christian Science Monitor* who had covered Geneva for that paper. Also in San Francisco were André Géraud (Pertinax) and Geneviève Tabouis, two noted French journalists, and Alvarez Del Vayo, a Spanish journalist, all of whom were familiar figures in prewar Geneva, as were two Hungarian caricaturists, Alois Derso and Emery Kelen.

Among many other respected correspondents for the U.S. media at San Francisco were Walter Lippmann, public affairs columnist for the

New York Herald Tribune and its syndicate; Bert Andrews, Joseph Barnes, George Fielding Eliot, and Archibald T. Steele, all of that same paper. In addition to James, the *New York Times* was represented by Arthur Krock, Anne O'Hare McCormick, James B. Reston, and John Crider. Walter Duranty, formerly in Moscow for the *Times,* was writing for the North American Newspaper Alliance. David Lawrence, of long experience in Washington, was writing a syndicated column. William Philip Simms, equally experienced, was writing for the Scripps-Howard Newspaper Alliance. Edgar Ansel Mowrer wrote for the *Chicago Daily News,* as he had for years past; Roscoe Drummond, Carlyle Morgan and Neal Stanford, wrote for the *Christian Science Monitor;* and Charles G. Ross, long Washington correspondent for the *St. Louis Post-Dispatch,* was just then named press secretary to President Truman.

Those at San Francisco included Thomas L. Stokes, Washington columnist for the United Feature Syndicate; Peter Edson, NEA; Demaree Bess, *Saturday Evening Post;* and George Creel, *Collier's,* who had headed the U.S. Committee on Public Information during World War I. Still others were Bruce Bliven, editor, *New Republic;* Alexander Uhl and I. F. Stone, *PM;* Mark Foote, Booth Newspapers of Michigan; Robert Elson, Washington bureau chief, Max Ways, Anatole Visson, and Sidney James, all for *Time* magazine; and E. B. White, the *New Yorker.*

Some who were returned from battle areas were Royal Arch Gunnison, Mutual Broadcasting System; Ray Henle, American Broadcasting Company; Carleton (Bill) Kent, *Chicago Times;* and Melvin K. Whiteleather, AP, and Carl W. McCardle, *Philadelphia Bulletin.* Present were Alexander Kendrick, *Philadelphia Inquirer;* Ludwell Denny, Scripps-Howard Newspapers; Blair Moody and Jay Hayden, *Detroit News;* Paul W. Ward and John W. Owens *Baltimore Sun;* Tom Reynolds, *Chicago Sun;* T. C. Alford, *Kansas City Star;* Barnet Nover, *Washington Post;* Sylvia Porter, *New York Post;* Paul Mallon, King Features Syndicate; and a host of other special correspondents.

The Associated Press had about twenty at the conference jointly directed by Paul Miller, head of the Washington staff, by Harold Turnblad, Western Division news editor stationed in San Francisco, and by T. M. Metzger, in charge of getting the news to the rest of the world. The staff included John Hightower, diplomatic news editor, and Jack Bell, political news editor, both of the Washington staff; John F. Chester, John A. Parris, Jr., Henry Cassidy, Joseph E. Dynan, and Charles H. Guptill, all with extensive foreign experience; Douglas Cornell, White House correspondent who had gone to Yalta with President Roosevelt, and others, including AP photographers, with Joe Rosenthal of Iwo Jima fame among them.

The United Press staff was directed by Lyle C. Wilson, chief of the Washington bureau, and included Frank H. Bartholomew, Western and Pacific news director, R. H. Shackford, Ralph E. Heinzen, Robert C. Miller, Harrison E. Salisbury, Russell Turner, Carroll Kenworthy, Sandor S. Klein, William H. Lander, John L. Cutter, James C. Austin, Robert L. Frey, and others, many with broad foreign experience.

The International News Service staff was headed by William K. Hutchinson, chief of the Washington bureau, assisted by John D. (Jack) Hanley, Pacific Coast manager, and included Leon Pearson, Pierre Loving, Robert Considine, Inez Robb, William Theis, Arthur Hermann, and others. With all of the correspondents mentioned above, it is not surprising that the U.S. media representation at San Francisco was the largest.

The British media were represented by forty-three correspondents, including a considerable group from the BBC. The press delegation was headed by Francis (Frank) Williams of the Ministry of Information, Charles Henry Campbell and Archibald Mackenzie, the first and second secretaries in the British embassy in Washington, and Jack Winicour, director of the British Information Service (BIS) office, also in Washington. Correspondents included Paul Scott Rankine, Reuters; Frank Oliver, the *Times;* Robert Waithman, *News-Chronicle;* Denys Smith, *Daily Telegraph;* Arthur Webb, *Daily Herald;* Guy Austin, *Daily Express;* and Clifford Hulme, *Daily Sketch.*

For the Soviet Union, F. R. Orekhov, press attaché in the USSR embassy in Washington, brought seven correspondents for Tass and *Pravda.* Among correspondents representing other countries there were Werner Imhoff, *Neue Zürcher Zeitung* (Zurich); Robert de Saint Jean, Agence France-Presse; H. A. McClure-Smith, *Sydney Morning Herald;* L. Fumasoni Bondi, *Il Globo* (Rome); B. Shiva Rao, *Hindu* (Madras); Ahmet Emin Yalman, *Vatan* (Istanbul); T. C. Wang, Central News Agency (Chungking); and Wang Tien-shin, *Sao Tang Daily News* (Chungking).

All of these correspondents reported the discussions and negotiations leading to the drafting of the Charter of the United Nations. This document, completed during the weeks in San Francisco, was printed by the University of California Press in Berkeley, across the bay from San Francisco. Using a new type face specially designed by Frederic William Goudy, it was produced in English, French, Russian, Chinese, and Spanish, and in 188 pages. Although done under pressure of time, it was a flawless example of typography, doing credit to master printer A. R. (Tommy) Tommasini, superintendent of the press, and his talented staff. Signed at the Memorial Opera House on June 25, 1945, its later ratification brought the United Nations into existence with fifty member nations. The first General Assembly meeting was in London in January 1946.

With so large a body of correspondents reporting World War II, it should have been covered thoroughly and well. Most commentators, while aware of flaws, seem to have regarded it as the most accurately and fully reported war in history. Faced with danger, sometimes ill-prepared to meet hardships or to grasp the full meaning of events and circumstances, frequently handicapped by censorship as well as by transportation and communications difficulties, and operating against propaganda campaigns, correspondents acquitted themselves extremely well.

General Omar Bradley of the U.S. Army spoke of their efforts in "hammering out on tired typewriters in the ruins of buildings throughout the world" those reports that gave to the people "a knowledge of where we were, what we were doing, and why we were doing it."

Mrs. Anne O'Hare McCormick, *New York Times,* already a Pulitzer Prize winner, upon returning from Europe and the Middle East early in 1945, described the correspondent's lot as one of "working long hours under maddening professional difficulties and a great deal of personal discomfort."

Hal Boyle, AP, also a Pulitzer Prize winner, took a somewhat lighter view of the difficulties. He called war reporting "the simplest job in journalism. All you need is a strong stomach, a weak mind, and plenty of endurance." Later, he added that it was no harder than police reporting, the only difference being that "you're a little closer to the bullets."

Robert Capa, *Life* photographer, who had seen battle at close quarters since the days of the Spanish Civil War, said in 1944 that "the tremendous toil and sweat being expended in the Italian campaign by correspondents and photographers, as well as the armed forces, is not sufficiently appreciated at home."

Most references to the work of the correspondents and to the general coverage were favorable and even flattering, but there were minority expressions. At the beginning of the European war an almost psychopathic concern developed in the United States. It stemmed from the literature of the 1920s and 1930s debunking events of World War I. People feared being misled by propaganda relating pro or con to the countries engaged in the conflict. Then as the war continued, there were objections to the censorship. There also were recurring criticisms of the manner in which the war news was presented, touching upon such points as the use of clichés, emphasis on personal experiences rather than issues or facts, and a softening of adverse aspects of the news, leading to a complacency about the war.

Fletcher Pratt, a writer on military subjects, took the extreme view that "instead of being the best reported war in history, it was very nearly the worst reported." Most Americans, he said, remained ignorant "of the larger issues of the war, of the way it was fought, of what actually happened both on the home and the military fronts." Robert S. Allen, former Washington correspondent and columnist, who became a colonel on General Patton's staff and who lost an arm, called the coverage "stupid," principally because "most of the correspondents were scarcely more than police reporters" and were either "lazy or ignorant."

After the war was over, Henry L. Mencken, *Baltimore Sun* staff member and perennial iconoclast, called the correspondents "a sorry lot." They were, he said, "either typewriter statesmen turning out dope stuff drearily dreamed up, or sentimental human-interest scribblers turning out maudlin stuff about the common soldier, easy to get by the censors. Ernie Pyle was a good example. He did well what he set out to do, but that couldn't be called factual reporting of the war. . . . Any honest effort to get the real news went out the window with the arrival of voluntary censorship. . . . The papers fell over themselves thinking up schemes for hobbling themselves that the military hadn't thought of." Mencken advanced the opinion that "the historian will find very little that is useful" in the news reports of the war, most of which he dismissed as "feature stuff."

Such views as those expressed by Pratt, Allen, and Mencken, and perhaps relating particularly to the work of U.S. correspondents, were ungenerous. Also, they ignored the remarkable work of news photographers and motion picture cameramen, and the effective contributions of certain radio correspondents.

It was true, as General Bradley said in a 1946 Overseas Press Club dinner meeting in Washington, that no correspondent could have seen the whole picture "clearly and unmistakably" because "that would have been impossible in as broad a panorama as war, even if there were no question of military security." But, he added, "all of you saw parts of it, vital parts that you reported with truth and accuracy." It was by constructing a mental mosaic of those parts that thoughtful persons were able to gain a reasonable understanding of the war when it was in progress. Similarly, historians, with access to documents and other source materials supplementing the news reports, are in a position to portray the war in three dimensions.

The portrayal of the war by British correspondents was applauded by Brenden Bracken, wartime minister of information. They also are favorably presented by Philip Knightley, a postwar member of the London *Sunday Times,* in *The First Casualty* (1975). His book devotes chapters to the coverage of the wars in Asia, Africa, and Europe from the 1930s to 1945 in a fair and balanced account of both praise and blame.

Knightley points out that correspondents were in no position to challenge the official version of events because they were "totally dependent upon the military to see the war at all." The Normandy landing, as he sees it, was so vast an operation that it overwhelmed most correspondents and radio may have done best because it could give the story almost unlimited time. Correspondents tended to become involved in military affairs, he believes, with some favored by commanding generals and chiefs of staff, and so contributing to public opinion figuring in "the generals' own power struggle." As in World War I, military successes were exaggerated to boost national pride, and setbacks were minimized to maintain morale.

In summarizing, Knightley quotes Charles Lynch, a Canadian-born correspondent for Reuters. Speaking thirty years later, Lynch called it "humiliating to look back at what we wrote during the war. . . . We were a propaganda arm of our governments. At the start the censors enforced that, but by the end we were our own censors. We were cheerleaders. I suppose there wasn't an alternative at the time. It was total war. But, for God's sake, let's not glorify our role. It wasn't good journalism. It wasn't journalism at all."[1]

Whatever criticism may be directed at news coverage during World War II, the system in vogue afforded correspondents more opportunity to display individual initiative than did the system in general effect during World War I. It must be said that the World War II system of gathering war news also seemed to result in more deaths and injuries among correspondents. Yet these were not always the result of the system. Apart from the many jeep accidents, most of the wounds and fatalities were attributed to airplane disasters and to bombings or torpedoings that could not be avoided if correspondents were in action at all, with or without military escorts.

The opportunities correspondents had to see the war resulted in numerous eye-witness accounts personalized at times to a point that Mencken seemed to find objectionable, and sometimes they contained more than factual interpretation. Yet the restrictions were such as to prevent the appearance of as many colorful reports as might have been expected in a war spreading over so much of the world—a war marked

---

1 Philip Knightley, *The First Casualty* (New York, 1975), p. 330.

by numberless dramatic events in which correspondents often participated.

During the course of World War II and thereafter, correspondents sometimes made their personal views and observations known by writing books or taking to the lecture platform. Aside, perhaps, from some radio correspondents, they had limited opportunity to do so through the media they served. Even then, their reward might be dismissal, as with G. E. R. Gedye and Douglas Reed, who wrote of Anglo-German relations in the Munich period.

The system of coverage meant that a high percentage of the first accounts to appear in print describing events or actions were prepared almost by necessity at headquarters or division points. They were put together by writers, far removed from the scene of the event, on the basis of communiqués, briefings, and possibly messages from correspondents in advanced positions.

Correspondents in those positions, however, did prepare substantial reports based on direct observation and knowledge. Many were used in the newspaper press, in magazines, and in radio reports. They were supported by photographs and motion picture films, whether as newsreels or in other forms. Because of delays in the transmission or delivery of some such matter from combat areas and from ships at sea, and sometimes because of added censorship delays, an account might not reach its intended audience before public attention had shifted to some later development, but even then most of these reports became available eventually.

The accreditation and field censorship system, the "voluntary" censorship regulations drafted with media cooperation, and the later censorship reviews gave correspondents and editors a thorough indoctrination in the concept of military security, which was more useful during wartime than Mencken allows. It was a lesson well learned over the years and one not easily set aside after the war by newsmen themselves, much less by military and government leaders.

Another wartime change related to the official use of radio in particular, while not excluding other methods to convey information, ideas, and impressions. Governments had begun to engage in the purposeful dissemination of news and ideas by such means in the 1930s, and the war years brought a growing use of such methods. This form of propaganda evolved into what became known as "psychological warfare" in its application by the military, but it was used also by civilian governments in a political context. The trend was difficult to reverse after the war and became an element in what was referred to as "the battle for the minds of men."

With the war at an end, some correspondents and other media personnel sought to maintain something of the spirit of comradeship that had developed during the critical war years. So far as these efforts prospered, they tended to do so through such existing groups as the National Press Club and the Overseas Writer's Club, both in Washington, D.C.; the Foreign Press Association and the Overseas Press Club of America, both in New York; Sigma Delta Chi, professional journalism society, with chapters throughout the United States; the Press Club, London; the Anglo-American Press Association, Paris; and other comparable organizations, old and new. These were supplemented later by such groups as the International Press Institute of Zurich and London.

Many of the correspondents of the war years remained with their newspapers, agencies, magazines, syndicates, and radio networks. They often continued reporting foreign affairs, sometimes from abroad as they had before the conflict. Others accepted assignments at home, moved to new posts, or became media executives. Still others became engaged in government information agencies, university teaching, and corporate or institutional public relations.

In midcentury, these correspondents of broad experience were joined by a new generation. The new medium of television was to make an impact upon the process of information gathering and to play a part in technological advances in publishing and broadcast communication affecting a world torn apart by more than a decade of war.

Bibliography

Abbe, James. *Around the World in Eleven Years.* New York, 1936.

Abend, Hallett. *Chaos in Asia.* New York, 1939.

──────. *Japan Unmasked.* New York, 1941.

──────. *My Life in China, 1926–1941.* New York, 1943.

──────. *Ramparts of the Pacific.* New York, 1942.

Aitken, Jonathan. *Officially Secret.* London, 1971. (Official Secrets Acts.)

Alcott, Carroll. *My War With Japan.* New York, 1943.

Allen, Frederick Lewis. *Since Yesterday.* New York, 1940.

[Allen, Jay Cooke]. "Allen, Hottelet Freed by Germans in Deal With U.S." *Editor & Publisher,* July 19, 1941, p. 8.

Alsop, Joseph and Robert Kintner. *American White Paper: The Story of the Second World War.* New York, 1940.

American Correspondents and Journalists in Moscow, 1917–1952: A Bibliography of Their Books on the USSR. Department of State Bibliography No. 73. Washington, D.C., 1953.

Andrews, Sir Linton and H. A. Taylor. *Lords and Laborers of the Press.* Carbondale, Ill., 1970.

Aronson, James. *The Press and the Cold War.* Indianapolis, 1970.

Austin, A. B. *We Landed at Dawn, The Story of the Dieppe Raid.* New York and London, 1943.

Baehr, Harry W., Jr. *The New York Tribune Since the Civil War.* New York, 1936.

Baillie, Hugh. *High Tension: The Recollections of Hugh Baillie.* New York, 1959.

──────. *Two Battlefronts.* New York, 1943.

Bainbridge, John. *Little Wonder, or The Reader's Digest and How It Grew.* New York, 1946.

Baldwin, Hanson W. *Great Mistakes of the War.* London and New York, 1950.

Baldwin, Hanson W. and Shepard Stone, eds. *We Saw It Happen.* New York, 1938.

Barnouw, Erik. *A History of Broadcasting in the United States.* 3 vols. New York, 1966–70.

Barns, Margarita. *The Indian Press.* London, 1940.

Bartlett, Vernon. *Intermission in Europe: The Life of a Journalist and Broadcaster.* New York, 1938. Published in London as *This Is My Life,* 1937.

Baum, Arthur W. "The Loudest Voice in the World." *Saturday Evening Post,* September 23, 1944, pp. 20–21, 90.

Beals, Carleton. *The Crime of Cuba.* Philadelphia, 1933.

———. *Glass Houses: Ten Years of Free-Lancing.* Philadelphia, 1938.

Beattie, Edward W., Jr. *Diary of a Kriegie.* New York, 1946.

———. *"Freely to Pass."* New York, 1942.

Belden, Jack. *Retreat With Stilwell.* New York, 1943.

———. *Still Time to Die.* New York, 1944.

Bellanger, Claude, with Jacques Godechot, Pierre Guiral, and Fernand Terrou. *Histoire Générale de La Presse Française.* 5 vols. Paris, 1969–76.

Benjamin, Robert Spiers, ed. *Eye Witness.* New York, 1940.

———, ed. *The Inside Story.* New York, 1940.

Bennett, Lowell. *Parachute to Berlin.* New York, 1945.

Berger, Meyer. *The Story of The New York Times, 1851–1951.* New York, 1951.

"Berlin Correspondents Have 'Harrowing, Nerve-Wracking Job.' " *World Press News,* July 13, 1939, p. 2.

Bernays, Robert. *"Special Correspondent".* London, 1934.

Bernstein, Walter. *Keep Your Head Down.* New York, 1945.

Bess, Demaree. "Tokyo's Captive Yankee Newspaper." *Saturday Evening Post,* February 6, 1943, pp. 22, 63–66.

Betts, T. J. "Chinese Public Opinion." *Foreign Affairs,* April 1933, pp. 470–77.

Bickford, Leland. *News While It Is News.* Boston, 1935.

Biddle, George. *George Biddle's War Drawings.* New York, 1944.

Bienstock, Gregory. *The Struggle for the Pacific.* New York, 1937.

Birchall, Frederick T. *The Storm Breaks: A Panorama of Europe and the Forces That Have Wrecked Its Peace.* New York, 1940.

Bisson, T. A. *Japan in China.* New York, 1938.

Blum, John Morton. *V Was for Victory: Politics and American Culture During World War II.* New York, 1976.

Bojano, Filippo. *In the Wake of the Goose-Step.* Chicago and New York, 1945.

Bolin, Luis. *Spain, the Vital Years.* London, 1967.

Booker, Edna Lee. *Flight from China.* New York, 1945.

———. *News Is My Job: A Correspondent in War-Torn China.* New York, 1940.

Bourke-White, Margaret. *Portrait of Myself.* New York, 1963.

———. *They Called It "Purple Heart Valley": A Combat Chronicle of the War in Italy.* Illustrated. New York, 1944.

Bourke-White, Margaret with Erskine Caldwell. *Russia at War.* Illustrated. New York, 1942.

———. *Shooting the Russian War.* New York, 1942.

Boveri, Margaret. *Mediterranean Cross-Currents.* London and New York, 1938.

Boyle, Andrew. *The Fourth Man: The Definitive Account of Kim Philby, Guy Burgess and Donald Maclean and Who Recruited Them to Spy for Russia.* London and New York, 1980.

Brandenburg, George A. "Press Wireless Makes Communications History." *Quill and Scroll,* December–January, 1944–45, pp. 5–6, 14.

Briggs, Asa. *History of Broadcasting in the United Kingdom.* 2 vols. Oxford, 1961, 1965.

Brines, Russell. *Until They Eat Stones.* New York, 1944.

Brock, Ray. *Nor Any Victory.* New York, 1942.

Brown, Cecil. *From Suez to Singapore.* New York, 1942.

Brown, Charles H. *The Correspondents' War.* New York, 1967.

Brown, D. and W. R. Bruner, eds. *How I Got That Story.* New York, 1967.

_____. *I Can Tell It Now.* New York, 1964.

Brown, Francis James, et al. *Contemporary World Politics; An Introduction to the Problems of International Relations.* 2d ed. New York, 1940.

Brown, James E. *Russia Fights.* New York, 1943.

Brown, John Mason. *To All Hands: An Amphibious Adventure.* New York, 1943.

Brown, Robert U. "1,800 in Press-Radio Corps as Conference Curtain Rises." *Editor & Publisher,* April 28, 1945, p. 7.

Brucker, Herbert. *Freedom of Information.* New York, 1949.

Bunnelle, Robert. "D-Day: How the AP Scored Sensationally on the No. 1 Story of Our Times," *Inter-Office,* June–July 1944, 3–8, 39. (AP internal publication, New York.)

Burchett, Wilfred. *At the Barricades: Forty Years on the Cutting Edge of History.* Introd. by Harrison E. Salisbury. New York, 1981.

_____. *Passport.* Sydney, 1969.

Burnham, Lord (Edward Frederick Lawson). *Peterborough Court: The Story of the Daily Telegraph.* London, 1955.

Burns, Eugene. *Then There Was One: The U.S. Enterprise in the First Year of the War.* New York, 1944.

Butcher, Harold. "Coverage of New Deal Is Big Job for Foreign Writers in U.S." *Editor & Publisher,* April 7, 1934, p. 16.

Byas, Hugh. *Government by Assassination.* New York and London, 1943.

_____. "Japan's Censors Aspire to 'Thought Control'." *New York Times Magazine,* April 18, 1937, pp. 4, 27.

Calder, Angus. *The People's War.* London, 1969.

Caldwell, Erskine. *All-Out on the Road to Smolensk.* New York, 1942.

Caldwell, Lewis G. *The American Press and International Communications.* ANPA Federal Laws Bulletin, no. 22–1945, April 9, 1945. Republished as a pamphlet by ANPA, New York, 1945.

Camrose, Viscount. *British Newspapers and Their Controllers.* London, 1939. Rev. ed. 1948.

Canham, Erwin D. "Diplomatic Gems at Golden Gate Sparkle from Settings Forged at Geneva." *Christian Science Monitor,* May 12, 1945.

———. *Commitment to Freedom: The Story of the Christian Science Monitor.* Boston, 1958.

Cant, Gilbert. *The Great Pacific Victory.* New York, 1946.

[Capa, Robert] "Capa—the Gay Cavalier of the Camera." *World Press News,* June 4, 1954.

———. *Slightly Out of Focus.* New York, 1947.

Carney, William P. "Fighting the Censor." *Scribner's,* June 1937, pp. 33–38.

Carpenter, Iris. *No Woman's World.* Boston, 1946.

Carroll, Gordon, ed. *History in the Writing.* New York, 1945.

Carroll, Wallace. *Persuade or Perish.* New York, 1948.

———. *We're In This With Russia.* Boston, 1942.

Carse, Robert. "We Fought Through to Murmansk." *Saturday Evening Post,* November 7, 1942, p. 9.

Casey, Robert J. *Cambodian Quest.* New York, 1931.

———. *I Can't Forget.* Indianapolis, 1941.

———. *This Is Where I Came In.* New York, 1945.

———. *Torpedo Junction.* Indianapolis, 1943.

Cassidy, Henry. *Moscow Dateline, 1941–1943.* Boston, 1943.

Chamberlin, William Henry. *The Russian Enigma.* New York, 1943.

———. *Confessions of an Individualist.* New York, 1940.

———. *Japan Over Asia.* New York, 1937. Rev. ed. 1939.

———. *Russia's Iron Age.* Boston, 1934.

———. "Soviet Taboos." *Foreign Affairs,* April 1935, pp. 431–40.

Chaplin, William W. *Blood and Ink: An Ethiopian War Diary.* New York and Harrisburg, 1936.

———. *The Fifty-Two Days: An NBC Reporter's Story of the Battle That Freed France.* Indianapolis, 1944.

———. *Seventy Thousand Miles of War: Being One Man's Odyssey On Many Fronts.* New York, 1943.

Charnley, Mitchell V. *News by Radio.* New York, 1948.

Chase, Francis, Jr. *Sound and Fury: An Informal History of Broadcasting.* New York and London, 1942.

Chester, Edmund A. *A Sergeant Named Batista.* New York, 1954.

Childs, Harwood L. *Public Opinion: Nature, Formation, Role.* Princeton, 1965.

Childs, Harwood L. and John B. Whitton, eds. *Propaganda by Short Wave.* Princeton, 1942.

Childs, Marquis. *I Write from Washington.* New York, 1942.

———. *Sweden, the Middle Way.* New York, 1948.

———. *Washington Calling.* New York, 1937.

Churchill, Winston. *The Second World War.* 6 vols. London and Boston, 1948–53.

Cianfarra, Camille. *The Vatican and the War.* New York, 1944.

Ciano, Count Galeazzo. *The Ciano Diaries, 1939–1943.* Ed. by Hugh Gibson. Introd. by Sumner Welles. New York, 1946.

Clapper, Olive Ewing. *Washington Tapestry.* New York, 1946.

Clapper, Raymond, "Hysterical Headlines!" *Quill,* September 1939, pp. 3–4.

―――. *Watching the World, 1934–1944.* Introd. by Ernie Pyle. New York, 1944.

Clark, Alan. *Barbarossa.* London, 1965.

Clark, Delbert. *Washington Dateline.* New York, 1941.

Clifford, Alexander G. *Conquest in North Africa.* Boston, 1943.

Close, Upton [Josef Washington Hall]. *Behind the Face of Japan.* New York, 1942.

Coblentz, Edmond D., ed. *William Randolph Hearst: A Portrait in His Own Words.* New York, 1952.

Cochrane, Negley D. *E. W. Scripps.* New York, 1933.

Cockburn, Claud. *A Discord of Trumpets.* New York, 1956. Published in London as *In Time of Trouble: An Autobiography.*

―――. *I Claud.* London, 1967.

Cockburn, Patricia. *The Years of The Week.* London, 1968.

Codding, George Arthur, Jr. *The International Telecommunications Union: An Experiment in International Cooperation.* Leiden, 1952.

Cole, Taylor. "The Italian Ministry of Popular Culture." *Public Opinion Quarterly,* July 1938, pp. 425–34.

Collier, Richard. *The Sands of Dunkirk.* London, 1961.

―――. *The City That Would Not Die: The Bombing of London.* London, 1960.

Commager, Henry Steele, ed. *The Pocket History of the Second World War.* New York, 1945.

Cook, E. T., Sir Arthur Willert, B. K. Long, and H. V. Hobson. *The Empire in the World.* London and New York, 1937.

Cookridge E. H. *The Third Man: The Story of Kim Philby.* New York, 1968.

Cooper, Kent. *Barriers Down: The Story of the News Agency Epoch.* New York, 1942.

―――. *Kent Cooper and The Associated Press: An Autobiography.* New York, 1959.

―――. *The Right to Know; An exposition of the evils of news suppression and propaganda.* New York, 1956.

"Correspondents in Japan Suffering Reign of Terror." *Editor & Publisher,* November 9, 1940, p. 14.

Coughlin, William J. *Conquered Press: The MacArthur Era in Japanese Journalism.* Palo Alto, 1952.

Cowles, Virginia. *Looking for Trouble.* New York and London, 1941.

Crawford, Kenneth G. *Report on North Africa.* New York, 1943.

Creel, George. *Rebel at Large: Recollections of Fifty Crowded Years.* New York, 1947.

Cremona, Paul. "Newspaper Restrictions Form Greatest of Difficulties for Student of Italian Conditions." *Christian Science Monitor,* October 30, 1931.

"Crisis Triples Press Coverage at State Department." *Editor & Publisher,* September 17, 1938.

Crow, Carl. *I Speak for the Chinese.* New York, 1938. (Pamphlet.)

Cummings, A. J. *The Press and a Changing Civilization.* London, 1936.

Custer, James. *Through the Perilous Night: The Astoria's Last Battle.* New York, 1944.

Dale, Edgar and Norma Vernon. *Propaganda Analysis: An Annotated Bibliography.* Columbus, 1940.

Daniell, Raymond. *Civilians Must Fight.* New York, 1941.

———. "Covering the News in London." *New York Times Magazine,* November 3, 1940, 16.

D'Arcy-Dawson, John. *Tunisian Battle.* London, 1943.

Darrah, David. *Hail Caesar!* Boston, 1936.

Darrock, Michael and Joseph P. Dorn. "Davis and Goliath." *Harper's Magazine,* February 1943, pp. 225–37.

Davis, Elmer. "Broadcasting the Outbreak of War." *Harper's Monthly,* November 1939, pp. 579–88.

———. "Elmer Davis: War News Boss." *United States News,* June 26, 1942, p. 13.

———. "Why News Is Censored: Elmer Davis Explains." *United States News,* December 11, 1942, pp. 19–20.

Davis, Forrest and Ernest K. Lindley. *How War Came: An American White Paper from the Fall of France to Pearl Harbor.* New York, 1942.

Davis, Frances. *My Shadow in the Sun.* New York, 1940.

DeForest, Lee. *Father of Radio: The Autobiography of Lee DeForest.* Chicago, 1950.

Dennis, Charles H. *Victor Lawson: His Time and His Work.* Chicago, 1935.

Denny, Harold, *Behind Both Lines.* New York, 1942.

———. "Soviet Ends Curb on Outgoing News." *New York Times,* March 5, 1939.

Desmond, Robert W. *Crisis and Conflict: World News Reporting Between Two Wars 1920–1940.* Iowa City, Iowa, 1982.

———. *Windows on the World: The Information Process in a Changing Society 1900–1920.* Iowa City, Iowa, 1980.

———. *The Information Process: World News Reporting to the Twentieth Century.* Iowa City, Iowa, 1978.

———. *The Press and World Affairs.* New York and London, 1937. Reprinted, New York, 1972; Tokyo, 1983.

_____. "200 Dailies Are Suppressed by Hitler." *Editor & Publisher,* April 1, 1933, pp. 8, 38.

Deuel, Wallace. *People Under Hitler.* New York, 1942.

Digby, George. *Down Wind.* New York, 1939.

Divine, A. D. (David Rame) *Dunkirk.* London, 1945.

Dodd, Martha. *Through Embassy Eyes.* New York, 1939.

Dresler, Adolph. *Geschichte der Italienischen Presse.* 2 vols. Munich and Berlin, 1933–34.

Drewry, John E. *More Post Biographies.* Athens, Ga., 1947.

_____. *Post Biographies of Famous Journalists.* Athens, Ga., 1942.

Driberg, Tom. *Beaverbrook: A Study in Power and Frustration.* London, 1956.

Driscoll, Joseph. *War Discovers Alaska.* Philadelphia, 1943.

"Duce's Instructions to Press Revealed by N.Y. Anti-Facist Editor." *Editor & Publisher,* November 30, 1935, p. 8. See *Editor and Publisher,* January 11, 1936; March 7, 1936; June 12, 1937; and *Current History,* July 1937. See also "Shop Talk at Thirty," *Editor and Publisher,* September 24, 1932; *Nation,* June 1, 1927; and *Editor & Publisher,* June 4, 1927.

Dunlap, Orrin E. *The Story of Radio.* New York, 1935.

Durant, Kenneth. "Russia." *Journalism Quarterly,* March 1937.

Duranty, Walter. *U.S.S.R.: The Story of Soviet Russia.* New York, 1944.

_____. *Duranty Reports Russia.* New York, 1935.

_____. *I Write As I Please.* New York, 1935.

Ebenstein, William. *Fascist Italy.* New York, 1939.

Eder, Joseph Maria. *History of Photography.* Trans. by Edward Epstean. New York, 1945.

Ehrenburg, Ilya. *The Tempering of Russia.* Trans. by Alexander Kaun. New York, 1944.

Eisenhower, Dwight D. *Crusade in Europe.* Garden City, N.Y., 1948.

Eldridge, Fred. *Wrath in Burma.* New York, 1945.

Eliot, Major George Fielding. *The Ramparts We Watch.* New York, 1939.

Elliott, William Yandell. *The New British Empire.* New York, 1932.

Elliston, Herbert B. "China's No. 1 White Boy." *Saturday Evening Post,* March 19, 1938, pp. 5–7, 31–40.

Elson, Robert T. *Time, Inc,: The Intimate History of a Publishing Enterprise, 1923–1941.* New York, 1968.

Emery, Edwin and Michael C. Emery. *The Press and America: An Interpretive History of the Mass Media.* 5th ed. Englewood Cliffs, N.J., 1984.

Enderis, Guido. "Reich Asks Pacts to Control Press." *New York Times,* March 13, 1938, sec. E, p. 5.

Ernst, Morris L. *The First Freedom.* New York, 1946.

Estes, Bernard et al., eds. *Deadline Delayed.* New York, 1947.

Faber, John. *Great Moments in News Photography.* New York, 1960.

Farago, Ladislas. *Abyssinian Stop Press.* London, 1936.

Farmer, Rhodes. *Shanghai Harvest: A Diary of Three Years in the China War.* London, 1945.

Farson, Negley. *Behind God's Back.* New York, 1941.

————. *Bomber's Moon: London in the Blitzkrieg.* Illus. by Tom Purvis. New York, 1941.

————. *A Mirror for Narcissus.* New York, 1956.

————. *Transgressor in the Tropics.* New York, 1938.

————. *The Way of a Transgressor.* London, 1936.

Fattorello, F. *L'origini del giornalismo moderno in Italia.* Undine, 1937.

Fenton, Charles A. *The Apprenticeship of Ernest Hemingway: The Early Years.* New York, 1954.

Ferguson, George V. *John W. Dafoe.* Toronto, 1948.

Fermi, Laura. *Mussolini.* Chicago, 1961.

Fernsworth, Lawrence A. "Correspondent in Spain." *Current History,* March 1938, pp. 31–34.

————. *Spain's Struggle for Freedom.* Boston, 1957.

Fessenden, H. M. *Fessenden—Builder of Tomorrow.* New York, 1940.

Fielding, Raymond. *The American Newsreel, 1911–1967.* Norman, Okla., 1972.

Fine, Barnett. *A Giant of the Press.* New York, 1933.

Finer, H. *Mussolini's Italy.* New York, 1935.

Fischer, Heinz-Dietrich and John C. Merrill, eds. *International and Intercultural Communication.* 2d ed. New York, 1976.

Fischer, Louis, *Men and Politics: An Autobiography.* New York, 1946.

————. *Soviet Journey.* New York, 1935.

Fisher, Charles. *The Columnists.* New York, 1944.

Fitzgibbon, Constantine. *The Blitz.* London, 1957.

Flannery, Harry W. *Assignment to Berlin.* New York, 1942.

[Fleisher, Benjamin.] "Fleisher Sells Japan Advertiser." *Editor & Publisher,* October 12, 1940, p. 32.

Fleisher, Wilfrid. *Volcanic Isle.* Garden City, N.Y., 1941.

Fodor, Marcel W. *Plot and Counter-Plot in Central Europe: Conditions South of Hitler.* Introd. by John Gunther. Boston, 1937.

————. *The Revolution Is On.* Introd. by Dorothy Thompson. Boston, 1940.

Forbath, Alex, ed. *Europe Into the Abyss.* London, 1938.

Ford, Cory. *Short Cut to Tokyo: The Battle for the Aleutians.* New York, 1943.

Forman, Harrison. *Report from Red China.* New York, 1945.

Forrest, Wilbur F. *Behind the Front Page.* New York, 1934.

Forsberg, Colonel Franklin S. "International Publishing Blueprint: Yank—The Army Weekly reveals how it produced 21 different editions covering 41 foreign countries in all continents." *Printers' Ink,* November 2, 1945, pp. 20–21, 136–47.

Fredborg, Arvid. *Behind the Steel Wall: A Swedish Journalist in Berlin, 1941–43.* Stockholm and New York, 1944.

Frédérix, Pierre. *Un Siecle de Chasse aux Nouvelles: De l'Agence d'Information Havas à l'Agence France-Presse, 1835–1957.* Paris, 1959.

Friedrich, Carl Joachim. *Foreign Policy in the Making—The Search for a Balance of Power.* New York, 1938.

From D-Day Through Victory in Europe: The Eye-Witness Story as Told by War Correspondents on the Air. New York, 1945.

From Pearl Harbor Into Tokyo: Documented Broadcasts of the Pacific War. New York, 1945.

Furman, Bess. *Washington By-Line: The Personal History of a Newspaperwoman.* New York, 1949.

Furneaux, Rupert. *News of the War.* London, 1964.

Furuno, Inosuke, ed. *Tsushinsha shi kankokai.* Tokyo, 1958. (History of news agencies.)

Gallagher, James Wesley. *Back Door to Berlin: The full story of the American Coup in North Africa.* Garden City, N.Y., 1943.

Gallagher, O'Dowd. *Action In the East.* New York, 1942. Published in London as *Retreat In the East.*

Gannett, Lewis, ed. *I Saw It Happen: Eye-Witness Accounts of the War.* New York, 1942.

Garratt, Geoffrey Theodore. "News-Hunting in Ethiopia." *New Statesman and Nation.* March 14, 1936, pp. 378–79.

Gayn, Mark H. *Journey from the East: An Autobiography.* New York, 1944.

Gedye, G. E. R. *Fallen Bastions.* London, 1939. Published in New York as *Betrayal in Central Europe.*

Gellhorn, Martha. *The Face of War.* New York, 1944.

———. *A Stricken Field.* New York, 1940.

———. *The Trouble I've Seen.* New York, 1936.

George, Alexander L. *Propaganda Analysis: A Study of Inferences Made from Nazi Propaganda in World War II.* Evanston, Ill. and White Plains, N.Y., 1959.

Gerahty, G. *The Road to Madrid.* London, 1937.

Gerald, J. Edward. "Aspects of Journalism in South America." *Journalism Quarterly,* June 1931, pp. 213–23.

Géraud André ["Pertinax"]. *Gravediggers of France.* New York, 1944.

Gerber, John W. "Berlin Signs Off." *New York Times,* May 6, 1945.

"Germany Spent £2,000,000 Bribing French Press, Editor Alleges." *World Press News,* December 29, 1938.

Gervasi, Frank H. *War Has Seven Faces.* Garden City, N.Y., 1942.

Gibbons, Edward. *Floyd Gibbons, Your Headline Hunter.* New York, 1953.

Gibbs, Philip. *The Pageant of the Years.* London, 1946.

[Goebbels, Joseph] *Final Entries: The Diaries of Joseph Goebbels.* Ed. by Hugh Trevor-Roper. Trans. by Richard Barry. New York, 1978.

Goralski, Robert. *World War II Almanac 1931–1945: A Political and Military Record.* New York, 1981.

Gorham, Maurice. *Broadcasting and Television Since 1900.* London, 1952.

[Gorrell, Henry T.] "War Reporter's Own Story of Facing Death in Spain." *Editor & Publisher,* September 25, 1937, pp. 7, 32.

Gossin, Albert. *La Presse Suisse.* Neuchatel, 1936.

Gould, Randall. *China In the Sun.* Garden City, N.Y. 1946.

Graebner, Walter. *Round Trip to Russia.* Philadelphia, 1943.

Gramling, Oliver. *AP: The Story of News.* New York and Toronto, 1940.

_____, ed. *Free Men are Fighting: The Story of World War II.* New York, 1942.

Grandin, Thomas. *The Political Use of Radio.* Geneva, 1939.

Greenwall, Harry J. *Round the World for News.* London, 1936.

Griffin, Frederick. *Variety Show.* Toronto, 1936.

Gruliow, Leo. "Red Star Gleams as Guide for Russia's Army Press." *Quill,* August 1942, pp. 10–13, 15.

[Gunnison, Royal Arch]. "Last Out, First In." *Newsweek,* March 19, 1945, pp. 109–11.

_____. *So Sorry, No Peace.* New York, 1944.

Gunther, John. *D-Day.* New York, 1944.

_____. *A Fragment of Autobiography.* New York, 1962.

_____. *Inside Asia.* New York, 1939.

_____. *Inside Europe.* New York and London, 1936. Rev. eds, 1937–40.

_____. *Inside Latin America.* New York, 1941.

Gurney, J. *Crusade in Spain.* London, 1974.

Hailey, Foster. *Pacific Battle Line.* New York, 1944.

Hamilton, Thomas J. *Appeasement's Child: The Franco Regime in Spain.* New York, 1943.

Handleman, Howard. *Bridge to Victory.* New York, 1943.

Hanighen, Frank C., ed. *Nothing but Danger.* New York, 1939.

Harlow, Alvin E. *Old Wires and New Waves: The History of the Telegraph, Telephone and Wireless.* New York, 1936.

Harris, Henry Wilson. *Life So Far.* London, 1954.

Harsch. Joseph C. *Pattern of Conquest.* New York, 1941.

Hartwell, Dickson and Andrew A. Rooney, eds. *Off the Record, The Best Stories of Foreign Correspondents.* Introd. by Bob Considine. New York, 1953.

Haslett, A. W. *Radio 'Round the World.* New York, 1934.

Hauser, Ernest O. "News of the Far East in U.S. Dailies." *Public Opinion Quarterly,* October 1938, pp. 651–58.

Hawkins, Desmond et al. *BBC War Report.* London and New York, 1946.

Hawkins, Eric and Robert N. Sturdevant. *Hawkins of the Paris Herald.* New York, 1963.

Hawkins, Lucy Rogers. "Helen Kirkpatrick Reports War News from the Fighting Fronts." *Quill and Scroll,* October–November, 1944, pp. 7–8.

Hemingway, Mary Welsh. *How It Was.* New York, 1976.

Hepp, Ernest A. "German Correspondents in America." *Foreign Press,* January 15, 1940.

Herd, Harold. *The March of Journalism: The Story of the British Press from 1622 to the Present Day.* London, 1952.

Herndon, Booton. *Praised and Damned: The Story of Fulton Lewis, Jr.* New York and Boston, 1954.

Herring, Hubert. *Good Neighbors; Argentina, Brazil, Chile and Seventeen Other Countries.* New Haven, 1941.

Herring, James M. and Gerald C. Gross. *Telecommunications: Economics and Regulations.* New York, 1936.

Herrmann, Lazar [Leo Lanis]. *Today We Are Brothers: The Biography of a Generation.* Trans. by Ralph Marlowe. Boston, 1942.

Hersey, John. *A Bell for Adano.* New York, 1944.

———. "Hiroshima." *New Yorker,* August 31, 1946.

———. *Hiroshima.* New York, 1946.

———. *Into the Valley: A Skirmish with the Marines.* New York, 1943.

———. *Men on Bataan.* New York, 1942.

Hetherington, John. *Airborne Invasion: The Story of the Battle of Crete.* New York, London, Melbourne, 1944.

Hibbs, Ben. "Journey to a Shattered World." *Saturday Evening Post,* June 9, 1945, pp. 20–22, 83–86.

Higgins, Marguerite. *News Is a Singular Thing.* New York, 1945.

Hill, Russell. *Desert War.* New York, 1942.

———. *Exchange Ship.* New York, 1942.

Hills, Lee and Timothy J. Sullivan. *Facsimile.* New York, 1949.

Hindle, Wilfred, ed. *We Were There.* New York, 1939.

Hindus, Maurice G. *Moscow Skies.* New York, 1936.

Hinton, Harold B. "Is Latin America News?" *Quarterly Journal of Inter-American Relations.* January 1939, pp. 41–49.

History of the Times. 5 vols. London and New York, 1935–48.

Hitler, Adolf. *Mein Kampf.* 2 vols. Munich, 1925–27. Annotated English translation in one volume, New York, 1939.

Hobson, Harold, with Philip Knightley, and Leonard Russell. *The Pearl of Days: An Intimate Memoir of The Sunday Times, 1822–1972.* London, 1972.

Hodson, I. L. *Through the Dark Night.* London, 1941.

Hohenberg, John. *Foreign Correspondence: The Great Reporters and Their Times.* New York, 1964.

———. *The Pulitzer Prize Story.* New York, 1959.

Hopkins, John A. H. *Diary of World Events.* 54 vols. Baltimore, 1948–49.

Hough, Richard. *Mountbatten: A Biography.* London and New York, 1981.

"How Press Covered Hitler's Austrian Coup." *World's Press News,* March 17, 1938, pp. 1, 4.

Howe, Quincy. *The News and How to Understand It.* New York, 1940.

Huddleston, Sisley. *In My Time: An Observer's Record of War and Peace.* New York, 1938.

Huergo, Maria C. "Argentina's Newspapers." *Independent Journal,* March 17, 1939, p. 1.

Huss, Pierre J. *The Foe We Face.* New York, 1942.

Hutchinson, William K. "When Cuba Ran Red With Blood." *Quill,* November 1933, pp. 3–4, 12.

Huth, Arno. *Radio Today: The Present State of Broadcasting in the World.* New York, 1942.

Hutton, Bud and Andy Rooney. *The Story of the Stars and Stripes.* New York, 1946.

Ingersoll, Ralph M. *Action on All Fronts; A Personal Account of the War.* New York and London, 1942.

_____. *The Battle Is the Pay-Off.* New York, 1943.

_____. *Report on England, November 1940.* New York, 1941.

Ireland, Gordon. *Boundaries, Possessions and Conflicts in South America.* Cambridge, Mass., 1938.

Irwin, Will. *Propaganda and the News.* New York, 1936.

Ito, Masanoir. *The Japanese Press—Past and Present.* Tokyo, 1949.

Iyengar, A. S. *All Through the Gandhian Eye.* Bombay, 1950.

Jacob, Alaric. *A Traveller's War: A Journey to the Wars in Africa, India and Russia.* New York, 1944.

James, Edwin L. "Nothing, Just Nothing—Red News from the Front." *New York Times,* February 4, 1940, sec. E, p. 3.

James, Rembert. "The Pacific War as an AP Reporter Sees It." *A P Inter-Office* January 1944, pp. 8, 18.

Japanese Press: Past and Present, The. Tokyo, 1949.

Jeffries, J. M. N. *Front Everywhere.* London, 1935.

Jeffrey, William H. *Mitre and Argentina.* New York, 1952.

"Jimmy Tells the World." *Time,* December 25, 1939, p. 50. (Talbot G. Bowen radio account of the scuttling of the *Graf Spee.*)

Johnson, Gerald W. *An Honorable Titan: A Biographical Study of Adolph S. Ochs.* New York, 1946.

Johnston, George H. *Action at Sea.* New York, 1941.

_____. *New Guinea Story.* London, 1943. Published in New York as *Toughest Fighting in the World.*

Johnston, Stanley. *Queen of the Flat-Tops.* New York, 1942.

Jones, Edgar L. "The Care and Feeding of Correspondents." *Atlantic Monthly,* October 1945, pp. 46–51.

Jones, Sir Roderick. *A Life in Reuters.* London, 1951.

Jones, Robert L. "So I Went to Spain." *Quill,* September 1937, pp. 3–4, 14.

Josephs, Ray. *Argentine Diary.* New York, 1944.

Jouvenal, Henri de, with Kingsley Martin, Paul Scott Mowrer, Sanin

Cano, and Friedrich Sieburg. *The Educational Role of the Press.* Paris, 1934.

Jullian, Marcel. *The Battle of Britain.* London, 1967.

Kahn, E. J., Jr. "The Men Behind the By-Lines." *Saturday Evening Post,* September 11, 1943, pp. 19, 96–98.

Kaltenborn, H. V. *Fifty Fabulous Years, 1900–1950.* New York, 1950.

_____. *I Broadcast the Crisis.* New York, 1938.

_____. *It Seems Like Yesterday.* New York, 1956.

Kato, Masuo. *The Lost War.* New York, 1946.

Kemsley, Viscount. *The Kemsley Manual of Journalism.* London, 1950.

Kendrick, Alexander. *Prime Time: The Life of Edward R. Murrow.* Boston, 1969.

Kennedy, Edward. "I'd Do It Again." *Atlantic Monthly,* August 1948.

Kennedy, Malcolm Duncan. *The Changing Fabric of Japan.* London, 1930.

Kent, George. "The Last Days of Dictator Benito Mussolini." *Reader's Digest,* October 1944, pp. 13–17.

Kernan, Thomas. *France on Berlin Time.* Philadelphia, 1941.

Kerr, Walter. "Berlin Men Got Break When Nazis Took Paris." *Editor & Publisher,* August 3, 1940, p. 28.

Kiefer, Alexander F. "Government Control of Publishing in Germany." *Political Science Quarterly,* March 1942, pp. 72–97.

Kinnaird, Clark, ed. *It Happened in 1945.* New York, 1946.

Kiplinger, W. M. *Washington Is Like That.* New York, 1942.

Kirk, Betty. *Covering the Mexican Front: The Battle of Europe Versus America.* Fwd. by Josephus Daniels. Norman, Okla., 1942.

Kirkland, Wallace. *Recollections of a Life Photographer.* Boston, 1954.

Kisch, Egon. *Sensation Fair.* Trans. by Guy Endore. New York, 1941.

Knauth, Percy. *Germany in Defeat.* New York, 1946.

Knickerbocker, Hubert R. *Is Tomorrow Hitler's?* New York, 1941.

_____. *Can Europe Recover?* New York, 1932.

_____. *Fighting the Russian Trade Menace.* New York, 1931.

_____. *The German Crisis.* New York, 1932.

_____. *The Red Menace—Progress of the Soviet Five-Year Plan.* New York, 1931.

Knight, Mary. *On My Own.* New York, 1938.

Knightley, Philip. *The First Casualty: From the Crimea to Vietnam: The War Correspondent as Hero, Propagandist, and Myth Maker.* New York and London, 1975.

Knoblaugh, H. Edward, *Correspondent in Spain.* London and New York, 1937.

Koenigsberg, Moses. *King News: An Autobiography.* New York, 1941.

Koestler Arthur. *Dialogue With Death.* New York, 1942. (Published London in 1937 as *Spanish Testament.*)

_____. *The Gladiators.* New York, 1939.

_____. *The Invisible Writing: An Autobiography.* New York, 1954; London, 1969.

Kert, Bernice. *The Hemingway Women.* New York, 1983.

Koito, Chugo. "The Foreign Press: Japan." *Journalism Quarterly,* December 1938, pp. 423–25; June 1939, pp. 210–11; September, 1939, 296–97; March 1940, pp. 59–63; September 1940, pp. 280–82; June 1941, pp. 189–92.

Koop, Theodore F. "Censors Saved Lives." *Quill,* July–August 1945, p. 9.

––––––. *Weapon of Silence.* Chicago, 1947.

Krieghbaum, Hillier. *Facts in Perspective: The Editorial Page and News Interpretation.* Englewood Cliffs, N.J., 1956.

Kreisman, Sergeant Irvin H. "Combat Correspondents." *Quill,* February 1943, pp. 10–12.

Krock, Arthur. "In Wartime What News Shall the Nation Have?" *New York Times Magazine,* August 16, 1942, pp. 3–4, 25.

Kuhn, Irene. *Assigned to Adventure.* Philadelphia, 1938.

Landry, Robert. *This Fascinating Radio Business.* New York, 1946.

Landstrom, Russell, ed. *The Associated Press News Annual.* New York, 1946.

Laney, Al. *Paris Herald: The Incredible Newspaper.* New York, 1947.

Langdon-Davies, John. *Behind the Spanish Barricades.* London, 1936.

Lansing, Bernard. "A Reporter at Large: Kopfwashen at the Adlon." New Yorker, February 15, 1941, pp. 41–50.

"La Prensa Opens $3,000,000 Plant Climaxing 65 Years of Progress." *Editor & Publisher,* July 14, 1934, p. 11.

Lardner, John. *Southwest Passage.* New York, 1943.

Lardner, Ring, Jr. *The Lardners; My Family Remembered.* New York, 1976.

Larson, Cedric. "The German Press Chamber." *Public Opinion Quarterly.* October 1937, pp. 53–70.

Lasswell, Harold D. *Propaganda Technique in the World War.* New York, 1927.

Laurence, William L. *Men and Atoms.* New York, 1946. Reprinted 1959, 1962.

"La vérité sur les 'fausses nouvelles'." *Le Moniteur de la Presse.* October 1938, p. 4.

Lauterbach, Richard E. *These Are the Russians.* New York, 1945.

Lawrence, David. *Diary of a Washington Correspondent.* New York, 1942.

Lazareff, Pierre. *Deadline: The Behind-the-Scenes Story of the Last Decade of France.* Trans. by David Partridge. New York, 1942.

Lazarsfeld, Paul F. *Radio and the Printed Page: An Introduction to the Study of Radio and Its Role in the Communication of Ideas,* New York, 1940.

Lee, Alfred McClung. *The Daily Newspaper in America: The Evolution of a Social Instrument.* New York, 1937.

Lee, Clark. *They Call It Pacific.* New York, 1943.

Leiding, Oscar. "How the European Crisis Was Covered" *Quill,* November 1938, pp. 8–9, 16.

Lenhoff, Eugene. *The Last Five Hours of Austria.* New York, 1938.
Leone-Moats, Alice. *No Passports for Paris.* New York, 1945.
LeSueur, Larry. *Twelve Months That Changed the World.* New York, 1943.
Levine, Isaac Don. *Eyewitness to History; Memoirs and Reflections of a Foreign Correspondent for Half a Century.* New York, 1973.
————. *Red Smoke.* New York, 1932.
Liang, Hubert S. *Development of the Modern Chinese Press.* Nanking, 1937.
Liebert, Herman. "Communications: International Communications." *Public Opinion Quarterly,* September 1940, pp. 507–12.
Liebling, A. J. *The Road Back to Paris.* New York, 1944.
Life's Picture History of World War II. New York, 1950.
Lindsay, Michael. *The Unknown War: North China 1937–1945.* New York, 1977.
Lindsley, Charles Frederick. *Radio and Television Communication.* New York, 1952.
Lin Yutang. *History of the Press and Public Opinion in China.* Chicago, 1936.
Lochner, Louis P. *Always the Unexpected: A Book of Reminiscences.* New York, 1956.
————. "News-Gathering in Nazi Germany." *Quill,* August 1939, pp. 5–6, 14.
————. *What About Germany?* New York, 1942.
Lockhart, R. H. Bruce. *British Agent.* Introd. by Hugh Walpole. London and New York, 1933.
————. *Comes the Reckoning.* London, 1947.
Lord, Walter. *Day of Infamy.* New York, 1957.
Low, David. *A Cartoon History of Our Times.* Introd. and text by Quincy Howe. New York, 1946.
————. *Low's Autobiography.* London and New York, 1957.
Lowenstein, Karl. *Brazil Under Vargas.* New York, 1942.
Lucas, Lieutenant Jim. *Combat Correspondent.* New York, 1944.
————. "That's How the Story of Tarawa Was Told." *Quill,* March–April 1944, pp. 7–8, 10.
Lyons, Eugene. *Assignment in Utopia.* New York, 1937.
————. *David Sarnoff.* New York, 1966.
————. *Moscow Carrousel.* New York, 1935.
————. *The Red Decade.* Indianapolis, 1941.
————, ed. *We Cover the World.* New York, 1937.
Macartney, M. H. H. and Paul Cremona. *Italy's Foreign and Colonial Policy, 1914–1937.* London and New York, 1938.
MacColl, René. *Deadline & Dateline.* London, 1956.
Macdonald, Roderick. *Dawn Like Thunder.* London, 1943.
Mackenzie, DeWitt. "Understanding the Problems of the Foreign Correspondent." *Journalism Quarterly,* March 1941, pp. 23–28.

Mackenzie, F. A. *Beaverbrook: An Authentic Biography.* London, 1931.

Maclaurin, W. Rupert. *Invention and Innovation in the Radio Industry.* New York, 1949.

MacLean, Robinson. *John Hoy of Ethiopia.* New York, 1936.

MacMahon, Arthur W. *Memorandum on The Postwar International Information Program of the United States.* Department of State Publication 2438. Washington, D.C., 1945.

McVane, John. *Journey Into War: War and Diplomacy in North Africa.* New York, 1943.

_____. *On the Air in World War II.* New York, 1980.

Mance, Brigadier General Sir Osborne and J. E. Wheeler, *International Communications.* London and New York, 1944.

Manchester, William. American Caesar: Douglas MacArthur, 1880–1964. Boston, 1978.

Manevy, Raymond. *Histoire de la Presse, 1914 à 1939.* Paris, 1945.

Marcosson, Isaac F. *Before I Forget: A Pilgrimage to the Past.* New York, 1959.

_____. *Turbulent Years.* New York, 1938.

Markham, James W. *Voices of the Red Giants.* Ames, Iowa, 1967.

Massock, Richard G. *Italy From Within.* New York, 1943.

Martin, Leslie John. "The Rise and Development of Agence France-Presse." *Journalism Quarterly,* Spring 1950, pp. 197–206.

Mathews, Joseph J. *Reporting the Wars.* Minneapolis, 1957.

Matthews, Herbert L. *Education of a Correspondent.* New York, 1946.

_____. *The Fruits of Facism.* New York, 1943.

_____. *Eyewitness in Abyssinia.* London, 1937.

_____. *Two Wars and More to Come.* New York, 1938.

_____. *A World in Revolution.* New York, 1971.

Mauldin, Bill. *Bill Mauldin's Army.* New York, 1946.

_____. *Up Front.* New York, 1945.

Mayer, Milton. *They Thought They Were Free: The Germans, 1933–1945.* Chicago, 1955.

McCormick, Anne O'Hare. *The World at Home: Selections from the Writings of Anne O'Hare McCormick.* Ed. by Marion Turner Sheehan. Introd. by James B. Reston. New York, 1956.

McKee, Alexander. *The Race for the Rhine Bridges.* London, 1971.

McKenzie, Vernon. *Here Lies Goebbels.* London, 1940.

_____. *Through Turbulent Years.* New York, 1938.

McMillan, Dick. "In the Great Days of 'Dateline Vienna'." *World Press News,* December 17, 1954, p. 10.

McMillan, Richard. *Mediterranean Assignment.* New York, 1943.

McNamara, John. *Extra! U.S. War Correspondents in Action.* Boston, 1945.

McNaught, Carlton. *Canada Gets the News.* Toronto, 1940.

Mee, Charles L., Jr. *Meeting at Potsdam.* New York, 1975.

Merrill, John C. *The Elite Press; Great Newspapers of the World.* New York, Toronto, London, 1968.

_____, and Harold A. Fisher. *The World's Great Dailies: Profiles of 50 Newspapers.* New York, 1980.

Michie, Allan A. and Walter Graebner. *Their Finest Hour.* New York, 1940.

Middleton, Drew. *Our Share of Night: A Personal Narrative of the War Years.* New York, 1946.

_____. *The Sky Suspended.* New York and London, 1960.

Miller, Lee G. *The Story of Ernie Pyle.* New York, 1950.

Miller, Webb. *I Found No Peace: The Journal of a Foreign Correspondent.* New York, 1936.

Ming-Heng Chao, Thomas. *The Foreign Press of China.* Shanghai, 1931.

_____. *My Fifteen Years as a Reporter.* London, 1944.

Minney, Rubeigh James. *Viscount Southwood.* London, 1954.

Misselwitz, Henry F. *The Dragon Stirs.* New York, 1941.

Mitarai, Tatsuo. *Shimbun Taiheiki.* Tokyo, 1950. (History of the press in Japan.)

Moats, Alice-Leone. *Blind Date With Mars.* Garden City, N.Y., 1943.

Monks, Noel. *Eye-Witness; The Journal of a World Correspondent.* London, 1955.

Moorehead, Alan. *Don't Blame the Generals.* New York, 1943.

_____. *The End in Africa.* New York, 1943.

_____. *A Late Education.* London, 1970.

_____. *Mediterranean Front.* New York, 1942.

Moreno, C. Galván. *El Periodismo Argentina; Amplia y Documentada Historia Desde sus Origenes Hasta el Presente.* Buenos Aires, 1944.

Morgan, Thomas B. *The Listening Post: Eighteen Years on Vatican Hill.* New York, 1944.

_____. *A Reporter at the Papal Court.* New York, 1938.

_____. *Spurs on the Boot; Italy Under Her Masters.* Philadelphia, 1941.

Morin, Relman. *East Wind Rising.* New York, 1960.

Morison, Samuel Eliot. *The Oxford History of the American People.* New York, 1965.

Morris, Joe Alex. *Deadline Every Minute: The Story of the United Press.* Garden City, N.Y., 1957.

Morris, John. *Traveler from Tokyo.* New York, 1944.

Morrison, Ian. *Malayan Postscript.* London, 1942.

_____. *This War Against Japan.* London, 1943.

Morton, John. *V Was for Victory: Politics and American Culture During World War II.* New York, 1980.

"Moscow News Ban Forces N.Y. Times to Withdraw." *Editor & Publisher,* September 14, 1940, p. 6.

Mosley, Leonard. *Down Stream: The Uncensored Story of 1936–1939.* London, 1939.

Mott, Frank Luther. *American Journalism: A History of Newspapers in the United States Through 260 Years: 1690 to 1950*. Rev. ed. New York, 1950.

———and Ralph D. Casey, eds. *Interpretations of Journalism: A Book of Readings*. New York, 1937.

———, ed. *Journalism in Wartime*. Washington, D.C., 1943.

Mowrer, Edgar Ansel. *The Dragon Awakes*. New York, 1938.

———. *Germany Puts the Clock Back*. New York and London, 1933.

———. *Triumph and Tragedy*. New York, 1968.

Mowrer, Lilian T. *Journalist's Wife*. New York, 1937.

Mowrer, Paul Scott. "Bungling the News." *Public Opinion Quarterly,* Spring 1943, pp. 116–24.

———. *The House of Europe*. Boston, 1945.

Munro, Ion. *Through Fascism to World Power*. London, 1933.

Murrow, Edward R. *In Search of Light*. New York, 1967.

———. *This Is London*. Ed. with introd. and notes by Elmer Davis. New York, 1941.

Murthy, Nadig Krishna. *Indian Journalism,* Mysore, 1966.

Mydans, Carl. *More Than Meets the Eye*. New York, 1959.

Nafziger, Ralph O. *Foreign News Sources and the Foreign Press: A Bibliography*. Minneapolis, 1937.

———. *International News and the Press: Communications, Organization of News-Gathering, International Affairs and the Foreign Press—An Annotated Bibliography*. New York, 1940.

———. "World-Wide War Wages With Words." *Quill,* July–August, 1943, pp. 3–4.

Newman, Joseph. *Goodbye Japan*. New York, 1942.

News Agencies: Their Structure and Operation. Paris, 1953. UNESCO publication.

"News Blackout Spreads Slowly Over Orient." *Quill,* July 1941.

"Newsmen Arrive from Orient: Tell Mistreatment at Jap Hands." *Editor & Publisher,* August 29, 1942, pp. 5–6, 30.

"Newsmen Seen 'Wasting Time' in Russia." *Editor & Publisher,* December 23, 1944.

Newspaper: Its Making and Its Meaning, The. New York, 1945.

New Yorker Book of War Pieces, The. New York, 1947.

Nichol, David M. "A Bleak Assignment." *Quill,* March–April, 1945.

Nichols, M. E. *(CP) The Story of The Canadian Press*. Toronto, 1948.

Oechsner, Frederick et al. *This Is the Enemy*. Boston, 1942.

Oestreicher, J. C. *The World Is Their Beat*. New York, 1945.

Oldfield, Colonel Barney. *Never a Shot in Anger*. New York, 1956.

Olson, Kenneth E. *The History Makers: The Press of Europe From Its Beginnings Through 1965*. Baton Rouge, La., 1966.

Orchard, J. E. *Japan's Economic Position*. New York, 1930.

Ortega y Gasset, José. *The Revolt of the Masses*. New York, 1932.

Orwell, George. *Homage to Catalonia*. London, 1953.

Packard, Reynolds and Eleanor Packard. *Balcony Empire.* New York, 1941.

Palmer, Colonel Frederick. "Re-enter the War Correspondent." *New York Times Magazine,* January 30, 1938, pp. 10–11, 25.

Palmer. Gretta. "Reds, Rebels and Reporters." *Today,* January 16, 1937, pp. 33–38.

Parker, Robert. *Headquarters Budapest.* New York, 1944.

Parris, John A., Jr. and Ned Russell, with Leo Disher and Phil Ault. *Springboard to Berlin.* New York, 1943.

Parrish, Thomas, ed. *Encyclopedia of World War II.* New York, 1978.

Patmore, Derek. *Balkan Correspondent.* New York, 1941.

Paulu, Burton. *British Broadcasting: Radio and Television in the United Kingdom.* Minneapolis, 1956.

Percival, A. E. *The War in Malaya,* London, 1949.

Pers, Anders Y. *Newspapers in Sweden.* Stockholm, 1954.

Peterson, Theodore. *Magazines in the Twentieth Century.* Urbana, Ill., 1956.

Pew, Marlen E., Jr. "China War Costs Services More Than Any Event Since 1917." *Editor & Publisher,* September 4, 1937, pp. 5–6.

Phillips, Cabell et al., eds. *Dateline: Washington.* Garden City, N.Y., 1949.

Pitcairn, Frank [Claud Cockburn]. *Reporter in Spain.* London, 1936.

Poliakoff, Vladimir ("Augur"). *Europe in the Fourth Dimension.* New York, 1939.

Political and Economic Planning. *Report on the British Press.* London, 1938.

Pollard, James E. *The Presidents and the Press.* New York, 1947.

———. *The Presidents and the Press: Truman to Johnson.* Washington, 1964.

Pollock, James J. and Harlow J. Heneman. *The Hitler Decrees.* Ann Arbor, Mich., 1934.

Porter, Robert P. *Uncensored France.* New York, 1942.

Potter, Jean. *Alaska Under Arms.* New York, 1942.

Powell, C. Arthur. "Victory-Mad Rebels in Brazil Wreck Newspaper Plants for Vengeance." *Editor & Publisher,* November 1, 1930. pp. 5–6.

Powell, John B. *My Twenty-Five Years in China.* New York, 1945.

Prando, Alberto. *A Century and a Half of Journalism in Argentina.* Austin, 1961.

Pratt, Fletcher. "How the Censors Rigged the News." *Harper's Magazine,* February 1946, pp. 98–105.

———. "Propaganda from Spain." *American Mercury,* August 1937, pp. 409–22.

Price, Byron. "The Censor Defends the Constitution." *New York Times Magazine,* February 11, 1945, pp. 11, 32.

Price, G. Ward. *Extra-Special Correspondent.* London, 1957.

————. *I Know These Dictators.* London, 1938.

————. *Years of Reckoning.* London, 1939.

Price, Morgan Phillips. *My Three Revolutions.* London, 1969.

Price, Warren C. *The Literature of Journalism: An Annotated Bibliography.* Minneapolis, 1959.

Pryce-Jones, David. *Paris in the Third Reich: A History of the German Occupation.* New York, 1981.

Pyle, Ernie. *Brave Men,* New York, 1944.

————. *Ernie Pyle in England.* New York, 1941.

————. *Here is Your War.* New York, 1943.

————. *Last Chapter.* New York, 1946.

Public Papers and Addresses of Franklin D. Roosevelt, The. 13 vols. Washington, D.C., 1941–50.

Raleigh, John McCutcheon. *Pacific Blackout.* New York, 1943.

Rame, David. [Arthur D. Divine]. *Road to Tunis.* New York, 1944.

Randau, Carl and Leane Zugsmith. *The Setting Sun of Japan.* New York, 1942.

Rechnitzer, Ferdinand E. *War Correspondent: The Story of Quentin Reynolds.* New York, 1943.

Reed, Douglas L. *Disgrace Abounding.* London, 1939.

————. *Insanity Fair: A European Cavalcade.* London and New York, 1938.

Reith, Lord. *Into the Wind: His Autobiography.* London, 1947.

Report on the British Press. London, 1938.

Reporting to Remember: Unforgettable Stories and Pictures of World War II. New York, 1945.

Reston, James B. *Prelude to Victory.* New York, 1942.

Reynolds, Quentin. *The Curtain Rises.* New York, 1944.

————. *Dress Rehearsal: The Story of Dieppe.* New York, 1943.

————. *A London Diary.* New York, 1941.

————. *Only the Stars Are Neutral.* New York, 1942.

————. *The Wounded Don't Cry.* New York, 1941.

Rhodes, Anthony. *Propaganda, The Art of Persuasion: World War II.* New York, 1976.

Riess, Curt, ed. *They Were There: The Story of World War II and How It Came About.* New York, 1944.

————. *Underground Europe.* New York, 1942.

Riegel, O. W. *Mobilizing for Chaos: The Story of the New Propaganda.* New Haven, Conn., 1934.

Rixon, Alex T. "Telecommunications of China with Foreign Countries." *Public Opinion Quarterly,* July 1938, pp. 478–83.

Robb, Arthur. "Shop Talk at Thirty." *Editor & Publisher,* June 12, 1937, pp. 48ff; July 17, 1937, pp. 52ff; July 31, 1937, pp. 48ff.

Robertson, Ben. *I Saw England.* New York, 1941.

Robertson, Terence. *Dieppe: The Shame and the Glory.* London, 1963.

Robinson, Pat. *Fight for New Guinea.* New York, 1943.

Robinson, Thomas P. *Radio Networks and the Federal Government.* New York, 1943.

Rolo, Charles J. *Radio Goes to War: The 'Fourth Front.'* New York, 1942.

Romulo, Carlos P. *I Saw the Fall of the Philippines.* New York, 1942.

Ross, Albion. *Journey of an American.* Indianapolis, 1957.

Ross, Ishbel. *Ladies of the Press: The Story of Women in Journalism.* Fwd. by Stanley Walker. New York and London, 1936.

Rosten, Leo. *The Washington Correspondents.* New York, 1937.

Roth, Andrew. *Dilemma in Japan.* New York, 1945.

"Russian Correspondents Write and Fight With Red Army." *World Press News,* June 8, 1944.

Ryan, Cornelius. *A Bridge Too Far.* London, 1974.

Saerchinger, Cesar. *Hello America! Radio Adventures in Europe.* Boston, 1938.

―――. "Radio, Censorship and Neutrality." *Foreign Affairs* January 1941, pp. 343ff.

St. John, Robert. *Foreign Correspondent.* Garden City, N.Y., 1957.

―――. *From the Land of the Silent People.* New York, 1942.

Salisbury, Harrison E. *Journey for Our Times: A Memoir.* New York, 1983.

―――. *The 900 Days: The Siege of Leningrad.* New York, 1969.

―――. *Russia on the Way.* New York, 1946.

Sarfatti, Margherita G. *The Life of Mussolini.* New York, 1926.

Schechter, Abel A. and Edward Anthony. *I Live on Air.* New York, 1941.

Scheffer, Paul. *Seven Years in Soviet Russia.* Trans. by Arthur Livingston. New York, 1931.

Schneider Walter E. "AP Launches Subsidiary to Sell By-Products of News-Gathering." *Editor & Publisher,* January 25, 1941, pp. 3–4.

―――. "Press Casualty Rate Exceeds Army's in Battle." *Editor & Publisher,* February 20, 1943.

―――. "U.S. Services and Dailies Spent Millions on First Year of War." *Editor & Publisher,* August 31, 1940, pp. 3–4, 35.

―――. "War in Europe Doubles Costs of U.S. Foreign News Services." *Editor & Publisher,* September 23, 1939, pp. 5, 32.

Schramm, Wilbur, ed. *Mass Communications.* Urbana, Ill., 1949.

Schumann, Frederick L. *International Politics.* Rev. ed. New York, 1937.

Schuster, M. Lincoln. *Eyes on the World: A Photographic Record of History-in-the-Making.* New York, 1935.

Scott, John. *Beyond the Urals: An American Worker in Russia's City of Steel.* Boston, 1942.

―――. *Duel for Europe.* Boston, 1942.

Seldes, George. *Sawdust Caesar.* New York, 1935.

―――. *Tell the Truth and Run.* New York, 1953.

―――. *The Vatican: Yesterday, Today, Tomorrow.* New York, 1934.

Seton-Watson, R. W. *Britain and the Dictators.* New York, 1938.

Sevareid, Eric. *Not So Wild a Dream.* New York, 1946. Rev. ed. 1977.

"Seventy-fifth Anniversary of La Nación." Bulletin of the Pan American Union. June 1945, p. 365.

"Seventy-fifth Anniversary of La Prensa." Bulletin of the Pan American Union. March 1945, p. 3.

Sharp, Eugene W. *The Censorship and Press Laws of Sixty Countries.* University of Missouri Bulletin. Columbia, Mo., November 1, 1936, pp. 20–23.

Sharp, Roland H. *South American Uncensored.* New York, 1945.

Sharp, Walter H. "Methods of Opinion Control in Present-Day Brazil." *Public Opinion Quarterly,* March 1941, pp. 3–16.

Sheean, Vincent. *Between the Thunder and the Sun.* New York, 1943.

———. *Not Peace But the Sword.* New York, 1939.

———. *Personal History.* New York, 1935. Published in London as *In Search of History.*

Sherrod, Robert. *On to Westward.* New York, 1945.

———. *Tarawa: The Story of a Battle.* New York, 1944.

Sherwood, Robert. *Roosevelt and Hopkins: An Intimate History.* New York, 1948.

Shirer, William L. *Berlin Diary: The Journal of a Foreign Correspondent, 1934–1941.* New York, 1942.

———. *End of a Berlin Diary.* New York, 1947.

———. *Midcentury Journal: The Western World Through Its Years of Conflict.* New York, 1952.

———. *The Rise and Fall of the Third Reich: A History of Nazi Germany.* New York, 1960.

———. *20th Century Journey: A Memoir of a Life and the Times of William L. Shirer; The Start, 1904–1930.* New York, 1976.

———. *20th Century Journey: The Nightmare Years, 1930–1940.* Boston, 1984.

Siebert, Frederick L. "Federal Information Agencies—An Outline." *Journalism Quarterly,* March 1942, pp. 28–33.

Siepmann, Charles A. *Radio, Television and Society.* New York, 1950.

Simon, André. *J'Accuse! The Men Who Betrayed France.* New York, 1940.

Simon, Lord. (Ernest D. C. Simon). *The B.B.C. From Within.* London, 1953.

Simonds, Frank L. and Brooks Emeny. *The Great Powers in World Politics.* Rev. ed. New York, 1937.

Simonov, Konstantin Mikhailovich. *No Quarter,* New York, 1943.

Singer, Kurt. *Duel for the Northland.* New York, 1943.

Sinclair, Gordon. *Cannibal Quest.* Toronto, 1934.

———. *Footloose in India.* Toronto, 1933.

Sington, Derrick and Arthur Wiedenfeld. *The Goebbels Experiment: A Study of the Nazi Propaganda Machine.* New Haven, 1943.

Slocombe, George. *A Mirror to Geneva.* London and New York, 1938.

———. *The Tumult and the Shouting.* New York, 1936.

Smedley, Agnes. *Battle Hymn of China.* New York, 1943.

Smith, Bradley F. *The Road to Nuremberg.* New York, 1981.

Smith, Bruce Lannes, Harold D. Lasswell, and Ralph D. Casey, eds. *Propaganda, Communication and Public Opinion: A Comprehensive Reference Guide.* Princeton, N.J., 1946.

Smith, Howard K. *Last Train from Berlin.* New York, 1942.

Snow, Edgar. *Battle for Asia.* New York, 1941.

———. *Far Eastern Front.* New York, 1934.

———. *Journey to the Beginning.* New York, 1958.

———. *The Pattern of Soviet Power.* New York, 1945.

———. *Random Notes on Red China.* New York, 1957.

———. *Red Star Over China.* New York, 1937.

Snow, Lois Wheeler. *Edgar Snow's China.* New York, 1981.

Snyder, Louis L., ed. *Masterpieces of War Reporting: Great Moments of World War II.* New York, 1962.

Snyder, Louis L. and R. B. Morris, ed. *A Treasury of Great Reporting: "Literature Under Pressure"from the Sixteenth Century to Our Own Times.* New York, 1949.

"Soldiers of the Press . . . ." *Editor & Publisher,* December 23, 1944, December 30, 1944. (List of killed and missing U.S. and British correspondents.)

Sokolsky, George E. *The Tinder Box of Asia.* Garden City, N.Y., 1932.

Sommers, Martin. "The War to Get the War News." *Saturday Evening Post,* March 25, 1944, pp. 26–27, 102–04.

"Soviet's 'Izvestia' Demands End of Censorship—But Is Forced to Retract." *World Press News,* March 28, 1939.

Stanford, Neal. "Ten-Million-Word Story." *Christian Science Monitor* August 18, 1945, p. 5.

Steel, Ronald. *Walter Lippmann and the American Century.* Boston, 1980.

Steer, George. *Caesar in Abyssinia.* Boston, 1937.

———. *Tree of Gernika.* London, 1938.

Steinbeck, John. *Once There Was a War.* New York, 1958.

Steinkopf, Alvin J. "Getting News Out of Germany." *Quill,* September 1942, pp. 3–4. 18.

Stevens, Edmund. *Russia Is No Riddle.* New York, 1945.

Stevenson, William. *A Man Called Intrepid: The Secret War.* New York, 1976.

———. *Intrepid's Last Case.* New York, 1984.

Stewart, Irwin, ed. "Radio." *Annals of American Academy of Political and Social Science.* Philadephia, 1939.

Stewart, Kenneth and Tebbel, John. *Makers of Modern Journalism.* New York, 1952.

Stokes, Thomas L. *Chip Off My Shoulder.* Princeton, 1940.

Stokesbury, James A. *A Short History of World War II.* New York, 1980.

Stone, Shepard and Hanson Baldwin, eds. *We Saw It Happen: The News Behind the News That's Fit to Print.* New York, 1939.

Storey, Graham. *Reuters: The Story of a Century of News-Gathering.* New York, 1951. Published in London as *Reuters' Century, 1851–1951.*

Stowe, Leland. *Nazi Means War.* New York, 1933.

———. *No Other Road to Freedom.* New York, 1941.

———. *They Shall Not Sleep.* New York, 1944.

Strong, Anna Louise. *I Change Worlds: The Remaking of an American.* New York, 1935.

Stuart, Graham H. *The Department of State: A History of Its Organization, Procedure and Personnel.* New York, 1949.

Sullivan, Mark. *Education of an American.* New York, 1938.

Sulzberger, Cyrus L. "Boom in Kuibyshev." *New York Times Magazine,* January 25, 1942.

———. *A Long Row of Candles: Memoirs and Diaries, 1934–1954.* New York, 1969.

———. *Seven Continents and Forty Years: A Concentration of Memories.* Fwd. by André Malraux. New York, 1977.

Swanberg, W. A. *Citizen Hearst: A Biography of William Randolph Hearst.* New York, 1961.

———. *Luce and His Empire.* New York, 1972.

Swindler, William F. "The AP Anti-Trust Case in Historical Perspective." *Journalism Quarterly,* March 1946, pp. 50–57.

Swing, Raymond Gram. "Hotel Room in Prague." *Ken* [Magazine], December 1, 1938, pp. 15–17.

———. *How War Came.* New York, 1939.

———. *Preview of History.* New York, 1937.

Tabouis, Genevieve. *Blackmail or War.* London, 1938.

———. *They Called Me Cassandra.* New York, 1942.

Tardieu, André. *France in Danger.* London, 1935.

Taylor, A. J. P. *Beaverbrook.* London, 1972.

Taylor, Edmund. *The Strategy of Terror: Europe's Inner Front.* Boston, 1940.

———. *Time Runs Out.* New York, 1942.

Templewood, Lord. *Nine Troubled Years.* London, 1954.

"This Is How the BBC Covered the War." *World Press News,* May 31, 1945.

This Is Our War. Baltimore, Md., 1945. (By six Negro war correspondents.)

Thomas, Hugh. *The Spanish Civil War.* London, 1961.

Thomas, Lowell. *Good Evening Everybody: From Cripple Creek to Samarkand. An Autobiography.* New York, 1976.

———. *Magic Dials.* New York, 1939.

Thompson, Charles A. H. *Overseas Information Service of the United States Government.* Washington, D.C., 1948.

Thompson, C. V. R. *I Lost My English Accent.* New York, 1939.

Thompson, Dorothy. *Let the Record Speak.* Boston, 1939.

Thomson, Rear Admiral G. P. *Blue Pencil Admiral: The Inside Story of Press Censorship.* London, 1947.

"The Times N.Y. Overcomes Argentine Censorship." *Little Times,* September 18, 1944, pp. 1, 4. (*New York Times* house publication.)

"Three War Correspondents Die as Shell Hits Their Car." *Editor & Publisher,* January 8, 1939, p. 8.

Timperley, H. J. "Makers of Public Opinion about the Far East." *Pacific Affairs,* June 1936, pp. 221–30.

————. *What War Means: The Japanese Terror in China. A Documentary Record.* London, 1938. Published in New York as *Japanese Terror in China.*

Tobin, Richard. *Invasion Journal.* New York, 1944.

Toland, John. *The Last 100 Days.* London, 1965.

Tolischus, Otto D. *They Wanted War.* New York, 1940.

————. *Through Japanese Eyes.* New York, 1945.

————. *Tokyo Record.* New York, 1943.

————. "What a Foreign Correspondent Wants These Days." *Editor & Publisher,* November 1, 1941, p. 9.

Tomlinson, John D. *The International Control of Radiocommunication.* Ann Arbor, Mich., 1945.

Tong, Hollington K. *Dateline: China, the Beginning of China's Press Relations With the World.* New York, 1950. Published in China as *China and the World Press.*

Treanor, Tom. *One Damn Thing After Another: The Adventures of an Innocent Man Trapped Between Public Relations and the Axis.* New York, 1944.

Tregaskis, Richard. *Guadalcanal Diary.* New York, 1943.

————. *Stronger Than Fear.* New York, 1945.

Tuchman, Barbara. *The Guns of August.* New York, 1962.

————. *Stilwell and the American Experience in China, 1911–1945.* New York, 1971.

"Twenty-seven Correspondents Leave Germany Under Pressure of Nazi Regime." *Editor & Publisher,* April 6, 1935.

"Twenty-two U.S. Correspondents Return After Five-Month Internment." *Editor & Publisher,* June 6, 1942, pp. 3–4.

Ullstein, Hermann. *The Rise and Fall of the House of Ullstein.* New York, 1943.

"United States Marines on Iwo Jima." *Infantry Journal,* 1945.

United States v. Associated Press. *52 Federal Supplement 362 (N.Y. 1943);* affirmed in *326 United States Reports* (1945).

"U.S. and World Communications." *Fortune,* May 1944, pp. 278–80.

"U.S. Recognition of Russia Has Aided Work of Correspondents." *Editor & Publisher,* November 24, 1934, p. 12.

Valdés, Miguel Valasco. *Historia del Periodismo Mexicano.* Mexico City, 1955.

Valenzuela, Jesus Z. *History of Journalism in the Philippine Islands.* Introd. by Willàrd G. Bleyer. Manila, 1933.

Van Passen, Pierre. *Days of Our Years.* New York, 1939.

Vaughn, Miles W. *Covering the Far East.* New York, 1936. Published in London as *Under the Japanese Mask.*

Victor, Walther. "Journalism Under Hitler's Heel." *Quill,* June 1943, pp. 10–13.

Villard, Oswald Garrison. *The German Phoenix: The Story of the Republic.* New York, 1933.

Von Wiegand, Karl. "I Cover the Spanish Front." *Cosmopolitan,* December 1936, pp. 26–27, 174–77.

―――. "King Features Gets Hitler Interview." *Editor & Publisher,* June 15, 1940.

―――. "Von Wiegand Tells Difficulties of Covering Spain's Civil War." *Editor & Publisher,* August 15, 1936, p. 6.

―――. "War Claims Confusing to Editors? 'Victories' Puzzle von Wiegand Too." *Editor & Publisher,* April 24, 1937, pp. 7, 32.

Wagner, Ludwig. "The Foreign Press: Germany." *Journalism Quarterly,* December 1941, pp. 409–10.

Walker, F. D. "Here is the News: The Growth of the BBC News Service." *World Press News,* March 5, 1954, pp. 17, 20.

Warburg, James P. *Unwritten Treaty.* New York, 1948.

"War Photographers." *Life,* November 5, 1945, pp. 97–113.

Waterfield, Gordon. *What Happened to France.* London, 1941.

Watson, Campbell. "10 Years After VE Day, History Vindicates Him, Kennedy Holds." *Editor & Publisher,* May 7, 1955. p. 16.

Waugh, Evelyn. *Waugh in Abyssinia.* London, 1937.

―――. *Scoop.* London, 1933.

Wecter, Dixon. "Hearing Is Believing." *Atlantic Monthly,* July 1945, pp. 37–43; August 1945, pp. 54–61.

Weddell, Alexander W. *Introduction to Argentina.* New York, 1939.

Wei Ma, Hsin-ye. "The Foreign Press: China." *Journalism Quarterly,* September 1939, pp. 284–87; December 1939, pp. 393–95; March 1940, pp. 77–80; June 1940, pp. 172–75.

Weigle, Clifford F. "The Press in Paris from 1920 to 1940. *Journalism Quarterly,* December 1941, pp. 376–86.

Weigley, Russell F. *Eisenhower's Lieutenants: The Campaigns in France and Germany, 1944–1945.* New York, 1981.

Weller, George. *Singapore Is Silent.* New York, 1943.

Wells, Linton. *Blood on the Moon.* Boston, 1937.

Wertenbaker, Charles Christian. *Invasion!* New York, 1944.

Werth, Alexander. *France in Ferment.* London and New York, 1934.

―――. *Moscow War Diary.* New York, 1942.

―――. *Russia at War.* London, 1964.

―――. *The Year of Stalingrad.* London, 1946.

Wheeler, Keith. *The Pacific Is My Beat.* New York, 1943.

————. *We Are the Wounded: An Epic of American Courage.* New York, 1945.

Whitaker, John T. *Americas to the South.* New York, 1939.

————. *And Fear Came.* New York, 1936. Published in London as *Fear Came to Europe.*

————. *We Cannot Escape History.* New York, 1943.

White, E. B. "A Reporter at Large: Beautiful Upon a Hill." *New Yorker,* May 12, 1945, pp. 42–45.

White, John W. *Argentina: The Life Story of a Nation.* New York, 1942.

White, Leigh. *The Long Balkan Night.* New York, 1944.

White, Llewellyn. *The American Radio: A Report on the Broadcasting Industry in the United States from the Commission on Freedom of the Press.* Chicago, 1947.

White, Llewellyn and Robert D. Leigh. *Peoples Speaking to Peoples.* Chicago, 1946.

White, Omar. *Green Armor.* New York, 1946.

White, Paul W. "Covering the War for Radio." *Annals of the American Academy of Political and Social Science,* January, 1941.

————. *News on the Air.* New York, 1947.

White, Theodore H. *Fire In the Ashes; Europe in Mid-Century.* New York, 1953.

————. *In Search of History: A Personal Adventure.* New York, 1978.

————. and Jacoby, Annalee. *Thunder Out of China.* New York, 1946.

————. *The View from the Fortieth Floor.* New York, 1960.

White, William Allen. *The Autobiography of William Allen White.* New York, 1946.

White, William L. *They Were Expendable.* New York, 1942.

Whiteleather, Melvin K. "The Foreign Press: Germany." *Journalism Quarterly,* December 1939, pp. 395–98; March 1940, pp. 80–83; June 1940, pp. 175–76.

Wildes, Harry Emerson. *Japan In Crisis.* New York, 1934.

Williams, Francis. *Dangerous Estate: The Anatomy of Newspapers.* London and New York, 1957.

————. *Nothing So Strange: An Autobiography.* London, 1970.

————. *Press, Parliament and People.* London, 1946.

————. *The Right to Know: The Rise of the World Press.* London, 1969.

————. *Transmitting World News.* Paris, 1953. (UNESCO.)

Williams, M. W. *The People and Politics of Latin America.* Rev. ed. New York, 1930.

Williams, Valentine. *World of Action.* Boston, 1938.

Wilmot, Chester. *The Struggle for Europe.* New York, 1952.

Wilson, Lyle C. "Covering the Capital." *Quill,* January 1941, pp. 10–13.

Wilson, Richard. "Reporting the Washington News." *Annals of the American Academy of Political and Social Science.* January 1942, pp. 127–31.

Windsor, Duke of. *A King's Story: The Memoirs of the Duke of Windsor.* London and New York, 1951.
Wohlstetter, Roberta. *Pearl Harbor: Warning and Decision.* Palo Alto, Calif., 1962.
Wolfert, Ira. *Battle for the Solomons.* Boston, 1943.
Wolff, Theodor. *Through Two Decades.* Trans. by E. W. Dickes. London, 1936.
Wolseley, Roland E., ed. *Journalism in Modern India.* Bombay, 1953.
_____. "Tainted Truth in the Tropics." *Quill,* October 1939, pp. 3–4, 14.
Wood, Alan. *The True Story of Lord Beaverbrook.* London, 1965.
Wood, James Playsted. *Magazines in the United States.* Rev. ed. New York, 1956.
Woodhead, H. G. W. *Adventures in Far Eastern Journalism: A Record of Thirty-Three Years' Experience.* New York, 1935. Published in London as *A Journalist In China.*
_____. *A Visit to Manchukuo.* Shanghai, 1932.
Wrench, John Evelyn. *Geoffrey Dawson and Our Times.* London, 1955.
"Writers in Japan Have More Difficult Job Than in Europe." *Editor & Publisher,* September 14, 1940, p. 14.
Wyant, Hubbard. *Fiasco in Ethiopia: The Story of a So-Called War by a Reporter on the Ground.* New York, 1936.
Wyden, Peter. *The Passionate War: The Narrative History of the Spanish Civil War.* New York, 1983.
Ybarra, Thomas R. *America Faces South.* New York, 1939.
_____. *Young Man of the World.* New York, 1942.
Young, A. Morgan. "Collisions With Japanese Authority." *Asia,* October 1937, pp. 753–56.
_____. "Japanese Press Censorship." *Asia,* August 1935, pp. 474–77.
_____. "The Press and Japanese Thought." *Pacific Affairs,* December 1937. pp. 412–19.
Young, Eugene J. *Looking Behind the Censorships.* New York, 1938.
Young, Gordon. *Outposts of War.* London, 1943.
Young, James R. *Behind the Rising Sun.* New York, 1941.
Young, Kenneth, ed. *The Diaries of Sir Robert Bruce Lockhart (1915–1938).* London and New York, 1973.
Yu'tang, Lin. *A History of the Press and Public Opinion in China.* Chicago, 1936.
Zacharoff, Lucien, ed. *The Voice of Fighting Russia.* New York, 1942.
Ziffren, Lester. "The Correspondent in Spain." *Public Opinion Quarterly,* July 1937, pp. 112–16.
Zobrist, Benedict Karl. "Edward Price Bell and the Development of the Foreign News Service of the Chicago Daily News." Master's thesis, Northwestern University, 1953.

Index